DEFEAT
AND
TRIUMPH

DEFEAT
AND
TRIUMPH

THE STORY OF A CONTROVERSIAL ALLIED INVASION
AND FRENCH REBIRTH

STEPHEN SUSSNA

To order additional copies of this book, contact:
Xlibris Corporation
1-888-795-4274
www.Xlibris.com
Orders@Xlibris.com
38770

Dedication

For Marian—wife, partner, friend—with love.

Acknowledgements

I am indebted to many people for a great deal of help in writing this book.

Marian, my wife, was of paramount importance during thousands of days in a variety of ways. Not only supplying me with lots of information (via the Internet), typing, and being a sounding board, she put up with an avalanche of papers and books in our apartment.

Special thanks are given to Professor Eric Neubacher and his colleagues Louisa Moy and Lloyd Parlato of the first-rate Newman Library at Baruch College, City University of New York. They rendered remarkable assistance in obtaining valuable material. Their help was of utmost importance.

In 1944, I was a sailor on the LST 1012, and my supervising officer was Reginald Charles "Chuck" Steeple Jr. At a fiftieth reunion of the commissioning of our ship, we met again. He inspired me to write this book, and he gave me valuable data and maps. He was always a very considerate and kind man.

Thanks to Geoffrey M. T. Jones for the detailed information re: the service he rendered as an OSS agent immediately before the invasion.

During his retirement, Adm. Henry Kent Hewitt wrote his memoirs. In the autumn of 2001, his daughter Mary Kent Norton and her son Randall sent me this material and other valuable items. I am very grateful for their assistance.

Commanding Officer (of the LST 282) Lawrence Edwin Gilbert's family (his son Terry, daughter Lauren, granddaughter Kirsten, and sister Susan) very graciously supplied me with photos and memorabilia. Kirsten even came to visit us in NYC. Many thanks to the family.

June Webb sent me important recollections and photos re: her father, Samuel Kimmel, who was the commanding officer of the LST 551.

Commanding Officer (of the LST 1011) Bob Wilson sent me very frank, insightful information concerning conditions at that time.

Robert Townsend, research director of the American Historical Association, gave me an extremely provocative publication concerning the rebirth of France.

Claude Bardin, who has encouraged French-American friendship, provided me with useful material concerning southern France.

Thanks to my LST 1012 friends—Ed Clowser, Charlie Cullen, Charlie Earle, Harold Larsen, Frank Lovekin, Bob Peck, and Ross Zimmerman. Their stories stimulated my memory.

Jim Connor Jr. sent me data concerning his father who won the Congressional Medal of Honor.

Grant Lee supplied me with extensive data concerning LST crew members who served during World War II.

I was given considerable assistance from Pat Osborne and his colleagues at the National Archives. Librarians from the U.S. Navy, Army, and Air Force and Columbia, Dartmouth, Princeton, and Stanford universities were very helpful.

Thanks to Robert Busch, editor of the LST *Scuttlebutt*. He provided me with the opportunity to obtain diaries, letters, and interviews from the following people: Tom Aubut, Bob Beroth, Clyde Bond, Howard Buhl, Ferris Burke, Ted Dunn, Tom Kronenberger, Lou Leopold, John McRea, Jeff Shatley (re: his father, Dean), Mike Sgaglione, and George Sweet.

Lewis Lapham helped me obtain 1940 and 1944 issues of *Harper's* magazine. Many of these articles were provocative and insightful.

Lindsay S. Krasnoff assisted in the editing process.

I apologize to anyone I mistakenly omitted. Please forgive me. Many thanks to all.

Who's Who

Americans

CLARK, Mark W.—Commanding general, U.S. Fifth Army in the Italian campaign.

DAHLQUIST, Maj. Gen. John E.—Commanding officer of the Thirty-sixth Infantry Division who landed on the Camel Beaches.

DEVERS, Gen. Jacob L.—Commanding general of the Sixth Army Group during Operation Dragoon. Before that command, Devers was deputy theater commander in the Mediterranean Theater. On September 15, 1944, General Devers formally took command of the Sixth Army Group consisting of General Patch's Seventh and General De Lattre's First. The Sixth Army Group was then no longer a part of the Mediterranean Theater. The Sixth would now answer to Gen. Dwight D. Eisenhower's Supreme Command Headquarters in Versailles, France, with Devers serving under Eisenhower.

DONOVAN, William J.—Head of the Office of Strategic Services (OSS).

EAGLES, Maj. Gen. William—Forty-fifth Infantry Division, landed on the Delta Beaches.

EAKER, Lt. Gen. Ira—Commander in chief of the Mediterranean Allied Air Forces (MAAF).

FAIRBANKS, Douglas E. Jr.—An actor who participated in Operation Dragoon; he commanded a mission to deceive the enemy as to the location of the invasion site.

FORRESTAL, James V.—Secretary of the navy.

FREDERICK, Maj. Gen. Robert T.—Commanding officer of the First Special Service Force. He and his parachute troops dropped into Le Muy, France, before the Dragoon landings to block German reinforcements. Duff Matson was Frederick's bodyguard.

GILBERT, Lawrence E.—Commanding officer of LST 282. Other LST 282 crew members mentioned in the book are Tom Aubut, Hans Bergner, and Bob Beroth.

HEWITT, Adm. Henry Kent—Naval commander of the North African invasion (Operation Torch, November 1942); the Sicilian invasion (Operation Husky, July 1943); the Salerno invasion (Operation Avalanche, September 1943); and the invasion of southern France (Operation Anvil/Dragoon, August 1944).

HIGGINS, Andrew Jackson—Manufacturer of amphibious craft.

HULL, Cordell—Secretary of state.

JONES, Geoffrey M. T. —OSS agent who played a big role in Dragoon (and friend of the author). Jones provided General Frederick with valuable information concerning German plans.

KIMMEL, Sam—Commanding officer of LST 551, a lawyer, and later a judge.

KNOX, Frank—U.S. secretary of the navy, 1940-1944.

LEOPOLD, Lou—An officer on LST 551, the author's source of good information.

LEWIS, Rear Adm. Spencer S.—Commanding officer of the Camel sector beaches of Operation Dragoon. Lewis replaced Rear Adm. Don P. Moon after the latter committed suicide shortly before August 15, 1944. The other Dragoon beaches were Alpha and Delta.

MURPHY, Robert D.—U.S. State Department officer used by President Roosevelt as his agent to deal with the French in North Africa.

O'DANIEL, John—Commanding officer of the Third Infantry Division, who landed on the Delta Beaches.

PATCH, Lt. Gen. Alexander M. Jr. —Commanding general, U.S. Seventh Army in southern France during Operation Dragoon.

PATTERSON, Robert P.—U.S. undersecretary of war.

PERSHING, Gen. John J.—Commander of American Expeditionary Forces in France during World War I.

STIMSON, Henry L.—Secretary of war.

TRUSCOTT, Maj. Gen. Lucian J. Jr.—Commander of the U.S. Army VI Corps composed of the Third, Thirty-sixth, and Forty-fifth Infantry Divisions. He was chosen for the assault on southern France.

LST 1012 Crew Members—Some of those who served on the 1012 were Marshall Flowers Jr. (commanding officer); R. C. Steeple Jr. (executive officer—second in command and also navigator); Jack Rushing (gunnery officer); Jim Duplessis (supply officer); Charlie Earle (petty officer in charge of gunnery); Charlie Cullen (radioman—petty officer); Frank Lovekin (radar—petty officer); Bob Peck (signalman—petty officer); and Petty Officers Frank Gruntkowski, Steve Sussna, Tom Hickey—navy quartermasters, helmsmen, and navigator assistants. (Navy quartermasters should not be confused with army quartermasters who have responsibilities concerning supplies.)

British

CUNNINGHAM, Adm. Sir John—He exercised overall control of naval operations; however, the on-the-spot commander was Vice Adm. H. K. Hewitt.

WILSON, Gen. Sir Henry Maitland—Supreme Allied commander, European Theater of Operations, and Allied commander in the Mediterranean.

French

AUMONT, Jean-Pierre—French actor and soldier.

DE GAULLE, Gen. Charles—French liberation leader.

DE LATTRE DE TASSIGNY, Gen. Jean—Commanded the units under French Army B during Operation Dragoon.

KOENIG, Gen. Joseph Pierre—Appointed military governor of Paris by Gen. Charles de Gaulle in August 1944. Koenig had been in command of the French Forces of the Interior. He was closely connected with the Allied liberation of Cherbourg.

LAVAL, Pierre—Vichy premier of France.

PÉTAIN, Marshal Henri Philippe Omer—Hero of World War I and titular head of the Vichy French government 1940-1944.

Germans

BLASKOWITZ, Col. Gen. Johannes von—Commander of the German Army in southern France.

GOEBBELS, Dr. Paul Joseph—Propaganda minister.

KLUGE, Field Marshal Guenther von—Commander of German forces in France.

Contents

Illustrations

CHAPTER 1

RETURN TO CAP DRAMMONT

On August 15, 1944, the daily newspaper of the United States Armed Forces, the *Stars and Stripes* (Mediterranean) observed,

> Two years ago today the Germans had the control of the Mediterranean within their grasp. Their armistice commissions were in French North Africa. They controlled southern France and had a friend in Franco's Spain. They had occupied Greece and Crete. Italy was still a trusted ally. And the Afrika Korps of Field Marshal Erwin von Rommel had driven eastward across Cyrenaica and deep into the western desert of Egypt to threaten the entire British position in the Middle East. Two years ago it would have been impossible for the Allies to do more than dream of landings on the coast of southern France. The turn of the tide which has now given the Allied navies virtually undisputed mastery of the Mediterranean began at El Alamein on Oct. 23, 1942. Since that date the Nazis have suffered an unbroken series of defeats in the Mediterranean theater.

By September 11, 1944, the troops that had invaded the beaches of southern France on August 15 had joined other Allied soldiers driving south from Normandy. And although it would not happen until May 8, 1945, the final defeat of German forces was made inevitable by the flood of more than 1.2 million Allied troops and their 4.5 million tons of equipment and supplies that poured through the beaches of southern France and the ports of Marseille and Toulon[1]—secured by the August 15 invasion.

A U.S. Army Command and General Staff College study prepared in May 1984 concluded that Operation Anvil/Dragoon—the August 15, 1944, invasion of southern France—"has drawn more fire from participants and observers than perhaps any decision during World War II." Though the study of this particular Allied invasion, known at

1

first as "Operation Anvil" and renamed, for security reasons, shortly before the invasion as "Operation Dragoon," is replete with controversy, importance, and interest, it has not received the scrutiny it merits, nor has it been situated in the context that it deserves.

Notwithstanding Prime Minister Winston Churchill's bitter and tenacious opposition and delay, Operation Dragoon took place on August 15, 1944—the Catholic holy day of the Feast of Assumption and also the birthday of Napoleon Bonaparte. On that day, a large combined military operation of mostly American and French army, navy, air force, and commando units used the same route to defeat their enemies that Napoleon took when he escaped from the island of Elba in 1815 and led his troops to Paris. The Allies began the successful assault of forty-five miles of French Riviera beaches.

Despite objections to the invasion, as historian Alan F. Wilt argued, "Most American leaders persisted in their belief that the operation was both necessary and beneficial to the Allied cause. To General Marshall, who was not given to overstatement, 'The southern France operation was one of the most successful things we did.' General Eisenhower echoed Marshall's sentiments when he wrote that 'there was no development of that period which added more decisively to our advantage or aided us more in accomplishing the final and complete defeat of the German forces than did this secondary attack coming up the Rhone Valley."[2]

The universal acknowledgment that Dragoon was a huge success, and a model case study for military planners, has not stopped leading historians and many others from insisting that the operation was a mistake and a wasteful diversion.[3] They claim that Churchill's alternative—to expedite victory in Italy and an Allied march east to the Balkans—could have blocked the Soviet Communist takeover of Eastern Europe and thus avoided the costly cold war.

After examining what has so far been made public, I concluded that the full story of Dragoon, the conditions that made it possible, and its results have not been told. Previously unpublished archival, anecdotal, and governmental materials are included in this book. Foreign periodicals, doctoral dissertations, diaries, and military reports are also used. These all help tell the story of Dragoon. In addition to collecting and analyzing new information, I am in a special position concerning Operation Dragoon. On August 15, 1944, I served as helmsman on LST 1012 (Landing Ship, Tank). Our ship was involved in the most dangerous, surprising, and tragic events of that day.

About two weeks before Operation Dragoon began, the admiral in command of the LST 1012 landing beach, Rear Adm. Don P. Moon, committed suicide (the landing beaches in southern France were divided into sectors, e.g., Alpha, Camel, and Delta). Moon was designated to be in charge of the Camel Beach sector. Badly overworked and exhausted, he worried that Dragoon would be a worse bloodbath than the invasion of Normandy in which he had participated. After his plea to postpone Anvil/Dragoon was denied, Moon killed himself. He was replaced by Rear Adm. Spencer S. Lewis who lacked the preparation of his unfortunate predecessor. LST 1012 was assigned to land in the Camel Beach sector. The original plan called for the ship to land on Camel Red Beach (264A). However, in the midst of the invasion, Lewis directed the LST 1012, LST 282, and other ships to land on Camel Green Beach (264B), at Cap Drammont,[4] believing it to be safer than Camel Red Beach, which was heavily defended by the enemy and dangerous. As a result, LST 1012 and nearly all the other ships benefited from Lewis's decision to reroute the landing to the Cap Drammont beach.

LST 282, many of its crew, and the soldiers that it transported as passengers were not as lucky. Toward dusk, following a day of successful landings, a German glider bomb hit and sank the ship, killing or wounding many. I remember seeing survivors on our galley tables when I left the wheelhouse after many hours of duty on the LST 1012 bridge. LST 282 survivors have helped in my research. The sister, son, daughter, granddaughter, and neighbor of the LST 282's heroic commanding officer, Lawrence E. Gilbert, have provided documents concerning him. The family of Adm. Henry Kent Hewitt, naval commander of four Mediterranean invasions, has also been generous in providing valuable information.

New, never-before-published information has been gathered from a wide assortment of sources. These materials include

1. Accounts provided to me by numerous crew members and passengers on a variety of ships and small craft—soldiers, airmen, OSS agents, commandos, and paratroopers—about their own experiences during Dragoon.
2. Accounts of the roles played by civilians, such as U.S. Secretary of the Navy James V. Forrestal and Assistant Secretary of War Robert Patterson, in Dragoon. Their participation, as well as

that of other civilians, among them Robert D. Murphy, a career diplomat chosen by President Roosevelt to be his special agent for French and North African affairs, and Isabel Pell, an American expatriate and humanitarian who aided the French Resistance, will receive attention, as will the actors who contributed to the success of Dragoon in the invasion of southern France, such as Alec Guinness, Douglas Fairbanks Jr., Jean-Pierre Aumont, and Audie Murphy. Another important player was the French author of *The Little Prince* and air pilot Antoine de Saint-Exupéry, who undertook mapping flights for the invasion. As a result of his air reconnaissance missions, important maps were prepared. Many of these unpublished maps will be included.

3. Significant unpublished information provided by my friend Geoffrey M. T. Jones, president of OSS-Veterans. Born in 1919, Jones grew up in a French Riviera villa near the Cap Drammont landing beach. As a U.S. Army officer and OSS agent, he parachuted into southern France to recruit and organize French Resistance members and to provide intelligence information via radio to England. He reported to Maj. Gen. Robert T. Frederick concerning German activity. His discovery of the German retreat plan was extremely helpful to Dragoon's commanding general, Alexander M. Patch Jr. Such knowledge of the German defense plan enabled Patch's troops to accelerate their Rhone Valley campaign. Jones also provided Admiral Hewitt with intelligence information concerning the Nice harbor facilities—a report that showed the location of enemy sentry towers, underwater nets, mines, and other dangerous devices that enabled precise targeting by the Allied fleet.

4. One of the many formerly secret documents obtained for this work is a debriefing analysis of the Allied intelligence operation in the area of the invasion of southern France. It does not pull any punches and candidly points out the conflicts between British, French, and American intelligence agents and other serious problems. The impact of other political animosities that plagued Operation Dragoon is also discussed.

5. Material obtained from Stanford University archivists concerning Major General Frederick. The heroism of Frederick and his troops in the Italian campaign was enacted in the movie *The Devil's Brigade*, with actor William Holden portraying Frederick.

In Operation Dragoon, the general commanded American and British airborne divisions, which he welded together with unprecedented speed. His First Airborne Task Force troops spearheaded the Dragoon assault to block off German attempts to rush reinforcements to the amphibious landing beaches.

6. An account of the bravery of Congressional Medal of Honor recipient Sgt. James P. Connor during the Dragoon campaign and the high points of his life.

7. U.S. Office of Naval Intelligence materials; U.S. Foreign Relations Reports and other federal government documents; a diversity of periodicals from 1944, such as *Time, Harper's, Atlantic Monthly, Progressive, New Yorker,* the *New York Times,* the *Stars and Stripes,* and French and German sources.

8. LST reports. Churchill recognized the crucial role of these ships in World War II, declaring that the destiny of civilization depended upon "some damn things called LSTs." Historians such as Samuel Morison, Stephen Ambrose, and others agree that the role of LSTs in achieving victory in that war needs to be better known. Readers will learn about the adventures of LST crews, the dangers they faced, and the life aboard these ships. Former LST 1012 crew members from all over the United States have been generous in providing me with log entries and war reports. Former crew members of other LSTs and other types of ships have also made available useful information.

To understand Dragoon, one must know the larger picture of the story: of events in France, the United States, and the Mediterranean. But for the defeat of France in June 1940 and the Pearl Harbor attack of December 7, 1941, there would have been no Operation Dragoon. Had the Allied Mediterranean invasions of North Africa (November 1942), Sicily (July 1943), and Salerno (September 1943) not occurred, there would have been no Operation Dragoon. By using a widely sweeping historical approach, one can reach a better understanding of the invasion of southern France, its consequences and results. The core story of Operation Dragoon has all the elements that ultimately combined to yield Allied victory in World War II.

Visiting Cap Drammont on November 18, 2000, I saw monuments honoring the U.S. Thirty-sixth Infantry Division, LST 282, and Admiral Hewitt, who had commanded the Operation Dragoon armada, as well as the three earlier Mediterranean invasions that were links in a chain that culminated in the invasion of southern France. His contributions will be discussed throughout this book.

Later that day, I visited a small museum in nearby Le Muy that contained photographs, equipment, and commentary concerning U.S. Major General Frederick and his First Airborne Task Force of parachutists. That day, I began to think about events and people I did not know of back in August 1944.

I doubt if any of us on the LST 1012 were concerned about American or French news during August 1944. Once aboard the ship, we were concerned with our duties, mail from home, diversions such as movies, reading, playing cards, gabbing, and eating. The liberties off the ship consisted of a little sightseeing, wandering around a strange place, boozing, and womanizing. We did not talk about what was happening outside the LST 1012. Despite my prenavy habit of being a "news junky," and being stationed in the wheelhouse near the radio room and receiving delayed copies of the *New York Times* from my father, I knew little of what was going on elsewhere—nothing about the origin or delays of Dragoon. In the United States and France, things were happening that were important to us. The LST 1012 was not an island unto itself, but it felt that way.

That November 2000 visit to Cap Drammont and the nearby places provoked my interest in Dragoon. I realized that in understanding the part that the invasion of southern France played in the liberation of France, I would need to learn about the events that began with the defeat of the French in June 1940.

With good cause, Gen. Jean-Marie de Lattre de Tassigny, commanding officer of the French troops that participated in Dragoon, called Drammont the symbolic heart of the invasion. The monuments on the beach corroborate his conclusion as to the extraordinary bravery that occurred during Dragoon. Among those who played important roles in the liberation of France were British forces, the goums of Morocco, and other North African troops. They were joined by soldiers, sailors, and airmen from all over the United States; and all of them assisted the French in removing the shackles of German occupation. After suffering more than four years of humiliating and devastating defeat and exile inflicted upon the French people, their troops' return to their homeland by landing on Cap Drammont and other Dragoon beaches was an indescribably glorious event.

The story of the people who brought about this victory, and how they did it, is the story of this book. My return to Cap Drammont beach provoked a fierce determination to tell the complex story of how French and American tragedies were transformed into victories on August 15, 1944. Vast improvements in military intelligence, logistics, and inter-Allied diplomacy brought about this triumph; but the price of victory was high. Some evidence of the cost of Dragoon is to be found in the Rhone American Cemetery in Draguignan, not too far from Cap Drammont.

Through the main gates of the Rhone American Cemetery is a sea of graves. Past the graves, at the northern end of the cemetery, sits the memorial, flanked by two flagpoles. Each tower reaches sixty-six and a half feet into the sky. In between the flagstaffs sits a bronze relief map that describes the military operations that occurred in the area in August 1944. Fashioned by Bruno Bearzi, a Florentine, the inscription, in both French and English, reads as follows:

On August 15, 1944 the Allied forces launched their campaign to assist the Normandy Operation and liberate southern France. The preparatory air bombardment had begun in July and had grown steadily in intensity. As the assault convoys assembled, the U.S. Twelfth and Fifteenth Air Forces struck at the beach defenses, as well as at the bridges astride the Rhone to isolate the battle area.

On the eve of the attack specially trained assault units landed to protect the flanks of the invasion beaches. Before dawn airborne troops dropped near Le Muy to seize highway junctions necessary to assure the Allied advance. At 0800 the U.S. VI Corps moved ashore under cover of bombardment by the Western Naval Task Force. Breaking through steel and concrete fortifications the U.S. 3rd, 36th and 45th Divisions pushed rapidly inland.

In a two-pronged advance the U.S. Seventh Army liberated Grenoble and within ten days was enveloping Montélimar to trap the enemy. Meanwhile French units had landed and thrust westward to Toulon and Marseille. By the end of the month the Allied ground troops were approaching Lyon preceded by the U.S. Twelfth Air Force whose attacks disorganized the fleeing enemy. By September 7th U.S. forces were moving on Belfort and Epinal. Four days later the Allied forces from

Normandy and southern France joined hands at Sombernon,
thus isolating all German units remaining in southwest France.
The Allies could now devote their efforts to the defeat of the
Nazis in Germany itself.[5]

In June 1940, and again in December 1941, there was no doubt that the enemies of French and American democracy were ready, willing, and able to use weapons of mass destruction. The Pearl Harbor attack immediately removed the option of American nonintervention. The country's small military force was quickly expanded by the many thousands who enlisted and the millions who were drafted. Grievous mistakes were made by Allied soldiers, sailors, and airmen, as well as by military and political leaders. But within a few years, military intelligence and Allied diplomacy and cooperation had vastly improved, and overwhelming manpower and logistical superiority was available. Abundant French allies were eager and rearmed to wipe out the shame of defeat and occupation. The cost for victory, and the debt owed to those who helped achieve it, cannot be calculated. However, it is worthwhile to remember how it happened, and those who made it possible.

On 15 August 1944, I did not calculate my survival odds or my fate. I did enjoy the glorious weather and the excitement in the LST 1012 wheelhouse. After leaving it, my observation of the LST 282 casualties on board was hasty. I was ignorant of the tragedy and did not know that the Allied invasion of southern France would play a substantial role in the destruction of Nazism. It took the passing of many years and belated study to appreciate that fact.

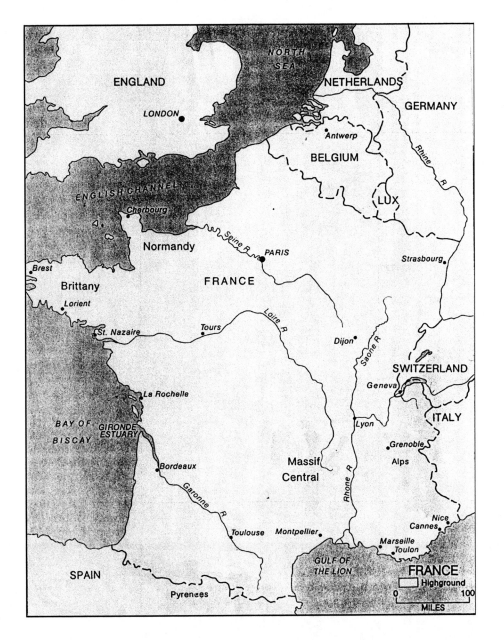

France

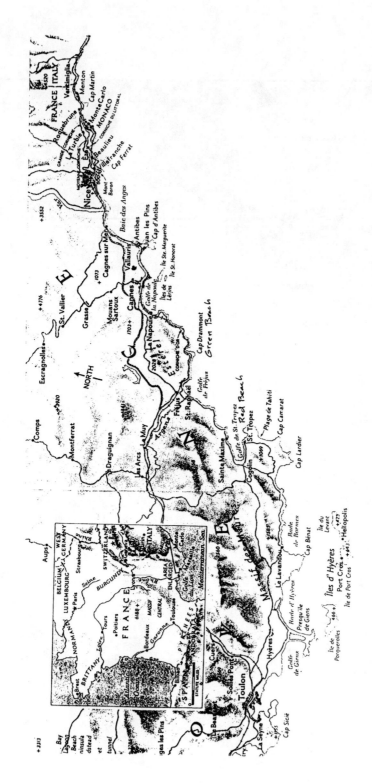

Map showing coast during Operation Dragoon

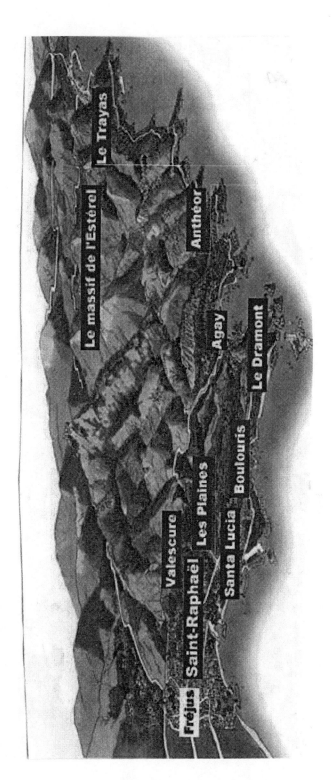

Cap Drammont and environs

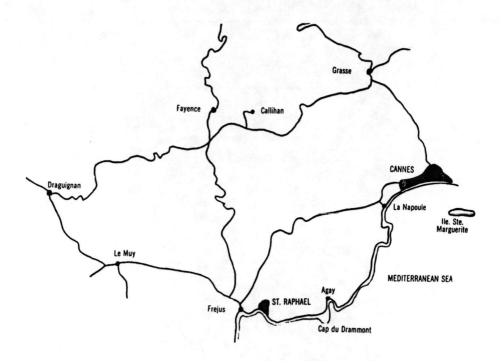

Cap Drammont and nearby municipalities

Ile d'Or, August 1944
The island's latter-day medieval-style tower was built in the
nineteenth century by the eccentric Doctor August Luthaud,
who proclaimed himself king of the island and received many
local personalities there.

Ile d'Or, November 2000

Steve Sussna on Cap Drammont mainland looking at the tiny
Ile d'Or and its conspicuous stone tower.

A small tribute to LST 282 on Camel Green Beach

A tribute to Adm. H. K. Hewitt on Camel Green Beach

CHAPTER 2

FRANCE BEFORE AND AFTER JUNE 1940

A page of history is worth a volume of logic.
—*Justice Oliver Wendell Holmes, U.S. Supreme Court*

Shortly before Adolf Hitler was elected chancellor of Germany in 1933, the renowned historian Arnold Toynbee concluded that "France was the dominant military power in Europe in the air as well as on land, she was executing a naval program . . . which was causing unease to the British Admiralty in Whitehall."[1] But long before the outbreak of World War II, German military leaders renovated their military intelligence, logistics, and strategies while the French and British disjointedly lagged behind, and Americans were ambivalent about their World War I allies, stressed neutrality and the protection afforded them by the Atlantic Ocean.

A primary cause of the French defeat of June 1940 was not that they lacked raw intelligence; rather, a lack of coordination, improper evaluation of intelligence, and decentralization of responsibility help explain the failure. This lack of alertness and imagination on the part of French military commanders and political decision makers caused their people irreparable harm. In addition to deaths and injuries, France's defeat resulted in the affliction of a host of other calamities: a huge number of prisoners of war and forced laborers taken to Germany; secret police and concentration camps in France; censorship; the intensification of anti-Semitism and internecine hostility; economic deprivation, hunger, humiliation, and many other plagues. Under the armistice agreement, the defeated government was divested by its conquerors of the power to make important decisions without German approval. France's economy was severely disrupted as Germany imposed on the country a charge of twenty million marks a day ($8 million at official rates) for the maintenance of German troops in occupied France. The French Treasury had to pay this money at the arbitrarily low exchange rate of twenty francs to the mark. Using this and other "reparation" devices, it was patent that the Germans were intent on bleeding France and emasculating its economy.[2]

17

Military intelligence failures to anticipate enemy attacks were largely responsible for the French defeat of June 1940 and the American losses at Pearl Harbor. A look back will help in understanding what happened after these two attacks to bring French and American forces together to undertake the invasion of southern France. World War II was a continuation of World War I, which started in August 1914 and ended with an armistice in November 1918. The earlier war contained the seeds for the second, which started in September 1939 and continued in Europe until May 1945. It is impossible to understand the French role in Operation Dragoon without gaining insight into what happened in the years that preceded it.

The Interwar Years

In 1917, a badly developed military offensive plan failed, crushing French hopes and depressing troop morale. News of the Russian Revolution, a widespread fear of communism, a mood of pacifism, and a staggering number of military casualties weakened the resolve of many French leaders to fight the Germans. French soldiers mutinied, and workers went on strike. French General Henri Philippe Omer Pétain gained a superb reputation as the defender of Verdun, a historic fortress town. He, along with the new prime minister, Georges Clemenceau, kept the punishment of soldiers to a minimum while executing some of the mutiny ringleaders. As a result of their reforms, living conditions in the trenches were improved, leaves for soldiers were increased, and the French people were inspired and organized to fight to the end. Clemenceau also used dictatorial powers to limit the Peace Party spokesmen in Parliament.

Between the wars, Pétain enhanced his image by appearing to be above petty political partisanship and by acting as a national unifier, and his compatriots were eternally grateful for his role in ultimately beating their World War I enemies. The French never forgot that a German offensive in spring 1918 succeeded in pushing Allied armies toward the Channel ports. The Allied troops held on, despite heavy losses, and, with American help and improved French morale, went on the offensive in the summer and autumn. The horrible four-year stalemate was broken, and Germany acknowledged defeat. On November 11, 1918, it signed an armistice; and in 1919, German representatives signed the Peace Treaty of Versailles.

The consequences of World War I were tragic. Frenchmen in the twenty- to forty-five-year-old age range in 1914 suffered a 20 percent death rate; 10 percent had to be supported; and 30 percent were periodically infirm due to gas warfare, shell shock, or other war-related causes. More than 1.25 million Frenchmen lost their lives during World War I.[3] The probability of another war with a bellicose Germany did not diminish the quest of many in France for peace. When war came again, its outcome was decided by the ineptitude of French military leaders. Their blunders and the outmoded Maginot Line defensive strategy doomed brave French troops and civilians to slaughter by German bombers using twentieth-century military technology and strategy. Moreover, economic difficulties fostered extremist practices in France, causing disunity throughout the country, and exacerbated the fear of many that France would be taken over by Communists. The prosperity begun in 1905 ended in 1931 as industrial activity declined and unemployment increased. Signs of economic recovery appeared in 1938, but production levels were about 20 percent lower than in 1928. From 1935 onward, there were more deaths than births in France; and in the two decades between the world wars, the population increase was small—only two million. Germany's population grew, in the same period, by ten million.[4] While the French, British, and Americans were mired in the depression of the 1930s, Germans were reaping the economic advantages of Hitler's National Socialist war production and public works programs. They were also benefiting from the theft of Jewish and other peoples' property. The French worried about German industrial and demographic superiority.

Compounding the economic depression in France were political corruption scandals. The political chasm that divided the French during the interwar years was enormous. The Right side of the political spectrum hated the Left as the harbinger of communism and atheism that would wipe out property rights and the Catholic religion. For their part, the Left viewed the Right as Fascists and Nazi emulators. Each camp viewed the other as the enemy within France—a "fifth column"—that was responsible for the country's alleged weakness. The French Left formed a political movement to resist fascism and to introduce social-economic reforms. Known as the Popular Front, this mélange of political parties gained electoral power in 1936 with 358 deputies (or legislators) against 222. Socialists were the largest party, and Léon Blum became premier. He persuaded employees and employers to develop social and economic policies to increase wages by 10 percent, reduce the workweek to forty hours, and resort to arbitration and meditation to resolve labor disputes. All employees were granted two weeks' paid holidays, and measures were enacted to help farmers by stabilizing grain prices.

When he became premier, Edouard Daladier sought the backing of employers by reinstating the forty-eight-hour workweek, adopting firm financial policies, and resuming French rearmament. Under Daladier, the Bank of France was made more accountable, children were required to attend school until they reached age fourteen instead of thirteen, and the French Fascist leagues were outlawed, but they continued underground. Despite popular social reforms, political infighting doomed the government, and by June 1937 Blum was unable to hold the Popular Front's political coalition of parliamentary parties united. His position of neutrality toward Spanish civil war combatants, a weak French economy that impaired the Popular Front's social reforms, a decline in production, and price increases diminished the effects of Blum's social reforms. He and his allies were unable to rely on the support of the Communists, and the Front's political parties were weakened by an unsuccessful Communist-inspired general strike. The loyalty of French Communists was put in doubt, and their political party was outlawed. Some Communists and rightists were united in preferring Hitler to the Jewish Léon Blum.

International tensions ignited by Benito Mussolini, Joseph Stalin, Adolf Hitler, and Japanese military leaders added to divisions within France. The absence of United States participation in the League of Nations in 1933 and Japan's and Germany's withdrawal from the organization in March and October 1933, respectively, increased the dangers of another war. French distrust of the British grew in 1935 when the latter agreed to a naval treaty that unilaterally eliminated Versailles' requirements for a limit on German naval expansion without consulting their French ally.[5] By 1936 it became clear that the League was failing to secure a lasting peace. Succumbing to the majority opinion, the U.S. Congress adopted legislation to preserve absolute neutrality in the face of future European conflict.

German Opinions

In an article for *Harper's* magazine that was completed before the successful invasions of 1940, Hans Schmidt wrote, "A Swiss paper stated that among the Germans there are from 10 to 15 percent full-fledged

National Socialists, men who would go with Hitler 'Durch Dick Und Duun' [through thick and thin]. On the other side of the scale there are from 10 to 15 percent equally determined anti-Nazis: Catholics, Liberals, Communists, Monarchists. The 'people', that is the remaining 70 to 80 percent, fluctuated back and forth according to the seasons. This is probably as good an analysis as any though one has to keep in mind that within each single German—including many German Jews—the 'pro and anti are in a state of conflict and fluctuation.'"[6] Schmidt wrote that Hitler's popularity was bad during the autumn of 1939 and early 1940 and that he was criticized personally for his impotent lust for naked dancers and his psychopathic outbursts at conferences with subordinates who expressed doubts about the wisdom of his policies.

Writing about the opening of the offensive against Belgium, the Netherlands, and France in 1940, Professor Ernest May of Harvard University quoted a letter from Germany's army chief of staff to his wife in which he observed that his fellow generals thought what they were doing was "crazy and reckless."[7] May also indicated that the German public had little or no appetite for entering into World War II and that Germany's generals believed that their nation was unprepared for war. Other doubts were expressed about unity in Hitler's Germany. In a November 1940 article entitled "Germany's Plans for Europe," Peter F. Drucker, a respected management author, claimed that the widespread assumption that Hitler had a definite plan for the organization of Germany's leadership in Europe was wrong. "There is the sharpest disagreement, the most violent quarrels between Nazi factions as to this future plan, its details as well as its essentials," he wrote.[8]

Of course not everyone in Germany during 1933-45 served or passively consented to Nazism. After their defeat, the Germans honored a courageous dissenter, Lisa Ekstein, who saved the lives of many French people and others. Ekstein was born in 1909 in Uzhgorod, at that time part of the Austro-Hungarian Empire and later part of Czechoslovakia following the land redistributions of the 1919 peace settlements.[9] Ekstein moved to Berlin with her family after World War I. In high school, Lisa joined a Communist organization. Her anti-Nazi activities led to pursuit by the Gestapo in 1933. Rather than submit to persecution, she and husband, Hans Fittko, also a leftist anti-Nazi, fled to Prague, then to Basel and Amsterdam. By 1938 she and Hans were in France.

New York Times reporter Douglas Martin noted that the Fittkos started helping refugees fleeing Germany long before World War II started. Once Germany invaded France, Lisa Fittko was detained in a concentration camp for women in Gurs, France, together with others from Germany. She helped her friend and fellow prisoner, Hannah Arendt, by giving Arendt a stolen release document. Once the Fittkos found each other, they traveled to Marseille, dodging Vichy officials collaborating with the Germans. They delayed their escape from France to help take other refugees to Spain. Ultimately, the couple escaped to Cuba and then to Chicago.[10]

Obviously, they were not the only German opponents of Nazism. Nevertheless, it was a serious mistake to deceive oneself about the anti-Hitler, anti-Nazi sentiment among the vast majority of Germans during the twelve years of the Third Reich. The hostility and dissent that did exist was almost entirely disorganized and too feeble to assert effective challenges. Nazi Storm Troops and Gestapo strength grew enormously, and in a short time, there were several hundred thousands of them. In addition to being terrorized by Heinrich Himmler's monsters, there was another reason why even Germans with strong feelings of discontent and hatred toward Hitler and his Nazis did not revolt: loyalty and discipline were traits that were instilled in Germans at an early age, and the Nazis counted on those traits to defeat their enemies. The country's military leaders energetically prepared for a second world war that demanded discipline and teamwork. Their infantry, artillery, tanks, and aircraft achieved the greatest mobility and launched bold, surprise attacks.

Nazi leaders didn't hesitate to use tactics such as attacking another nation without bothering to declare war or invading neutral nations like Belgium. Their mechanized thrusts into foreign countries depended on a tightly knit organization of military transport, ammunition supply, refueling, and other logistical considerations. Many in France and Britain were not busy with war that first winter of 1939 because the Germans appeared to be dormant and nothing much happened. What they did not know was that during this so-called phony war period, Hitler and his military leaders were carefully preparing for the April 1940 invasions of Denmark and Norway. When Britain and France tried to help the Norwegians, they did not have the troops needed for an amphibious landing. The lack of the types of equipment needed for the weather conditions and for adequate protection against German aircraft attacks was a prime cause for the failure of the Allied troops in capturing Troheim.

The Disastrous French Defeat of June 1940

In spring 1940, Germany defeated Norway, the Netherlands, Belgium, and Denmark. These calamities shocked the French, especially the defeat of Holland and the surrender of Belgian King Leopold two weeks afterward.[11] These latter victories freed Hitler's military to concentrate on defeating French and British forces.

By early May, the best French troops had been sent north of the Ardennes Forest because their military high command, led by Marshal Pétain, had expected the main German offensive attack to invade through Belgium. As minister of war before the outbreak of the war, Pétain had insisted on the impenetrability of that sector because of its alleged barriers of the Meuse River and the dense Ardennes. He refused to acknowledge the potential danger posed by the Ardennes, even though the area was weakly fortified and inadequately protected by ill-equipped reserve troops who were no match for a massive, mechanized German attack.

The illusion of French military invulnerability persisted even after the swift defeats of Denmark, Norway, Belgium, and Holland. The debacle became clear when German tanks reached the French border. Hitler had recognized that the primary French defense, the Maginot Line, was no longer a deterrent to his conquest of France. On May 10, 1940, the German Army surprised the French by attacking through the Ardennes Forest; and by June, German forces launched attacks on other parts of France: Marseille was bombed on June 2, there was an air raid on Paris the following day, and by June 10 the German Army was within thirty-five miles of Paris. That city was intentionally left undefended and was declared open to German occupation so that it would not be destroyed. Paris surrendered, and the French armies disintegrated. The northern anchor of the Maginot Line fell to the Germans, the entire rear line was open to enemy attack, and Hitler's forces capitalized on this weakness, swerving toward the sea and the rear of the Maginot Line. This intelligence lapse proved fatal for the French, compounded by faltering military planning. The French Army fell apart in the face of repeated strafing by German planes and an onslaught by German tanks, armored motorcycles, and infantry equipped with machine guns. Some French soldiers retreated, but most continued to fight.

A mass exodus of the French population ensued. As they fled the invader, German air bombardment, panic-stricken refugees were mowed down with machine guns. The fleeing population clogged roads and added to the crippling of France's military defense. The June 10 decision to move the French capital added to the confusion and dismay of Parisians. Two million people fled Paris. Premier Paul Reynaud tried to shore up his authority by appointing Marshal Pétain to his administration as vice premier. When Reynaud sought to appoint a middle-aged brigadier general as deputy war minister, one staff member referred to the forty-nine-year-old Charles de Gaulle as a mere child.

Before World War II, de Gaulle had urged French military leaders to improve strategies and tactics by stressing mechanized warfare. He advocated the coordinated use of tanks and aircraft and the use of combined army, air force, and naval operations; surprise and shock techniques; and a more imaginative and better-coordinated military intelligence system. His advice was not adopted to the extent that it should have been by his French superiors. In spring 1940, however, German military leaders took full advantage of de Gaulle's ideas. Jenny Vaughan's biography of de Gaulle discusses his 1934 publication, *The Army of the Future*, and his suggestions concerning mechanization of troops, specialized army divisions, and the opposition he faced from the French military establishment.[12]

Once the French lines were broken, the fallaciousness of the Maginot Line mentality became only too obvious. Gross inadequacies of the French High Command's strategic thinking were in large part the fault of a miserable performance of the French intelligence service. By June 14, the Germans had marched into Paris. They then swept through Dijon, Lyon, and, eventually, Bordeaux and the Spanish border. Mussolini opportunistically declared war on France and Britain, as the Italian Army occupied Menton, a short distance from Nice.

Although they were overwhelmed and surrendered in Flanders, the Allied troops fought bravely though their backs were against the water of the English Channel. German radio broadcasters boasted that their Luftwaffe aviators would sink every vessel that attempted to escape to Britain. Nevertheless, many British and French soldiers were evacuated and lived to fight another day—returning to France in June and August 1944. The British Expeditionary Force that was pushed back to Dunkirk crossed the Channel in a variety of vessels, fishing boats, ferries, tugboats, cargo boats, and more. A total of 338,226 troops were safely removed from Dunkirk, 139,097 of them French. However, the French Navy complained that they were not given enough advance notice of the intentions of the British forces.

Rear Adm. Paul Auphan and Jacques Mordal, both of them firsthand Dunkirk observers, claimed that the British moved quickly toward the evacuation of their army without even informing their French allies of their decision. At a meeting of the Franco-British War Council held on May 2 at Vincennes, headquarters of French commanding general Maxime Weygand, Churchill did not utter a word about British intentions during the conference.[13]

Weygand and the head of the French Navy, Adm. Jean Louis Xavier François Darlan, were outraged by the unilateral British decision, convinced that such an evacuation would disorganize the entire French defense. According to Auphan and Mordal, "When two or three weeks later, the question of a separate Franco-German armistice arose, it was the opinion of the majority of French leaders that after such a breach of trust and disregard for the spirit of teamwork, France was not required to make a greater sacrifice for the common good than England had."[14]

Hundreds of miles of territory and the Channel ports were lost to the Germans. The pride and will to resist remained alive in many French people, but the defeat of spring 1940 was massive. Writing in *Harper's* magazine a short time after the event, Robert de Saint Jean observed that "the defeat of France which for many years to come will be a theme of discussion is a unique happening in history for very precise reason. Up to the present the world has never seen military events entail political consequences involving so many nations and *in so brief a time*."[15]

The German blitzkrieg overwhelmed the French and British armies in spring 1940 because of superior military preparation, intelligence, and generalship. Intelligence mistakes were abetted by French hostility toward the British. The defeatism of Marshal Pétain, politician Pierre Laval, Admiral Darlan, and others added to the political Tower of Babel chaos and instability that disrupted French unity. The Germans defeated the French after six months of fighting a "phony war." The French suffered ninety thousand dead and two hundred thousand wounded between September 1939 and June 1940.[16] The British too sustained heavy losses but continued to fight with the help of their dominions and colonies.

After the French calamity, the British people were issued hand grenades to counter German parachute invaders and told not to run away lest they be machine-gunned from the air, as had happened to civilians in Holland, Belgium, and France. British citizens were also warned not to believe rumors, not to supply any Germans with food, gasoline, or maps, and to go to the police if they noticed anything suspicious. In an article,

"Letter from London" dated June 29, 1940, *New Yorker* commentator Mollie Painter-Downes observed that "the best news of the week for most people was the appointment of Mr. Stimson and Colonel Knox to President Roosevelt's Cabinet."[17] The British people were informed that both U.S. Secretary of War Henry Stimson and U.S. Secretary of the Navy Frank Knox were prominent Republicans who were pro-British. Unlike most Republicans, Stimson and Knox were interventionists rather than isolationists. Both of these exceedingly competent and brave men were vilified at the 1940 Republican Presidential Convention, yet these American patriots were instrumental in transforming a militarily weak United States into the strongest nation on earth.

Another result of the German 1940 spring offensive was the belated closing of ranks in the Allied political field. According to the *Economist* of May 18, "While a conservative British Cabinet was expanding Leftward, a French cabinet, originally perhaps very slightly left, was assuming a broader national basis by taking in two prominent representatives of the extreme Right, M. Louis Marin and M. Jean Ybarnegaray."[18]

Too Little, Too Late

One explanation for the Allied defeats of spring 1940 was that their "too little, too late" military preparation policies ignored the mushrooming of Hitler's war machine. According to World War II historian John Keegan, France had about three thousand tanks compared with Germany's two thousand four hundred, they held the upper hand concerning important military weapons, and their tanks were technically better.[19] However, the French economized on the Maginot Line after deciding that it was too costly to extend the fortifications from Luxembourg to the sea. The Dutch nation's policy of neutrality resulted in the skewed numbers of fifty Dutch air bombers against five thousand German bombers. But while Holland's population was one-tenth that of Germany's, the Dutch had several times more wealth per capita than the Germans. Norway had the fourth largest merchant marine in the world, but this fleet was rendered futile since Norwegians had not built good warships that might have defended their forts.[20] The Germans, by contrast, did not hesitate to build up their military might; they had air superiority over the French and were also better prepared in carrying out coordinated operations that combined the use of infantry, armor, artillery, and aircraft.[21] Once British and French leaders sold out Czechoslovakia to appease Hitler, his generals used French plans to build tanks for Germany, in Czechoslovakia's Skoda plant.

Statistical comparisons dealing with the military strength of the Axis powers versus the Allies became skewed after the German victories of spring 1940. Allied losses included thousands of lives and vast amounts of equipment. Churchill spelled out losses of seven thousand tons of ammunition, ninety thousand rifles, two thousand three hundred guns, one hundred twenty thousand vehicles, and eight thousand antiaircraft guns, most field artillery, and nearly all of the new cannons used by the British in northern France. He described Britain's plight thus: "Never has a great nation been so naked before her foes."[22]

As the French military machine neared its end, Premier Reynaud entreated Britain and the United States to help France. Churchill agreed to help, but efforts to enlist United States support were less successful. *Time* magazine reported in its June 24, 1940, issue that American Fascists, Communists, and isolationists discouraged military preparedness in the United States and help to France and Britain and that American military leaders doubted whether the British alone could stop Germany long enough for America to rearm.

It took French military leaders four days in June 1940 to realize that they had made grievous mistakes in sending their best forces to Belgium and not anticipating massive German attacks through the poorly defended Ardennes Forest. The French High Command had deluded itself by believing the legend that the Ardennes would be inaccessible and impenetrable and safe from a German onslaught. Many years earlier, French military leaders had been warned. One such warning came in 1928 from British military historian Capt. B. H. Liddell Hart who had traveled the alleged impassable Ardennes Forest and found that it was "well-roaded and most of it rolling rather mountainous country" but that "the impassability of the Ardennes has been much exaggerated," he warned in *The English Edition of the Battle of France 1940.*[23]

French military reports were not properly evaluated. Professor Ernest May, in his *Strange Victory: Hitler's Conquest of France,* published in 2000, provided many examples of French and British intelligence failures that ignored warnings of a German attack through the Ardennes. French counteraction plans were inadequate. They did not identify or test their critical presumptions, did not pay attention to abundant information that showed what the Germans were planning, and overlooked the consequences of German military surprises. The shifting of the main German attack from Belgium and Holland to the Ardennes should have alerted French military leaders to reconsider their impenetrability presumption and lead to better preparation. They lacked a system of collecting and analyzing intelligence to serve their decision-making needs. May attributed the German success to a system for mating intelligence and decision making to generate an effective plan and action. Presciently, he wrote, "And it must be added that, in these respects, the United States and most other democracies today resemble France and Britain of 1940, not Germany."[24] The events of December 7, 1941, and of September 11, 2001, attest to May's sagacity. In 1940, French generals neglected to adequately prepare for a surprise attack from a patently dangerous enemy. No attempt was made to understand how or why their foe's thinking might vary from their own and how to promptly react to it. The German leadership, by contrast, identified major weaknesses of the French High Command—the lack of imagination, negligence in preparing for the possibility of surprise attacks, and slowness of corrective response. These failures of a small number of Frenchmen led to the horrible plight of millions of their compatriots, and of thousands of others who fought for French liberation.

Examining the cause of France's defeat sixty years later, May found ample evidence to conclude that "overall, France and its allies turn out to have been better equipped for war than was Germany, with more trained men, more guns, more and better tanks, more bombers and fighters. On the whole, they did not lag even in thinking about the war tanks and airplanes. A few German military men may have been ahead in this respect, but not many. The Allied Commander-in-Chief, General Maurice Gamelin, had worked to increase and improve France's tank forces. The German Army Commander-in-Chief, General Walter von Brauchitsch, by contrast, had tolerated the formation of all-tank divisions but said to his staff that this was wasteful—wars would continue to be decided by foot soldiers and horses. In computer simulations of the war of 1940, if the computer takes control, the Allies won."[25]

This was not how France's defeat was explained shortly after it happened. Repeatedly, the loss was attributed to the neglect of France and other European democracies in falling behind in the production of war equipment, such as enough aircraft. For example, a *Time* magazine reporter claimed that the Germans built "the world's most magnificent military machine in six short years under fanatical Adolf Hitler."[26] While claiming the importance of Germany's superiority in weaponry, the article also noted that "what made the German Army perform as it did was primarily a matter of its leaders' brains and its nation's morale."[27]

Germany's defeat in World War I led to the replacement of its elderly Prussian military officer corps with younger officers capable of developing new military strategies that were carried out by young soldiers, sailors, and airmen. German military forces were energized by Hitler and his coterie. While the French were plagued by economic, political, religious, and social divisiveness, German nationalism was whipped up by Nazi propaganda: that the German people were superior, they were the victims of Jewish treachery and Allied rapaciousness, and they were unified by lies and hatred to avenge undeserved defeat and subsequent hardships. Young men who served Germany's war machine were thus instilled with a distorted and deformed ideology, and a string of victories in June 1940 increased their veneration of National Socialism. Hitler achieved these victories by using a variety of deceptive and innovative tactics: German parachute troops poured down, disguised as French peasants and as women, to set fires in rear area villages; they mixed delayed action bombs with contact bombs, and their dud bombs caused terror; German bombers filled the skies above Allied columns moving along highways. They came down in ear-shattering power dives to bomb and machine-gun civilians on roads.[28] These tactics succeeded in creating hysterical refugees who jammed roads and hampered military movement.

The German military machine was far from invincible, however. Its heavy loss of ships during the 1940 assault on Norway seriously impaired the German Navy's ability to try to obstruct the British troop withdrawal from Dunkirk and its plans for an invasion of Britain. Even at the zenith of its military successes in spring 1940, the mighty German war machine was vulnerable. British pilots were sent to bomb large oil depots in Cologne, Düsseldorf, Aachen, and Hamburg; and Royal Air Force bombing frustrated German plans to invade Britain. In his report of the war, General George C. Marshall wrote that "according to Col. General Jodl, Chief of the Operations Staff of the German High Command, the campaign in France had been undertaken because it was estimated that with the fall of France, England would not continue to fight. The unexpectedly swift victory over France and Great Britain's continuation of the war found the General Staff unprepared for an invasion of England . . . no orders to prepare for the invasion of Britain were issued prior to July 2nd. Field Marshal Kesselring stated that he urged the invasion since it generally was believed in Germany that

England was in a critical condition. Field Marshal Keitel, Chief of Staff of German Armed Forces, however, stated that the risk was thought to be the existence of the British fleet. He said the army was ready but the air force was limited by weather, the navy very dubious. Meanwhile, in the air blitz over England the German Air Force had suffered irreparable losses from which its bombardment arm never recovered."[29]

Gen. Charles de Gaulle followed the June 14, 1940 German occupation of Paris with a radio broadcast from London on June 18 to his compatriots, in which he urged a continued struggle against the Germans. His plea that "France had lost a battle but had not lost the war" was ignored by the vast majority of his demoralized and distressed people. With defeat, France was divided in two—the northern Occupied Zone, under German domination, and the southern Unoccupied Zone, under the jurisdiction of the new French regime, located in the town of Vichy. A French delegation of politicians negotiated the terms of defeat and signed an armistice on June 25. After a long history of democracy and republicanism, conservative leaders sought to reconstruct France into a nationalist and authoritarian state that would resemble its Fascist neighbors. French historian Henry Rousso wrote that "eventually, the line came to be clearly drawn between the Collaboration and the Resistance, groupings diverse in themselves, though clearly differentiated."[30] The Vichy regime called itself the French State and was hostile to republican institutions that were created after the French Revolution, to the Popular Front of the 1930s, and to France's Jewish community. It did not owe its anti-Semitism to the Nazi occupation. It was instead a homegrown French product.

In Fréjus, following the defeat of their nation, French officers toasted Germany's victory. At a railroad station in Nice, one Frenchman reportedly told another, "Thank Christ we lost the war; otherwise, we might, after defeat, still be governed by those left-wing motherfuckers of the Front Populaire."[31] The relief at their nation's defeat was widespread across France in 1940. Many remembered that during the previous war, France lost a quarter of its men between the ages of eighteen and thirty.[32] The French campaign from September 1939 through June 1940 was responsible for the deaths of ninety-two thousand Frenchmen.[33] Returning French soldiers complained that their ammunition had been sabotaged, that ambulances had been transformed into accommodations for officers' lady friends, and declared, over and over, "Nous avons été vendus" or "On nous a vendu"[34] until one could have made a popular song of it—the words and the music of defeat.[35]

All Was Not Lost

From their defeat, the French salvaged two important possessions, both of them outside the country: their Mediterranean fleet and their colonial territories in Africa and Asia. French ships were required, by the terms of the surrender, to return to their home ports, having exacted from the enemy an assurance that these ships would not be used by Germany against France's former allies. Neither Roosevelt nor Churchill wanted to see the French Navy in German hands, concluding that the danger of a German takeover of French ships was too great to risk. Without consulting de Gaulle or any other French official, Churchill decided that drastic action was necessary to prevent Marshal Pétain and his fellow Vichyites from handing the French fleet to the Germans. British intelligence indicated that the French would not do this voluntarily. However, it was assumed that the Vichyites would try to gain Hitler's approval. Churchill did not want to gamble on losing this important asset; and so on July 3, 1940, the British fleet attacked the French squadron base at Mers-el-Kebir, Algeria, without warning. Squads of British military men boarded all French vessels in British ports, forcing naval officers and sailors off the ships and interning them—a devastating blow to French pride. To assuage a furious de Gaulle, the British allowed him, on July 8, to use BBC Radio to denounce the takeover. De Gaulle asked his countrymen to realize that there was not the slightest doubt that the Germans would have used French ships against England or against the Free French, and he claimed that it was better that the British destroy the ships than for them to be used by the Germans.

After the defeat of France, there were intense differences within the French Navy as to the disposition of the national fleet. Admiral Hewitt, in his introduction to Auphan and Mordal's *The French Navy in World War II*, wrote the following: "I understand the regret of the authors that the British and ourselves did not rely on [French Naval Chief] Admiral Darlan's word that the French fleet would never be surrendered intact to the Axis . . . . That Darlan would have been true to his promise, I now firmly believe . . . . Unfortunately, however, conditions at the time were not such as to inspire confidence on the part of the British, nor, later, of their American ally. With an aging Marshal Pétain at the head of the government and such men as Laval[36] wielding political power, who could be sure that Darlan, even were he determined not to give up the fleet, would remain in power? And, for that matter, Darlan himself was suspect, owing to his apparent dealings with the Nazis—dealings which, it is now revealed, had the aim of securing the best possible bargain for France without sacrificing her Navy."[37] Some French naval officers preferred a handover to the Nazis over the Allies. In one instance, several officers tried to sabotage their ship, the *Emile Bertin*, a light cruiser, "rather than see it enter the war on the side of the Allies."[38]

After the British sunk the French fleet and humiliated its navy, full powers were granted to Marshal Pétain whose Vichy government retaliated by severing diplomatic relations with the British. Britain imposed a naval blockade against France and French possessions. President Roosevelt's State Department agent, Robert Murphy, later wrote, in *Diplomat Among Warriors*, that "the British attack [at Mers-El-Kebir] was unnecessary and cost much more than it gained. Perhaps this was the most serious British mistake of the war. Simultaneously it undermined the influence of the pro-British moderates in Vichy and of de Gaulle in London."[39]

French enmity of the British stemmed from more than the British attacks on the French fleet. France blamed its defeat on the British, arguing that more British planes should have been provided during their battles with the Germans. French animosity toward their former British allies was provoked by Britain's refusal to surrender, their withdrawal to their home islands, and Churchill's support of de Gaulle and his determination to continue fighting the Germans. The British blockade worsened the shortage of food in France. Admiral Darlan told the U.S. Ambassador to Vichy France, Adm. William Leahy, that the Germans had released two hundred thousand tons of wheat from their warehouse in northern France. Leahy observed that Darlan did not tell him what the Germans had gotten in return. Pétain did not trust Darlan, nor did Leahy. However, Leahy did request that Roosevelt order the shipment of necessities to the French.[40] The Vichyites and the Nazis used the Mers-El-Kebir incident, where nearly one thousand three hundred French sailors were killed, to their considerable propaganda benefit: Vichyites insulted de Gaulle with impunity; recruitment efforts to strengthen the struggle against the Axis were frustrated; recruitment of Resistance fighters diminished, as did financial support; and French Anglophobia soared.

Adm. Jean François Darlan

Adm. Jean Louis Xavier François Darlan served the Vichy government as its military commander in chief and premier. From 1936 to 1940,

Darlan was chief of France's Navy and, in 1940-41, his nation's minister of marine. He was a nationalist who despised the British and their navy and was certain at first that the Germans would defeat Britain. However, Darlan considered the French Navy his property and vowed not to surrender it to the Germans. He was an opportunist who lived in a lavish manner during the Vichy era. Before Admiral Leahy was sent to Vichy, President Roosevelt told him that Pétain did not trust Darlan and instructed him to tell Pétain what Darlan and other Vichy ministers were keeping from the Marshal.[41] Darlan told Leahy in August 1941 that if the Americans would invade southern France with six thousand planes and five hundred thousand troops, he would welcome them.[42] It is doubtful that Leahy reported that conversation to Pétain.

When Admiral Hewitt was asked about Darlan, the American answered, "I heard much about Admiral Darlan from a friend in whose admiralty house he was staying at the time he was assassinated, and also from other leading French officers, who were very loyal to him, and they all without exception said that Admiral Darlan was thinking of France first, and that he would never have turned over the Toulon fleet to the Nazis. There were great doubts about him, before the landing [of North Africa]. He seemed to be leaning towards the Germans. But all his people say 'No, he was just trying to do the best for France.'"[43]

France's naval fleet became its main weapon after the surrender to the Germans in June 1940. Darlan, who helped to strengthen the navy, became his nation's military leader. His pragmatism served his shortsighted opportunism, but he did not promote technological improvements, such as aircraft carriers, antiaircraft defense, and radar. Preservation of the French Empire was paramount to Darlan, but that did not stop him from making a deal with General Eisenhower that ran counter to official Vichy policy concerning French North African colonies, thereby double-crossing his superior, Marshal Pétain. Frequently Darlan acted completely on his own without bothering to discuss important issues with Pétain or anyone else. Despite his conciliatory overtures toward the Germans, they did not trust him either.

Neither Darlan nor Pétain nor any other Vichy leader controlled the calumny of the Parisian press. It spit sulfurous criticism at Leahy, who was portrayed as a tool of Jewish bankers, a former British agent, and a Freemason who forced Pétain to appoint his "sailor friend" Darlan to his number two position. Pétain did not have confidence in Darlan, but he also confided to Leahy that he did not have anyone who would be better.

For their part, the Americans wanted to use Darlan to achieve their goals and then get rid of him. On one occasion, Roosevelt sent a message to Churchill in which he said, "It is impossible to keep a collaborator who is a Fascist in civil power any longer than is absolutely necessary."[44]

Darlan's likes and dislikes are also germane. He pried money from a reluctant French parliament to build up a powerful navy under his command. Notwithstanding his contempt for the British, there was little doubt about his handing over the French fleet to the Axis. Despite his collaboration with the Germans, Ambassador Murphy claimed that Darlan was more anti-Nazi than he was anti-British.[45]

Playing Games with the Vichy French-German Armistice Treaty

Augustin Leon Guilliame was a French Army officer who deceived the German and Italian armistice commissioners in Morocco. A 1914 graduate of France's military academy Saint-Cyr, he was assigned to frontline duty in World War I. Guilliame was captured and imprisoned in German prison camps and was released in 1919. His next assignment was in Morocco where he commanded Moroccan troops known as the goums—an elite native army paramilitary police who were trained, armed, clothed, and equipped by the French. They served as guides and scouts and often led combat units. In difficult mountain terrains, such as the Atlas Mountains of Morocco from which they hailed, goum troops were especially helpful. Extreme weather conditions did not bother them; and they were praised for their endurance, cheerful disposition, and marksmanship. Guilliame and other French Army officers liked them because of their loyalty and military abilities. After the surrender of French forces in June 1940 and the subsequent armistice, Guilliame developed a plan to use the goums for continuing the war and redeeming French honor.

The armistice agreement permitted the French to keep one hundred twenty thousand troops stationed in North Africa. Much of the equipment had to be surrendered to the German or Italian armistice commission or destroyed. Guilliame succeeded in convincing the commission that the goums were a police force, not soldiers—a claim supported by the fact that the budget classification showed that the goums were financed as a police force necessary in maintaining order among warring Moroccan tribes and in preventing gun smuggling at Moroccan borders. The German and Italian armistice commissioners accepted Guilliame's story. He also succeeded in having rifles, machine guns, and ammunition hidden in the Atlas Mountains, on the farms of French settlers, and buried in Morocco's rocky terrain. The French also used the mountains and deserts of Algeria and Tunisia to hide weapons, ammunition, and other supplies.

Edward L. Bimberg's *The Moroccan Goums: Tribal Warriors in a Modern War* explains that "the mountains and deserts of Morocco, Algeria, and Tunisia formed far too great an expanse for the inspection teams to explore. Besides, the cafés and bordellos of Casablanca, Algeria, and Tunisia were far more interesting than the barren wastes of [Africa] and that's what the conquerors preferred to inspect."[46] The German and Italian armistice commissioners saw the goums as small dark-skinned men wearing bathrobe-type uniforms, with sandals and turbans, armed only with knives and rifles; and they were not viewed as a military threat by the Axis inspectors. Nazi and Fascist supermen did not take the goums, who marched leading their goats, as serious fighting men and agreed that they were only what Guilliame represented them to be—rustic, primitive policemen and not potentially dangerous enemy soldiers. Later events proved that the goums were underestimated by their foes and others.

The Vichy Regime

When Marshal Pétain was authorized to create a new French regime on July 10, 1940, in a gambling casino in Vichy, the French Chamber of Deputies also voted 568 to 80 to replace the 1789 watchwords of "liberty, equality, fraternity" with "work, family, and fatherland." Pétain and his followers wanted a fundamental change of French politics and society and considered themselves free to abolish the Third Republic and repeal the 1875 constitution. Many Frenchmen were disgusted by their nation's political instability, disorder, and scandals during the 1930s and were eager for a reign of order and stability that Hitler supposedly provided the Germans. A national revolution would return France to its traditional values of patriotism and authoritarianism and would curb freedom's excesses and disorder, political instability, and corruption. It soon became apparent, however, that many Vichyites were, in reality, more intent on settling old scores, informing on people of contrary views, and hunting for scapegoats such as the former premiers of the Third Republic—Blum, Daladier, and Reynaud.

Pierre Laval, a fifty-seven-year-old lawyer and politician, was the Vichy government's second in command. He was viewed as the evil genius of the highly respected Marshal Pétain but lacked the Marshal's prestigious standing in the eyes of the public. Laval was the son of a Chatelaine village innkeeper and butcher who became rich representing trade union members. In 1914, he was elected to parliament as a Socialist and delivered his first parliamentary speech in 1917 on behalf of French Socialists who wanted to attend a meeting in Stockholm to discuss peace terms to end World War I. Defeated in the 1919 parliamentary elections, Laval returned to government a few years later after being elected mayor of a working-class town. Representing the people of the same constituency, Aubervilliers, Laval was reelected to parliament.

As Laval's law career prospered, his political inclinations progressed to the right. Within a short time, he bought a newspaper and radio stations, and his career flourished. In 1930, he was appointed France's minister of labor; and by 1931 he became premier, heading a conservative government. His use of money, flattery, and intrigue enhanced his personal standing. Ideological integrity was of little importance to him, with one exception: neither a pacifist nor an idealist, Laval believed that war was senseless. He was not a supporter of Benito Mussolini, but after the Italian invasion of Abyssinia in 1935, he opposed the French leftists who wanted to drag France into war to halt Italian expansionism. Laval believed that the abilities he had used to become rich and socially prominent should have been deployed to prevent France's entry into World War II. The Pétain-Laval political leadership was a marriage of convenience; the revered military hero needed the disreputable but highly successful politician, and together they negotiated the terms of France's surrender in June 1940.

French soldiers were assigned to ensure internal order following the collapse of the French State; otherwise, French troops were expected to return to civilian life. The armistice excluded Negro troops and the Senegalese battalions that remained in France, awaiting repatriation to Africa. They were placed in special camps. Some 1.5 million French prisoners of war remained in Germany as hostages. No drastic alterations were taken in terms of realignment of the French military until 1941 and 1942, when Jews and members of Masonic orders were ousted from the French Officer Corps.[47] Freemason and Communist organizations were outlawed by October 1940. The regime's anti-Semitism policy denied French Jews employment opportunities in public service, teaching, movies, and the press. These exclusions were expanded in July 1941. Foreign Jews were to be interned. The powerful French media elite rallied against Communists, foreigners, and the British. A witch hunt was orchestrated, and Léon Blum and the Popular Front leaders were reviled. Pétain sought to distance himself from Nazi anti-Semitism in public; yet he insisted that Jews be excluded from national, education, and justice positions, confessing to the French chief rabbi that the Germans compelled him to be anti-Semitic.[48] The terrible plight of Jews and other so-called non-Aryans under the control of zealous French toadies seeking to ingratiate themselves with the Nazis was far worse for its victims in French areas than those administered by Italians. Italy had no historical tradition of racism or anti-Semitism. Mussolini and others in his government were less eager than many of the French to cooperate in executing Nazi atrocities.

Recognizing that he could not force the French to continue fighting the Germans, Roosevelt in 1940 decided to recognize the Vichy regime as legitimate, treating it as an independent sovereign nation. While not approving many of the regime's policies, the Roosevelt administration did not condemn them. FDR sought to maintain a good relationship with the Vichy government as well as with the various French Resistance groups, trying to gain whatever benefits the United States could from the opposing factions. Roosevelt therefore disapproved of de Gaulle's appeals for direct economic and military assistance but instructed the British to transfer help from what they received under the Lend-Lease program. At the start of the Lend-Lease program, de Gaulle's popular standing in France and North Africa was slight while Marshal Pétain and Admiral Darlan had the overwhelming support of the French people and their military chiefs. By the time of the invasion of North Africa in November 1942 (Operation Torch), the desperate economic condition of the people of North Africa was only too obvious; German economic exploitation and the lack of assistance resulted in widespread misery and the threat of political upheaval.

Roosevelt knew that many Americans wanted to support a French leader whose goal it was to defeat the Germans, but General de Gaulle was deemed unacceptable. His insistence that France be looked upon as a great power, despite its defeat, was one reason for Roosevelt's disapproval of de Gaulle. FDR distrusted the haughty, self-anointed, nonelected de Gaulle, whose lack of condescension and effacement added to his unpalatability. His courage, patriotism, and his great military and political abilities were outweighed by unfavorable perceptions of his personality and his supposed dictatorial ambitions. De Gaulle was also the victim of vicious criticism from French leftists and rightists, as rumors spread that he and his followers were intent on establishing a dictatorship. Repeatedly, de Gaulle insisted that he was the leader of a proud and important nation that he would help regain its democracy and prestige. But Roosevelt and his ambassador to Vichy France, Admiral Leahy, pursued a policy toward the regime that regarded temporary recognition of Pétain's government as indispensable. The president was also intent in having the French people choose their leader.

Realizing the importance of having an ambassador whose ability and integrity he trusted, Roosevelt had selected Leahy to represent the U.S. at the difficult post of Vichy. Leahy's record of service was a distinguished one: he climbed to the top post in the navy as chief of naval operations; served as governor of Puerto Rico; and, starting in 1942, was chief of staff to Presidents Roosevelt and Truman. In 1941, Leahy was sent as ambassador to Vichy on the condition that Vichy would not join the Germans' military. Such a policy made sense since there were indications that many Vichy stalwarts opposed fighting the United States. Leahy suggested to the British that if they removed their support from de Gaulle and his followers, Pétain might move closer to Britain. Roosevelt did not want to change his recognition of Vichy until the French had been liberated and had decided who should lead them.

Pétain and other Vichy leaders were eager to maintain good relations with a neutral United States for a number of reasons. First, the U.S. was a source of supplies. Second, American recognition of the Vichy government legitimized its international status. Third, Vichy leaders believed that a neutral U.S. could serve French interests well as a potential arbitrator to end a fruitless war. Fourth, the U.S. was seen as a counterbalance to Germany, and to Japan in Indochina. The Vichy leaders did their utmost to convince the United States that France would remain autonomous and neutral under its armistice treaty with Germany, and their propaganda chief told the American Press Association on November 15, 1940, that a break with the United States would be horrible.[49]

Controversies developed between Americans and French government leaders concerning various facets of assistance programs. For example, the United States demanded that the French pay cash for civilian goods while allowing Britain, Russia, and China to receive assistance on credit or a Lend-Lease arrangement. The alleged inequity, according to

American policymakers, stemmed from France's failure to pay its World War I debt to the United States. Another disagreement stemmed from American businesspeople trying to take advantage of France's distress in some of its colonies where there were opportunities to pluck profits for private enterprise.

David Schoenbrun, the distinguished American journalist and radio commentator, in his biography, *The Three Lives of Charles de Gaulle*, viewed Leahy's appointment as U.S. ambassador as unfortunate, claiming that he had virtually no political or diplomatic experience and was not temperamentally suited for such an assignment. Critics of his tenure claimed that Admiral Leahy was unable to evaluate the French sentiment in favor of the Gaullist movements; he was blinded by Vichy flattery and falsehoods; he provided erroneous reports to Roosevelt; and he retained outdated and wrong opinions of French conditions in 1943 and in 1944 when he returned to the United States. Despite such criticisms, Roosevelt elevated Leahy following his Vichy assignment.[50] His alleged political inexperience was offset by his unquestioned loyalty to Roosevelt, and it was reasonable for the president to assume that the respected admiral could deal with French military leaders such as Pétain and Darlan better than a civilian diplomat.

Roosevelt also turned to a career diplomat, Robert D. Murphy, to carry out his policies. Endowed with ample talent for maneuvering in turbulent and politically dangerous waters, Murphy was FDR's point man in politically treacherous North Africa. Murphy had two objectives: to ensure that the French fleet and French Africa remained out of Nazi hands and to establish a link with North African French forces to earn their support for a potential United States involvement in North Africa on the side of the Allies. Compounding the difficulties in achieving these objectives were American opponents of the Vichy government, who with good cause looked upon it as a Nazi tool. American supporters of the Vichy regime preferred this traditionalist, conservative, and authoritarian administration to its turbulent, scandal-ridden parliamentarian predecessor. Americans on the political right, left, and in the center were dissatisfied with Roosevelt's policies toward the French in the early 1940s.

It is arguable whether Roosevelt merited the criticism of not being a model manager, of making hash out of organization charts, and of following wasteful delegation procedures. But he was vigilant concerning Vichy policymaking, North African politics, economics, and military intelligence. He assigned naval attachés to keep an eye on the Vichy government. He grasped the big picture, realizing that the regime controlled about one hundred thousand troops and a fleet and that these were potentially powerful Allied assets. FDR did not hesitate to bend management and other rules to achieve his objectives. He let Secretary of State Cordell Hull serve as a lightning rod and receive the harsh criticism of anti-Vichy critics. He ordered Murphy to bypass the State Department and to send his reports directly to the president. Both the State Department and the de Gaulle forces were to be kept in the dark, and Roosevelt disregarded their sentiments. He was more concerned about protecting the lives and limbs of American soldiers and sailors who were to invade North Africa and France. His son, Franklin Roosevelt Jr., served as a naval officer in the invasion of North Africa; and his other sons also served in the U.S. Armed Forces during World War II.

Murphy's many important services included the implementation of the groundwork for the invasion of North Africa in November 1942. Its success greatly facilitated Allied victories in the Mediterranean. Murphy completed political, economic, and intelligence surveys of North Africa; helped obtain the cooperation of Arabs; and diminished the harmful effects of German propaganda. American suppliers shipped cotton cloth to Arab leaders—an important gesture to Muslims who buried their dead in cotton robes so that they could enter heaven. Muslims also liked tea, and the Americans provided it.

Murphy was not only taken into President Roosevelt's confidence, he was also informed about Allied military action in North Africa. He conducted continuous public opinion surveys to find out who was for the Allies and who was for the Axis powers. He was exceedingly shrewd and admirably suited for his task. Before the November 1942 Allied invasion, Murphy suggested to General Eisenhower that cooperation between the American military and French military supporters could be facilitated by a conference in North Africa. The meeting had to be arranged in the utmost secrecy, using both an airplane and a submarine, to safeguard the lives of the participants. Eisenhower's deputy, Gen. Mark W. Clark, and a small American staff were chosen to represent the United States. Local suspicion was raised, and the pro-Allied French delegates to the meeting fled. Clark and his team were forced to hide until they could return to the submarine, made difficult by bad weather. As a result of the meeting, American leaders gained some understanding of the political coloration of a number of French officials and military men. Most importantly, Murphy discovered that the American people and their government were highly regarded by the French.[51] Murphy carried out Roosevelt's diplomatic policy and exaggerated his characteristics by becoming nearly every French leader's friend, with the exception of de Gaulle who detested him.

De Gaulle never forgave Roosevelt or Murphy and persisted in holding them personally liable for their purported arrogance and ignorance in humiliating him and his forces during France's lowest historical ebb tide. To carry out FDR's policies during that period, Murphy was involved in an OSS proposal to subsidize a secret anti-Gaullist newspaper published by another French Resistance faction. Pro-de Gaulle American media and other supporters persisted in their criticism of Murphy in 1944 and thereafter. Less than a month after Operation Dragoon, the influential *Washington Post* published a series of articles by A. Mowrer, a *Chicago Daily News* war correspondent in both wars, and Emanuel Celler, who represented the Brooklyn, New York, congressional district where the author's family lived. Mowrer attacked Murphy's fitness to advise General Eisenhower on German problems—a strong critique that was based upon Murphy's alleged connection with "the reactionaries" in North Africa. Murphy asked whether *Post* publisher Eugene Meyer had anything against him personally. Meyer acknowledged that he did not know Murphy but that he approved the critical articles and took responsibility for them. Murphy went further by asking the paper's editor whether Gaullist pressures had influenced the articles. Meyer reprimanded Murphy for his crude approach in questioning him and accused Murphy of acting in a manner unfitting a professional diplomat and that he could not conceive how Murphy could discharge his duties efficiently.[52] Joining in the vicious attacks against Murphy was the left-leaning, short-lived Marshall Field-financed newspaper, *PM*. Murphy's mother was of German origin, and he was concerned about that fact being used against him. He subsequently served as United States ambassador to Belgium during the Truman administration and as ambassador to Japan under Eisenhower's administration.[53] In 1958 when Eisenhower was president, he appointed his good friend Murphy to a special mission in North Africa. According to Schoenbrun, "this appointment of his personal enemy [Murphy] to a consultative post with France embittered de Gaulle and soured his otherwise excellent relations with Eisenhower."[54]

Franco-American Relations

Before and during World War II, French Anglophobia exceeded their anti-Americanism. Prior to World War I, Professor Julian Jackson of the University of Wales, in Swansea, wrote, "The French attitude towards America was one of mild condescension"; and when the United States entered into that war, it took the French time to appreciate that Americans might have independent policies that differed from theirs.[55] French refusal to accept the reality that Americans would want to pursue policies that did not coincide with French interests persisted during World War II. One illustration is a September 27, 1939, report provided by an American naval attaché stationed in Paris, reporting to the U.S. Office of Naval Intelligence. Outlined in this document are the attaché's observations that "French hopes of Americans joining war [Reliable]. It is surprising to hear from many French people, some through ignorance and others through press propaganda, the question, 'What is America going to do; when is she going to decide?' A good many people mistook the president's address to Congress on the neutrality law for a clear-out demand for American participation in the war. This was partly due to the headlines in the French press: 'America Announces Tomorrow!' A member of this office, who went to a nearby store the day prior to the president's message, was immediately accosted by the proprietor, who said, 'When is America going to decide—now is the time before it is too late—I see Roosevelt has postponed his message until tomorrow.' This man actually believed that the president's address was to be a demand for American participation in the war. When I explained that it was merely to remove an embargo so that we could sell war supplies, he nearly keeled over and remarked, 'You're out for business.'"[56]

Frenchmen might be disgruntled at American independence, excesses, uniformity, mechanization, and boorishness; but during World War II, as the leader of France's primary benefactor, Roosevelt had acquired an attitude of contempt as extreme as his admiration for China. He considered France a source of decay in the world, a politically and socially sick nation that lying down before Hitler and giving way to Japanese in Indochina had forfeited the right to be respected. Roosevelt saw de Gaulle as a pompous adventurer who represented only a clique of followers and who secretly intended to assume the dictatorship of his country after the liberation, according to Julian Hurstfield.[57] Yale University's Gaddis Smith's portrayal of Roosevelt's view of the

French and their devastating defeat is similar to Hurstfield's. Diverse American observers rebuked the French for their internal weaknesses, their complacency, their self-indulgence, and the collapse of their willpower.[58]

An example of the torturous relationship between the American government and de Gaulle's Free French troops occurred on September 23, 1940, when Free French troops, backed by a British naval squadron, attempted to seize Dakar, a base on the western coast of Africa. Their attempt was unsuccessful, much to the delight of Hitler, as Pétain had sent reinforcements to secure Dakar in advance of the Allied attempt. Marshal Pétain also had Gibraltar bombed as further retaliation for the failed maneuver. The importance of these actions was that they clearly indicated to Hitler that Vichy, with Pétain's defense of the colonies, could successfully thwart any future Allied attacks in Northwest Africa. It also appeared plausible that Pétain might be convinced to fight the British. By not allowing Spain to take over French Morocco, Hitler hoped that France would join anti-British forces. On October 24, 1940, Hitler assured Pétain that if France would help Germany accelerate the defeat of Britain, France would get a peace settlement on easier terms and would also benefit by the repatriation of British-owned African colonial possessions. Although Pétain agreed to share in the spoils of an Axis victory, he did not commit France in the active engagement of war against her former ally.

Although Marshal Pétain was a traditionalist who viewed the divisive politics of the French Third Republic with contempt, that did not prevent him from engaging in Machiavellian machinations. As long as his regime was not threatened by the United States, he was amenable to getting along with the Americans. De Gaulle was regarded by Vichyites as a British puppet.

Secretary of State Cordell Hull had little enthusiasm at first for de Gaulle and his Free French organization. One explanation that was widely cited at the time was that de Gaulle sympathizers described Hull in an insulting manner on the radio and in the press. This feather ruffling had to do with the Saint Pierre and Miquelon incident—two stony little islands off the coast of Newfoundland, Canada. De Gaulle's supporters had been successful in winning over the residents of these twin islands, whose strategic importance was that they possessed weather and radio transmitter equipment that could relay signals to German submarines.

After the painful and humiliating naval losses at Pearl Harbor on December 7, 1941, Admiral Leahy was opposed to the prospect of the French Navy, controlled by the Vichy government, fighting the Free French for these strategic coastal islands. About a week later, on December 13, 1941, Roosevelt notified Pétain that the United States desired that the status quo be maintained. On Christmas Eve, Secretary Hull was notified that French naval forces friendly to de Gaulle had seized the islands despite de Gaulle's promise otherwise. Hull issued a communiqué, letting the world know that he deemed de Gaulle to be a liar and a cheat and that he would have nothing to do with him. The Frenchman did not suffer slights to his honor or that of his motherland lightly and was furious at the communiqué. Eventually tempters cooled, but both men had irritated Churchill and Roosevelt. After this episode, FDR excluded Hull from top-level discussions when French matters were considered and relied more on Robert Murphy, the State Department's representative in North Africa, who became his emissary concerning French policymaking.

For a considerable period, Roosevelt was wrong concerning some of his French policy conclusions: that civil war would develop in France, that de Gaulle would establish a dictatorship and sided with the Communist faction of the Resistance, and that de Gaulle would frustrate United Nations policies to create trusteeships in Indochina and other colonial areas. One explanation for FDR's mistakes is that he gave credence to reports from Admiral Leahy, his ambassador to Vichy, France, and to French General Henri Giraud, among others. Even after D-day and Operation Dragoon, FDR persisted in his antagonism toward de Gaulle and his forces, despite the pro-de Gaulle advocacy of the major American newspapers, magazines, and radio. Secretary of War Henry Stimson, Secretary of State Hull, and Ambassador Murphy later supported de Gaulle. Despite his dislike of the Frenchman, Roosevelt and American military leaders increasingly recognized de Gaulle's importance in winning the war in Europe.

Some Findings

Untangling the complex web of the confusing history of relationships between American and French leaders during the first half of the 1940s, of who was correct and who was mistaken, we find the following:

1. There were good reasons supporting President Roosevelt's recognition of the Vichy regime despite the cries of opposition in the media. (The author recalls newspaper, magazine, and radio commentators belittling FDR as an appeaser of the French Fascist government.) However, the president did succeed in retaining an American presence in Africa and imposing pressure on Pétain, Laval, and Darlan and helped thwart Vichy France becoming a complete ally of Hitler.

2. The benefits gained from Roosevelt's policies were enormous: Vichyites were prevented from harming American interests after the U.S. provided economic assistance to the French; the Allies were rewarded with the pivotal control of the Mediterranean; and they gained a substantial part of the French Navy, their bases, and maintenance of the status quo in the West Indies.

3. Airfields on both sides of the Mediterranean were under German and Italian control at the beginning of World War II, and the British Navy was confronted with the serious problem of maintaining communication with Egypt and the Suez Canal. By August 15, 1944, and the Allied invasion of southern France, the Germans were divested of their position in the Mediterranean through sea and air mastery; were prevented from establishing bases in Dakar that would allow their surface ships, submarines, and aircraft to threaten the Allies; and were deprived of the opportunity of endangering American hemispheric safety.

4. More was involved than American diplomatic and economic policies. The Allies were lucky that Hitler ignored his naval advisors, who understood sea power strategy and urged control of the Mediterranean. When the Germans could have seized this important route, Hitler diverted the attention of his military forces, declaring war on the Soviet Union on June 21, 1941. To a considerable extent, the pressure on the French and North Africa was reduced. The balance of strength at sea that had been upset by the collapse of France was restored by Allied victories in the Mediterranean. And, of course, Hitler was wrong when he proclaimed that the Allies were incapable of solving the problem of amphibious landings. Later, he claimed that the successful Mediterranean invasion had proceeded "only with the help of traitors."[59] Hitler also predicted that Americans would be ineffectual warriors and no match for proven Nazi superiority.

CHAPTER 3

UNITED STATES—BEFORE AND AFTER
PEARL HARBOR

T his chapter is primarily concerned with American military intelligence and war preparation before and after the Pearl Harbor attack. President Franklin Roosevelt's penchant for the gathering and analysis of French and other foreign national military intelligence began many years before the outbreak of World War II. Adm. Henry Kent Hewitt and U.S. naval attachés stationed in major capitals throughout the world were engaged in this undertaking. While seeking to remedy the worst economic and social depression that befell a huge proportion of Americans, and when an overwhelming percentage of American voters wanted parsimonious military expenditures, neutrality, and nonintervention in foreign conflicts, Roosevelt tried to guide his people toward strengthening the woefully weak American military forces and rearming World War I Allies.

Among the many brave American leaders of the Republican Party who assisted the president and their fellow citizens were Henry L. Stimson, Frank Knox, Wendell Willkie, and William J. Donovan. Another patriot who disliked Roosevelt, his New Deal and most of its economic policies was the prodigious James V. Forrestal. He served as U.S. secretary of the navy and was a firsthand witness of the Dragoon landing. This modest man used his extraordinary abilities and energy to lead a vast American naval expansion.

The American production of ships, tanks, aircraft, and other war necessities have been justifiably heralded as phenomenal. But the record indicates serious shortcomings, such as inadequate planning, outrageous war profiteering, war production stoppages, and a variety of flaws. World War II reports from the General Accounting Office and findings of Senator Harry S. Truman's War Production Investigation Committee provide particulars of many ignoble practices that have been swept under the rug.

The development of amphibious operations in the Mediterranean and elsewhere during World War II by a master of this specialty, Admiral Hewitt, merit examination. He provided a valuable and meticulous record of his initial experience in amphibious operations. An account of the history and development of LSTs and other amphibious craft built after December 7, 1941, that were vital to the success of the Dragoon invasion and other operations deserves discussion.

Rebecca Robbins Raines's addition to the vast literature dealing with the Pearl Harbor attack has not received adequate attention. Her account of one of the important failures of military communications that led Americans into World War II centers on an unfortunate decision by then Col. George S. Patton in 1939 to block the improvement of a communications facility on an army post located in Fort Myers, Virginia. Patton's magnificent leadership during World War II should not, and will not, be overlooked in this book, nor will it ignore his aborted designation to command the Seventh Army's invasion of southern France, his friendship with Gen. Alexander Patch who was ultimately chosen to lead Dragoon, and their subsequent joining of forces to invade Germany.

Another American military commander who made enormous contributions to World War II victory in Europe, through his administrative and diplomatic contributions to the successful invasions of Normandy and southern France, was Adm. Harold R. Stark. However, he has not received the favorable recognition due him for his important service as the U.S. naval commander in Europe. The cognoscenti are aware of his splendid logistical and alliance-building record, but Stark happened to be chief of naval operations on December 7, 1941, and his reputation was unjustly tarred. But that's another story that's readily available elsewhere.[1]

A Presidential Request for Information

Below is a copy of President Roosevelt's letter[2] of July 14, 1943, to Navy Secretary Frank Knox, and a copy of Knox's memo[3] to the director of U.S. Naval Intelligence, Rear Adm. H. C. Train.

These letters generated voluminous responses from U.S. naval attachés stationed in nine countries mentioned by the president. The author has obtained copies of these dispatches and has included some in this work.

July 14, 1942

Dear Frank: S07 16 99

    I should like to have copies of the despatches of our Naval Attaches which estimate or express any opinion regarding the probability or improbability of an outbreak of war, or which refer in any way to the estimates of potential military strength of any of the countries involved. I am concerned with those despatches dating from January 1, 1937 until such time as our Naval Attaches left the following countries:

    Germany, Japan, Italy, Bulgaria, Austria
    Occupied France, Belgium

    I should also like the similar despatches from England, dated from January 1, 1937 to the outbreak of the war in September, 1939.

    I should like our despatches bearing on this subject from Russia from January 1, 1937 until the present time.

Sincerely yours,

Franklin D Roosevelt

The Honorable Frank Knox,
Secretary of the Navy
Navy Department,
Washington, D.C.

THE SECRETARY OF THE NAVY

WASHINGTON

July 15, 1943

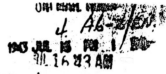

S07 16 99

MEMORANDUM FOR: REAR ADMIRAL H. C. TRAIN, USN

My dear Admiral:

Please note the attached letter from
the President which clearly expresses what he
desires. Will you take steps to have this data
gotten together at once and sent down to me so
that I can comply with the President's desires?

Yours truly,

Frank Knox

Attachment

There was precedent for Roosevelt's use of U.S. naval attachés to gather military information concerning foreign nations. Capt. Wyman H. Packard, USN (Ret.), wrote that as early as May 1866, Navy Secretary Gideon Welles instructed Assistant Navy Secretary Gustavus Fox to collect information concerning foreign navies. "Fox was to observe foreign methods of building, repairing, and laying up naval vessels and to compare European naval vessels with those of the United States. Fox visited ports in England, France, Denmark, and Finland on his way to Russia; the return trip included stops in Sweden, Germany, France again, and various Mediterranean ports during the winter before arriving in the United States in May 1867."[4] Seventy years later, naval intelligence reports remained crucial to gathering information on foreign sentiment.

On September 12, 1938, an American naval attaché reported from Berlin that "at a dinner for attachés, the Germans made the statement that the United States would never send another army to Europe. There could never be another war between Germany and the United States."[5] This statement implied that Germany felt that it could act as it pleased in Europe, regardless of U.S. opinion. Other naval attaché reports of the late 1930s and early 1940s warned American authorities of potential enemy plots against the U.S. and its leaders. On January 16, 1941, a naval attaché reported that "Mussolini and Hitler have planned and ordered the murdering of Roosevelt in addition to sabotage activities in America, especially New York." Nearly a month later, the U.S. naval attaché stationed in Germany reported that a "German landing will be attempted in England after six weeks of intensive submarine and air warfare—not before. If pressed, this government is so ruthless that if they consider it necessary they will wage a Bacillus war." A June 1941 report from the U.S. naval attaché in Rome stated the following: "Contact states a major act of sabotage against United States Army sometime during August. Place and character not stated. American codes believed to have been broken in that it has been stated that copies of all code dispatches from U.S. Embassy at Rome are being forwarded to Berlin."[6]

A Weak United States

Half a world away, the American naval attaché in Tokyo reported in March 1941 that "Japanese Army opinion appears to be that British defeat is a foregone conclusion. The United States will therefore be forced to retain her fleet in the Atlantic. This will provide an opportunity for Japan to execute her designs in Southeast Asia unhampered. The United States is thought to be seriously disorganized and incapable of exercising decisive efforts in a war."[7] Put bluntly, German and Japanese military leaders had a low opinion of American military ability.

The Axis powers were aware of American military weakness during the interwar period and exploited this to their advantage. Hitler's opinion of Americans was that they combined the possession of vast material power with a vast lack of intelligence, saying, "This evokes the image of some child stricken with elephantiasis. The United States was a giant with feet of clay."[8] His view of American military capability reeked with contempt, namely, that the United States was weak with a loud mouth. Shortly after Pearl Harbor, Hitler proclaimed, "I'll never believe that an American can fight like a war hero. I don't see much future for the Americans. In my view, it is a decayed country."[9] Hitler was certain that U.S. soldiers were inferior to his tough veterans, and his top-level advisors concurred with his low opinions of American military personnel.

Most of his Army High Command believed that the United States had not contributed much to Germany's World War I defeat, and so when Hitler declared war on the U.S. on December 11, 1941, his military advisors did not consider America to be much of a military threat. German Admiral Erich Raeder was "positively eager for the fight, while the army and Luftwaffe paid hardly any attention at all" to American armed capability.[10] Hitler's reaction to the Japanese attack on Pearl Harbor was that "we're now to a certain extent protected on the flanks," quoted Ian Kershaw. "The United States will no longer be so rashly able to provide England with aircraft, weapons, and transport space, since it can be presumed that they will need all that for their own war with Japan."[11]

The Japanese shared these assessments regarding the military capacity of the United States. A Japanese rear admiral claimed that the United States was weak in the Far East, and the Allies were overawed by Japanese strength; that the Allied powers, according to Japanese intelligence, had only three hundred thousand army troops, one hundred fifty warships, and one thousand planes in this area; and concluded that the inferior quality of American planes precluded their reaching Japan from Kamchatka or the Philippines.[12] A similar Japanese naval evaluation of American naval personnel and ships concluded that since it took three years to properly train sailors, and the United States lacked necessary materials to build needed ships, Japan would defeat the United States in a war. According to Eric Larrabee, Gen. George C. Marshall stated that the U.S. had an army of one hundred seventy-four thousand personnel before World War II.[13] General Eisenhower wrote that "two increases, authorized during the summer and fall of 1939 raised the active army at home and overseas to 227,000. But there it remained during the eight months that Germany, brutally triumphant over Poland, was readying herself in full might for the conquest of Western Europe."[14]

The Japanese Army, by contrast, consisted of 2.4 million trained men and 3 million partially trained reserves. They had manufactured 2,675 first-grade planes in a month and were training 2,750 pilots a year. The Japanese did not accept the inferior naval role assigned to them by Britain and the United States and in 1934 denounced naval agreements reached in 1922 and 1930. Secretly, the Japanese increased the strength of their navy to 230 major ships. They had gained considerable amphibious operations experience in fighting the Chinese during the 1930s, learning how to coordinate land, sea, and air power.[15] On the other side, Allied operations in 1942 and 1943 lacked close coordination and planning, which led to disaster in Dieppe and serious problems in North Africa, Salerno, and other Allied amphibious operations.

With tensions brewing globally, military intelligence became more important to democracies. From spring 1933 through January 1936, Eric Philipps, Britain's ambassador to Berlin, supplied important reports to British Foreign Secretary Anthony Eden for confidential examination by members of the British cabinet. These detailed reports severely criticized the programs and activities of the Nazi regime. In the introduction to these reports, Eden observed that "Hitler's foreign policy might be synthesized as the destruction of the order established by the peace treaties and the restoration of Germany to her dominant position in Europe."[16] He stressed the importance of accelerating British rearmament to counter German expansion.[17]

President Roosevelt was also concerned about Nazi and Fascist subversion of U.S. military and economic power in Hispanic America. Admiral Hewitt's role in carrying out FDR's hemispheric defense policies are described in his letters to the director of naval intelligence, obtained from the Library of Congress and from Hewitt's memoirs.

Hewitt and Military Intelligence

Toward the end of Herbert Hoover's presidency, Hewitt was offered a position with U.S. Naval Intelligence in Peru, South America. He declined the offer in order to remain in the States, near to his elder daughter, Floride, who had just started studying at Vassar College. After the November 1936 presidential election, Hewitt was placed in command of the heavy cruiser *Indianapolis,* which carried President Roosevelt to the Pan-American Conference in Buenos Aires, Argentina. This Pan-American good—neighbor trip lasted a month. In letters to his mother, Hewitt described the many ceremonial, diplomatic, and intelligence activities that took place in Argentina, Brazil, and elsewhere in the region. In a letter dated November 27, 1936, he wrote, "While confidentially my politics are unchanged, I must freely admit that the president is a most delightful person to be with."[18] In another letter dated December 10, it is evident that although the trip was replete with elaborate diplomatic gatherings, dinners, luncheons, receptions, and cocktail parties, there were also meetings with South American military leaders that Hewitt attended.[19]

Roosevelt and his military chiefs were concerned too about eliminating commercial airlines owned, controlled, or maintained by the German, Italian, and Japanese governments. One remedy was to demonstrate American military power in such areas as the Panama Canal Zone. The United States tried to replace Axis-controlled commercial airline companies with American—or locally controlled ones. Known as the Pan American Airways system, this strategy succeeded in attaining a foothold in Latin American commercial aviation by 1938.

In a September 11, 1940, letter to Rear Adm. W. S. Anderson, director of naval intelligence, Hewitt reported that there was "evidence of a strong fifth column organization [in Ecuador] but to date it appears to have been unable to get away with anything extensive."[20] He cautioned that Ecuadorian Fascist agents "would undoubtedly break out if given the opportunity." Hewitt suggested that "the most urgent thing at present is to take whatever steps are necessary to secure the elimination of SEDTA"—the *Sociedat Iana de Transportes Aereos.*

Created in Ecuador in July 1937 by the German government airline Lufthansa, SEDTA was to serve as a Nazi stalking horse. Hitler and his cohorts had used such subversive agents to overturn democratic governments in Europe. To eradicate the SEDTA movement, Hewitt suggested subsidizing an Ecuadorian group, the Panagra, which supported U.S. policies. He also recommended that the U.S. pay for the training of Ecuadorian army and navy officers in the United States, changing the policy of having such training take place in Fascist Italy. To encourage U.S. Army and Navy officers to serve in Ecuador, Hewitt suggested "they could live well on their salaries since the cost of living there appeared to be surprisingly low. They could save most of their American pay."[21] Hewitt wrote that he found this intelligence assignment very interesting and that he "hoped to develop it into something of real value in the matter of hemispheric defense and of the defense of the [Panama] Canal in particular."[22] These security recommendations were aimed at ousting German aviation from Ecuador and Colombia, and they enabled the American government to improve the security of the Panama Canal and helped to reduce Axis influence in Latin America.

From Isolation to Intervention

There are many accounts of how the American people were transformed from isolationism and neutrality during the 1930s to a state of war starting on December 7, 1941, and ending in August 1945. The proximate cause was the Japanese attack on Pearl Harbor and the killing of 2,403 people and the destruction of much of the U.S. Navy and aircraft. However, the complex events and conditions that preceded the Pearl Harbor attack are relevant and should at the least be mentioned.[23]

After World War I, a substantial majority of Americans was disillusioned with the results of intervention in what Woodrow Wilson had labeled "the war to end all wars." Approximately fifty thousand American soldiers had died in France; thousands more were maimed and the victims of gas warfare before an armistice was reached on November 11, 1918, and fighting ended. The United States also did not become a member of the League of Nations in 1919. The American people, in November 1920, elected Warren G. Harding, Republican U.S. Senator of Ohio, as president and Massachusetts Governor Calvin Coolidge as vice president. A reign of Republican probusiness and pacifism dominated the 1920s. The United States Navy had less than one hundred thousand men—less than was allowed under international treaties—while the United States Army averaged about one hundred thirty-five thousand men.[24] American isolationism led to diplomacy that ratified treaties requiring the United States to destroy about a million tons of warships and to limit naval construction.

The findings of a U.S. Senate Munitions Investigating Committee headed by North Dakota's isolationist and Anglophobic senator, Gerald P. Nye, intensified American antagonism toward international involvement. At well-publicized Senate hearings, many witnesses claimed that American financiers and munitions manufacturers had connived with the British to fraudulently manipulate the United States' entry into World War I. An outraged American public approved congressional legislation in the 1930s to ensure neutrality in future European wars. Initially, a major feature of the neutrality acts was to forbid American sales of munitions and other war goods to belligerents. A few months after the defeat of France in 1940, the America First Committee was organized to oppose United States help to the British. That committee included isolationists in the Congress, prominent businesspeople such as Robert E. Wood, head of Sears-Roebuck, and about eight hundred thousand other ardent nationalists opposed to the U.S. getting entangled in war. Wood had been the general in charge of providing supplies in World War I and an early supporter of Roosevelt's New Deal policy. He and other America First members favored selling military equipment to the British on a cash-and-carry basis and building up the United States military. They did not view Nazi Germany as a threat to America and believed that the British would capitulate to the Axis. Many of the leading America Firsters were Republicans from the Midwest who opposed the New Deal, but some were progressives, like Philip LaFollette, governor of Wisconsin. Whether conservative or liberal, America First members and millions of other Americans believed that the more than three thousand miles of the Atlantic Ocean would shield Americans from their enemies.

The isolationists had plenty of arguments against U.S. involvement. One was hostility toward the British—America's enemy since revolutionary times. Some isolationists argued that America had been dragged into World War I because of British manipulation, that British policies and practices were offensive (e.g., their class and colonial system). Some Americans disliked Britain's strong competitive financial and commercial status. There were also Americans of German, Italian, Irish, French, Spanish, and other national origins who were hostile to the British and disinclined to help them—especially when respected men such as aviator Charles A. Lindbergh and U.S. Ambassador to Britain Joseph P. Kennedy warned their fellow citizens that the invincible

German air force would decimate the British population with its bombing raids and reduce the survivors into submission.

Lindbergh, one of America's best-known heroes of the 1920s, opposed helping Britain in its 1940 struggle against Hitler. He and others in the America First movement—which included, among its members, Gerald R. Ford, later a U.S. president; Potter Stewart, later a justice of the United States Supreme Court; Kingman Brewster Jr., later a president of Yale University; and perennial Socialist Party presidential candidate Norman Thomas—demanded that Congress refrain from helping the British and remain neutral. Lindbergh and his wife, Anne Morrow Lindbergh, viewed Hitler's Germany as a necessary counterweight to safeguard the United States against communism. Lindbergh maintained that the New Dealers, the British, and the Jews were pushing the U.S. into war. Isolationists argued repeatedly that the Atlantic Ocean and the great distance between Europe and the United States provided Americans with an impenetrable shield and that the British were doomed to the fate of the French, Dutch, Belgians, Norwegians, Poles, and others who had succumbed to German might.

Influential senior military officers, such as Maj. Gen. Stanley D. Embick, had no confidence in Churchill's ability to deal with the mighty German war machine. He and most Americans opposed war with Germany. Military chiefs Adm. Harold Stark and Gen. George C. Marshall also opposed giving away American military equipment to the French and British. They suggested, on June 22, 1940, that President Roosevelt discontinue his attempts to strengthen Britain—the same day the French agreed to an armistice with Germany. Until the Pearl Harbor attack, Col. Robert R. McCormick, publisher of the *Chicago Tribune* newspaper, and Father Coughlin, a Roman Catholic priest and anti-Semitic radio broadcaster, regularly lashed out at those who sought to help the British. A huge gathering of Nazi sympathizers convened at New York City's Madison Garden to urge neutrality. America Firsters of varying political persuasions and others made it obvious that the United States should remain clear of involvement with the British and their empire. Even after Hitler declared war on the United States and placed America on the side of the British as U.S. Allies, the distaste and distrust for war continued for many Americans.

Doubt was cast on the isolationists' assertion that the Atlantic Ocean would protect America from Europe when four Germans from a submarine reached a beach in Long Island, New York, on June 13, 1942. They were under orders to cause communications and transportation havoc, blow up New York City's water supply, and cripple industrial plants. Another four-man team landed in Florida four days later. All eight were caught before they could do harm; and following military tribunal trials, six of the invaders were executed, a seventh was sentenced to life imprisonment, and the eighth man to thirty years.[25] That such an occurrence could happen demonstrated that the three-thousand-mile alleged Atlantic Ocean shield was defective.

Not all Americans were prone to isolation, however; many realized that buying time to prepare for war could be achieved by helping democratic Allies defeat the Fascist dictatorships and ward off the United States being the next Axis victim. To overturn isolationism, Roosevelt sought the help of some Republican and independent leaders. Two of his most trusted allies were Secretary of the Navy Frank Knox and Secretary of War Henry Stimson. A third important proponent for U.S. interventionism was the man who ran against Roosevelt in the 1940 presidential election, Wendell Willkie. A fourth was staunch Republican William J. Donovan. These men provided FDR with bipartisan support for rearming in the event of potential conflict. James V. Forrestal, a politically independent investment banker who disliked Roosevelt, became his secretary of the navy after Knox's death in May 1944.

In the summer and autumn of 1940, there was little doubt about international turmoil. On August 11, the devastating Battle of Britain had begun, and the horrors descending upon the British people were regularly reported on U.S. radio and depicted in American newspapers. In addition to a coalition cabinet, Roosevelt had at his disposal other levers of government power. He began the process of seeking the first peacetime draft in United States history and won authority to call up the National Guard to strengthen the country's small army. Congress passed a record-breaking appropriation defense budget of $17 billion for 1940. Fifty overaged destroyers were leased to the British in exchange for bases to protect United States shores.

Before December 7, 1941, Roosevelt had avoided actions and statements that were too far ahead of American public opinion. But he did take war preparation steps seriously, including a bill to Congress that established the first peacetime compulsory military service in September 1940. It passed by only one vote, thanks to strong antiwar public sentiment. It was imperative for Roosevelt to secure bipartisan support for interventionist and rearmament policies. Once war was declared in Europe in September 1939, the need for military preparations was increasingly evident, and the defeat of France accentuated this. The mounting pressures from the

Allied governments were also intense. The British and French clamored for American assistance. The British, who found themselves increasingly divested of allies on the Continent, helped propel FDR's thinly veiled agenda to prepare America for entry into the war on the Allied side.

A native of Indiana and of German descent, Wendell Willkie, who had been a liberal Democrat for decades, won the 1940 Republican presidential nomination. A talented lawyer who fought for civil rights, Willkie was president of Commonwealth and Southern Corporation, a utilities holding company, prior to becoming the Republican presidential candidate in 1940. After his defeat by Roosevelt, Willkie became an important ally, giving the president his support for the Lend-Lease Act. Although political opponents, both men believed in many of the same objectives, such as aiding the British people in their need to combat Hitler and Nazism.

In February 1941, Roosevelt sent Willkie as his emissary to England. Willkie delivered to Churchill a handwritten letter from FDR that quoted lines from the American poet Henry Longfellow:

> Sail on O ship of State!
> Sail on O Union strong and Grand!
> Humanity with all its fears
> With all the hopes of future years
> Is hanging breathless on thy fate!

Both Roosevelt's and Willkie's sympathies were on the side of the British, and they both believed that the American people would be in grave danger should Hitler's forces defeat Britain as they had done to France and other nations in 1940. The German air blitz on the British people in the winter of 1940-41 left many leading Americans certain that British defeat was inevitable. However, there were many others who did not know what was at stake and simply did not care.

Willkie not only knew, but he cared as well. As early as 1941, he showed his empathy toward the British people; and throughout his extensive travels within Britain, he found devastation and also a determination to win. His visit was cut short when requested by Secretary of State Hull to testify on behalf of the Lend-Lease Bill before the U.S. Senate Committee on Foreign Relations. Among those opposing Lend-Lease were Lindbergh, Kennedy, Socialist Norman Thomas, Alfred Landon—FDR's 1936 opponent—and many others. When Willkie left England for Washington, D.C., the important *Times* of London pronounced him the most interesting personality in American public life in thirty years, with the possible exception of FDR.[26] Willkie later was the guest of General de Gaulle, on September 10, 1942, a visit that was viewed by both men as unfavorable. Willkie, like Roosevelt, found his host to be arrogant, defiant, and stubborn while de Gaulle complained about the American's ignorance of the Middle East, being misrepresented by Willkie as a latter-day Napoleon, and Willkie's emulating Roosevelt, who shared his dislike of de Gaulle.

Navy Secretary Frank Knox was a man who enjoyed an enviable record of achievement. One of President Teddy Roosevelt's "Rough Riders" who served in World War I, Knox had developed careers as an industrialist, a journalist, and a politician in New Hampshire and Michigan. He became the publisher of the *Chicago Daily News* in 1931 and gained political fame, running in 1936 as Alf Landon's vice presidential candidate. FDR was drawn to Knox because of his support of interventionist policies, opposing the bitter onslaughts hurled at the Democrats by isolationist *Chicago Tribune* publisher Robert McCormick. Once Roosevelt satisfied Knox's condition of appointing another Republican, Henry L. Stimson, to his cabinet, Knox agreed, in July 1940, to serve as secretary of the navy.[27] (Both Knox and his successor, James V. Forrestal, had to deal with Adm. Ernest J. King's fierce hostility toward civilian authority. As chief of naval operations, King had enormous power at his disposal but still chafed at having to defer to civilian superiors.)

Stimson agreed to serve as secretary of war under Roosevelt, having previously served Republican presidents in the same capacity and as secretary of state. He had served as secretary of war from 1911 to 1913 in the Taft administration. In World War I, he served as a field artillery colonel in France. In the 1920s, he was governor-general of the Philippines and later secretary of state in President Hoover's cabinet. In the 1930s, he was a staunch foe of Nazism and neutrality. As secretary of war in the Roosevelt administration, Stimson chose competent assistants and developed an excellent working relationship with U.S. Army chief Gen. George C. Marshall.[28] Both Stimson and Knox were skilled in dealing with a fractious Congress and an apathetic citizenry. While Knox's knowledge of navy customs and bureaucracies was scant at first, he quickly gained the respect and gratitude of knowledgeable Americans of various political persuasions by the end of his service in 1944. Both Knox and Stimson served their nation well.

The terrible plight of the British people after the defeat of France, and their strong resolve to continue fighting Hitler's forces, evoked American sympathy and Lend-Lease help.[29] Prime Minister Winston Churchill pleaded with President Roosevelt that it was crucial for Britain to obtain shipments of steel, destroyers, and the latest types of aircraft, antiaircraft equipment, and ammunition. FDR was warned that Italy's joining Germany would increase the danger to British shipping by adding one hundred Italian submarines and that U.S. steel was necessary because Britain's own ore supply from North Africa, northern Spain, and Sweden would be curtailed. Churchill concluded his appeal, saying, "We shall go on paying dollars as long as we can, but I should like to feel reasonably sure that when we can pay no more you will give us the stuff all the same."[30]

In the midst of overwhelming isolationism, FDR succeeded in obtaining congressional approval for a program to provide weapons and supplies to Britain with the agreement that repayment would be made after the war. Declaring that the defense of Great Britain was of crucial importance to the United States, Roosevelt signed the Lend-Lease Act into law on March 11, 1941. It passed through Congress only after considerable effort by Roosevelt, Secretary of State Hull, War Secretary Stimson, Navy Secretary Knox, and Willkie. This legislation authorized the president to supply military and other goods to any country whose interests were deemed vital to the defense of the United States. Isolationists in Congress and throughout the nation denounced FDR's interventionism and whipped up the horrors of American boys dying in a foreign war that was of no concern to Americans. FDR and Stimson downplayed the likelihood of war and sold the Lend-Lease program as a preventive measure that would provide the Allied combatants necessary supplies to continue fighting the Axis powers. Willkie's forthright and constructive criticism before and during the war targeted isolationism, race and religious hatred, wasteful war production, and colonialism.

Naval equipment vital to the defense of sea-lanes was made available to the British. They and the French had contracted with American truck and aircraft companies in 1939 and 1940, and by March 1941 large amounts of these and other war items were being produced in the United States. However, not all of the items requested by the British were manufactured economically, according to Senator Harry S. Truman's War Production Investigation Committee. Bureaucratic bungling and inefficiency were responsible for procurement problems. However, by the end of May, forty-four American cargo ships were assigned to the British in the Middle East; and by July, forty-one ships were ready for use. British military officers—Gen. I. S. O. Playfair, Capt. F. C. Flynn (Royal Navy), Brig. C. J. C. Molony, and Air Vice-Marshal S. E. Toomer—found that by the end of July 1941, American aid to Britain consisted of nearly ten thousand trucks, eighty-four tanks, one hundred sixty-four fighter aircraft, ten bombers, twenty-four antiaircraft guns, a few howitzers, and a huge amount of machinery. Tools, equipment for road-building engineering, and communications were delivered from America to Britain. After July, an average of sixteen American ships arrived every month for the remainder of the year.[31] Other Allied powers also received American aid as a result of the Lend-Lease agreement, among them Greece, which got fifty field guns, a huge supply of ammunition, and thirty Grumman fighters.

The quantity of critical materials to be released under Lend-Lease was subject to U.S. Army and Navy scrutiny. In autumn 1941, the Soviet Union requested $33 million worth of machine tools for shipbuilding without any explanation concerning their use. Navy Secretary Knox denied this release because of a critical shortage of such machine tools in the U.S. William S. Knudsen, an immigrant's son who had advanced through the assembly line of General Motors to become prosperous and famous as GM's production genius, became an important advisor to FDR's Commission to the Council of National Defense. Responding to Willkie's criticism that the United States was being inadequately served by an antiquated defense organization, Roosevelt appointed Knudsen to advise on industrial production for war. When Knudsen concluded that the release of shipbuilding machine tools to the Russians would not delay the U.S. Navy's own program, Secretary Knox's decision was reversed. And when the Russians requested eleven million pounds of aluminum, Knox objected again, on the grounds that the United States desperately needed this metal for aircraft production; he was again overruled, even though the Russian government had not supplied information requested by the United States concerning its aircraft production. Writing in 1951, Robert H. Connery reflected that "history will decide whether the President's lenient policy toward the Russian request was wise or not."[32]

When Lend-Lease became law, President Roosevelt proclaimed that "the end of compromise with tyranny" had arrived, and the United States would help Britain until it won.[33] The Lend-Lease program contributed to the subsequent successful Allied invasions of North Africa, Sicily, Salerno, Corsica, Elba, and southern France that wiped out Axis forces in the Mediterranean. Once the Mediterranean became a corridor controlled by the Allies and safe for shipping, Lend-Lease aid could be also provided more easily to the Russians to fight the Germans, as noted by Douglas Porch, professor of national security affairs at the Naval Postgraduate School in Monterey, California. He claimed that the Allies cleared the Mediterranean for Lend-Lease.[34] Domination of the Mediterranean saved shipping time and provided air and naval bases for the Allies. Achievement of these and other objectives also saved the lives of Allied soldiers, sailors, and airmen.

FDR and Europe

Although Roosevelt was cautious about his commitment to the Allied cause prior to the Pearl Harbor attack and sensitive to noninterventionist opinions, the reactions of Europeans upon learning of his reelection in 1940 was astounding. One reader of *Time* magazine, Maurice Barber, a member of the American Field Service in France (American Red Cross), wrote in the January 8, 1941, issue, "I, an American citizen, homeward bound, had the impression of being swept along the road between Paris and Lisbon on a wave of enthusiasm and affection—all of which was meant for Mr. Roosevelt . . . . I took the cheers—I heard the pleas—which tried to ascend the wall of tragic and unnatural silence behind which the French people are imprisoned, which were directed toward the President of the United States—and toward the American nation. The French are enormously grateful to the American people—'for being *chic,* you know, for showing, *et si largement,* to the best man that they knew how to appreciate his merits . . . .' As the French see it, the American people have made a gesture of friendship for France in electing *their* President, their first—and last—friend."[35] Through a slow but carefully orchestrated prodding, FDR and his allies attempted to steer American public opinion toward the cause of the Allied side and the survival of democracy.

Roosevelt tended to operate with sensitivity to the views of others; his diplomatic style was not unilateral and threatening. After the defeat of France, his concern for a victorious Britain heightened, and he started in earnest to prepare Americans for combat. One example was his creation, on June 27, 1940, of the Defense Research Committee, which was assigned to enlist the best scientists to protect the nation. Another example of FDR's belief that the United States had to reinforce the Allies as much as it could in the growing world conflict was the implementation of neutrality patrols. Launched in early 1941, these patrols used the

U.S. Atlantic Fleet to provide American naval escort and protection of merchant vessels—both Allied and neutral—crossing the Atlantic with critically needed supplies. The U.S. Navy and British Admiralty convoys provided safety throughout the one thousand five hundred sea miles between the North American coastline and Britain. Rear Admiral Hewitt was assigned to the patrols and commanded the Atlantic Fleet's Cruiser Force that was used to implement the Lend-Lease program.

One result of the August 1941 conference between Churchill and Roosevelt aboard the U.S. naval cruiser *Augusta* and the British battle cruiser *Prince of Wales,* when these ships were anchored off the Newfoundland coast, was pivotal in that the United States government agreed to protect shipping to Britain. In cooperation with the Royal Canadian Navy, the U.S. Navy took responsibility to protect convoys of ships bringing Lend-Lease goods to the British people. In September and October 1941, the U.S. Navy was involved in battles involving Canadian-escorted slow convoys. An undeclared naval war between Germany and the United States resulted. A German submarine torpedoed the U.S. destroyer escort *Kearny* on October 17, 1941; and German submarines sank another American ship, the *Reuben James,* on November 1. These two incidents were not used by the United States or Germany as causes for war.[36]

American Mobilization

The United States Army prepared a series of mobilization plans. Its publication, *Mobilization,* outlined the importance of production planning. The army's mobilization plans bridged two gaps: they sought to mesh production schedules and the early needs of the army and to bring together the rates of troop and matériel mobilization. They also made provision for a small and well-equipped emergency force, called the initial protective force, to provide security during general mobilization. This force of four hundred thousand troops consisted of the then available Regular Army and National Guard. Overall, the 1939 version was sound enough to become the permanent basis for mobilization.[37] With most of Western Europe forced into submission by the Nazis, and Japanese dominance of Asia, the American plans for mobilizing Allied assistance grew more crucial with each passing day. Neutrality patrol convoys were critical to the endurance of the Allies; and Hewitt, commander of the Atlantic Fleet's Cruiser Force in 1941, oversaw the Atlantic crossings. In his memoirs, the admiral described little-known facets of American preparation for war. In the following entry, Hewitt described his initial experience in amphibious operations. The last sentence of this entry is especially interesting:

> During the first week in August 1941, the newly formed Amphibious Brigade, which had been spending some time exercising in the Caribbean, carried out a major amphibious exercise on the North Carolina coast at New River. This brigade which consisted of the First Marine Division and the First Army Division, under the command of Major General Holland M. Smith, U.S.M.C. embarked in attack transports of the Atlantic Fleet Base Force. The Transport commander was Captain R. R. M. Emmett, U.S.N. General Smith was an old friend and shipmate, having been Fleet Marine Officer when I was Pacific Fleet Operations Officer, and having worked closely with me in operations planning.
>
> Admiral King ordered all the available flag officers of the Atlantic Fleet to witness the exercise—a far-sighted move. So it was that on August 1 I preceded westward from Bermuda to New River with my current Task Group, *Savannah*, escort carrier *Long Island* (a converted oiler), and two destroyers. In order to get the best view of the landing, I decided to watch it from the air, which I did in one of the *Savannah*'s two-seater observation planes. It was a new and very strange sensation to be catapulted off a ship. After the beach landing was completed, I joined General Smith in his headquarters on shore to observe the purely military part of the exercise. It was all most interesting and rewarding. And while I was certain of the future probability of such operations, I little realized what was to be my own close connection with them.[38]

An American neutrality patrol commanded by Rear Admiral Hewitt in the beginning of September 1941 provoked concern about the start of a war between the United States and Germany. Hewitt wrote,

> After the New River exercise, there was another patrol across the Atlantic, followed by a return to the area off the Virginia Capes for target practice. My final neutrality patrol in early September with Task Group 26, flying my flag in the carrier *Wasp*, with the *Savannah* and the two destroyers, proved to be rather exacting. Somewhat east of Bermuda, eastbound,

we intercepted a dispatch from a Canadian man-of-war to the northward of us, reporting the sighting of what she thought to be a German cruiser proceeding on a southerly course at high speed. What she had seen had disappeared in the haze to the southward before positive identification could be made. The rest of the position given, and the probable courses and possible speeds, showed that the supposed raider might well come into our search area. Speed was increased and group course and aircraft search were oriented accordingly. One plane, returning in the afternoon from the first search flight launched, made a message drop on the bridge before being recovered. Strict radio silence, except in emergency, had been enjoined. The message stated that the pilot had sighted a suspicious vessel at the extreme safe limit of his flight, but he had to turn back before making a close approach. The silhouette sketch he drew bore a strong resemblance to one of the German cruiser types. The pilot's testimony after landing seemed to confirm this although he stated he was far from sure.

At this time the Atlantic Fleet had orders from the President to destroy any Axis raider found in the Neutrality Zone proclaimed by him. No time was lost, therefore, in launching another search flight to confirm the original contact. And a squadron of torpedo-bombers was brought up to the flight deck and armed in readiness. I began to wonder if it was to be I who in carrying out my orders would be first to involve the United States in war. However, the scouting planes returned at dusk without further contact.

The search was continued the following day without result. It was conjectured that the raider, if there was one, might be making for British Guiana, with the object of destroying some of the bauxite supply, so important to our own and the British construction program.[39]

Pearl Harbor and Its Aftermath

On December 7, 1941, when effective alarms were needed to safeguard American lives and ships and aircraft, there was no alarm to prevent or mitigate a devastating enemy attack. Much has been written about the United States military bureaucracy's communication failures that were responsible for the losses that Sunday. The toll: 2,403 dead; 1,178 wounded; 6 battleships sunk and 2 others damaged; 3 destroyers, 3 light cruisers, and 4 other ships destroyed; and 164 planes destroyed and 128 damaged. Japanese forces had attacked Hong Kong, Guam, the Philippine Islands, Wake Island, and Midway Island.[40] This outrageous sneak attack occurred without any declaration of war while Japanese military leaders used fraudulent tactics to deceive Americans. The tactical victories that the Japanese enjoyed because of the success of the Pearl Harbor attack were substantial, and the harm caused to their victims should not be underestimated. However, by August 1945, Japanese military successes were transformed into an indescribably painful defeat. The big German victories in spring 1940 were also reversed, and German military leaders surrendered in May 1945.

An important work by Rebecca Robbins Raines, *Getting the Message Through: A Branch History of the U.S. Army Signal Corps,* was published in 1996. In her carefully documented account of the Pearl Harbor disaster, Raines alleged that in 1940 Roosevelt transferred the U.S. Pacific Fleet from bases on the West Coast to Pearl Harbor on the Hawaiian island of Oahu in the belief this would act as a deterrent to Japanese aggression. The Oahu air warnings system was incomplete on December 7, 1941. Although the United States Signal Corps attempted to improve strategic communications for Pearl Harbor, "the Army had only a limited ability to communicate with its garrison in Hawaii."[41] The islands' Japanese-American inhabitants were viewed as potential saboteurs, and precautions were taken against their doing harm. The wrong perception was communicated; in reality, nearly all Japanese-Americans were loyal to the United States, and many served valiantly in the army.

In 1939, when Col. George S. Patton was commander of the army's Fort Myer, Virginia, post, he was requested to implement a Signal Corps plan to improve communications by installing new high-frequency radio transmission facilities that would enable receipt of point-to-point communication from the West Coast. According to author Raines, "The new antenna would encroach upon the turf he used as a polo field and the radio towers would obstruct the view."[42] Patton therefore not only prevented installation of the new communications equipment, he also stymied a navy proposal to locate a radio station near Fort Myer. Instead of providing the Signal Corps with an opportunity to improve its facilities, Patton was intent in using the facilities to house his enlisted men. Raines believed that the expanded Fort Myer facilities blocked by Patton could have perhaps eliminated the communications problems confronting Army Chief of Staff General Marshall on the morning of December 7, 1941. He could not call Lt. Gen. Walter Short, army commander at Pearl Harbor, directly because the scrambler telephone available to him was not considered secure from interception. Instead, Marshall had to resort to a radio message that was beset with heavy static and did not get through to General Short. Finally, a message was sent via commercial telegraph to San Francisco and from there by radio to the RCA office in Honolulu, which had a teletypewriter that was not yet functional. Consequently, General Short did not receive the vital information until the afternoon of December 7, many hours after Japanese bombs descended at 0755 hours.

Despite the prevailing isolationist public opinion and a strict Neutrality Act prohibiting further involvement in the escalating global conflict, the American armed forces began some preparations for war. Admiral Hewitt wrote in his memoir manuscript that in the spring of 1941,

> the Pacific Fleet was acutely conscious of the possibility of an air attack on it while in Pearl Harbor. Consequently, frequent air raid drills were held with the ships in port. The various berths were divided into air defense sectors, with a flag officer in charge of each. The Naval District participated in these exercises, but, insofar as I know, the Army, which had the major responsibility for the defense of the Fleet at its base, took no part. An Air Defense Board, headed by Rear Admiral P.N.L. Bellinger, at that time in command of Naval Air based on Oahu, prophetically suggested that an enemy carrier attack would be delivered shortly after dawn from the north.[43]

In July 1945, after the Allied victory in Europe to which he contributed so much, Navy Secretary Forrestal assigned Hewitt the task of heading an investigation of the Pearl Harbor attack. Henry C. Clausen, who served as the U.S. Army's counsel to the Pearl Harbor Committee, stated that he "always believed that the Hewitt investigation was the best one that the Navy had . . . Hewitt bore down on intelligence matters . . . his work should be reevaluated by historians in light of his probing into previously unexplored areas."[44] Clausen, a distinguished lawyer, added that "like myself, Hewitt reached some conclusions that were not to the Navy's liking. He, too, concluded that Navy personnel had made mistakes that contributed to Pearl Harbor. He also found that Admiral Kimmel did have sufficient information in his possession to indicate that the situation was unusually serious."[45]

For most of 1942, Americans were confronted with enemies who were flushed with victory. It took time before the U.S. military could assert itself. Before the military's phenomenal increase in strength, Americans suffered because they lacked seasoned, experienced military forces that were well led and properly equipped. The American Army and Navy had separate logistics at the beginning of World War II, and each service had separate ports of embarkation for overseas movement. The army had its own shipping, and the Army Air Corps and Naval Aviation had their separate systems of procurement and supply. Although the army procured small arms ammunition for itself and the navy, and a joint army and navy munitions board had been created to prepare plans for industrial mobilization, the U.S. Government Accounting Office (GAO) audits of war production found serious war production waste and corruption, as well as instances of commendable efficiency and patriotic teamwork.

On March 23, 1942, an advance decision was requested from the Coordinator of Inter-American Affairs, Nelson A. Rockefeller, by the comptroller general (head of the General Accounting Office or GAO). It was the rule that requests for decisions in advance of any payment would be disposed of, if practicable, within ten days of receipt. On March 24, 1942, a decision was rendered allowing the creation of corporations to strengthen the bonds between the United States and other American republics.

As a result of subsequent close cooperation amongst the military branches, the U.S. Treasury Department, and the GAO, bureaucratic hurdles affecting the war effort were cleared with unprecedented promptness. On one occasion, forty-seven requisitions for dispersing funds and related documents were received with informal advice that it was of utmost importance to the navy. Monies had to be available at the earliest possible moment. Every qualified person was immediately put to work, and the warrants and requisitions were cleared in a matter of minutes. The imperative need to develop, build, and operate a fleet of amphibious vessels benefited from the herculean efforts of GAO personnel.[46]

Despite the 25 percent decrease in auditing staff during war, the GAO continued to scrutinize war production. Among the many irregularities criticized were duplicate payments, purchasing materials at excessive profits, unauthorized payments of salaries, improper bonuses, failure to purchase under the General Schedule of Supplies, purchase of items such as typewriters and vehicles in excess of prices fixed by statute, reimbursement for various types of unauthorized fees, unauthorized premiums on accident insurance policies, subcontracting a part of the prime contractor's obligation without a corresponding reduction in the fixed fee, excessive valuation of rented equipment resulting in exorbitant rental rates and an excessive recapture prices, reimbursement for obsolete plans and specifications and manufacture of articles hereunder, and excessive overhead or indirect charges.[47] The annual report of the comptroller general for the fiscal year ended June 30, 1943, added fourteen additional irregular practices by the U.S. Maritime Commission and the war shipping administrator.[48]

A formal army agreement of June 13, 1942, between Maj. Gen. Brehon Somervell and Mr. Lewis Douglas, deputy war shipping administrator, stated that "henceforth Navy requirements for merchant shipping to bases and staging areas would be met in large measure by the allocation to the Naval Transportation Service of civilian-manned vessels under the control of the War Shipping Administration . . . . Commissioned vessels of all types, the 'fleet auxiliaries,' would generally be assigned to the Service Forces, where they would be employed in deliveries directly to the fleet, or, in the case of vessels designed for assault uses, would be assigned to the Amphibious Forces."[49] General Somervell was responsible for helping get supplies from the U.S. over to joint military forces. It is clear now that Somervell's leadership contributed greatly to the torrential supply of weapons and other necessities of war that resulted in the Allied victories of 1945. But when William Harlan Hale wrote the following immediately after the devastating Pearl Harbor attack, Allied victory was far from certain. In an article entitled "After Pearl Harbor," Hale predicted that "time is given to us to mass and deploy our huge, far-flung forces. What happens from now on will involve the frontal clash of metal on metal. And our metal is heavier."[50]

An Overlooked Benefactor

Adm. Harold R. Stark was an American who played a major role concerning the administration of war supplies in Europe. As head of the U.S. Navy on December 7, 1941, Stark was scapegoated and wrongly blamed for the mistakes of others. He was succeeded, as chief of naval operations, by Adm. Ernest J. King and assigned to command naval forces in Europe. His logistic, diplomatic, and other World War II contributions warrant better recognition than they have received. Stark's abilities and efforts in planning and preparing the naval assaults on North Africa in November 1942, and Normandy in June 1944, were commended by General Eisenhower, Prime Minister Churchill, General de Gaulle, and other Allied war leaders.[51]

Once the United States was at war with Germany, it sought to strengthen its relationship with French Resistance forces. The strongest French faction opposed to the Germans was led by Gen. Charles de Gaulle. Roosevelt's attempt to replace him with another French general, Henri Giraud, failed because FDR's choice lacked de Gaulle's political skills. The policy differences between Roosevelt and de Gaulle were made worse by their incompatible personalities. Fortunately, these tensions were mitigated by the intervention of Admiral Stark. One of Stark's responsibilities was to consult with de Gaulle's faction concerning the conduct of the war, and Stark soon became a de facto ambassador on political and military questions. Due to his rank, status, diplomatic personality, and firmness, Admiral Stark achieved both a working and a good personal relationship with General de Gaulle, which ultimately facilitated war aid to the French.[52]

De Gaulle and his faction disrupted the shipping needed for supplying the war effort, recruiting seamen from North African French ships to serve as soldiers. Secretary of State Hull asked Admiral Stark to discuss this problem with de Gaulle, but the talks went nowhere. To avoid a stalemate, Stark ordered an American armed guard placed on board a French ship chartered by the Allies, the *Jamaique,* which was located in the River Clyde. This move infuriated de Gaulle and his followers who saw the issue as being the right to control a French crew. Admiral Stark's view centered on the operational requirements of the ship. Although the policy differences between the Gaullists and the Americans were not completely resolved, the careful observations and reports of Admiral Stark, combined with his strong personal friendship with de Gaulle, reduced impasses and aided the flow of supplies.[53]

Clearing the Oceans of Enemy Submarines

The menace of German submarine warfare posed a serious danger to the survival of Great Britain and an Allied victory. Before Allied amphibious forces could successfully invade Axis occupied territories, deadly enemy submarines had to be rendered impotent. British and American officials held secret meetings early in 1941, in Washington, D.C., to consider the possibility of forming an alliance in fighting Germany, Italy, and Japan. They understood that war in Europe would ultimately require an invasion of Europe and that unless they could protect their ships from German submarines, there would be no invasion and the Allies would lose.

Once the United States was at war with Germany, Hitler ordered an intensification of submarine warfare against the U.S. shipping critical resources to its Allies. German submarines (or U-boats) destroyed merchant ships and tankers carrying American supplies to the British under the Lend-Lease program. In entering World War II, the United States was grossly unprepared for antisubmarine war, according to A. Timothy Warnock.[54] The United States did not have trained manpower, specialized surface vessels, and aircraft with requisite flight ranges. The U.S. Army Air Corps had more demands placed on it than it had sufficient combat aircraft. Its supply was about three thousand. This lack of preparedness, for example no specialized detection personnel and equipment such as radar, was immediately exploited by the Germans. According to Warnock, "Within a month of the U.S. declaration of war, the first German submarine arrived in American waters. Between mid-January 1942 and the end of June, U-boats sank 374 ships—171 off the East Coast of the United States, 62 in the Gulf of Mexico and 141 in the Caribbean Sea. Many of these vessels were tankers . . . . By June (1942) the U.S. Navy, supported by the Army Air Force, had driven most of the U-boats from the East Coast but enemy submarines continued to wreak havoc on Allied shipping in the Gulf of Mexico and the Caribbean Sea. The Allies lost three million tons of shipping and five thousand men, mostly in American waters, during the first half of 1942. The loss of cargo grievously endangered Britain's ability to continue the war."[55]

Professor Kathleen Broome Williams's statistical report of the human costs involved in the German submarine warfare campaign is permeated with tragedy. "Of the approximately 41,000 Germans engaged in operation, 27,378 were killed (including German Naval Chief Admiral Donitz's two sons) and 4,945 became prisoners. The Allied losses were even greater: 30,249 men of the British Merchant Navy; 73,642 men of the Royal Navy; 1,965 from the Royal Canadian Navy; 2,000 Americans lost in Atlantic waters, 36,950 drowned in the Pacific by Axis submarines;

and 6,883 American Merchant Marine crew members dead. Allied airplane crews were also killed because of submarine warfare."[56]

German submarines were withdrawn from the Atlantic Ocean by the spring of 1943.[57] This was the result of a well coordinated Allied antisubmarine strategy which used aircraft, the Ultra System, to break the German code, direction finding and other technology. When German radio operators sent messages they exposed their ships. Allied direction-finders located enemy submarines and sunk them.[58]

Clearing the oceans of enemy submarines was a top Allied priority, and achievement of this objective helped win a global war that was accomplished by immense sacrifice. An armed force was developed that increased to twelve million personnel in uniform. American productive capacity that had been comatose during ten years of economic depression was rejuvenated. It supplied guns, bullets, tanks, planes, ships, and other items of destruction for the American military and its war-ravaged Allies. War production in the United States went from 2 percent of the budget in 1940 to 40 percent in 1944. Between 1940 and the end of 1945, $183.1 billion was spent on ammunition production. Less than six thousand airplanes of all types were manufactured in 1939 at a cost of $279.4 million. By 1944 the number of aircraft plants in the United States had doubled, and nearly all the 96,369 planes that were built were for combat. The American aluminum industry in 1935 consisted of one company, which produced mostly appliances and cooking utensils. By 1944 there were more than a dozen aluminum producers, turning out 2.3 billion ingot pumps—all of which was being used for aircraft and other military items. In 1940, synthetic rubber in the U.S. was a laboratory curiosity. The enormous Japanese military successes in late 1941 and early 1942, in capturing sources of natural rubber, caused the United States serious worry. Without sufficient tires for a totally motorized army, there was a real possibility that the United States would lose the war. From having practically no synthetic rubber in 1942, the U.S., in a short period, had produced nine hundred thousand tons. The navy ended up with 1,200 new combat vessels and 64,546 assorted landing crafts. Steel, coal, and the use of other materials made the United States the world's arms supplier. The statistics are impressive: 12 million rifles, carbines, and machine guns; 47 million tons of artillery ammunition; and 3.5 million vehicles (from jeeps to tanks). The innovative weaponry that was produced included armor-piercing shells, bazookas, recoilless rifles, devices using radar, computers, and atomic bombs.

The military goals for World War II were astronomical. General Marshall and Admiral King led a military effort that sought to provide U.S. armed forces with the best arms equipment and the most comfort. Enemies of FDR's New Deal furiously attacked annual budgets of $7, $8, or $9 billion. Critics claimed frantically that Roosevelt's administration was leading the U.S. to financial disaster. During fiscal year 1940, $34 billion was spent; in 1943, $79 billion; in 1944, $95 billion; in 1945, $98 billion; and in 1946, $60 billion. From $19 billion of national debt in President Herbert Hoover's last year in office, the debt had risen to $40 billion in 1939. The concentration on massive and fast military production with little attention to costs resulted in winning a global war. America helped defeat strong and vicious enemies without going bankrupt. Raising money for the war effort, and deficit and inflation reduction, was to be achieved by voluntary means—by buying war bonds. Celebrities, movie stars, professional athletes, and war heroes appeared at bond rallies to stimulate patriotic buying. Roosevelt and others thought such volunteerism would be more palatable than additional taxation and would also have the virtue of stronger civilian participation in the war effort. The one flaw in this reasoning was that the people did not buy enough war bonds; the sale of bonds in 1942 raised a mere $10 million, when the government's war expenditure was $160 billion.

To pay for the huge costs of war, and to siphon off the surplus money as a means of preventing inflation, Congress passed a $10 billion tax bill and gave President Roosevelt broad power to carry out the war without referring to Congress for specific authority. Legislation was passed to train civilians for possible air raids; bombing insurance against possible damage was made available. Congress provided money for needed government agencies; and it monitored war production by investigating corruption, waste, and inefficiency and exposing shortages and war contract profiteers. Instead of waiting until the war was over, as had happened in the previous war, Senator Truman's committee sought to minimize graft and inefficiency while the war was in progress.

One dispassionate review of the efficiency and effectiveness of American military production and procurement during World War II provides both accolades and scathing criticism of serious flaws. Dr. Alan L. Gropman's study, *Mobilizing U.S. Industry in World War II*, describes realities and myths that have been ignored. In the following extract, Gropman discusses an American war production record that was replete with extraordinary achievement and serious problems.

At a dinner during the Teheran Conference in December 1943, Joseph Stalin praised United States manufacturing:

"I want to tell you the Russian point of view, what the President and the United States have done to win the war. The most important things in this war are machines. The United States has proven that it can turn out from 8,000 to 10,000 airplanes per month. Russia can only turn out, at most, 3,000 airplanes per month .... The United States, therefore, is a country of machines. Without the use of those machines, through Lend-Lease, we would lose this war."

It was more than airplanes, of course. The Soviets received, in addition to thousands of tanks and airplanes, hundreds of thousands of trucks from the United States, which vastly enhanced the mobility of the Soviet ground forces. The United States also supplied Stalin's factories with millions of tons of raw materials and thousands of machine tools to assist the Soviet Union in manufacturing trucks and all the other implements of modern war including tanks.

World War II was won in largest part because of superior allied armaments production. The United States greatly outproduced all its enemies and, at its peak in late 1943 and early 1944, was manufacturing munitions almost equal to the combined total of both its friends and adversaries. The prodigious arms manufacturing capability of the United States is well known by even casual readers of World War II history, if its decisiveness is not as well understood. But myths provoked by sentimentality regarding United States munitions production have evolved in the half-century since the war ended, and these have become a barrier to comprehending the lessons of that era.

When viewed in isolation the output is indeed impressive. United States Gross National Product grew by 52 percent between 1939 and 1944 (much more in unadjusted dollars), munitions production skyrocketed from virtually nothing in 1939 to unprecedented levels, industrial output tripled, and even consumer spending increased (unique among all combatants). But United States industrial production was neither a "miracle" nor was its output comparatively prodigious given the American advantages of abundant raw materials, superb transportation and technological infrastructure, a large and skilled labor force, and, most importantly, two large ocean barriers to bar bombing of its industries. Germany, once it abandoned its *Blitzkrieg* strategy, increased its productivity more than the United States, Britain, and the Soviet Union, and despite German attacks on Britain and the Soviet Union, these states performed outstandingly too.

This is not to say that United States logistics grand strategy was not ultimately effective. The United States and its allies were, of course, victorious, and we lost far fewer lives than any of our adversaries and fewer than our main Allies. Stalin was correct when he hailed American production. But the halo that has surrounded the era needs to be examined because there were enormous governmental, supervisory, labor-management relations and domestic political frictions that hampered the effort—and there is no reason to think that these problems would not handicap future mobilization efforts. With enormous threats looming in the mid 1930s and increasing as Europe exploded into war at the end of the decade, the United States was in no way unified in its perception of the hazards, nor was there any unity in government or business about what to do about it. In the end, America and its allies were triumphant, and logistics played the decisive role, but the mobilization could have been more efficient and America could have produced more munitions more quickly and perhaps have ended the war sooner. A nostalgic look at United States industrial mobilization during World War II will not make future mobilizations of any size more effective.

Certainly none of the major World War II adversaries was less prepared for war in 1939 than the United States. There were fewer than 200,000 men in the Army, only 125,000 in the Navy, and fewer than 20,000 in the Marine Corps. Those troops on maneuvers in 1939 and 1940 used broomsticks to simulate rifles and trucks to represent tanks. Despite war orders from Britain and France in 1939 and 1940 and Lend-Lease shipments to Britain, the Soviet Union, China and elsewhere after Lend-Lease took effect in March 1941, there were still five million Americans unemployed at the end of the year. Hitler's Germany had long since absorbed its unemployment by building arms and German infrastructure. In the United States, great progress had been made by the time production peaked in late 1943, compared with the situation in 1941, but output could have been even higher. The fact that it took from August 1939, when the first federal agency designed to analyze mobilization options—the War Resources Board—was inaugurated, to May 1943, when the final supervisory agency was put in place—the Office of War Mobilization—should be instructive. Because it had been less than effective in World War I, industrial mobilization was studied throughout the interwar period—a fact that should be sobering. Certainly the interwar planners hoped to improve on the World War I experience with industrial mobilization and they believed because of their efforts the next round would be more efficiently and effectively executed. They were wrong.[59]

Amphibious Warfare

Invasions by sea of enemy-occupied land date back to 490 BC and the Battle of Marathon. Modern amphibious methods were used by the Japanese in 1937 when they landed troops at Tientsin, China. The Japanese built specialized landing craft; and they used aircraft, intelligence gathering, and planning to surprise their Chinese victims. The Germans used an amphibious attack to invade Norway in April 1940.[60]

Amphibious warfare, which combined air, sea, and ground forces, involved many people and much equipment over great distances. It depended on effective logistics. The United States used a strategy that invested in developing an infrastructure of factories that would provide for a long war. Hitler, however, expected a fast victory, and so Germany did not develop an extensive logistic infrastructure. A United States Industrial College of the Armed Forces study, published by the National Defense University Press, pointed out that Hitler used materials to build new munitions but not enough new munitions factories. Germany mobilized more men for its army than did the United States and used about as many men in its armed forces, even with a much smaller population than the U.S. Germany spent a greater part of its gross national product on the war than did the United States and had a higher percentage of its women working in war industry, but it did not produce enough armaments and was drowned in a sea of Allied munitions.

The survival of the Allies depended upon United States Merchant Marine shipping. The U.S. Maritime Commission and the War Shipping Administration rebuilt the nation's merchant marine. Its workers built more than 600 new tankers to carry 64.7 million tons of oil, gasoline, and other desperately needed commodities. They reduced the time it took to build a merchant ship by one-half.

In February 1942, Admiral King established the Amphibious Force, Atlantic Fleet, with headquarters at Hampton Roads, Virginia. It was recognized that offensive Allied action required major landings in the face of fierce opposition. Therefore, the responsibility for the training and planning for an invasion required a commander. To his surprise, Admiral Hewitt received dispatch orders, detaching him, upon arrival in port, from command of Cruisers Atlantic Fleet and Cruiser Division Eight and directing him to proceed to Hampton Roads immediately to assume command of an amphibious force.

Hewitt's role in commanding amphibious invasions was to increase by exponential proportions as American involvement in the war grew. Thomas B. Buell, author of a biography of Fleet Adm. Ernest J. King, wrote that "perhaps the most important thing that King did was to appoint Rear Admiral Henry Kent Hewitt as the Naval Amphibious Commander. Hewitt was magnificent. Through his leadership and organizational genius, the United States Navy was ready for its first major amphibious assault of the Second World War" (Operation Torch, the November 1942 invasion of North Africa).[61] Hewitt's account follows:

> Early on April 28, 1942 the *Philadelphia* arrived at the Navy Yard, New York, and at about 8:30 in a brief ceremony I turned over command of Cruiser Division Eight to Rear Admiral Lyal A. Davidson. I hated to leave my cruisers, my fine flagship, and my loyal staff personnel. But even more interesting work lay ahead. Accompanied by my flag lieutenant, I drove immediately to Floyd Bennett Field and took off promptly in a two-engine plane for the Naval Air Station, Hampton Roads. By noon, I was in command of the Amphibious Force, Atlantic Fleet. This was the most rapid change of duty I ever made.
>
> Having been established only two months before, the Amphibious Forces was in its infancy. Already, however, its responsibilities were many and varied, with initially few means with which to meet them. Headquarters had been established in a small building near one of the Naval Base Forces, which itself needed more room. The Commander of Transport Ships, Captain Emmett, was on his flagship.

AmPhioLant, to use its abbreviated title, was charged with (1) the training of the assault transports and cargo ships and the crews of landing craft carried by them, (2) the training of crews for the larger beaching amphibious craft—tank landing craft, infantry landing craft, and tank landing ships, the construction of large numbers of which had already been begun in the United States, and (3) the training of assigned army units in amphibious operations. The last included not only embarkation and disembarkation, but the principles of combat loading, of joint communications, and of joint handling of operations on assault beaches where navy responsibility and army responsibility met. This was a considerable task. To make matters worse, all our Marines, our amphibious experts, were detached to the Pacific, soon to be followed by General Holland Smith himself—not, however, before I had been able to profit by his experience and advice.

Adequate training of naval crews in beaching and retracting their craft under surf conditions required the use of exposed beaches. These were available outside of Cape Henry, an area which could be reached by craft operating from Little Creek. But training of troops and of transport crews and boat crews, in execution of landings from the open area, was not practicable without unjustified risk, on account of the presence of enemy submarines off the Capes and the unavailability of escort craft, which were fully occupied in the protection of trans-Atlantic and coastal convoys. Consequently, all training involving transports had to be carried out in the smooth waters of Chesapeake Bay, using beaches north of the mouth of the Patuxent at Solomon's Island, and the Lynnhaven Roads beaches between Little Creek and Cape Henry. To meet these needs, a training base was established on the west side of the Little Creek estuary, and a smaller one at Solomon's Island. These schools were set up in hastily constructed wooden buildings in an area (a potato field when I first saw it) immediately adjacent to the landing craft piers already constructed at Little Creek. Fortunately, we were able to have initially considerable Marine Corps help, and, on the Navy side, the assistance of many officers who had participated in previous amphibious exercises. For guidance, there were a series of "Standard Operating Procedures", which had been established as a result of Navy-Marine Corps experience, procedures which subsequent experience proved to be thoroughly sound.

Quite early in the game, I met in Washington the then Vice Admiral (who was also Lieutenant General and Air Vice Marshal) Lord Louis Mountbatten, son of the Admiral of the Fleet Prince Louis of Battenberg, who at the beginning of World War I had been removed from his post as First Sea Lord, because of his German name (thus the subsequent Anglicization of the name). In March of 1942, Mountbatten had been appointed Chief of Combined Operations with the rank of Vice Admiral and, to emphasize the necessary coordination of services, given a corresponding rank in the other two. Thus he was, in a sense, my trans-Atlantic "opposite number". He had come over to press the construction of the specially designed landing craft, to obtain allocation of as many as possible to British use, and to further allied cooperation in planning for the future, particularly with regard to European landings. He was considerably younger than I, but I found him to be a man of great personal magnetism and very able. This encounter was followed a month or two later by a visit on my part to "Combine Operations" activities in Britain.

An efficient and successful amphibious operation, however, involves more than the mere leading of troops on a transport, embarking them and their equipment in landing craft in boats, and setting them ashore on a selected beach. It includes the proper loading of transports so that the weapons, equipment, and supplies may be unloaded in the order required (combat loading). It involves the naval gunfire, and its control, needed to support the landing and the first advance inland to secure a beachhead. It includes a Joint Organization on the assault break, where naval responsibility ends and army responsibility takes over; a Navy Beachmaster to handle the beaching and retraction of landing aircraft, to repair and salvage craft that have been stranded or disabled, to maintain communications to seaward, and to take care of casualties for return to ships; and an Army Shore Party Commander to prepare beach exits and route traffic forward, to unload craft and dispose of their cargoes, to maintain communications forward to the front line, and to receive and turn over to the Navy casualties to be returned seaward. There also had to be joint training for navy radio and signal personnel and army signal corps crews, because communication systems of the two services differed considerably, and they had to be brought into harmony.[62]

Hewitt also stressed the need to create training programs for the American armed forces so that they would be better equipped to fight the enemy with the new technology that was being produced. "The immediate need," he wrote, "was for the establishment of joint schools, one for communications, one for gunnery, one for the study of branch organization problems, and, last but not least, one for the training of army transport quartermasters and navy transport cargo officers in the technique of combat loading."[63]

The initial amphibious vessel design work was British. The building of LSTs and other types, like the LCIs (Landing Craft, Infantry), was primarily an American accomplishment. Some of these landing crafts were large enough to cross the ocean.[64] There was a substantial difference in size and crew composition between the oceangoing LSTs, the LSDs (Landing Ship Docks), and the shore-to-shore amphibious crafts. An LST carried a crew of about one hundred.

LSTs

We will never know how many lives LSTs saved during World War II. We do know that in World War I, when the Allies tried to attack Germany's ally Turkey in the Dardanelles, more than one hundred thousand troops (mostly Australian and New Zealanders) were killed, wounded, or missing. The Gallipoli plan urged upon the Allies by First Lord of the Admiralty Winston Churchill was a disaster because of the lack of amphibious vessels that were oceangoing with the ability of beaching, and Prime Minister Churchill continuously pleaded for the production of more and more LSTs during World War II. The spectacle of having the British Army stranded on the beaches of Dunkirk, France, in June 1940, after its attempt to rescue its Allies, must have added to Churchill's concern about the need for amphibious vessels and the need of their crews.

Early in World War II, Allied military leaders realized that they needed large oceangoing ships that could deliver tanks and vehicles in amphibious assaults. In November 1941, before the United States entered the war, officers of the U.S. Navy Bureau of Ships met with a delegation from the British Admiralty. A few days later, John Niedermair of the U.S. Bureau of Ships provided a basic design for LSTs. His concept satisfied two conflicting objectives: it met the requirement of a deep draft for ocean voyages and the design satisfied the mandate of providing a vessel with a shallow draft for beaching. The essence of the Niedermair design was that the ship would have a large ballast system that could be filled for ocean travel and that would be pumped out for beaching operations. British naval leaders immediately approved the design.

By early 1942, final working plans were developed that incorporated the chief features of LST 1012 and other ships in its class. LSTs could carry a 2,100-ton load. The width of the bow door and ramp accommodated most Allied vehicles. Ventilation of the tank space was provided to allow the running of tank motors. An elevator was installed to lower vehicles from the main deck to the tank deck for disembarking.

The construction of LSTs was ultimately given high priority. By the end of 1942, there were twenty-three in commission. The urgent need for LSTs resulted in unique building practices. Even before the completion of a test vessel, contracts were entered into and construction started. Preliminary orders were expedited by oral contracts, telephone calls, telegrams, and airmail letters. Materials were ordered before the design work was completed. Procurement of materials was handled pragmatically. Some items, for example main propulsion machinery, were provided by the navy. To avoid having the many private builders in the LST manufacturing program bid against one another, an adjunct unit of the Bureau of Ships, the Material Coordinating Agency, was created; and procurement was centralized. There was careful monitoring of the materials by the Material Coordinating Agency, which expedited construction schedules. LST 1012 and similar ships were completed in a little more than a month. There was an urgent need for LSTs. The keel of an aircraft carrier was hastily removed to make place for several LSTs to be built instead.

Most of the existing shipping facilities were located in coastal cities. They were used for the construction of large deep-draft ships. New construction facilities for LSTs were created along inland waterways. Some of the new shipbuilding yards were located in navy industrial plants, such as those that fabricated steel. LST 1012 and many others were built at the Bethlehem Steel Company, in Fore River, Massachusetts. Bridges posed the main obstacle in transporting the completed LSTs from the inland shipyards to deep waters. To tackle this problem, the navy completed a program of modifying bridges. It developed a ferrying program to move the newly constructed LSTs to coastal ports for final installation of missing parts. Of the 1,051 LSTs completed during World War II, 670 were built by five major inland "cornfield" shipyards. For example, the LST 282 was built in 1943, in Ambridge, Pennsylvania, by the American Bridge Company.

Although LSTs made their combat debut in the island-hopping campaigns of the Pacific War, they played important roles in the Italian and French campaigns. Enemy military leaders knew that LSTs were valuable and saw a special need to target them for destruction. However, most remained intact: twenty-six LSTs were lost to enemy action, and thirteen were victims of reefs, weather conditions, or accidents.

Building the LSTs

Andrew Jackson Higgins played an important role in the development and production of the landing craft that helped the Allies defeat the Axis power in World War II.[65] In the 1930s, he was a successful boat builder in Louisiana. Before the Pearl Harbor attack, Higgins was in the business of importing and exporting lumber. After Pearl Harbor, he became internationally known as a builder of a variety of landing craft (LCMS or Landing Craft, Mechanized; LCVPs, or Landing Craft, Vehicle, Personnel; LCPs, or Landing Craft Personnel; and other types). Jerry F. Strahan wrote that "Higgins claimed that his Atlantic tank carrier was the 'Grand-Daddy' of the LST, which he had originally developed in 1940."[66]

His company designed, developed, and rapidly built nearly twenty-one thousand different types of boats. Higgins later claimed that his LST design was stolen by competitors and that a large part of blame lay with then Undersecretary of the Navy Forrestal, Admiral King, and William Francis Gibbs, a supervisor/coordinator of shipbuilding for the War Production Board and also head of a shipbuilding company.

LSTs moved to and from shore by the skillful use of stern anchor and winch (handle of a revolving machine). The stern anchor was dropped before the LST hit a beach. To back away, the winch and the anchor rope were used to pull the ship from the shore.

The bottom of an LST was flat so that the ship could beach itself and then withdraw to the water. The bow drew about three feet of water and the stern from eight to ten feet. LSTs were not designed to cut through water, and they rode the surface. This subjected the craft to the movement of the sea, and even moderate movement resulted in the LSTs rocking and rolling; seasickness was prevalent. Heavy seas meant that the ship listed twenty-five to thirty-three degrees and concurrently pitched ten to twelve degrees. The ship would ride the crest of a wave and then crash down into a trough between waves. It was imperative to brace oneself to offset the results of a rolling ship. Equipment had to be tied down and secured. Negligence, such as the improper securing of heavy equipment on the top and tank decks of LSTs, resulted in accidents, such as loose equipment going overboard.

Many LSTs were 346 feet in length and 54 feet wide. Four or six LCVPs—landing craft for vehicles or personnel—were carried on davits—cranelike devices used for supporting, raising, or lowering boats. Each could carry thirty-six men, seven thousand five hundred pounds of cargo, one jeep, or one 105-mm gun. The LCVP was about thirty-seven feet in length and the beam nearly eleven feet. While their troops were being evacuated from Dunkirk in spring 1940, the British Admiralty started planning the invasion of Europe. They and American Navy engineers worked together on the design and development of different types of amphibious vessels, using features of existing craft. Shallow draft tankers were used as models in the design of LSTs. The LCTs (Landing Craft Tanks), which carried tanks, or nine trucks or one hundred fifty tons of cargo, were a variation of continental river barges.

STATISTICS CONCERNING LST 1012 AND OTHERS

Length overall	328 feet
Length in waterline	316 feet
Extreme beam	50 feet
Beaching displacement	2,366 tons
Full load displacement	4,980 tons (displacement at limiting draft)
Tons per inch immersion	33 tons (at beach displacement)
Trial speed	11.6 knots
Number of propellers	2
Manufacturer type of engines and model	GM Diesel 12-567A
Shaft horsepower	1,700
Total accommodations	13 officers, 106 enlisted
Type of drive ship's service generator	Diesel

Capacity each   230 DC
Fuel capacities (diesel oil)   4,320 barrels[67]

Life Aboard an LST

Life aboard an LST during World War II was often difficult. But those who served on them have fond memories of their peculiarities. Claude Miller of East Moline, Illinois, is well qualified to describe the ship. He was a crew member of LSTs 313, 229, and 621. His ode, "The LST," follows:

THE LST

> An ugly duckling to some
> She 'nay well have been,
> Slow of speed
> And her armor plate thin.
>
> Not graceful like a cruiser
> Nor slim like a can
> And when entering a port
> Was never met with a band.
>
> No keel to slice thru
> The waves of the sea.
> Never sharing in the glory
> Of crossing a '71.
>
> No songs were ever sung,
> No stories every told
> Of battles she won
> With deeds that were bold.
>
> No broadsides to fire,
> No torpedoes on deck,
> To blast enemy ships
> And reduce them to wrecks.

United States—Before And After Pearl Harbor

No name in the headlines,
No mention in the dispatches,
Just storming a beach
With battened down hatches.

Storming hostile beaches
Was the name of her game
And winning a war
Not seeking out fame.

Just plodding along
With warriors on board
As she headed for the beach
And the enemy horde.

Large slow targets,
They were called with a grin
as with flank speed ahead
They barreled on in.

Oh! there were grander ships
That sailed in the seas
And we sailed in their shadow
In the LSTs.

But to me, she was a lady
Of beauty and grace,
Broad in the beam
And never winning a race.

But I have no regrets.
I'm as proud as can be
To have been one of the crew
Of an LST

—Claude Miller [68]

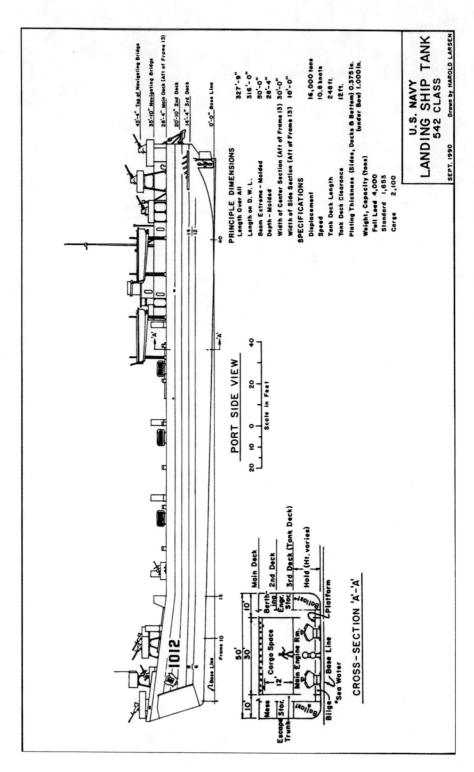

LST 1012 drawing by Harold Larsen, crew member LST 1012

LST 1012

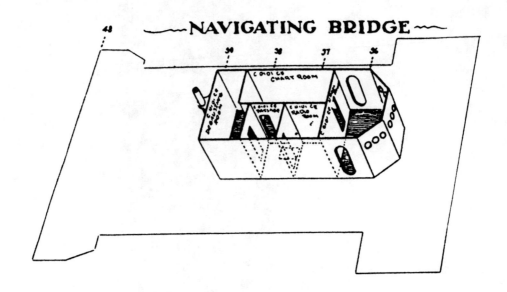

Navigating bridge of the Landing Ship, Tank 542 Class

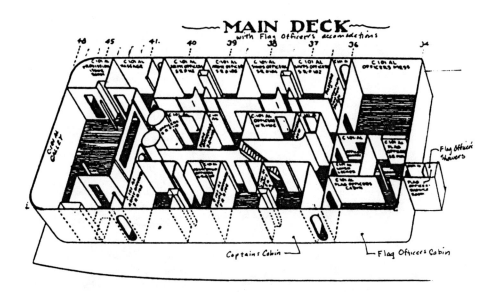

Main deck of the Landing Ship, Tank 542 Class

Opera-tional use	Ocean-going ship designed to land waterproofed tanks or vehicles over a low ramp on a 1/50 beach slope.
Description	An American design now the United Nations standard. Elevator and hatch service main deck where miscellaneous vehicles and cargo are stowed. Starting with LST-513 and excepting LST-531, main deck ramp is substituted for elevator. For inaccessible landings, sectional pontoons are used, or earth causeways built. LCT(5) or (6) may be carried in sections or as a unit on main deck. UK Designation—LST(2).
Capacity	Ocean-going load is limited to 2,100 tons on LST(1) class and 1,900 tons on LST-542 class. Of this maximum, main deck load is 350 tons. Main deck is designed for concentrated load of trucks having 10-ton gross weight. When this load is exceeded, as in case of LVT's, vehicles should be loaded over short span side beams with planking to distribute load. Tank deck load is designed for concentrated load of heaviest tanks. The limiting height from deck to underside of lights in this space is 11'3''. Volume is 92,765 cubic feet. 1,060 tons of Diesel oil can also be carried.

Endurance	6,000 mile radius at 9 knots. Speed—10.8 knots (maximum).
Displace-ment	Sea-going (full load of 2,100 tons) 4,080 tons. Draft, 8' fwd. 14'4" aft. Landing (full load of 500 tons) 2,160 tons. Draft, 3'1" fwd. 9'6" aft. Light, 1,490 tons. Draft, 1'6" fwd. 7'5" aft. Tons per inch immersion Landing Displacement 33.3 Tons per inch immersion Ocean-going 33.5 LST-542 class has a light displacement of 1,623 tons. The increased displacement is a result of the additions of authorized armament, a distilling plant (4,000 gallons per day), and other miscellaneous weight increases. Payload to maintain designed landing draft is decreased accordingly.
Dimensions	Length, 328'0" o.a. Beam, 50'0"
Armament	U. S. 1–3"/50 cal. D. P. BRITISH: 1–12 pdr. (omitted when 40's are available) 6–20 mm 1–40 mm. (7 authorized). 4–FAM 6–20 mm. (12 authorized).
Armor	15-lb. STS splinter protection.
Crew	(2 davit)—7 officers, 204 men. Troops—16 officers, 147 men. (6 davit)—9 officers, 220 men. Troops—14 officers, 131 men.
Propulsion	Two 900-hp. Diesels; twin screw.

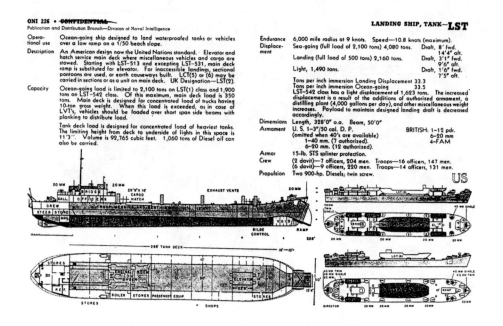

Landing Ship, Tank

CHAPTER 4

THE STRUGGLE FOR THE MEDITERRANEAN

A lthough they were not available for use in the North African invasion (Operation Torch, November 1942), LSTs were prime performers in the later invasions commanded by Admiral Hewitt—Sicily (Operation Husky, July 1943) and Salerno (Operation Avalanche, September 1943). What prompted these combined amphibious operations? How were they planned and executed? How were they connected? What did Allied army, air force, and naval commanders of the Dragoon invasion learn from the preceding Mediterranean invasions? Why did American military and diplomatic leaders, who made most of the preparations for the invasion of North Africa, pass over de Gaulle and deal instead with Adm. Jean François Darlan, commander in chief of Vichy forces? How did Roosevelt's State Department agent, Robert D. Murphy, serve as a catalyst for a successful North African invasion? How was the rehabilitation and rearming of anti-German French forces achieved? Many other provocative questions concerning differences between the North African, Sicilian, and Salerno invasions also require answers. For example, what impact did the 1943 ouster of Benito Mussolini and his Fascist government have on the subsequent Mediterranean invasions?

The Significance of the Mediterranean

British and French military leaders, before the start of World War II, recognized the strategic importance of the Mediterranean and prepared plans to protect the Suez Canal and French colonies in North Africa jointly. Allied leaders believed that Mussolini would join Hitler, in which case the safety of Britain's lifeline to the Far East would be endangered. The French considered the Mediterranean the vital passageway to their colonies in Algeria, Tunisia, and Morocco. Within a few weeks in the spring of 1940, the defeat of France rendered a vast blow to Britain's superiority of the Mediterranean. The armistice between Germany and the Vichy government mooted the British partnership with the powerful French Navy. Added to the agony of the Allied situation in the Mediterranean was the challenge posed by a large Italian Navy, which aspired to control this large inland sea. Soon after the Pearl Harbor attack, the editors of *The New Republic* magazine wrote that "it might . . . be a wise though uncomfortable policy to [concentrate the American] Navy in the Mediterranean."[1]

The British had a strong Mediterranean fleet, including a major base in Alexandria, Egypt, and others of strategic importance, such as Malta. However, German and Italian naval strength was formidable. The havoc wrought by German submarines on Allied shipping in the Atlantic was frightening and required enormous Allied resources. Italian naval power was also impressive. Since the Italian invasion of Abyssinia (Ethiopia) in 1935, Italian Navy crews had been gaining valuable experience and preparation for war against the Allies in the Mediterranean. Mussolini was intent on restoring Roman glory and controlling the Mediterranean, despite the fact that his army was not ready to fight a war. Only two of Italy's six battleships were in service; its navy, however, had seven heavy cruisers, twelve light cruisers, fifty destroyers, and one hundred eight submarines. The Italians also modernized two old battleships and built four more, which were faster and more modern. Taranto was one of the main Italian naval bases; and those at Naples, Spezia, Brindisi, Augusta, Palermo, Cagliari in Sardinia, and Tripoli and Benghazi in Libya provided the Italian Navy with key tactical positioning into the eastern and western reaches of the Mediterranean.

Italy's entry into the war triggered serious concerns for the British. Could they maintain control of Malta? Its proximity to Italian territory posed problems. By the end of summer 1940, the British sent a convoy to Malta. On October 28, ignoring his naval strategists, Mussolini issued orders to invade Greece, instead of strengthening Italy's position in the Mediterranean. The British came to the aid of the Greeks to bolster their own Middle East position, sending money, munitions, and the Royal Air Force to help the Greek government. The Italian invaders were pushed back to Albania; and Mussolini's army, with its inadequate planning and support, was subjected to ridicule. The British regained their positioning and power in the Mediterranean.

The German High Command wanted to help Italy, but Hitler's decision to invade the Soviet Union required extensive planning and preparation. German energies were focused on the eastern front instead of one to the south via Greece. This did not mean that the German High Command was oblivious to the importance of the Mediterranean; it implemented many measures to help Italy regain Greece.[2]

Allied ships sailing the Mediterranean were subjected to immense dangers from German aircraft and submarines. In the first few months of 1941, the British Mediterranean Fleet was subjected to considerable losses from German attacks. In March, Italian ships were able to safely transport Gen. Erwin Rommel's "Afrika Korps" across the Mediterranean to North Africa. Providing supplies to fighting forces in North Africa was much easier for the Axis powers than for the Allies; the Germans and Italians needed only a three-day voyage to reach North Africa while the British had to undertake a much longer voyage around the Cape of Good Hope.

Allied supply requirements increased following the German invasion of Russia in June 1941. The United States decided to provide Lend-Lease help to the Russians, who had few ships to transport war supplies. Churchill and Roosevelt met in Argenta, Newfoundland, in August 1941, to resolve this and other problems. Plans were also laid by their respective chiefs of staff for the escort of Allied convoys. By September 20, Rear Admiral Hewitt received orders that directed him to command a convoy on to Argenta, which the United States acquired as a base under the Churchill-Roosevelt deal.[3]

Although service disputes developed between British and American political and military leaders concerning the Mediterranean and other theaters of war, the degree of cooperation between the wartime Allies was remarkable. Despite the serious, long-drawn-out controversy between those who favored and those who opposed the invasion of southern France and many other disputes, Fleet Adm. Chester W. Nimitz and editor E. B. Potter asserted that "seldom in the history of coalition warfare has there been more complete trust and cooperation between Allies than there was between Britain and the United States in World War II."[4]

Dealing with the French

Charles R. Anderson, writing for the U.S. Army Center of Military History, noted that "Casablanca was of particular concern to the U.S. Navy covering force off Fedala since it harbored French naval units including cruisers, destroyers, submarines, and the uncompleted battleship *Jean Bart,* whose 15-inch guns could easily reach both transport and landing beaches to the north."[5]

Several secret efforts were undertaken by President Roosevelt, General Eisenhower, State Department agent Murphy, and other Americans to persuade the French in North Africa not to harm the Allied invaders; but no such guarantee was provided. With their loyalties divided, many French military officers faced a moral dilemma: whether to follow Vichy dictates to oppose the Allies or to dismiss Vichy authority.

The invasion of North Africa, on November 8, 1942, was the first major European theater offensive action by Americans in World War II— the first time that American troops were stationed in the Mediterranean theater of war. These actions provided a shift in France's relationship with the United States since the 1940 armistice. American political and military leaders realized that they needed someone to lead French North Africans. Apprehensions existed that General de Gaulle could not help the Allies because most French military officers considered him disloyal to Pétain, to whom they had allegiance as head of the French nation. Therefore, the United States, which was designated to play a major role in the invasion, selected the highly regarded general Henri Giraud as commander in chief of the French Army of North Africa.

The Allied commander in North Africa, General Eisenhower, was confronted with several difficult problems. These included securing the extensive invasion areas with minimum losses; getting the cooperation of the French civil authorities; and, perhaps most important, persuading the French military not to oppose the Allied landings. If the Allies could be joined by the French in North Africa without the vexatious de Gaulle, it was likely that Roosevelt would rejoice. Much has been written about the political and diplomatic issues and the events surrounding the Allied invasion of North Africa. These included Robert Murphy's delicate task of getting the cooperation of General Giraud, who was in France and ignorant of Allied North Africa plans, and Murphy's having to deal with French Admiral Darlan, which led to the controversial Darlan-Murphy deal. Samuel Morison and other historians have presented ample coverage of events.[6] However, this author doubts whether Murphy's spirited defense of the United States policy in North Africa during that period is well known.[7]

OSS agents contacted Allied sympathizers throughout North Africa who, in turn, gathered and helped analyze crucial information. Admiral Hewitt's staff also made good use of army, navy, and army air force intelligence services. According to Professor Morison, Hewitt's staff, headed by Leo A. Bachman, utilized information from the OSS, the hydrographic office, weather bureaus, tourist photos, and movies.[8] To prevent a possible German attack through Spanish Morocco into the Allied rear, Allied intelligence agents organized Arabian tribesmen into a guerrilla force.[9]

While the Middle East was important to American foreign policy before December 7, 1941, the Mediterranean, especially French North Africa, was of greater immediate strategic significance. American foreign policy leaders were aware of the economic problems facing Vichy, France and French Northwest Africa after the France's 1940 defeat. The Americans considered economic aid to these regions important to the defense of the United States. The costs of the Lend-Lease program amounted to over $40 billion, and the great majority of the French Northwest African population relied heavily upon the generosity of the United States. However, the amount of aid was far below the level needed to further American and Allied war interests. One of the main obstacles in the delivery of U.S. aid was the refusal of the British to take a lenient attitude toward giving assistance to the Vichy regime. That "stubborn" British policy resulted in reduced American aid, according to author James Dougherty, who also believed that U.S. economic aid to French Northwest Africa severely undermined French authority. The Americans came to be seen as liberators from French rule, and Arab dislike of the French increased throughout the war years. By November 1942, wrote Dougherty, "the Americans in North Africa were in an unusual, if not ludicrous, situation; they had aroused the suspicions of the French and Nazis."[10] The Allies learned that in order to campaign against the Axis powers in Northwest Africa, it was essential to obtain the cooperation and support of its native population. Thus, the rearmament and training of Allied forces was extended to the French colonies in the region, where the lines between allegiance to the Vichy regime or the Free French were often blurred.

The rehabilitation of anti-German French forces in Northwest Africa was a remarkable achievement, wrote Brig. Gen. Monro MacCloskey. Both the Americans and the British realized the importance of utilizing a French colonial force that was sympathetic to the Allied cause; and "with both the Americans and the British maintaining their positions, the French were forced to scale down their initial aspirations and let the rearmament progress at a pace determined by the global supply and equipment demands of the war. That was the basis on which successive rearmament programs were formulated and conducted, but the French still continued to press for fuller reestablishment of their military forces."[11] These colonial troops proved to be important in defeating the German Army in the Mediterranean theater of war. The French military was five-hundred-sixty-thousand-men strong by September 1944; of that number, North and West Africa provided roughly two hundred ninety-five thousand colonial soldiers and two hundred fifteen thousand Frenchmen, for a combined estimated total of five hundred ten thousand.[12]

The majority of these troops originated from Tunisia, Algeria, and French Morocco. The language barrier was a problem, as were customs, food, and clothing size differences. "Most acute were shortages of various kinds: of Allied shipping, of port facilities for receiving, stocking, and distributing equipment; and of French technical personnel necessary to man depots, repair shops, and base units and to provide combat and service support troops. Then there was the lack of familiarity on the part of the French with the newer weapons and with American technology and working methods. For these or other reasons the French were persistently reluctant to accept fully the importance of logistics and by the same token found themselves excessively dependent on American logistical support in combat. Foremost among the factors in-fluencing Franco-Allied relations, particu-larly in the field of rearmament, were the language barrier and a dearth of qualified liaison officers on both sides."[13]

"Considering all aspects of the undertaking," wrote MacCloskey, "the United States received good value for the time, money, and effort expended in the rearmament program. Certainly the project presented many difficult problems, and absorbed the attention of countless individuals. Nevertheless, it made it possible for the United States to reduce its outlay of combat manpower in the Mediterranean and European theaters by 8 to 10 divisions and 19 air squadrons—perhaps more, considering that U.S. troops used in place of the French would have been relatively inexperienced. For the same reason, U.S. forces suffered fewer losses in those two theaters. French losses from the beginning of the Tunisian campaign to V-E Day, for the ground forces, were estimated at 23,500 killed and 95,500 wounded in action.

"Most important, however, is the fact that the U.S. rearmament program made it possible for the French to regain the honored position they had so long held but had temporarily lost. Although a small group of General de Gaulle's followers had kept the French flag flying during the dark months following the June 1940 armistice, it was the large-scale re-entry of the French into the common struggle, such as took place in mid-November 1942, that enabled them to regain the esteem of the Allies and a place among the democratic nations of the world."[14]

Relations between the French Northwest African colonies and the French mainland deteriorated as Arab nationalism grew. Nevertheless, a common consensus emerged on how best to attack the Axis stronghold in the Mediterranean. It would have to be done by an army with strongly equipped armored divisions landing safely on hostile enemy beaches.

The North African Invasion (Operation Torch)

President Franklin Roosevelt's decision to undertake the amphibious operation that secured French Morocco in November 1942 was important and advantageous. This invasion was coordinated with combined Anglo-American operations that were conducted in two sections, Atlantic and Mediterranean; but they shared the same objectives, planning, and command. The North African campaign succeeded in preventing Germany from controlling the French Empire in Africa and also in preventing the Axis from controlling the French fleet.

FDR's decision to recognize and deal with the Vichy government, despite venomous and widespread protests of appeasement against his administration, helped achieve the success of Operation Torch. Maintaining an American presence in Africa, and placing pressure on Vichy leaders to not completely capitulate to Hitler, helped the Allies dominate Algeria and French North Africa less than a year after the Pearl Harbor attack. Roosevelt's controversial diplomatic policy made possible the occupation of Algeria and French Morocco by the Allies in 1942, with a minimum of bloodshed, according to naval historian Samuel Morison.[15]

Allied leaders preparing for the invasion of North Africa were faced with a serious dilemma: would French military commanders remain loyal to Marshal Pétain and his Vichy regime, or would they align themselves with the invaders? A few realities had to be taken into account: first, the sworn allegiance of French military officers to Pétain and his government; second, many French people detested the British and were unlikely to peacefully welcome them, and there were plenty of Frenchmen who held little admiration for Americans; a third Allied worry was the respect and awe with which some French military officers viewed the German brand of discipline, efficiency, and success.

However, Allied apprehensions about this potentially dangerous mix of French sentiments was mitigated by the OSS, naval intelligence, and other sources of information, all indicating that opposition to Operation Torch would be slight. Roosevelt's agent in North Africa, Robert D. Murphy, reported to him that anti-German French citizens were prepared to assist in the invasion.[16] Murphy mistakenly assumed that French General Henri Giraud would be effective in issuing orders to French military forces not to shoot at Allied troops as they landed in North Africa. But Giraud lacked the necessary political and popular influence to achieve this. Nevertheless, the information gathered revealed that Gen. Alphonse Juin, the French North African commander in chief, was more likely to gain the necessary cooperation to minimize bloodshed between the French and the Allies. Unfortunately, Murphy never approached Juin.[17]

General Marshall, Admiral King, and War Secretary Stimson opposed Churchill's proposal to include North Africa in the invasion plans, preferring a decisive cross-Channel attack on France and not the end-run peripheral North Africa attack favored by the British. President Roosevelt opted for the British plan. By fighting the Germans in North Africa, the Allies compelled them to withdraw crucial troops from the Russian front. This, the first significant combined Allied campaign, provided much-needed experience for American troops and their commanders. Admiral King was against the invasion of North Africa. His biographer, Thomas B. Buell, provided King's reasoning—the admiral did not want urgently needed American ships diverted from an imminent Guadalcanal campaign, nor did King want an American convoy exposed to dangerous German submarine attacks.[18] News reporter and commentator Charles Collingwood suggested that the North African phase of the war was a rehearsal for the successful landings in France in 1944. In a foreword to Peter Tompkins's *The Murder of Admiral Darlan: A Study in Conspiracy*, he observed that, politically, the North Africa phase of the war was a prelude to the subsequent struggle for political power in France.

For two weeks Rear Admiral Hewitt zigzagged a huge armada across the Atlantic Ocean without serious mishap. Three major North African ports were chosen for the Torch invasion—Casablanca on the Atlantic side and Oran and Algiers inside the Mediterranean. The Allied planners of Operation Torch did not know the extent of potential French North African resistance to the invasion, the reaction of the

German High Command, or what the winds and waves on the landing beaches would be like.

Hewitt was in command of the Western Task Force, an all-American unit, whose goal was to capture Casablanca, 190 miles south of Gibraltar on the Atlantic Coast. Maj. Gen. George S. Patton was in charge of the thirty-five thousand assault troops that arrived from the Hampton Roads Naval Air Station, in twenty-nine transport ships. Lieutenant General Eisenhower, who was in command of U.S. troops in Britain, was designated as the supreme Allied commander for North Africa.

The other Torch forces dispatched to take Oran, 280 miles east of Gibraltar, and Algiers, 220 miles farther east of Oran, were a mix of British and American troops who arrived from Britain. Because of French hostility toward the British for sinking their ships in North African ports, the Allied military chiefs decided that Operation Torch would have to be, to a large extent, at least in the early stages, an American endeavor. The Americans were to provide the administration of services and logistics, and they demanded to command Torch. The number of Allied troops involved in the landings was sixty-five thousand.[19]

Admiral Hewitt's Memoirs on the Invasion of North Africa

The following abbreviated account from Admiral Hewitt's memoirs covers preparations for the North African invasion and its implementation and eloquently explains the context of the situation.

> [We] began the tremendous task of collecting all possible information about the Atlantic Coast of Morocco, off-shore and on-shore, including weather and surf conditions, beaches, beach approaches and exits, adjacent terrain features, coast defenses and local defense forces, army and navy. This required examining all sources of information in a highly secret manner so as to give no inkling of the objective. Were this to leak out and pass on to the enemy, a concentration of submarines might not only result in heavy losses but even defeat the operation as a whole.
>
> July 1942 was a period of intensive preparation, with a staff working in cramped quarters. There was much travel back and forth for conferences with the high command in Washington, and there, on July 25th, we received the "Go ahead", for Torch,

the North African landings. Our Army leaders had long favored a limited invasion of northern France in 1942. The British, who realized the difficulties and lack of readiness as our army did not, were opposed. We, in the Amphibious Force, who saw it much as did the British, were greatly relieved at the final decision to undertake the North African alternative.

It was unfortunate that we should not have had an organization such as the British Combined Operations to coordinate the activities of all services in the training, planning, and the providing of material for the landing of ground forces against opposition on an enemy shore. We would have been spared such mistakes as an Army purchase of wooden Chesapeake Bay Line steamers for prospective European use as cross-Channel transports. One of these was even fitted with special bulwark and moved in convoy to Britain, where it was probably soon scrapped. No thinking seaman would have ever considered risking troops in such an unseaworthy and inflammable craft where it might be subject to submarine or air attack or gunfire. Another mistake, from the amphibious point of view, was the training at Camp Edward, Massachusetts, of Army Engineer boat crews for surf landings. These crews were employed in the Algerian landings and performed efficiently, but they were engaged in what, to us, was properly a navy function. After Torch they were soon drawn off for other engineer duties and were never used as boatmen in other Mediterranean operations. At a time when the Amphibious Force was exerting every effort to recruit any one with marine experience for landing craft crews—fishermen, yachtsmen, etc.—it was distinctly annoying to read advertisements in leading newspapers addressed to the same sort of people, "Join the Army's Navy." And it was still more annoying to have some of our best Guard officers and surf men taken away from us to instruct these soldier crews. This was partly the Navy's own fault, for the Bureau of Personnel, depending on voluntary enlistment, did not feel that it could guarantee boat crews in what the Army thought was sufficient number. So the Army, taking advantage of the draft, went ahead on its own . . . .

Amphibious training of naval transports, boats' crews, shore parties, and army elements, as they became available, went on apace. Everywhere, we tried to instill the idea that no matter what uniform an officer or man wore, he was a member of one team working toward the same objective. To illustrate this, when later on we were able to establish our own Headquarters in Ocean View, guarded by military police and blue jackets, the guard to honor a visiting dignitary was always paraded with alternate files of soldiers and sailors . . . .

The worst task, however, was the planning for there were so many uncertainties involved. Not until almost the end was it known what naval units would be available. Many transports reached us just in time for final rehearsals and had little or no other training. Yet Navy plans and Army plans had to be closely coordinated.

By the time the Nansemond headquarters had been set up, the general features of the overall plan were beginning to take shape. The mission assigned to the Western Naval Task Force was "To establish the Western Task Force on beachheads ashore near Mehedia, Fedhala, and Safi, and to support subsequent coastal operations, in order to capture Casablanca as a base for further military operations." The plan had to be based on the assumption that the French forces would resist, although it was devoutly hoped that they would not. The strong fixed defenses of Casablanca, the presence of French Naval forces in the port, and the absence of suitable landing beaches ruled out any direct attack on that city. Fedhala, a small port up the coast at the extreme range of the Casablanca batteries had practicable beaches and only minor defenses. It was chosen as the site of the main landing.

Since the British air facilities at Gibraltar would be fully occupied in supporting the Algerian landings, the only air support initially available to the Western Task Force and Naval Task Force was naval air. Therefore, the early seizure of an airfield was considered essential. Such a field existed at Port Lyautey on the Sebou River, some eighty miles up the coast from the principal objective. Not only was it an airfield but a French naval hydroplane base, since the windings of the river permitted smooth water landings into almost any wind. There were good beaches on both sides of the Sebou River mouth, at Mehedia, and the fixed defenses there were minor. Port Lyautey would be the objective for a Northern Attack Group . . . .

Contact between naval and military command in the three attack groups was also essential to the formulation of their more detailed plans which involved the exact points of beaching, the number, size, and timing of boat waves, and the units that were to go in each. Accordingly, arrangements were made to effect this, as early as possible . . . .

The task of establishing the Western Task Force ashore in Morocco included not only its landing at the selected points, but the safeguarding of its movement to those areas against any enemy attack, submarine, surface, or air. Axis submarine or raider attacks might be expected at any point during the passage. At Casablanca, and also at Dakar, there were substantial French light forces and a number of submarines had to be guarded against if the French decided to resist. Also there were two new partially completed battleships, of unknown mobility, the *Jean Bart* at Casablanca and the *Richelieu* at Dakar, which might be brought into play. The French also had a considerable number of air units at nearby fields whose opposition might have to be combated. To meet these threats required more than the cruisers, old battleships, and destroyers, which were to be assigned to the various attack groups to furnish gunfire support and raider and submarine protection. Accordingly, two additional groups were formed: a Support Group consisting of the new battleship *Massachusetts* and the heavy cruisers (8") *Wichita* and *Tuscaloosa* and an Air Group consisting of the carrier *Ranger* and four auxiliary carriers (converted oil tankers), each with a submarine screen of destroyers. The former was to be commanded by Rear Admiral R.C. Giffen, and the latter by Rear Admiral E.D. McWhorter, both classmates and old friends upon whom I knew I could count on for anything. In fact, I knew all my principal subordinate commanders well and had the utmost confidence in them—a most comforting thought . . . .

The British, in some of their combined operations had made good use of submarines to observe selected landing areas, to fix their positions and then to act as beacons to lead transports in to the disembarkment area. Our intelligence indicated the probability of suitable conditions for landing on the Moroccan Atlantic Coast only one day in five in November and December. The Eastern and Center Task Forces in the

Mediterranean would not be faced with such a problem. Accordingly, one submarine division of five boats was assigned to Task Force 34. This would give a beacon for each of the three landing areas, one to observe Casablanca, and one to watch Dakar for any reaction by the French forces there. The Division Commander, Captain Norman S. Ives, would ride my flagship with me . . . .

Most of the transports originally assigned to the Amphibious Force, Atlantic Fleet, had come from the Old Army Transport Service in various degrees of material condition. All had to be converted to attack transports by being fitted to carry beaching craft for personnel, vehicles, and light tanks, and by being made able to lower them in water which might not be entirely smooth. To obtain transports in adequate numbers to carry and land General Patton's Western Task Force, the Pacific Fleet had to be drawn on, and the conversion and manning of other merchant vessels had to be rushed. Not until very late was it possible to determine just how many would be available, and some reported barely in time to participate in a final rehearsal. Except for Coast Guard manned transport crews, boats crews left much to be desired, but the date set for the landing, November 8th, was a *must*. We had to do the best we could with what we had.

The time had not yet come when the Army was to develop confidence in the accuracy of naval gunfire against land objectives. Consequently the Supreme Commander, General Eisenhower, and other army commanders were insisting on landings under cover of darkness and sufficiently before daylight to give reasonable time for the establishment of a beachhead. The zero hour for Torch as a whole was set at midnight, at which time a message to the French from President Roosevelt, announcing the landing and its purpose, and asking that the Allied Forces be received as friends, was to be broadcast. This hour was satisfactory for the Eastern and Center Task Forces, which would be proceeding close along the Algerian coast as if en route to Malta. But the hour was entirely too early for the Western Task Force, which would be approaching its destination from seaward. For the reason that the state of training and the distance boats would have to travel from transport area to beach, it was estimated that at least four hours would be required between heaving to in the transport area and beaching of the first waves. This would mean that transports would necessarily be heaving to at 8:00 p.m., and thus in sight of shore before dark. Thus the surprise considered essential to success would be lost. As a result of urgent representations, a zero hour of 4:00 a.m. was authorized for the Western Task Force.

Submarines, French as well as Axis, were a great source of anxiety. In an effort to provide protection to anchored transports beyond that which could be afforded by a mobile destroyer screen, a mine detachment consisting of three large mine layers (named for Old Navy monitors), five fast mine layers (converted from old destroyers), and several minesweepers were added to the force. The sweepers and fast mine layers would augment the anti-submarine screens underway. A fleet tug was also added to provide for a possible breakdown or other emergencies.

With the addition of five naval oil tankers to insure adequate fuel supplies, the Western Naval Task Force would comprise a fleet of 102 vessels of all types of which the most important were 3 battleships, 3 heavy and 4 light cruisers, 1 fleet and 4 converted carriers, 38 destroyers, 23 assault transports, and 6 assault supply ships . . . .

Off the Virginia Capes the shoal water of the continental shelf extends out for something like 100 miles. To avoid mines which might be laid by enemy submarines, outgoing and incoming shipping was restricted to a long narrow channel constantly swept by navy minecraft. The major shipping of the Western Naval Task Force proceeding out this channel single file as it would have to do, would make a column some 30 miles long. In order to form a proper convoy disposition at the end of the channel the leading ships would have to maneuver back and forth off the entrance for some two hours or more waiting for the rear ships to catch up. This would have provided such a rare opportunity for lurking submarines that it could not be accepted. It was decided to reduce this risk by dividing the force into two detachments, the advance detachment under Rear Admiral Kelly composed of the Port Lyautey and Safi Groups, departing a day ahead, on the 23rd of October, to rendezvous later with the following detachment.

In view of the submarine menace, it was not desirable to let the advance detachment proceed at slow speed; so it was to be directed initially on a southerly course as if destined to the West Indies. To promote this deception, the Haitian government was very secretly asked for permission to hold amphibious exercises in the Gulf of Gonaives, in the hope there might be some leak of information in Port-au-Prince.

Since the preservation of radio silence by all the force during the voyage to Africa would be of the utmost importance, rendezvous and alternative rendezvous had been set for the advance Detachment, the Covering Group, and the Air Group.

Hampton Roads and AmphibFor Headquarters at the Nansemond were centers of great activity throughout October, particularly towards its last week.

In the midst of this, on October 20th, I received a secret dispatch directing me to report to President Roosevelt at the White House, the next day, at 11:00 a.m.

General Patton, already in Washington, was also to be present. There were so many last—minute matters requiring my attention that I did not feel able to leave until the next morning. If flying weather was good, I could make the appointment easily by taking off not later than 9:00 a.m. Predictions were favorable. But, since an appointment with the President of the United States is something for which one just does *not* arrive late, I decided to play safe by having my car moved over to the Old Point and directing that I be called at 5:00 a.m., and given the latest weather report so that if necessary I might start for Washington in ample time by automobile.

The early morning report to my Hotel Chamberlin apartment convincing me that I could safely count on flying I rolled over gratefully for a little more much needed rest. But, while breakfasting at the Nansemond, I received word that adverse visibility conditions were setting in, and if I wanted to get away I had better get over to the airfield as soon as practicable. I broke all records getting there, only to encounter considerable delay while my pilot was awaiting clearance. My feelings may be imagined. At last, to my relief, we were permitted to take off. But that relief was short-lived, for hardly had we passed over Fortress Monroe, when the plane winged-over and headed back, the pilot reporting he had been ordered to return, why he did not know. That was almost the last blow. But it developed that he had been called back merely to get his secret weather code, which he had forgotten. We were soon once more on our way.

Arrived over Washington with a low cloud ceiling. We were directed to circle while some plane in trouble was coached in to a landing, I becoming more and more impatient. At long last, we came down through the overcast—my delight at finally seeing Anacostia Field below me being indescribable. Whisked to the White House by a car with one of Admiral King's staff, we arrived just in time—a narrow escape.

General Patton and I were brought into the White House by separate entrances in such a manner as not to be seen by any of the usually waiting reporters, who might have smelled a rat, meeting only in the anteroom of the President's office.

Ushered into the sanctum, I was able to greet the President as an old friend of *Indianapolis* days, and then to present General Patton, whom he was seeing for the first time. We were greeted cordially and waved to seats. Then the President, leaning back in his chair, with his cigarette and holder in hand, said, "Well, Gentlemen: what have you got on your minds?" Whew! As if we did not have plenty! But I know that was said just to put us at our ease. Both the General and I discussed our plans at length, and assured the President that we would carry through to the best of our ability. After a hearty handshake and a "God Speed", we departed as we had come. By mid-afternoon, I was back at my desk at the Nansemond, trying to tie up some loose ends.

(A bit of postlogue—Back in my apartment after a late dinner at Chamberlin, I was sitting in a lounge chair trying to catch up with the day's news in the paper, when I suddenly caught myself falling out of the chair. Thoroughly alarmed, my good wife marshaled me into bed, and despite all my protests, insisted on calling up my medical officer, who in response came dashing across the Roads in my barge to see me. After giving me numerous tests and finding that my eyes and other parts of my anatomy reacted properly, he merely prescribed more sleep.)

And so the great day approached. At a conference held on-shore the details of the plans, Army and Navy, were gone over by General Patton and me and members of our staffs, with the principal commanders, many of whom were being let in on the secret for the first time.

By October 22nd, the ships of the Advance Detachment had all been moved out into the Chesapeake Bay or LynnHaven Roads, some holding last-minute rehearsals. On the 23rd, Admiral Kelly and his group departed, as planned, ostensibly for the Caribbean. And on that day, General Patton and I, and those of my staff who were to accompany me on the operation, moved aboard the *Augusta.*

As dawn broke on the 24th, a long column of ships mostly transports, with army trucks on deck and soldiers hanging over the rail started filing out past Fortress Monroe bound for the Capes of the Chesapeake. The destroyers of the screen had already gone ahead to patrol the assemblage area off the entrance to the swept channel. In the midst of this sortie was the *Augusta,* and as we passed the Hotel Chamberlin, I wondered what my wife, and the other service wives there were thinking. I had merely told my wife that I was to go out on an exercise, and that it might be some time before I got back. Being a good Navy wife she asked no questions.

As we passed out the channel we felt well protected, for the air overhead, was well filled with navy patrol planes and a guardian blimp, and our destroyers were all around us. By nightfall we were well on our way to the northeastward in five parallel columns of large ships, the *Augusta* leading the center one and the cruisers of my old Cruiser Division heading the other four. We were off to a new adventure; the plans had been made and were in process of execution, and one could only pray for the best.

General Patton was quite impressed with the orderliness and smoothness of a fleet sortie, something which he had not seen before; but the getaway was not entirely without a hitch and last-minute problems developed, requiring a hasty solution.

The most serious was the breakdown of the *Harry Lee,* an old transport taken over from the Army, which had acquired the nickname of "Leaning Lena" from its tendency to assume a list and retain it. This casualty occurred after the ship had been loaded and the troops embarked. The transport *Calvert* had to be hastily substituted. The latter was brought into a mooring across the dock from the *Lee*. Thus the *Lee* had to be entirely unloaded before the loading of the *Calvert* could commence. It was impossible to get her ready in time to sortie with her group. The destroyers *Eberle* and *Boyle* were left behind as an escort; and she was given necessary rendezvous instructions. She sailed one day after the Main Body . . . .

Most of the first day out was spent in exercising the ships of the Main Body in maneuvering by flag signal, using the prescribed allied convoy signal book (called Mersigs), and in the various zigzags. One oil tanker, due to engineering casualty, was forced to drop back, but was able to regain station well after dark. There were similar incidents on the following day, the 26th, but fortunately all ships concerned were able to rejoin before dark.

General Patton and his staff had little to do during the voyage except to amuse themselves as best they could. The General, for one thing, spent some time in reading the Koran. He wanted to be thoroughly acquainted with the Moslem religion and customs so that neither he nor any of his troops would do anything to antagonize the native Berber population.

As for myself, I spent my time regularly on the flag bridge, or in my bridge cabin. With plans all made and promulgated, there was little to do except to study the intelligence and weather reports broadcast to us, to watch reported concentrations of submarines, to plan the changes of course necessary to avoid such danger spots and to throw off possible trailing submarines, and to be ready to take suitable action in the event of an emergency. Ships were still breaking down now and then, but fortunately resuming station after affecting repairs.

A commander should always try to plan ahead what his action should be in the event of possible emergencies. With such advanced decisions in mind, valuable time can be saved in taking decisive and sound action when the emergency actually arises. One decision which I tried to face was, "In the event a transport is torpedoed, how many destroyers do I dare to leave behind to pick up survivors, without weakening the screen so much as to unduly endanger the remainder?"

When I considered my responsibility for the lives of some 35,000 soldiers, and of as many more naval personnel, and the fact that the screen was none too strong as it was, it was a most difficult decision to make, one that I never solved to my satisfaction. I thank God that the occasion did not come when I had to implement it. There were occasional alarms but no actual attacks throughout the voyage . . . .

General Lucian K. Truscott Jr.,—desiring further opportunity to indoctrinate some of his subordinate commanders, asked and received permission to visit several ships of the Northern Attack Group during the operation, transferring via motor whale boat. This was accomplished safely and to his satisfaction, and to my relief when he returned to his own ship . . . .

By November 2nd, we were well south of the Azores, in fact almost between them and the Cape Verde Islands, and still heading on southeasterly courses. We were warned of three submarines to the northwest of the Cape Verdes, four to the west of the Azores, and four more not far from our line of advance. There were several submarine sound contacts reported during the day, some of which may have been authentic, and a German shore station was overheard broadcasting what we knew to be contact report. It looked as if we might have been spotted.

After dark that night, the night of November 2nd-3rd, several very radical changes of course were made which, by the morning of the 3rd, found us heading to the northeastward so as to pass to the northward of the Azores. It may be difficult for the layman to appreciate, but large changes of direction at night, fully darkened by such a huge body of ships in close formation is a "tricky" maneuver. That it was accomplished without untoward event is a testimonial to the training and skill of the officers primarily concerned.

The enemy submarine estimate received during the early morning of the 3rd indicated a possible concentration off Dakar, which led us to hope that our ruse of heading in that general direction might have been successful. These submarine position estimates were the result of allied radio direction finder bearings taken during the night, when the submarines habitually surfaced and reported by radio to their higher command. We were now moving toward the Strait of Gibraltar.

It was planned to start the "topping off" fueling on the 3rd, but the weather became too rough, the convoy wallowing in the trough of a moderate swell from the North Atlantic. Even proposed anti-air-craft practices had to be called off. One of the planes from the carrier *Ranger* crashed, but the pilot and crew were picked up by the destroyer *Wilkes*. One transport dropped back as the result of engineering casualty, but rejoined.

The weather on the 4th, if anything, was worse, and the fueling again had to be postponed. The auxiliary carrier *Suwanee* had an engineering casualty, and the mine layer *Miantonomah* was unable to keep up on the prescribed course due to an excessive roll. The latter was directed to proceed independently and given a rendezvous for the following day. We were having our troubles.

On the 5th we still could not fuel, and some of the shorter-ranged small craft were getting so dangerously low that the possibility of towing had to be considered. We were also approaching an area where we were liable to encounter north and southbound European-African traffic. In fact, after dark that night, an emergency turn had to be executed to avoid being sighted by a lighted vessel, which upon being investigated by a screening destroyer turned out to be a Portuguese passenger steamer bound to the Cape Verde Islands. She was directed to maintain radio silence for twelve hours. Other contacts were made on the following day, but none saw the convoy.

On the 6th, with somewhat more favorable weather, the scheduled refueling was carried out. By that time, it was a *must*. All weather reports were now receiving more careful attention than ever. There was an alternate plan by which, if a Moroccan landing ultimately proved impracticable, the Western Task Force would be landed inside the Mediterranean, in western Algeria near the Moroccan border. This, however, was an undesirable alternative since it would greatly delay, if not defeat, attainment of Casablanca as a supply port for the Allied Armies in North Africa. After dark, a destroyer was detached to take station well to the southward for the transmission of important dispatches to the beacon submarines, to the *Miantonomah*, which had not yet rejoined, and to the Supreme Allied Commander in Gibraltar. The beacon submarines were directed to report surf conditions. Transmission by a single vessel well away from the convoy itself would not destroy the convoy position to enemy direction finders.

In order to effect a timely arrival in their assigned areas it would be necessary for the various attack groups to begin breaking off shortly after daylight on the previous day. Therefore a decision as to whether to carry out the attack on November 8th, as scheduled, had to be made early on the 7th. All night long, on the 6th-7th, General Patton and I studied the incoming weather charts, covering all the North Atlantic.

As previously mentioned, the latter had spent most of the summer studying the relationship between weather in the North Atlantic, where the swells which broke on the Moroccan coast were generated, and in the surf conditions in that area. We were receiving independent surf predictions from the War and Navy Departments, but from our knowledge of the backgrounds of the experts involved, we placed greater confidence in the latter.

There were many factors which had to be weighed. An attempted landing through over-rough seas might spell disaster—an entire failure, or undue loss of life. On the other hand, delay would undoubtedly mean loss of surprise, serious exposure to gathering submarines as the Task Force cruised up and down off the coast awaiting favorable weather, lowering of fuel supplies, and finally perhaps entire abandonment in favor of the alternate plan.

Army predictions were entirely unfavorable. The Navy report was slightly more optimistic, but not too encouraging. Mr. Steere was of the opinion that the landing would be practicable. Furthermore, he felt that the conditions would be much less suitable on the following day, the 9th. I still had one "Ace in the Hole." If later on unfavorable reports were received from the beacon submarines, I could halt the operation by radio.

I decided to go ahead, and General Patton concurred. Divine Providence was with me, and it was one of the most important decisions of my life. Conditions for 60 days after the 8th were highly dangerous.[20]

Several years later, a Russian general with whom I became associated in connection with the United Nations and who had apparently been studying my background told me he was interested in Professor Morison's account of the foregoing incident. He said "You decided to proceed with the attack without asking the General?" Yes, said I, "General Patton was consulted, but I was the seaman and it was my responsibility to decide whether a landing would be practicable." The Russian just shook his head in disbelief. Apparently, it was incomprehensible in the Russian Army that an admiral should make a decision involving a general.

As soon as it was sufficiently light for signaling, the signal "Execute Attack Plan One" was transmitted to the Task Force by flag, and by light. By 0700, the flag signal "Proceed on Service Assigned" was directed to the Commander of the Southern Attack Group, in the *Philadelphia.* Admiral Davidson immediately assumed charge of the ships assigned to his group and moved off to the southward toward Safi. He was joined by the auxiliary carrier *Santee,* detailed to him from the Air Group to provide his air support. The destroyers assigned to the remainder of the Main Body realigned themselves as an anti-submarines screen, and a change of course more to the northeastward was made . . . .

Broadcasts of President Roosevelt's message announcing the landings were intercepted from Washington and London. For better or for worse, the operation was underway.

During the morning watch off Fedhala, November 8th, all was quiet on shore. In fact, no sounds other than that of slow running circling landing craft and the voice of Captain Emmett over the TBS (short range ship-to-ship radio) giving orders to his transports were heard in the transport area. Reports did not reach me until later, but all the other groups had arrived at their stations exactly on time. Our eminent naval historian, Professor (Rear Admiral) Samuel E. Morison remarks, "So closely was the timetable executed that the Northern Attack Group arrived at its planned position off Mehedia at 2400, the Southern Attack Group made Safi at 2345, and the Center Group was in Fedhala Roads at 2353. For precision planning and faultless execution, this on-the-minute arrival of a large, complicated task force after a voyage of about 4500 miles merits the highest praise." These are kind words, but the planning was easy. Past experience (the *Indianapolis* Presidential Cruise, e.g.) indicated the desirability of always having ample "velvet" to reach a destination on time, regardless of weather, etc. Credit for faultless execution belongs to the various group commanders.

The details of the landing in Morocco have been so thoroughly covered by historians, both on the American and the French sides, that I shall endeavor in these reminiscences to limit myself to the events which I was an eyewitness or to those in which as the Task Force Commander I was intimately concerned.

At about 0130, our radio intercepted reports from both London and Africa of the midnight scheduled landings in Algeria. It was of course assumed that this information would be transmitted from Algiers and Oran to the French command in Morocco, which might result in a military alert. We were hoping against hope that, when discovered, the searchlights on shore would be elevated to the vertical, the signal that there would be no resistance and that we were to be received as friends. All of our units were under strict orders not to fire unless fired on, or other positive signs of hostile reaction were shown. In each case an immediate report was to be made via the chain of command, and there would be no general engagement except by the order of the commander of the particular group concerned. In order to expedite such reports and orders, resort was had to American baseball terminology: "Batter up," over the TBS, meant "I am being fired on"; "Play ball," from a commander, was the order for the unit addressed to go into action.

The Center Group, on account of the depth far off shore, could not anchor in the transport disembarkation area but had to heave to, occasionally maneuvering to counteract the effect of the current. This, coupled with the darkness and the inadequate training of some transports, resulted in delays which early made it evident that the Zero Hour of 0400 could not be met. About 0300, Captain Emmett postponed H-Hour to 0430, and shortly thereafter set it back another fifteen minutes. Radar plot showed the first wave of boats starting in about 0415, but they did not land until 0505, a little over an hour late.

As the first wave was approaching the beach, or just after it had landed, a searchlight was turned on from the Chergui or Pont Blondin Battery, on the northeast flank of the landing area, and immediately turned upward. The hoped-for signal? No: It was at once brought down to the water's edge, picking up the advancing boat waves. Then we heard the sound of machine-gun fire, apparently from the shore, immediately followed by a stream of tracer bullets from one of our scout or support boats directed toward the searchlight, which immediately went out—either shot out or turned off.

The destroyers assigned to the special duty of furnishing gun fire support were in position, well inshore, clear of the boat lanes, and the cruiser *Brooklyn* was also on station to cover the Chergui Battery on the left flank of the landing. The *Augusta* was in position on the right flank, more toward Casablanca. The minesweepers and the destroyers of the screen were maintaining an active patrol on the flanks and seaward side of the transport area. About 0530 a coastal convoy, consisting of two small French steamers escorted by the corvette *Victoria*, blundered into the left flank screen, with unfortunate results. Not knowing what he was up against, the officer of the little corvette, ignoring the minesweeper *Hogan's* warning to stop, opened fire and attempted to ram. The *Hogan's* 20 mm. return fire swept the *Victoria's* bridge, killed the captain, and brought the little convoy to a halt. This gunfire was noted from the *Augusta* and the incident was promptly reported over the TBS. Boats returning from the beach reported, via Captain Emmett, that there appeared to be little opposition on shore, but that many boats had been damaged on landing.

At about 0600 faint outlines of the shore and heights above Fedhala began to appear in the early morning twilight. This was followed by flashes of gunfire from the shore batteries as they became able to distinguish the shipping offshore. By this time, there had been numerous reports "Batter up." With the gunfire support vessels under fire, "Play ball" was soon given for the Center Group, and the action became general. The *Brooklyn*, delivering a rapid fire on Chergui with her 15-gun 6th battery, was a sight to behold, and the shore battery was soon silenced. The cruisers had launched their observation planes at daylight. It was not all one-sided, however, for the destroyer *Murphy* received a hit in an engine room, which killed three men and disabled the engine.

The fire of the *Augusta* and right flank support destroyers similarly silenced the defenses on Cape Fedhala, the tip of the little peninsula which, with its outlying breakwater, formed Fedhala Harbor. Unfortunately, however, one of the oil tanks of the tank farm there which we had especially planned to conserve for our future use, was hit and set on fire. The silencing was only temporary, for these batteries came to life later and once more had to be taken in hand.

By 0800 firing between shore and ship at Fedhala had died down, and the *Augusta* closed the transports, again, to be prepared to furnish anti-aircraft protection. It was well that she did, for soon a few French planes flew in and strafed the Fedhala beaches. Little or no damage was done and no transports were hit. The planes of Admiral McWhorter Air Group were already in the air: fighters, torpedo-bombers, and scouting planes, furnishing air cover and information, and standing by to attack. The French submarines in Casablanca Harbor constituted such a dangerous threat that the air group had been given orders that any attempt by them to sortie was to be considered hostile. This, however, was unnecessary because the anti-aircraft fire delivered against the planes circling over the harbor was sufficient evidence of French resistance. The *Jean Bart*, and the anti-aircraft batteries were accordingly bombed. French airfields in the vicinity were also worked over, but the French air took little part on the whole.

In the meanwhile, Admiral Giffen with his Covering Group had similarly gone into action against the ancient Table d'Aoukasha Battery to the northeast of Casablanca, the *Jean Bart* with its one completed quadruple turret alongside a dock, and the modern El Hank battery to the southwest of the harbor entrance.

Reports of these actions reached me fairly promptly, but the anxiously awaited news of events in the North and in the South was slow in coming. Later it was learned that everything had proceeded at Safi in accordance with the plan. A scout boat had found and marked the entrance buoy, the *Cole* and *Bernadcu* had dashed in alongside the selected docks and landed their rangers successfully; other elements had landed on small beaches, one inside the little harbor, one at the entrance, and one to the southward. Surprise had been complete and resistance negligible. The *Lakehurst* was seen disembarking her tanks.

In the North, however, things had not gone quite so well. Troops had been landed at or near the proper beaches, but with some confusion. Errors had occurred similar to some in the Fedhala area, where, in one case, a small unit was landed well to the northeastward, and, in another, a group of boats groping along the coast for its proper beach finally found itself in Casablanca Harbor, there promptly to be captured. Also, as at Fedhala, surf conditions off Mehedia were bad and many boats were stranded and disabled. Unlike Fedhala and Safi, where military resistance was minor, strong opposition from shore was encountered. It was the Navy, which, under French defense organization is responsible for the manning of coastal fortifications as well as ships, put up the spirited fight at Fedhala and Casablanca.

An ancient fort called the Kasba, at Mehedia, high on a hill commanding the entrance to the Sebou River, was manned by a strong detachment of the famous Foreign Legion. The other defending forces in that area were also legionnaires and two regiments of the Moroccan Tirailleurs, the cream of the French colonial army.

General Truscott,—fearing that inaccurate naval gunfire would endanger his troops, had elected to carry the Kasba by storm. He wished naval gunfire to be used only when called for by the troops by shore. The *Texas* and the *Savannah* could have demolished the old stone fort in short order, but unfortunately they were not called on to do so. Consequently, there were serious delays in cutting the barrier net, with its French river pilot (secretly smuggled to the United States in time to our convoy), ultimately reached its up-river destination on D + 2, after ramming the net.

Returning to the Fedhala story. As soon as it became light enough and the shore batteries had been for the most part silenced, the transports moved close in to the beach to reduce the boat run, and there they were able to anchor. The mine layers, as planned, proceeded to lay an anti-submarine flank of the transport area, and the vessels of the screen continued their active patrol of the other two sides.

The Naval War College, and staff experience during Fleet Problems, had taught me that lack of adequate information from subordinate commanders was not only annoying to superior commanders, but often made sound decisions difficult. I had learned to ask myself what I should want to know were I in my superior's shoes. The whole world now knew where we were; so there was no need further for radio silence. Accordingly, I directed Captain Bachman, my intelligence officer, to prepare a situation report on operation of the Western Task Force every two hours for transmission to the Supreme Allied Commander (General Eisenhower) and the Commander in Chief, Mediterranean (Admiral Cunningham) at their headquarters at Gibraltar. This was done religiously, so I felt I was doing everything possible to keep these officers informed of developments as I knew them. It was not until three days later, when the Supreme Allied Commander dispatched a staff officer to me from Gibraltar in a British destroyer to find out what was going on, that I discovered that none of these dispatches had been received. I have never been able to learn what was the reason. It may be that British communication and decoding facilities at Gibraltar were so overloaded that my reports were lost in the shuffle. There was no doubt of their having been broadcast from the *Augusta.*

As it happened, General Patton and I were to experience something of the same difficulty with reports from the Northern Task Force—so much so that ultimately, at the request of General Patton, Brigadier General Cannon of the Army Air Force, who was with us, was sent up to Mehedia to investigate.

Shortly after 0800, General Patton having expressed a desire to go ashore at Fedhala, a Higgins personnel landing craft, carried on the well deck of the *Augusta* for just such a purpose, was swung out by the aircraft recovery crane and lowered to the port rail. While some of the General's equipment was being loaded into it, a report was received from an observation plane that a number of French destroyers were sneaking close along the coast, under cover of a smoke screen, toward the Fedhala transport area. Since these immobile transports would soon be within torpedo range of these attackers, no time could be lost in driving them off. The *Augusta,* the *Brooklyn,* and the two nearest destroyers swung into action, the cruisers opened fire on their unseen targets from bearings and ranges given them by their observation planes. With a target sharp on the port bow, the blast of the *Augusta*'s after a turret completely wrecked the fragile landing craft and it had to be cut away, contents and all.

The gallant little French ships were soon forced back toward their harbor, but not without loss. The Covering Group, firing at El Hank, had drawn too far to the westward to counter the sorties of these light forces, and I had to call Admiral Giffen back. During this action, and subsequent ones during the day, the two cruisers had to dodge torpedoes several times. Whether these came from the surface ships or from the French submarines which had escaped being sunk in harbor and succeeded in getting out has not been entirely established.

We finally succeeded in getting the General ashore about three hours late (and not three days as stated in some accounts). Instead of being annoyed at the delay, as alleged, he stood beside me on the bridge and watched the action with keen interest. The incident, however, emphasized the undesirability of joint command being exercised from a flagship which might have to be diverted from that function. Steps were immediately taken by our Navy Department to convert a number of transports to command (or, in British terminology, headquarters) ships, and this was the last time a cruiser was so employed in one of our amphibious operations.

The day was not over before my subsequent good friend, Contre Admiral Gervais de la Fond, who commanded the French High Forces, made repeated skillful, courageous attempts to torpedo the Fedhala transports, in the course of which practically his entire command was either sunk, beached, or otherwise disabled, including the gallant little admiral himself, who was wounded. A Ranger plan reported that the *Jean Bart*, as the result of bombing, had been gutted by fire.

Resistance at Safi having ended, and the *Massachusetts* and cruisers of the Covering Group having expended considerable ammunition, the *New York*, which had done little firing, was ordered up from the Southern Group as a reinforcement.

During the 9th, very little happened from the naval point of view, except that unloading was continued from transports now anchored well inshore, but as a result of the many casualties, with fewer boats . . . .

On the morning of the 10th, General Patton came out for a conference with me in the *Augusta*, to plan the final joint assault on Casablanca. Disembarking from a bobbing landing craft, he had to climb a rope embarkation net up the high side of the ship to the well deck. Although he was a well-known athlete, he was so slowed up by fatigue and by the equipment he wore that I momentarily feared for his safety. If he had ever let go, he would have sunk like a stone. Captain Hutchins and I, who were waiting to receive him, got down on our knees, reached over the side, and, as soon as we could, grabbed his arms and literally hauled him aboard. As we walked up to my cabin, I noted that the General did seem pretty well worn out; so I sent my orderly to summon the ship's medical officer. When he arrived I said, "Doctor, I think the General is very tired and I wish you would prescribe for him. And," I added, "you might prescribe for me, too." Forever after, General Patton claimed that I had saved his life on that occasion.

Hardly had the General left the ship on his return to shore, when there was a report from an observation plane that several small enemy vessels off shore were apparently firing into our troops advancing from Fedhala. This, naturally, could not be allowed. So the *Augusta, Brooklyn,* and two accompanying destroyers took off once more down the coast. This was somewhat of a surprise, for we had been led to believe that all the light forces in Casablanca were by this time, *hors de combat.* The attackers were only two small corvettes, which were soon driven back into port, but not before we had received a surprise of another sort.

As we came down the coast to close the range, our proximity to the *Jean Bart* caused us no concern, for we knew that she had received hits from the *Massachusetts* and had been heavily bombed. Her turret, trained in the *Massachusetts* on the 8th, had not been moved since that day, according to reports from the air. Suddenly two huge orange splashes rose, so close alongside the bridge of the *Augusta* that I and others on the flag bridge were dowsed with the spray. It was no place for the *Augusta* to be. We promptly rang up full speed, put the rudder full right, made smoke, and zigzagged away, but not before we had been near-missed several times more by the *Jean Bart's* two-gun salvoes. The French gunnery was excellent. It was a close call. Later I was to learn the French side of that episode from a rugged Breton, who as her captain was responsible for sneaking that half-completed ship out from under the noses of the Germans when France fell and who, promoted to Contre Admiral, was in command of the Casablanca defenses at the time of our landing. This was Pierre Jean Ronaré, a gruff man with a keen sense of humor, who became a very good friend. Said he, "On Sunday (the 8th), the *Massachusetts* made a hit on the barbette which jammed the turret in train. The crew, after working diligently for thirty-six hours, finally got it free. I ordered it left trained as it was. So it happened, when you ran down the coast on Tuesday after our little corvettes, the gunnery control officer sat up the top beckoning and saying, 'Come a little closer: Come a little closer:' *And* you *came.*"

In the early evening of the 10th, I issued the necessary orders for the naval participation in the final assault on Casablanca. This was to consist of the bombing and bombardment of targets, selected by the Army, but executed by naval planes and the batteries of the *Augusta*, the *New York*, and the *Cleveland* at long range, and of four destroyers closer in, commencing at 0715. The *Cleveland*, which had been the cruiser escort for the Air Group, was brought in because she still had a full allowance of ammunition. Shortly after midnight of the 10th-11th, word was received from General Patton that Casablanca might capitulate at any time, and directing that we be prepared to suspend hostilities at short notice. This information was promptly passed on to the naval forces, and they were directed to be ready to cancel the proposed bombardment upon the receipt of "Cease Fire," broadcast *en clair.*

By 0700, the bombardment vessels were on station with their guns loaded and elevated, and bombing planes were in the air proceeding toward their targets. But at that very moment the welcome word arrived from shore, and the "Cease Fire" was broadcast to all stations. It was in the nick of time, for fingers were already on firing keys and bomb releases. Down came the guns, and back went the bombers to their carrier. Fittingly, it was the twenty-fourth anniversary of the Armistice Day of World War I. That date now for me has a double significance.

Returning to our position off Fedhala, we learned that there was to be an armistice conference with French officials that day at the Hotel Miramar in Fedhala, and Admiral Hall went ashore to get the details. He sent back word that General Nogues, the Governor General, and other military officials would not arrive until afternoon, but that Admiral Michelier would lunch with General Patton at a Fedhala restaurant—the hotel's kitchen having been put out of commission by a destroyer shell intended for the Batterie du Port. My presence was requested. I got ashore about 1230, and found quite an assemblage at a pleasant "brasserie", some dozen in all consisting of General Patton, Admiral Michelier, and me, together with leading members of our staffs. Colonel Wilbur, who had attended the Ecole de Guerre, and Marine Major Rogers of my staff were there as interpreters, but none more was really needed for most of the French officers spoke excellent English.

I was a little uncertain how to approach Admiral Michelier, whom I found to be a fine-looking man of medium height. The desire to establish friendly relations was uppermost in my mind; so I put out my hand, which he took, and I said that we had come as friends and old allies, and that it was with the greatest regret that we were forced to fire on the "tricolour." He looked me in the eye, and said, "Admiral, you had your orders, and you carried them out. I had mine, and I carried them out. Now, I am ready to cooperate in every way possible." I am happy to testify that he kept his promise faithfully.

During the course of a very amicable conversation at the luncheon, the subject of our urgent need for the facilities of the port of Casablanca arose. Admiral Michelier replied, "You have not seen it! C'est une cimitiere!" And so it was, as we later discovered.

The later conference at the Miramar was more formal and certainly stiffer. General Nogues was received with all the honors due his rank by a guard of military police. General Patton, having succeeded to the overall command after establishing his headquarters ashore, presided. General Nogues, pending receipt of awaited orders from Admiral Darlan, would make no formal agreement other than the "Cease Fire" then in effect and a release of prisoners by each side. In order to avoid loss of French prestige with the restive native Berber population and to take advantage of the service of the French military in preserving order, this was a wise decision. The Governor General sought permission to take disciplinary action against certain subordinates who, he claimed, had been guilty of not obeying orders. This was refused by General Patton, who had been informed that General Bethouart, one of the French officials secretly advised of Torch in advance, had been placed under arrest by General Nogues, early in the morning of the 8th, for attempting to isolate the Governor and forestall resistance to the landing. The impression was gained that General Nogues was one of those who had become firmly convinced of the ultimate success of the Axis and was afraid to offend the Nazis . . . .

Darkness closed in early on that evening of November 11th, and, except for the loading and movements of boats, all was quiet with the totally darkened shipping in transport area. With some of my staff I was on the flag bridge apprehensively looking at the blaze of light from the now illuminated Casablanca, the glare from which was certainly silhouetting my ships from seaward. Hardly had I drafted a message to the Army requesting action to obviate this hazard, when there was the boom of an underwater explosion nearby.

It was the transport *Joseph Hewes*, torpedoed on the port bow. The time was 1948. A few minutes later, the oil tanker *Winooski* and the destroyer *Hambleton* were hit on their port sides. All available boats in the vicinity were promptly dispatched to the *Hewes*, which was wildly signaling by blinker for help. Unfortunately she sank in less than an hour, taking down her gallant captain, a splendid officer, Robert McL. Smith—a loss which grieved me greatly. I believe he voluntarily stayed with his ship. Fortunately, her troops had been landed, and her crew; except for several killed by the explosion, were rescued. A large part of her cargo, however, was lost. The hit on the

Winooski was in an empty fuel tank, and did not prevent the further discharge of her fuel nor her return home for repair. The hit on the *Hambleton* was more serious. She was struck in an engine room and fire room, and lost twenty of her crew. The others, however, succeeded in keeping her afloat. She was towed into Casablanca the following morning, where with French assistance she was repaired sufficiently to enable her later to return with a west bound convoy . . . .

Influenced by a desire to insure the safe and timely arrival in port of the following convoy, to avoid interruption in the delivery of supplies and munitions to General Patton's forces, and to expose only partially discharged ships to the major risk, I ordered the unloading day and night of supplies and munitions but, at the first sign of further trouble, to take our ships promptly to sea.

I then proceeded into port with the *Augusta*. As we passed in through the entrance, it was rather "tricky" to see the French sailors standing by their anti-aircraft guns. Had there been any breach of faith on the part of the French, we should have been in for trouble.

There proved, however, to be no cause for uneasiness. We could not have had more perfect cooperation than that which was shown us. The *Augusta*, with the aid of a French pilot and tugs, was placed alongside the phosphate pier, just inside the entrance along the northeast breakwater. Here we were able to survey the conditions in the harbor, which was indeed a "cimitiere." The hull of a capsized French destroyer lay there. Opposite us, alongside the main pier, was a line of sunken merchant vessels. On the other side of this pier, partly hidden by the damaged dockhouse, was the badly damaged *Jean Bart* resting on the bottom. At the end of this pier was a capsized passenger vessel that had arrived from Dakar on the 7th carrying women and children, fleeing that port in fear of attack there. Fortunately, they had been taken ashore before the shelling of the *Jean Bart* began. The long-range bombardment of that ship had been responsible for all the surrounding damage.

Contact with Admiral Michelier's staff was established early through his Chief of Staff, Rear Admiral Misoff, who came on board with the news that his commanding officer had established a special "Bureau des Affaires Americaines," through which we could deal directly in obtaining needed services. Plans were made for the reception of the D + 5 Convoy the following morning, November 13th, the French exerting every effort to clear a maximum number of berths.

A problem of protocol engaged my attention. We had defeated a gallant French resistance, and were more or less taking charge. But Admiral Michelier was a Vice Admiral, I a Rear Admiral. Furthermore, we had not come as conquerors but as friends and allies. It was important to restore that relationship. I sent my flag lieutenant to the "Amiraute" to inquire when it would be convenient for Admiral Michelier to receive my official call. After some delay, I received word that the Admiral would be happy to welcome me at the Admiralty at 5:00 p.m. the following day. I sensed the French were surprised and wanted time to prepare a proper ceremony.

This day, November 12th, however, ended far from happily. At about 1800 (6:00 p.m.), while it was still daylight three of the transports at Fedhala, the *Edward Rutledge*, the *Hugh L. Scott*, and the *Tasker H. Bliss* were torpedoed. The first two sank within a short time, but the *Bliss*, on fire, hung on until after midnight. It was a daylight attack, in spite of our minefield and our surface and air patrols. Unfortunately there were no salvage vessels available, but with the exception of those killed in the explosion or trapped below by fire, most of the crews were safely brought ashore where they were cared for by Army, French civilians, and their own surviving medical personnel. Later, it was learned that this attack was the work of a skillful U-boat commander, who had sneaked down from the northeast, so close to shore that he passed safely inside the anti-submarine minefield.

In accordance with his orders, Captain Emmett promptly got the surviving vessels of his force underway and took them to sea. There was no question now but that these Center Group ships would have to be brought into Casablanca the next morning for final unloading, instead of the D-5 Convoy, due at the same time. Orders had to be radioed to Rear Admiral Bryant, in U.S.S. *Arkansas*, to cruise with his convoy well off shore and out of sight of land until further orders.

Hardly had the above catastrophe occurred than a British destroyer, H.M.S. *Welshman*, arrived, bearing Rear Admiral Bieri and some Army members of General Eisenhower's staff seeking information as to the situation in Morocco. As previously related, the Supreme Allied Commander had received none of my carefully prepared intelligence reports. General Patton, whose headquarters had not yet moved to Casablanca, was sent for, and we conferred well into the night. At about 0200, with the flames of the burning *Bliss* being quenched as she finally went under, the visitors departed for Gibraltar to report the latest sad news. Our attention was then turned to the plight of the survivors. There was no rest for the weary . . . .

My call on Admiral Michelier the afternoon of the 13th was most pleasant. I was greeted by a very smart guard of honor of French bluejackets, dressed in blue coats and white trousers and white caps, topped by the traditional "pompon rouge". As I passed down the line on my formal inspection, I studied their faces for signs of resentment, which I could well have pardoned, for many had lost friends and shipmates at our hands. But all was quite military correct. As I proceeded up the steps to the entrance, I noted two major caliber projectiles, one mounted on each side. These, I later learned, were unexploded shells from the *Massachusetts*, mounted especially for my benefit— truly a French touch. The many shells from the "Massy" which failed to detonate indicated faulty fuses, which in time became the subject of a Bureau of Ordinance investigation.

The Admiral welcomed me politely, and since his English was very good, we had no need for an interpreter. At first, I was a little uncertain of him, because I knew he had once been the French naval attaché in Berlin and thus might have some Axis leanings, but I was soon disabused of that idea. Among other things, he urged me to take every possible precaution to combat air attack. Said he, "I know these Germans. I expect they will attack us with everything they have . . . ."

The *Jean Bart* had an anti-torpedo net around her to protect her from an attack like the one at Pearl Harbor. He called my attention to this, and said, "Le *Jean Bart*, c'est fini." Let me place the net around shipping your *Augusta*. I felt there was little danger because of the way the *Augusta* was moored with other ships protecting her. Moreover, the net would have interfered with very necessary boat traffic. So I declined this very thoughtful and kind offer.

Admiral Michelier returned my call promptly the following morning, when he was received aboard the *Augusta* with all the honors due his rank (barring a salute, not customary in wartime). The basis for a lasting friendship had been laid . . . .

By the morning of the 16th, General Patton had established his headquarters in Casablanca, in the midtown Shell Oil building. This made for more effective liaison, and I promptly visited him there. The *Brooklyn* and three destroyers, short of fuel and having been prevented by rough weather from fueling at sea, entered port and were berthed at the Jete de Lure alongside tankers, of which the torpedoed *Winooski* was one. The British hospital ship *Newfoundland,* coming in at nightfall to pick up the survivors of the *Hecla,* having unaccountably failed to receive any word of our minefield, and ignoring the frantic signals of our patrols, was damaged by a mine. Fortunately, since she was of light draft, and the field was deep laid to protect against submerged submarines, the damage was minor.

The following two dispatches received in November, and later transmitted to the Western Naval Task Force as a whole, were sources of great satisfaction and pride, both to me and the splendid officers and men who were primarily responsible for the successful accomplishment of the task assigned. I quote:

"FOR ADMIRAL HEWITT FROM EISENHOWER X WITH SUCCESSFUL COMPLETION OF YOUR TASK UNDER ALLIED HEADQUARTERS AND YOUR RETURN TO NORMAL AMERICAN COMMAND I WANT TO EXPRESS MY GRATEFUL APPRECIATION OF THE SPLENDID SERVICES YOU AND THE FORCES UNDER YOUR COMMAND HAVE RENDERED X I AM MAKING IMMEDIATE OFFICIAL REPORT TO WASHINGTON TO THIS EFFECT BUT IN THE MEANTIME I HOPE IT IS PROPER FOR A SOLDIER TO SAY TO A SAILOR QUOTE WELL DONE UNQUOTE"

And this, from General Eisenhower's Supreme Naval Commander, Admiral of the Fleet Sir Andrew B. Cunningham, R.N., to the Commander of the Western Naval Task Force:

"ON DEPARTURE OF WNTF[21] I SEND YOU MY CONGRATULATIONS ON A FINE JOB WELL DONE X THE PROBLEMS FACED WERE IN MANY WAYS THE MOST DIFFICULT AND I HAVE ADMIRED THE ENERGY AND RESOLUTION WITH WHICH YOU AND ALL UNDER YOUR COMMAND HAVE TACKLED THEM X I SEND VERY GOOD WISHES TO YOUR FORCE FOR SPEEDY PASSAGE AND GOOD LANDFALL."

Darlan and Operation Torch

During Operation Torch, the highest-ranking Vichy official in Algiers was Adm. Jean François Darlan, who was eager to travel with his wife to the United States because his son Alain was undergoing treatment for infantile paralysis (polio) at Warm Springs, Georgia. President Roosevelt arranged for the son to be treated there for an extended period. Roosevelt recalled his time at Warm Springs with great fondness, believing that the treatments there helped him with his polio. Never forgetting this, Roosevelt poured a considerable portion of his wealth and energy into making Warm Springs a first-class facility and prodded others to contribute. Once Ambassador Murphy told Admiral Leahy about the condition of young Darlan, it didn't take much urging to have Roosevelt make the necessary arrangements. In return, Darlan and his wife were eternally grateful, and she was able to visit her son as a guest of the American government. Nevertheless, the Americans kept Darlan in the dark about the pending invasion of North Africa. And on that night, it was Darlan alone, as the highest-ranking French government official present in Algiers, who had to act instead of Marshal Pétain. His initial hostility toward Operation Torch subsided because of its success. Even though some soldiers landed on the wrong beaches, and there were fights between the French and the Allied invaders, Allied troops moved quickly inland with little resistance. Calm weather and enemy confusion helped as well. FDR's considerable diplomatic and communication skills placated some French and stiffened their hatred of the Germans. He spoke to them eloquently in French and accentuated their self-interest. His efforts to gain French cooperation were partially successful.

Darlan agreed to the surrender of Algiers shortly after the invasion. Elsewhere, the situation was very different. In Oran, the French resisted the onslaught of Allied troops and hampered their rapid progress ashore. Some of the landings were again poorly planned and executed and were permeated with procrastination and confusion. American troops were met with heavy gunfire as they advanced. U.S. Navy warships fired on an unlucky French fleet and sank thirteen ships.

The fighting between the Americans and French only complicated the already-hazardous political situation between the two historic allies. Eisenhower's deputy, Gen. Mark W. Clark, arrived in Algiers on November 9, with the mission of ending the fighting. Clark met with Darlan on November 10 and pressured him to issue orders, in Pétain's name, to French commanders in Oran and in Morocco to cease-fire. Darlan continued to carry out Pétain's policy of noncapitulation and delayed cooperation with the Allies.

While Clark and Darlan negotiated, Hitler met with Vichy leader Pierre Laval in Munich and insisted that Tunisian ports and air bases be made available to the Axis. Laval responded that only Pétain could approve Hitler's demand. On November 11, Hitler ordered German and Italian troops to occupy southern France and Corsica.

On November 12, an agreement between General Clark and Admiral Darlan recognized Darlan as head of the government of French North Africa. This deal generated an explosion of criticism in the United States, where many believed that it weakened democratic resistance against the Axis and diminished de Gaulle's status and the morale of his followers. What at first appeared to be a reasonable military solution was later deemed to be a horrendous political blunder. Recognizing that Darlan's support was important to the U.S. Army at that time, Admiral Leahy advised FDR to include him, but to watch him carefully. Darlan was important, and there was no need to alienate him when such behavior could very well cost the lives of thousands of American soldiers and sailors and add to the difficulties of the North Africa campaign.

Admiral Darlan's claim to legitimacy resulted in bringing French forces to further American objectives. However, Roosevelt adhered to his policy of not recognizing any French government that was not in accord with the free choice of its people. The French overwhelmingly wanted Pétain in June 1940, and when they later made it clear that they chose de Gaulle as their leader, FDR and his administration agreed. One outcome of the Clark-Darlan agreement was a massive military aid program that was vastly important to the Allies. According to Ambassador Murphy, American largesse included

1. Equipment and training for eight French divisions in North Africa.
2. Partial outfitting and training of more troops in France.
3. North Africa was supplied with equipment for nineteen air squadrons, and the French Navy was reequipped; this included one thousand four hundred aircraft, thirty thousand machine guns, three thousand artillery guns, five thousand tanks and self-propelled weapons, and fifty-one million rounds of ammunition.[22]

Gen. Charles de Gaulle, in his *War Memories*, viewed the agreement differently. He wrote, "No one paid attention to the Darlan-Clark agreement. The Committee of National Liberation considered it as null and void. I had openly declared on the rostrum of the Consultative Assembly that in the eyes of France it did not exist. That the failure of his policy in Africa had not been able to dispel Roosevelt's illusions was a situation I regretted for him and for our relations. However, I was certain that his intentions, venturing this time into metropolitan France, would not even begin to be applied in fact. The Allies would encounter no other ministers and officials in France than those of which I was the leader. Without any presumptuousness, I could defy General Eisenhower to deal lawfully with anyone I had not designated." According to de Gaulle, Eisenhower admitted to him that he was dependent on the cooperation of the de Gaullists, that he had to have their help. His response to Ike was, "Splendid, you are a man! For you know how to say 'I was wrong.'"[23]

Without untangling the complex web of the confusing history of relationships between American and French leaders during the first half of the 1940s as to who was correct and who was mistaken, we know some of the consequences:

1. That, ultimately, Americans and the French of all political persuasions demolished the heinous foe.
2. That Generals de Gaulle and Eisenhower became the political heads of their governments.

Aftermath

Shortly after the North African invasion, President Roosevelt assured the world that he deemed the defense of any French province, colony, or any other territory not under the control of the Axis as vital to the defense of the United States. He understood that the extensive German exploitation and influence required complex approaches. In Morocco, Arab nationalism could be stirred by adept Nazi propagandists, causing devastation to Allied forces. Besides, there were indigenous leaders in France's far-flung empire who were ready and willing to remove the colonial yoke. Roosevelt sympathized with their aspirations toward independence and was concerned that de Gaulle would persist in continuing French imperialism after the war—one of several reasons for FDR's distaste for de Gaulle. Rebellious North Africans posed a serious threat to the Allies; and ways were found to reduce disagreements between American and French officialdom concerning the distribution of medicine, food, clothing, and other commodities. To deal with the haggling that resulted over goods already in French territory, it was agreed that distribution problems could be resolved more efficiently at dockside in the United States rather than when the goods reached overseas warehouses. This approach had several advantages: it would reduce the number of agents in Africa, require less complex accounting, and result in fewer disagreements between civilians and military officials.

Despite the implementation of this system, black marketing did not disappear. French colonial discrimination in North Africa resulted in the huge native population receiving far less than its fair share of foreign aid goods. James Dougherty wrote that since the French refused to sell European goods to native retailers, some people purchased such materials through the flourishing black market. They obtained goods through bribery or political favors. Allied soldiers and sailors helped expand black marketing, and theft from docks and warehouses was rampant.[24]

One of the glaring problems that emerged was the complete and utter failure of the communication systems during Operation Torch. The shock of naval gunfire destroyed many shipboard radios, and because the message centers remained aboard when the troops landed, there was a serious communications failure. Heavy truck and trailer radio sets had been stowed deep in the bowels of convoy ships, and only one set could be unloaded for use during the initial invasion. Inadequate waterproofing was responsible for salt water damaging much of the signal equipment while insufficient training hampered signalmen from using communications equipment properly. Another major communication problem resulted from the use of conflicting codes by the British Army and Navy, the Royal Air Force, and the United States Army Air Force.[25]

Other communications problems included garbled signaling, poor services, severe static conditions, and poor circuit discipline. Radio sets were unsatisfactory because their range was too short, and radio operators too often were incompetent. Communications between shore fire control and bombarding ships were established only in about 60 percent of the cases during Operation Torch.

The Torch operation clearly demonstrated the need for a headquarters ship with adequate communications, aerological photography, and other facilities. Hewitt's flagship, the *Augusta*, was inadequate in providing facilities for amphibious operations. By the time Operation Dragoon was launched, the admiral's flagship, the *Catoctin*, was equipped with the facilities he had recommended at the end of 1942. The Torch invasion also demonstrated the importance of intelligence gathering, analysis, and usage.

Hewitt thought that naval and amphibious communication planning, "although seriously handicapped by conditions during the planning period, was in general adequate. The plan was executed reasonably well—better than might have been expected, considering the unusual complications involved, the last-minute receipt of instructions, material, and personnel, and the inadequate training of personnel. Army communications, insofar as they affected the assault phases of this operation, were generally not in accordance with the Army communication plan. It is considered that the Army plan would have been satisfactory if carried out."[26]

The experience that Admiral Hewitt gained from Operation Torch was instrumental in achieving the great success of Operation Dragoon. His twenty-eight-page "Torch Operation Comments and Recommendations," submitted to Admiral King, the commander in chief of fleet and chief of naval operations, demonstrated Hewitt's thorough analysis and study of the various operations carried out by personnel, individual ships, and task groups in Operation Torch.

Under the heading "Naval Gunfire Support," Hewitt presented eight major findings and provided seven specific conclusions and findings. They were

(a) Light cruisers of the *Savannah* and *Cleveland* type, by virtue of their great volume of fire, long range, accuracy, high performance of ammunition, and maneuverability, are the most effective gunfire supporting ships for landing operations.

131

(b) Destroyers are extremely effective in delivering close supporting fire, direct fire on beaches, and direct fire on targets of opportunity.

(c) Plane spotting is the most effective method of controlling accurate naval gunfire on designated targets ashore.

(d) Cruiser and battleship spotting planes must either have fighter protection or be capable of considerable more speed.

(e) The procurement of the new high-capacity ammunition will greatly increase the effectiveness of naval gunfire.

(f) One or two bombardment practices should be scheduled each year for all types of ships capable of giving gunfire support in landing operations in order to ensure their readiness for this particular gunnery mission.

(g) At least one ship's gunfire support dress rehearsal should be conducted prior to any landing operation. This should include actual bombardment of land objectives and the employment of shore fire control parties and plane spot. A conference of all units involved should be held before and after such a rehearsal.[27]

The "Ammunition" section found that "the 16-inch armor-piercing projectiles fired by the [battleship] *Massachusetts* were unsatisfactory . . . as many proved to be duds. The performance of 100-pound bombs dropped from naval aircraft was only mediocre as a number of them failed to explode. It is believed, however, that these duds were caused by dropping the bombs from too low an altitude."[28] The failure to use the proper bombardment ammunition resulted in a loss of about 50 percent efficiency in destroying the enemy's shore installations.

While praising the benefits of radar for navigational and gunnery purposes, Hewitt noted that "unfortunately, radar sets as now installed are too complicated and touchy for the conclusion and shock caused by ships' gunfire . . . A study should be made of the effect of shock on all our radars and equipment . . . . [29] All future instruments should be shock tested and vibration tested before installation."[30]

Landing boats were afflicted with serious problems during Operation Torch and were remedied by the time of Dragoon. These included improving the ramp operating mechanisms of small landing craft that carried troops and vehicles, the installation of mechanically driven ramp hoists that prevented unloading problems at the various Dragoon beaches. Mechanical aids and equipment accelerated unloading. Hewitt urged that "items such as gasoline and ammunition must be removed quickly to less exposed locations so that they do not become a menace to further operations in the event of an enemy bombing attack."[31] These recommendations were followed in the separate invasions of Sicily, Salerno, and southern France.

Practical suggestions abound in Hewitt's critique, such as "cast propellers should not be used on landing boats as they shatter on striking solid objects."[32] Realizing that these small amphibious craft would be operated by young men who lacked the required expertise, he urged that "landing boats should be provided with a simple type of directional gyro compass."[33]

"Psychological warfare may prove to be a potent factor in amphibious operations," wrote Hewitt; and he recommended that "it be planned and executed only by experts with a thorough knowledge of the religious, social, economic, historical, political, and linguistics backgrounds of the countries involved."[34] Operation Dragoon adopted this recommendation in its reliance on French expertise in various fields.

To mitigate the perils of performing crucial tasks in pitch-black nights aboard warships and amphibious craft in the midst of battle, Hewitt recommended that "some system of shielded low-power lighting should be used on transports, or a luminous paint or luminous composition should be applied to parts of cranes, booms and transport equipment in a way that will facilitate night loading of boats."[35]

Professor Williamson Murray of Ohio State University, an officer in the United States Air Force Ready Reserve, found that the relocation of German transport aircraft from the Mediterranean and the closing of German instrument and bomber transition schools beneficial to the Allies. Nevertheless, in November and December 1942, German transport squadrons flew 41,768 troops, 8,614.8 tons of equipment and supplies, and 1,472.8 tons of fuel into North Africa. Williamson concluded that Operation Torch severely weakened the Germans: their air force lost 128 Junker planes in November and December and an additional 36 in January 1943 (13.9 percent of the Luftwaffe's total transport strength). He found that "the North African invasion forced the Germans to shut down attacks on the Murmansk convoys and to send additional anti-shipping units into the Mediterranean."[36] By May 1943, the Germans had lost 40.5 percent of their total air force, or 12,422 aircraft, in the Mediterranean.[37] Nevertheless, a German submarine commanded by a daring commanding officer eluded Allied defense and sank a transport ship and damaged a tanker and destroyer.

Another enemy submarine destroyed three other transport ships under Hewitt's command. In addition to these losses, many amphibious craft were devastated along the Moroccan beaches. (No LSTs were available for Operation Torch.)[38]

French military resistance during the November invasion cost the United States Army and Navy 337 dead, 637 wounded, 122 missing, and 71 captured. French losses were much greater.[39] The mission in Northwest Africa commenced a Mediterranean journey that immersed American forces for almost three long years of struggle. Together with their Allies, American airmen fought from the deserts of North Africa to the Italian Alps. Winning air supremacy at the cost of the loss of many young lives and expensive equipment, Allied airmen contributed mightily to the success of four major Mediterranean landings—North Africa, Sicily, Salerno, and southern France.[40]

Hewitt's letter of August 26, 1944, to Vice Adm. Randall Jacobs, chief of naval personnel, referred to Operation Dragoon as "a very successful operation with minor losses. I attribute this to lessons learned from past operations, which lessons have permitted us to eliminate *faulty* practice and approaches . . . ."[41]

The invasion of North Africa exhibited inadequacies of Allied training and preparations. The feasibility of invading France in 1943 was demolished by the terrible results of the Canadian assault of Dieppe, France, on August 19, 1942. The 3,369 casualties among the 5,000 Canadian military men who participated demonstrated the lack of preparation for this assault.[42] However, the victorious outcome of the invasion of North Africa provided the Allies with a surge of confidence.

From Enemies to Allies

The U.S. Office of Naval Intelligence reported that

> by January 1943, less than 2 months after the Allied landings in North Africa, French convoys consisting of French warships and merchantmen began moving between the ports of North and West Africa and patrols of these ports were instituted by French naval units. For the first time since the Armistice a French convoy from Africa arrived in a British port. It was composed of vessels placed at the service of the Allies in Dakar.

In April 1943, a French cruiser on patrol in the South Atlantic intercepted and sank one of the few remaining German blockade runners, outward-bound with goods destined for the Far East. Two months later this cruiser, en route from Dakar to the United States, fired upon an unidentified submarine with unknown results. Another 6-inch cruiser, on her first patrol from Dakar, intercepted a Spanish merchant vessel which was sent into port for contraband examination.

Two heavy destroyers, rearmed in the United States early in 1943, have been operating in close cooperation with Allied forces in the Mediterranean. These units took part in the bombardment of the Italian coast in the early stages of the operations against Italy and played an important role in the landing at Ajaccio. While this occupation of Corsica was navally an inter-Allied venture, the French Fleet took an important part in the liberation of the island. Two 6-inch cruisers, two heavy destroyers, two destroyers, and three submarines participated in this action, debarking troops and material, bombarding land installations and barring the way for enemy planes. One of these submarines alone unloaded some 40 tons of arms on the coast of Corsica prior to the island's deliverance. This submarine, which arrived in Algiers on 30 November 1942, after a dash from Toulon to escape scuttling, has been especially active. In May 1943, she was credited with sinking a French merchant vessel and an escorting destroyer, and later in the year reportedly sank a submarine chaser and a large cargo vessel.

French vessels based in the Levant took part in the operations against the Dodecanese islands of Kos and Leros in October 1943, transporting material for the occupation troops and protecting Allied shipping. During a violent aerial attack the French vessels were credited with downing two Axis planes, with two other probably destroyed.

French corvettes have been performing outstanding service in escort work in the North Atlantic. One was credited with the probable destruction of a submarine in February 1943, and in March another rammed a German submarine which was forced to surface by depth charges from a British destroyer. A few hours later she destroyed another submarine by ramming.

In June 1943, a third corvette, escorting a convoy bound for Russia, braved heavy seas and floating mines in rescuing 179 members of crews of vessels sunk by mines. A French sloop, operating in the Indian Ocean, was credited with the probable destruction of an enemy submarine.

French vessels participated in the bombardment of German coastal installations at Nettuno and Anzio and will no doubt continue to play an active and important role in present Italian operations.[43]

The Sicilian Invasion (Operation Husky)

In January 1943, Prime Minister Churchill, President Roosevelt, and their Combined Chiefs of Staff met in Casablanca, Morocco. Most of North Africa, with the exception of Tunisia, was in Allied hands. The Allied leaders discussed the coming invasion of Sicily, scheduled for July under the name of "Operation Husky." Nearly all the senior officers who had served in the North African campaign were to participate in Husky. The question arose as to whether the Allies would invade Sicily or Sardinia; and Admiral King, U.S. Navy chief of staff, made it clear that the decision should be to invade Sicily, where "he would find the necessary escorts."[44]

A major problem that confronted the planners of Husky centered on providing enough escort shipping for both the Sicilian invasion and the transatlantic and artic convoys. Lt. Gen. Brehon B. Somervell, the U.S. Army's chief logistics officer, and Lord Leathers, the British minister of war transport, worked together to resolve this problem. They were helped by the fact that there were Allied troops already in North Africa, eliminating the need to cross the Atlantic.

General Marshall viewed the Sicilian invasion as a means of saving the turnaround time of several hundred ships from the long Cape Horn route to the more direct Mediterranean route. Churchill and Roosevelt assumed that the invasion of Sicily would placate Stalin's urging of a second front to be opened in the West while also expecting the action to help bring about the collapse of Mussolini's Fascist regime.[45]

After the victorious landings in Algeria and Morocco, American warships withdrew from the Mediterranean. The decision to invade Sicily made it necessary for United States personnel, ships, and equipment to return to the North African region. By mid-March 1943, Admiral Hewitt's command became known as the U.S. Eighth Fleet. Lieutenant General Eisenhower gave Hewitt his military orders; and Admiral King supplied Hewitt with men, ships, and equipment. When Hewitt had commanded the naval arm of Operation Torch, he was responsible for the transportation of about thirty-five thousand soldiers, thirty-five thousand sailors, and one hundred two ships. They sailed from Norfolk to Africa through thousands of miles of German submarine-infested Atlantic Ocean. Hewitt's command of Operation Husky included over one hundred thousand troops and one thousand two hundred fifty ships.[46]

The American military chiefs, General Marshall and Admiral King, intended to invade Sicily and learn from that outcome before tackling other Mediterranean targets. The benefits anticipated were numerous, including increasing the safety of Mediterranean communications, reducing German pressure on the Russian front, and escalating pressure on Italy.

German submarines were a serious threat to Allied troop and supply ships in the first half of 1943. In June, there were still almost forty-five Italian submarines in good operating condition. Although these did little harm to Allied shipping, their potential impact could not be ignored. Enemy aircraft raised a more serious threat, because it was easy for German airplanes to attack convoys from well-placed bases in Sardinia, Sicily, southern Italy, and Crete.

The American Joint Chiefs were also concerned that Allied forces in the European theater were being kept idle. They and their British counterparts agreed that a successful invasion of Axis-dominated territory would electrify morale. But, first, a variety of planning and preparatory obstacles had to be overcome.

Command headquarters of the different British and American teams were widely dispersed across North Africa. Communication between navy and air force commanders was also hampered. Senior officers, such as Generals Alexander, Patton, Montgomery, and others, were heavily involved in the Tunisian campaign and, at the outset, could not give Husky much attention. They did reach agreement concerning various objectives. Reconciling the strategic and tactical requirements of the American and British military leaders proved to be exceedingly difficult. Speedy seizure of the Straits of Messina was deemed as a wise objective by all of the military commanders because it would protect the major supply artery and also trap enemy Italian and German forces. But the invasion beaches to be used in the Straits of Messina could not be effectively protected by Allied air cover because the beaches were beyond the range of their aircraft. Ultimately, a compromise was developed.

The arrival of recently built LSTs and hundreds of amphibious cargo-carrying trucks enabled an army attack across the southeast Sicilian beaches. The availability of a few ports helped implement a massive Allied assault. July 10, 1943, was selected for D-day and 0245 for H-hour. Army commanders chose this timing to provide moonlight for paratroops. Assault troops were to reach their beach landings in complete darkness. The designated H-hour exposed the fleet to moonlight and enemy attack. Navy planners recommended a later approach, preferring that the landings take place after dawn. Naval gunfire to neutralize enemy beach defenses was to precede the landings. These suggestions were ignored by army commanders, who insisted that ship-to-shore movement under the cover of darkness was crucial for surprise. They also claimed that naval gunfire would not be effective since it was designed for bombardment at sea and not on land.

Admiral Hewitt's fleet was organized into three parts. The landing front was almost one hundred miles, the widest in World War II. (Even the assault on Normandy in June 1944 was not as extensive as the Sicily invasion.) Fleet Adm. Chester W. Nimitz and coauthor E. B. Potter provided the following statistics: (1) more than 470,000 troops were assigned in the initial landings, half of which were British and the other half American; (2) an American armada of 580 ships and 1,124 amphibious craft sailed from Bizerte and other North African ports to Sicily; (3) the British fleet consisted of 818 ships and beaching craft and 715 landing craft that arrived from the eastern Mediterranean and Tunisia.[47]

Preparation for the Sicilian invasion was impaired by the Allied Air Forces' lack of coordination concerning the use of tactical air power. Air force doctrine required the blasting of Axis communications to halt movement into or out of beachhead areas. Axis airfields were attacked to reduce Allied damage, but Allied Air Force personnel did not participate in joint planning, and pilots were prohibited from answering calls for support from ship-based or ground stations except those approved by Air Force Headquarters in North Africa. This prohibition deprived some Allied sailors and soldiers of important air force help.

Allied army and navy commanders demanded the type of air support that had been provided by the U.S. aircraft carrier *Ranger* off the coast of Casablanca during the invasion of North Africa. British Royal Air

Force marshal Arthur W. Tedder prevailed in having a tactical air force assigned to support the landings, but it was controlled from North Africa with no guarantee of priority to army-navy calls for help. General Patton argued that aircraft carriers assigned to assault forces be immediately available to provide aircraft strikes. Admiral Hewitt disagreed, claiming that there was a great demand for his carriers to serve elsewhere and that there were plenty of land-based Allied air power sources within easy range of the beachheads. The landing attack therefore was without a clear plan that was acceptable to all the military planners. Air support was doomed to be either too slow or unavailable. To neutralize and diminish enemy resistance, American Rangers would neutralize major German installations. Important airfields and bridges were to be seized by Allied paratroopers before H-hour.

It was important to deceive the Axis defenders and convince them that the Allied objective was not the invasion of Sicily. Therefore, elaborate schemes were undertaken to persuade the enemy that the principal attack would be in Greece and the secondary assault in Sardinia. One deception entailed dropping a carefully prepared corpse into the sea off the Spanish coast. It washed ashore near Cadiz. The corpse of a "Maj. William Martin" carried a briefcase full of misinformation that ended up in the hands of German agents. The Italian and German commanders at the scene were not deceived by this ruse, but Hitler and his high command were. German armed divisions and torpedo and mine vessels were dispatched to Sardinia and Greece while Sicilian waters were mined by slow and antiquated Italian minelayers.

Upon arrival in the Mediterranean to participate in the Sicilian campaign, new LSTs, LCTs, and LCIs were subjected to training exercises, which had not been possible for the North African mission. There were plenty of tasks that needed rehearsal. Along the coasts of Sicily there were dangerous sandbars, almost a hundred yards of which shoaled too much to allow the passage of large beaching craft or LSTs. To remedy this problem, Rear Adm. Richard L. Conolly designed pontoon causeways. These were standard pontoon units that were shackled together to form a bridge to shore. A ferry service of sorts was developed to run between LSTs anchored offshore and the beach.

Training exercises took place in North African ports. Army troops and the crews of the new LCVPs (Landing Craft, Vehicle, Personnel) worked together to properly land through surf waters. Practice exercises were undertaken to prevent problems that had occurred in North Africa.

Inexperienced sailors, soldiers, and officers rehearsed amphibious assaults. Admiral Hewitt and his British colleague, Adm. Sir Bertram Ramsay, saw to it that such critical tasks as evacuation of the wounded and directing gunfire were rehearsed.

Hewitt, Ramsay, and other Allied military leaders were well aware that the Germans and Italians were also preparing and training. The thrust of the Axis defense was based on plans for surprise ground and air attacks. Axis mobile forces were stationed at strategic locations. With about three hundred fifty thousand Italian troops and more than fifty thousand Germans, they waited for an attack by four hundred seventy thousand Allied invaders.

Hitler had offered Mussolini three more German divisions. But *Il Duce* refused them. All major ports defenses were strengthened and anti-invasion exercises completed. Both the Germans and the Italians expected an Allied landing at Gela. The betting odds substantially favored an Axis victory, because as Nimitz and Potter put it, "To military men acquainted with that sort of war, the Allied plan to invade with only a slight numerical advantage over the defenders would have seemed an invitation to disaster."[48]

The key to understanding the Allied victory in Sicily is easily found. Mussolini assigned Sicilian reservists to defend their homeland. They hated the Germans and were far from being devoted Fascist admirers. The Sicilians and the overwhelming majority of Italians on the mainland realized that the Fascist government had led them into a war that did not serve their interests and that it was futile and unwinnable. By July 1943, it was clear that most Italians welcomed the Allies and wanted the Germans out. But Mussolini and the German commander in Italy, Field Marshal Albert Kesseling, were certain that the Allied invaders would be wiped out at the water's edge.[49]

British Air Force Commander Tedder ordered the Mediterranean Allied Air Forces to destroy nearly all of Sicily's airfields, forcing the Germans and Italians to base the surviving planes on the Italian mainland. Even though Tedder's planes did not gain total control of the targets' airspace, they ruined the Sicilian transport system. Italian troop morale was depressed by this and other hardships.

North African ports were tightly packed on July 8, as the large Allied armada went to sea. The weather was good at first, and the convoys skirted heavily mined waters and appeared to be headed toward Greece and Sardinia. No enemy planes attacked. But the weather changed a day later, and Allied convoys were confronted with heavy seas and noisy winds. Sailors and soldiers became seasick, and commanding army and navy officers started to worry. Large transport ships were flooded, and small beaching craft were shattered. Admirals Hewitt and Ramsay assumed that their aerologists were correct in predicting subsiding winds and allowed the invasion to continue, despite navigation difficulties. Fortunately, the slowing down of small craft such as LCTs did not ruin the armada's approach pattern. Mostly it was followed, and the ships arrived as planned. They were aided by British beach submarines that blinked signals seaward with good luck messages.

If the intricate Allied invasion plan was to be successfully executed, it was vital to place the troops on the correct beaches. Small boats placed scouts on beaches to verify exact landing points for the invading soldiers. Poor landmarks made this task difficult, and there were other serious problems. Stormy weather confused and overwhelmed many of the Allied transport ship captains. It was difficult to land the small landing craft, such as those carrying vehicles and personnel (LCVPs). Troops were compelled to descend on moving, drenched nets to small boats rolling on a heaving sea.[50]

The first assault waves remained quiet that frightening black night. Hewitt's plea that a predawn bombardment precede the infantry hitting the beach was vetoed by the Allied army commanders who insisted that the tactical surprise of getting men ashore in the darkness outweighed the horrors confronted in the pitch-black night as soldiers and sailors were bedeviled by seasickness and fear. The less fortunate soldiers drowned by falling from hazardous ship ladders while trying to get into the small assault boats. Many of those vomit-, water-, and fear-soaked soldiers did end up on their assigned beaches and accomplished their missions. Not only did they survive the enemy's fierce force, they gradually wiped out all of the Sicilian beaches. Authors Nimitz and Potter found that "enemy fire gradually lessened on all beaches as the invaders rapidly overran enemy pillboxes and gun emplacements, or as supporting destroyers and gunboats blasted hostile positions one by one. For several hours enemy shells fell sporadically on the various American areas, but by 0800 most enemy artillery was silent. The Americans climbed the hills towards their D-day initial lines well ahead of schedule."[51]

The Allied success in Sicily was due in large part to naval gunfire against shore targets. Admiral Hewitt had obtained permission to have Allied destroyers, gunboats, and rocket-firing craft open fire once the enemy discovered the assault wave. Shortages of tanks, antitank guns, and tank destroyers on D-day were remedied the following morning.

A couple of days after the start of the Husky invasion, German tanks broke into a beach taken by the Allies. The Germans, according to British naval historian Bernard Fergusson, "were engaged by Admiral Hewitt almost personally, since he took a cruiser *Savannah* and a destroyer *Shubrick*, close ashore and helped restore the situation by opening fire at point-blank range with their 36-inch guns."[52]

Immediately after he received word of the Allied landings, Italian general Guzzoni ordered counterattacks by armored forces. It was then that the U.S. Seventh Army, General Patton, and other Allied generals became convinced of the importance of coordinated, precise naval gunfire against shore targets. Hewitt's ships battered retreating tanks, infantry, and other enemy targets. But the failure of Allied Air Force commanders to participate in joint planning led to disaster. According to Nimitz and Potter, "Through faulty identification, 23 of the Allied transport planes were shot down by anti-aircraft guns on shore and in task force."[53] During the night of July 11-12, 144 transport planes carrying American paratroopers were scheduled for descent behind the Gela, Sicily, landing beach. No one in Hewitt's armada was informed of this in time to notify antiaircraft crews. The arrival of Allied planes coincided with the end of an Axis raid, and some U.S. anticraft gunners failed to properly identify the friendly planes. Two nights later, this tragedy was compounded by the downing of eleven planes by friendly fire.[54]

Despite the terrible aircraft identification and other errors, the Sicilian invasion was a major victory for the Allies. It demonstrated effective applications of sea power in support of land operations. The invasion planners adopted the wise policy of not staging the amphibious assault beyond the radius of land-based support. There was not enough air support available in the Mediterranean. All U.S. fleet carriers were in the Pacific in July 1943. The news of Allied success in Sicily and a 560 plane raid in Rome hastened the dissolution of the Axis coalition. King Victor Emmanuel of Italy removed Mussolini from office; and his successor, Marshal Pietro Badoglio, did not continue the war against the Allies. Conditions in Russia prevented Hitler from sending enough troops to seize Italy; he could only move German troops into Italy from France and Germany.

In a little more than a month, Operation Husky accomplished most of its goals: communications were secure for the Allies in the

Mediterranean, and further opportunities to defeat the enemy were created by the Allied victory. People in neutral nations learned about the Anglo-American success, and it soon became clear that the Germans would be fighting alone in Europe against heavy odds. Allied casualties of the Sicilian invasion were seven thousand eight hundred killed and fourteen thousand wounded.[55] Bob Jagers, of Farmington, Michigan, who served as a crew member of LST 351 during Husky, wrote that the first-wave troops shouldered the worst of the invasion, adding, "Most of the soldiers on our ship had never been exposed to real action and many of them were 18, 19, and 20 years old."[56] Through summer 1943, troops and supplies were unloaded in Sicily by Allied soldiers and sailors. The LST 335 made six round-trips from North Africa during July and August.[57]

George H. Sweet Jr. became, at the age of twenty-three, the commanding officer of LST 358. He participated in all the amphibious invasions in the Mediterranean theater, earning five battle stars. Before becoming captain of LST 358, he served its crew as stores officer, gunnery officer, and executive officer (second in command.) A book that he wrote with his brother Donald (who also served in the navy during World War II), *Lightning Strikes: A Story of Amphibious Actions during World War II: The Adventures of LST 358 in the Mediterranean Sea during World War II*, reflects an LST crew member's observations of the invasions of Sicily and Salerno. Sweet noted that LST 358 crew members were more confident after the success of the Sicilian invasion. "It was not that we were so overly confident of our abilities, but we did feel that we now had a 'handle' on the way such an effort was to be performed."[58]

The authors also observed that the characteristics of the various beaches differed. In Sicily, for example, the beach was about one hundred yards wide and running up to cliffs and hills. They had roadways and paths that entered inland. This was important to the Allied soldiers who were able to move into the interior of Sicily quickly. The landing of heavy equipment, such as tanks, trucks, jeeps, howitzers, and emergency items, preceded a troop landing. Commanding Officer Sweet, who later in civilian life rose from an assistant purchasing agent to become president and CEO of a large leather company in Philadelphia, praised the logistics for the Sicilian invasion. He claimed that "the planning and the execution of the logistics were beyond belief. The smoothness with which it was carried out was totally unreal. Had it not been . . . for amphibious vessels, the back-up of the troops would not have been possible."[59]

After the initial July 1943 landing, the LST 358 made many other trips from Bizerte to Sicily. Once the Allies secured the island, Palermo became a new base for LST sailors to visit when the war afforded the pleasures and hangovers of liberties. But the LST 358's first trip to Sicily was a rough one, with many soldiers and sailors getting seasick during the pitching and tossing of the ship. The Sicilian landings were comparatively low in casualties; but some U.S. paratroopers were the victims of inexcusable Allied negligence, miserable pre-Husky invasion planning, and trigger-happy inexperienced anticraft gunners.[60]

The biggest threat to LSTs and other ships was enemy air assaults. This danger diminished as German air power was destroyed, but the threat never disappeared. Often Allied ships were anchored in large numbers, and enemy divers often attacked LSTs at the rising morning sun or twilight. Barrage balloons, fifty feet above Allied landing ships, offered some protection. Increasing Allied air superiority provided an even better shield. Allied air power was markedly better for the sailors by the time of the Dragoon invasion. But death did not take holidays during any of the Mediterranean invasions. [61]

Torch-Husky: Some Comparisons

One of the big differences between the North African and Sicilian invasions was the use of amphibious craft in the latter. Landing Ship, Tanks (LSTs) were cursed as Lousy Stinking Tubs and Large Slow Targets by the men who sailed in them; but their capacity to make landings more efficient by being able to ground directly on a beach and lower their large bow ramps so that vehicles, tanks, guns, and personnel could disembark more safely was a considerable advantage. It became increasingly obvious that LSTs were critical in all fifty World War II amphibious campaigns.

Another important feature of the Sicily invasion was that LCIs (Landing Craft, Infantry Large [or LCI(L)s]) were used for the first time. Initially, they were about 155 feet long, could carry roughly 200 troops who could disembark by gangways that were lowered. The first landing craft arrived at Sicily on July 10, 1943. Transport ships anchored about six miles out and parallel to the beach. Behind them, LCIs and LSTs were anchored. Five navy cruisers and destroyers lay on either side of the amphibious vessels to provide fire support. Allied invasions planners repeated the practice used in the North African invasion of not allowing prelanding or air bombardment on the assault beaches. Again they hoped that the troops would get ashore under the cover of darkness and thus surprise the enemy.

Allied troops, vehicles, and equipment reached the Sicilian beaches; but they collapsed when heavy equipment was set down on them. More and more amphibious craft brought huge piles of supplies. A supply glut caused a backup on the beaches, compelling the landing craft to wait in the surf. In Admiral Hewitt's December 22, 1942, report to Admiral King, entitled "Torch Operation Comments and Recommendations," he discussed the problem of unloading at beaches thus: "Considerable delay was caused by congestion of boats and difficulty of unloading heavy weights at beaches. The need for mechanical aids, improved methods, and equipment for unloading boats is apparent. Once on the beach, equipment and supplies must be quickly unloaded and carried out of the tidal wave to prevent loss of cargo and stranding of boats."[62] While waiting to come ashore and unload, some of the landing craft became stranded.

Within a month, the Allied Sicily landings were all successfully completed. The German and Italian troops retreated across the Straits of Messina, and Sicily came under Allied control.

Salerno (Operation Avalanche)

The impressive evacuation of German forces from Sicily intensified General Marshall's desire to deploy American soldiers and equipment to Britain to invade Normandy. General Eisenhower was left in an awkward position by his mentor, General Marshall, and was compelled to carry out the September 9, 1943, invasion of Salerno (Operation Avalanche) with reduced resources and with the small amphibious fleet that was available for the invasion of Sicily. Marshall's reduction of forces for Avalanche was exacerbated by the squabbling between the British and Americans over differing objectives and logistical competition.[63] The invasion of Salerno was poorly planned because military commanders involved in Avalanche were either heavily occupied with the Sicilian invasion or dispersed throughout the Mediterranean area.

On August 30, 1943, less than two weeks after the subjugation of Sicily, General Eisenhower presented a plan that chose Salerno as the place for the landing because it had good beaches and sparse enemy coastal guns. But it was thirty-five miles southeast of Naples, and the difficult road connecting it with that magnificent city was carved through a rocky promontory. It was clear that Allied troops attempting to use this road could be victims of heavy artillery from the heights. However, Allied planes from Sicily and naval bombardment could weaken the German defenders. The invasion of the Gulf of Salerno on September 9 was at the extreme attack radius of Sicily-based Spitfire aircraft fighters equipped with droppable fuel tanks. Lt. Gen. Mark W. Clark led the newly organized U.S. Fifth Army in the drive for Naples.

Complicating the planning for the Salerno invasion was the wide geographical dispersion of the principal commanders and their troops. Another problem was the uncertainty over military force allocations, with only a short interval between the Sicilian and Salerno invasions. Tower of Babel confusion resulted when complicated plans were poorly executed. The navy was confronted with the withdrawal of landing craft from the Sicilian operation, repair work had to be done so that the vessels would be seaworthy, and disputes between army and navy commanders arose. Describing one army-navy dispute, Admiral Hewitt wrote, "These [landing] craft, particularly the LSTs, had been found to be so useful in Sicily ferrying motor vehicles, supplies, and troops, that the Army was exceedingly reluctant to let them go. It took the very strongest of representations on our part to effect the release, and that at the very last moment."[64] The landing craft performed well because of the efforts of maintenance workers at Bizerte, Algiers, the U.S. shipyard at Palermo, and the crew of the Vulcan, a fleet repair ship. Many Allied army commanders connected with the Salerno invasion were amphibious combat novices. The army service command assigned in Oran to load assault transports and cargo ships of the Thirty-sixth Division was unfamiliar with amphibious techniques and combat loading. Arguments and wastes of time resulted from such inexperience. The people who were specially trained for this type of work, army transport quartermasters, were ignored. Ammunition and cases of inflammables were loaded in the same cargo holds of merchant ships. Proper loading practices would have prevented many deaths and injuries.

The air planning for the Salerno invasion did benefit from lessons learned during the Sicilian invasion. The Salerno invasion armada was better protected from German submarines by Allied aircraft vigilance. However, not all the defects of the previous operation were remedied in time for Avalanche. The commander of the forward area did not have adequate control over aircraft coordination with ship movement. During morning and twilight periods when the reliefs between land-based fighters occurred, there was insufficient aircraft protection of Allied ships.

Superiority of Allied sea power depended on effective air supremacy. Hewitt's armada was big and powerful, but it was vulnerable. The planning and preparation to resolve complex problems such as assemblage, transportation, and safety required utmost care. Uncertainties were generated by political and military changes in Italy. Mussolini's ouster and the defeat of his Fascist party did not immediately result in a stable democratic government that Allied military leaders could trust.

On September 6, 1943, Vice Admiral Hewitt left Algiers to lead his armada to the beaches of Salerno. He received a message while at sea that Italy had surrendered. The assumption that this capitulation would be a boon to the Allies proved incorrect. Italian soldiers were disarmed by the Germans, who also seized all Italian communication centers.

Mussolini's successor, Marshal Pietro Badoglio, wanted to turn Italian allegiance to the Allied side without the humiliation of a formal surrender. Remembering the hostile public relations that had occurred in November 1942 when the Darlan-Murphy deal was undertaken to assist the Allied invasion of North Africa, Roosevelt and Churchill refused to treat the Italians too gently. An agreement was reached between Badoglio's government and the Allies that, at the landing at Salerno, Italians would surrender and would fight the Germans instead of the Allies; and the Italian Air Force and fleet would place themselves under Allied control. Because German troops continued to enter Italy, Badoglio suggested that the Allied landing take place north of Rome and that an Allied airborne division be dropped into Rome. He also promised to have Italian troops join the Allies near the landing area and closer to Rome. Uncertainty, shortages of Allied forces, and lack of trust doomed Badoglio's plan.

German troops occupied Rome during the night of September 8, and the flagship of the Italian fleet was sunk by German aircraft. The Italians admitted British airborne troops carried in warships to Taranto, but Allied plans were frustrated when the planned airborne assault of Rome was cancelled. British general Harold Alexander had rejected Eisenhower's airborne assault of Rome, claiming that the Germans still occupied the airfields.

British forces and U.S. Rangers were assigned the tasks of capturing the port and city of Salerno, the Monte Corvino airport, and passes through the hills that would lead to Naples. The Salerno landing site combined good and bad features. Guides were provided to Allied assault forces; but mountains presented the nightmare of good observation opportunities for the foe, defensive gun emplacements, and staging areas to assault Allied forces. However, the Salerno beaches were suitable in some instances for LSTs to land directly, because they had better gradients than those in Sicily. There were also fewer offshore bars than in Sicily.

In some ways, the planning for the Salerno invasion was better than that of Sicily; not only was air support better, but cooperation was improved between the air force and the army and navy, and communications were superior. For example, Admiral Hewitt's flagship, *Acun,* was equipped with sophisticated radio and radar equipment. An air force general in command of a fighter-director was aboard the *Acun.* Two fighter-director ships were also present for standby purposes. One of the first things that Maj. Gen. Lucian Truscott,—U.S. Army, did early in September 1943 was to have his division signal officer establish a radio intercept net on wavelengths of the Allied Fifth Army. Reports of the actual landings on September 9 were to be transmitted to him.

Truscott—contended that his division had done all it could after participating in the Sicilian invasion and the capture of Messina to prepare for Salerno. He noted that his division was "hot and ready" but acknowledged that it was about two thousand officers and men under the authorized strength. At first the news about the landings was good. Then, according to Truscott, "there were fragmentary messages intercepted by improvised and incomplete radio intercept system that some of the beaches were under fire and that one could not be used for landing. Appeals for help, for naval gunfire, and the like came over the ether but we never received information to permit us to know what was taking place on shore."[65]

There were difficulties in attacking an enemy that had important advantages, including topography, landings site intelligence information, and flexibility of fast movement. It was important to the Allies that air power be coordinated with sea power. The inadequacies of Allied air coverage did not endanger the outcome of the Salerno invasion, nor did it cause Hitler to strengthen the Mediterranean sector. The Germans most likely knew the range and characteristics of Allied shore-based aircraft and realized that Salerno was within the reach of Allied aircraft. The enemy also had vigilant submariners and radar operators. The Germans were improving their defenses, and Admiral Hewitt proposed

Allied bombardment to weaken them. The enemy had undertaken anti-invasion maneuvers a couple of weeks before the actual invasion.

As things turned out, the Allied generals who believed that the German defenders could be surprised by the Salerno landing turned out to have been correct. Bernard Fergusson, an eminent British authority on the Mediterranean amphibious invasions during World War II and an admirer of Admiral Hewitt's abilities, wrote, "The Army believed there was a chance of winning surprise, and proved to be right . . . the Germans alerted their troops only fifty minutes before the first landings; even though thinking an attack likely, they strengthened the defenses two days earlier."[66] The naval assault commander of the Salerno invasion was correct about the extent of the defender's knowledge, but he did not assume its negligence. He did, however, anticipate serious German opposition.

The Allied assault forces approached their destinations late at night. The weather was warm and pleasant, and there were no surf problems. Mussolini's resignation and his replacement by the seventy-one-year-old Marshal Badoglio had lulled many of the Allied invaders into the mistaken belief that they would only encounter surrendering Italians at the beaches. The fear that was present at the Sicilian invasion was absent. General Eisenhower and other Allied leaders knew that the Italian garrison in the Salerno Bay area was now in the hands of the best German troops, and Allied intelligence had predicted enemy strength. But this knowledge did not filter down to the lower echelons. In his book *Crusade in Europe*, Eisenhower wrote this about Salerno: "The landing and succeeding operations developed almost identically to G2 (Intelligence) predictions. There was a sharp but relatively short fight in getting ashore and with minor exceptions, the actual landing proceeded well. The enemy, as was his custom, immediately began to counterattack and by September 13, 1943, had gathered up to sufficient strength to make a major effort to throw us into the sea. German propaganda was ridiculing the operation as a great mistake and pouring out over the radios of the world predictions of a complete defeat of the Allied invasion."[67] A serious German attack ensued. The American Thirty-sixth Division was confronted with a surprise attack that resulted in many deaths and injuries. It did recover, however. General Clark made plans for reembarking and going back to sea. He was criticized severely for his weakening of resolution. In his 1948 book, Eisenhower wrote that Clark never faltered.[68]

American military leaders assumed that the Allies would not need a large amount of landing craft. "This was a most unfortunate assumption, as events were soon to prove," according to Chester Wilmot.[69] The Allied forces assaulting on a front of three divisions almost faced disaster. The insufficiency of LSTs for Operation Avalanche nearly resulted in failure. The prospect of the assaulting forces being thrown back to the sea was real.[70]

There was no gunfire bombardment of the Salerno beach. There wasn't even fire in the American sector as assault waves approached the beach. Admiral Hewitt's suggestion that the landing be made in the light of day and with prelanding naval bombardment was again rejected by Allied army commanders. His argument that complete surprise was impossible, and that darkness led to confusion, was overruled, despite clear evidence that he was correct. The Axis had twice raided Bizerte— the major assembly place for amphibious vessels. Their reconnaissance planes had most likely detected assault forces on their way to the landing area. The German High Command was well aware that Salerno was the probable invasion site because it was the key to Italy's best port—Naples. The army commanders' thesis, that a little surprise was better than none at all, prevailed.

The Germans were ready and waiting in Salerno. The enemy mined and wired the beaches and the gulf, doing everything possible to create a hellish reception for the invaders. Guns were placed in positions from the hills and down to the water. Tanks were deployed for counterattack, and plans for manning other German divisions were put into action. In the beginning, it appeared that there was a chance that the Germans might push the Allied forces back to the water. It also looked as if the enemy would be able to reinforce their troops faster than the Allies. An effective German counterattack seemed to be on the horizon.

The Allied assault forces enjoyed perfect weather. Allied troops on the amphibious craft and transport ships became euphoric when they heard that the Italians had surrendered and mistakenly assumed that they would be welcomed by friendly Italians. They were wrong, because there were plenty of hostile Germans. As American troops, overcome by tension or seasickness, neared their assigned beaches in small amphibious craft, they heard a loudspeaker call out in English, "Come on in and give up! We have you covered."[71]

Despite a hail of German rifle, machine gun, mortar, and tank fire, the Allied assault troops continued ashore. These first troops bypassed

German strong points and assembled at prearranged areas. Armed with howitzers that were brought ashore, the Allied soldiers blasted German infantry and tanks. Allied sailors were busy placing pontoons for landing tanks while shells burst around them. By the afternoon of D-day, the U.S. Southern Attack Force beaches were under the precarious hold of the Americans. To the north, the British sector of the beachhead was tenuously occupied by the Fifth Army. The Allied army's restriction against prelanding naval fire support was cancelled once the Germans fired on LSTs before they could anchor to launch their LCVPs. Rear Admiral Conolly, USN, ordered three destroyers into position a mile off the beach. Destroyers fired onshore installations, and rocket-firing amphibious vessels defended the first assault troops as they ran for the beach. German resistance was fierce, and small amphibious vessels were badly battered by shelling. Admiral Hewitt's ships used hundreds of rounds of ammunition in response to Allied army commander calls for firepower.

LST 358 crew members were less fortunate during the Salerno invasion than in Sicily. While directing the unloading of his ship, the first commanding officer was gunned down on the bow ramp and killed by a German mortar. Other members of the ship were exposed to more danger than they had encountered in Sicily. The Germans were in elevated positions, with good defenses and good firing capabilities. Allied forces approaching the beaches were exposed to enemy gun and mortar fire. George Sweet's ship lost its stern anchor at Salerno. "We burned out the clutch on the wench on our way to the beach and we were unable to use the anchor to pull ourselves off," he wrote of the incident. "Fortunately, by the use of one of our engines and the rapid shifting of ballast, we were able to leave the beach and the severed stern anchor cable, which is probably still laying on the bottom of the Mediterranean at Salerno."[72] The LST 358 crew was happy to get out of the Salerno assault beach fast!

Operations Husky, Avalanche, and Dragoon

The invasion of Sicily (Operation Husky—July 10, 1943) and Salerno (Operation Avalanche—September 9, 1943) are linked to the invasion of southern France. The Sicilian invasion achieved the important objectives of (1) making the Mediterranean safe for Allied shipping, (2) toppling Mussolini and his Fascist government, (3) realigning Italy's allegiance from siding with the Axis to joining the Allies, and (4) diverting German forces from the eastern front where the Soviet Union was engaged in a battle of survival. By the spring and summer of 1944, crews of American ships, including the LST 1012, were enjoying the pleasures and sights of Palermo, Rome, Naples, and many other Italian cities.

The invasion of Salerno had been spearheaded by the U.S. Fifth Army commanded by Lieutenant General Clark. The campaign started well but got mired down. German troops fought vigorously, helped by the Italian mountains and mud. Their skilled defense and the arduous Italian topography were aided by bad weather. Allied communications efforts were frustrated by mountain peaks that impeded radio transmissions. It took the Allies a little more than a month to rout the Germans out of Sicily. But the Salerno campaign lasted into winter, with icy and deep mountain streams adding to the Allied hardships. The communication equipment used for the Sicily invasion was waterproofed (unlike being damaged during the North African invasion). Amphibious trucks (DUKWs) sheltered equipment so that it could be used on vessels or on land. However, the Salerno invaders were beset with other communication problems. Erratic Italian terrain hindered the installation of wires and telephone lines, and Allied military vehicles were useless; mules, carts, and bicycles had to be used instead. Homing pigeons became popular and flew hundreds of missions. Author Rebecca Raines wrote that "at Colvi Vecchia in October 1943, the Signal Corps pigeon, G.I. Joe, saved a British brigade by flying twenty miles in twenty minutes to deliver an order to cancel the bombing of the city, which troops entered ahead of schedule. (The bird later received a medal for gallantry from the Lord Mayor of London.)"[73]

Salerno invasion forces fought their way to Naples while the British Eighth Army, under General Alexander, defeated the enemy at the bottom of the Italian Peninsula. Rome was conquered by the Allies shortly before the invasion of Normandy, and sailors from LST 1012 and other ships enjoyed liberty in the Eternal City in July 1944.

Despite all the problems, complications, and communications confusion that accompanied Avalanche, the three invasions—Torch, Husky, and Avalanche—provided Admiral Hewitt and other Allied commanders with sufficient concrete examples to heed lessons for the fourth, and final, Mediterranean assault—Operation Dragoon. One example was the commendable performance of the French colonial goum troops in the Sicily campaign. The U.S. Naval Intelligence report found that these troops rendered superb service.[74]

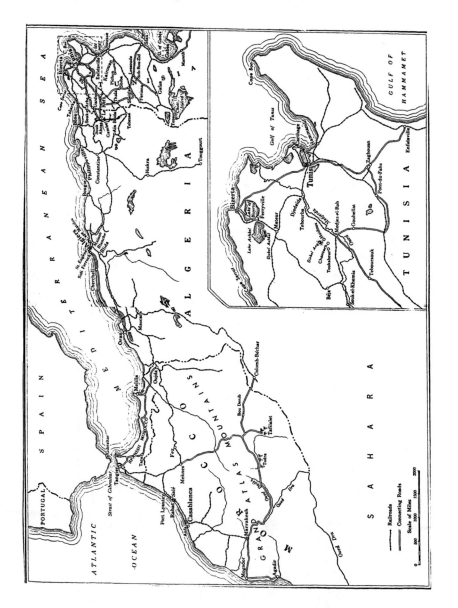

North African Invasion, November 1942 (Torch)

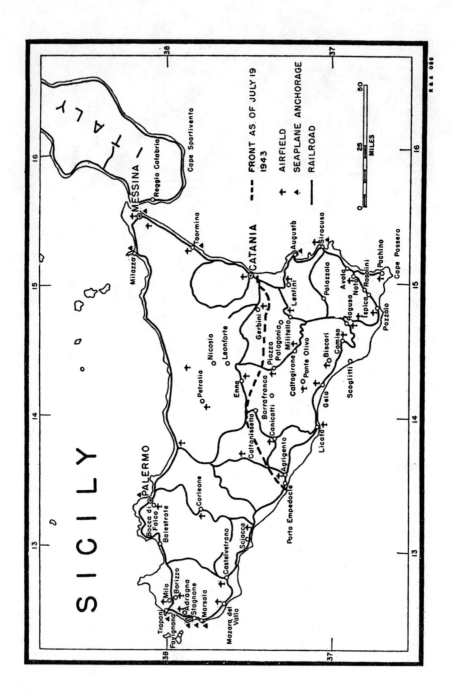

Sicilian Invasion, July 1943 (Husky)

Invasion of Sicily and Salerno

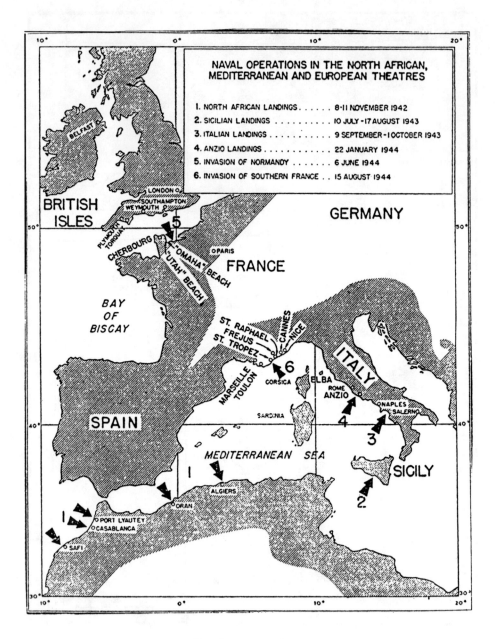

Combat operations

CHAPTER 5

THE LAST AND BEST

The last link in the chain of Mediterranean invasions was the most contentious and also the most successful of the four combined amphibious operations. Examination of the pros and cons of Dragoon, the consequences of the impasses, the invasion's planning, execution, and its aftermath are still provocative and instructive.

Under the direction of Maj. Duncan Stewart, a dozen U.S. Army majors attending the U.S. Army Command and General Staff College prepared, in May 1984, a study of Operation Anvil/Dragoon. They found that "the highly controversial decision resulting from the debate to invade southern France (Operation Dragoon/Anvil) has drawn more fire from participants and observers than perhaps any other decision during the war."[1]

Origin of Anvil/Dragoon

In August 1943, at a Quebec conference, the combined British and United States chiefs of staff discussed the operation against the southern coast of France in support of the cross-Channel invasion. Three objectives were sought: first, to engage about eleven German divisions deployed in southern France, to prevent their movement against the Allies near Cherbourg; second, to compel the movement of additional German reserves from central and northern France; and third, a surprise landing, in a double envelopment, to liberate the whole of southern and central France. Late in November 1943, the combined Allied chiefs of staff met in Cairo and decided that the operation should be undertaken. President Roosevelt and Prime Minister Churchill approved the proposal in Cairo, and Premier Stalin later approved it at Teheran. General Eisenhower was directed to prepare the plan for the invasion of southern France with about ten divisions. These were to consist of rearmed French troops in North Africa and Italy. American units that could be made available would be added. The availability of assault craft and shipping influenced the planning for Anvil/Dragoon.

The strategy to crush the Germans between two forces coming from the north and south was delayed by Churchill's subsequent objection to Anvil/Dragoon and because of a shortage of LSTs and other landing craft. Norman Polmar and Thomas B. Allen portrayed Churchill's frustration over the scrambling for LSTs as "probably the most important ship in the Allied war effort. The landing ship tank or LST was the backbone of amphibious landings in the Mediterranean, European, and Pacific areas. In 1944 Prime Minister Churchill declared: 'The whole of this difficult (strategy) question only arises out of the absurd shortage of the LSTs. How is it that the plans of two great empires like Britain and the United States should be so hamstrung and limited by a hundred or two of the particular vessels will never be understood by history.'"[2]

At the November 1943 Teheran conference, Stalin told Roosevelt and Churchill that he considered an attack in southern France to be much more important to the achievement of Allied victory than the capture of Rome. Adm. William Leahy, FDR's chief of staff, who was present, later wrote about Stalin: "We knew at once that we were dealing with a highly intelligent man who spoke well, knew what he wanted, and was determined to get it. No professional soldier or sailor could find fault with that. The Marshal's approach to our mutual problem was direct, agreeable, and considerate of the viewpoints of his two colleagues—until one of them advanced some point that Stalin thought was detrimental to Soviet interests. Then he could be brutal to the point of rudeness."[3] Both General Marshall and Admiral Leahy supported the Soviet position, but British general Lord Alan Brooke insisted that all available Mediterranean forces be used in the Italian and eastern Mediterranean campaigns, despite previous British agreement to undertake Anvil/Dragoon.

By January 1944, General Eisenhower was assigned to the Allied Expeditionary Force in England, and British General Sir Henry Maitland Wilson was selected as his successor in the Mediterranean. Gen. Jacob L. Devers was named deputy theater commander and commanding general of the North African Theater of Operations. Gen.Alexander M. Patch Jr. replaced Gen. George S. Patton as commander of the Seventh Army, which was to undertake Operation Dragoon. Patton's slapping of two hospitalized soldiers had led to Patch replacing him. Patch's superb record, as a commander against the Japanese in Guadalcanal, had impressed Marshall.

The June 6, 1944, invasion of Normandy (Operation Overlord) required all available shipping. The Italian campaign had exacted more troops and supplies than anticipated. Despite Churchill's opinion to the contrary, American military planners viewed the Normandy invasion as confirming the need for Dragoon. The clashes between the proponents and opponents of Operation Dragoon were based on differences about the overall strategy. One of Churchill's arguments was that fighting in Italy was at last going in favor of the Allies, and concentrating resources there would lead to gaining all of Italy before the start of winter. Weighing the strategic importance of Dragoon against the limited value of the Italian offensive, General Eisenhower persisted on a speedy invasion of southern France. Churchill and his faction might be displeased, but Roosevelt was facing a presidential election in 1944. Ending the war in Europe as soon as possible and satisfying the wishes of America's French and Russian allies were more important to Roosevelt than following Churchill's agenda.

Timing and Arguments

The date of August 15, 1944, was pivotal. Any delay beyond it was courting danger. Bad weather would descend on the Riviera in early autumn, including mistrals—cold, dry, northerly winds common in southern France and neighboring regions. This danger and the type of stalemate that occurred at Monte Cassino, Italy, had to be avoided. Churchill argued that Allied troops should be transported via ports in Brittany rather than the Mediterranean ports. Eisenhower rejected this proposal, claiming that he expected the Brittany ports to be stubbornly defended and destroyed by the Germans, but did not expect the destruction to be so extensive at Marseille. He knew that a large portion of defending forces had been drawn northward to meet Allied attacks. Eisenhower concluded that "the entry of a sizable force into southern France provided definite tactical and strategic support to our operation."[4] Churchill was certain that the southern France invasion would result in a bloodbath. Early in August 1944, British General Bernard Montgomery withdrew his opposition to Anvil/Dragoon, agreeing with Eisenhower to proceed with it. Only four days before the August 15 landing did the British conclusively agree with their American counterparts that Dragoon should become a reality. After observing the landings, Churchill telegraphed Eisenhower, saying, "I watched this landing from afar. All I have seen there makes me admire the perfect precision with which the landing was arranged and intimate collaboration of British-American forces."[5] Nevertheless, Churchill and some American generals, such as Mark W. Clark, continued to have strong views opposing Dragoon because they were convinced that it was a waste of manpower and equipment.

Gen. Ira Eaker of the U.S. Army Air Force and Gen. John Slessor of the British Royal Air Force headed the single combined operational staff of the Mediterranean Allied Air Force (MAAF) during the summer of 1944. General Eaker opposed the withdrawal of Allied divisions from Italy so that they could fight in Operation Dragoon. He contended that such action would prevent General Alexander's armies in Italy from breaking the German defensive line from Pisa to Rimini and would frustrate the plans for the capture of the Po Valley as a base for Allied planes—a base that would have been much nearer to Germany. General Marshall rejected Eaker's argument against Dragoon, dismissing his objection with this comment: "I think you've been with the British too long."[6]

President Roosevelt had rejected Churchill's repeated and strenuous opposition to Dragoon and supported the U.S. chiefs of staff. He disapproved the British proposal to use nearly all Mediterranean resources for an advance into northern Italy and continued advancing to the northeast. He also vetoed Churchill's strategy to preempt Stalin's troops from heading west. Churchill ignored American admonitions to cease his opposition to Dragoon and persisted in his attempts to thwart it. One of the reasons Roosevelt chose Eisenhower as the supreme commander of Allied military forces in Europe was that he was widely recognized as having diplomatic ability. He did not antagonize the British by nationalistic confrontational behavior, and the relationship between the British people (including their king and prime minister) and Eisenhower was one of reciprocal admiration. But his insistence on the Anvil/Dragoon invasion almost caused an irreparable breach between the British leaders and Eisenhower and his superiors—General Marshall and President Roosevelt.

Eisenhower's determination to launch Dragoon was based on military grounds. He wanted to crush the Germans by confronting them with attack forces from the south of France as well as from the north. He concluded that France was the pivotal European war theater and that the speedy concentration of maritime force against the Germans in France was crucial. This could only be accomplished by winning the ports of Marseille and Toulon. His cable of July 1944 to his British counterpart,

General Wilson, spelled out the American objectives for the invasion of southern France:

1. Contact and destroy enemy forces that would otherwise oppose the Normandy invasion.
2. Secure a major port in southern France for entry of additional Allied forces.
3. Advance northward to threaten the southern flank and rear communications of the enemy forces opposing Overlord (Normandy).
4. Develop lines of communication for the support of an Allied advancing force (Dragoon) and for the development and support of additional forces to be introduced through the ports as reinforcements for Wilson's command.[7]

Churchill's opposition to Anvil/Dragoon led to Eisenhower's refusal to reinforce British troops in Italy. The prime minister urged an attack toward the Ljubljana Gap, Austria, and southern Germany. This was vetoed by the Americans. Churchill was mindful of both military and political considerations. The success of the Normandy invasions convinced him that Allied victory was not only foreseeable, but it would happen soon. His focus was on postwar possibilities and dangers. In World War I, Churchill had been concerned about Soviet threats to Western interests, and that concern emerged again in 1944. He realized that Stalin's forces would be positioned to seize and control the nations of Eastern and Central Europe and that this takeover by the Red Army of neighboring nations could happen before the defeat of Germany. If American and British armies accelerated their conquest of the Italian Peninsula by beating determined German resistance, the Allies could cross the Alps through the Ljubljana Gap. Then a move into Austria and parts of the Balkans could preempt Stalin's control and deny him this satellite region. Churchill's strategy, however, left General Marshall totally unconvinced; he believed that the Allies in Italy were mired in an impasse, and both he and Eisenhower lost patience with Churchill's stalling of Dragoon.

American military leaders were intent on ending the war as fast and as decisively as possible and rejected Churchill's alternative to Anvil/Dragoon and his political entanglements. The U.S. Army's case against Churchill's opposition to the Dragoon operation was concerned about the following:

a. "We get into political difficulties with the French.
b. Overlord will lose at least ten fighting divisions.
c. Our service forces continue to support the western Mediterranean.
d. Our divisions and the French divisions will be committed to a costly, unremunerative, inching advance in Italy. The people of both the United States and France may or may not take this indefinitely.
e. Once committed to Italy, we have our forces pointed towards southeastern Europe and we will have the greatest difficulty in preventing their use for occupation forces in Austria, Hungary, and southern Germany."[8]

General de Gaulle's fervent advocacy for Dragoon was founded on substantial French commitment. French military and Resistance forces contributed mightily to Dragoon's success. The Allies armed about fifteen thousand Resistance fighters in southern France, and they supplied crucial intelligence and effective sabotage. From July 1942 onward, de Gaulle regularly advised Generals Marshall, Eisenhower, and H. A. Arnold and Admirals King, Hewitt, Stark, and others of French military activities.[9]

George H. Sweet, the commanding officer of LST 358 who participated in the Mediterranean invasions (Husky, Avalanche, Dragoon), provided an example of de Gaulle's hands-on interest concerning new military technology: "One day while docked in Bizerte, General Charles de Gaulle and his staff came aboard—not to inspect but out of curiosity about the ships they had heard so much about, the LST. Of about ten officers, he, of course, stood out among the rest of his entourage with his six-foot-six-inch frame. He was a tall man but not too heavy—extremely military and important in demeanor and appearance. His curiosity in the LST and its capabilities was very interesting. He did not miss a thing and wanted to tour the entire ship, which he did. He was aboard for about an hour and was very gracious to all of the officers and crew with whom he came in contact. We will always remember him as a very domineering character."[10]

De Gaulle's LST inspection was not an isolated incident of French military involvement. Carl R. Morin Jr., a 1942 West Point graduate, provided, in his master's thesis entitled "The Strategic Consideration of the Allied Invasion of Southern France, 1944," many examples of French military and Resistance cooperation with their Allies after the June 1940 defeat. He cited numerous French efforts to assist the Allied landing of North Africa and their participation in the Italian campaigns.[11]

Had the Allies followed Churchill's proposal that their military forces in the Mediterranean push the Germans north up the Italian boot into Venetia, Giulia, and Istria and then continue via the Ljubljana Gap through Yugoslavia into Hungary, would the "iron curtain" have been prevented from falling outside Austria, Hungary, and the Balkans? Professor Morison is doubtful. He pointed out that even if a dangerous amphibious landing at Trieste could have been avoided, the difficulties of sending a military force from the Adriatic to the Hungarian plains were huge. For example, a pivotal but steep twenty-foot road was winding and barely surfaced and crossed two two-thousand-foot passes that were dominated by high mountains. The region's topographic, vegetation, and weather features were much more favorable to the German defenders than to the Allied invaders. Allied vehicles would have to deal with narrow roads with steep gradients, heavy rainfall, and dense forests. Morison scoffed at Churchill's characterization of the "rugged nature" of the Rhone Valley, which faced Dragoon troops, observing that "the route north from Marseille is an open speedway compared with the Ljubljana route to Vienna."[12] The Germans were ready to repeat their strong defense of Anzio against a landing near Trieste, and they were building defensive positions on each side of the Ljubljana Gap. By the end of August 1944, Russian armies had reached Bucharest. The likelihood of Anglo-American troops beating the Russians to Vienna was remote. Even when British and Americans advances to the outskirts of Prague in April 1945 had conquered other enemy-held territory in Eastern Europe, the Russians managed to subjugate neighboring people.

President Roosevelt rejected Churchill's claim that the Dragoon advance up the Rhone Valley was replete with great hazards, difficulties, and delays and that the southern France invasion route was most formidable. Roosevelt stressed the role of the French Resistance and the logistical needs of deploying in France thirty-five American divisions that were waiting for shipment. French objections to the use of their troops other than in France could not be ignored. Roosevelt did not hesitate to let Churchill know that "for purely political considerations over here, I should never survive even a slight setback in Overlord if it were known that friendly forces had been diverted to the Balkans."[13] In addition to the serious geographical obstacles and logistical difficulties, Churchill's Ljubljana Gap plan would have resulted in a battered Allied army in Slovenia. It is also likely that this Churchill strategy would have triggered a horrendous civil war in Yugoslavia, which in turn would have extended the war.[14]

Criticism of Churchill

Field Marshal Lord Alanbrooke was not alone in his severe criticism of Churchill's military strategic thinking. H. P. Willmott, the eminent British military historian who taught in the Department of War Studies and International Affairs at the Royal Military Academy Sandhurst, England, wrote, "It was a sign of Churchill's continuing poor judgment that he persisted in his opposition to Anvil after Eisenhower revealed his hand, and on 28 June and again on 1 July (1944) he appealed directly to Roosevelt for support against J.C.S (U.S. Joint Chiefs of Staff Generals George C. Marshall, Henry Arnold, and Adm. Ernest J. King). It was only when these entreaties were rejected in a somewhat dismissive manner that he conceded temporary defeat with as much poor grace as he could muster. Indeed, Churchill continued to snipe at Anvil until 8 August, just one week before the operation was carried out."[15]

Britain's highest-ranking army officer, Lord Alanbrooke, did not think much of Churchill's ability as a military strategist. Alanbrooke's *War Diaries* is replete with criticism of the prime minister. Accusations of strategic lunacy, administrative incompetence, senility, and alcoholism were some of the many charges Alanbrooke hurled at Churchill.[16]

President Roosevelt had little military knowledge and relied on General Marshall and listened to his advice. Churchill, according to Lord Alanbrooke, thought that by being a descendant of the great general Marlborough, he had inherited his ancestor's military genius. As a result, Churchill sought to impose his often wild, dangerous ideas upon his top generals, interfered with their plans, and too readily removed them as if they were mere chess pawns. It appears to this author that Churchill's alternatives to Operation Dragoon were dreams devoid of reality.[17]

Lord Alanbrooke was not alone in questioning Churchill's competence as a military strategist. Lord Hankey, one of Britain's leading professional civil servants responsible for coordinating his nation's secret services, had a similarly low opinion of the prime minister's military abilities. While recognizing Churchill's great gifts as a leader, Hankey found that he had a long record of failures as a master of war. These included Churchill's disastrous Gallipoli venture in Italy in World War I, the failed expedition to help the White Russians after the end of that war, obstructing the construction of new ships in 1925, mistaken appraisals of the competence of French generals and French military methods, adherence to the myth of the invulnerability of the Maginot Line, failed strategies in Normandy and Greece, and a disaster in Crete.[18]

Morin's comprehensive and thoughtful study of the arguments for and against the undertaking of Operation Dragoon revealed that "postwar attempts to establish the antecedents of the cold war have settled upon the Anvil [Dragoon] decisions as one of the contributing factors."[19] Churchill and those who still support his alternative to the invasion of southern France claim to have foreseen the post-World War II Russian takeover of Eastern Europe and the resulting cold war. Churchill's persuasiveness was powerful during World War II and thereafter, and he used his great gift of communication to spur distrust of communism.

Was the United States so naive about Russian aims? Morin asked. To answer the question, one must first determine Soviet aims during World War II—aims that have not been definitely established and that appear to have been obscure as late as September 1944. Herbert Feis, Richard Leighton, Maurice Matloff, and other military historians have argued convincingly that, within the framework of 1944, U.S. political and military decisions were based on sound U.S. interests. The necessity to get on to the defeat of Japan demanded an early defeat of Germany. In order to be able to rapidly transfer troops to the Pacific after the defeat of Germany, the U.S. could not afford to get involved in Balkan politics that promised to require occupation duty if civil war was to be averted. Further, Soviet Russia had borne the brunt of the German attacks, was behaving reasonably, and was believed to be needed in operations against Japan. President Roosevelt had established cordial relations with Stalin and, believing that mutual cooperation would continue after the war, was reluctant to damage these relations.[20] The extra pressure applied in Dragoon was instrumental in convincing Hitler to withdraw German troops from France.

Add to the above the opportunity for French military forces to participate in the liberation of their own country, thereby relieving a goodly portion of the stain on their national pride. The French forces acquitted themselves well and, problems notwithstanding, proved a valuable addition to the Allied forces. The support of the Maquis in southern France was more certain than that of Tito's partisans especially after the Normandy landings. The influence of these forces was considerable on the final decision for Anvil. Finally, the practical difficulties inherent in the alternatives to Anvil had been shown. The Italian campaign succeeded admirably without the forces in Anvil. It held some twenty-six German divisions away from other fronts during the time when the appearance of half that number on the Western Front could have proven decisive. The advocates of the Ljubljana proposal were blinded to the difficulties in its implementation by the prospects it held out and personal desires that Italy should be more than a secondary theater.[21]

President Roosevelt's support of Dragoon was based on both military strategy and politics. He was intent on bringing the war to a speedy end with the least casualties. His Joint Chiefs of Staff had made it clear to him that the Italian campaign had already cost more American lives and resources than it should have, and it was time to strike the enemy elsewhere. Eisenhower's insistence on Dragoon was supported by his colleagues in Washington who warned him not to cave in to the unrelenting pressure from the British. Accusations against Eisenhower's possible capitulation to the British were so strong that he had to assure Marshall that these rumors were false. The Dragoon controversy became the most troubling diplomatic/military problem that confronted this gifted military diplomat. Eisenhower stuck to his position despite the barrage of persistent pressure from Churchill, who went so far as to threaten to resign as prime minister if Dragoon was not aborted. We will never know whether the adoption of Churchill's strategy and the abandonment of Dragoon would have been the better course to follow. What we do know is that Roosevelt had to be mindful of political considerations as well as military strategy. We also know that he believed that the United States could get along with the Soviet Union after the war. Many American voters in 1944 agreed with the president.

Churchill's fury and his predictions about the spread of communism throughout Europe did not deter the Americans from reassigning three divisions from the Italian campaign to participate in the landing of southern France. The blow to Britain and Churchill's position as Allied partners was severe. The British had gallantly fought the Germans since September 1939 and had stood alone until Pearl Harbor, suffering death and destruction. Now they were being relegated to a secondary role: Dragoon would be primarily an American and French undertaking, and British air and sea support would only supplement the American and French thrust. Many Republicans wanted de Gaulle and his forces to crush the Germans and win back France. In August 1944, Roosevelt was in the midst of another presidential campaign, and a victorious invasion would help.

Before Operation Dragoon, the French ports that were available to the Allies were too distant for the effective pursuit of retreating Germans. Allied pursuers and their equipment had to be hauled long distances by trucks. The success of the invasion of southern France changed that by opening up the ports of Marseille and Toulon. Marseille, with its artificial harbor that was useful in all types of weather, was also fully serviced by rail. It had canal connections to the Rhone River. In addition to the port of Toulon, the Allies wanted to acquire Port de Bouc, primarily a fuel-handling facility with good handling equipment.

Results of Decision Impasse

One result of the complex on-again, off-again history of Operation Dragoon was that this lengthy indecision frustrated the planning of civil affairs administration for the people of southern France. The Civil Affairs Section of General Patch's Seventh Army had about 16 percent of the administrative personnel for southern France than were available for a much smaller area in northern France. The French were given far more power to administer their public affairs in southern France than they had in northern France—thirty-one departments compared to eighteen—due to the shortage of Anglo-American administrators. Dangerous fighting between French Communists and Socialists competing for political power in Toulouse was mitigated by British officials after August 15, 1944. Frequently Allied groups assisted in the mediation of disputes. Coordination between the Anglo-Americans and various French groups yielded favorable results, such as providing needed drugs, food, and clothing faster.

When American parachutists dropped into the small French town of Le Muy early in the morning of August 15 virtually unscathed, the wisdom of the American position was confirmed. When later that day LST 1012 and other ships landed on the beach of Cap Drammont, there was cause for greater satisfaction over how well Allied planning had succeeded. Roosevelt quashed Churchill's dogged opposition by proclaiming that "Anvil/Dragoon should be launched as planned at the earliest practicable date and I have full confidence that it will be successful."[22]

Among the many views concerning whether Operation Dragoon should have been undertaken are the following comments from Admiral Hewitt:

In substance, the Prime Minister and the British Chiefs of Staff advocated abandoning Anvil in favor of concentrating on pushing the German forces facing the Italian front back into plains of north Italy, with possible auxiliary operations in the Adriatic and elsewhere in the Balkans, and an eventual drive into Austria. The American Chiefs of Staff, and General Eisenhower, on the other hand, insisted on concentrating on the campaign in Western Europe, as the best means of accomplishing the final defeat of Nazi Germany at the earliest date. Furthermore, General Eisenhower argued that the port of Marseille was urgently required for the support of the Allied Forces in the north of France.

To me, who naturally had no part in the foregoing argument, it seemed, in addition, that Anvil would provide opportunity for the immediate employment of considerable French forces in an operation which would raise their morale to the highest pitch, the liberation of their own country. Furthermore, Allied occupation of the south coast of France would deny to the enemy the only remaining submarine bases and air fields from which he could direct attacks against shipping in the western Mediterranean. And, of course, it would have been a bitter disappointment to all those who had worked so hard over such a long period in planning and preparing for Anvil to see the results of their efforts thrown overboard at the last moment.

It required a determined stand by President Roosevelt to carry the day. And even after the final "Go Ahead" had been given, a last-moment desperate effort was made to have the troops assigned to Anvil carried around and landed in the Bay of Biscay instead. Sir Winston relates that, shortly before D-day, the code name for the operation was changed because the enemy might have become cognizant of the significance of the old name. Unfortunately, he does not confirm the story, at that time prevalent at Allied Mediterranean Headquarters, that he himself renamed it Dragoon because he had been "dragooned into it."[23]

The immediate results of Dragoon were the addition of another Army Group to the Allied Forces driving toward the Rhine, including a new French army of high morale, the liberation of southern and central France, and the availability of Marseille as a supply port, badly needed because of the unexpectedly low capacity of the badly damaged ports of Cherbourg and Brest. But these were not all. The enemy had been deprived of all means of attacking shipping in the Mediterranean. The Strait of Gibraltar had already been blocked to submarines by effectively coordinated U.S. naval air and British surface patrols. The loss of the south coast of France made further submarine operations in the Mediterranean impossible. Furthermore, the north shore of the Mediterranean could no longer be used as a base for aircraft preying upon the convoy lanes. Soon ships in the Mediterranean were enabled to proceed independently, burning navigation lights, with a saving of time and of shipping which was inestimable.

Sir Winston Churchill still argues that Dragoon was a mistake. And one American writer has classed it as one of the three big errors of the war. This is certainly debatable. To me, the strongest argument against it was not military, but political—that, by adopting the course proposed by our British allies, we would have forestalled the Soviet forces in the Balkans, and thus pushed back what was to become known as the "Iron Curtain." Had we postponed the defeat of Hitler, as I believe would have been the case, to attain this political end, one can but ponder the ultimate result. Would it not have been the establishment of freely elected governments under Anglo-American aegis, followed by prompt troop withdrawal under the urge of demobilization, and then, the initiation of the usual communist procedure of infiltration, military pressure, and outright aggression.[24]

CHAPTER 6

IT HAPPENS

How did the invasion of southern France happen and who was involved? Men such as the American General Alexander M. Patch Jr., British General Henry M. Wilson, and German General Johannes Blaskowitz deserve recognition, as does the Cap Drammont quarry owner, Louis Marchand, a French Resistance fighter. But the innocent people who were killed because of German reprisals and Allied air bombing of French cities in preparation for Dragoon remain unknown.

According to the Seventh Army Plan, on December 19, 1943, Seventh Army Headquarters in Palermo received a message that interrupted a four-month period of comparative inactivity. It was a telegram from Allied Force Headquarters that read, "An estimate is required as a matter of urgency as to the accommodations which you would require for your planning staffs should you be asked to undertake the planning of an operation of a similar size to Husky . . . ."[1]

Since the capture of Messina on August 17, 1943, which terminated the campaign in Sicily, the Seventh Army had been reduced from a tactical force of six divisions to a headquarters with a skeleton force of a few remaining service units. In Washington and London, the Combined Chiefs of Staff had made plans for an all-out offensive in the Mediterranean Theater to eliminate Italy from the war. As preparations for the invasion of the Italian mainland got under way, the Third and Forty-fifth Infantry Divisions, the Eighty-second Airborne Division, and most of the Seventh Army service units were assigned to the Fifth Army. At the same time, the focus of coming events was also centered on the invasion of northern Europe. The First and Ninth Infantry Divisions and the Second Armored Division were ordered to the United Kingdom for training as major assault units in the contemplated cross-Channel invasion. The remainder of the Seventh Army force bivouacked in and about the city of Palermo to continue its training and conditioning, as the headquarters went through a series of command post exercises and completed tactical and historical reports of the summer campaign.

Now, an operation similar to Husky, which had hit the beaches of Sicily, was to be planned. During the last week of December 1943, preparations were made to move and organize the nucleus of a Seventh Army planning staff in the Ecole Normale of Bouzareah in the city of Algiers. Other units remained in Sicily.

Instructions from Allied Force Headquarters to the planning staff on December 29, 1943, indicated general direction and objectives. The operation, which was to be known by the code name Anvil, would be launched with a target date during May 1944 against the south coast of France.[2] In conjunction with the Overlord invasion of northern Europe, Anvil was to establish a Mediterranean bridgehead and, subsequently, to advance toward Lyon and Vichy. The forces engaged were to be American and French, although the proportion and total strength were as yet uncertain.

Lt. Gen. George S. Patton was relieved from command of the Seventh Army as of January 1, 1944. Lt. Gen. Mark S. Clark retained his Fifth Army command but was also charged with planning Operation Anvil. He was to replace Patton.[3] Five months were available for planning and revising the tactical details of Anvil and for organizing and training the striking force against southern France.[4]

Although Generals Marshall, Eisenhower, and Devers wanted Patton to command Anvil/Dragoon, the assignment was given to Patton's friend, Maj. Gen. Alexander M. Patch Jr.[5] Before Patch, the command of Dragoon was offered to General Clark. Clark's many admirers praised his intelligence, great planning, and training abilities, all of which made him an ideal candidate to lead the coming invasion of the southern French coastline. Critics, however, belittled his battlefield competence, the high rate of casualties his troops suffered, and his failure to work effectively in conjunction with the British forces. Historian Douglas Porch of the U.S. Naval Postgraduate School described an example of Clark's weakness as a military commander as follows: "Clark's near panic at Salerno and increasing criticism of his stubborn, poorly conceived, and inadequately supported attacks on the Cassino Line in the winter of 1943-44 caused Eisenhower to consider relieving him, a step he never took. So disappointed had Eisenhower been in Clark, however, that he was never included on Ike's short list for a command in Overlord the Normandy invasion."[6]

Early Indecision

From the outset, the plans for Anvil were handicapped by stipulations, varying assumptions and possibilities, and special considerations, all of which pointed to the lack of clear decision from higher headquarters. The number of assault divisions available, the buildup force to follow, the influence of the Italian campaign, and likely objectives in southern France once a successful landing had been made were among the many unanswered questions.[7]

During the mid-January 1944 meetings in Algiers, an amphibious operation known as Shingle was being mounted for a landing on the Italian coast in the area of Anzio-Nettuno. The success of this move would determine for some time to come the shipping and troops available for future operations. There was as yet no decision by the Combined Chiefs of Staff on the scale of Anvil, or even the approval of the general outline plan. Planning proceeded, however, on the basis of a one-, two-, or three-division assault with a seven-division follow-up. The supply sections began the preparation of logistical requisitions so that the loading of ships in the United States would not be delayed. Initial steps were taken to arrive at a tentative troop list. Supply and tactical planning progressed concurrently, but both were beset with the same fundamental difficulty, namely, the absence of definite decisions. Preliminary studies on the beaches, coastal defenses, inland terrain, and the disposition of enemy troops were made by the various subsections.

It became apparent that the Third and Forty-fifth Divisions, which were a part of the Anzio beachhead forces, would not be available for immediate transfer.[8] Two fronts in Italy had to be supplied continuously by shipping troops and necessities. All service and supply facilities were heavily taxed. What could be made available for a third operation elsewhere? A historian of Anvil recorded, "The failure of the Shingle operation to develop as it was expected is having a direct effect . . . . It is very difficult to make sound decisions under such uncertain conditions."[9]

The task of planning Anvil became more complex and more confused. On February 10, 1944, the Combined Chiefs of Staff announced that D-day for Overlord would be postponed about three weeks. Shipping requirements were proving to be enormous; and the commander of the Mediterranean Theater, Gen. Maitland Wilson, was to arrange for the immediate return to Britain of all LSTs not vitally needed. As the Italian campaign developed, higher headquarters became "loathe to risk a change in commanders of the Fifth Army either now or in the near future." The decision not to replace Clark was General Wilson's, and General Devers concurred as of February 28. Clark's Italian campaign's "grave burdens" made impossible the close supervision of the Anvil operation, which was now becoming necessary.[10]

General Patch Assumes Command

General Devers chose General Patch to command the U.S. Seventh Army in the invasion of southern France, replacing Patton. In Devers's opinion, Patch proved to be a great commander, if not the best.[11] Generals Patton and Patch were good friends but had very different personalities. Patch (who was called Sandy) had conquered his fierce temper and was a considerate, modest man, who detested profanity. Patton was an intemperate man who often used profanity.

An event that illustrates personality differences between Patton and Patch took place in London on February 3, 1944. After seeing the husband-and-wife acting team of Alfred Lunt and Lynn Fontanne perform in Robert Sherwood's *There Shall Be No Night* at the Haymarket Theater, the generals were invited to dine with the actors at the Savoy Hotel. A German buzz bomb had descended on a roof near the Theater during the performance of the play. The war was on everyone's mind, and one of the actors asked the generals why they were fighting. Patch answered that he was fighting to resist enemy aggression, defend America, and preserve its way of life. Patton's answer was that Patch was talking through his hat and that he, Patton, was in the war because he loved fighting.

The secretary of the Seventh Army General Staff, William K. Wyant, published a definitive biography of the commander of the Dragoon invasion force. He concluded that Patch was an admirable man who was very popular and well esteemed among those in the military profession, especially among enlisted men. They saw in him qualities they looked for in officers but did not always find, namely, integrity. He was brutally honest; it was difficult to imagine him doing anything cheap or self-serving; he was brave and tended to value that quality in others; one of his outstanding traits as a commander was his concern for the lives of his soldiers. Wyant quoted one of Patch's staff officers as saying that "Patch was compassionate, more than any other commander, in his love and care of the soldiers . . . lovable, kind and a modest man. I loved that man."[12] General Eisenhower called him an outstanding troop leader, a soldier's soldier, and a brilliant leader of the Seventh Army. Even General Marshall, who was not given to bestowing casual accolades, said that Patch rendered magnificent service to the country.

Unlike a number of other World War II generals and admirals, Patch shunned publicity. When a public information officer rushed into his office to deliver the August 28, 1944, issue of *Time* magazine, which featured the general's picture on the front cover and praised the success of the Seventh Army, Patch did not read the story. Military historians Williamson Murray and Allan R. Millett, in their *A War To Be Won*, acknowledged Patton's great ability as a general but wrote, "His personal weakness lay in an inability to control either his emotions or his mouth."[13] Patch, on the other hand, controlled his fierce temper, his emotions, and his mouth. He detested the bullying that he had to endure as a plebe (or freshman) at West Point, and he tried not to bully freshmen when he became a senior. Other upperclassmen sought to ingratiate themselves to their superior officers by being harsh to plebes, but not Patch. His demonstration of independence in not catering to the harsh dictates of his superiors earned him the respect and affection of his peers. They elected him class cheerleader.

The son and father of West Point graduates, Patch at first wanted a civilian career as a businessman or engineer. At his father's insistence, he accepted an appointment to West Point and a military career. As a cadet in March 1909, there was doubt as to whether he would be allowed to graduate. His conduct record placed him last in a class of 93 students. His attitude was inflamed by alcohol. A fight with an army cook led to Patch's arrest, with his future in the military endangered. Fortunately, his popularity with fellow officers and their petition for leniency saved his career, and the incident was reduced to one week's arrest and a pledge to refrain from getting drunk. When asked why his punishment was so mild, Patch answered, "Well, I was pitching on the regiment baseball team."

After graduating West Point in 1913, he served with his brother Joseph and George Patton, among others, under the command of Gen. John Pershing on the Mexican border to enforce American neutrality during battles between warring Mexican revolutionary armies. When the troops of one of the armies led by Pancho Villa raided the town of Columbus, New Mexico, U.S. Army efforts to capture the Mexican general were evaluated by German military observers who concluded that there was not much to fear if the Americans intervened on the side of the Allies in Europe. German military experts thus had a low opinion of American fighting ability long before World War II.

Shortly after his service on the Mexican border, Patch was part of the American Expeditionary Forces (AEF) sent to fight the Germans in France during World War I. Writing to his wife after being hospitalized with pneumonia in a field hospital near the front, he observed, "I have been about as much help to the government . . . as your dog. The difference between the dog and I is I expect to do better and the dog won't."

General Patch appreciated the modesty of other men. A trim, unobtrusive man who dressed in simple, unadorned khakis was General Patch's fellow passenger on a crowded ship in August 1944. James V. Forrestal, secretary of the U.S. Navy, was on board Admiral Hewitt's command ship *Catoctin,* which took Patch and other top brass to the Dragoon invasion shore. Patch's estimate of Forrestal was glowing: "One of the most attractive and appealing men whom I have ever met, completely unspoiled, natural, direct, unostentatious, intelligent and with a sense of humor. I believe him to be one of our ablest type of man." Patch and Forrestal avoided the limelight while seeking praise for others.

After being promoted to the rank of lieutenant colonel five years after graduating from West Point, Patch answered his father-in-law's congratulations letter by stating that the promotion "resulted from the fact that the colonel of this regiment is a very old friend of mine." He said he felt guilty about accepting congratulations on his promotion and that his service did not warrant it.

Between the two world wars, Patch taught for ten years and received more training at advanced military schools. He taught military science and tactics at Staunton Military Academy in the Shenandoah Valley of Virginia, a private secondary school. One of his students in 1923 was fourteen-year-old Barry M. Goldwater, the future Arizona senator and 1964 presidential candidate. Goldwater remembered that Patch stuck to the rules but also on occasion bent them and used his own judgment. The day Goldwater was to graduate from Staunton, he pulled an outrageous prank. Patch, who was then a major, scared the teenager by telling him, "You might not graduate." After he was allowed to graduate, Patch told the teenager, "You know I used to do things like that." According to Goldwater, Patch was stern but not mean. He took his duties at the school seriously.

Before Pearl Harbor, Patch continued his vocational education by studying military history and mastering infantry and tank weapons. He improved the Browning automatic rifle and graduated from the Army

Command and General Staff School (1925) and the Army War College (1932). At the direction of President Roosevelt in mid-January 1942, Patch was assigned the difficult job of defending New Caledonia and the neighboring islands in the South Pacific. Military superiors, peers, and troops were effusive about Patch's service in Guadalcanal from October 1942 to February 1943; and his reputation continued to soar.

Gen. George C. Marshall was usually parsimonious in dispensing praise. But Marshall's praise of Patch's Guadalcanal role emphasized his organizational and training abilities, his handling of difficult political problems involving relationships with the French in New Caledonia, and his commendable cooperation with U.S. Navy leaders. Patch was seriously sick with tropical dysentery and malaria during his Guadalcanal service. He also was afflicted with pneumonia as he had been in France during World War I. The brutal six-month fight for Guadalcanal was won, although the losses on both sides were staggering. About 1,600 American soldiers and marines, out of a total of 60,000, had been killed in action; and 4,245 were wounded. Japanese military losses exceeded 14,800 killed or missing, and 9,000 were dead of diseases. About 1,000 Japanese prisoners were taken. The severity of losses can be gauged by the fact that the total Japanese force was comprised of about 36,000 men.

After exemplary South Pacific service in the midst of death, disease, and physical deterioration, Patch was ordered back to the United States in spring 1943. Following a month in Washington, on May 25, 1943, he was assigned command of Fourth Corps at Fort Lewis, Washington. One of his responsibilities was to prepare an infantry division for combat duty overseas.

General Patch confined himself to the role that he was assigned in Operation Dragoon. His role was not the assault phase of the invasion. He delegated that to other generals. Periodically, there were jurisdictional disputes between generals. In June 1944, General de Lattre argued with Patch about the possibility of the French Army being assigned to Patch's Seventh Army in Italy for a campaign in Austria. Before the Dragoon invasion, de Lattre rebuked the Dragoon assault commander, General Truscott,—for inspecting French troops without the French general's permission. Although in this instance Patch admonished de Lattre for not talking to him before he argued with Truscott, Patch tried to reduce the tensions between the French and the Americans. He followed French suggestions that involved knowledge of their homeland. Deferring to French pride, General Patch allowed their military leaders to savor their victories. He individually thanked his officers and enlisted men for their efforts. Unlike his friend, General Patton, Patch did not engage in interservice flare-ups. Working unobtrusively with U.S. Navy and French Army commanders, he sought ways to minimize Allied casualties while fulfilling his responsibilities. His planning sought to deceive the Germans by the use of diversionary tactics. To confuse the enemy, he ordered that electronic transmissions concerning troop movements be sent out. After the Dragoon invasion, when German prisoners were taken, it was learned that these tactics had, indeed, fooled the enemy.

Gen. Sir Henry Maitland Wilson

He was a tall, corpulent man who was nicknamed "Jumbo" because he looked like Colonel Blimp. Gen. Sir Henry Maitland Wilson was a graduate of Eton and had served in World War I as an infantryman, where he gained the reputation as a good staff officer. Between the two world wars, he served in India and taught at a military college. His calm demeanor hid his steely determination and ability. He was, at age sixty-three, older than the other Allied officers in the Mediterranean Theater; but he had mastered the arts of offensive operations and military leadership. Wilson refused to be used by Churchill in the prime minister's scheme for British domination of the Mediterranean.[14]

On May 11, 1944, the all-out offensive of the Fifth and Eighth Armies got under way in Italy. The linkup of the Anzio beachhead with the main front led to the capture of Rome. The release of troops from Italy for Anvil had been dependent on a turn of events in the Italian campaign. On June 4, the supreme Allied commander in the Mediterranean agreed that three American divisions and one French division could be released at an early date.

Gen. Maitland Wilson, in his turn, now felt that Anvil could not be launched in time to be of use to Overlord and therefore could be eliminated. As an alternative operation, he recommended an advance to the Ljubljana Gap with an amphibious operation against Trieste at a later date.[15] At a conference in London of the Supreme Headquarters Allied Expeditionary Force and Allied Force Headquarters, which ended around June 25, Operation Anvil was given the final go-ahead signal. Southern France would be invaded. Plans, supplies, and a definite assault date would be provided. It was apparent that the Combined Chiefs of

Staff had taken the view that France would be the decisive theater for operations during 1944. General Eisenhower concurred, explaining that the resources of Britain and the United States would not permit them to maintain two major theaters in the European war, each with decisive missions. He recommended that Anvil be launched not later than August 30 and preferably by August 15, with sufficient strength to give it reasonable chances of success. Otherwise, all French divisions, plus one or two American divisions previously allocated to Anvil, would be made available for Overlord as soon as shipping could be secured.

Supplying and Training the French

By August 1944, the United States and its Allies were able to provide enough tanks, planes, and men to soundly defeat the Germans in Marseille and elsewhere in France. But there was no early peace. From November 8, 1942, to January 8, 1943, Allied vessels delivered more than four hundred thousand men, forty-thousand war vehicles, and one million tons of supplies to North Africa, according to the British first lord of the Admiralty, A. V. Alexander.[16] By January 1944, most of the equipment for eight French divisions had arrived and had to be properly distributed, and many of the French soldiers and sailors had to be trained to use the equipment before they would be ready to participate in Anvil. General de Lattre was in charge of this training. His son Bernard enlisted in the French Army at sixteen, having been granted special permission from General de Gaulle. The young soldier was seriously wounded in battle. De Gaulle was eager to return to France as soon as possible. He wanted French troops experienced in the Italian campaign to participate in Dragoon, and if he could have had his way, it would have been a French operation with a French commander in charge. The American military chiefs did approve the use of French troops who were veterans of the Italian campaigns.

Nearly three thousand French Resistance fighters were organized by the end of May 1944. On June 2, a few days before the Normandy invasion, it appeared that the French had begun their own liberation. A premature alert from a radio broadcast from London on June 5 had called for an uprising by the French underground. This was one of a number of liberation efforts by the French to regain their homeland by themselves during the months of June through August 1944. German reprisals and atrocities followed each such attempt. By June 10, the Germans returned in force and exacted reprisals. The Gestapo killed hundreds of people and buried them in common graves and ditches. De Gaulle had appointed Gen. Koenig to serve as a special aide to General Eisenhower. In June, while the Normandy landings were taking place, Koenig ordered sabotage operations and uprisings throughout France. The Resistance fighters were few in number and inadequately armed. By August 1944, they were greater in number, better equipped and organized, and intent on not showing any mercy to their enemies. A variety of measures were taken to safeguard Resistance security: radio operators sent their messages from different locations nearly every day, the groups operated under tight compartmentalization, and weapons were delivered by parachutes.

German fortification of Le Drammont (called Camel Green Beach on the Allied invasion maps) was obstructed by Resistance fighter Louis Marchand. Le Drammont beach stretched over a quarter mile at the base of quarries filled with blue-gray porphyry, a type of rock used to pave streets. The rock was also the object of a German bureaucratic struggle over who would appropriate it from the quarry owner, the Marchand family. Louis Marchand took advantage of German internecine squabbling to delay the burying of dangerous mines on the beach. He also notified Allied invasion planners that the Camel Green Beach was without mines and bunker guns.

Reprisals

Richard Cavell Fattig's doctoral dissertation, "Reprisal: The German Army and the Execution of Hostages during the Second World War," found that

1. The occupation of southern France in November 1942 greatly magnified the problem of security for German troops.
2. German defeats during the winter of 1943 persuaded most French people that they would be liberated soon. This encouraged them to attack entire units of the German Army.
3. In February 1944, Field Marshal Gerd von Rundstedt, commander of German forces in Western Europe, designated French coastal areas to be under the jurisdiction of combat commanders. They

were authorized to seize and execute hostages, without consulting military administrators in Paris or Belgium. German troops were permitted to shoot innocent people in retaliation against terrorism attacks.

4. Shortly after the Allied landing in Normandy, French Resistance fighters attacked small detachments of German troops in southern France. Field Marshal Rundstedt ordered his troops to take the "sharpest possible measures" to intimidate the people in these "bandit-infested regions."

5. On June 9, 1944, during a struggle between German troops and French Resistance fighters for the small town of Tulle, a number of German soldiers were killed. German wounded were treated in a French hospital. After the French guerrilla fighters responsible for the killings and injuries had escaped, the Germans arrested all French males in the town capable of bearing arms. Ninety-nine Frenchmen were killed, and their bodies hung from lampposts and balconies. Frenchmen who were deemed to be "economically indispensable" were spared; students were not. Only the decent treatment accorded to the German wounded, the SS commander assured the French, had spared them an even more horrific reprisal.

6. On June 10, 1944, German troops entered the small French town of Oradour-sur-Glane after French Resistance fighters sabotaged a major rail artery, attacked German motor convoys, and captured a high-ranking German officer. There was no evidence to suggest that the residents of the town were connected with these anti-German acts. Indeed, French sources claim the contrary. The German reprisal destroyed the town and killed 642 men, women, and children after SS troops set fire to the church in which they were incarcerated.[17]

Gen. Johannes Blaskowitz, who had complained about his fellow Germans' atrocities toward Polish civilians in 1939, urged his troops to distinguish between French combatants and noncombatants. Under his orders, innocent French women, children, and men who had not harmed Germans were not to be victimized, nor should their homes be destroyed without justification. Another German general, Karl Heinrich von Stulpnagel, also tried to get his troops to protect innocent French people. He and Blaskowitz were aware that circumstances made it difficult for German soldiers to distinguish between friend and foe, but both generals tried to protect the innocent. Blaskowitz complained to his superior, Rundstedt, about German atrocities; and von Stulpnagel forfeited his life when he conspired in the failed attempt to kill Hitler on July 20, 1944.

In summer 1944, French Resistance fighters were provided with more money than previously. A Jesuit priest, Father Chaillet, was in charge of the movement's finances. He lived humbly in a small servant's room at 185 rue de la Pompe in Paris. For transportation he rode a bicycle. A senior Treasury official named Bloch-Laine provided him with banknotes that the priest carried in his bicycle. Bloch-Laine was inspector of finance and also a member of the Financial Committee of the Resistance. The banknotes he handed over came from the reserves of Gaullist banks outside of France.

The funds were produced through a parachuting system that was organized throughout France's countryside. Frenchmen in Algiers organized and directed this program. Before the Normandy invasion, there were great difficulties in converting Treasury bonds issued by the Algerian government into cash to be used by the Resistance. These bonds did not generate confidence because they did not carry a presentation date, and potential underwriters who might wish to change them into Bank of France notes were leery of making risky investments. However, in summer 1944, when it became clear that France would be liberated, there was a clamor for the Algerian Treasury bonds. Expectations of profit spread as the likelihood of Allied victory became clearer.

De Gaulle's Concerns

In a telegram sent to Prime Minister Churchill on May 12, 1944, President Roosevelt observed, "I have no objection whatever to your inviting de Gaulle and others of the French Committee to discuss your association in military or political matters; however, you must consider in the in-terest of security keeping de Gaulle in the United Kingdom until the Overlord landing has been made. It is my understanding that General Eisenhower now has full authority to discuss with the Committee all matters on a political level. I do not desire that Eisenhower shall become involved with the Committee on a political level and I am unable at this time to recognize any government of France until the French people have an opportunity for a free choice of government."[18]

On the eve of the Normandy invasion, Roosevelt tried to placate de Gaulle by having him invited to London from Algiers. This attempt failed when de Gaulle rejected speaking last on a radio proclamation announcing D-day. Rather than speaking with Eisenhower and heads of state of occupied European nations, de Gaulle opted to do his broadcast at another time. He also threatened to prevent Free French liaison officers from participating in Normandy; however, 120 of them did land with the Allies on D-day. The relationship between de Gaulle and his Allies was bad on June 6, 1944. As a result, there were no French troops present when the Allies landed in Normandy that day. In June 1944, French men and women joined the Resistance in droves without the necessary preparation. They lacked training, equipment, and were unorganized and unprepared; and many paid the price for the rash of premature uprisings with their lives.

De Gaulle was suspicious of American intentions. He was furious because they would not discuss French political issues with him as the British did. On the Italian battlefront, a good relationship had existed between French and American fighting forces. Secretary of State Cordell Hull was informed "that the nerves of a majority of Frenchmen in North Africa are frayed to the breaking point with anxiety and suspense. Many of them suffered from an unfortunate inferiority complex resulting from long exile. They are suspicious of everyone and everything. Once the military operations begin this psychology should disappear."[19]

President Roosevelt's telegram of June 14, 1944, to Prime Minister Churchill provided clues as to his pragmatism and playfulness:

> To the Former Naval Person. Your 703. I can see no objection to your action in permitting de Gaulle to visit France and feel that his visit may have the good effect of stimulating that part of the French underground over which he has authority or which he can influence to work against the common enemy.
>
> In my opinion we should make full use of any organization or in-fluence he may have insofar as is practicable without imposing him by force of our arms upon the French people as their government or giving recognition to his outfit as the Provisional Government of France. After all, the Germans control over 99 per cent of the area of France.
>
> His unreasonable attitude toward our supplementary French cur-rency does not disturb me.

I join with you in a hope that the Italian situation will clear up to the advantage of our military effort in Italy and elsewhere, and I regret exceedingly that it was not possible for me to be with you on your visit with our splendid soldiers who have made the first breach in Hitler's "citadel of Europe." But don't do it again without my going with you."[20]

From the outset, the French were single minded in their arguments in favor of Anvil. "It is inadmissible," de Gaulle contended, "for French troops at this stage of the war to be used elsewhere than in France." At times, as a matter of "prestige," the French sought as representation for their forces an army under their own command. They even went so far as to suggest that all Allied forces taking part in the southern invasion might constitute a single army under French command.[21]

To the French, it was of vital importance that in a campaign for France's liberation, native forces should be under French command. As a matter of national pride and honor, they wanted a French army under a French general on French soil. They agreed, however, that although it meant placing a full French general under an American lieutenant general, they would be willing for the Americans to handle all administration, supply, and the overall tactical planning. The French were seriously perturbed to hear that alternatives to Anvil were being considered.

On March 15, 1944, General de Gaulle visited General Wilson at his headquarters in Italy to declare his full cooperation for the coming battle of France. Three important elements were involved: the regular army, the Resistance groups, and the administration of French territory as soon as it was freed from the enemy. General Wilson expressed satisfaction with these offers but pointed out that the Combined Chiefs of Staff had given priority to the battle of Italy. Rome would have to be taken before the Battle of France could be begun. The fact that it would be difficult to use French troops during the assault phase of the landing in southern France was also pointed out; but General Wilson indicated that after a beachhead had been secured, there was no reason why French troops could not be landed to participate in the ensuing battles. De Gaulle agreed.[22]

One month later, Gen. M. E. Bethouart, chief of staff of French National Defense, called on General Wilson to say that de Gaulle had named General de Lattre de Tassigny to command French forces in Operation Anvil. Wilson stated that while he was glad to hear that a choice had been made, it would, however, be difficult to fit a French

Army commander into the scheme of things at that particular time because there were already too many staff involved in planning.[23]

General de Lattre had a history of arguing with American generals. He had Patton's and MacArthur's egomaniacal and flamboyant qualities but admired General Patch's lack of pretension and his concern for his troops. But when de Lattre was informed that the invasion of southern France might not be undertaken, and that French troops might be assigned to an American Seventh Army Company in Italy for a drive on Austria, he was furious with Patch. Once Roosevelt confirmed the decision to carry out Operation Dragoon, de Lattre made it clear to his troops that they were part of an Allied coalition. French dependence upon the Americans and the British for supplies was an inescapable reality. Because of this dependence, de Lattre urged his troops to follow Anglo-American orders. That was the price French patriots had to pay to participate in the liberation of their people.[24]

From its inception, preparations for Operation Dragoon were subjected to the vagaries cast by the bitter Italian campaign and the overwhelming preparations for the Normandy invasion. Logistics were consequently confined to certain hypothetical propositions, which had to be constantly revised. There was the reluctance to withdraw any of General Alexander's divisions from Italy until after the breakthrough and capture of Rome. Nor could troops be diverted from any other theater. These were the principal factors involved in the postponement of the Anvil target date from early May until mid-August 1944.

By mid-June, according to General Wilson, supreme Allied commander, Mediterranean Theater, a firm decision had been reached to mount an amphibious operation in southern France. Headquarters of the Allied armies in Italy was notified on June 15 to release the headquarters of the U.S. Sixth Corps "at once"; the Forty-fifth, Third, and Thirty-sixth Divisions; two French divisions; and certain auxiliary combat troops, such as tank destroyers, tank battalions, and antiaircraft units. But there were still several "possible courses of action," including an amphibious operation "at the head of the Adriatic." In a message to Generals Wilson and Eisenhower, the Combined Chiefs of Staff simply stated that "preparations for an amphibious operation should go forward on the greatest scale for which resources can be made available and at the earliest date."[25] By the end of June, the decision had been made. General Eisenhower had insisted, and General Wilson concurred, that Operation Anvil/Dragoon would be undertaken.

CHAPTER 7

FINAL PLANNING

Dragoon's military commanders and planning chief were placed in an awkward position. Detailed, comprehensive planning, coordination, and training were crucial for Allied success; but such preparation was frustrated by uncertainty over whether this contentious invasion would ever happen. Strenuous opposition from Prime Minister Churchill, British General Harold Alexander, American General Mark W. Clark, and others stalled final approval to proceed with Dragoon while Allied troops were fighting still-formidable foes elsewhere in France and in Italy. Ultimately, these and other difficulties confronting the Dragoon invaders were overcome.

In this chapter, note the communications between the naval commanders of the Normandy invasion (Rear Adm. Alan Kirk) and the Dragoon invasion (Vice Admiral Hewitt). This chapter also describes the tactful, firm, and successful effort by Hewitt to ensure Anglo-American joint naval planning and operations; the liaison assignment of Commodore Ziroli, a graduate of Annapolis, to work with Italian navy officers; and the transformation of the political and military allegiance of Spain's dictator, Gen. Francisco Franco, from Axis supporter to Allied benefactor.

Less dramatic but more important tasks were also undertaken before August 15, 1944. Allied commanding officers with extensive teaching experience, among them, Generals Patch, Truscott,—and Frederick, oversaw carefully prepared training exercises that were undertaken under difficult conditions.

Admiral Hewitt's concern for intermilitary coordination resulted in resolving jurisdictional issues such as the use of Allied aircraft before and during the landings and invading southern France during daylight rather than during the far more accident-laden nighttime. Objections by army commanders who favored night landings because of the alleged surprise factor had to be overcome, as was General Truscott's worry about deadly enemy underwater obstacles planted by the enemy. Hewitt deemed it important to inspect galleys (navy term for kitchens) and mess halls (dining facilities) in which his sailors were fed, and if their ships were destroyed and they were rescued, he saw to it that these men were outfitted with navy clothing. These and other details were scrutinized while Hewitt orchestrated a large combined amphibious invasion that entailed ten convoy routes for different types of ships with different speeds and starting from several Mediterranean ports.

A variety of tasks—some requiring considerable imagination, others more prosaic—had to be dealt with expeditiously and efficiently: the use of American and British paratroopers to block the entry of enemy troops into the Allied landing zone and learning the characteristics of many miles of deadly invasion beaches—vegetation, topography, infrastructure, land use, defenses, and defenders. Among Allied apprehensions were the German radar stations and batteries. Ways and means had to be devised of protecting invading soldiers, sailors, airmen, and French men and women from deadly obstacles. Fortunately nearly all were unharmed.

Operation Dragoon had been forced to compete for troops and supplies with Normandy, the most important operation in 1944, and with the Italian campaign that, until the capture of Rome, absorbed the greater part of the military resources of the theater. From the very beginning, a feeling of uncertainty and indecision hampered progress. Valuable preliminary work was accomplished by the Dragoon planning staff during the first half of 1944. Once it was decided that the operation against southern France would be mounted in mid-August, final planning was completed with remarkably little confusion and delay.

The headquarters of Force 163 (the planning group) moved from North Africa to the Naples-Salerno area in Italy during the first week of July 1944 in order to keep in closer contact with the training program. Each army division was to receive about three weeks of amphibious training. The training program was to culminate in a landing exercise simulating conditions of the coast of southern France. Admiral Hewitt was intent on achieving effective intermilitary cooperation, and he carefully monitored the various facets of the forthcoming invasion.

Busy Admirals

In 1943, Rear Adm. Alan G. Kirk, Normandy's naval commander, had relieved Vice Admiral Hewitt as commander of the Amphibious Force, Atlantic Fleet. The exchange of letters between Kirk and Hewitt in April and May 1944 revealed Kirk's regrets about cutbacks in Hewitt's armada.[1] His prediction about the price that the invasion of Normandy would exact was tragically prophetic. Hewitt's regret was that the invasions of Normandy and southern France were not undertaken simultaneously.[2]

File No.
CTF122

Serial

SECRET

**UNITED STATES FLEET
TASK FORCE ONE TWO TWO**

Navy 803
Care Fleet Post Office
New York, N. Y.

18 April 1944.

Dear Kent:

     Thank you very much for your good letter of
February 11th, which I have allowed to go a long while unanswered.

     You can imagine we are pretty busy here. The
trend of events has forced you to take a temporary cut in
some respects. I am sorry about this, but, of course, you
will realise that it is none of my doing. The main thing
from your point of view, it seems to me, is that I should
pass on what was originally intended to be yours. On this,
I am not sure I can make you any promises. The fact is
that some of the big boys will have to go in and take it
on the chin, if we are to put the soldiers where they want
to go.

     Our enemy is toughening up all along and I
expect this party will exact a larger price than any yet
put on - either here or in the Pacific.

     People come through here from home and go
onward to you so frequently that I hope you get some of
the messages and greetings I send. The return voyagers
always say you are in fine form and excellent health.

     Good work! Good Luck!

                Sincerely,

                Alan Kirk

Vice Admiral H. K. Hewitt, USN,
U.S. Naval Forces, North West African Waters,
c/o Fleet Post Office,
New York, N.Y.

SECRET

1 May 1944

Dear Alan,

Thank you for your letter of the 18th. It was good to hear from you and know that things are going all right. I can imagine that you are busy.

I have tried to give you all possible support from this end and to pass everything along in the best of shape. From my own point of view, I also regret some of the decisions which were made because I feel strongly that we could be of the greatest assistance with a simultaneous push from here. We are going ahead with plans and will be prepared to do our stuff as soon as we get the means.

In the meanwhile, I want you to know that we will all be with you I in spirit and wishing you the best of luck and success.

Sincerely yours,
H. K. HEWITT.

Rear Admiral Alan G. Kirk, USN,
Commander Task Force 122,
Navy 803,
Care Fleet Post Office,
New York, N.Y.[2]

Admiral Hewitt's report of April 21, 1944, addressed to British admiral Sir John Cunningham, supreme naval commander of the Mediterranean Theater of Operations, mentioned that U.S. Navy leaders were dissatisfied about their underrepresentation on the staff of the supreme Allied commander Mediterranean Theater of Operations, commanded by Cunningham. Hewitt noted that, as of January 22, 1943, there had been sixty-seven meetings concerning the development of a system of unified command in combined U.S.-British operations. Ever the diplomat, he continued, "Relations have been extremely cordial and have been marked, in my opinion, by mutual confidence, understanding, and friendship. However, the U.S. Navy has never had direct representation on the staff of the Supreme Command as referenced."[3] Hewitt assured Cunningham that there was no question of the U.S. Navy attaining undue influence in Mediterranean matters.[4] The absence of representation meant that Hewitt was often not provided with important information by the British. He made it clear that the U.S. Navy was entitled to be represented in the Mediterranean Theater of Operations. Such representation was justified, he believed, because of a prior agreement; the scale of the U.S. naval effort in the Mediterranean theater; and the American rearmament, supply, and upkeep of the French fleet operating in the Mediterranean. Hewitt requested that U.S. naval representatives be members of Admiral Cunningham's staff and would deal with planning, operations, intelligence, and logistics.

May 1944 Events

The following description of Hewitt's activities, inspections, and remarks covering the period from May 12 to 17, 1944, were among his papers deposited in the Library of Congress. Starting at 9:00 a.m. until 5:30 p.m. on May 12, 1944:

1. Conferred with Rear Admiral Frank Lowry, who participated in the Dragoon invasion.
2. At 10 a.m. Hewitt inspected a Navy barracks housing 120 of the ship's company and 60 construction battalionmen. He found the "heads"[5] filthy and lacking in storage space and adequate refrigeration.

3. In the basement of the barracks, Hewitt found an accumulation of supplies for Navy men who might become survivors after their ships and boats were destroyed. He commented that, "prior to this, survivors had to be outfitted in Army clothing."

4. By 10:45 a.m., he had inspected a new ship's company barracks and construction battalion workshop that had been a former stable in a villa. Hewitt found that the "head" and facilities were excellent and had already been installed.

5. Fifteen minutes later, the Admiral inspected radio equipment, other supplies, and dispensary facilities.

6. He used an hour (from noon to 1 p.m.) to have lunch with his officers and inspect the recreation facilities. From 1 p.m. to 5:30 p.m., he undertook eleven other tasks.

On Saturday morning (May 13), Hewitt called on Alexander Kirk, the U.S. envoy to Italy, who later was U.S. Ambassador to Italy until March 1946. Before leaving for Salerno, he officiated at a decoration ceremony honoring four landing craft officers. Shortly after his 7 ½-hour trip from Naples to Salerno, Hewitt had dinner with three Navy Captains, including Captain Robert Morris. In his memoirs, Hewitt wrote that Captain Morris "had done splendid work throughout the Mediterranean campaign in amphibious training and operations."[6] A Naval Academy, Class of 1923, graduate, Morris retired as a Rear Admiral and died in 1984 at the age of 83.

The next morning (Sunday, May 14), Hewitt called on Marshal Pietro Badoglio, who had replaced Mussolini as head of the Italian government. Hewitt and Captains Morris and Simpson then met at the former Fascist headquarters building. The Admiral concluded that this building provided "excellent accommodations for the administration building—centrally heated and ample space." It was subsequently converted into an Allied administrative building.

After the Admiral drove around the Salerno port area, he inspected a small boat base that had 18 landing craft. He noted that an Army unit, consisting of drafted skilled mechanics, was assigned to small boat repairs at a time when the Navy was very short of this type of personnel. Hewitt found that the skippers appeared to be very familiar with the equipment in the landing craft, but Captain Morris said that they needed training in seamanship and amphibious problems. Forty-eight crew members were housed in tents. Between 11:30 a.m. and noon, the Admiral inspected an old school building that had been converted into very adequate barracks, with clean galleys[7] and living conditions that were generally good. About 850 men lived in the barracks. From noon to 12:30 p.m., Hewitt visited a recreation hall, and remarked that it was an excellent set-up. The Fourth Beach Battalion was in a tent situated in an old stadium. Hewitt observed that excellent use was made of the apartments under the stadium for galleys, mess halls, showers, and recreation rooms. The officer-in-charge, Commander Walsh, was carrying on a rather energetic training program. By 2:30 p.m., Hewitt returned to Naples. At 8 p.m., he had dinner with Admiral Lowry on board the USS *Duane.*

At 9 a.m. on May 15 and 16, Hewitt held conferences with Commodore Humbert W. Ziroli another Naval Academy graduate, Class of 1916. An able officer of Italian descent, Ziroli had been chosen by Hewitt in October 1943 to serve as a liaison officer with the leaders of the Italian Navy. Ziroli's ability to speak Italian well was an important asset for the United States. He was promoted to the rank of Rear Admiral and died in 1979 at the age of 86.

The other actions mentioned on Hewitt's list of activities for the same two days included: a press conference, dinner with Army and Navy officers, a conference with U.S. envoy Kirk and Admiral Davison, and inspections of many American ships. At 4:30 p.m. on May 16, Hewitt presented a Purple Heart to Claude F. Maston, Gunners Mate Third Class, USNR, at the 118 General Hospital, Naples.

At 11:30 p.m. on Wednesday, May 17, Hewitt left Naples for Palermo. After a brief lunch with Captain Nichols, the Admiral inspected the enlisted men's club there. By 3 p.m., he left Palermo and arrived at Algiers at 7 p.m.[8]

On July 8, when the Supreme Headquarters was transferred to Naples, Admiral Hewitt and General Patch and their staffs moved together to their new headquarters. There, it was possible to gather in one old Italian barracks all the assault force commanders and the division and corps commanders involved in the operation. The air command, under Brig. Gen. G. P. Saville, United States Army Air Corps, established headquarters in the same city. For the final planning period, General de Lattre de Tassigny, commanding general of the French Army B (II Corps), and his staff also set up headquarters in Naples. The close association, as Admiral Hewitt reported, helped achieve an effective invasion.

Combat elements of the French II Corps were scheduled to arrive in the Naples area around July 8. They were to refit and then go promptly to Taranto for loading. Since the French had only a skeleton staff of their II Corps in Italy, it was advisable that the remainder be summoned from North Africa in order to supervise properly troop movement and combat loading. The French were short on replacement personnel, but it was understood that they expected to recruit locally after entry into the target area. This was a matter of serious importance for future planning inasmuch as the use of American equipment was involved.

Commodore Benjamin L. McCandlish was commander of the Moroccan Sea Frontier and the Naval Operations Base in Casablanca. His letter of July 11, 1944, informed Admiral Hewitt of various significant items. These included (a) the increase of business in the port of Casablanca; (b) relationships with the Army Air Transport Command; and (c) a meeting with General de Gaulle, who McCandlish found gracious, and not a cold Calvin Coolidge type.

Informing Hewitt about affairs in Spain, McCandlish wrote that Gen. Francisco Franco had reported that the Germans were unable to transport the chemical wolfram (tungsten—a rare metallic element that has a high melting point and is used in alloys and electric lamp filaments) from Spain to France; that Franco had said that damage to French railroads as a result of bombings and sabotage was such that the Germans had to use all their transport facilities to move troops against the Normandy landing; that Franco also told U.S. ambassador to Spain Hayes that his "debt to Germany and Italy had long ago been paid." According to McCandlish, "Mr. Hayes believes that Franco never had been pro-German but always and now is pro-Spanish. When Germany seemed all-powerful, Franco apparently believed that it was expedient to collaborate. At the present time the shift to show proper consideration for the Allies has been marked. He stated that he had no trouble in getting our aviators who have been forced down in Spain out of the country with no payments. The naval attaché told about the same thing in regard to rescuing our aviators. We have had no firings on our planes from Spanish Morocco since May 20. There have been some recent firings down in the Canary Islands, but in one case we were inside the three-mile limit. I gathered from the ambassador that he believed that the Spaniards would cause us less and less trouble as the war continued to go against the Germans."[9]

Special Allied troops included in Operation Dragoon accelerated Germany's defeat. The Invasion Training Center was notified that the First Special Services Force would engage in a training program to end with a two-day final exercise from July 5 to 20. Brig. Gen. Robert T. Frederick, appointed to command the Provisional Airborne Division, began temporary planning, organizing, and training, pending the arrival of an airborne division staff from the United States. The Second British Independent Parachute Brigade, which was to be incorporated into the Provisional Airborne Division, now came under the operational command of Force 163. On July 8, the Seventh Army Airborne Division (Provisional) received training orders.[10]

Robert T. Frederick

Robert Tryon Frederick's father was an eminent San Francisco physician, and his mother had been a nurse. One of his ancestors, Maj. Gen. William Tryon, was England's governor to North Carolina before the Revolutionary War. His maternal grandfather, McCurdy, migrated from Canada to fight in the Civil War.

His parents tried to make him a competent cello player, and he did try to please them. But even long hours of practice did not help, and his sounds from the bow were awful. As a lad, he was more successful at learning how soldiers drilled and wandered into San Francisco's Presidio to watch the soldiers drill there. So eager was he to join them that at age thirteen he enlisted in the National Guard by claiming he was sixteen. At age fourteen, Frederick joined the crew of a ship that sailed to Australia. Just after turning seventeen, he received an appointment to West Point and was the youngest cadet in his class.

Frederick graduated 124th out of a class of 250. *The Howitzer*, the West Point yearbook's description of him was not glowing; it merely indicated that Frederick had a modest personality. However, he had an above-average ability in mastering military tactics and developing loyal friendships. His record at West Point was mediocre. On the day that he graduated in 1928, he also married his longtime sweetheart, the daughter of a Brooklyn physician. They were the parents of two daughters.

He started his army career as an artilleryman and gained experience in dealing with harbor defense and anticraft weapons. In 1930, he attended flight school and flunked out. For six months in 1933, Frederick administered the Civilian Conservation Corps (CCC) in Oregon—one of FDR's New Deal programs to mitigate the consequences of the Depression. Its objective was to give unemployed young men from urban areas an opportunity to work outdoors in the West, building needed public improvements such as dams, roads, reforestation, and other useful projects. For their labor, the CCC volunteers were fed, sheltered, clothed, and given a little money. Army officers, such as Frederick and George C. Marshall, helped destitute young men live healthier and more disciplined lives. President Roosevelt later chose Marshall to head the U.S. Army. One reason for his choice was Marshall's competence in training these young civilian men. Later, of course, Marshall was responsible for the expeditious and effective training of millions of Depression-era civilians.

On a smaller scale, Frederick did the same. As a battery officer stationed at Fort Shafter, Oahu, he outlined the requirements for adequate defense of Hawaii. He wrote that "barrage balloons should be obtained to supplement meager anti-craft artillery . . . Primary targets for attack are Pearl, Hickham Field . . . no ship to be in Pearl . . . raiding forces will stream toward Oahu during night, releasing planes about daylight . . ."[11] Frederick's daughter, Anne Frederick-Hicks, also wrote that the entire outline was "eerily accurate." Dated February 24, 1941, her father presented his recommendations that morning to the planning committee at Fort Shafter, hoping it would be passed on to the commanding general of Hawaiian command. Later in the day, he dejectedly entered his quarters with the returned six typewritten pages and a note attached that read, "Maj. Frederick, we are not much impressed with your ideas."[12]

By the end of summer of 1941, Frederick's request for an assignment to the operations division of the U.S. War Department was granted. His job was to critique proposed new warfare methods. Nathaniel Pyke, an innovative British thinker, suggested a way to destroy Hitler's control of electronic power resources in Norway. Pyke's idea of deploying paratroops and transportation to traverse Norway's snow-covered electric power installations intrigued Lord Louis Mountbatten. Prime Minister Churchill asked President Roosevelt to review Pyke's proposal, which FDR passed along to General Marshall, who turned it over to his war plans chief, Dwight Eisenhower. At the end of the bureaucratic chain was Frederick, who was made responsible for evaluating Pyke's proposal.

Frederick spent twenty days thoroughly examining it. He demonstrated its lack of practicality. Nothing in existence at that time could carry snow vehicles. Gliders could not be used because they required too much manpower, and a sea approach would diminish the element of surprise. What bothered Frederick most about Pyke's proposal was that damaged snow vehicles would leave commando troops stranded in the snow and easy targets for slaughter by the enemy. The absence of a way to rescue Allied troops angered Frederick the most.

When the army needed an officer to organize, train, and command a mobile unit of American and Canadian troops, Generals Marshall and Eisenhower chose Frederick, having been favorably impressed by his thorough analysis of Pyke's proposal. The military group, consisting of Canadians and Americans, was to be known as the First Special Service Force (FSSF) and its soldiers trained at Fort Harrison, Montana. The story of the FSSF was told in the movie *The Devil's Brigade*, with actor William Holden portraying Lt. Col. Robert T. Frederick. Holden's performance accurately depicted Frederick's soft-spoken, shy, but determined demeanor.

Frederick was given the opportunity to carry out the American-Canadian guerrilla assignment as he saw fit. He recruited strong, resourceful outdoorsmen—lumberjacks, hunters, and forest rangers—men who were single and were between the ages of twenty-one and thirty-five. The Canadian volunteers were their nation's best soldiers. American commanders, however, were not inclined to have their best soldiers leave for duty with Frederick's force. Frederick offered imprisoned American soldiers their freedom if they would volunteer to serve under his command and stay out of trouble. He saw to it that all of his men, including the chaplain, were subjected to physical fitness training all day and lectures for most of the night. His men became adept in the use of various weapons and experts in knife fighting. Their training also included skiing and parachute jumping.

His analytical mind was supplemented by great physical courage. After only fifteen minutes of parachute jump instruction, he made his first jump. He later acknowledged that he had been frightened but realized that he needed to show his troops that it could be done without harm. Throughout World War II, Frederick led his men by examples of his own courage. In doing so, he was severely injured on several occasions and earned eight Purple Hearts. When his troops departed for Kiska, in the Aleutian Islands, Frederick was concerned about the durability of their uniforms and their having to keep dry in tents placed on knee-high damp Aleutian tundra. When they were wounded, he quietly prayed over them; and when they could not walk, he carried them. He was not the garrulous, cheerleader type. But this unobtrusive leader inspired his men, and they were devoted to him during and after serving under his command.

The FSSF left the Pacific for service in Italy and then southern France. *The Devil's Brigade* shows Frederick and his mountain-climbing commandos at Monte La Difensa in Italy. For two weeks its thirty-one-thousand-foot rise halted an Allied advance. In December 1943, Frederick developed and carried out an unorthodox rear approach up the mountain's sheer side. His superior officers anticipated at a minimum three days of fighting. Climbing at night for three hours, Frederick and his men destroyed German control of the mountain and the highway below it. He was shot and hit by shrapnel. His resourcefulness and courage were recognized by Gen. Mark W. Clark and others. In February 1944, Frederick was promoted to the rank of brigadier general.

At Anzio, his troops were subjected to a deafening, screaming German noise campaign. Frederick devised an anxiety retaliation scheme. He had stickers printed that read, "USA-Canada. The Worst Comes Yet." His men used a special knife that Frederick had designed to pin the stickers on the bodies of enemy soldiers they killed. This fierce aggressiveness earned his troops the name "the Devil's Brigade."

Often without fanfare, General Frederick would go out on night patrol through enemy lines. Tired one night, and alone in his bunker, he tried to complete a letter to his wife and daughters. The charcoal heater filled his quarters with carbon monoxide, causing enlargement of his heart. According to his daughter, Anne, it was this accident that was the cause of her father's early death in 1970, at the age of sixty-three.

Moving northward in June 1944, Frederick and his troops were supported by Allied armored forces. They were the first to reach

Rome and to secure its entrances. The communication system was not working, and Frederick and his troops were under constant fire. Once Allied forces captured Rome, Frederick got into a half-track to find out which roads over the Tiber River needed demolition. Frederick's driver was killed by an enemy sniper near the Rome boundary. An eyewitness described the scene this way: "Frederick was a bloody mess crawling along a bridge, bleeding from the neck and arm, his pants soaked with blood. I wanted to bandage him up but he kept saying he was okay—here I was an AWOL soldier with a general that I thought was going to die."[13]

Frederick refused to go to a hospital and spent the night deploying his men to seize Roman bridges. After two days he received medical attention and twenty-eight stitches for his wounded leg. A week later he was notified that he had been promoted. He was thirty-seven and the youngest major general in the ground forces. Frederick was also informed that he was to be in charge of a complex new assignment in southern France. Before undertaking this new command, Frederick and his men earned some rest and relaxation. In early June 1944, they were sent to Lake Albano, near the pope's summer home at Castel Gandolfo. Before long, each of his men was driving his own jeep, each of which had been "appropriated" from another Allied army unit. Author Flint Whitlock pointed out that a lot of furniture from the pope's home was removed by American soldiers.[14]

Maj. Gen. Robert T. Frederick

Tactics

On July 20, Troop Carrier Groups allocated to Operation Dragoon began arriving at Italian bases from Britain. There was much to do: erecting gliders, completing training, and mounting the operation. At the conclusion of the joint army-navy landing exercises, three American assault divisions moved directly from their training area to Naples for mounting.

The army's tentative Dragoon plan was flown to VI Corps Headquarters on June 26. In a cover letter to the commanding general, Gen. Alexander Patch explained, "It has not as yet had the approval of the Supreme Allied Commander, and therefore is subject to change. However, it will at least give you and your staff a basis for planning . . . .

Please submit any changes you may wish to suggest as early as convenient and feel utterly free to comment."[15]

A reply arrived the next day. There were apparently many points of disagreement, and General Truscott—found some of the Dragoon information to be "most disturbing." Truscott wrote, "It has been my understanding up to this time that I am to command the actual assault . . . I think it would be highly desirable for me to be present when this plan is presented to the Supreme Allied Commander." In the first place, the proposed chain of command seemed to be taking "a grave risk." Until a beachhead was established, it was felt that assault troops should be under the assault force commander and only afterward revert to army control. "I have no doubt that much of the difficulty that attended the Salerno landing was due to the confused command organization during the assault phase. I sincerely hope that we will not repeat that mistake . . . ." Finally, General Truscott—warned against an overextension of the beachhead line in an effort to take in too much of the coast. Fearing a repetition of an Anzio error, he warned against any overextension that would make impossible the massing of sufficient strength for the advance to the west.[16]

There were some other points of disagreement, but Truscott admitted that his own criticisms were based on a rather hurried study. After receiving Truscott's critique, General Patch invited VI Corps planning officers to accompany their commanding general to Force Headquarters for a more detailed study of the problem. It was felt desirable that these disagreements be examined and clarified before the plan was submitted to the supreme Allied commander, Mediterranean Theater, Gen. Henry Maitland Wilson, for his approval.

The employment of French forces and French channels of command was considered during several planning conferences in July, and it was decided that, in the early phase of the operation, Headquarters Force 163 would exercise command functions over the U.S. VI Corps and such French contingents as were ashore. Channels of command would thus be direct from Force 163 to the French Army commander. However, when a total of two French Corps had been landed, the French Army Headquarters would assume tactical command of them; and Headquarters Force 163 would assume the normal tactical and strategical functions of headquarters, army group, retaining at the same time logistical and administrative functions for the entire Dragoon force.

The plan to attach the First French Armored Combat Command to the U.S. VI Corps during the assault phase was also considered and clarified. General de Gaulle had only "reluctantly consented to this employment under American command." General de Lattre expected the return of this combat command not later than D plus 3, as it was being counted on in the operation against Toulon.[17] However, it was obvious that the VI Corps would need armor not only for the assault but also for its subsequent advance to the northwest; and if there were any questions of command authority or limitations on its employment, this arrangement would not be satisfactory. General Truscott—suggested that this matter be taken up with the supreme Allied commander, Mediterranean Theater, without delay.

When the Dragoon outline plan with the latest revisions had been presented to General Wilson on June 28, he had given his general approval, suggesting only that further study be given to the most effective use of the airborne division to determine whether it should be used in one concentrated area rather than at three scattered points as was proposed in the outline plan. However, in a subsequent message to General Eisenhower, General Wilson showed some concern over the amount of airborne lift to be made available. Since the decision had been made to increase the assault to three divisions, the boundaries of the target area would likewise be expanded, and more extensive airborne operations were designed to block the movement of enemy reserves into the assault area. General Wilson asked for "not less than 384 operational aircraft in addition to those at present in the Mediterranean . . ."[18]

Allied Force Headquarters issued a directive on July 8 notifying the commanders of the navy, air, and ground forces in the Mediterranean Theater that Dragoon was scheduled to be mounted and launched with a target date of August 15. Its twofold mission was to establish a beachhead east of Toulon as a base for the assault, to capture Toulon and then Marseille, and to exploit northward toward Lyon and Vichy. Its conduct was to conform to the principles of joint command in that the commander in chief, Mediterranean, would provide the naval forces and appoint the naval task force commander. The latter would assume command of the entire seaborne expedition from the time of sailing until firmly established ashore. The ground force commander would then take charge of all ground forces participating in the operation. The air commander in chief would nominate an air task force commander who would be responsible for full air support for the operation.

A conference held on July 12 took up the following topics with relation to Operation Dragoon: air action prior to and on D-day, assault loading, further development in the use of airborne troops, and the relation of the battle in Italy to the invasion of southern France. Two days later, Admiral Hewitt informed General Truscott—of a new naval dissent to the Dragoon proposals. He wrote, "I believe that the proposal to land the second assault from LCI(L)'s is unsound. It is going to run into trouble when any sort of resistance exists, as experience at Elba only too well showed. When an LCI(L) gets hit you lose about 200 soldiers. If an LCVP gets hit you lose only about 30. At Elba the initial wave in the smaller craft got in. The LCI(L)'s attempting to follow-up waves in the operation against the Mediterranean island on June 17, 1944, were vulnerable targets for artillery fire."[19]

Throughout the remainder of July, tactical planning centered on what was to be accomplished by the preinvasion air and naval bombardment and the final coordination of the various outline plans. For example, the enemy-held islands of Levant and Port-Cros were a definite menace to the Third Division beaches on the Bay of Cavalaire. The navy was insistent that these hostile shore batteries be neutralized or else -assault shipping in this area would be within easy enemy gun range. This assignment was given to the First Special Service Force, which was to land under cover of darkness just before D-day.

The pre-D-day bombing plan envisioned attacks on enemy lines of communications in northern Italy and southern France. The target area was to be isolated by the destruction of road and railroad bridges. At the same time, a general bombardment was to be kept up along the whole Mediterranean coast. The enemy was to be given the impression that the main assault might come either in the Genoa area or at Séte near the Spanish border. On D minus 1, the bombing attack was to shift to the islands of Levant and Port-Cros and on D-day to the assault area to neutralize coastal batteries and support ground operations.

Some questioned the advisability of postponing the invasion from 0800 to 0900 hours, the contention being that "an effective naval bombardment could not be carried on simultaneously with that from the air." Dust and smoke would interfere with the observation of spotting planes, causing spotters to mistake bomb bursts for shell bursts and consequently confuse the control of naval fire. There were, however, many disadvantages to prolonging the preinvasion neutralization effort. It was decided that the 0800 H-hour should be the start and that the air attack and naval bombardment must be concurrent.[20]

By direction of the Combined Chiefs of Staff, effective August 1, the word "Anvil" was no longer to be used, as the operation would henceforth be known as "Dragoon." So-called "bigot" security instructions and procedures remained in force. On the same date, the supreme Allied commander's conference lay down several important decisions regarding preinvasion activities. It had previously been suggested that the forest regions in the Maures Mountains northeast of Toulon should be burned by the air corps prior to D-day. The extreme dry timber, heavy underbrush, and prevailing winds constituted a great fire hazard. It was decided at the conference that there would be no intentional burning of these forests. Plans were to be drawn up to cover a twenty-four-hour delay in H-hour "which might be necessitated by unfavorable weather conditions." Further details for the deceptive bombing plan of the Mediterranean area were discussed, and it was decided that Séte should receive an additional attack by heavy bombers on D minus 5.[21]

Whether the invasion force could actually make the landing without drastic interference by underwater obstacles was a question that troubled General Truscott.—On August 1, he told Admiral Hewitt, "I do not believe we can justify sending an assault onto a beach until we have ascertained by actual reconnaissance that assault craft can actually reach the beach . . ."[22]

"I believe," Admiral Hewitt replied the next day, "that the menace of underwater obstacles has been somewhat exaggerated . . . ." Last-minute reconnaissance would disclose, he argued, only little new information and would "seriously risk disclosing the *exact* beaches in which we are interested." The difficulties of Overlord, which had been a special condition of the English Channel and the Normandy coast, had now become a mental hazard. The admiral felt that neither factors of bathymetry nor tidal range nor the crucial element of tactical security substantiated the new fears and suggestions. "I know of no preliminary reconnaissance, other than actually running boats through the obstacles, which will *ensure* that boats can beach . . ." he wrote.[23] In the event that LCVPs could not push through, LCTs would most certainly be used to ram any remaining obstacles in order to ensure a successful landing.

During the first weeks of August, tactical planning was brought to its final conclusion. Instructions to the commanding generals of the U.S. VI Corps and French Army B were completed. The pre-H-hour attack on the islands of Levant and Port-Cros was changed from 0100 hours on D-day, with vessels twenty-six miles off shore. If they came in too close, enemy radar might be alerted or movement observed visually. On the afternoon of August 11, the chief of staff and other Seventh Army Headquarters, personnel went aboard the USS *Henrico* in the Bay of Naples. Here the Seventh Army set up its command post afloat. General Patch and key officers comprised the Advanced Seventh Army HQ aboard the USS *Catoctin.*

In a message of commendation to the officers and enlisted men of the Seventh Army HQ, General Patch said,

> "I desire at this time to express my appreciation for the painstaking zeal, initiative and high devotion to duty displayed by all officers and men of my staff in formulating the plan for the forthcoming operation . . .
>
> I recognize the patience and perseverance demonstrated by all members of the staff in following through with the planning despite obstacles and delays resulting from factors beyond their controls, and upon which the progress of the planning was dependent. I deeply appreciate the constant effort, tireless application, and attention to duty displayed by all in completing the planning phase of the operation."[24]

Army Ground, Airborne, and other Missions

Dragoon's general mission was to establish a beachhead east of Toulon as a base for the assault, to capture Toulon and then Marseille and proceed toward Lyon and Vichy. This mission was to be accomplished by the following military forces:

Kodak Force consisted of the Third, Thirty-sixth, and Forty-fifth Infantry Divisions plus one French Armored Combat Command and supporting troops. Kodak's mission was to land three infantry divisions (reinforced) at H-hour over the beaches between Cape Cavalaire and Agay. Le Muy was to be seized on D-day, and a rapid advance into the inland would contact the airborne task force. As soon as the beaches were cleared, the French Armored Combat Command would land. The boundaries of the beachhead were to be extended to the prearranged "blue line" and airfield sites secured in the Argens Valley between Fréjus and Le Muy. Further advances to the west and northwest would protect the right flank of the army; after the French II Corps was established ashore, contact was to be maintained. Kodak would be prepared to release the French Armored Combat Command, the French Groupe de Commandoes, and all airborne forces to army control on army order.

Garbo Force consisted of detachment, HQ French Army B, French Corps with the First French, Third Algerian, and Ninth Colonial Infantry Divisions plus the First French Armored Division (less one combat command), and supporting troops. Landing over beaches in the Saint-Tropez-Cavalaire area on D plus 1, it was to pass through the left of the U.S. VI Corps and capture Toulon. By D plus 9, the Ninth Division and two attached groups of tabors (goums) were to be landed in the Le Lavandou-Hyères area. The remainder of the First French Armored Division was to land by D plus 25, and after the capture of Toulon, the attack was to be continued against Marseille and the northwest. Contact on the right would be maintained with the U.S. VI Corps.

Rugby Force consisted of the Seventh Army Provisional Airborne Division with the Second British Independent Parachute Brigade, one parachute combat team, two parachute battalions, one infantry glider battalion, and supporting troops. It was to land on the high ground north and east of Le Muy and on the high ground north of Grimaud. The primary mission was to prevent the movement of enemy forces into the assault area from the west and northwest. Prior to darkness on D-day, Le Muy was to be cleared of enemy forces and the area secured for subsequent glider landings. Rugby Force would be assaulting enemy positions from the rear and also be of assistance to the advance of seaborne forces by neutralizing enemy installations to the east within the range of weapons. Bridges in the airborne division area were to be prepared for demolition, but no bridges were to be blown up except on order of the task force commander. When the contact was made, the Rugby Force was to come under U.S. VI Corps control and would revert to army reserve on army order.

First Airborne Task Force (FATF), commanded by Maj. Gen. Robert T. Frederick, was part of the U.S. VI Corps, commanded by Lt. Gen. Lucian K. Truscott Jr.—On July 11, 1944, less than five weeks before the scheduled invasion of southern France (Operation Dragoon), General Frederick started organizing the FATF near Rome. Many of the men in this unit had never before seen a parachute or a glider, and many had never seen battle. Some of the task force troops were from Britain; others were from different U.S. airborne units serving in the Mediterranean Theater. Thirty-six airborne staff officers were flown to Italy from Camp Mackall, North Carolina, to help Frederick with organizational and preparation work. General Frederick was assisted by a veteran parachute specialist, Brig. Gen. Paul L. Williams, who had planned parachute drops in Sicily, Salerno, and Normandy, and whose assistance in designating drop zones was an important factor in blocking German forces attempting to move into Dragoon's assault area.

Sitka Force, or FSSF, was to land under cover of darkness on the night of D minus 1 and neutralize all enemy defenses on the islands of Port-Cros and Levant prior to H-hour. It would subsequently be prepared to withdraw to the mainland and reorganize as the **Satan Force** for the capture of Porquerolles Island.

Romeo Force, or the French Groupe de Commandoes, was to land under cover of darkness on the night of D minus 1 and destroy enemy defenses on Cape Negre. The coastal highway in the vicinity of the cape was to be blocked and the high ground two miles to the north seized. It would protect the left flank of the assault and, when contact was made, would come under control of the U.S. VI Corps and revert to army reserve on army order.

Parachute assault troops were well prepared. Precise orders of what to do upon landing were issued to officers and enlisted men. They were provided rations, water-purification tablets, shoulder patches, United States or French flags to be sewn on their insignia, and a pocket guide on French customs and cultural differences. Condoms and VD preventive devices were handed out to everyone, including chaplains.[25]

On the night that he and his men were to jump into southern France, General Frederick's men were served jelly sandwiches, ordered by the general himself. After a steam bath and massage in Rome in the afternoon, Frederick arrived at the airfield at 11:00 p.m. to jump in the first wave. He landed thirty miles from where all the equipment had been dropped. In an interview many years later, he stated, "There was nothing I could do so I just lay down and went to sleep for a few hours. I had been up for three days before that."[26]

The parachute units of the First Airborne Task Force (FATF) received final briefings on the night of August 14. Aircraft for the mission were ready at ten airfields north of Rome. Three pathfinder teams that were to jump ahead of the main parachute assault to mark drop zones in the Le Muy area were getting ready for takeoff. The pathfinders carefully packed and waded their equipment and checked their sensitive radar guidance instruments.

The island of Elba was the first checkpoint for the pathfinder aircraft, after which they were to fly over north Corsica. After Corsica, and the Ligurian Sea, the aircraft were to fly straight for a point east of Cannes. Three C-47 planes carrying FAFT pathfinders were in the air at 0100 hours on August 15. Two and a half hours later, they approached France's dark and foggy coast. Nothing could be seen below on the first overhead pass of the aircraft. A second and third pass over the designated drop zone did not help either. Ground fog had thickened, and the drop zone was not visible. A fifth pass did not help the Allied pilots find an opening in the fog.

When the pilots decided to guess the location of the pathfinders' drop zone, they seriously misjudged it, and the misdropped pathfinder teams were left wandering through the hills of southern France by 0430 hours—the same time most of the parachute-assault troops were coming over southern France. Using dead-reckoning navigation and aided by luck, the pilots made "the most accurate night-combat drop of the war without aid of ground guidance. Nearly 85 percent of all paratroopers jumped directly on their assigned drop zones."[27] The pilots' record in landing their vulnerable gliders amidst parachutes that had been left by earlier jumpers was better than expected. Their skill saved their passengers from being killed, despite the gliders' landing speed of ninety miles per hour. Some gliders hit trees, and other gliders, and troops, hit poles. Eleven glider pilots died trying to land, and thirty were badly injured. By August 16, the town of Le Muy was attacked by an Allied force of glider infantrymen, British paratroopers, and men from the 509th Parachute Infantry Battalion. Le Muy fell under Allied control before noon, and more than seven hundred enemy prisoners were captured. Early the same evening, American tank units linked up with the paratroopers in Le Muy, and the airborne phase of Operation Dragoon ended.[28]

Frederick had an uncanny ability in judging people. As his bodyguard, he chose a strong, intelligent soldier with a terrible army record for getting into trouble and who was imprisoned for serious crimes. Frederick's trust in the young soldier, Duff Matson, was amply rewarded. Matson later became a very wealthy businessman. Frederick had other hard-core criminals released from prison to serve in his command. He, and they, benefited from the second chance that he gave them.[29]

American and French troops benefited from Allied air superiority. The Luftwaffe's two hundred estimated aircraft were opposed by almost five thousand Allied aircraft. On August 15, the procession of 204 Allied planes towing two gliders each stretched more than a hundred miles from takeoff areas near Rome, over Elba, and into southern France. There were no losses due to German air action, yet the Rugby operation glider incurred casualties because the Germans had planted a profusion of dangerous poles that impaled the flimsy gliders and paratroopers that landed in the fields of Le Muy, fifteen miles inland from the Camel Green assault beach.[30]

General Frederick's parachute troops each carried about one hundred pounds of supplies, including gas masks. Frederick flew in the lead plane, two stars on each shoulder, and a .45 auto pistol on his hip. Once he hit the ground, his blue-lens flashlight was to be ready to signal his men. As Allied planes flew over the French coast, German anticraft flashes disturbed the beautiful black night. At 0430 hours on August 15, it was time to jump. Frederick quietly said, "Follow me," and bodyguard Matson jumped. They were dropped almost five hundred feet from where they should have been and on mountainous terrain. Matson landed on top of a sharply pointed pole and broke a leg. He was worried about finding Frederick but soon saw the general's blue flashlight beaming. As Matson was assembling his rifle in a mist of flying tracer bullets, a newspaper reporter nearby was searching for his typewriter. Running toward Matson and Frederick were several men who were shouting guttural phrases. Matson fired several times, a couple of heads fell back, and the other intruders fled. The bodyguard had done his job. An unarmed medical corps major helped Matson limp along to a ditch filled with Scottish paratroopers. When a German machine gunner started firing at the ditch, the Scots pursued the enemy, leaving Matson behind. He kept crawling in the ditch and heard the moans of a paratrooper who had fractured both legs. Matson relieved the man's pain by injecting morphine into his arm, and he fell asleep. Two German soldiers were also in the same ditch, and one of them shot Matson in the same injured leg. Scottish paratroopers shot the German in the back. A Scottish medic carried Matson to a farmhouse in the midst of more German shooting. He was taken to a barn where Scottish paratroopers were drinking tea, which they shared with their American guest. He was later transferred to a church near Le Muy that was being used as a hospital, was treated for his injuries, and was able to get to Frederick's Le Muy headquarters after a few days of recuperation. Glider pilots provided him with chickens that they had machine-gunned. Matson used his helmet to clean some of the chickens and asked for some for General Frederick and other officers. Diced tomatoes spiced up the taste of the chickens.

After it was unloaded from a plane, Frederick's men used a jeep to forage for food and supplies. The vehicle was equipped with devices that cut wire stretched across roads, removing dangerous traps. Piles of hair from the heads of women covered the streets—women who had been accused of "horizontal collaboration" with Germans. American soldiers took special note of women wearing wigs. Food, clothing, and many other items were difficult for most French civilians to obtain, leading some Frenchwomen to trade their bodies to American soldiers rather than Germans.

The FATF suffered 450 casualties (killed, captured, and missing) during the D-day fighting; another 300 men were wounded. The actual parachute drops and glider landings resulted in an additional 250 casualties. Only 47 of the 407 gliders used in the D-day Dragoon assault survived for future use.[31]

On D-day, there was a dense fog over the designated zones, but most of the parachute elements dropped on or near their objectives. No air opposition was encountered, and the paratroopers drifted down safely through the fog. On the ground, the enemy was alerted immediately; but resistance was light, primarily small arms fire. Defensive lines were established at all zones, and all enemy forces driven out, except in the village of Le Muy. Preparations were made for the arrival of the glider-borne elements.

The first glider unit landed in Zone O about 0930 hours. Throughout the day, other units arrived, and by late afternoon the entire Rugby Force had landed. Contact with all elements within the force was established and the command post set up by 1800 hours. By the end of D-day, the villages of La Mitan, La Motte, Castron, and Les Serres had been occupied and 103 prisoners taken. A protective screen had been established over the road network connecting the invasion coast with the interior. The enemy counterattacked in the vicinity of Les Arcs but was repulsed by the 517th Regimental Combat Team.

The Second Independent Parachute Brigade had successfully blocked the highway at Le Muy but had been unable to take the town. Its capture was then assigned to the 550th Glider Infantry Battalion. During the early morning of August 16, an unsuccessful attack was launched. The airborne troops continued to attack and overcame determined resistance at about 1500 hours. During D plus 1, other elements of the force fanned out and consolidated their positions. Later the same day, contact was made with reconnaissance elements of the Forty-fifth Division. At the close of D plus 1, the FATF had destroyed all enemy resistance in its assigned zone of responsibility and had taken 493 prisoners of war.[32]

With the exception of the operation of the French Marines at Theoule-sur-Mer, all pre-H-hour activities were successful. While the transport and landing craft were approaching the beaches, the enemy in the assault area was cut off from reinforcements, and his defenses were pounded and seriously damaged. A prisoner of war interrogation report later found that enemy officers believed they were deliberately left to their fate.

The embarkation of troops and loading of equipment of the Seventh Army within a short period was an extraordinary achievement. It had to be spread from ports ranging from Bari in the Adriatic to Oran in North Africa (some 260 miles west of Algiers). At the same time, an airborne division had to be formed by collecting British and U.S. parachute battalions scattered about the theater. The operation had to fit in with Eisenhower's plans for the advance in the north.

Most of the FATF's men who landed in southern France achieved their objectives.[33] One unfortunate jumper was eighteen-year-old Henry Wilkins, who fractured his leg parachuting near Le Muy. He was the son of German-Jewish parents who had escaped Nazi Germany. At age seventeen, Henry had changed his name from Wikinski to Wilkins and volunteered for parachute duty. After his injury, other soldiers tried to make him comfortable before continuing on their mission. When they returned, they found Henry's body, pockmarked with bullets, hanging from a tree, with his penis shoved in his mouth.[34]

The parachute troops moved through enemy lines with black-and-green painted faces. Toting their machine guns, they wore helmets covered with branches, and grenades hung from their chests. The unit's chaplains, a Catholic priest and a Protestant minister, parachuted with the soldiers. It helped that the priest, Father Alfred J. Guenette, was of French descent. He was told that he and the other Americans had landed thirty-five miles from where they should have. The minister, Charles L. Brown, broke a leg on landing; and French women hid him in a hayloft. When a French child was killed by dynamite, which he believed to be food, Chaplain Brown officiated at the funeral.

General Frederick's airborne campaign at Le Muy destabilized the Germans and rendered them ineffective. The ambush of a German command car by Frederick's soldiers led to the discovery by Geoff Jones and his troops of a knapsack containing important combat plans. This interception helped General Patch's Seventh Army as it swept up the Rhone River. Frederick's troops attacked enemy soldiers who were left behind to obstruct the Allied movement toward Germany. The men of the FATF defeated an enemy that had observation, terrain, and defensive advantages. About one-third of Frederick's task force was killed or wounded. German losses were far greater—four thousand captured and unknown numbers injured and killed. This was accomplished with almost no motor transport, no light weapons, and a difficult terrain favoring the specially trained and equipped enemy.

Rosie Force consisted of the French Naval Assault Group, a demolition party that was to land in the vicinity of Pointe des Trayas on the night before D-day. Its mission was to execute demolitions on the Cannes-Saint-Raphael and Cannes-Fréjus roads and then fall back on the army right flank.

The Eighth Fleet's mission was to establish the Seventh Army firmly ashore and to support its advance westward for the capture of Toulon and Marseille. The fleet was responsible for the army buildup and maintenance on the beach until no longer required after the capture and utilization of ports. It was to be subdivided into six forces, each with a specific mission.

The Control Force was to provide naval beach control and establish and operate naval fuel facilities on shore and in the assault area. Navigational markers and air beacon markers were to be established and diversionary operations conducted. Control would screen the attacking forces from hostile surface or submarine forces and would provide convoy control and escort for shipping outside the assault area.

Alpha Attack Force was to establish the Third U.S. Infantry Division on selected beaches in the Pampelonne-Cavalaire area beginning at H-hour on D-day. By D plus 1, it would be prepared to land French Army B. It was to receive and place five pontoon causeways on Beach 261 and five on Beach 259 and, at the earliest possible opportunity, to unload special air force equipment on the island of Port-Cros. Its naval gunfire would neutralize enemy batteries threatening transports, landing craft, or the beaches themselves.

Delta Attack Force was to establish the U.S. Forty-fifth Infantry Division on selected beaches in the Saint-Tropez-Bougnon area beginning at H-hour on D-day. Five pontoon causeways were to be delivered that day to Beach 261 and the port facilities of Saint-Tropez exploited. By D plus 1, Delta Attack Force was to be prepared to assist Alpha in landing French Army B over selected beaches in the Saint-Tropez area.

Camel Attack Force was to establish the U.S. Thirty-sixth Infantry Division and one combat command of the First French Armored Division on Saint-Raphael-Antheor beaches beginning at H-hour on D-day. As soon as the beaches were cleared, Camel Attack Force was to prepare to land another French combat command. The force was to ensure that the proper number of pontoon causeways were delivered to Beach 259 for unloading French armored equipment, ensure the safety by special measures of troop-carrier aircraft, and expedite the unloading and turnaround of LST shuttles from Corsica. Its naval gunfire was to neutralize threatening enemy batteries.

Support Force was to establish the First Special Service Force (**Sitka**) on the islands of Levant and Port-Cros and the French Groupe de Commandoes (**Romeo**) in the vicinity of Cape Negre. Its bombardment would support the military operations, and after the initial assault phases, the force was to support the army's westward advance and assign necessary sweeping forces.

Aircraft Carrier Force, the sixth of the Eighth Fleet's subdivisions, was to provide the maximum fighter protection, spotting aircraft, and close support missions. It was to be prepared to transfer aircraft to captured airfields and to provide its own protection against enemy air and submarine forces.

Admiral Hewitt's "Invasion of Southern France Report"[35] provides details of the meticulous preparation that was undertaken in planning and carrying out Operation Dragoon. One chapter deals with intelligence, prisoner of war interrogation, and press relations.

Another chapter concerns a variety of aircraft operations. The forty-two problems anticipated in the execution of this invasion are covered in Naval Planning Memo #21, among them "Precaution of looting by naval personnel."[36]

The commanding general of the XII Tactical Air Command, Brig. Gen. Gordon P. Saville, was designated the air task force commander and charged with all detailed air planning for Operation Dragoon. From a time element point of view, air operations were broken down into four phases: (1) air offensive operations prior to D minus 5; (2) period D minus 5 to 0350 hours D-day, known as Operation Nutmeg; (3) period 0350 hours D-day to H-hour (0800 hours), known as Operation Yokum; and (4) period after H-hour, known as Operation Ducrot. From the functional approach, air operations were further subdivided into (1) offensive operations; (2) defensive operations; (3) air-sea rescue operations; (4) tactical reconnaissance, artillery reconnaissance, and naval gunfire spotting; and (5) troop carrier operations.

To deceive the enemy about the point of actual assault and to prevent undue enemy concentration on the Allied assault, several special operations were planned. One such diversion was called "Rosie" and simulated a task force headed for Genoa. It was led by Douglas Fairbanks Jr., who then held the rank of lieutenant commander in the United States Naval Reserve. He was the son of the famous actor Douglas Fairbanks Sr. and was himself a successful actor and businessman. He played a leading role in striking panic among the Germans the night before the Dragoon invasion. Fairbanks and his men at the opposite end of the landing area created a diversionary threat that appeared to be so real—thousands of dummy doll parachutists were dropped to confuse the enemy—that the erroneous report of the German officer in charge of the area provoked a panic in Berlin. German radio broadcasts reported landings west of Toulon and east of Cannes.

Fairbanks's summation report to Vice Adm. Henry K. Hewitt on Special Operations covered the period from January 1943 through September 1944. Fairbanks was instructed to develop experiments and tactics that would apply to commando-like raids, assaults, and amphibious operations. Deceptive radar and radio-traffic devices, inflatable dummy paratroops (demolition charged), dummy landing craft, sonic, and other devices were developed by his Special Operations unit.

Vice Admiral Hewitt, Lt. Douglas Fairbanks Jr. and
Mr. French at Amphibious Trial Operations

In March 1943, Fairbanks was put in charge of training personnel in the use of deceptive and secret offensive weapons. After the Sicily and Salerno landings, his Special Operations unit assisted in prisoner-escape agent, landing, and rescue missions. Fairbanks reported that "while beginning to plan for Dragoon and the landings in southern France, plans were made and forces allocated for the diversionary and special assault phases of the Elba invasion."[37] The Special Operations unit was responsible for three major amphibious operations (Sicily, Salerno, and southern France), two smaller ones, and more than twenty minor operations such as raids and assaults, four over major plains, and many other operations in the Mediterranean, Adriatic, Dodecanese, Spain, Turkey, and the Middle East. However, according to Fairbanks, "the largest cover and diversion plan was used for the invasion of southern France."[38] When he was appointed Admiral Hewitt's Special Operations officer,[39] Fairbanks developed close coordination with General Eisenhower's headquarters and the army air force.[40]

Phase I of the air offensive operations in support of Dragoon actually began as far back as April 28, 1944, when heavy bombers attacked Toulon. Between then and August 10, during the preliminary air phases of Dragoon, MAAF had dropped more than nineteen thousand five hundred tons of bombs on southern France.[41] Phase II (Operation Nutmeg) beginning on August 10 was to continue attacking enemy coastal batteries and radar stations and harassing coastal defense troops while at the same time isolating the target area by destroying highway bridges across the Rhone River.

In order not to jeopardize tactical surprise, this phase was to be carried out simultaneously with a cover plan that included the bombardment of identical targets between Viareggio in Italy and Béziers near the French-Spanish border. It was hoped that the intensity of the cover plan would be sufficient to conceal true Allied intentions until about 1500 hours the evening of D minus 1.

Phase III (Operation Yokum) would begin one hour after the conclusion of Nutmeg and last until H-hour. Its purpose was to cause maximum destruction to enemy coastal and beach defenses utilizing all available forces. Twelve groups of escorted heavy bombers plus all available medium bombers and fighter-bombers were allocated for the attack. These bombers were to attack enemy coastal guns seen still firing while formations of heavy and medium bombers carried out attacks against the assault beaches with the object of destroying underwater obstacles and beach defenses.

Phase IV (Operation Ducrot) beginning after H-hour would continue the offensive to interdict enemy communications started in Phase I. This was not only to complete the destruction of bridges on the Rhone and Isère rivers and to extend the area of isolation outward but also for fighters and fighter-bombers to give close tactical support to ground forces.

The plan for air defensive operations was a constant air cover, by day and night, of fighter and night-fighter aircraft. Escorts were also to be furnished to bombers and troop carrier planes unless specifically charged to another command. Fighter sweeps and area cover were to be provided in accordance with the demands of the situation and the availability of fighter aircraft.

For purposes of air-sea rescue, MAAF assigned two high-speed launches to operate within a fifteen-mile radius of the fighter control ship. In the event that pilots were forced down at sea, they were to attempt to contact the fighter control ship, if possible; if not, their names and locations would be reported by observing aircraft that would continue to circle over the spot until the rescue launch arrived.

Plans for tactical reconnaissance and aircraft spotting emphasized both the rapid transmittal of information by broadcasting in "the clear," the size and location of enemy concentrations, and accurate observation and direction of naval gunfire. Naval spotting missions were also to be used for field artillery until the army's own observers were in a position to take over the work.[42]

The Provisional Troop Carrier Air Division was assigned the mission of lifting the Seventh Army Airborne Division, consisting of both parachute and glider-borne troops. Subsequent missions were to include resupply of airborne units and air evacuation. From home bases in Italy, thirty-two squadrons of troop-carrier planes totaling 415 aircraft flew to the target. Beaufighters and Spitfires were assigned to provide air cover. The first jumps were to be made just before daylight on D-day, and the first resupply mission was to be planned for the late afternoon of the same day. For purposes of identification, some troop-carrier aircraft were painted with black-and-white stripes underneath the fuselage and wings. They were also to show amber-colored recognition lights up to forty miles from the French coast en route to the dropping areas.

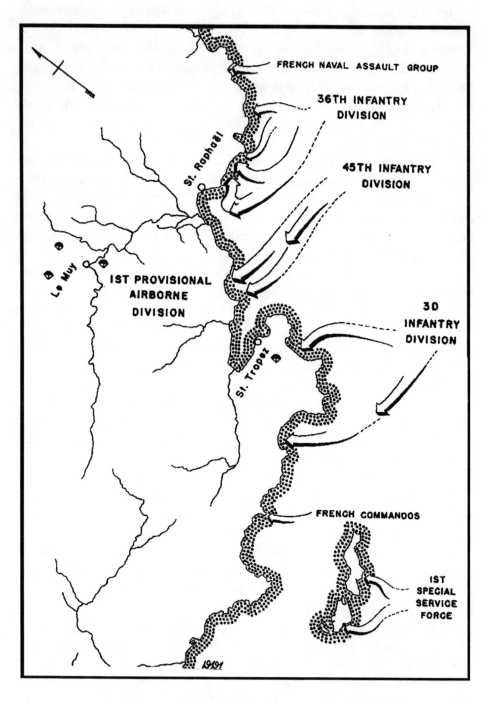

The initial landings in southern France on August 15, 1944

With the target date less than a month away, little was known initially of the French troops' supply status or readiness for combat, and French commanders had not been completely briefed for the operation. Though French planning personnel were available March 22, 1944, complete liaison was not secured until July 1; and discussions with them and their supply agencies had been forbidden until late July. Lower echelons of the French elements lacked information about Dragoon and needed orientation on the complicated American supply system and nomenclature.[43] Language was also a problem.

Inspections disclosed that the French were very short of supplies. On June 21, only 30 of 133 units had more than 30 percent of their authorized equipment. Based on U.S. standards, the French were not ready for combat.[44] Except for medical and ordnance, however, the French considered themselves capable of their own support. They were to be equipped from stocks of supplies available to the French Army through the Joint Rearmament Committee. Deficiencies would be made up from American stocks and charged to the French Lend-Lease account. As the target date approached, all units were inspected for serviceability of equipment. Final shortages were filled. Loading plans were completed down to the detail of each person and each vehicle and weapon. In ports on two continents and on the island of Corsica, Americans assisted in filling shortages, forwarding emergency supplies, and providing intelligence.[45]

Donovan, OSS, SOS, and SOE

William Donovan, a.k.a. "Wild Bill Donovan," founder and head of the Office of Strategic Services (OSS), the U.S. World War II intelligence organization, was a phenomenal man. Although the record of his poor grades as an undergraduate and law student at Columbia University do not reflect academic brilliance, Donovan's analytical ability and intelligence were widely recognized.[46] He founded one of America's great law firms and successfully argued many cases before the U.S. Supreme Court, gained political prominence in the Republican Party, and served President Roosevelt as a military observer and fact finder. He was a voracious reader of scholarly books dealing with history, sociology, public affairs, philosophy, and, of course, law.

In addition to his intellectual prowess, Donovan was a good athlete and a courageous man of action. During World War I, he served in the Rainbow Division. He was one of two men to receive the nation's three highest awards: Distinguished Service Cross, Distinguished Service Medal, and the Congressional Medal of Honor. France gave him the Croix de Guerre and made him a Chevalier of the Légion d'honneur. Donovan was without physical fear and went ashore after the Normandy invasion. Hollywood made a movie, based on his World War I exploits, starring George Brent as Donovan.

He was born in Buffalo, New York, on New Year's Day 1883, the son of a freight-yard foreman. Before attending Columbia University, Donovan worked as a laborer. He worked his way through school and played on its football team. After graduating law school, he returned to Buffalo, practiced law, joined the National Guard, became active in Republican politics, and married the beautiful Ruth Rumsey—a member of the richest family in Buffalo.

As commander of the Rainbow Division, the "Fighting Sixty-ninth," during World War I, Colonel Donovan toughened his soldiers by making them engage in difficult cross-country and harrowing obstacle exercises. He organized his intelligence section and frequently raided German territory. His interrogation of prisoners of war was thorough but fair. He also developed an extraordinary talent of learning what the Germans were going to do, where, and when.

The first of his many foreign diplomatic, military, and humanitarian missions came in 1916, as a member of the American Relief Commission of the Rockefeller Institute to provide aid to the Polish people. After World War I, he accompanied the U.S. ambassador to Japan, Roland Morris, on an expedition to investigate the Kolchak government in Siberia. Back in the United States, he became, successively, U.S. attorney for Western New York, assistant U.S. attorney general, and assistant to the attorney general. He was also chairman of the Rio Grande River Compact Commission. Donovan, a Republican, lost the race to be governor of New York in 1932.

During the 1930s, his regular activities were punctuated by a constant succession of foreign missions, mostly secret, which were designed to inform the U.S. government on the military and political significance of the explosive series of events engineered by the Axis powers. As an impartial observer, he witnessed the Italian invasion of Abyssinia (Ethiopia) and the campaign of Franco's forces in Spain, thereby gaining a clear concept of the changing techniques of warfare.

In 1940 and 1941, his friendship with the president and secretary of the navy sent him as a special fact-finding envoy to England, the Balkans, and the Middle East, to study the military situation and complex political, economic, social, and psychological issues. In July 1941, Donovan was asked by President Roosevelt to organize and direct the nation's secret intelligence, the OSS. Much of OSS work is still secret, but it is known that the office employed, both at home and abroad, the ablest scholars and investigators in history, psychology, ethnology, and communication; that it trained and employed units to work behind enemy lines; that it aided and fostered underground movements in occupied countries; and that its network of agents and operatives circled the world.

The Office of Strategic Services began its organizational life as Coordinator of Information under Executive Order 8826 on July 11, 1941. The order was signed by President Franklin D. Roosevelt. William J. Donovan was designated the Coordinator of Information. In June 13, 1942, the Office of Strategic Services was formed under Roosevelt's military order, with Donovan as its director. The order follows:

By virtue of the authority vested in me as President of the United States and as Commander-in-Chief of the Army and Navy of the United States, it is ordered as follows:

1. The Office of the Coordinator of information, established by Order of July 11, 1941, exclusive of the foreign information activities transferred to the Office of War information by Executive Order of June 13, 1942, shall hereafter be known as the Office of Strategic Services, and is hereby transferred to the jurisdiction of the United States Joint Chiefs of Staff

2. The Office of Strategic Services shall perform the following duties: a. Collect and analyze such strategic information as may be required by the United States Joint Chiefs of Staff b. Plan and operate such special services as may be directed by the United States Joint Chiefs of Staff

3. At the head of the Office of Strategic Services shall be a Director of Strategic Services who shall be appointed by the President and who shall perform his duties under the direction and supervision of the United States Joint Chiefs of Staff

4. William J. Donovan is hereby appointed as Director of Strategic Services.
5. The Order of July 11, 1941 is hereby revoked

> Franklin D. Roosevelt
> Commander-in-Chief

The White House
June 13, 1942.[47]

Eventually the OSS consisted of five major parts: (1) Secret Intelligence (SI), which was engaged in spying; (2) Secret Operations (SO), whose agents parachuted into France and elsewhere; (3) Research and Analysis Branch, where agents were academics who gathered and analyzed intelligence data such as the impact of aerial bombing on industrial plants used for military production; (4) Morale Operations (MO), which was the propaganda unit that sought to discourage enemy civilians and military people; and (5) X2, the counterintelligence unit that was responsible for protecting American intelligence from enemy spies and attempted instead to plant American spies into enemy espionage organizations.

Alfred H. Paddock Jr. described OSS activities and the French Resistance for the National Defense University Press. His findings and conclusions follow:

> The major OSS effort during the war was directed at France. Here U.S. Army personnel made a significant contribution to the three groups of OSS operational units that worked behind enemy lines in direct support of the French Resistance. The first group consisted of 77 Americans who worked in civilian clothes as organizers of secret networks, as radio operators, or as instructors in the use of weapons and explosives. Thirty-three members of that group were active in France before 6 June 1944 D-day. The second group consisted of 98 people who were mem-bers of the "Jedburgh teams," organized in Great Britain or Algiers and parachuted into France beginning on D-day. Jedburgh teams were composed of a British or American officer, a French officer, and a radio operator. These teams, usually working in uniform, coordinated Maquis activities under the aegis of Supreme Headquarters, Allied

Expeditionary Force (SHAEF), obtained supplies for the Resistance groups, reported significant intelligence, and as a secondary role en-gaged in guerrilla warfare and attacks on German lines of retreat or communication.

The largest OSS group in France consisted of some 356 Americans who were members of OSS "Operational Groups" (OG). All recruits for the OGs were French-speaking volunteers from U.S. Army units, primarily infantry and engineer (for demolition experts). Medical technicians were procured from the Medical Corps, radio operators from the Signal Corps. Working in uniform, these teams parachuted behind the lines after D-day to perform a variety of missions. They cut and harassed enemy communication lines; attacked vital enemy installations; organized, trained, and sustained the morale of local resistance groups; and furnished intelligence to the Allied armies. Interestingly, Donovan distinguished between the missions of Rangers and Commandos and those of the OGs, even though some aspects of their tactical operations were similar. The crucial difference in his mind was that the OGs fitted into the pattern of OSS activities behind the enemy lines.

Actually, the mission of the OGs was distinct not only from that of the Rangers and Commandos, but also from that of other OSS activities. The OG Branch had been established on May 4, 1943; then, on Nov. 27, 1944, the OG Command was activated as a separate entity within OSS. In addition to basic military training, OG recruits received specialized instruction on such subjects as foreign weapons, operation and repair of enemy vehicles, enemy espionage organizations, communications, demolitions, organization and training of civilians for guerrilla warfare, parachute jumping, and amphibious operations. Their basic function was to organize resistance groups into effective guerrilla units, equip them with weapons and supplies, and lead them into attacks against enemy targets, in concert with orders from the theater commander. As for how the concept of their mission differed from those of other Special Operations activities, an OSS general orientation booklet published in 1944 described it this way: "OG personnel activate guerrillas as military organizations to engage enemy forces. They always operate in uniform as military units and are not primarily concerned with individual acts of sabotage." Clearly, the OGs were primarily designed for guerrilla warfare, and the principles that they embodied were to significantly influence the Army's effort to develop a similar capability in later years.

A less enthusiastic analysis of the role of the OSS was rendered by the G-2 Division, War Department General Staff (WDGS), in a "Summary of French Resistance, 6 June-31 August 1944". The opening paragraph of that summary reads as follows: "It must be borne in mind that so-called resistance activities in France were the combination of the efforts of the local French themselves under the organization and direction of American, British, and French agents infiltrated from the United Kingdom and North Africa. In the majority of cases, the specific acts of sabotage were committed directly by the local French; and it is to them for their courage and daring, that the greater portion of credit for the end results accomplished must be given. However, it is not at all out of place for OSS in general, and SO particularly, to take credit for its share in the planning and directing of the overall scheme of sabotage."

Once again, this evaluation reveals more about the low regard accorded unconventional activities in general, and the OSS in particular, by many Army officers, than it does about the value of the resistance itself.

While the success of OSS and SOE [British Special Operations Executive] efforts in France is difficult to estimate, General Eisenhower, commenting on how effectively the Maquis cut enemy lines of communication in support of the Normandy landings, stated that the French Resistance forces were worth 15 divisions to him in his invasion of the Continent.[48]

In 1944, the combined headquarters of the American OSS and the British SOE were renamed Special Forces Headquarters (SFHQ).

The British sabotage and intelligence agencies, known as SOE (Special Operations Executive) and SIS (Secret Intelligence Service), were not active in France after its defeat in June 1940. French opposition to the German victors was led by an unknown brigadier general who had little following. Charles de Gaulle at first led a small number of French people who wanted to continue fighting the enemy. He was considered a self-appointed, obscure saviour, not a French government exile who merited diplomatic recognition. Vichy generals had court-martialled him in absentia for deserting the legitimate French government and condemned him to death. However, by early 1944, both the SOE and OSS had to acknowledge the reality of Gaullist political strength in France. The level of cooperation that developed in Algiers between the SOE and OSS was superb by August 15, 1944.

Both organizations supported de Gaulle and Gaullist operations. The French Resistance strength by that time was so evident that one SOE agent dared to place the British flag on the hood of an automobile in southern France and blow up a road. SOE teams crippled the Route Napoleon from Cannes through Digne and Gap to Grenoble. This helped Allied troops outflank German counterattacks from the lower Rhone Valley. When SOE agent George Starr was captured by the Gestapo, another agent who was originally from Poland, Cristine O. Granville, managed to convince the Germans to release him. She saved Starr's life by warning his captors that the arrival of American troops was near and that they would exact terrible revenge on the Germans. M. R. D. Foot's account of the work of the British Special Operations Executive in France, entitled *SOE in France,* stated that about one hundred thousand German troops near Limoges insisted in surrendering to American captors rather than being captured by French Resistance fighters, because they dreaded surrendering to the French who had understandable hatred and little food for the despised occupiers. To the dismay of the French, the Americans frequently offered their German prisoners food unavailable to the French, such as oranges.[49] Foot lists fifty-two women agents who entered France from May 1941 to September 1944, their method of entry—often by parachute—and their destiny. Most of these valiant women survived; thirteen were executed by the enemy. "Some of the blackest passages in the black record of Nazis crimes cover their dealings with SOE women,"[50] Foot observed.

American and French women demonstrated courage in gathering information as spies, undertaking dangerous sabotage missions, and killing enemies. One of them, Virginia Hall, was an OSS agent. She had one leg amputated because of an automobile accident but convinced General Donovan to send her into Nazi-occupied France with an artificial leg. Legend has it that she parachuted into southern France in March 1944 with her artificial leg under her arm. Her physical handicap did not prevent her from undertaking myriad training, sabotage, ambush, derailing, demolition, raiding, and communications assignments. After Donovan interceded on her behalf, Hall was awarded the Distinguished Service Cross, becoming the first civilian woman in World War II to receive military honors. Another heroine deserving of the highest commendation was a beautiful young French woman, Helene Vagliano. A member of a prosperous and prestigious family, she was also a spy in the French underground. She was arrested by the Gestapo, was violated and tortured, but she never betrayed any of her accomplices.

Pearl Witherington, a British citizen, was born in France in 1914 and became one of the few women to command a French Resistance group. She helped provide weapons, supplies, and money for the men. In summer 1944, her group harassed German troops retreating from France after the Operation Dragoon landing. Once, when she learned that some twenty tank cars loaded with gasoline were being transported by rail, her message to headquarters was relayed to bombers who destroyed the fuel. She viewed her role as that of a liaison officer between Allied Headquarters in London and the French Resistance in the field. The French honored Witherington with various medals. When her British superior officers recommended her for the Military Cross, she was considered ineligible because of her gender. When the British government presented her with the MBE (Member of the Order of the British Empire), Witherington refused. According to Margaret L. Rossiter, Witherington refused, "observing that she had done nothing civil." Ultimately, the British Air Ministry offered her the MBE, a military honor; and this she accepted.[51]

In April 2006, at the age of ninety-two, and sixty-three years after first complaining at the injustice of not getting her wings, Pearl received her Parachute Wings at her retirement home in Chateauvieux, France. After being presented the highly regarded award by the squadron leader of the parachute regiment, she responded, "This is more important to me than receiving the CBE or MBE."[52]

Under-draft-age French teenagers often worked for the OSS. Because the French Signal Corps needed radio operators, those who were of military conscription age were not allowed to assist the Americans. The French did supply submarines and other assistance to the OSS, such as documents for cover stories. After landing on the coast of southern

Spain, two OSS agents were picked up by Spanish police. They were jailed and interrogated. Using fluent French and false documents, they were able to convince the Spanish police that they were Vichy supporters who had been engaged in anti-American activities in North Africa and had escaped to France's pro-Fascist Vichy government. They were subsequently released and ended up working with the Allies. Infiltration into France by OSS and other Allied intelligence agents by air and sea was not always successful. An OSS report, *The Overseas Targets*, volume 2, pointed out that between January and May 1944, three infiltration missions out of eleven ended tragically because of Gestapo vigilance. OSS casualties behind the lines in France were higher in 1943 than in 1944. In summer 1944, it was clear that the Allies were winning the war. Proportionately, statistics for OSS agents killed or wounded were higher than those for combat troops in the Dragoon operation. Of 523 OSS agents working behind the lines in France, the total casualties were 86, or 16.5 percent.[53]

Before the invasion of southern France, OSS agents risked their lives to obtain enemy fortification data concerning the Camel Beach area on which LST 1012 landed. Secret Intelligence agents provided thirty reports. An example of the detailed information gathered included the sand content of the concrete Fréjus wall and the name and address of the Italian engineer who designed it in 1942. General Patch estimated that 50 percent of the operation's intelligence information was gathered by the OSS, 30 percent by the French, and 20 percent by the British. The Dragoon intelligence operation benefited from lessons learned in North Africa and Italy. Techniques of recruitment, infiltration, radio transmission, and security precautions were improved. Intelligence gathering, subversion, and resistance were far more efficient. From its very beginning, OSS personnel exhibited imagination and sophistication. Professor of anthropology, Carleton S. Coon, who was recruited by General Donovan, developed explosive animal turds for antitank use. The OSS recruited Arabs, Catholics, Jews, Protestants, atheists, Communists, Royalists, a variety of nationalities, professionals, laborers, Gaullists and anti-Gaullists, rich and poor, young and old, Republicans and Democrats, male and female, and police officers and criminals. Assisting OSS activities in Tangiers were English-speaking Muslim agents, an important tribal Arab chief, and a powerful religious leader. One result was that "tens of thousands of Muslims from every walk of life were ready to obey unquestioningly the will of their leader." They were able to penetrate areas forbidden by the Vichy French authorities. Muslim farmers and shepherds relayed valuable intelligence without raising suspicions. A fisherman was able to report the movements of a German submarine, and an Arab tribesman helped to debunk a false report about the existence of an aircraft facility.[54] Information concerning the location of firepower at Toulon and Marseille influenced the Allied decision to take these cities from the rear. Intelligence for Operation Dragoon was established early and continued to the last minute.

Information was effectively used. Some of the sources were in Lisbon, Madrid, and Istanbul. Spurred on by General Donovan's competitive, irrepressible, and innovative OSS, American military leaders reformed the quality of their own intelligence branches. General Marshall and Admiral King realized that they needed bright, enterprising individuals to undertake intelligence as well as operational assignments. Innovative thinking was needed for both tasks rather than traditional, unimaginative, inept, territorial, stultifying, and bureaucratic approaches.

By the time of the invasion of southern France, the OSS had grown to fifteen thousand men and women. It had a budget of $57 million for 1944, and most of that money did not require any accounting. The OSS was officially part of the United States military service. But the special and unconventional services that OSS agents were required to perform often resulted in conflicts with West Point and Annapolis-trained career officers. Regular military officers often had good cause to resent brash OSS agents who were either well-connected members of the American elite, Ivy League academics, or members of prestigious law firms. However, in fairness to Donovan and his subordinate recruiters, the OSS was inclusive and pragmatic enough to include nonglamorous people who served its objectives, such as individuals who spoke foreign languages, were competent labor organizers, radio operators, engineers, statisticians, teachers, psychologists, or printers, and Germans opposed to the Nazi regime. In spring 1944, there were over one thousand four hundred OSS agents in the south of France. Joseph E. Persico found that by the time the French and American invaders arrived on August 15, they were aware of virtually all transportation and troop movements, coastal defenses, battle orders, and the precise location of minefields, roadblocks, artillery, even searchlights. OSS's richly detailed anatomy of the enemy defenses won this campaign the designation "the best briefed invasion in history."[55]

Intelligence information disrupted German troop movement from southern France to the Normandy beachhead. Expectations that the French Resistance would be able to cause a sudden disintegration of enemy forces in southern France were too optimistic. The Resistance was at a disadvantage in fighting the Germans directly in stand-up battles because the enemy had heavy weapons and controlled a terrain not suitable for guerrilla warfare. During the summer and autumn of 1944, the Allied High Command substantially increased supplies to Resistance fighters. The number of aircraft serving the special forces was increased. Between the Normandy landings and the beginning of September 1944, Britain and the United States flew in seven thousand tons of arms and ammunition. French Resistance fighters were supplied with one hundred jeeps.

OSS Director Donovan ordered a dramatic daylight flight of more than three hundred planeloads of supplies for people in central France on Bastille Day, July 14. The French underground and secret intelligence benefited by the placement of almost three hundred British and American agents behind German lines to assist Operation Dragoon. More than one hundred intelligence agents from the Resistance were added to the U.S. Forty-fifth Division when its troops landed on the Dragoon beaches. During the operation, British, Free French, and American OSS sources provided precise information concerning German military activities.

Edward Gamble, the director for OSS operations for the Dragoon invasion, had been the manager of a New York brokerage company that dealt with capitalist government bonds. Other wealthy young Americans, graduates of Ivy League universities, served as OSS operatives in southern France, among them, David Rockefeller, Arthur Schlesinger Jr., and Geoffrey M. T. Jones. Wall Street lawyer Alan Dulles and labor-management lawyer Arthur Goldberg were also OSS men. Many achieved national prominence: Dulles later headed the Central Intelligence Agency and Goldberg served as an associate justice of the United States Supreme Court and as United Nations ambassador. Differences of backgrounds of Americans in the OSS were widespread— academics, Mafia members, playboys, idealists, scientists, conservatives, and communists.[56]

When the Hitler-Stalin partnership pact was in effect at the beginning of World War II, the French Communists followed Soviet dictates and were, for the most part, nonresisters. From the June 1940

German defeat of France to their June 1941 invasion of Russia, there were French Communists who worked with the Nazis. Following the German onslaught of the Soviet Union, however, French Communist Resistance (known as the FTP—France-Tireurs et Partisans) started killing collaborators and Germans. Members of the Communist and Socialist parties, and Germans opposed to Nazism, were recruited by the OSS for missions in France. Given the incendiary political mix of Communists, Socialists, Capitalists, Monarchists, and some Fascists within the diverse factions of resisters, saboteurs, spies, and intelligence agents opposing the Germans in France, their wasteful skirmishes, unsanctioned and uncoordinated acts of sabotage, competitive power grabbing, and intramural rampages of violence were understandable. It's unlikely that an acceptable scientific study will be forthcoming of how the aforementioned difficulties and differences were overcome and why the Allied resistance, intelligence, and sabotage efforts ultimately yielded successful results. Some conjecture, however, may be useful. French men and women of different political and socioeconomic coloration realized that the Germans were their primary enemies—aristocrats such as Pierre de Benouville, a French conservative and capitalist who was also a patriotic nationalist and fierce enemy of the Nazis. Starting after the defeat of France, de Benouville became an expert in organizing escape routes for Resistance fighters of all political persuasions and nationalities. (Eric Pace's account of de Benouville's extraordinary life and death, at age eighty-seven, is described in a *New York Times* article.[57]) It is also possible that some French factionalism was reduced by the outsiders—British and American young men and women who were risking their lives to restore a free France. During the first Operation Dragoon assault, Lt. Col. Edward Gamble led a unit of twenty-three Americans who spoke French. They were on the dangerous beaches of southern France, and this was no time for factional squabbling.

Before August 15, 1944, the Allies were worried about the extent of Resistance cooperation concerning landings in France. In a July 12 communiqué to General Marshall, OSS director Donovan informed the army chief of staff that "all factions are united against the Germans and that unity creates a strong base for a stable, democratic France with little danger of a civil war or extremist control."[58] Donovan said that the influence of the French Communist resisters was due not to their communism but to their effectiveness as resisters and that they were not planning to take over the French government. General Patch gave the French greater authority in Operation Dragoon than Eisenhower had allowed them at Normandy. In the south, administrative power was ceded to the French.

German intelligence agents were eager to find out the destination of Dragoon convoys, and OSS director "Wild Bill" Donovan discovered a security problem that could have provided the enemy with this crucial convoy information.

In his book *Last Hero,* about Donovan and Dragoon, Anthony Cave Brown wrote that Robert Murphy, who was the U.S. political advisor to the supreme Allied commander in the Mediterranean, Gen. Henry Maitland Wilson, became romantically involved with the princess de Ligne, the representative in French North Africa of the comte de Paris, pretender to the French throne. Murphy's entanglement grew out of his wife's incurable manic depression, his daughter's suicide, and his own emotional vulnerability. The princess was associated with a Syrian international antique and jewel dealer, David Zagha, who had moved to Buenos Aires. Zagha was retained by the OSS for information and money laundering. He also served various French factions, including Vichy collaborators friendly to the Germans. Donovan perceived the potential danger of Zagha possibly informing Nazi agents about the location, timing, and strength of the Dragoon invasion and so saw to it that Zagha was shipped off to Argentina. Brown called it "one of the wisest moves of Donovan's career."[59]

The OSS supplied French-speaking American agents to the French and British who used them in the field to assist the French Resistance teams. They were trained, equipped, and transported by the OSS. The inclusion of a French person was designed to provide the non-French members of the team with information unfamiliar to strangers—for instance, that in France the Feast of Assumption (August 15), a most solemn Catholic holiday, could not be disrupted by worldly tasks. One OSS team forgot that August 14-16, 1944, was to be celebrated as the Feast of Assumption; consequently, the radio operator could not get needed assistance because his helpers were observing the feast. Thousands of crucial radio intelligence messages did reach OSS headquarters in Algiers, however. These dealt with the location of German coastal fortifications, minefield traps, roadblocks, antiaircraft guns, lighting, airfields, aircraft, and enemy troop disposition in southern France.

Donovan's agents kept him informed as to the morale and attitude of French civilians as well as provided him with military information. Pierce

Martinot, the first OSS agent in southern France, and his radio operator, a young man from Poland, worked with the French Resistance and reported German troop movements and destinations to Donavan. This team also disrupted enemy communication and deprived the enemy of overall local command, and the OSS disrupted a continuous line of defense around the beaches. Instead of a coordinated German counterattack, the invading Allied forces were faced with haphazard opposition that was inadequate to hamper American and French advances. German troops in the invasion area had no tanks and mobilized antitank weapons, which had been sent to defend the German front. When the German defenders of southern France sent messages to their Berlin headquarters, the Allies intercepted them by using the code-breaking machine known as ULTRA.

When Donovan was appointed as director of OSS but with no specialized personnel, he had to contend with British and Free French who had skilled and experienced agents in the field and with American political and military officials who viewed the OSS as hostile competition. Robert Murphy often supported army intelligence policies that were opposed by Donovan, and their staffs were frequently in conflict. The Army Military Intelligence Division chief, Gen. George V. Strong, a West Pointer who also had a law degree, disliked Donovan's ability to procure funds and detested his associates, especially leftists. Strong was determined that military intelligence be withheld from the civilians in Donovan's OSS, and he sought to place a straitjacket on the OSS and Donovan's mandate to create a semicivilian organization to obtain civil and military information from countries occupied by the Axis and to use enemy agents. General Patch's staff, however, cooperated with OSS agents; and after careful screening and training in sabotage, they successfully completed their sabotage assignments.

G. M. T. Jones

Geoffrey M. T. Jones parachuted into occupied France shortly before the invasion of southern France. His mission was to organize the Maquis forces and provide intelligence information via radio to England. After the Allies landed at Normandy, Jones coordinated information from Resistance fighters he recruited and provided hundreds of reports of German activity from behind enemy lines. This important mission carried out by Jones was known as Operation Rabelais.

The following "Report on Operation Rabelais," an official account of this covert maneuver, was obtained from the National Archives:

> After one unsuccessful attempt on the night of 5/6 August 1944, followed by bad weather, Captain Geoffrey M.T. Jones parachuted into the Upper Var, France, on the night of 10/11 August 1944. His mission assisted entry of the Allied airborne invasion.

1. Captain Jones was parachuted in civilian clothes with Commandant Allain (French) of BCRA Mission Lougre. After spending one hour in the hold, following five unsuccessful passes over the point, he finally ordered the pilot to make the drop and landed on top of Mont Malay, north of Fayence. Jones lacerated his left leg and Allain was badly cut on the right ankle in their mountain landing, making initial movement physically most difficult.

2. With Commandant Allain, Jones helped to arm and reorganize the regional Maquis groups, especially the Mons Maquis. With receipt of his action message, a conference was held on the evening of 14 August 1944, with Captain Fontes, Chief of the FFI of Drauignan, Lieutenant Silvani of the FFI at Montauroux, Commandant Blanc of Les Arcs, and Joseph of the FTP Mons Maquis, following which the prearranged targets and orders were reviewed and coordinated. They planned the eventual taking of Draguignan, Bargemon, and Montauroux by the FFI, and the attacking during the night of 14/15 August 1944 by the Mons Maquis of the German observation and DF radio station at Fayence.

3. Having been previously briefed on the landing area for the airborne invasion, Jones proceeded with Commandant Allain, Commandant Blanc, and seven gendarmes from different towns in the area (having been sent to the Maquis especially to serve as guides for the Airborne Task Force) through German-held territory on foot and in a truck, some 50 km south to the valley of Le Muy.

4. After having been bombed by unidentified aircraft on the Bargemon Plain, the party arrived in the valley between La Motte and Trans-en-Provence where initial contact was made with Allied soldiers at approximately 0500 hours on the morning of 15 August 1944 . . . .

  In the succeeding few hours of the initial confusion of landing, individual assistance was given by members of Jones' party in general orientation, intelligence, and guiding.

5. Because of a heavy fog, a confused situation continued until approximately 0830. Jones then contacted and helped to establish headquarters in the Chateau de Ste. Rosseline, between Le Muy and Les Arcs. With the organization and centralization of the command, all possible assistance was given to Colonel Graves. Jones was told the exact location of the parachute and glider landing fields for the subsequent airborne drops. He organized the clearing of the glider landing fields by 1600 hours. This facilitated the landings of a Parachute Battalion and the Glider Battalion Combat Team and attached units.

During the day of 15 August, Captain Jones' party accomplished the following:

1. The seven gendarmes served as guides for reconnaissance, patrolling, and attacking units. The two gendarmes who spoke German were extremely helpful in interrogating initial prisoners of war, and all were most helpful in giving local intelligence on terrain, population and enemy dispositions.

2. Commandant Blanc rallied local FFI forces, whose notable achievements were the taking of Les Arcs (and helping to hold the town with U.S. troops against subsequent German attacks) and the clearing of the above-mentioned landing fields of all anti-landing obstacles.

3. Commandant Allain as a French regular officer greatly assisted in the organization of and liaison with the

local population, and, in spite of his wound, led and fought with strayed American soldiers he picked up along the way.

4. Maj. Gen. Robert T. Frederick and his paratroopers had landed northeast of Le Muy. They were temporarily cut off from the intelligence Jones provided to General Frederick.

5. During the morning of the 16 of August 1944, General Frederick ordered Captain Jones and his team of four gendarmes to bring back Commandant Allain from Les Arcs, which was being attacked by German reinforcements. When they reached Les Arcs, Jones and his team escaped an erroneous Allied bombing and a German barrage. He and his team succeeded in removing Commandant Allain and they also provided valuable information that led to the recapture of Les Arcs.

6. From a small headquarters set up by Captain Jones in collaboration with Commandant Allain and Captain Stuyvesant, services were rendered to Frederick's troops, such as interpreting, guiding troops, and running supply missions of arms to the Resistance groups fighting in the north. In conjunction with the local resistance, several short and long-range reconnaissance patrols were made giving intelligence for the successful attack on Le Muy on the following morning of 17 August. All available arms and ammunitions captured from the Germans, and American reserves from glider pilots, dead and wounded, were provided to the Resistance groups.

On the morning of 17 August Captain Jones assisted in the taking of Le Muy and moved his headquarters into town and continued to render all services requested by the high command.

This ended Mission Rabelais.[60]

As Mr. Jones pointed out in the following critique of his mission, not everything in the official version of Operation Rabelais was correct. In a statement he provided to the author, Jones wrote the following:

This "Report on Operation Rabelais" was also just recently discovered at the U.S. National Archives (when the reports were declassified). It was not written by me. It does give a more official outline for the mission. From reading this report, I feel that the basic facts were probably supplied by Commodore Allain (and/or Commodore Blanc) to an American officer who was assigned to getting such reports. (One such came to see my at my HQ in Nice later in September, but I was too busy working for Gen. Frederick to attempt to detail that earlier action—plus, I did not want to get anyone in trouble for breaking security regulations).

1. "Badly cut on the right ankle" is an understatement of Allain's wound. "Crushed" would be a better description, as I remember we ran out of morphine for his pain, and he had to ride a small mule/horse to be moved to the Maquis several days after his jump.
2. Allain—his mission impossible to perform due to his accident—helped Jones.
3. Whoever wrote this Report did not know that Jones already knew (in Algiers) of the landing area. ("Previously briefed on" is what Jones writes in his letter).
4. Obviously, it was Jones who was able to make "initial contact with the soldiers of the Parachute group."
5. Again, Jones already knew "the exact location of the parachute and glider landings." (See 3 above.)
6. Commandant Allain's mission was to neutralize the French Fleet at Toulon. It was difficult to get aircraft at that time. When Allain was badly hurt—and not able to travel to carry out his mission—he joined me and was most helpful in assisting in carrying out my mission.[61]

French Forces and Civil Affairs

Seeking the maximum cooperation from France's civilian population and a minimum of interference with operations against the enemy, Gen. Alexander Patch on March 1, 1944, ordered that a Civil Affairs detachment of two hundred officers and four hundred enlisted men would be necessary to administer efficiently the area assigned to the invasion of southern France. Such a body had been created previously and had trained near Algiers. Every effort was made to coordinate the work with the parallel organization in Britain, which was preparing to administer northwestern Europe.

The main objective of the contemplated Civil Affairs program was to relieve combat troops of such civilian administration as they might otherwise be called on to perform. There would be, at the same time, cooperation with the appropriate staff section or military agency in the maintenance of public order and the restoration of the health, welfare, and internal economy of the liberated regions. The Civil Affairs detachment was charged with making available for military use all local resources and manpower necessary to support the operation.

The responsibility for Civil Affairs direction was to remain with the commanding general, but this direction was to be exercised through the senior Civil Affairs officer. The Civil Affairs Regiment was largely American and British. French officers would handle most of the liaison work with the local authorities, particularly with regard to directing the functions of services needed for military operations.

In addition to the administrative sections, there were to be a number of specialist branches—civilian supply, public health, welfare, finance, refugee control, a legal department, transportation, price control, property control, monuments, fine arts, education, industry, commerce, utilities, and communications—each of which was to be under a chief who might serve as a specialist staff officer with Army Headquarters. Detachment personnel were to be assigned specific territorial or functional responsibilities or might be attached for supplementary service to operational military units to meet special problems or be assigned to rear-area duties. Of necessity, plans for Civil Affairs personnel had to be kept flexible and closely integrated with the tactical situation.

Probably the most important aspect of the anticipated Civil Affairs program was that of civilian food and medical supply. The situation in southern France was critical, and the plan was to bring in three Liberty ships per convoy from D plus 10 until D plus 40 and, thereafter, four ships per convoy until D plus 80. All shipments were to come direct from the United States except edible oils, which had been stockpiled in North Africa. French local authorities would distribute the supplies, under the supervision of Civil Affairs officers.

Topographic, Infrastructure, Demographic, and Other Realities

To appreciate the difficulties confronting the planners of Dragoon, it is necessary to describe in some detail the topography of the target area, the enemy strength and capabilities, the enemy defense system, and the invasion beaches prior to D-day. If it followed its usual defense tactics, the enemy would plan to annihilate the invading forces before any landing could occur and, if unsuccessful in this attempt, to counterattack with the greatest possible strength to drive the invader into the sea.

France's Mediterranean coast consists of three main mountain masses separated by two corridors. Along the Spanish border lie the Pyrenees, to the north of which is the Carcassonne Gap, formed by the valleys of the Garonne and Aude rivers. Northeast of the Pyrenees is the Massif Central, which presents its steepest face to the Mediterranean. Farther east, toward the Italian-Swiss border, is the great mass of the Alps-Jura system. The latter two mountain masses are separated by the valley of the Rhone River, which is the great natural corridor from the Mediterranean coast to the Paris Basin. The Rhone flows through a series of narrow valleys and broad basins, which are frequently openings into important corridors to the east. There is, for example, the valley of the Isère, leading to Grenoble, and the valley of the Durance, which separates the Provence Alps from the Dauphine Alps.

Below Avignon the Rhone Valley widens into a broad delta that merges with the lowlands of the Carcassonne Gap to form a long stretch of marshy coast extending from the base of the Pyrenees to Marseille. The beaches in this area were suitable for large-scale landing, but the delta was not a good entrance to the Rhone corridor because of the many watercourses that intersect it. The general bogginess of the terrain would create difficulties for both tracked and wheeled vehicles deploying off the roads. East of Marseille, the coast is rugged and irregular where the mountain masses reach to the sea, leaving only narrow sand beaches and small deltaic plains. Passage into the interior was possible only through a few narrow river valleys, such as the Argens, which led into the Durance corridor and was the best approach to the Rhone Valley from the south. It was a portion of this eastern coast, from the Bay of Cavalaire to the Rade of Agay, which was chosen as the target area for Operation Dragoon.

In this particular area, there are three outstanding topographical features—the Massif des Maures, the Toulon-Saint-Raphael Corridor, and the Provence Alps. The massif is a hill mass about thirty-five miles long, about ten miles across at its widest point, and rises to an average height of one thousand to one thousand five hundred feet. At the base of the Maures were the invasion beaches. The corridor that lies behind the massif is formed by the valleys of the Real Martin and Argens rivers and varies in width from one to six miles. Farther inland are the Provence Alps, slightly higher than the coastal massif but marked by the same steep slopes with broader valleys connected by low passes. On the east this range runs to the Alps proper, but on the west it drops off to the Durance River.

The target area comprised a portion of the famed Riviera resort coast with a traditionally mild climate and sparse rainfall, particularly during summer. Most of the time, light winds prevail, and gales or complete calm are rare. Cloud ceilings are usually unlimited, though haze over the coast occasionally limits visibility to five or six miles.

Soil in the target area varies from rocky to sandy; much bedrock at the surface makes foxholes difficult to dig. Streams running from the mountain masses into the coastal area frequently dry up in summer, and even the larger rivers reach an extreme low-water stage. However, during the summer, occasional thunderstorms create the danger of flash floods. The original forest cover was almost entirely gone, and uncultivated areas were covered with patches of woodland: evergreen oak, cork oak, pine, and chestnut, or low scrub growth of juniper, broom, box, and myrtle, the latter frequently referred to as "maquis." Cultivated portions support olive, fig, almond, mulberry, and citrus trees and vineyards, though the poor quality of the soil allowed for agriculture on a less extensive scale than in other parts of France.

The population was sparse in this region of Mediterranean France and was concentrated mostly in the immediate coastal strip. Because there were many Italians on the Riviera, the proportion of native French was lower than in other regions of France. In the target area proper, there were no large cities. The adjoining towns of Saint-Raphael and Fréjus, having together a population of nineteen thousand, were the largest settlements.

The road net in the target area was adequate for military operations. Two main highways crossed the area—the coast road from Marseille to Nice and the inland route from Fréjus to Aix-en-Provence. There were also a number of secondary roads formerly suitable for military traffic, but many of which had deteriorated since the 1940 defeat. Roads that ran through narrow defiles were commanded by high ground on the flanks and could thus be easily blocked. Road surfaces were generally satisfactory, but bridges were often old and narrow. In the towns, many important roads became narrow and winding, permitting only one-way traffic.

The railroads, like the highways, were also limited in the coastal area of southern France. A main line passed from Italy by way of Nice and Cannes and connected with the main north-south trunk line at Marseille; lesser lines crossed the immediate beach area and connected the small coast towns with the main east-west line in the interior.

Though the Mediterranean coast of France had four major and four secondary ports, only three minor ports—Saint-Tropez, Sainte-Maxime, and Saint-Raphael—were in the immediate target area. These could be used to supplement the tonnage unloaded over the beaches until Toulon, Marseille, and Nice could be made available to handle ten-thousand-ton "Liberty ships."[62]

Enemy Strength and Capabilities

Enemy capabilities, disposition, and defense strategy were constant influences on Allied decisions. By the end of July 1944, the Mediterranean Sea was almost completely cleared of German naval power, now reduced to a few destroyers, a few torpedo and escort boats, and approximately ten U-boats.[63] The Germans had hoped to augment their U-boat fleet by construction and repair activities at Marseille and Toulon, but Allied air attacks not only crippled production facilities but also destroyed those U-boats that were in their pens awaiting repair. In the main, German naval craft were considered to have only a nuisance value and could offer no serious interference to the invasion of southern France.

Intelligence information indicated that by the middle of 1944, the German Luftwaffe had definitely reached a state of decline. Yet its disposition on airfields throughout southern France allowed it to enjoy speed of movement and a certain tactical surprise. Immediately prior to D-day, the most reliable estimates placed German air strength at approximately two hundred airplanes either in or adjacent to the target area.[64] It was also assumed that in the event of invasion, the Germans would be able to draw additional air strength from either Italy or northern Europe, if the squadrons there were not already committed elsewhere. Of these two hundred planes, about three-fourths were especially designed for ship bombardment or reconnaissance. This functional distribution of the Luftwaffe suggests that German air strength was concerned mainly with efforts to embarrass Allied shipping in the Mediterranean and thereby impede any attempt at invasion or to discover by reconnaissance the scale and exact location of any landing in southern France.[65]

By mid-May 1944, increased German reconnaissance activity was observed over the Corsica-Sardinia sea-lanes while during the same period, antishipping operations showed a marked decrease. This change in functional activity seemed to suggest that for the period immediately prior to D-day, the Luftwaffe had abandoned all hope of forestalling any invasion by attacking shipping and was now merely attempting to discover the time, place, and scale of the invasion.

The Allies estimated the possible air force available to Germany in Dragoon and the adjacent area to be 1,515 planes of all types. Of this number, 1,085 were thought to be on airfields in northeastern France; southern France accounted for another 240; and Italy had 190.[66] The fact that there were great distances to be covered and that practically all available planes in northern Europe were already committed in Normandy or attempting to defend German factories and internal supply lines made it highly unlikely that any additional planes could be spared for southern France. The most likely possibility seemed to be that forty to fifty planes might be sent from northern Italy if the tactical situation permitted.

However, to checkmate enemy air activity during the critical period of the invasion, planning had to take into account three distinct possibilities: the sending of strong reinforcements into the assault area by withdrawing air power already committed elsewhere, the immediate withdrawal of most of the aircraft stationed in southern France to prevent their destruction by a superior Allied air force, or the sending of minor reinforcements from Italy and southwest Germany for restricted use over the immediate assault area.[67]

The presence of any large-scale reinforcements would indicate a German willingness to risk heavy air losses in order to defend what they considered as vital territory. An immediate withdrawal of the greater part of their aircraft would suggest an opposite attitude on the part of the German High Command. Minor reinforcements sent into the area would merely convey the impression that the Luftwaffe was putting up a token defense aimed at doing whatever damage possible and then withdrawing to safety.

On the basis of Allied pre-D-day intelligence, the general opinion was that enemy air activity would soon dissipate. On D-day, and shortly thereafter, the usual antishipping activities and sorties against Allied ground forces were expected, in an attempt to impede the establishment of a beachhead. However, it was thought that these activities would be so costly to the Germans that after three or four days the Luftwaffe would confine itself to isolated sneak raids and strafing of Allied forward positions. Finally, even this would degenerate into routine reconnaissance patrols for purposes of intelligence.

The utilization of the most advantageous terrain positions was the prime consideration in German ground force defense plans. In general terms, the delta of the Rhone River was considered as a focal point for lines of communication running in all directions. The route northward up the Rhone Valley has always been the principal avenue of entry from the Mediterranean into the heart of France. At Lyon, this route branched into roads northwest into the Loire Valley, north to the Paris Basin, and northeast into the Belfort Gap.

Prior to D-day, the Nineteenth German Army had at its disposal for the defense of southern France nine divisions stationed along the Mediterranean coast and at strategic points in the interior. The precise location at which the Allies would debark was unknown to the enemy, and so the entire coast required complete defensive coverage. Moreover, once an Allied landing point became known, it would be necessary to move troops quickly to repel the invasion and also to occupy certain strategic locations in order to protect flanks and internal supply lines.[68]

The lack of German strength and firepower could be remedied only by the introduction of troops and equipment from outside the immediate area of southern France.[69] However, German commitments on other fronts, and the lack of sufficient reserves in Germany proper, made it quite unlikely that reinforcements in sufficient strength could be counted on.[70] It was thought that one German reaction to Allied landings would be a withdrawal from the immediate coastal area to the Rhone Valley, with a serious attempt to defend Marseille and Toulon. Because the terrain of the beach area was such as to preclude the effective use of mobile troops, the logical withdrawal plan would be to fall back to the Rhone Valley and take up defensive positions. The prediction of a stubborn defense at Marseille and Toulon was based on the assumption that denying the Allies the use of large ports would delay a rapid buildup. This delay might allow the Germans to gain sufficient time to assemble their forces to a major defensive stand in the lower Rhone Valley or to withdraw them northward to safety.

Any Allied landing between Marseille and Nice would probably encounter elements of the 148th Infantry Division along the eastern segment of the Mediterranean coast and units of the 242nd Infantry Division in and about Toulon. As soon as the focus and magnitude of the invasion became clear to the German High Command, defense divisions would be maneuvered to meet the initial thrust and to modify the pattern of divisional distribution to prevent isolation or encirclement of those elements not yet actively committed to combat.

Between November 1942 and September 1943, southern France was divided into German and Italian zones of defense. The demarcation line between these zones ran east of Toulon and left the Germans responsible for defending the two principal French ports on the Mediterranean. After Italy's collapse in September 1943, the Germans faced the problem of defending the entire French Mediterranean coast. Defenses were quickly installed to make the chain of fortifications from Spain to Italy complete.

In the event of an Allied landing, the German High Command would immediately put into operation its alert plan that embodied the following main points: (1) order all troops to their assembly areas; (2) proclaim a state of siege; (3) forbid the civilian population to circulate except certain special classes of workers and officials; (4) requisition all able-bodied men and serviceable vehicles; (5) guard all railroads and other communications facilities; (6) demolish all machine shops, garages, and other installations that might be of service to the Allies; and (7) require the French to abide closely by the terms of the armistice of 1940. In addition, trustworthy Todt workers and collaborating French were to be formed into defensive detachments, and it was even reported that certain North African prisoners of war were to be turned loose to create disorder.[71]

The Germans implemented a general policy on laying mines along the coast, and the Allies encountered some difficulty during the early phases of the landing. Although as early as April 1944 it was reported that the construction of underwater obstacles was actually under way, those turned out to be only of minor hindrance to the assault boats. Offshore defense measures were used chiefly in and around the big ports and included antitorpedo and antisubmarine booms and nets, fire barges, and warning devices such as hydrophones and infrared barrages.

The enemy made the maximum use of artillery for coastal defense purposes. Batteries included railroad guns, heavy coast artillery, German field pieces, old French and Italian equipment, and even naval guns transferred from French warships scuttled in Toulon Harbor. German policy in the target area was to allot coast defense responsibility to the division charged with defending that sector. Multipurpose guns near the beaches were positioned so they could be fired at sea targets as well as cover dead spaces between the more important coastal batteries. There was a system of antiaircraft searchlights throughout the target area, and the whole coastal strip was covered by radar stations.

In general, local defenses along the Mediterranean coast were not deep. They were constructed around a system of strong points that involved concrete pillboxes and subsidiary features, such as barbed wire and minefields. The whole system of defensive works embraced blockhouses, pillboxes, personnel shelters, and command posts, often very skillfully camouflaged as normal buildings. There was also considerable improvisation; tank turrets were mounted on concrete as pillboxes or tanks were almost completely buried with only the top of the turret and the gun exposed above ground. The system of beach defenses generally extended inland only as far as was necessary to take advantage of the terrain.

Roadblocks and antitank obstacles were positioned where tank or vehicular traffic might be expected. Tank obstacles included sand ditches, concrete cubes, cones, pyramids, dragon's teeth, steel rails, timber, and antitank blockhouses. Roadblocks in the beach area were frequently defended by machine guns and light artillery. In many places, previously prepared obstacles were in readiness along the side of the roads to be put into use if the situation required.

From experience gained in Italy and Normandy, it was expected that the Germans would make extensive use of mines and demolitions. Mines were planted in antipersonnel and antitank minefields, blocking all obvious avenues of approach, and in roadbeds that ran from the beaches to the main lateral highways. Demolition charges were prepared for highway and railroad bridges, viaducts, dams, tunnels, and in banks along sides of roads where landslides could be started.[72]

The Invasion Beaches

The main assault area extended approximately forty-five miles along the coast from the Bay of Cavalaire to the Rade of Agay. It included sixteen individual beaches numbered serially from west to east and divided into the principal divisional assault areas known as Alpha, Delta, and Camel. The individual beaches varied from five hundred to four thousand five hundred yards in length and from ten to fifty yards in width, each landing area presenting an individual topographical problem.

On the extreme western flank along the Bay of Cavalaire and the Bay of Pampelonne were the Alpha beaches—259, 260, 260-A, 261, and 261-A. Beaches 259 and 260 were backed by a narrow belt of tree-covered dunes, behind which ran a highway and a narrow-gauge railroad. To the southwest were wooded slopes and the village of Cavalaire and to the east cultivated fields. Several small streams traversed the area but presented no obstacle to the advance of infantry. However, because of soft-sand preparation, it was necessary to ensure that wheeled vehicles could negotiate the first fifty yards from the water's edge and gain the hard ground and highway beyond.

The defenses in the Alpha area were considered moderate. There were three or four casemates, a dozen or so pillboxes, and seventeen machine guns. In the high ground beyond were located eight light antiaircraft guns and at the extreme western end four batteries of fixed guns of medium caliber. Parallel to the shoreline of Beach 259, about sixty yards out, were concrete pyramids covered by fire from batteries and machine guns. Barbed wire extended some eight hundred yards in the center of the beach, and the whole area was thought to be thoroughly mined. Intelligence reports prior to D-day indicated that there were probably two companies of one hundred men each manning the defenses.

Beach 261 stretched along the Bay of Pampelonne for a distance of four thousand five hundred yards between the rocky points of Cape Pinet and Bonne Terrasse. The terrain consisted of soft sand with a wooded slope in the center and a flat plain on either end. The gradient was sufficient for small landing craft, such as LCVPs, to nose up to the shore; but larger craft required pontoons for a dry landing. Enemy defenses were considered moderate and consisted of a single row of piles about 150 feet offshore, pillboxes, wire, and minefields. Roadblocks were placed across all exits and two coastal batteries some distance to the rear. It was estimated that there was an understrength enemy battalion of four hundred men defending the area.

Beaches in the Delta assault area—262, 262-A, 263, 263-A, 263-B, and 263-C—were in the vicinity of Saint-Tropez and Sainte-Maxime. Those on the northern shore of the Gulf of Saint-Tropez were partially protected from the surf. Off shore was a single line of floats designed to support an antisubmarine net and block the channel into the harbor of Saint-Tropez. The north end of Beach 262 was strongly defended, though there were pillboxes and casemates at the southern end as well. Between these two strong points the Germans had placed a double apron of barbed wire to be covered by fire and supplemented by minefields. Behind the beach itself, the terrain was flat and swampy and interspersed by small streams. This area was covered by a series of small minefields staggered in such a way as to block all obvious exits. The main arterial highway that ran from Marseille to Nice along the northern shore of the gulf was also heavily mined.

A few miles to the east, at the seaward end of the Gulf of Saint-Tropez, were two beaches near the town of Sainte-Maxime. From the point of view of topography, composition of the soil, and fortification, they were similar to those at the other end of the gulf, though perhaps less strongly defended. One of the beaches was flanked by a seawall, and on the other the Germans had constructed an antitank wall nine hundred feet long and six feet thick. Its height was insufficient to hamper infantry in a scramble landing, but it had to be breached before tanks and vehicles could reach the coastal highway. A line of floats blocked the entrance into the harbor of Sainte-Maxime.

East of Sainte-Maxime along the inner curve of Bougnon Bay were three small sand and shingle beaches backed by the usual belt of dunes, which ran up to the coastal road and narrow-gauge railroad. Beyond this were steep wooded slopes that merged into cultivated areas when the terrain became more level. At Garonnette Plage, Beach 263-C is cut in two by the Garonnette River. Because of an almost vertical embankment forty to fifty feet high, all vehicular traffic would have to be routed to the high ground by way to the extreme eastern end, where the terrain offered an exit to the coastal road. These three beaches were considered to be lightly defended but were well mined, flanked in part by an antitank wall, and protected by wire. Pillboxes were located at strategic points, and several batteries of coastal guns covered the approaches from the sea.

The third and final group of beaches—264, 264-A, 264-B, 265, and 265-A—made up the Camel assault area and extended from Point Saint-Aygulf to Antheor. Beaches 264 and 264-A, in the Fréjus-Saint-Raphael area, were heavily defended by underwater minefields and offshore concrete obstacles. On all roads leading from the beach area, on important streets in the two towns and even on the coastal highway itself, there were carefully planted minefields, antitank ditches, and roadblocks consisting of dragon's teeth and concrete pillars.

Beach 265, at the head of the Rade of Agay, was considered strongly defended. It was semicircular in shape and bounded on the west by a small boat harbor and on the east by a low, rocky point. Directly behind was the coast road and railroad, and the connecting terrain was flat and cultivated. All types of landing craft could come up to the beach, but soft sand would make it necessary to prepare a road necessary for tracked and wheeled vehicles.

Six batteries of light coast defense guns were augmented by well-camouflaged pillboxes, wire, and mines, located to take advantage of excellent defensive terrain features. The Rade of Agay was reported to be mined to a vertical depth of from twenty to fifty fathoms, and a series of floats was anchored offshore to support an antisubmarine net. A 150-yard antitank wall in the center of the beach was protected from the sea approach by a minefield three hundred yards long. Behind the wall was another minefield, and still farther back on the high ground adjacent to the highway and railroad was a third. Three highway bridges opposite the beach area had been destroyed previous to D-day, and the railroad bridge over the Agay River prepared for demolition. The Germans had installed two radar stations a few hundred yards to the rear of the highway.

West of the Rade of Agay and facing south, Beach 264-B extended from Cap Drammont, a steep red cliff, to the west. Quarried rock rose behind the sand and shingle beach. The main coastal road and railroad ran close to the shore; the best exit to the road was at the extreme eastern end of the beach. At Antheor on the other side of the Rade and facing southeast was 265-A, a small beach of fine sand one hundred yards long and thirty yards wide at the head of a cove with steep and rocky sides. The beach was backed by the road and a sharply rising coastline, behind which was a high viaduct carrying the main railway line. Infantry could land without difficulty and move on to the coast road, but for vehicles extensive preparation would be necessary. These two minor beaches, because they were considered lightly defended, were chosen for Camel assault at H-hour.

About seven miles off the coast of the target area were the islands of Levant and Port-Cros. By their strategic location, they were a menace to convoys approaching the beaches, and their neutralization was considered essential. For the most part, these islands were beachless with steep cliffs dropping down to the water's edge. The interior consisted of scrub-covered hills broken here and there by small patches of cultivated land. On the western end of Port-Cros, the enemy was reported to have a coastal battery protected by antiaircraft and machine guns. The island of Levant, which lies northeast of Port-Cros, was an even greater threat because of its closer proximity to the invasion beaches and convoy route. The most significant fortifications were constructed on the northeastern tip of the island and consisted of three or four 164-mm guns, machine guns, pillboxes, and a searchlight. Four medium coast defense guns were thought to be in position on the other end of the island.

The terrain of southern France and the constantly shifting disposition of enemy forces caused those planning for Dragoon to periodically reconsider the tactics and the logistics of the contemplated operation. After the launch of Operation Overlord, the German High Command was forced to shift to the Normandy front certain divisions previously designated for the defense of southern France. Because replacements in personnel and equipment were difficult to obtain, the defense of the Mediterranean coast, as D-day approached, was probably not on the scale that the Germans had originally planned.

If the assaulting forces were successful in breaking through the German coast defense system and establishing a permanent beachhead, the enemy's best course would be to take advantage of the defensive terrain, fight delaying actions, and attempt to withdraw its main force to safety. The possibility of a complete German collapse with the immediate cessation of hostilities or, on the other hand, a series of vigorous counterattacks supported by armor and mobile troops were the two extremes contemplated by those planning the invasion.[73]

Training

No units were assigned to the Seventh Army until the middle of June 1944. Up to that time, troop requirements for the Italian campaign had first priority. Some service units did not come under Seventh Army control until just prior to loading the assault ships. Consequently, the time available for training in preparation for the Dragoon operation was very limited. However, there was sufficient time for the principal combat elements of each of the three American subtask forces to undergo a three-week refresher course in amphibious assault.

The training program was adequate because most of the divisions, both American and French, as well as the service units, had combat experience. The United States Third Infantry Division had participated in the Moroccan, Sicilian, and Italian campaigns. Overall, General Truscott—had played an important role in training the troops of the Third Division for these previous campaigns. The Forty-fifth United States Infantry Division received its first battle experience in the Sicily campaign. The Thirty-sixth United States Infantry Division made the initial landing at Salerno in the Italian campaign and fought along with the Third and Forty-fifth in the breakthrough at Anzio and in the subsequent advance through Rome northward toward the Pisa-Rimini line.

Of the immediate follow-up forces, the First French Infantry Division and the Third Algerian Infantry Division had been in the line during the winter months of the Italian campaign and had taken an important part in the May breakthrough. The Ninth French Colonial Infantry Division, also part of the follow-up forces, had made an amphibious assault against the island of Elba and had overcome stubborn resistance in capturing the German garrison. The other French units had undergone a period of approximately twelve months' training in North Africa.

The service units of the newly constituted Seventh Army were, to a great extent, those that had worked with the divisions mentioned above in the three previous campaigns. Their training placed special emphasis on the organization of various service troops into three shore groups to operate the beaches in the three-division assault areas until this function could be taken over by the base section. Using three experienced engineer regiments as miniature base sections and adding components of all branches of service and supply troops, the command trained these groups as teams.

Naval and air force units of the Mediterranean Theater had been actively engaging the enemy since the beginning of the invasion of North Africa. This action included participation in amphibious landings in North Africa, Sicily, Salerno, and Anzio. The Naval Western Task Force organized the convoys to transport the Seventh Army or trained special groups to assist in the assault and to direct naval gunfire support. The Mediterranean Allied Air Force organized and prepared the airborne task force and regrouped air strength to assist the assault.

The initial success and rapid advance of the Allied invasion of southern France can be attributed, in part, to amphibious training that was designed to prepare troops for the actual problems of landing. The program's mission was to acquaint them with the use and care of new equipment and techniques, to coordinate the maximum usefulness of the several arms of the service, and to review the best practices of modern warfare. Every effort was made to be as realistic as possible.

As early as March 13, 1944, the commanding general of Force 163 recommended the creation of a Joint Army-Navy Beach Obstacle Board, composed of one member from the Invasion Training Center, two from the navy, and three from Seventh Army Headquarters. The board's mission was to investigate possible means of breaching underwater and beach obstacles, to make recommendations to corps and division commanders, and to assist in the procurement of the necessary demolitions and equipment to perform this work as efficiently as possible. A detailed study was made of Beach 264-A (Saint-Raphael) as a basis of training. That beach had been previously recommended by General Davidson and approved by General Patch as one possible site for an initial landing. However, Beach 264-A was considered one of the most heavily defended in the target area.[74]

On June 20 and 21, a demonstration of equipment and techniques was conducted at Salerno. The air corps showed the results of hitting beach defenses with showers of small-sized serial bombs, specially designed with fuses on sticks attached to the nose of the bomb. These bombs exploded several feet above the ground, effectively cutting wire obstacles and detonating mines. The navy shelled beach defenses with heavy guns and sent in Apex boats, drone boats, Reddy Foxes, and rocket ships. The Apex boat was a small radio-controlled craft that towed, at an angle, two drone boats. The latter were small craft filled with explosives that were detonated from the control radio of the Apex boat. Reddy Foxes were a nautical adaptation of the Bangalore torpedo, consisting of a section of pipe filled with explosives floated into position over underwater obstacles, sunk, and then detonated by remote control. Rocket ships were LCTs equipped with launchers for up to one thousand rockets, to be fired in mass at beach defenses by the crew.

In the actual course of Operation Dragoon, these devices were used with the exception of Reddy Foxes which, though available, proved unnecessary. Their "combined efforts," it was later noted, "added to the softening process of the pre-H-hour bombing and made the assault landing easier."[75]

The Invasion Training Center (ITC), commanded by Brig. Gen. Henry C. Wolfe, was moved from Port-aux-Poules, Algeria, to Salerno, Italy, during the spring of 1944. In compliance with an order from Allied Force Headquarters, the ITC established a school for weeklong instruction in waterproofing, principally for officers from Mediterranean and northern base sections, from which Dragoon units were to be mounted. At the completion of the course, they were to return to their sections to conduct schools to instruct officers and key noncommissioned officers (NCOs) in Seventh Army service units. During their stay at the center, personnel from all divisions during their stay at the center were to attend the waterproofing school. For the troops scheduled to arrive in the assault area after D-day, weatherproofing rather than waterproofing instruction was given.[76]

The Salerno site was well selected. The memory of former experiences on this terrain created an atmosphere of grim realism and a thorough appreciation of the necessity for proper preparation. The proximity of the sea was ideal for practice in loading and unloading vehicles and personnel, beach assault exercises, and swimming both for training and recreation. The nearby mountains were practically perfect for instruction in patrolling, wiring, and radio mapping. They were also used for hikes and general physical conditioning. Ranges were available for firing all types of weapons. Rubber models of terrain features, along with sand and clay tables, helped make vivid the assault objectives. Combat sports and infantry tactics were emphasized in order to weld replacements into the fighting team.

The nine infantry regiments comprising the Third, Thirty-sixth, and Forty-fifth Divisions were given a brief review of regular infantry warfare and specialized training in demolitions and amphibious assault. Their training period also served to refit and restore equipment lost or worn out during the Italian campaign and to receive and absorb replacements. As much rest and recreation as could be fitted into the brief period was allowed.

The general schedule for demolition training consisted of a ninety-minute lecture by officers preceding demonstrations by engineer troops that covered the general field of military explosives. This course introduced the types and nature of American and British explosives, fuses (safety and instantaneous), the handling of caps, the preparation of charges, the use of Primacord, the nature and fusing of Bangalore torpedoes, the preparation of pole and satchel charges, and the application and effect of shaped charges. This phase was followed by another ninety-minute period of practical work; under the supervision of the engineers, each soldier prepared a charge.

After basic principles of handling explosives, the program continued with a lecture and demonstration of underwater obstacles, beach obstacles, and the neutralization of obstacle-defended beaches. Work was also done on special demolition charges and special equipment to be used with armor. Practical demonstrations were given in the destruction of tetrahedrons, dragon's teeth, pillboxes with doors of wood or steel, German wire obstacles, double-apron barbed-wire fences, and concertinas. Experiments were carried out with placed charges to breach antitank walls, destroy concrete tubes or horned s\u200bscullies, and fill antitank ditches.

The men already had a grim familiarity with the use of mines in modern warfare. Problems involving antitank and antipersonnel mines, minefield patterns, marking of minefields, methods of neutralizing mines, use of various types of mine detectors, probing, and mine-lifting methods were anticipated.

Boat teams were given assault training, demonstrations and "dry runs," and critiques of "lessons learned." Special attention was paid to the clearance of both underwater and beach obstacles. The methods recommended by the Joint Army-Navy Beach Obstacle Board were introduced: eight-man DUKW (amphibious trucks) teams from the engineers were to be used to widen and to mark gaps through underwater obstacles. Infantry boat teams that were to land in the first wave were taught to destroy beach obstacles with wire cutters, pole chargers, and Bangalore torpedoes and to assault pillboxes with demolitions and flamethrowers.

The artillery units of the Thirty-sixth and Forty-fifth Divisions received training at the Invasion Training Center between July 1 and 17. This training consisted primarily of the use of artillery weapons under amphibious conditions and involved the loading and unloading of 105-mm howitzers from DUKWs, firing from DUKWs both on land and on water, and the use of A-frames in unloading howitzers. Other phases included the firing of small arms and machine guns at aerial-towed targets, reconnaissance, and occupation of positions. Classes were held in security, communications, surveying, photo interpretation, map reading, swimming, and physical conditioning.

Combat engineer outfits went through particularly rigorous and thorough training because of their key role in dealing with enemy defenses. They were to clear the way for the infantry's advance and establish initial supply dumps and depots. Attached to each division would be an engineer regiment reorganized into a beach group. The composition of these beach groups was such that each was a base section in miniature. The chief aim of the training was to practice engineer assault duties. The training period was so organized as to give special training to the beach groups as units.[77]

Of the beach group personnel, only the engineers, a small detail from the chemical warfare troops, and the naval beach battalions were to participate in the initial landing. Their technical training program included extensive practice problems in demolition work. The teams experimented with different types of obstacle demolition. One snag that proved temporarily difficult was the impracticability of the new type of mine detector, which was too heavy and far too sensitive. Engineers reported that the detector "picked up air pockets, roots, wood, stone, and small particles of iron and metal as well as box mines."[78]

All service troops received training in the use of their authorized weapons, in waterproofing and dewaterproofing vehicles, and in loading and unloading procedures. They attended lectures on gas warfare, security, sanitation, orientation, map reading, and special subjects according to their respective duties. A physical conditioning program that included road marches, swimming, and calisthenics was followed by all troops.

Lucian King Truscott Jr.

The man responsible for leading and training troops in their assault of the beaches of southern France had acquired a unique military and teaching record. He was chosen for top combat command in the U.S. Army during World War II. Through successive battle commands of regiment, division, corps, and field army, Lucian K. Truscott Jr. had been promoted in rank from colonel ultimately to four-star general. In summer 1944, Major General Truscott—was commander of the U.S. VI Army Corp.

Born in Chatfield, Texas, on January 9, 1895, the son of a country doctor, Truscott grew up in Norman, Oklahoma. For six years he taught school during the winter and studied at various teachers' colleges during summers. When the United States declared war against Germany and its allies in April 1917, Truscott was attending the Cleveland Teachers' Institute. He enlisted in the U.S. Army and became a cavalry officer. After the war, he remained in the army. The years between the two world wars were devoted to learning and teaching. In 1925, he was assigned to the cavalry school at Fort Riley, Kansas, to take advanced courses. He subsequently taught there for four years. His next assignment was to command troops for three years. After completing his studies in the Command and General Staff School at Fort Leavenworth, Kansas, he was again retained as an instructor for four years.

After service at Fort Knox, Kentucky, and Fort Myer, Virginia, Truscott—was selected by Gen. George C. Marshall for assignment to Adm. Louis Mountbatten's Combined Operations Headquarters in London. After studying the operations of the British Commandos, Truscott helped organize an American equivalent, the Rangers. Truscott's planning and organizational talents, and his superb battlefield leadership during the invasion of North Africa, led to his promotion as major general and award of the Distinguished Service Medal.

In preparation for the invasion of Sicily, Truscott—carried out a strenuous training program; one element was dubbed the "Truscott Trot." He demanded that his troops undertake an accelerated pace over considerable distances. It saved the lives of countless American soldiers who had to march over rugged, difficult terrain full of tough enemy troops. Truscott won Patton's praise for his remarkable leadership.

Gen. Mark W. Clark selected Truscott to become the Army VI Corps commander because of his outstanding ability and skill in "inspiring confidence in all with whom he came in contact."[79]

Truscott's—experience in ascending the heights of the U.S. Army's officers' ladder without being a West Point graduate demonstrated his fierce determination. He had both the intellectual capacity and the physical strength to succeed. One of the many accolades to Truscott can be found in the *Dictionary of American Military Biography*, which states, "His knowledge of men, skill in conditioning, and training them and interest in their well being brought high morale to his command. He was a great soldier who contributed measurably to the success of the Allied effort in World War II."[80]

When the amphibious training schedule had been completed, two of the three divisions moved from the Salerno area to new bivouac areas north of Naples. Physical conditioning and regular combat training continued, and equipment was brought up to standard. As much recreation as possible was allowed.

Under the direction of VI Corps, each division participated in a realistic "dry run" assault on a division scale, with naval and air support, simulating as closely as possible conditions to be expected in southern France. Everything was done to make the exercises simulate exact conditions of the coming invasion. On August 5, a field order arrived from the division headquarters for an exercise by the Forty-fifth Division on the Bay of Salerno. Sealed overlays and maps were put aboard the ships. Embarkation took place in and near Naples from the same points, which were later used in the departure for France.[81]

The training program of the airborne troops, whose role Lt. Gen. Ira C. Eaker, commanding general of Mediterranean Allied Air Force, called of "great historical importance," had one aim: "To mechanize each man in his job so as to insure that he would carry out his mission under the most difficult circumstances."[82]

A school for glider training was established near Rome. Between July 20 and August 5, nine ground units from artillery, chemical, infantry, engineer, signal, medical, and ordnance branches completed the course. The training team was provided by the 550th Glider Infantry Battalion. Instruction included the loading and lashing of equipment, two operational flights, and basic training in the technique of assembly after landing under simulated battle conditions. It was not an easy task to convert ground force troops into glider-borne units within the short time available. However, the team had previously conducted glider training in the States, and their work was successfully accomplished.

The First Special Service Force, which was to assault the cliff-bound islands of Port-Cros and Levant, had already had considerable combat experience. Originally organized from carefully selected Canadian and American personnel, it had been given varied forms of combat training, including parachute jumping, demolitions, mountain fighting, and amphibious tactics. This force, commanded by the intrepid Robert T. Frederick, had led the American drive into Kiska in the Aleutians, had seen action in the mountains around Cassino, and had played an important role in the Anzio beachhead action, including the breakthrough and march on Rome.

The Invasion Training Center program included organizing boat teams and infantry demolition squads; wire breaching by boat teams; using rockets, flamethrowers and infantry weapons; adjusting individual equipment for debarkation; waterproofing signal equipment and weapons; and handling mines and booby traps. The navy offered instruction in the care and use of rubber boats. Under joint army-navy sponsorship, classes were conducted in loading and unloading from naval vessels and in approaching precipitous shores with rubber boats. Practice in scaling cliffs was emphasized in day and night landing exercises against beachless shores. After each, critiques were held, and the training director made comments and suggestions in order to improve amphibious and other special techniques.

In addition to the Invasion Training Center programs, the Special Service Force carried out such activities as swimming instructions for nonswimmers, special methods for swimmers, route marches over hilly terrain, infiltration marches from beaches to inland objectives, compass problems, and a study of aerial photographs of the beaches.[83]

On the night of August 7-8, 1944, in the final practice assault called Operation Bruno, the troops landed on the islands of Ponza and Zannone, off the Italian coast. Terrain features and conditions closely resembled those to be encountered in the coming operation. Sheer cliffs extended down to the water's edge, and strong winds were creating hazardous surf conditions. The cliffs were scaled, and the enemy was theoretically taken by surprise from the rear. Apparently the Bruno intelligence report was correct when it stated that the defending troops were "non-German recruits, largely Caucasian Russians," who appeared to be indifferent and lax. The only difficulty of the assault occurred when the engines of one of the landing craft broke down and Gen. Jacob Devers had to be "rescued" in a midnight midsea transfer by the USS *Greene*.[84]

The French Commandoes were given an intensive training program similar to that of the Special Service Force. In an area on the Italian coast near Agropoli, they participated in small craft drills and practiced landing on beachless shores. The navy furnished ships for rehearsals of ship-to-shore assault by teams using rubber boats. The main emphasis during the training was on night operations, trying to preserve to the utmost the element of surprise. The final full-scale practice assault took place on the night of August 7-8 on the Italian coast near Mondragone.

Although the period of training for the Seventh Army's invasion of southern France was necessarily brief, it was realistic and sufficient. New techniques were introduced and old ones reviewed. Seldom had an army moved from combat to training and then into combat again with so little loss of time. The Seventh Army returned from its final dress rehearsal on August 8 and began loading into transports. In less than a week, the troops were putting into actual practice the lessons they had learned.

At the completion of training rehearsals in early August, various elements of the Seventh Army were waiting at ports of embarkation in Italy, Corsica, and North Africa. In the Naples-Salerno area were the Third Infantry Division, commanded by Maj. Gen. John W. O'Daniel; the Thirty-sixth Infantry Division, commanded by Maj. Gen. John E. Dahlquist; and the Forty-fifth Infantry Division, commanded by Maj. Gen. William W. Eagles, together with the headquarters of the VI Corps and Seventh Army. In ports on the "heel" of Italy was the French II Corps, under the command of General de Larminat, consisting of the First French Infantry Division, commanded by General Prosset; the Third Algerian Infantry Division, commanded by General de Goislard de Montsabert; and attached troops. In Corsica were the First Special Service Force, commanded by Col. Edwin A. Walker, and the French Groupe de Commandoes, commanded by Lt. Col. Georges Bouvet, both of which had been moved, combat loaded, from the Naples area on August 11. Near Oran, Algeria, were minor elements of the French II Corps and General Sudre's Combat Command One of the First French Armored Division. Troop ships and naval escort vessels waited in the harbors of Pozzuoli, Naples, Salerno, Taranto, Brindisi, Palermo, Malta, Oran, andAjaccio.[85]

The island of Corsica lies one hundred miles southeast of the assault beaches, but its ports were insufficient to accommodate ships for a major naval operation. The greater portion of the forces forming the initial assault were marshaled near the excellent anchorages, beaches, and restored docks in the Naples area, including the harbor facilities of Cuma, Baia, Pozzuoli, Bagnoli, Nisida, Portici, Castellammare, and Salerno. This area lies some 430 miles southeast of the assault beaches. Nevertheless, it was obvious that the pre-D-day assault by the Special Service Force and French Groupe de Commandoes would jump off from nearby Corsica and that the main D-day assault by three divisions would come from the Naples area. For the subsequent buildup, all available Allied-held ports would be used.[86]

Naval convoys that transported the forces were to follow the regularly prescribed routes or channels; these prearranged routes were to be swept of mines and efficient air protection given by regular and coordinated aerial patrols. Deviations for the purpose of deception were to be made from the formal convoy lanes, but in general there were ten arterial routes of communication between the mounting areas and the coast of southern France.

Convoy Routes

Of the ten routes, Route No. 1 from the Naples area was the most important, since it was to be used by the main force of the assault. It proceeded from Naples in a northwesterly direction, passing through the Straits of Bonifacio, which separate the islands of Corsica and Sardinia, and thence followed the western coast of Corsica in a northerly direction until abreast of the middle of the island. It was here where the main route was joined by routes from the "heel" of Italy, Sicily, Sardinia, and North Africa. This point served as a naval assembly area, from whence convoys were to proceed to the invasion beaches.

Route No. 2 originated at the port of Taranto and joined Route No. 4 at a point off the southeastern coast of Italy. Route No. 4 came around the "heel" from the port of Brindisi, and the two routes then passed north of the islands of Malta and Pantelleria to join the Naples route at the assembly point off Corsica.

Two routes originated in the harbor of Oran. One of these, Route No. 3, went eastward along the North African coast, passed Algiers, where additional ships would join in, and then continued along the coast for some two hundred miles before turning northward to join the Taranto-Brindisi routes at a point off the southwestern coast of Sardinia. The other, Route No. 5, proceeded northwestward from Oran between the Balearic Islands and Sardinia, thence due north into the region of the assault.

Route No. 6 originated in the port of Palermo, Sicily, and proceeded westward, eventually joining the Oran, Taranto, and Brindisi routes off the southwestern coast of Sardinia. At this same point, Route No. 7, from the southern Sardinian port of Cagliari, also joined the other southern routes. Route No. 8 started in the Bay of Ajaccio, Corsica, and passed westward a short distance to join the Naples and southern routes at the naval rendezvous.

Route No. 9, the shortest of the ten, ran from the harbor of Calvi on the northwestern coast of Corsica directly to the invasion beaches, approximately 105 miles away. The tenth and final route, beginning at Ajaccio, kept to the west of the assault approach corridor and was used by the Special Service Force in its attack on the islands of Levant and Port-Cros.[87]

To accommodate the two pre-D-day assault forces, a special naval task force of high-speed ships was organized. This was known as the Support (Sitka-Romeo) Force and was commanded by Rear Adm. L. A. Davidson, USN. The naval complement consisted of five transports (APDs) and three medium and two small infantry landing ships, making a total of ten, escorted by the French battleship *Lorraine,* one heavy cruiser, five light cruisers, three destroyers, sixteen motor torpedo boats, and fifteen small craft. The Sitka Force (First Special Service Force) included 2,057 troops, and the Romeo Force (French Commandoes) was approximately one thousand strong. The former had come from Santa Maria de Castellabate and the latter from Agropoli, both in Italy. On August 11, they both transferred to Propriano near Ajaccio. Here they remained for two days, cleaned equipment, and were briefed with the most recent intelligence concerning their objectives.

Naval Task Force No. 87, commanded by Rear Adm. Spencer Lewis, USN, transported the Camel Assault Force from Italy and Combat Command Sudre of the First French Armored Division from Africa. In the Naples area, the Thirty-sixth Division, the 540th Engineer Beach Group, and attached troops, 31,355 men and 4,313 vehicles, were loaded between August 10 and 12 on twenty transports and ninety-one landing ships and craft. The nine combat battalions of the Thirty-sixth Division were loaded in the same manner as those of the Forty-fifth Division, but special arrangements had to be made for the loading of vehicles. This was necessary because an H-hour assault over the heavily defended Camel Red Beach (264-A) presented too great a risk, and the first LST and LCI landings were to be made on the nearby Agay beaches. Red Beach was to be attacked by ground forces first and by naval gunfire at H plus 6 hours, and the loading of vehicles was planned to fit this anticipated delay.

Shore control officers also served to check on the operation of the base sections, to ensure that Seventh Army units carried out the mounting plan fully and on schedule. This steady, uninterrupted flow of troops and supplies according to priority changes based on the tactical situation continued until all major units of Seventh Army had been dispatched and a base of supply created in France. Through this means, more than one hundred twenty-five thousand troops, thirty-four thousand vehicles, and one hundred sixty-five thousand tons of cargo reached southern France by August 31, 1944.[88]

The Naval Western Task Force commander conducted his final briefing for key commanders on August 6. On August 9, General Truscott, the VI Corps commander, briefed his staff, in the presence of Navy Secretary Forrestal, Admiral Hewitt, the division commanders, commanders of the naval task forces, General Frederick of the airborne task force, and General Saville of the XII Tactical Air Command. On the evening of August 12, General Truscott and his staff then boarded the USS *Catoctin*. On August 11, General Patch conducted his final briefing at Seventh Army Headquarters, Naples.

The vessels of the Alpha, Delta, and Camel attack forces left the Naples area on August 11, 12, and 13, the slower vessels sailing first. Seventy-two hours prior to embarkation, maps in sealed packages, and the Seventh Army map identification code and key in a sealed envelope had been delivered to commanding officers. These were to be opened four hours after sailing and all assault troops carefully briefed. First the unit officers were briefed; and they, in turn, instructed the enlisted men under their commands. Through the use of charts, pictures, blackboards, and sponge rubber models showing terrain, the exact mission of each assault team was explained in detail. Prior to debarkation, all watches were synchronized with ship's time.

Shoulder patches and appropriate flag brassards, both American and French, were distributed. Soldiers sat about the deck sewing on their insignia and reading the "Pocket Guide to France." Rations for the first days were issued, with each man receiving one "K" ration, one "D" ration, a small bottle of halazone tablets to purify water, one bottle of salt tablets, and two packages of cigarettes. Units were issued two rations of either "C," "10-in-1," or "B," plus one of "D" on a basis of strength. The voyage was uneventful. There was no enemy opposition by submarine, surface craft, or aircraft. The convoys sailed northward along the western coast of Italy and passed through the Straits of Bonifacio. On the evening of August 14, the following message from General Patch was read over the ships' loudspeakers:

> Soldiers of the Seventh Army:
>
> We are embarking for a decisive campaign in Europe. Side by side, wearing the same uniform and using the same equipment, battle experienced French and American soldiers are fighting with a single purpose and common aim—Destruction of Naziism [*sic*] and the German Army. The agonized people of Europe anxiously await our coming. We cannot and will not fail. We will not stop until the last vestige of German tyranny has been completely crushed. No greater honor could come to us than this opportunity to fight to the bitter end in order to restore all that is good and decent and righteous in mankind. We are an inspired Army, God be with us.

At approximately 1900 hours on August 14, 1944, off the western coast of Corsica, the Dragoon convoy met in rendezvous and turned toward its objective.[89]

Softening the Targets

The strategy of Operation Dragoon included plans to soften the beach defenses by concentrated bombing and to isolate the assault area by special landings prior to H-hour. To accomplish this isolation, the specially trained American Special Service Force, the French Commandoes, and the French Naval Assault Party were to land at midnight August 14-15 on the flanks of the invasion beaches. The First Airborne Task Force was to be dropped before dawn August 15 in the rear of the target area, thereby preventing the enemy from reinforcing its coastal defenses. The air force was to step up its regular offensive operations against enemy lines of communication and military installations in southern France and Italy, turning attention to the invasion as D-day and H-hour approached. The fire support ships of the navy were to shell the beaches just prior to H-hour. The air corps started the execution of the preinvasion bombing during the first week in August.

While the embarkation of the ground forces was in progress, the XII Tactical Air Command under General Saville was softening the enemy for invasion. Fighter bombers from bases in Corsica and Sardinia were attacking coastal defense guns, beach defenses, lines of communication, airfields, and radar installations. Assigned air support included six groups of P-47s, three wings of RAF Spitfires, one squadron of A-20s, one squadron of Beaufighters, two squadrons of tactical reconnaissance Spitfires, one squadron of P-51s, and one squadron of photographic reconnaissance aircraft.[90]

Their offensive support of Operation Dragoon was divided into four phases: Phase I—the period August 5 to five days prior to D-day; Phase II—from D minus 5 to 0350 hours D-day, known as Operation Nutmeg; Phase III—0350 hours D-day to H-hour, known as Operation Yokum; and Phase IV—the period after 0800 August 15, known as Operation Ducrot.[91]

Operation Nutmeg opened on August 10 with attacks by P-47s on gun positions on Cape Esteral, Cape Benat, Levant Island, and Camarat. Radar installations from Marseille to Cannes were attacked with explosives dropped during the course of 410 sorties on the following day. As Nutmeg was essentially a cover plan, on August 12 the strategic air force dispatched 139 B-17s and 94 B-24s against Séte and a small force against gun positions at Marseille. Fighter bombers of the

Eighty-seventh Fighter Wing flew 384 sorties against communications, destroying bridges at Arles, Tarascon, and Avignon. As the convoys began to sail, the air assault increased accordingly. Gun positions, bridges, and communications were blasted by 626 heavy bombers escorted by 241 fighters. Four Wellington bombers scanned the convoy route for two U-boats reported at sea.

During the twenty-four hours prior to D-day, the attention of the air force was directed more specifically at the invasion coast. Bombers ranged inland to strike fuel dumps and water transport, radar installations, coast-watching stations, and gun positions on the coast itself. Fighter planes flew over two hundred sorties to cover the assembling invasion convoys off Corsica. During the entire Nutmeg phase, the enemy offered merely token resistance, limiting its air activities to fast reconnaissance trips to watch convoy movements.

To add to the enemy's confusion, the cover operation, Ferdinand, was carried out during the night of August 14-15. Two naval diversion "forces," including heavy ships, sailed at 1800 hours on August 14 to feign assault west of the selected beaches in the Ciotat area, which is between Marseille and Toulon, and to the east between Cannes and Nice. To simulate an airborne assault, five aircraft left Corsica after midnight (0115 on August 15), each carrying 5,780 pounds of parachute dummies, rifle simulators, and window (strips of paper covered with metallic paint to confuse enemy radar). This material was dropped from a height of six hundred feet in a zone near Ciotat. The enemy was alerted immediately. Pilots reported many flashes, colored lights, and small explosions. The success of the operation was later established from prisoners taken on D-day.[92]

The naval fire support ships commenced long-range bombardment of prearranged targets at 0630. Until 0800 this fire was almost continuous, lifting only when bombers were over the targets. Following behind the minesweepers, ships approached the shore and laid down a drenching fire on beach fortifications. In all, naval guns threw over fifteen thousand nine hundred projectiles into the beach defenses. Phosphorous shells were included and were reported very effective. The aerial bombing had ceased at 0730 to allow the smoke over the area to clear and to enable the naval gunners to fire without interference on observed targets and positions revealed by gun flashes. The shelling continued until 0750; and then it shifted to the flanks, for the hour of the major assault was at hand. Meanwhile, the pre-H-hour assault forces had landed and begun the isolation of enemy forces in the strategic area.[93]

Final Steps

Plans to isolate the invasion area by commando assaults on the flanks went into operation on the night of August 14-15. Ships of the support forces (Naval Task Force No. 86) moved from Propriano, Corsica, at 1130 hours on August 14. Shortly after darkness, the sharp outlines of the cliffs of Levant and Port-Cros appeared in the offing.

French officers and others with local knowledge advised that a landing over the south coast of the islands was impracticable or impossible. This situation was just what was wanted, since the Germans would probably believe likewise and make little or no effort to defend the cliffs. The troops had been especially trained for the task. After they had scaled the cliffs, they were to destroy all enemy defenses, particularly coastal guns that might threaten the invasion fleet. When relieved by French troops on the evening of D-day, the Special Service Force was to withdraw with its prisoners to the mainland.[94]

As the assault boats were being paddled toward the beach, scouts in kayaks and electric surfboats preceded them to mark the landing spots with small lights. The First Regiment, of approximately 650 men, landed on Port-Cros; and the Second and Third Regiments, about 1,300 strong, debarked at midnight on Levant Island. Both groups included attached Naval Shore Fire Control Parties. These landings were unopposed, and all groups reached assembly areas without interference.[95]

Surprise was complete. Although the enemy had been alerted for an assault on August 15, reports from prisoners revealed that the Germans did not expect an attack up the cliffs on the seaward side of the islands. Resistance on Levant was scattered and moderate, and the enemy shortly withdrew to the port of Levant, where it put up a stiffer fight. By dawn a beach was cleared, supplies landed, and the wounded evacuated. The coastal defense battery at the eastern end of the island was found to be a cleverly camouflaged dummy. During D-day, mopping up continued on Levant; but because of radio failure, regular reports could not be sent to the Force Command Post aboard the USS *Catoctin*. During the afternoon, General Patch sent his aide-de-camp to Levant to investigate and report. Energetic and athletic Navy

Secretary Forrestal accompanied Patch's scout. They found only snipers and small pockets of resistance still active. By 2234 hours on D-day, all resistance on Levant ceased.[96]

To protect and secure the left land flank of the invasion coast, Romeo Force was landed by the Naval Support Force at Cape Negre prior to H-hour. This force of French Commandoes, under Lieutenant Colonel Bouvert, landed from three LSIs shortly after midnight on August 14-15, west of the Alpha beaches. Their mission was to destroy all enemy coastal defenses on the cape, to establish a roadblock on the coastal highway, and to seize and hold the high ground two miles to the north. Two advance light detachments were sent in small boats as an initial assault force.[97]

The first detachment of seventy men beached from rubber assault boats at the eastern base of Cape Negre, scaled the steep banks, and took the enemy by surprise. They destroyed the gun emplacements and established a tank block in a pass on the coastal highway. This operation was successfully and quickly accomplished. The second detachment was to land in two sections on either side of Le Rayol Beach, two miles east of the cape, to surprise and knock out the pillboxes believed to exist in that area. Afterward, they were to prepare the beach for the landing of the main force from LSIs. Because of the difficulty of locating Le Rayol Beach in the darkness, a small reconnaissance party preceded the detachment and marked the beach with a guide light. In spite of this precaution, one section landed near Cape Negre, where it was fired upon and suffered some casualties. The main body followed at about 0100 hours and, failing to observe the guide light, also landed in the wrong area, this time at Le Canadel between Le Rayol and Cape Negre. Since time was of the utmost importance, the LCIs proceeded to land on the beach at Le Canadel. The enemy was found to be confused and disorganized, and the landing was accomplished without a single shot being fired.

Taking advantage of the enemy's disorder, the force hastened to accomplish its mission with little interference. By morning, the beaches were cleared and a junction effected to the west with the detachment holding the tank block at Cape Negre pass. During the morning, the enemy reorganized and launched several violent counterattacks, but these were repulsed. The commandoes continued to advance inland, clearing the towns of Le Rayol and La Mole of Germans and mopping up all pockets of resistance in the area.

At approximately 1300 hours on August 15, a combat patrol from the U.S. Third Division that included the French actor and soldier Jean-Pierre Aumont contacted the French Commandoes. This brought the force under the command of VI Corps; at 2000 hours, the commandoes received orders to resume their advance westward to Le Lavandou.[98]

To sever German communications to the east between Cannes and the right flank of the assault area, a roadblock was to be established on the coastal highway prior to H-hour. A demolition party of eighty-seven French Marines was organized, known as the Rosie Force or the French Naval Assault Group. The force was to land in the vicinity of Pointe des Trayas on the night of D minus 1 and to block the roads from Cannes to Saint-Raphael and Fréjus. The block was to be constructed by the downing of trees and telegraph poles and by laying mines in critical areas. During the night of August 14-15, the party was landed from four torpedo boats in seven rubber boats on the beach south of Theoule-sur-Mer. In the darkness, the marines ran into barbed-wire defenses and antipersonnel mines. The explosions and confusion alerted the enemy, who immediately opened fire with deadly effect. The party dropped their demolition equipment and attempted to withdraw. However, the operation failed completely; and on the afternoon of D plus 1, the survivors made contact with the Thirty-sixth Division. Twenty-two wounded were evacuated by the Fifty-sixth Medical Battalion; the rest had either been killed or captured.[99]

To isolate the assault area completely, it was necessary to cut the coastal highway on each end of the projected beachhead and to block enemy movement from the rear. The coastal highway was bisected, at Fréjus, by a road leading from the interior down a defile to the coast. The First Airborne Task Force, or Rugby Force, was to land at various hours on D-day beginning at 0430 near Le Muy and Le Luc to establish the necessary roadblocks, to prevent enemy movement toward the beaches, and to help reduce the defenses in the Fréjus area.[100]

The Provisional Troop Carrier Air Division was detailed to transport the force. To avoid convoy routes to the target area, aerial routes were set up east of the assault corridor and marked by beacon ships. Three drop zones—O, A, and C—were chosen along the Nartuby and Argens rivers near the towns of La Motte, Trans-en-Provence, and Le Muy. Zone A and Zone O were either flat, cultivated fields or gently rolling ground suitable for both parachute and glider operations. Zone C was a broken, rocky area.

Dragoon's commanding general, Sir Henry Maitland Wilson, made this observation:

> The timing and coordination of the pre-D-day bombing program, the bombardment tasks for naval and air forces to cover the assault, and the air landing operation raised a multitude of problems to sort out, for which I held a series of conferences in Naples; the former had to be worked out to deceive the enemy as to the point of assault and at the same time knock out certain coast defense batteries which covered the beaches; the bombardment tasks required special timings as between the fleet and air forces while the mission of the airborne division which, starting from the Rome area, also required a special timing and routing. It was the toughest bit of coordination I had been faced with during the war and I had at times to crack the whip over the staffs of the different services to get them to swallow their objections and pull together. Eventually everything was settled satisfactorily and as a final session Admiral Hewitt, who commanded the Western Task Force, and his admirals gave a clear presentation of the naval programme and the specific tasks for each beach. At the conclusion of the conference, I thanked everyone for their cooperation in working out the plan and reminded them that Fréjus was the place where Napoleon had launched from Egypt in 1799 and urged them to bear in mind one of his well-known sayings: "*Activité, Activité, Activité, je commande à toi.*"[101]

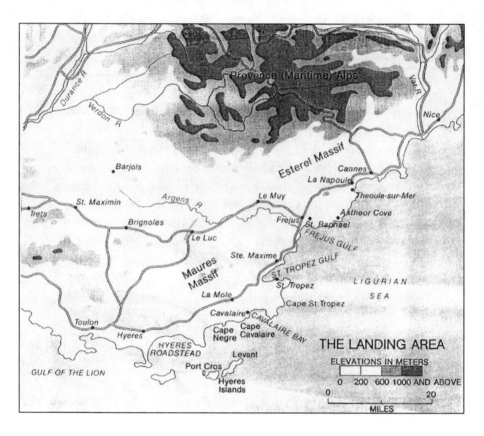

The landing area

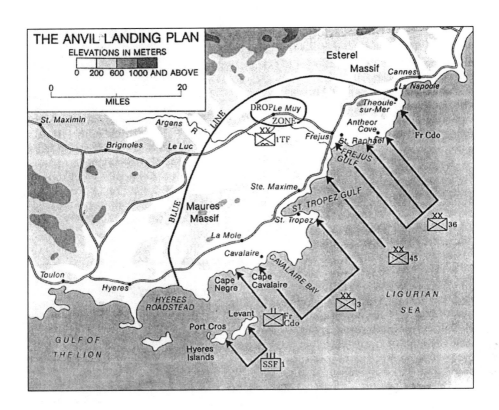

The Anvil landing plan

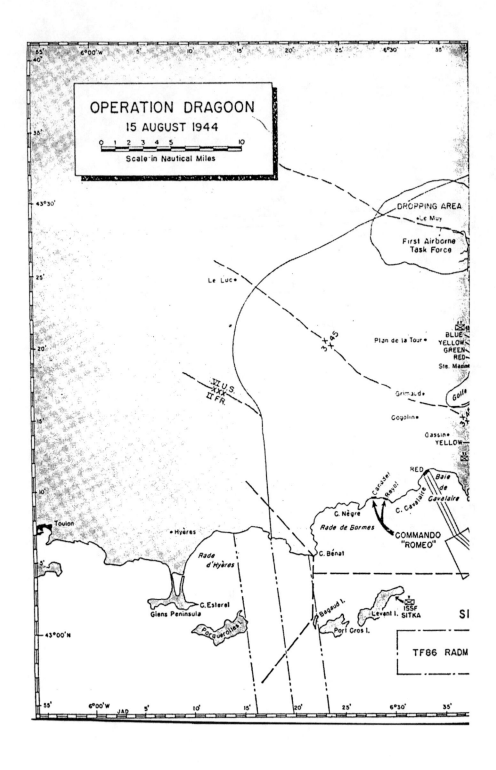

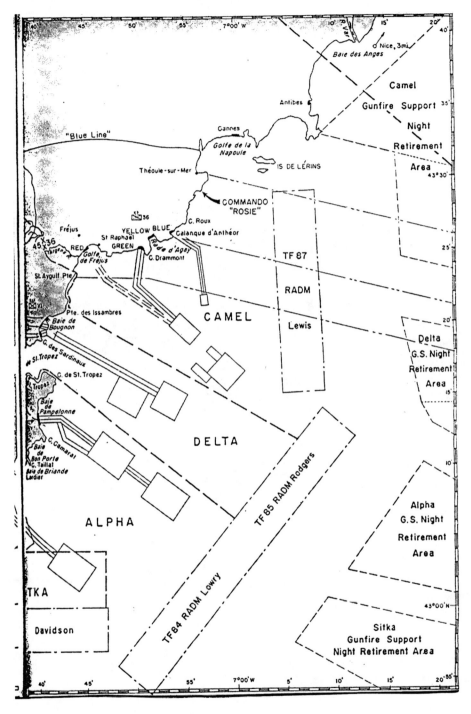

Alpha, Delta, and Camel assault beaches
Task force assignments

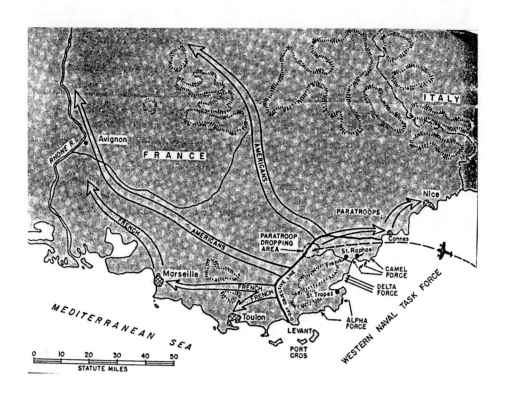

Invasion of southern France, August 15, 1944

CHAPTER 8

EN ROUTE TO DRAMMONT

Before Operation Drammont, Allied military leaders tried to deceive the Germans regarding the forthcoming invasion, and the German defenders reciprocated with their own trickery. But the Germans could not deceive their enemies concerning some significant realities: Anglo-American victories generated by the Normandy invasion; Russian military ascendancy; the reverberations of the attempt to assassinate Hitler; and the debilitation of the German army, navy, and air force—none of which could be hidden.

These and other serious weaknesses did not change German reserves of strength and determination. German reprisals to prevent outbreaks of French sabotage and the killing of occupation troops were forceful and unconscionable. Too often the killing of one German soldier by the French resulted in the disproportionate killing of a great many innocent, unfortunate Frenchmen. Air bombing added to the toll of the hapless. As their liberation was approaching, the French people suffered horrible Allied air attacks. Their country's coasts, communication centers, railway lines, and marshalling yards were devastated. Between Paris and Le Havre, the railway system had been bombed in fourteen places. All bridges between Paris and the sea and all bridges over the Seine had been destroyed. Nearly three thousand civilians were killed by mass bomber raids in one June 1944 week.[1] German civilians also were killed by air raids. U.S. Army Air Force planes dropped seventy-three thousand tons of bombs on people in Munich, Friedrichshafen, Metz, and Belfort. Royal Air Force bombs on German targets dropped fifty-seven thousand tons of bombs on German targets that included Stuttgart and Hamburg. Attacks on Wesseling, Bohlen, Merseburg, Vienna, and Ploesti were undertaken to destroy German oil supplies.[2] The British people were not spared death and destruction from the air. Prime Minister Churchill's review of the war to the House of Commons on August 3, 1944 reported that "the weight of flying bombs launched upon the country from the evening of June 15th to the evening of July 31 is estimated to be some 4,500 tons. During the same period Allied air forces dropped approximately 48,000 tons of high explosive bombs on Germany. Of course we try in the main to aim at military objectives, but it may be that loss of life occurs in particular places. But these [German] weapons have no other object than indiscriminate slaughter of the civilian population."[3]

Opportunists in France (and elsewhere) were vigilant and prudent. Frenchmen who had been staunch Vichyites shed their allegiance and became overnight fans of the Americans. The reasons for this change on the part of both opportunists and the multitude of nonpartisan people were apparent: the masses of well-fed Americans, equipped with overwhelming weapons, tanks, ships, money, etc., were quite visible to a people occupied by an enemy that appropriated vast amounts of their necessities and wealth. It was also apparent that the Americans shared their logistical prowess by rearming the French and other Allies.

It was also true that a workable Franco-American military relationship had been formed. Gen. Charles de Gaulle's July 1944 meeting with President Roosevelt had gone well enough to ensure a workable political relationship. But the general's insistence on full recognition of France's prerogatives remained unresolved. His demand that France play a major role in Operation Dragoon was realized, but de Gaulle's struggle to have France placed on par with other Allies was to continue for many years after World War II.

In July and August 1944, American, British, and French political and military leaders were primarily concerned with the planning and execution of an invasion whose outcome depended on both veterans of other Mediterranean and the Normandy campaigns as well as novices such as the crew members of the LST 1012. Their adventures, and misadventures, are described later.

It Was No Secret

The impending invasion of southern France became steadily more obvious. The transfer of Allied close-support aircraft to Corsica and Sardinia was a clear sign, and the withdrawal of seasoned American units from the Italian front was conspicuous. So too were the actions of the French units—including some Moroccan divisions—in North Africa, which were being readied for shipment. It was impossible for German soldiers in the streets of Italy not to notice the evacuation of civilians from the coastal areas. Preinvasion fever in early August 1944 was high; and rumors of an Allied attack on Napoleon's birthday, August 15, were rampant. When German air reconnaissance spotted the Allied fleet streaming north from Corsica on August 13, the German Army went on full alert.[4] The waters surrounding Naples were jammed with Allied ships and large overhead barrage balloons.

LSTs loading invasion supplies and vehicles at Nisida, Italy, on August 9, 1944, just prior to the southern France operation.

Under the hot Italian sun, soldiers of the Third, Thirty-sixth, and Forty-fifth U.S. Infantry Divisions were trained for the invasion of southern France. For many who survived the invasions of North Africa and Italy, the plague of mosquitoes required medicine to avoid malaria. Their training curriculum included beach fortification and barbed-wire blasting, boat-wading skills, and waterproofing vehicles. Soldiers used their precious free time for boozing, whoring, and sightseeing. Some visited the magnificently decorated Italian churches and the ruins of old Pompeii, where they bought phallic symbols. Ugly scenes took place in the streets of picturesque Naples: young boys touted their "beautiful virgin sisters" for sale; on one street corner, sailors from LST 1012 witnessed an American soldier fornicating with an Italian girl; and there was no shortage of sordidness and Allied drunkenness. There were also opportunities to see *Faust* and *Tosca* at the opera house, according to actor Alec Guinness, who was in Naples awaiting shipment to Britain after two and a half years on duty as the commanding officer of a British amphibious vessel serving in the Mediterranean.[5]

By August 1944, Neapolitan docks were full of American ships being loaded with troops and massive equipment and supplies. Italian Fascists on German payrolls were reporting a pending Allied invasion. Even amongst the locals it was obvious that France was the next target of the Allied forces. Journalist David Schoenbrun, who participated in Operation Dragoon, wrote that an Italian boy who was hustling for handouts from American soldiers and sailors asked him, "You going to France?"[6]

Blaskowitz

Col. Gen. Johannes Albrecht Blaskowitz was charged with the German defense of the Atlantic and Mediterranean coastlines of France, from the Loire to the French-Italian border. The German security of this area was concentrated upon the areas of La Rochelle, Mouth of Gironde, Séte, Marseille, and Toulon. As early as May 10, 1944, the Germans knew of an impending Allied invasion. "The ever increasing indications of an intended Allied landing in southern France," Blaskowitz wrote, "led to a fusion of command for the two Armies (The First and Nineteenth Armies) located between the Loire Estuary and the French-Italian border. With myself as commander-in-chief (being familiar with conditions there), they were at first organized into an Army Group; i.e., purely an operational staff without territorial authority."[7]

Born on July 10, 1883, in the east Prussian town of Pateswalde, with a population of seven hundred, Blaskowitz was instilled with Christian values from an early age—his father was the local Protestant minister. His mother died a week before he was sent to a Prussian cadet school to improve the family's meager financial position. From that young age until his death, he was subject to Prussian restrictions, regimentation, and discipline. German professional soldiers obeyed the orders of their government, even a Nazi government.

Blaskowitz's command of the Polish campaign in September 1939 displeased Hitler but commended by German Army chiefs. The creation of the Polish Corridor by the Treaty of Versailles after World War I ripped out a vital part of Prussia to provide Poland a path to the sea. This was resented by nearly all of Germany's officer corps, including Blaskowitz, even though Nazi acts of brutality toward the Polish people were repugnant to his ethical and religious beliefs. These values overpowered his oath to serve anti-Christian cruelty. He made his disgust, outrage, and disapproval of the *Schutzstaffel,* or SS, Nazi atrocities toward the Polish people known in language that was unprecedented in German military history. Concerned about the treatment of Polish Jews in the Warsaw Ghetto, Blaskowitz assigned Major General Langhaeuser the task of stopping the atrocities. Appeals were made to the German High Command's army commander in chief Colonel General von Brauchitsch, who was too weak willed to confront Hitler. Blaskowitz's only avenue for protest, von Brauchitsch, was not able to stop the monstrosities of the SS, who carried out Hitler's policies. Blaskowitz nevertheless continued to protest the arrests of the Jews, the forming of ghettos, the raids upon Jews, and their deportation by the SS. He objected to Nazi violations of laws that deprived Poles, Christians, and Jews of life and property.

Blaskowitz also sought adequate nourishment and necessities for the Polish people, writing reports about their plight even after he was ordered to desist. This extraordinary disobedience was tantamount to mutiny, and yet Blaskowitz persisted in behaving in accordance with Christian principles. In Richard Giziowski's thorough and detailed review of Blaskowitz's life, the author concluded that Blaskowitz was not quiet about Nazi crime, that he protested and tried to change orders, that he risked his life, and that he secretly sabotaged criminal orders.[8]

His courage in disagreeing with Hitler before World War II over the role of tanks and his efforts to bring Nazi atrocity perpetrators in Czechoslovakia to trial fanned Hitler's fury. However, although Blaskowitz flaunted German Army protocol, Hitler continued to retain his services for he recognized in Blaskowitz a loyal and superb army commander. He knew that Blaskowitz would loyally and professionally perform his military duties—the German war machine needed him. Hitler took his revenge upon Blaskowitz by often removing him from duty and denied Blaskowitz promotion to the highest rank of field marshal, which he bestowed on far less able but subservient German generals. Blaskowitz's love for Germany and its people superseded his hatred of Hitler and the Nazis.

Months prior to Dragoon, the Germans suspected an Allied assault against the southern French coastline. Blaskowitz wrote in May 1944, "The ever-growing preparations by the Allies for their invasion of Western Europe obviously were being concentrated in southern England, even though there were reports of troop-assemblies in Algiers to an extent (about 30 Divisions) which were in excess of the current needs of the Italian Theater of War."[9] He concluded that the most probable course of invasion would be in the area north of the Loire and that if this Allied thrust were successful, then the French combat area would be divided. Thus, at this early stage in 1944, Blaskowitz had deduced that the main Allied landing points would be in the bay that separates Normandy and Brittany, with a secondary debarkation point in the area south of the Loire Estuary, an area patrolled by Army Group G. He believed that this plan would allow the Allies the opportunity to quickly annex Brittany and that their main reasons for this course of action was that if they landed on the Mediterranean coastline along the Mentone-Rhone Estuary area, their invasion would be successful since this region held nearby well-secured embarkation facilities in Sardinia and Corsica. He considered that the roads through Grenoble and the Rhone Valley would allow the Allies a means for easy advance inland; that a secondary landing on the French Riviera, in conjunction with a primary landing in the Bay of Genoa, would allow for an Allied push toward the Brenner Pass; and that simultaneous landings in the Bay of Biscay and the Golfe du Lion would erase German contact with Spain in addition to preventing the Germans from transferring troops to the main invasion area in the north and spurring on the French Resistance in southern and central France.[10]

Blaskowitz wrote,

> As to the time-element, the Army Group at first would have its northern wing tied down at the Atlantic coast (case a). Only later the operational pincer-movement of the Allies would develop in the Mediterranean area (case b). It would then be important whether the Allies would limit the invasion area to France or whether they were intending to expand, by means of an encirclement of Upper Italy, through the Brenner Pass to southern Germany in the Upper Danube Valley (case c). The latter would have unhinged both the Westwall and the Rhine Front at the same time. This operation, of course, was depending on the available forces and landing facilities (case d).
>
> Although fortification and armament of the Atlantic coast had made progress—especially around La Rochelle, to both sides of the Gironde Estuary, around Arcachon and near

Bayonne—the defenses of 450 km. of coastline could still not be safeguarded by four divisions. These forces would at least have to be doubled. While, on the other hand, the 550 km. of the Mediterranean coast were manned by seven divisions, there were, in that sector, hardly any fortified positions worth mentioning as there had not been any time for such preparations. Thus, even along that coast at least ten divisions would have been required.

The armored reserves on hand were sufficient. There remained, however, the question (in view of the enemy air superiority and the vastly extended landing areas) as to whether these forces could be moved up fast enough for a counterattack.

Additional reserves of motorized GHQ Artillery, antitank— and AA-Artillery would have been needed as the danger increased. Fully fit units with up-to-date equipment are the prerequisite for such a calculation. These conditions did not exist. The Coast Defense Divisions suffered from the lack of mobility, the reserves from insufficient training.

Wherein lay the weakness of the ordered rigid coast defense? It tied down locally many weapons and their ammunition. It also tied down at these localities their crews with the necessary supply facilities. It caused the Divisions which had become committed for the defense to expand in such a way that they were unable to form local reserves. It necessitated a widely ramified organization for command and supply. And finally, it aggravated and hindered assembly—and later on timely fusion—of the reserves of the higher command.

This may have been one of the considerations that led the supreme command of the Wehrmacht to this decision for a rigid defense. Aside from any political reasons, as well as those concerning the war-economy, for holding on to the French soil, it was undoubtedly the vast obstacle of the sea which prompted the decision to link up with the outer edges of the coastline. The debarkations of the enemy could furthermore be handicapped and prevented by means of shore—and underwater—obstacles. Constructions of such obstacles, however, which would also be sufficient for periods of low tide, required much time and manpower.

He understood the need for additional German fortification of the French Mediterranean and Atlantic coastlines. His failure to secure such forces from the German war machine proved to be one of the decisive factors in the Allied success of Operation Dragoon.[11]

Gen. Johannes Blaskowitz (center)

Elba—Operation Brassard, Alec Guinness, and de Lattre

Another factor in the success of Dragoon was the "dress rehearsal" for the August 15 invasion. This trial exercise was the invasion and occupation of the island of Elba, near the Dragoon landing beaches, known as Operation Brassard. Here, on the island once occupied by an exiled Napoleon, the Allies refined their operational and strategic maneuvers. During the night of June 16, 1944, French shock battalion commander Major Gambiez and his troops seized seven German shore batteries, with help provided by British and American pursuit and bombardment squadrons, including U.S. Air Corps air support out of Corsica.

Minesweepers tried to create a safe channel for the Elba invaders. One landing craft was destroyed and another damaged. British actor Alec Guinness commanded a British Navy amphibious ship that participated in the invasion of Sicily in July 1943 and Elba in June 1944. Serving in the Royal Navy throughout World War II, Guinness started as a seaman in 1941 and was later commissioned as an officer. (In a theater, movie, and television career that started in 1934 and ended in 2000, he played eighty-two roles. He was awarded the Best Actor in the Oscar and the Golden Globe awards. for his role as Colonel Nicholson in the 1957 film *The Bridge on the River Kwai*. In 1980, he was given an Honorary Academy Award for advancing the art of screen acting in many memorable performances. Guinness wrote four superb books, was awarded a CBE [Commander of the Order of the British Empire] in 1955, and knighted in 1959 in recognition for his acting and wartime service.)

Captain Guinness's ship survived the heavily mined waters around the island of Elba early on June 17, 1944. A French amphibious landing force of 14,999 men, commanded by French general Jean de Lattre de Tassigny, was transported from Corsica forty miles away. After fierce fighting and casualties on both sides, French Commandoes captured the battery guarding the entrance to the bay. They took two thousand three hundred prisoners and seized sixty canons and a great deal of equipment. By June 18, French troops destroyed the German garrison and secured all of Elba within forty-eight hours. Possession of Elba was an important step to further northward advance in Italy and for Operation Dragoon. The Allied landing on Elba was relevant to the success of Operation Dragoon, according to de Lattre from the point of view of the configuration of land and Elba's defensive system. The Elba invasion was a virtual rehearsal. De Lattre also claimed that Operation Brassard would deprive the Germans of the opportunity of driving up the Italian Peninsula.[12] He telegraphed de Gaulle from Elba once the island was captured and reminded the leader of the Free French that it was the anniversary of de Gaulle's great call to honor and resistance in 1940.

De Lattre was born in 1899. He attended the Saint-Cyr military academy and served during World War I. Before World War II, he was assigned to various staff and command positions. Before the June 1940 defeat of France, his troops fought well. De Lattre then served the Vichy government in Tunisia from September 1941 to September

1942. When he opposed the German occupation of all of France in November 1942, de Lattre was imprisoned by the Vichy government and given a ten-year sentence. He succeeded on his fourth attempt to escape prison. In October 1943, British agents helped him reach Free French forces in England. He arrived in North Africa on December 20, 1943. Early in 1944, he was assigned to the position of commander of the Free French II Army. He encouraged his subordinates to argue military strategy with him and was a tough taskmaster and a good teacher with a dramatic flair and little vanity. This dynamic and creative individual was to lead the French forces once the landing was accomplished. General de Gaulle described de Lattre as "emotional, flexible, farsighted and widely curious, influencing the minds around him by the ardor of his spirit and winning loyalty by the exertions of his soul, heading toward his goal by sudden and unexpected leaps, although often well-calculated ones."[13] After his troops captured Elba in June 1944, de Lattre played an important role in the preparation and execution of Operation Dragoon.

The Germans attempted to thwart Allied invasion plans with false intelligence information. In order to persuade them that it would be impossible to successfully invade any part of France, German agents in Paris and Switzerland tried to convince the French that German troop reinforcements were being sent to the Riviera. At Cap Drammont and elsewhere on the beaches of southern France, a plethora of signs warned of minefields. The Germans even supplied false information and maps to the Japanese ambassador to the Vichy government to assure Japan and other Nazi sympathizers of German invincibility.

German deceptions were supported with steel and concrete fortifications, buried deadly mines, mile after mile of barbed wire, trenches, and gun nests. Below the tide lines were abundant killer obstacles. On land there were antiaircraft searchlights, radar stations, roadblocks, antitank obstacles, and demolition devices to welcome and destroy young Americans and Frenchmen. The German defense of southern France consisted of two hundred fifty thousand men, from the excellent Kriegsmarine to the mediocre conscripted foreign legion. De Lattre found these troops to be of "a very good average." They manned a powerful defense system of a continuous coastal barrier that included bunkers, air-raid shelters, minefields, obstructions, wire entanglements, and other dangerous devices. Toulon and Marseille were well defended. General de Lattre concluded that "to the east of the Rhone, besides divisional artillery, there were 45 coastal batteries; between Cavalaire and Agay 150 guns were counted of 75mm or more."[14]

But Allied intelligence greatly diminished the hazards, real and false. Their use of ULTRA—their device to decipher many of the German codes—was of help to General Patch and Admiral Hewitt in separating German defense realities from fiction. American military leaders, using ULTRA and other means of intelligence, learned before the Dragoon D-day that the German defenses on the coast of southern France were a chain of fortifications—a thick layer of defenses, that this defensive crust was not deep and was incapable of resisting a substantial Allied invasion. Hitler's ravings about not surrendering French territory and fighting till his last soldier died ignored overwhelming Allied air and naval superiority and the dramatic increase of French Resistance power. Nevertheless, German defense capabilities were still formidable. The coast that was being guarded was rugged, with many hidden and protected batteries. The enemy had strengthened these with 450 heavy and 1,200 light antiaircraft guns.[15] In the summer of 1944, Hitler and his forces were permeated with a variety of weaknesses.

On July 20, German generals of the staff corps of the Wehrmacht attempted to assassinate Adolf Hitler. Their frustration stemmed from subordination to the Nazi Party and SS. Even though the attempt failed, Hitler was severely shaken. The disciplinary measures taken reverberated throughout the German armed forces: they had been at war for nearly five years; more than one-third of German soldiers had been wounded in battle at least once; young boys and old men were forced into the army, with one unit composed of deaf enlisted men, who were commanded by sick officers. Inadequate food, clothing, and bad news from Germany further depressed morale. The tables had turned; and many German civilians, as well as those serving in the military, had lost their confidence in Hitler and his war. His alleged invincibility in August 1944 was severely damaged. The French, in victory, regained their confidence; and American strength was palpable. The *ONI Weekly* of August 9, 1944, published Prime Minister Churchill's "Review of the War." In a speech to the House of Commons, Churchill stated, "The Germans have certainly had remarkable opportunities of revising the mocking and insulting terms which they put upon the military value of the American Army at the time they declared war on the Great Republic."

It was estimated by the U.S. Naval Intelligence that there were about thirty thousand enemy troops in the zone that the Allied soldiers were to invade, with an additional two hundred thousand German troops nearby.[16] Admiral Hewitt strengthened his armada with two groups of escort carriers, five British carriers commanded by Rear Admiral Troubridge, and four American carriers.[17] Two weeks before August 15, these air groups had spotted naval gunfire targets; however, the Allied escort carriers and their aircraft were not attacked by the Germans. Enemy submarine attacks on Allied vessels had diminished greatly in a few years because of radar detection and increased aerial bombing.[18]

German Submarines

British and American officials held secret meetings early in 1941 in Washington, D.C., to consider the possibility of forming an alliance in fighting Germany, Italy, and Japan. They understood that their war in Europe would ultimately require an invasion, but unless they could protect their ships from German submarines, there would be no invasion. Once the United States was at war with Germany, Hitler ordered an intensification of submarine warfare against American merchant ships and tankers that provided needed supplies to U.S. Allies under the Lend-Lease Act. When it entered World War II, the United States was grossly unprepared for antisubmarine war, according to A. Timothy Warnock,[19] as it had neither trained manpower, nor specialized surface vessels, nor aircraft with requisite flight ranges. The U.S. Army Air Corps had more demands placed on it than it had combat aircraft to supply—about three thousand. This lack of preparedness and other weaknesses (e.g., no specialized detection personnel and equipment such as radar) were immediately acted upon by the Germans. Warnock wrote that within a month of the U.S. declaration of war, the first German submarine arrived in American waters between mid-January 1942 and the end of June 1942; and German U-boats sank a total of 397 ships—off the East Coast, in the Gulf of Mexico, and in the Caribbean Sea, many of them tankers.[20] "By June (1942) the U.S. Navy, supported by the Army Air Force, had driven most of the U-boats from the East Coast but enemy submarines continued to wreak havoc on Allied shipping in the Gulf of Mexico and the Caribbean Sea. The Allies lost three million tons of shipping and five thousand men, mostly in American waters, during the first half of 1942. The loss of cargo grievously endangered Great Britain's ability to continue the war."[21]

Germany's defeat of Norway and France in 1940 provided the victor's submarines easier access to the North Atlantic. The range of German U-boats was extended by the location of French Bay of Biscay ports. Grand Adm. Karl Donitz protected U-boat bases with strong concrete berths at various Biscay ports. The result was to extend the safe range of U-boats operating in the Atlantic. They could patrol areas far from land with less fear of being destroyed by the limited supply of British aircraft, which were desperately needed to fight Luftwaffe raids over Britain. Professor Kathleen Broome Williams's description is worth noting: "The conquest of France solved the problem of extending the range of the U-boats into the Atlantic away from Allied raids. But lack of cooperation from the German Air Force in the location of targets was a continuing source of aggravation for Donitz. Hitler increased the normal friction between the various services and encouraged counterproductive competition by his practice of having conferences . . . with each service chief individually. This made it more difficult for Donitz to secure the cooperation of the Air Force."[22]

On May 24, 1943, about a year before the LST 1012 and other ships crossed the Atlantic Ocean, German submarines were withdrawn from the North Atlantic[23]—the result of an effective Allied antisubmarine strategy. It should be recalled that the human costs involved in the German submarine warfare campaign are replete with tragedy. About 41,000 Germans engaged in submarine operations, 27,378 were killed and 4,945 became prisoners. Allied losses were even greater: 30,249 men of the British Merchant Navy; 73,642 men of the Royal Navy; 1,965 men of the Royal Canadian Navy, and 2,000 Americans lost in Atlantic waters.[24]

By the summer of 1944, the Allies had removed the German submarine menace in the Atlantic Ocean and controlled the Mediterranean. They had also gained what the United States Office of Naval Intelligence called "a secret army." Earlier that spring, Prime Minister Churchill declared that the French had "a powerful underground army of the interior which may be called upon to play an important part before the end of the war."[25] That secret army was a product of the French National Council of Resistance. After the failure of French Communists, from 1941 to 1943, to unify all of France's contentious resistance groups, de Gaulle's National Council of Resistance was successful in creating liaison among the many French military units. The coordination of these disparate groups caused the Germans considerable trouble: their trains and transportation networks were wrecked and their soldiers killed and

German communications were disrupted and their food reserves and ammunition destroyed. Advancing Allied invasion troops were helped by French workers in strategic positions.[26]

Resistance groups, many under the sway of Communist leaders, began to organize resistance to the German occupation, especially in and around Paris. One such agitator was Henri Rol-Tanguy, leader of the Francs-Tireurs et Partisans (Snipers and Partisans) resistance group.[27] Credited with building the main underground movement in the Anjou area, Rol-Tanguy became a captain in the FFI (French Forces of the Interior), a group that was often at odds with de Gaulle's FFF.

The Resistance movement had also gained enormous power in the rural areas of southern France, and this was another significant factor in the success of Operation Dragoon. But although the Vichy government was being displaced in rural France—weakened by the Germans and by Resistance opposition—the Germans were still powerful in the urban areas. A German minder constantly watched Marshal Pétain; and Hitler's war production czar, Albert Speer, demanded ninety-one thousand Frenchmen to work in the German fatherland. In the first third of 1944, however, less than twenty thousand French workers ended up in Germany. Many members of the *Millice*—the Vichy government's police force—were people who joined up to escape forced labor in Germany; others were criminals. They intensified their viciousness toward suspected opponents and Jews.

Vichy propagandists presented their police state government as the French people's defender against anarchy, chaos, and revolution; and they tried to frighten the populace by portraying Resistance fighters as terrorists and Communists. *Millice* members joined German troops in killing French Resistance members and civilians. Before the invasions of Normandy and southern France, it was easy for German propagandists and their French adherents to enflame hatred against the Allies. German massacres and Allied aerial bombing devastated the French before their nation was liberated.[28]

Unlike spring 1940, by the summer of 1944, French forces were led by competent commanders, such as Gen. Alphonse Juin, Philippe Leclerc de Hauteclocque, and Jean de Lattre de Tassigny. French troops and commanders learned quickly how to use modern weapons and tactics to defeat the enemy. General Leclerc's Second Armored Division fought the Germans at Normandy, and French troops returned in far greater force during Operation Dragoon.[29]

Lt. Gen. Ira C. Eaker, the U.S. Air commander in chief in the Mediterranean Theater, interceded in allowing a forty-three-year-old French pilot to continue flying after he had been grounded in 1943 after crash-landing his plane in Tunis. That pilot was none other than Antoine de Saint-Exupéry, author of the aviation classic *Night Flight* and the world-famous *The Little Prince*. Eaker encouraged training and equipping of the French Air Force. He was, according to playwright Clare Boothe Luce, a talented writer. In the early 1930s, he requested that the U.S. Army Air Force allow him to attend the University of Southern California so that he could get a degree in journalism. Gen. Douglas MacArthur, then chief of staff of the U.S. Army, denied his request; yet Eaker persisted and succeeded in convincing MacArthur's superior, the acting secretary of war, to overturn the decision. For a year and a half, Eaker pursued his studies at USC. For eighteen years after he retired from the air force, Eaker wrote a weekly column that appeared in hundreds of newspapers throughout the United States. In all those years, he missed only one week.[30]

French Resistance members carried out 960 acts of railway sabotage in the first week after the Normandy invasion (June 6, 1944). Overconfident French men and women boldly and often recklessly confronted German troops who were far stronger militarily. In the town of Tulle, the French killed some German prisoners alleged to be Gestapo members. In retribution, German soldiers herded all the male inhabitants into an armament factory and hung them from the town's lampposts and balconies.[31] Despite this and other atrocities suffered by the French people during 1944, many former Nazi sympathizers realized that the Germans would lose the war and that it was time to transfer their allegiance to the Allies.

Gen. Francisco Franco of Spain was one such opportunist who took steps in May 1944 to ingratiate himself and the Spanish government to the Allies. British foreign secretary Anthony Eden told the House of Commons that Spain was taking measures to expel German and Japanese agents from Tangiers and that measures to limit Spanish exports, including wolfram (tungsten), to Germany would soon be put in effect.[32] (Wolfram is a rare metallic element used in alloys and electric lamp filaments.) Franco's cooperation also included releasing Italian ships under Spanish control to the Allies.[33]

General Franco was not the only one who transformed his loyalties in 1944; Bulgarian, Turkish, and other pro-Axis leaders also deserted the Germans. An OSS report about the French underground concluded that a phenomenal change had occurred between the time of the country's defeat in June 1940 and 1944. Whereas in 1940 there was only a weak, scattered, disorganized, and fractious French Resistance, a remarkable transformation had occurred in four years. The OSS found that "at least 90 per cent of the French people are anti-German and prepared to support the underground."[34] Leading the movement toward this remarkable national unity was none other than the remarkable Charles de Gaulle.

De Gaulle Visits America

On July 6, 1944, General de Gaulle, at Roosevelt's invitation, visited the United States. The visit went well. Adm. William Leahy recommended that the U.S. should recognize de Gaulle's government, and the U.S. accepted the French Committee of National Liberation as the working authority for civilian administration in the liberated areas of France. The Soviet Union had previously accorded the group full recognition.[35]

Brigadier General de Gaulle arrived in Washington, D.C., at 4:00 p.m., where the temperature was a steamy ninety-four degrees. A platoon of French air cadets and three squadrons of U.S. airmen greeted him with an honor guard and a seventeen-gun salute. After a band played "The Marseillaise" and "The Star-Spangled Banner," he shook hands with U.S. Army chief of staff Gen. George C. Marshall; Gen. Hap Arnold, head of the air force; Lieutenant General Vandergrift, head of the U.S. Marines; Adm. Ernest J. King; and a number of State Department and White House officials. De Gaulle was then whisked away to the Oval Office, where Roosevelt met the general's icy reserve with a flurry of charm and chitchat.

A tired, aging Cordell Hull hosted a gold-plate dinner early that evening for the exhausted de Gaulle, but it was a subdued affair. De Gaulle appeared thinner to guests than his photographs. He consumed a vast quantity of manhattans and French, Portuguese, and American wines. Then he finished off a dinner of squab and asparagus tips. Other than a brief comment about the history of French and American relationships, the general said little. At 10:42 p.m., he strode the lobby of the Canton Hotel amidst applause of loungers who rose to their feet.

On July 7, de Gaulle and his committee worked on French liberation plans at the elegant home of Henri Hoppenot, his representative in the United States. He made it clear that the shame of France's defeat would be eradicated, that Germans must be destroyed or driven out of France, and that the French must depend upon themselves. On July 10, Roosevelt sent Churchill a telegram that read,

> I am prepared to accept [De Gaulle's] committee as temporary de facto authority for civil administration in France provided two things are clear—first, complete authority to be reserved to Eisenhower to do what he feels necessary to conduct effective military operations, and, second, that French people be given opportunity to make free choice of their own government. I have asked officials here to take British drafts as a base and modify them to insure these points, and they will shortly be in touch with your people here. Suggest you authorize your political and military officials here to work out details immediately with our officials for final clearance through the Combined Chiefs of Staff. General De Gaulle is leaving behind officials qualified to deal with this matter. I urge that no publicity be given these arrangements until they are finally cleared. The visit has gone off very well.[36]

On July 8, President Roosevelt and General de Gaulle met for a third and last time. Neither disclosed the results of their discussions. But undisputed reports indicated that the French were highly gratified by the results of the conference. President Roosevelt announced, on July 11, that the United States recognized de Gaulle's provisional government as the de facto authority for the civil administration of the liberated territory of France.

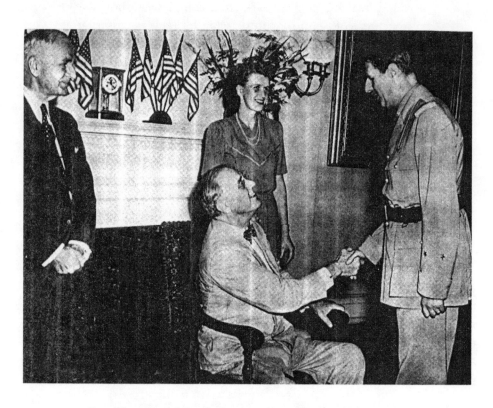

President Franklin D. Roosevelt welcomes General de
Gaulle to the White House on July 6, 1944.

When de Gaulle arrived in New York City, he mentioned comforting talks with President Roosevelt. Mayor Fiorello H. LaGuardia gave the general a tremendous reception. De Gaulle was hailed as the symbol of a free France by the mayor and others. Prime Minister Churchill also claimed that the great improvement in relations between the government of the United States and the French National Committee headed by de Gaulle was due in large part to this visit.[37]

Over a four-day visit, de Gaulle accomplished much in addition to social and cultural visits. He visited Mount Vernon, held a press conference, and succeeded in obtaining Roosevelt's acceptance of his Committee of National Liberation as a working tool to foster harmony between the United States and France. By extending every possible courtesy toward his guest, and assuring de Gaulle that the United States did not intend to usurp any French colonial territory, Roosevelt reduced the hostility that had existed between them. De Gaulle's contribution to this thawing of an initially cold relationship was also laudable. He reciprocated courtesy and was appreciative of the gracious hospitality shown him. But he made it clear to his hosts that in peacetime France would have a national status on par with the United States, Britain, and the Soviet Union.

Admiral Hewitt pointed out that General de Gaulle "was very anxious that we [Anglo-Americans] should give adequate support to the French Army as it advanced along the coast of Toulon and Marseille, and that we would utilize French cruisers and battleships for that purpose. I was able to assure him that we would do that, to the very best of our ability."[38]

As de Gaulle and French Resistance forces gained in strength, Vichy's political control and effectiveness was weakened in the area where Operation Dragoon was to take place. Pressure from their constituents caused the mayors of the Var and other departments to resign. After the collapse of the Vichy-controlled municipal governments, Resistance leaders stepped in to provide essential services for the populace. By Bastille Day 1944 (July 14), some municipal police forces had been neutralized and were no longer a threat to the Resistance movement. As the likelihood of a German defeat became more apparent, some of Vichy's austerity policies changed. For example, sensual music and public dancing that, according to the aged Marshal Pétain, were responsible for the degeneracy of pre-World War II France, and had been prohibited, were now overlooked in the summer of 1944. Also, once the Germans replaced the Italian occupiers in southern France, curfews and blackouts had been enforced, and the sheltering of Jews and deserting soldiers was severely punished.

De Gaulle chose General de Lattre de Tassigny as commander of the French troops that would participate in the invasion of southern France. His troops were to come ashore on the Delta beaches east of Sainte-Maxime. General Patch later approved of de Lattre's tactical plan to attack Toulon, according to which French troops, consisting of French, Algerian, Senegalese, and Moroccan forces, would encircle, isolate, and penetrate both Toulon and Marseille. Generals de Lattre, Patch, and Truscott—were dynamic and aggressive leaders who promoted coordination between French Resistance groups and Anglo-American troops.

Resistance fighters in southern France were directed to attack rail, electrical, telegraph, and other military installations; and by August 10, all secondary rail lines in Grenoble and west of the Rhone River between Limoges and Marseille were destroyed. Allied military planners expected the enemy's destruction of important military installations and crucial infrastructure; therefore, on August 14, groups of OSS teams were sent to protect vital sites in southern France. One such site was an important hydroelectric power plant at Eguzon. The OSS team that undertook this mission was dispatched to the field in five planes and was equipped with an abundant supply of arms and devices to accomplish its objectives. They also had five hundred ninety thousand French francs and $1,250 for bribes.

Also in August, OSS Operational Group Patrick, consisting of twenty-five men—three officers and twenty-two enlisted men—was sent to the Indre region of France for this type of work. Some of the men landed a mile or more from the parachute-dropping zone. For those who suffered sprains after jumping from the five Liberator planes, there was a carefully organized reception committee that provided doctors for the injured and food and shelter for the entire team in a nearby farmhouse.

French Resistance groups of some 3,220 men had a total of 1,000 weapons among them, some stolen from the Germans. Clearly, the Resistance fighters were poorly armed. There had been numerous requests for rifles to be parachuted to this group, but these pleas went unanswered.[39] OSS head Major General Donovan and his lieutenants looked for opportunities for French Resistance members to take on the Germans. The OSS, however, was a comparatively new and inexperienced organization obstructed by jurisdictional and bureaucratic disagreements and hindered by inter-Allied political squabbles, inadequate training, and transportation. Recognizing that the British had more experience in developing shadow warfare organizations, Gen. Jacob Devers in 1943 ordered that OSS special operations and secret intelligence activities be merged with those of Britain, thus placing OSS operations under British control.[40] By the June 6, 1944, invasion of Normandy, OSS and Resistance strength had increased substantially.[41] The supplies provided by the U.S. Lend-Lease program played an important role in the liberation of France, notwithstanding their repackaging by British and French Allies, which misrepresented the true source of weapons and other necessities.

People from all walks of life helped to free France. Nuns from religious nursing orders, Jewish doctors, Protestants, and people with first-aid experience often worked in hospitals to treat wounded Resistance fighters and perform emergency surgery. Evacuating injured fighters was often difficult because they had to be transported through areas dense with German soldiers.

The mobility and widespread presence of French Resistance fighters across southern France hampered German response to Dragoon, which compelled the enemy to remain in their fortifications until the last minute, forcing them to improvise their retreat. German troops were the targets of French Resistance fighters and Allied aerial bombardment, leading, in one instance, to the surrender of four thousand German soldiers. Resistance fighters reported to General de Lattre about civilian hardships. From November 24, 1943, to August 6, 1944, for example, Toulon was heavily bombed eight times, its people subjected to both Allied Air Force bombing and German demolition. The Germans cut off Toulon's electricity, forcing frightened residents to sleep outside the city, under pine trees, in olive groves in the countryside, or in cellars. To ease Toulon's hardships, seven canteens were opened, bakeries were established, flour and vegetables were rationed, and the injured and sick were treated. De Lattre's request to the Allies to relieve the suffering of the people of Toulon was promptly approved by Generals Devers and Patch. French troops and Resistance fighters subsequently defeated the enemy in Toulon and elsewhere later in August. The cost of liberation: two thousand seven hundred French dead and wounded, thousands of enemy troops killed, and seventeen thousand German prisoners captured.

After the Dragoon invasion, no German column of troops crossed to the south unscathed. Free French forces serving on the Mediterranean coast swiftly liberated eastern France, from Provence to Burgundy. In the town of Saint-Pons, the hospital consultant tended both French and German wounded. This humane act led the German commander to revoke his order to kill the entire population of the town. On August 17, when their commander ordered the execution of fifty hostages in retaliation against Resistance action, recuperating German soldiers in another hospital persuaded him to revoke the order. Resistance members were not blameless either; some robbed pro-German French families, and French women reported to have had sex with Germans were unjustly punished while many male collaborators went unscathed.

Geoffrey M. T. Jones, Moe Berg, and the OSS

Geoff Jones was instrumental in helping the French regain their country from the German occupiers. He worked as an OSS agent to gather intelligence related to the invasion of southern France. Jones was flown to Algiers on May 22, 1944, to begin preparations for his mission on mainland France. Jones remembered that en route to Algiers,

> there were maybe 10-15 of us in the front [of the plane] but I didn't pay attention because it was a short flight and you don't want to talk to somebody 'cause somebody's going to ask what you do and you don't want to talk or tell them anything. But when we were about an hour out someone said we should be getting in soon. We all looked at our watches and, as I looked up from my watch, I looked across the way and the guy's looking at his watch—an OSS watch. You know who it was? Moe Berg, the professional baseball player. [Moe Berg went to Princeton and later to Columbia. He was not only a ballplayer with the Boston Red Sox but also a lawyer recruited by the OSS. Jones recalled that Berg "communicated in five or six languages," and due to his height and girth, he stuck out in a crowd.]
>
> He was a big lumbering guy, he was about 6'2" and weighed about 210-220 pounds . . . . I didn't know who he was at the time [of the incident onboard the plane to Algiers], but we looked at each other and laughed.
>
> At one point he [Berg] said, "What are you going to do?" I said I hadn't been told yet. I was supposed to go to the Vercors. This was a plateau in the middle of France with big mountains nearby. French Resistance fighters were called upon prematurely to rise up, without preparation or equipment.

The idiots on the plateau on the Vercors raised the French flag, which the German general in Lyon could see through his binoculars. It was only a matter of time before they got wiped out. I was supposed to go in there with some field artillery and parachute in. There was only one way to get there by car. It was a terrible road and it was easy to jam up. Luckily for me, British General Sir Henry Maitland Wilson cancelled my assignment.

Right after I got there [and the assignment cancelled], Moe Berg said, "Why don't you come with me?" . . . I learned later on that Moe became one of the Allies' most important atomic energy spies. He gathered crucial information on the most important German scientists. His assignment was to find out just how near the Germans were to deploying an atomic bomb. As a disguised OSS agent, Moe went to Switzerland to hear Werner Heisenberg give a lecture in Zurich and concluded that the Germans were not close to developing an atomic bomb.

I was to put French agents from Algiers in southern France before the invasion of Aug. 15, 1944. In my apartment in the Casbah, there was a full closet with all sorts of clothes from different places for our agents. So, if someone had to go to Lyon, we had clothes, shoes, hats from Lyon. I didn't have documentation—that was a whole other group, but I did have a big rack of shoes.[42]

To prepare the French Resistance for the forthcoming Dragoon invasion, Jones was to organize French agents where Allied troops were to land on August 15. He was to lead them in destroying a radar station in the Cap Drammont area and oversee the clearing of glider landings and drop-zone areas. It was important to remove the tall, dangerous sharply pointed stalks and the horrible German barbed wire and bombs designed to kill or cripple Allied paratroopers. These monstrosities were called Rommel Spargel or Rommel's Asparagus.

In order to blend in with the French country dwellers, Jones wore an old blue suit, similar to what French workers wore in the fields or factories. He let his hair grow out so that it was unruly, and he grew a "substantial moustache." The identification document that he was given stated "that I was a mute and so exempt from military service and only fit to help farmers in the field."[43]

Capt. Geoffrey M. T. Jones, 1944

Forged identity card of Geoffrey M. T. Jones

Jones was one of ninety-three liaison teams, known as Jedburghs, who were trained to parachute into France. Each team included two officers and a sergeant who was a radioman. Many of the radios were damaged because of incompetent packing. The Jedburgh teams provided French Resistance groups with additional weapons, training, and sabotage instruction. Frequently, the Jedburgh teams supplied valuable liaison assistance to the Allied High Command. When he was to be parachuted into France (into the Basses-Alpes) prior to Dragoon, Jones had orders to destroy the only radar station in the area, organize the French Resistance, and help to clear and secure the planned airborne drop-zone and glider-landing areas. Once on the ground, he was put in contact with the Marquis de Mons, the group he was responsible for training.

Jones almost didn't make his mission, having originally been considered to have known too much about the planned invasion to be risked parachuting into enemy territory. But the agent who was initially assigned the duty was captured by the Gestapo, and Jones was the only available and able agent to conduct the mission. Women were assigned to missions as well; among them was Betty Lussier, who helped to set up a double-agent network in Perpignan, France.[44] Isabel Pell was also involved in the Resistance, helping to organize a female network that staffed Jones's OSS headquarters.

Operating out of the countryside and using weapons and intelligence provided in part by the Allies, the French Resistance demolished the German logistical lines. M. R. D. Foot claimed in his 1966 work, *SOE in France,* that "so thoroughly had the termites of resistance eaten away by now the pillars that German authority rested in southern France that the whole structure crumbled to powder in days."[45]

OSS networks established in southern France under Henry Hyde worked closely with the Seventh Army's Col. William W. Quinn, assistant chief of staff for intelligence. Hyde was based in Algiers, North Africa; and from the reports of his agents, the Seventh Army was able to piece together a detailed picture of German disposition and strength.[46] Raised in France, Hyde was recruited to the OSS by its founder, Maj. Gen. William Donovan. Hyde's fluency in both French and German was of crucial importance to his work during the war. His intelligence network in France, known as Operation Penny Farthing, gleaned valuable information that helped the Allies plan Operations Overlord and Dragoon.

Dr. Stanley Lovell was an OSS chemist in charge of developing devices and underhanded tricks. Members of the French Resistance used his inventions in Operation Dragoon. On one occasion, two German divisions ordered to stop the Allied attack were moving in trucks on French highways. Manning the gasoline filling stations on the highways were French Resistance groups. Lowell explained what happened: "As the gasoline station attendant inserted his hose in the filling pipe—or as he withdrew it—he dropped a 'firefly' into it. This was a small plastic cylinder into which was placed an explosive charge. The device would explode after several hours, when the German vehicle was far away from the gasoline pump." Lovell attributed much of the success of Dragoon to the little "firefly."[47]

After August 15, 1944, the U.S. Seventh Army, working with the OSS, sent into Germany thirty-seven German agents. They had been recruited from prisoner-of-war camps, trained, and equipped to fight against Hitler inside Germany. They did good work, but two went missing and were presumed to have been killed.[48]

One U.S. Army captain, John Ball, known by his war name Capitaine Niveau, assisted the Maquis and was well liked and respected. Ball led the Maquis in sabotage and guerrilla stings against the German units stationed in his area. He had an affinity for the area; and after his discharge from the army, he decided to remain in France, in Annecy, where he was stationed. There, he married one of the local girls and became a hotel restaurant owner.

Agents such as Geoff Jones who obtained intelligence were questioned by their superiors after completing their missions. Lt. Col. Kenneth H. Baker of the U.S. Army prepared a final report for the Special Projects Operation Center for a debriefing of Allied intelligence operations in southern France. Based upon statements from all the personnel who operated in the area in summer 1944, the report found that the composition of this intelligence group was 15-20 percent American, 30-35 percent British, and about 50 percent French; that the chief of the major French Resistance organization (FFI Vaucluse) was responsible for keeping southern French intelligence operating by providing transportation necessary for the delivery of necessities; that access to air transport into and out of France was difficult "because of the very rudimentary and disorganized state of air transport at the time"; that while the conflicts between the officers and men and women of the three nationalities seemed serious at the time, in retrospect it appeared that the frictions that did develop were unavoidable and did not injure the execution of the entire operation as was feared at the time; that the briefing of personnel sent to various missions was often inadequate in that proper priorities were not attached to each target—intelligence and sabotage agents admitted to a tendency to attack wrong targets since these were unimportant to the Germans. "The net result," wrote Baker, "was that targets were sometimes attacked in reverse importance to the enemy" and that intelligence was not recent enough in some instances. For example, an agent would be briefed concerning the attack of a railroad only to discover, upon arrival there, that the railroad in question had not been operational for several months.[49]

The Steadfast Countess and Other Aristocrats

Countess Frances Gruiociardi started out as Frances Hyde from New Jersey. In 1928, she visited her sister who was living in Paris. A banker friend invited Frances to dine with him and Count Horace Gruiociardi, and a few months later she was a countess. When the U.S. Seventh Army liberated southern France in August 1944, the countess was discovered on an invasion beachhead. The *Stars and Stripes* staff correspondent, Sgt. Stan Swinton, reported that when the countess first encountered her fellow Americans, she asked, "Have you got a Lucky Strike? I'm dying for one."[50]

For four years she had sought safety for herself and her family in a small Riviera farm buried in the vineyards, far from any major city. Her family had pleaded with her to return to the United States, but she insisted on remaining with her husband. He stayed with the family until the money ran out, then he left for Paris. Their two children, François, 14, and Mary, 11, stayed with the countess. There was little food. They received 150 kilograms of bread a day—enough for only one meal. There was no milk—the countryside was too dry for cows. Black markets provided food for the rich; for the rest there was nothing. She weighed only ninety-five pounds, but the countess and her son plowed the earth to dig a garden and grow potatoes. Sergeant Swinton reported the countess's words: "All day I did nothing but scramble for food for my children. In the morning I would get on the bicycle and ride everywhere until I found food. Now you soldiers have given me food. But it was very hard . . . . the Germans? They were very correct. And they were lonely—always they wanted to show pictures of their children and family. When they began to trample through my living room to use the telephone they paid half of the telephone bill. They were very correct

298

but they were the enemy. Ten days ago many of them left for the north. We knew that if you invaded you would have little trouble here. But we thought you would not come to this little, forgotten village."[51]

Another French aristocrat from Provence assisted in the mapping of the coastal area of southern France. Existing maps were checked against photographs, and it became obvious that they were inaccurate and not acceptable for combat use. Continuous photography, however, was impossible, in part because cloudy wintry weather frustrated flight. As American, French, and Russian leaders became more insistent upon the invasion of southern France, the need for reliable mapping and reconnaissance became urgent. Toward the end of July 1944, a French reconnaissance group took off from Corsica. Maj. Antoine Marie Roger de Saint-Exupéry and his colleagues knew nothing about the Anvil/Dragoon landing—where it was to take place and when—nor did he know that the invasion was to occur where his sister lived. All he knew was that he had enough fuel for six hours of flight and that he was supposed to return to Corsica at 1430 hours after fulfilling his reconnaissance emission in the Grenoble and Annecy regions. Saint-Exupéry never returned from that mission.

According to Jacques Robichon's *The Second D-Day,* pages 50-51, his mother, Countess Marie de Saint-Exupéry, that afternoon, was on her way to share her food ration coupons with a worker's family in Grasse, less than two miles from the village of Cabris where she lived. The countess, sixty-nine, had been widowed when she was twenty-nine. Her young son, François, had died in the Great War. She had not seen Antoine in four years, as he had gone to the United States. There, he and pilot-author Anne Morrow Lindbergh were lovers. She was the wife of aviator Charles A. Lindbergh and the daughter of J. P. Morgan's partner, Ambassador Dwight Morrow, for whom a ship was named.

Completion of the mapping and reconnaissance of southern France by aerial photography and other means provided Allied military planners with life-saving information: suitable locations for the landing of paratroopers and other airborne units were identified; photographs were provided to the strategic air force concerning roads, railroads, and marshalling yards and manufacturing centers; the tactical air force was able to target bridges, dams, and road junctions; the selection of suitable beaches for the landing of troops was based on the mapping; and thorough aerial photography helped to determine the water depth and pinpoint underwater obstacles.

Maps drawn by OSS agents noted enemy fuel stations, ammunition depots, and transportation bottlenecks. The Eighth and Fifteenth Army Air Force used these maps to the advantage of Allied soldiers and sailors. On August 12 and 13, the OSS was still transmitting information to Admiral Hewitt's flagship, the *Catoctin*, dealing with enemy gun emplacements, airport data, and antiparachute stakes at Le Muy. This crucial information was sent to General Patch, who was on board the *Catoctin*. It also helped paratroopers under the command of Maj. Gen. Robert T. Frederick. Secret intelligence reports to the OSS continued to provide life-saving information even after the August 15 landing. Behind German lines, valiant men and women sent detailed information concerning German troop strength and locations; and in less than two hours that valuable information was transmitted to OSS headquarters in Algiers, relayed to London, and then to aircraft bomber pilots. An entire German division was destroyed using such information.

The rearmed French Air Force, under the command of General Bouscat, consisted of fighter planes, bombers, and reconnaissance aircraft. Skilled French pilots, navigators, bombardiers, gunners, mechanics, and other technicians were part of the Mediterranean Allied Air Force (MAAF). There were one thousand aircraft in the MAAF, under Gen. Ira Eaker, and two hundred planes aboard Allied aircraft carriers. The Germans had one hundred air bombers, and their sea-power strength consisted of about ten submarines and about thirty small surface ships. The French Navy contributed a battleship, five cruisers, five light cruisers, five destroyers, and almost fifteen small vessels.[52]

The chief of the French Naval Mission in the United States, Vice Adm. R. Fenard, sent a secret letter to Vice Admiral Hewitt dated July 18, 1944. After expressing his gratitude for Hewitt's many kindnesses and courtesies, Fenard continued, "Your keen understanding of our problems and your friendly cooperation have meant so much to me, as they show that you have the interests of France at heart. It has reassured me greatly to learn that you approve assigning an aircraft to the French Navy. The addition of such a vessel to our fleet should obviously be of greatest importance, particularly in view of the increasing strength of the French Naval Air Arm, and also as it will enable us to take a much greater part in the war effort."[53]

In the weeks before Dragoon, the war was going well for the Allies. They broke out of Normandy on July 31, 1944, and General Patton's Third Army moved through Brittany while other Allied troops advanced eastward and headed through the Seine. The military wing of the Resistance, the FFI (French Forces of the Interior), consisted of thirty thousand armed troops, ready to fight. Their success in defeating the enemy at various French naval bases and their other victories so impressed British and American generals that the role of the Resistance was expanded for Operation Dragoon.[54]

Once OSS Director Donovan informed General Marshall that Communists in the movement were not planning to take over the French government, General Eisenhower and his Supreme Headquarters Allied Expeditionary Forces (SHAEF) staff were eager to have the French Resistance work with Allied Armed Forces planners and the OSS. Donovan's suggestions to his military superiors were based on reports provided by OSS agents Joseph R. Starr and David Rockefeller. According to these agents, Communist resisters were motivated by patriotism and nationalism. Increased trust in the loyalty of Resistance members led to improved cooperation between them and the OSS. Hundreds of agents were sent into southern France from January to July 1944, with orders to send back military reports to headquarters. From the beginning of August 1944, Anglo-American agents were instructed to supply political information. Foreign agents were told to inform the French people that they were serving the French military commander, General Koenig.

Serious disagreements between de Gaulle and American leaders persisted because of his sensitivity to slights to French honor, such as providing Allied troops with counterfeit French currency before the Normandy landing. Roosevelt viewed de Gaulle as someone who was more concerned about satisfying his ambition than serving France's best interests. This hostility was shared by many American civil and military leaders. They were infuriated by de Gaulle's initial refusal to allow 120 French liaison officers to leave for France during the Normandy invasion, because he had argued that liaison officers were trained for administrative duties and that the Allies would use them for other purposes. They did go to France, in the end, but a little later than originally scheduled and after much confusion and acrimony. Secretary of State Cordell Hull was informed by the acting American representative to the Free Committee of National Liberation on June 4 that de Gaulle was "full of suspicion concerning American intentions and furious because it appears in London the Americans will not be prepared to discuss French affairs with de Gaulle on a governmental level as will the British . . ." U.S.

representative Chapin let de Gaulle's representative know that the United States was "making a very important contribution at great expense of blood and treasure toward the liberation of France and its people."[55] Chapin acknowledged that on the front in Italy, which he had visited,

> perfect harmony reigns between French and American forces that are fighting side by side. In Algiers, however, the effects of a French inferiority complex . . . are manifest at every turn and have been since arrival in this area of General de Gaulle, marked by suspicion of Anglo-American motives and hardening criticism of our military, economic, financial, and political performance.
>
> The facts are that the United States has rearmed and helped train a new French Army, is rebuilding the French Navy, is supplying this theater of operations with the bulk of its supplies, has cooperated loyally with the FCNL in territories acknowledging jurisdiction, has publicly declared that its political purpose in France is to see a free and happy French people at full liberty to choose its own governmental institutions and personalities and to cooperate with the French in the relief and rehabilitation of the country—these do not seem to satisfy.
>
> I also referred to the fact that in London de Gaulle has access to General Eisenhower who has the President's confidence and authority, as well as Ambassadors Winant and Phillips on the civil side both of whom surely have adequate rank and prestige to satisfy General de Gaulle's sense of proprieties. Should General de Gaulle decide to proceed to Washington after London he would unquestionably receive a dignified and appropriate reception. But the difficulty in all this, my contacts agreed, is that de Gaulle insists on American recognition of himself as head of Government of France. At that point his ideas and American policy seem to clash. Is the reason for this unsatisfactory state of affairs that one man seeks to dominate the French picture and if not permitted to have his own way in all things he proposes to gain his points by employing a technique of blackmail and threats on the slightest provocation? Frenchmen who disagree are ruthlessly suppressed as witness yesterday's order consigning Senator

Mallarmé at seventy years of age to forced residence in Algeria. We know that de Gaullist elements in North Africa for months have carried on a subtle campaign against Americans casting suspicion on American motives for example the whispering campaign that the United States intended to keep Morocco and that American troops would never leave there. When our troops left Morocco the same circles commenced stories that the Americans were buying up railways and public utilities and intended to dominate the economic life of French North Africa. The press under de Gaulle's influence frequently maintains a subtle anti-American line and has done so for a long time. We fared at least as well under the Vichy press as rotten as it was. Under the present system of course we are permitted to supply the newsprint. Men like Massigli and Puaux[56] are fully conscious of these things. They advance the reason, which I believe correct, that the French are torn by anxiety regarding their homeland, and suffer from the tortured mentality of exiles whose nerves are frayed as a result of humiliation and fears of uncertainty and privation. They suggest that even de Gaulle once his feet are planted again on French metropolitan soil will relax. Right now Franco-American relations suffer and it is to be recommended that we be as tolerant and kind as is our tradition.[57]

Many Allied intelligence operations were imaginative and effective. For instance, the OSS established a dummy broadcast circuit that operated on a twenty-four-hour basis from July 13 to August 9, 1944, to confuse the Germans concerning Operation Dragoon landing sites.[58] Fleet Admiral Ernest J. King, in his official report to the secretary of the navy concerning Operation Dragoon, wrote,

About eight hours before the main landings, French Commandoes and units of the First Special Forces were landed near Cap Negre and the Hyères Islands by forces under command of Rear Admiral L.A. Davidson. Rear Admiral T.E. Chandler (subsequently killed in the Philippine Islands in January 1945) commanded a group of Gunfire Support ships. Of this force no resistance was met on the islands, and only inaccurate machine-gun and small arms on the mainland.

In the meantime, diversionary groups were operating to the eastward in the Nice-Cannes area and in the westward between Toulon and Marseille, where a mock landing and repulse were staged at La Ciotat, producing considerable enemy reaction. The bombings, in tactical support of the landing, commenced before daylight on D-day. This was followed at dawn with heavy and medium bombing for one hour and twenty minutes, by more than 1,300 aircraft along a 40-mile front. The execution of this plan in conjunction with naval gunfire and barrages of rockets appeared to paralyze the enemy defenses on the initial, assault beaches.[59]

A special operations group, under the command of Capt. Henry C. Johnson, (USN), carried out several diversionary operations. This group consisted of one U.S. destroyer, the *Endicott*, two British gunboats, two British fighter director ships, thirteen high-speed airplane rescue crafts, eight motor torpedo boats, and eight motor launchers. For D-day operations, this force was to be divided into two units. The eastern unit departed from Ajaccio, Corsica, on the morning of August 14 and took a northerly course as if it was headed toward Genoa. The eastern unit was provided with the fighter cover to keep reconnaissance planes away. During the night, north of Corsica, it was joined by twelve motor torpedo boats from Bastia. Upon making this rendezvous, three PT boats headed toward Nice to form a shield against enemy high-speed, armed motorboats. Four PT boats proceeded to the Gulf of Naples. The objective was to land seventy French naval commandoes at Theoule-sur-Mer. These commandoes destroyed the road leading from Cannes toward the Camel area, where various Allied vessels, including LST 1012, were to land. To prevent the enemy from learning about the assault area, various confusion and deception tactics were deployed. One was the use of sound devices to simulate a landing: gunboats simultaneously bombarded the defenses of this nonlanding area; reflector balloons were streamed to simulate a twelve-by-eight-mile-wide convoy moving to La Ciotat (which lies between Toulon and Marseille); a German radar station near Toulon, Cap Sicie, was intentionally left unmolested by Allied bombing so that it would be able to observe and report false information. To prevent the enemy from bringing up reinforcements to the assault beaches, commando raids destroyed shore batteries at Cavalaire Beach, Cap Negre, and Le Trayas.

As the assaulting armada was proceeding along the west coast of Sardinia and Corsica, a command headquarters was arranged for Gen. Henry M. Wilson and his colleagues on board a ship in Ajaccio Harbor. In his magisterial *Eight Years Overseas*, General Wilson admitted to anxiety concerning the possibility of early morning fog and other misfortunes. All went well, however; and it was a marvelous sight—the different echelons, each with its escort vessels containing a progressively larger landing craft, from LCIs in front to LCTs and LSTs farther astern. Finally, there was the bombardment fleet and troop and supply ships.

The proud Allied armada was confronted with threats of enemy gunnery. The Germans had salvaged two 340-mm guns from the scuttled French battleship *Provence* in Toulon Harbor and had replaced two guns there. Courageous workers at the Toulon navy yard sabotaged one gun, and Allied air attacks put the other turret out of action. When the Allies sought to silence the Toulon shore battery, only a single 340-mm gun was in condition to return fire. Allied planners believed that a dangerous enemy battery of 164-mm guns was located on the extreme eastern end of Levant Island, one of the Hyères group, but the French had sabotaged this battery in November 1942. The Germans repaired and later removed it, replacing this battery with four dummy guns made of wood. Allied reconnaissance planes photographed these guns, and despite evidence from the French submarine *Casablanca*, the belief lingered that these dummy guns were real. Moreover, an Allied reconnaissance flight had closed to within ten thousand meters of the alleged battery on the night of June 8, 1944, and had not been fired upon.

One diversionary operation was called "Rosie." Commanded by Lt. Cmdr. Douglas Fairbanks Jr., Rosie simulated a task force headed for Genoa. Fairbanks played a leading role in striking panic among the Germans the night before the Dragoon invasion when he and his men, at the opposite end of the landing area, created a diversionary threat that appeared to be so real that the erroneous report of the German officer in charge of the area provoked panic in Berlin.

The courage demonstrated by Fairbanks during Rosie was preceded by his willingness to risk ruining his career as a Hollywood movie star during the pre-Pearl Harbor attack period when the vast majority of Americans wanted their nation to stay out of the war. He antagonized the members of the politically powerful America First and other isolationist organizations. One America First leader, the highly respected and influential Gen. Hugh Johnson, a top New Deal administrator in the 1930s, ridiculed Fairbanks in newspapers throughout the nation. Johnson claimed that Fairbanks's broadcast of pro-British propaganda would drag Americans into war. He belittled young Fairbanks as someone with "a long heroic and varied celluloid military and diplomatic experience—in all parts of the world that can profitably be imitated on photographic film in Hollywood."[60] Fairbanks's response to such widespread verbal abuse led to his quest to become a naval reserve officer. He succeeded on April 10, 1941, when Navy Secretary Frank Knox signed his commission as lieutenant junior grade. Although a friend of Roosevelt's and of the president's son, Franklin Jr., Fairbanks had to satisfy difficult requirements, such as obtaining the equivalent of a college degree within a short time, mastering complex naval regulations, and learning Spanish and Portuguese. His first assignment as a naval intelligence officer in South America was to find out if the United States Navy would be welcome to use the ports in that hemisphere for possible emergency repair bases.[61]

Zigzagging to Camel Beach

After leaving their safe Mediterranean ports in early August 1944, LST 1012 and the rest of the Allied armada zigzagged and shifted course to confuse German planes. On August 14, a few hours before dusk, Admiral Hewitt saw a German spy plane checking the positions of his ships. Wanting the Germans to believe that the Allies were intent on attacking from the rear, the admiral ordered the armada to head toward Genoa. A German spy plane was allowed to take photos and to plot the Allied fleet's course. Once night fell, Hewitt swung his fleet back around and ordered full steam ahead toward the planned invasion beaches of Dragoon.[62] That evening, a Mediterranean haze started to gather, which shielded the Allied armada from German reconnaissance aircraft. General Devers described the Allied reaction thus: "With the precision of a mechanical toy, this tremendous seaborne fleet was whirled around by Hewitt. It was no longer headed north toward Genoa, now a scant few hours away. It was headed southeast at top speed towards the selected landing areas."[63] To further confuse the Germans, the Allies prevented enemy use of radar observation of the position and size of the invasion armada by employing jamming and deception devices.[64]

Rear Adm. Spencer S. Lewis, who was commander of the naval task force that was assembled and prepared for the assault on Camel Beach, wrote in his "Action Report—Assault on the Beaches of Southern France" about operations in the Saint-Raphael-Antheor area of the Mediterranean:[65]

> Task Force (#87) was assembled and prepared for Operation Dragoon in a minimum of time. It was formed of units from three separate theaters, those already in Mediterranean waters, those which had just participated in Operation Neptune,[66] and recent arrivals from the United States. Commander Task Force 87 (Rear Adm. D. P. Moon) and his planning staff, having just completed Operation Neptune, arrived from the United Kingdom in Naples on July 1, setting up headquarters in the same building with the other two Assault Force Commanders, all three Assault Division Staffs, and the Sixth Corps Headquarters. This concentration led to a cooperative and harmonious relationship without which the preparation of plans for Dragoon would have been extremely difficult. Training for Task Force 87 and the embarked troops of the 36th Division was conducted in the Salerno area during the period July 8-22, under the administrative organization in effect in the theater prior to the activation of the Dragoon Task Forces on July 30. Task Force 87's rehearsal was conducted on Aug. 7, concurrently with, though in a different area from, that of Task Force 85. The rehearsal was not as profitable as desired because:
>
> 1. Personnel landings, only, were conducted. It was not possible to land vehicles and cargoes and reload them in the brief time available prior to the actual operation.
> 2. Because of late availability, many ships and craft assigned to the Task Force could not participate in the rehearsal.
> 3. Firing areas were not available. The landings were, therefore, dry runs.
> 4. There was not time enough between the rehearsal and the operation to conduct a critique nor to correct errors and discrepancies discovered in the rehearsal.
>
> The training period, rehearsal, and actual operation were blessed by excellent weather, thereby simplifying landing and unloading problems tremendously."[67]

The general plan comprised three main assault forces. Each was under the overall command of a rear admiral, United States Navy, and each landing force consisted of one American combat division of troops with its division commander. The corps commander of the three United States Army divisions was Maj. Gen. L. K. Truscott, VI Corps United States Army. Left to right along the invasion coast of southern France, the three assault forces were assigned as follows: on the left, the Alpha Attack Force, Rear Adm. F. J. Lowry, CTF84; in the center, the Delta Attack Force, Rear Adm. B. J. Rodgers, CTF85; and on the right, the Camel Attack Force, Rear Adm. Spencer S. Lewis, CTF87. H-hour for these three landings was set for 0800, which, as Admiral Hewitt stated, "was the first occasion in which zero hour was made after daylight."[68]

Rear Admiral Moon

Rear Adm. Spencer S. Lewis succeeded Rear Adm. Don P. Moon to the command of Group Two, VIII Amphibious Force, designated CTF87 Camel Force, the most difficult section of the target coast. Initially, Moon was assigned the task of landing and supporting the Thirty-sixth Division, which was to protect the right flank of the assault. The Thirty-sixth Division was to land in the Golfe de Fréjus, in Agay region, and capture Saint-Raphael and Fréjus. Seizing Le Muy and airfields in the Argens River valley, it was to link up with the Forty-fifth Division on the left and secure the right flank. Rear Admiral Moon returned after murderous Utah Beach Normandy invasion duties to lead the Dragoon Camel Attack. Admiral Hewitt later wrote that he and his colleagues did not realize how thoroughly worn out Moon was by the ordeals of Normandy. Nevertheless, Moon was ordered by the chief of naval operations to command an assault force for the invasion of southern France shortly after Normandy.

Admiral Moon had a penchant for first-rate technical performance. He was first in his graduating class (1916) at the Annapolis naval academy. In addition to his naval gunnery and ordnance expertise, Moon was a versatile athlete, good at fencing, wrestling, swimming, diving, tennis, and golf. On September 28, 1923, he married Sibyl Peaselee, the daughter of Charles Mason Hall, a New York City marine insurance broker. The couple had four children: Meredith Whittier, Don Pardee,

David Peaselee, and Peter Clayton Moon. In 1923, Don Moon received an MS degree from the University of Chicago for his work in perfecting the oscillograph, a device used to measure the trajectory of gunfire. He installed this device at the Dahlgren, Virginia, Naval Proving Ground. At the Naval Gun Factory in Washington, D.C., in 1929, he worked out plans for modernizing the gun turrets of the older battleships. He designed a revolving loading platform, which facilitated the loading of guns under bad weather at sea. This substantially increased the rapidity of fire. His many sea-duty assignments during World War II included command of a destroyer squadron, protecting convoys on dangerous duty between Iceland and Murmansk. To combat the menace of German submarines in the North Atlantic, Moon developed several antisubmarine devices, perfecting these devices for years until they proved most effective.

In November 1942, he was given invasion command of a destroyer division at Casablanca. When he was assigned to command a Normandy invasion assault in June 1944, he supervised the loading of every landing vessel so that none would sink with its own load. Every step was planned with precision. When the assault force he commanded was approaching the Normandy shore, Allied scout planes reported a massing of German guns behind the target Utah Beach. Moon quickly took this new information into account and changed course, leading his force to a landing that was a complete surprise to the enemy. This corps, the U.S. Seventh Army, landed successfully near Saint-Martin-de-Varreville with a very small casualty loss. Later, it captured Cherbourg, the first major French town taken by the Allies. After his Normandy success, Moon was assigned to northern Italy for additional work in preparation for the Dragoon invasion. He labored day and night to get his men and ships ready.

The extent of Admiral Moon's physical and mental exhaustion seemed to have been underestimated by his superiors, Admirals King and Hewitt, who were unaware that while on the bridge of his flagship, the USS *Bayfield* at sea late in July, Moon had accidentally injured his head during darkened ship operations. Although seamen got accustomed to walking and climbing on their ships' ladders on pitch-black nights, it was dangerous even for a rested young sailor. Admiral Moon was fifty at the time of his accident, worn out, preoccupied with a host of concerns, and worried about the forthcoming August 15 invasion. Moon's head injury induced recurring periods of violent headaches so severe that his mind would go blank. He repeatedly mentioned his apprehensions about the lack of adequate preparations of his task force and the many naval units, which were arriving late, and he worried about the inadequacy of assault training.[69]

Admiral Hewitt, in his July 1954 report to members of the United States Naval Institute concerning Operation Dragoon, wrote, "He (Admiral Moon) spent some hours with me on Aug. 4, 1944 . . . begging me to have Dragoon postponed. I explained the urgency of meeting the date set by the higher commands and gave it as my opinion that the state of readiness, while not as complete as we would like, was still not as bad as he seemed to think. Eventually, it was agreed that we carry on the rehearsal, which I would observe personally, and that if that did not prove to be satisfactory, I would then take up with the Supreme Commander the question of postponement. Admiral Moon left my office, apparently satisfied and in good spirits. The next morning after what was undoubtedly a sleepless night, he took his own life."[70] In his suicide letter, Admiral Moon gave as the reason for his act the fear that one of his headache seizures would occur while he was on the bridge of his flagship giving commands to the immense invasion fleet and cause him to issue a wrong order that would jeopardize the lives of the men under his command. The admiral died aboard the *Bayfield* at sea off the coast of Naples on August 5, 1944. His death by suicide was kept secret at first. The need to replace him promptly, however, was only too evident.

With Admiral Moon's death, Camel Attack Force was left without a commander, and there was little time to procure another flag officer to replace him. Even if one could be found, he would be confronted with the difficult problem of suddenly taking over a complex responsibility whose intricacies had to be mastered in a short time. Of the flag officers available in Hewitt's Eighth Fleet, only his chief of staff, Rear Adm. Spencer S. Lewis, knew to some extent the Camel Attack plan. Hewitt therefore assigned him to take over command of Moon's staff on the *Bayfield*. Lewis, a widower, had recently married a woman serving in the British Navy's Women's Auxiliary. Before becoming the flagship of Rear Adm. Spencer Lewis, the *Bayfield* had participated in the Normandy landing, where she had put all of her combat troops ashore successfully. The war diary of the *Bayfield* shows that Maj. Gen. John E. Dahlquist, commanding general of the Thirty-sixth Infantry Division, and his staff were aboard the ship on August 6-7, 1944, for training exercises, and again on August 13 when the *Bayfield* was under way from Naples for the assault on the southern coast of France. Other ships, such as the LST 282 and LST 1012, were also under the command of Rear Admiral Lewis.

In his biography of Fleet Adm. Ernest J. King, who was Hewitt's and Moon's superior, Thomas B. Buell provided a disturbing account of this tragic event. He pointed out that it was Admiral King who precipitately decided to detach Moon from the Normandy invasion and send him to the Mediterranean to assist Hewitt. King was impressed by Moon's amphibious expertise, and "disregarding objections that Moon was needed at Normandy, King made his decision without fully considering the consequences."[71] In fairness to Admiral King, it should be noted that Buell also wrote this about him: "It was in (King's) nature to ponder complex problems and to weigh all relevant information with a life-and-death matter at stake, King avoided premature decisions."[72] In recognition of his distinguished services rendered during World War II, Admiral Moon received high military honors from the governments of the Soviet Union, France, Great Britain, and the United States.

Capt. John A. Moreno, U.S. Navy (Ret.) was Rear Admiral Moon's air officer and assistant for planning during the preparation for the Dragoon invasion. In his article "The Death of Admiral Moon," in a book entitled *Assault on Normandy*, Moreno provided details about Admirals Moon and Lewis that are not widely known. These discuss Moon's suicide and Lewis's remarkable decision to change the landing plan in the middle of the invasion. Moreno acknowledged some merit in Hewitt's contention that "perhaps it was Admiral Moon's worry over the southern France landings that pushed him over the edge." However, Moreno argued that the more likely cause of Moon's suicide was what had happened in Exercise Tiger.[73]

Exercise Tiger, a rehearsal for the Normandy invasion, was held on the night of April 27-28, 1944, at Slapton Sands, England. German torpedo boats sank two LSTs and damaged a third during Exercise Tiger, and some losses resulted from "friendly fire." Allied soldiers were in tanks that were pitching erratically in choppy water, firing unstabilized guns on Allied troops on the beach. The major cause of the tragic events, however, was a failure of communications: there was no common radio frequency for the escort ships to talk to the LST convoy they were supposed to protect, and hundreds of men lost their lives. Rear Admiral Moon was not responsible for this communications breakdown, for the failure to properly instruct tank gunners, and to provide for stable guns in choppy water; but as the officer in charge, he was blamed. Moon's record as an exceedingly hardworking, hard-driving officer who regularly worked an eighteen-hour day, and who disapproved of the work ethics of subordinates who worked less, was ignored by Rear Adm. Arthur Struble, who disliked Don Moon.

Captain Moreno had firsthand knowledge of the bad relationship between Moon and Struble. According to Moreno, Adm. Ernest King gave Moon an important Normandy invasion command assignment that Struble wanted, and so there was bad blood between the two. It was Moon's misfortune that Struble was put in charge of investigating the Exercise Tiger calamities at Slapton Sands. In the presence of Moreno and another junior officer, Struble leveled a venomous reprimand at Moon, charging that this paragon of responsibility and conscientiousness had failed to do his duty. "I think this is when Moon really broke down," Moreno observed.[74] After the humiliation that Moon was subjected to, a thorough investigation revealed that he was not at fault because he had no way of learning about the grievous errors made by the British officers that caused the Exercise Tiger tragedies.

Rear Adm. Donald P. Moon

LST 282 before Dragoon

The LST 282 suffered its first accident on its trial run of October 27, 1943 (Navy Day and President Theodore Roosevelt's birthday). This ship was one of 147 LSTs built by the American Bridge Company at Ambridge, Pennsylvania, eighteen miles down the river from Pittsburgh. Fifty guests were aboard the LST 282 as it cruised down the Ohio River.

A bit of paint had splashed on the switch box of an electric rudder control. Dropping on the fuse connection, the paint became hot and burned on to the fuse, which automatically threw the steering gear of the ship out of control. Although the engines were reversed to full speed astern, the ship headed for the shore and a forty- to fifty-foot concrete retaining wall. As the ship approached to within a few feet of the wall, its bow settled into an underwater mud bar and stopped. The pilot, an experienced riverman in temporary command of the LST 282, switched the steering gear to emergency control and accelerated the reverse power.

The LST 282 participated in the Normandy invasion of June 6, 1944. Sometime after the Normandy landing, the LST 282 was delivering cargo when a military photographer, who was on board, snapped a photo of the unloading. He used a carrier pigeon to return the film to England, but instead of flying west, the bird got confused and flew east to Germany where the film was captured. On June 28, the photo was published in a German newspaper, with the accompanying article claiming that soon after the photo was taken, the LST 282 was sunk. That was pure hype, but prophetic.[75] For both the Normandy and Dragoon invasions, the commanding officer of the LST 282 was Lt. Lawrence Edwin Gilbert, USNR.

Gilbert was born on November 13, 1917, in New York City. His father, Abbey Edwin Gilbert, left Natchez, Mississippi, to seek his fortune in New York City and became vice president of the Hanover Fire Insurance Company, headquartered in downtown Manhattan. His mother, Laura Feldstein, emigrated from Russia and was an accomplished musician. Lawrence Gilbert grew up in the Sheepshead area of Brooklyn, near Coney Island and the water.

After graduating from James Madison High School, Gilbert attended Dartmouth College, where he was a member of the Theta Chi fraternity. He and some friends wanted to drop out of college to volunteer for service in the Spanish civil war of the 1930s. His father caught him before he left the United States and sent him back to Dartmouth. In 1939, Gilbert received his BA degree in political science. After graduation, he worked for a group of insurance companies in Havana, Cuba. On November 20, 1941, he married Frances Grace McGovern in Havana, where her father, M. T. McGovern, was president of the General Electric Company.

Shortly after Pearl Harbor, Gilbert enlisted in the U.S. Navy.[76] Almost immediately he was flown to Antofagasta, Chile, for naval intelligence duty, from January 1942. His father responded to an inquiry about his son from Bertram R. MacMannis in a letter dated December 23, 1942: "On Sept. 3, 1942, his wife who returned to live with her parents in Havana, gave birth to a baby girl, Grace Ellen.[77] Larry, being about nine thousand miles from all of us, has neither seen us, his wife, nor his child since entering the service."[78] In a letter home, Lawrence wrote,

> You know, I've been thinking (I've managed to find time to think today). Reading Dots'[79] letter sort of made me get a lump in my throat. I sure am happy for her, but at the same time, her news sort of brought home to me just how Mom and Dad must feel. Must sort of seem to them like their whole private world is falling to pieces great chunks at a time. First I get married and then go away to war, a grandchild waiting to greet them any day now. And now Dots is all ready to leave the nest. Susie growing up so fast. I'll bet that down deep you feel a little scared. Well, don't worry. You raised some pretty good kids, and we've had one heluva lot of fun. Honestly I've stopped wishing for "things as they used to be." You just work yourself up into a lather for nothing, doing that. It's going to be a fine new world after this "spring-cleaning" is done with, and we all as Americans are going to have a heluva lot to do in putting the House in order. Petty, individual things won't matter so much, and we will all be a lot closer in the future even though at present things might indicate that everything is disorganized or in the process of same. What we're fighting isn't as important as what we're fighting for. The latter is the thing that sort of unifies and makes a coherent picture of what is happening in the world. You are fighting one thing, I'm fighting another. Tom, Dick, and Harry are fighting different things in different parts of the world . . . and we are all fighting in different ways . . . but to

the same end. That, for me, is enough. Of course we all might call what we are fighting for by different labels or explanations, but as far as I am concerned, it's all fundamentally the same thing. Things aren't going to Hell . . . far from it. We are all getting a chance that few generations are privileged to have, and I mean all of us. It doesn't matter how much shaking up our old values get. It's damgood for them.

In the light of the new perspectives which we are gradually getting, a re-evaluation should take place. The really good, old values will still be with us, never fear, but that will be because they've stood the test. "Spring-cleaning" . . . a lot of musty old relics have been dragged out of all the attics. Odds and ends swept out of dark corners in the closets. There's some damgood stuff there that was carefully put away. Now is the time to see if we still want to keep them. That ball of twine that was put away ten years ago and dragged out today might still be of use . . . if it was made of good stuff. We may find that it has rotted. Well then, whyinell keep it? I guess you see what I mean even though I don't think I'm expressing myself very well . . . I haven't had the time or the inclination to think this way for a long time and now I'm just sort of letting it all out on you. All it means is that I love you all very much and I'm trying to tell you that everything is going to be ok, for us and everybody else."[80]

After completing his service in Chile in September 1942, Gilbert was assigned to a destroyer in the southwest Pacific. By June 1944, he was serving as the commanding officer of the LST 282. According to Bob Beroth, a member of that crew,

> Lieutenant Gilbert was a superb ship handler and a good man. He was a very friendly person and easy to communicate with. Over the nine months I served under him, we developed an understanding that most of the crewmembers were there to do the job they were assigned and were not seeking a career. While we were in New Orleans, in December 1943, Lt. Gilbert had his wife brought aboard for the Christmas dinner. I had been dating a nurse from the Catholic Hospital and was given permission to bring her aboard along with another nurse, who was dating Ensign Peterson.

I had access to the LCVPs to make mail pick-up and to exchange the 35mm movie films, since I was the projector operator. I learned to operate the LCVPs with respect and protection, as I did the ship when I was operating the helm in rough seas and entering and exiting harbors. Lt. Gilbert had the carpenter shop make a surfboard for him, which could be towed behind an LCVP. While awaiting orders in the English harbors, I towed Lt. Gilbert many times, especially while we were anchored in Falmouth. When we made our third shuttle trip to Normandy, we delivered English troops and equipment to Gold Beach. We had trouble with the Gold Beach English Beaching Master giving orders to come in and unload and then rescinding those orders when we were about ready to drop the stern anchor. After we beached and unloaded, Lt. Gilbert and I were standing on the ramp discussing the beaching problem and Lt. Gilbert stated, "I hope I never have to take orders from an Englishman again." When we returned to England, we were assigned to the convoy destined for the Mediterranean Sea and Italy, so Lt. Gilbert received his wish. Lt. Gilbert was a down-to-earth person, but ran a controlled ship; which was liked by all crewmembers.[81]

LST 282

Lawrence E. Gilbert, commanding officer, LST 282

Food and Other Needs

Lt. Laurence Gilbert also ran a well-fed ship. His granddaughter, Kirsten, recounted, in May 2004, that he was a good cook. Gilbert didn't cook on the LST 282, but as the following menu indicates, his crew had plenty of food. One of the many duties of an LST commanding officer was to approve the bill of fare for the general mess. Lieutenant Gilbert approved the following menu for the LST 282 for the week of June 26, 1944.[82]

Bill of Fare for the General Mess
USS LST 282
Week beginning 26 June 1944

Day	Breakfast	Dinner	Supper
Monday	Fruit juice Cereal—milk Baked corned beef hash French toast Hot sirup—catsup Butter—coffee	Grilled rib steaks Brown gravy Roast potatoes Buttered corn Chocolate cake Bread—butter Coffee	Fresh beef stew Macaroni & cheese Pickled beets Chilled fruit Bread—butter Coffee
Tuesday	Tinned fruit Cereal—milk Creamed ham on toast Fried potatoes Butter—coffee	Roast loin of pork Brown gravy— applesauce Mashed potatoes Buttered asparagus Mincemeat pie Bread—butter—coffee	Fried hamburger steaks Fried potatoes Brown gravy Boiled navy beans Sweet relish Fruit cocktail Bread—butter—coffee
Wednesday	Tomato juice Milk—cereal Hot griddle cakes Pork sausage Hot sirup Butter—coffee	Pot roast of beef Vegetable gravy Boiled potatoes (jacket on) Buttered peas Plain cake Bread—butter—coffee	Fried pork chops Brown gravy Lyonnaise potatoes Buttered carrots Sugar cookies Bread—butter—coffee

Thursday	Fruit juice Milk—cereal Fresh minced beef on toast Fried potatoes Butter—coffee	Cream of tomato soup Fried ham steaks Brown gravy Mashed potatoes Fried string beans Pear pie Bread—butter—coffee	Chili con carne Kidney beans Pickled beets French fried potatoes Bread pudding Bread—butter Tea
Friday	Tinned fruit Cereal—milk Scrambled eggs Fried crisp bacon Hot toast Butter—coffee	Beef broth Boiled beef Boiled potatoes Boiled cabbage and carrots Sliced pickles Marble cake Bread—butter—coffee	Beef fricassee Fried potatoes Steamed spinach Oatmeal cookies Bread—butter—coffee
Saturday	Fruit juice Milk—cereal Baked pork and beans Tomato catsup Hot toast Butter—coffee	Swiss steaks—gravy Mashed potatoes Buttered corn Fresh vegetable salad Chilled fruit Butter—bread—coffee	Ham & macaroni au gratin Welch Rarebit Buttered string beans Sugared doughnuts Bread—butter—coffee
Sunday	Tomato juice Milk—cereal Hot griddle cakes Fried crisp bacon Hot syrup Butter—coffee	Cream pea soup Roast young chicken Giblet gravy—dressing Baked sweet potatoes Sweet relish Ice cream Bread—butter—coffee	Asst. cold cuts of meats Potato salad Cold baked beans Sliced cheese—pickles Cinnamon rolls Bread—butter Hot Ovaltine

Total estimated cost: Total estimated rations:
Estimated ration cost per day:

Respectfully submitted,
Approved: L. E. Gilbert, Lieut. USNR—R. F. Meilinger[83]

As this bill of fare indicates, there was a wide choice of food on LST 282. This was also true on LST 1012. But there was no special dietary provisions for observant Jews or Muslin crew members.[84]

Rear Admirals Worral R. Carter and Elmer E. Duvall, in their valuable *Ships, Salvage, and Sinews of War,* prepared an account of the provision of food and other logistical support for Operation Dragoon.[85] The following excerpts from their book describe (a) the special features of logistic support for Operation Dragoon, (b) the feeding of army personnel, (c) the saga of food ship *Yukon,* and (d) providing clothing to survivors.

The logistic support planned for the invasion of southern France was far more extensive than in previous operations in the Mediterranean due to the following conditions: Greater distance from major repair yards; anticipation of large-scale enemy action from shore batteries and aircraft; probability of extended period of unloading over assault beaches prior to the capture of Toulon and Marseille; and the expectation that such ports would be severely damaged and would require extensive harbor clearance.

Army personnel embarked in Allied naval ships, including LSTs, were fed by such ships except that in some cases the number of troops embarked in LSTs required a modification in the Navy ration and augmentation by the Army. The Navy provided hot soup and coffee where practicable.

Throughout the entire operation United States Navy provisioning facilities were made available to Allied ships and craft when necessary. This applied particularly to craft assigned for unloading duties and to auxiliaries which remained off the assault beaches without relief until the closing of such beaches.

One of the food ships which arrived prior to the invasion was the *Yukon.* On 10 July 1944, at the Naval Supply Depot, Bayonne, New Jersey, the provisions stores ship *Yukon,* Lieutenant Commander A.L. McMullan, completed loading 2751 tons of cargo and the next day she sailed for Hampton Roads. There she joined a convoy for the Mediterranean; and on 30 July she reached Mole Jules Giraud, Oran, Algeria, and soon thereafter commenced discharging cargo from all holds. The next day she fueled, loaded 175 tons of miscellaneous radio gear for Naples, and, after having discharged 650 tons of food at Oran, secured all holds, and got underway for Naples. On 4 August, D-minus-11 day, ships and craft were making ready for the assault, and the *Yukon* anchored in Castellammare anchorage where she discharged cargo from all holds to various landing craft. The next day, having shifted to an anchorage in Naples Harbor, she unloaded for 6 ½ hours into landing craft alongside. The total amount of provisions discharged in the Naples area was 842 tons. Less than three hours after completion there she got underway to Palermo, Sicily. On 6 August, shortly after mooring at Pier No. 6, the *Yukon* commenced discharging food and by 1230 the next day had completed her issue of 941 tons. She lost no time in clearing port for Bizerte. There, on 8 August, at Pier No. 3, she discharged the remaining 493 tons of her initial cargo of provisions, took fuel from a Dutch tanker, the motor ship *Agatha,* and prepared to return to the United States. On 20 August the *Yukon* moored to the Commonwealth Pier, Boston, Massachusetts. In her voyage of about five weeks she had done important provisioning at four Mediterranean ports just prior to the invasion of southern France.

The lessons learned in previous operations regarding the need of keeping on hand ample stocks of survivor clothing did not go unheeded, for a supply was maintained at various points: Oran, Naples, Bizerte, Palermo, and Ajaccio. Limited stocks were carried in attack transports, cargo ships, merchant transports, LSIs, LSTs, and LCI(L)s assigned as mother ships.[86]

Food shortages in France during the German occupation were a widespread reality. Most of the population was limited to food rationing of 1,327 calories per day, and even this small ration was hard to get. Rationing and long waiting lines became part of everyday life for millions of French people, accustomed to eating an average of three thousand calories per day prior to the war. German requisitioning of food, British blockades, and shortages of labor, fertilizer, and livestock were responsible for causing hunger throughout France.

Operation Dragoon took place on the coast of the Var department, which was not a region of mixed agricultural production. As a result, civilians there suffered much greater hunger than elsewhere in France, and there were food demonstrations. Starvation did not enhance the popularity of Vichy leaders Pétain, Laval, and others. Friendships with farmers were, therefore, very important.[87] All French Christian troops received the same emergency rations as Americans, supplemented by wine and brandy on a scale that was determined and furnished by the

French. Special rations were supplied to French Muslims. The gratuitous issue of tobacco, candy, and toilet goods to all French troops was the same scale as Americans for the first thirty days.[88] Spiritual needs such as religious services were also available to Allied forces before invasions and at other occasions.

In addition to ensuring that the troops were well fed, there were a number of chaplains available to perform wedding services for servicemen and their fiancées at opportune times. In 1944 alone, four chaplains officiated more than one hundred marriages each: Chaplain W. N. Thomas (Naval Academy, 149); Chaplain C. L. Glenn (Midshipmen School of New York City, 157); Chaplain J. E. V. Carlson (Third Naval District, 122); and Chaplain C. R. Ehrhardt (Anacostia, Washington, D.C., 107).[89] Several marriages were even performed via telephone when the bride and groom were in different states. The navy, as a whole, advocated marriage, believing the institution would negate potentially unusual/delicate circumstances.[90]

Reports from LST Crew Members

LST 282 crew member Bob Beroth wrote that "after participating in the Normandy invasion, the LST 282 was assigned to a convoy being formed for a voyage to Naples, Italy, in early July. All ships were loaded with Army equipment and personnel for the planned invasion of southern France, Operation Dragoon. The convoy sailed through the Straits of Gibraltar and along the northern coast of Africa to an area north of Bizerte, where the convoy turned and sailed to Naples. On August 11, the 282 received her cargo of equipment to be transported to the coast of Southern France for Operation Dragoon. The cargo consisted of six 155mm Hawsers,[91] four 105mm Hawsers, and support trucks loaded with ammunition for the artillery guns, all secured in the tank deck. On the main deck were six 40mm anti-aircraft guns secured to the deck, with three located on each side. Support trucks were secured to the deck between the anti-craft guns, lined up between the elevator and the cargo hatch. On the cargo hatch were secured four jeeps. Army personnel on board were assigned to monitor the equipment being transported. In the late afternoon of August 12, the 282 departed the harbor of Naples and joined the convoy for Operation Dragoon. The convoy sailed through the straits between Corsica and Sardinia and arrived off the coast of southern France at the location for the planned Operation Dragoon, before daylight on the morning of Aug. 15, 1944."[92] Accounts from crew members of other ships en route to the Dragoon invasion provide a variety of details worth remembering.

Mike Sgaglione, an LST 350 crew member, described the intermingling of sailors and troops aboard his ship: "The stories we swapped about home life and towns and cities; I met a few soldiers from my beloved Brooklyn and remember we got kidded a lot about our New York accents. Most of us were on the average of seventeen or eighteen years old and were unaware of what might lie ahead. Most were unmarried and lots of talk and photos shown of moms, dads, sisters, and younger brothers. One soldier I remember played the guitar and he was a great player—he entertained us in those pre-invasion days. It was very crowded; an LST is not too big a ship, and quarters were very tight. It brought us into closer contact, and for that I am grateful. I have no way of knowing how many of those brave souls made it."[93]

There were serious problems on some LSTs headed toward the Dragoon operation beaches. In addition to the ships' crews of one hundred, there were three hundred to three hundred fifty extra people on board for six days. Water shortages, long lines for food, and poor sanitation conditions added to the apprehensions of the troops.[94]

George Sweet, age twenty-three and a veteran of earlier Mediterranean invasions, was commanding officer on the LST 358, which had participated in the invasions of Sicily, Salerno, and Anzio, prior to southern France. Sweet described Gen. Charles de Gaulle's visit aboard his ship when it was docked in Bizerte. As a morale booster, Sweet stressed the fact that de Gaulle was very gracious to all of the officers and crew with whom he came in contact.[95] Regarding his ship's participation in Operation Dragoon, Sweet recalled that on August 12, 1944, the LST 358 and the ships of the Alpha Attack Force that were to carry out the assault on the southern coast of France, in the vicinity of Cavalaire Bay, left anchorage at Torre Annunziata, Italy. The voyage to the landing site was uneventful.

On December 7, 1941, Irving "Chet" Noyes was a lucky young naval officer. His ship had left Pearl Harbor a day before the Japanese attack. After dangerous Pacific Ocean duty on four ships, Noyes was selected to command the LST 494 and to train its inexperienced crew. He subjected his men to rigorous training exercises. Six decades later, USS LST 494 Association crew members expressed their sentiments about him, "We have never forgotten how much Captain Noyes meant to us during those difficult days of intense training and combat. We have always remembered his skill, leadership, and outstanding judgement under fire. He cared greatly about his men."[96]

The LST 494 crossed the Atlantic Ocean in March 1944 and was one of the twenty-four LSTs that arrived at Omaha Beach on June 6, 1944, for the D-day landings at Normandy. One of its crew members, Howard H. Buhl, now of Lakeland, Florida, was a "plank owner" of the LST 494—which meant that he was a member of the original crew when the ship was commissioned on December 18, 1943, in New Orleans. Three doctors were aboard the LST 494, and they had twenty-three assistants. The tank deck of the ship was fitted for the wounded. Bunks in the crew quarters were used for the injured, and tables in the mess (or dining) area were used for surgery. Resourceful crew members improvised makeshift lighting and other facilities for medical personnel. During LST 494's seven shuttle trips across the English Channel, it delivered thirty-seven litter cases to a hospital at Southampton, England, before joining twenty-four other ships in convoy to the Mediterranean. While LST 494 was in the convoy to the southern France invasion, the ship had to thread its way through German minefields without a minesweeper escort. On August 15, 1944, LST 494 participated in the Dragoon invasion.

Shortly before that, on July 25, while on its voyage from England to the invasion of southern France, LST 494 was the column leader of column three (port, or left, side). LST 284, the leading ship of the second column (center column) turned starboard (right) on a port emergency turn and collided with LST 504, the column leader of the first column (convoy commodore). After this collision, LST 494 then collided with LST 284. LST 494 suffered only minor damage, but the 504 and 284 were badly smashed up and required substantial repairs. Within a short period, however, both vessels were repaired and ready for Operation Dragoon duty. The bow doors from an LST that was beached and incapacitated during the Normandy invasion were used to replace the smashed ones of the LST 504, and the deep gash in the middle of the LST 284 disappeared. In his e-mail of January 18, 2003, Buhl wrote that the July 25, 1944, events were recorded in the LST 494 ship's log and that he had been on watch in the auxiliary engine when the accident occurred. Buhl was a motor machinist who was the lead engineer on LST 494.

On August 12, 1944, LST 494 left Naples with soldiers of the Forty-fifth Division. They were headed toward Blue Beach, Delta Landing Area, Operation Dragoon. The LST 494 made a total of 15 shuttle trips, carrying 3,318 soldiers and 717 tanks, trucks, and other vehicles from August 15 to November 24, 1944. LST 494 landed American, Free French, and French Moroccan goums and Senegalese soldiers. Two hundred mules that belonged to the goums troops were also transported to France. On September 9, 1944, LST 494 carried a group of French nurses, and on the twelfth the passengers were American nurses.[97]

On September 30, 1944, the LST 494 was in a convoy with five other LSTs, starting from Sardinia to Marseille. A few days later, the LST convoy was in the midst of a fierce storm with forty-foot waves and seventy-five-foot sprays. A small crack appeared on the left side of the LST 494 tank deck. Commanding Officer Noyes requested permission from the commodore (convoy commander) to maneuver his ship to ride out the storm and continue on to the port of Marseille. When his request was denied, Noyes ignored the convoy commander. The ships that followed the convoy commander's order to return to Sardinia were badly damaged and nearly sunk, according to Mike Guarino who has completed a history of LST 494. He wrote that "as the 494 drew close to the Commodore's LST, Noyes saw the commodore's signal light blink out a message to the 494: 'Operate independently, proceed to destination. Good luck.'" The LSTs that obeyed the commodore's directives were severely damaged and had to return to Sardinia for repairs. The LST 494 completed its mission and arrived in Marseille. Noyes was not punished for his failure to obey the convoy commander.[98]

Lou Leopold, an officer on the LST 551, participated in Operation Dragoon and provided, for this book, diary entries and comments concerning people and events before the invasion. He wrote,

> I was a reasonably new Ensign USNR during the June 1944-August 1944 period. I was commissioned Oct. 30, 1943, at the same time as I was graduated from the University of Pennsylvania Wharton School with a B.S. in economics. The commission was earned at the then-new U of P NROTC program that started with my freshman year October 1940.
>
> The informality aboard many LSTs was not always appreciated by those few old-time regular Navy types who were assigned to some command posts. There was a laxity toward

uniform of the day regulations. Nevertheless, the civilians turned sailors ran the LST 551 well.

Richard George Fritzmeier was a natural leader and organizer in the deck gang. He was quickly promoted to Bosun's Mate and was leader of section one of the deck gang. He is credited as the artist who designed and organized the painting of our ship's symbol the "T.S. (Tough Ship of course) Vulture." You probably do remember the TS cards that any chaplain or pharmacist mate could punch for you (while giving you an aspirin). Fritz by profession was a field organizer for the Phil Murray Steel Workers Organizing Committee of the CIO and a friend of Murray's. On LST 551 he worked hard organizing a strong voter turnout in the 1944 presidential election. He encouraged the crew to get their military ballots, to vote on them and to return them promptly. CIO election campaign literature was all around the ship. While we were still training in and out of Baltimore aboard LST 32 Fritz got in trouble with the executive officer who discovered that Fritz had used his 24-hour liberty in Baltimore to visit Phil Murray, labor union leader, in Washington. Technically we were not allowed to go out of the Navy District without special orders. Given the regular and fast rail service between Washington, Baltimore, Wilmington, and Philadelphia, almost everyone in the LST Bay training program ignored the ruling. When Fritz was threatened with court-martial several of us appealed to the captain with a list of many of our key people who had also been riding those trains, including us. Indeed, I had been to a fraternity party in Philadelphia that night. Captain Sam Kimmel, knowing that the next visit to Baltimore would be our takeoff to get our own ship, announced his policy. In the future we would all follow the District rule and District boundaries would be announced for each new district. Fritz was saved.[99]

We learned quickly that Captain Sam had been the executive officer of a 300-numbered LST in the early wave of LSTs sent over for the invasion of Sicily and then went on to take part in the invasion of Salerno. When he was training to be an exec, I suspect that no one had any overseas combat or other experience about running LSTs. He had done well under tough conditions in both operations and was sent home to be skipper of one of the new 541 class LSTs. At Salerno his LST took German artillery shells in its open bow doors. In Sicily his LST was one of those caught in the German air raid. Allied ship gunners shot enemy planes and through carelessness Allied planes were also destroyed.

By profession he was a Baltimore attorney. I do not know whether he had been a Baltimore boatman as he grew up or not. He was a remarkable ship handler. LSTs in tight quarters and in wind and/or sea were tough to handle. I never saw any LST handled better in docking, beaching and maneuvering than 551 with Capt. Sam on the Conn. He had a very low opinion of many of the LST unit, division, group and flotilla Annapolis-trained commanders who had no LST knowledge and had been transferred from other more prestigious duties surrounded by rumors that they were on elite ships—and later relegated to lowly LSTs. Kimmel's legal training and his belief in getting war objectives accomplished combined with his ship handling and his LST knowledge made him a great skipper to serve under. But he was unwilling to put up with arrogance and stupidity. When we were right he would really back us up as I learned as early as our training days out of Solomon's Maryland.

On the legal side, he expected us to enforce censoring rules and as I learned this included photography. He knew that I was an avid 35mm photographer and that my communication duties included security and censorship, so he ordered me not to bring my camera when we got our own ship. He kept the ship's cameras locked in his safe when not needed. It was much easier for me to enforce the rules when I was not taking pictures myself.[100]

Captain Sam Kimmel himself was something special. As executive officer on the first wave of the brand new LSTs to the Mediterranean, he had been in the invasions of Sicily and Salerno and experienced much combat including taking German 88mm shells into open bow doors. Since he had also been involved in the shooting down of the Allied Airborne C-47 planes at Sicily that resulted from bad planning and communication failures by Air and Navy Corps, he insisted that we follow fire control discipline. He also learned by experience how to drop stern anchors and made sure we all learned. With Sam's supervision we had a guide to the ports and customs of the area. He probably knew as much about LST ship handling as anybody in the Mediterranean and he knew what problems were likely and some options to survive them. Maneuvering an LST under windy conditions in tight quarters is something special and constant tiny collisions in busy but damaged ports were frequent. The real challenge was to avoid real damage that would keep you from carrying out missions. I never knew where Sam learned these skills, but perhaps boating in Baltimore Inner Harbor helped. He was good and he was fair.

As communication officer I was blessed with radio, radar, flag-communications including mersigs, running the coding board and acting as chief censor. He knew how hard my job of censoring, controlling, and confiscating photos would be. It took me ten years after the war before I again picked up my cameras and went back to taking pictures, after his order prohibiting my taking photos.[101]

Once while loading a Canadian tank unit that was being moved from Italy to France the system broke down. The Canadians had just been issued two months' back whiskey allowance before a night boarding our ship. The officers showed up in the wardroom with open bottles of the best Canadian. Below deck likewise. They were a friendly change from the Indian Army, the Brazilians, and the French Colonials. We were lucky to be able to get the ship underway for France at daybreak.

Ashore beverages were freely available to all in bars and clubs, and the heavy drinking was a major problem. We had a senior petty officer die from bad alcohol.[102] Most of us drank far too much. Except on invasion beaches, open bars were available in almost all ports. We were seldom out of port more than 30 hours at a time. Allied Officers Clubs offered quality drinks, if a little exotic in the Brazilian Officers Club in Piombino, Italy. Lacking our own vehicles we did not drink and drive but walked or conned rides. Often we worked with British ships and when we tied up near them we would be invited to join them in their wine mess for fine drinks. As fair exchange we provided Camels and Lucky Strikes.

In the Mediterranean we picked up from the British "Bless Them All." There will be no promotion this side of the ocean so "bless" them all. The Brit 8th Army brought us a Lilli Marlene song which they borrowed from the German Africa Korps. Especially in France and Corsica we heard it sung in French. We met a French Resistance leader named Alstone who was returning to his musical comedy world. He produced a new musical review "Hello Marseille Hello" which he once performed for us down on our tank deck. It was a great party. He wrote the French hit song, "C'est Fini", mistranslated into symphony by Tin Pan Alley.

At prayer services with a variety of clergy at rear bases and prior to our major invasion, religious convictions were expressed. Pre-invasion services did attract a good crowd. A Jewish seaman asked to be sent to a seder Services inland up in Florence, suggesting that our German captain was anti-Jewish. I replied that our Jewish captain and I both would enjoy sightseeing in Florence, too, even though neither he nor we had gone to services when available in Naples, but time did not allow.[103]

About life at sea aboard the LST 551, prior to Dragoon, Leopold wrote in his diary,

25-27 June—Our convoy for Salerno mixed up with a convoy off Palermo. LST 906 in collision June with tanker. 906 had its bow crushed and put into Palermo for major repairs. During the rough seas that night on LST 551 LCVP#2 broke loose and smashed davit secured in time to prevent detonation (551 was carrying a mixed load of high explosives and pyrotechnics and the cargo detonators had been stowed separately in the LCVPs).

About 24 June—Our convoy one Group of LST Flotilla 20 under command of Commander LST FLOT 20 Captain Murphy USN was en route Bizerte to Salerno passing by Cape Bon-Egadian Islands-Palermo-Eolian Islands-Gulf of Policastro laden with a large variety of ammunition of various types being moved from the old Bizerte depots up to the new depots in preparation for the invasion of southern France. For the trip we were given special orders on loading/handling mines and detonators with the detonators being stowed in the LCVPs. Captain Murphy a regular Navy type who had recently been transferred from submarines was apparently making a major effort to instill order and discipline in an almost all-reserve relaxed LST force many of whose Navy Reserve skippers had been successful executive officers on the first wave of LSTs. These officers knew what was to be known about LSTs and were focusing efforts to get their young officers and crew to run their ships. Rumors suggested that meeting between the skippers and Murphy were heated, leaving the skippers convinced that he was a slow learner about what LSTs could do and how they could do it, and Murphy convinced that he had to whip his command into order as soon as possible. While lying to and forming up off Bizerte, Captain Murphy busied himself with his "long glass," tightening up topside discipline on ships two miles away. Emphasis was on the prescribed uniform of the day, especially on sailors' hats being strictly regulation. The officers of the deck of all offending ships were ordered "into hack for two weeks."[104] On LST 551, Ensign Fritz Graf had the conn as OD (Officer on Duty). Skipper Sam Kimmel very angry at interference with ship's internal discipline, especially as the Skipper thought Murphy should really concentrate on LST handling group maneuvers, essential drills, and even learning something about how LSTs functioned. Capt. Sam told Ens. Graf that Graf was to be in hack for two weeks just as Capt. Murphy (Dracula was the nickname) ordered but that the two weeks were to commence on June 26, 1946 or sometime thereafter, as just now we were too busy to have the assistant navigator and one of the four underway watch officers out on two weeks' vacation. LST 906 being the first ship asked who was at the conn responded that the skipper himself was at the conn. Murphy then ordered the skipper of LST 906 in hack for fourteen days. Our skipper at that time commented that he would not have obeyed without first being relieved of responsibility for his command. Capt Kimmel's favorite response became, "if you don't like relieve me of my command."

During the night the wind and sea rose. On the flagship was Capt. Murphy penning a note to his "buddy" Capt Opie, Chief of Staff of the 8th Amphibious Force, also known as LANDCRABNAVNorthwestAfricanWaters (we really did not know whether they were Annapolis classmates) reporting the success of his drive against sailors who were not wearing prescribed headgear while lying several miles off Bizerte. While off Palermo and proceeding northeastward the flagship apparently did not notice that our convoy was on a collision course with a merchant convoy apparently proceeding into Palermo Harbor. The night was dark, the merchant convoy may have lacked radar and apparently was not aware of us until they were upon us. Our flagship failed to order any course change despite radar. At the moment the two convoys were almost ready to meet. Murphy ordered an emergency colored light signal from mersigs or WIMS (Wartime instructions to merchant shipping) to his LST group to scatter on a fan-shaped pattern right into the oncoming convoy, increasing probability of collisions. Would a simultaneous turn on several possible courses avoided collisions? (I thought so at the time when I was well informed on such actions.) The result was mass confusion and almost every LST was involved in a long series of emergency course and speed changes to avoid collisions. We missed two merchants each by much less than twenty yards. Several ships bumped while LST 906, with her skipper ordered in hack, smashed in her bow on the side of a tanker and was forced to limp into Palermo and was out of action for about one month.

29 June—Sail by Capri and Mt. Vesuvius to Nisida (just north of Naples which was to be our normal Naples area amphibious base).

30 June-5 July—Five hits inside windy, wreck-strewn Naples Harbor.

Naples and Nisida. Going into Naples we hit a tanker and a liberty ship in high winds, low speed, and tight quarters. LST 659 becomes our bouncing buddy. We became division flagship and then hit (lightly of course) a liberty ship and tug leaving on way back to Nisida. Liberty time includes great places on the Posillipo promontory with 3-star Michelin views and the clubs and restaurants of great fame. In 1944 they were the Orange Grove Allied Officers' Club, British run; the Allied Naval Officers Club, also Brit; the Rotunda with another grand view (on this and other Naples/Nisida/Bagnoli/Pozzuoli visits saw Phlegrean Fields and Solfatara, a still active crater which seen steaming by moonlight with vision slightly blurred was something).

6 July—Sailed past Procida, Istria, Gaeta, Anzio to Civitavecchia (I had become an avid long-glass sightseer) carrying a mixed load of Fifth and Eighth Army replacements and returnees from around the world.

7-24 July—Running between Civitavecchia (the port of Rome, then very badly smashed up) and Porto Vecchio, Corsica (beautiful enclosed bay long famous for malaria) moving US 12th Tactical Air Force units and RAF units of Mediterranean Allied Tactical Air Force to Corsica in preparation for the invasion of southern France and moving the French II Army Corp from Corsica to Italy so they too could prepare to return to France. Stores Officer Jim Olney and Lou Leopold were unofficially allowed to hitchhike to Rome although the rules said colonels and above only. We were not allowed to stay at U.S. places but ended up at the Pension Monaco, cheap and ok. Did much sightseeing, including the Vatican and Broadway Bills. We became Axis Sally listeners to get the German view of what we were all doing. A German ME 210 late one night flying back from a likely recon over Naples flew low just over our main deck only two or three feet in front of our middle small boat davit. From my superconn position I was actually looking down on him and from his reaction he seemed as startled as I was. While in the ruined almost macabre port of Civitavecchia, air raid condition red was almost normal but apparently mostly recon flights. We lost our stern anchor in high winds at CV and Jack Osborne earned the name "Rigging Jack" in getting the replacement into service in adverse circumstances. (Rigging Jack was later to be a fatal casualty of poison whiskey which was investigated as deliberate hostile action.) The division commander left LST 551 in anger, shifting the flag to another ship. The skipper indeed was not unduly friendly to flag and staff and was always glad to encourage them to go. We tended to support the skipper in this effort.

24 July—We regularly shared harbor space with a good bunch of British escorts and minesweepers, with whom we shared U.S. tobacco and British scotch and gin as the Brits still had a wine mess. The captain of the LST 659 kept up his good work at the Corsican end, hitting the wooden pier at full tilt. (On 14 July we were moving some senior French staff to Italy and to help the French celebrate we declared the wardroom to be temporarily part of France and broke out the medicinal supply of classical American whiskey in honor of Bastille Day.) [105]

25 July—All ahead flank speed for Nisida and invasion preparations.

26 July—11 August—Prep for southern France.

Naples area inc. Nisida, Bagnoli, Pozzuoli. (Was that really a very young Sophia Loren bumming food at the bow doors?) Torre Annunziata (Did I really swim ashore there after we lost the use of our LCVPs and before we got APEX boats for D-day? Yes, and we were anchored out much further than I thought; it was a long swim back so I inflated my life belt.) Next to Pompeii at Castellammare di Stabia we took turns manning the shore communication station. We loaded the U.S. 3rd Infantry Division including DUKWs full of field artillery; the whole area filled with people, ships and notables as the forces massed and we all loaded and rehearsed landings with nightly German recon flights and lots of busy smoke pots, searchlights and AA firing. When ashore there was a good supply of gin, juice and ice. King George VI waved at us.

12-14 August—Operation Anvil [Dragoon] underway, we are in convoy sailing through the Straits of Bonifacio (between Corsica and Sardinia) past Ajaccio toward the south of France. Winston Churchill reviewed us as we sailed out of Naples from a speedboat and again off Ajaccio with good luck from the halyards of his destroyer. On the 13th Axis Sally, a spokesperson for Germany, let us know that she would be waiting for us as we beached on the 15th.[106]

Samuel Kimmel's daughter, June Webb, provided the author some particulars concerning her father's German-born mother and other biographical matters. Mrs. Webb wrote,

> My father's mother, Fredia Blumenthal, age twelve, came from Memel, Germany, alone on a ship in 1878. Her father, Max Blumenthal, had married twice and Fredia was child of his first marriage. She came to her father and second wife in Maryland after her mother died very young in Memel.
>
> Fredia married Joseph Kimel and they had nine children. Joseph was born in New York City and died in his late forties. The children changed spelling of "Kimel" to Kimmel. The change in the spelling stopped my father years later from joining the Secret Service section of the Navy. Fredia raised her children with the help of a pedal sewing machine doing piecework for a men's clothing store, working in her kitchen. As the children grew up they worked at an early age to help the family. While he was very young, Samuel sold newspapers on the streets.[107]
>
> My father and mother (Viola Pearce) married in York, Pennsylvania, on Sept. 11, 1928. Two years later they had a daughter and eighteen months later a son. They bought a cottage in Baltimore County, Maryland, for $350. My father then started working at night as a postal sorter and attending the University of Baltimore during the day. He would return home in the morning, have a few hours' sleep, then go to school and received his law degree.
>
> I remember Dec. 7, 1941, Sunday, and the radio news [that] Pearl Harbor was bombed. Soon war was declared. A few days later my father announced to my mother that he was taking his best friend Morris Bevins to the Navy Recruiting Office. Only Morris was going to sign up, not my father. A few hours later Dad returned. Morris could not pass the health exam. My father did pass and now belonged to the U.S. Navy. My mother was not happy. My father was thirty-five years old with

two young children and a new law practice. My father came out of boot camp as a yeoman then went on to petty officer 3rd class. Soon he was made a line officer and was made captain of his first ship, LST 356.[108]

A crew member of Sam Kimmel's second LST (551) described how his skipper learned from his daughter. While his ship was at sea, Ens. Bland Bounds of the LST 551 ordered a sailor to knock a dent out of the ship caused by a tug while in port. The sailor fell into the water. After a frantic couple of tries to get a line to the sailor, it was apparent that the 551 would have to stop and launch a boat to recover the sailor. Seaman Gertz ran to the superconn to deliver the message. Seaman Gertz stuttered badly when excited. After several moments of stuttering and hissing in front of skipper Kimmel, the skipper, being impatient, ordered, "Dammit, boy, if you can't say it, sing it!" At that, to the tune of "Auld Lang Syne," Seaman Gertz replied, "A sailor fell overboard. He is now one mile behind." With that the 551 had to launch an LCVP and recovered the bosun's mate.[109] Kimmel's daughter, June, had stuttered as a child; and thus he knew that singing would remedy the problem.

There are other stories that attest to Captain Kimmel's alertness. One night while the LST 551 was moored to a dock in Palermo, Sicily, crew member Shatley was on watch. He saw a truck being unloaded and several barrels left near his ship. When Shatley saw the first group of his shipmates returning from liberty, he called their attention to the barrels.

"After much grunting and straining, a barrel was deposited on the fantail (rear of ship). Seaman 1st Class Berford Pope, using his elbow, bashed in the lid to find black olives. At this discovery, Shatley calls to the crewmembers on the dock, saying 'Dammit! Shake'em till you find one that sloshes!' After a few shakes, one sloshed. More grunting, barrel deposited on fantail. Barrel contains red wine. Barrel is then hidden under the fantail's 40mm mount and a tarp placed over it. Two days later the 551 receives orders to get underway. A week later Shatley is standing the second watch once again, only this time his watch station is in the fantail 40mm mount. Sometime during the watch, Shatley hears someone near the notorious barrel. Looking over the side of the gun tub, Shatley sees the skipper, with a pitcher, getting a share of the red wine. Nothing is ever said, and no one knows to this day how Sam Kimmel knew the wine was hidden under the fantail 40mm."[110]

As the LST 282 was hit by a bomb, LST 551 antiaircraft gun crews started shooting at overhead aircraft, without orders from Kimmel, their commanding officer. Kimmel raised hell, and gunners heard him on their headphones yell, "For every piece of [ammunition] brass in the [gun] tub you spend a day in the brig." All the evidence was thrown overboard while the tanks were being unloaded.[111]

Samuel Kimmel, commanding officer, LST 551

Ted Dunn, of Richardson, Texas, served as executive officer of the LST 561. Dunn had participated in the invasion of North Africa against French forces and in the invasion of Sicily on Admiral Hewitt's staff aboard the USS *Monrovia*. In September 1943, Dunn again served on Admiral Hewitt's Salerno invasion staff on the flagship *Ancon*. Dunn also participated in the invasion of southern France. His diary entries follow:

> The invasion of southern France was one of the most bloodless landings in WWII. I was by then a Lt. (jg) and executive officer on LST 561. We had no personnel casualties. The only personnel casualty I knew of was a seaman from another LST. He ventured ashore and onto an enemy

landmine, suffering a wound to his legs. Dr. G.A. Neufeld, a U.S. Navy physician assigned to LST 561 for the invasion, helped get him to an army field hospital ashore.[112]

On July 25th we were ordered to Pozzuoli, Italy, which is about the same distance north of Naples as Salerno is south of Naples. We arrived in the morning of July 25th and anchored out. Later we were ordered into the harbor, berth six. No sooner than securing everything we were reordered to berth two. We moved to that berth and offloaded our army passengers, vehicles, and gear.

The following day we were ordered back to Salerno. On arriving we practiced beaching and landing our LCVPs on the same beach I had landed on a year earlier. We spent the next three days there practicing landings with the Army's 45th Division on and off several times.

At this time Naval Intelligence found that the Germans had planted oyster mines along the coast. These are mines that lie on the bottom and after a predetermined number of ships pass over them they automatically arm themselves. The next ship that passes is the victim. Hence an area thought to be free of mines because ships have passed over it will become deadly. We were ordered to Bizerte, Tunis, for further degaussing. This is a process in which electrical cables are put around the hull and the magnetic influence of the hull is neutralized. To prevent damage to them, all clocks and watches must be removed to a remote spot ashore while the cables are energized. The process takes several hours and must be rechecked from time to time to insure it has not lost effectiveness. When completed all compasses must be recompensated. This took a second day to complete. Although we used the gyrocompass most of the time, it was necessary to have the magnetic compasses in reserve. They were used when the gyrocompass went down due to power interruption or some other cause.

Our frequent trips to French North Africa for cargo and troops brought us into a bubonic plague zone. This was the black death of the Middle Ages. A regulation had been promulgated that on entering any North African port all personnel would be given an anti-plague shot, or inoculation. Great if you came and remained. After entering North African ports three or four times in a month it became a burden. We had enough shots to stop a dozen plagues. Our medical staff, Dr. G. Neufeld, and Pharmacist Mate John Kuzma, were not pleased, but Lt. Foster ordered the shots stopped. We were fortunate as only one LST in each division of six ships was allowed a medical doctor.

John Kuzma, our Pharmacist Mate, was a mortician in civilian life. He was also the best mechanic on the ship, a quality which disturbed the engineering section greatly. He could usually fix what they could not. This included our fog generator. This was a device mounted on the fantail to make fog or smoke in case of attack. We eventually put John in charge of the machine in addition to his sick bay duties.

Coming into Pozzuoli Harbor one afternoon a small sailing craft of about fifty feet, loaded with gravel and stone, crossed our path. Sailing craft have the right of way over powered vessels, but usually they defer to naval vessels—but not this fellow. We were empty and without ballast, giving us fifteen or sixteen feet of freeboard along the full 327 feet of our hull. This was, in effect, a big sail pushing us sidewise. On the public address system we requested any Italian-speaking crewman to report to the forecastle to tell the small boat to move out of our way. One man volunteered. Our mistake. All he could do was swear in Italian. The balance of his speech was in Pig Latin English. The sailboat finally got out of our path and we docked. We did not ask for linguist help again. We took on water for our evaporators. After watering we found an Italian civilian barber who was brought aboard and everyone got a haircut. He must have cut a hundred heads that evening and worn out his hands and scissors.

Our stores officer also found a tile setter who we hired to cement our showers.[113] This involved making a bowl shaped floor over the flat shower deck, which drained poorly and tended to slosh water over the sill in a rough or rolling sea. He had a pushcart full of tile and cement and did four showers for us. Both the tile setter and barber were aboard when we closed the bow doors and went out to the anchorage. We used some of the profits from our canteen to buy cigarettes to pay them both. This was preferable to lira as cigarettes brought fancy prices on the black market. When they finished we put one of our boats in the water, lowered the pushcart and two men in the boat and took them ashore.

In Naples we had a soup run. Each day an LCVP would visit each ship dockside or anchored to pick up leftover food, which was saved in clean GI cans and poured together to make a soup. Everything except mashed potatoes was accepted to make a soup. This was given out to the impoverished civilians, many of whom lived in caves above the city.

We were at anchorage near Naples, at Castellammare Bay, on Aug. 12, 1944, when we were advised we would take part in Operation Anvil. We loaded some extra ammunition from an ammunition ship and at 1615 were underway for the invasion of southern France. The destroyer DD396 was our escort for the balance of the night, leaving us at dawn. We made nine knots, arriving at Ajaccio mid-afternoon, beaching on an army hard at 1500. A hard was an area of the beach with a hard road from the high water mark inland to a regular highway. They were usually packed clay or earth on sand and were sure free of mines.

Pontoons were huge square structures welded together to form a floating roadway. Each pontoon was about 100 feet long and 8- or 10-feet wide. One was carried fixed to our port side and another to our starboard side. They had quick release shackles for easy release, but were secure for a sea voyage. Before beaching we flipped them over into the sea, towing them alongside. Beaching momentum carried them to the beach. Our LCVPs maneuvered them into position in the shallow water so vehicles could exit the bow ramp onto the pontoon and hence onto the beach. Thus it was not necessary to get wet. They were of shallow draft and, after a few vehicles ran on them, settled into the sand well enough to be used as a landing hard.

The French Ninth Division had a one-star general as commanding officer. He turned out to be an arrogant, haughty fellow who demonstrated by actions and attitude why the Germans had defeated the French Army. The general who had the guest seat at the officers' mess was late for meals. When we refueled the LCVPs in their davits, the smoking lamp was out, that is "No Smoking". The general lit up. When asked to put it out, he would not. He made a pest of himself in the chart room and was generally condescending to all. We were glad when he left the ship at Bay Cavaliere, France, where we beached and offloaded the French on Aug. 18, 1944.[114]

Capt. John Opie replaced Rear Admiral Lewis as Admiral Hewitt's chief of staff. Ted Dunn worked under Opie and wrote, "Captain Opie was a career naval officer who lived by the book, that is, 'Navy regulations were his chart and compass'. He was held in high esteem by his subordinates."[115] (Captain Opie's evaluation of the performance of the LST 1012 gunnery during D-day is discussed in the next chapter.)

John T. McCrea, of Miami, Florida, was gunnery officer of the LST 655. He recalled that "as all 78 of the LSTs lined up as we made our way out of Naples, toward France—39 ships in each of two columns—we saw a motor craft moving back and forth from one column to the other, and on the prow sat a heavy figure with his hand up to form a 'V'—and we realized it was Winston Churchill—come to bid good speed to the Forces."[116]

Thomas J. Kronenberger, boatswain's mate second class,[117] provided the author with a copy of his diary on LST 914. His ship left the United States on June 24, 1944; it crossed the Atlantic in a large convoy and proceeded through the Straits of Gibraltar into the Mediterranean. It was a pleasant and quiet trip except for a few submarine alerts. As the LST 914 passed through the straits, Kronenberger wrote, "Gibraltar looks the same as shown in books. As we enter the Mediterranean Sea everyone is on the lookout for planes. So far, everything is going along smoothly. Between one and two in the morning, while on our way just off the coast of Oran, N. Africa, general quarters sounded. This was our first air raid. I guess we were all pretty nervous when all the firing started. It was just like a Fourth of July. One of the planes was knocked down; it was believed to be a German JU-88. Next morning a destroyer notified us that survivors had been picked up from one of the downed planes. After this everything has been pretty quiet except for a few air raid alerts."

The LST 914 reached Bizerte, Tunisia, on July 14; and the crew had liberty there. Kronenberger wrote, "The Arabs will buy anything you have to sell. They wanted skivvy shirts in a bad way for which they gave 150 francs, or $3, so we always had some spending money. Later, when we transported French Moroccan soldiers, we made $5 to $10 profit on a carton of cigarettes. Bizerte was bombed up pretty well, so there wasn't too much doing there maybe, except to go to a grille and get a few drinks. After unloading our passengers and equipment in Bizerte, we set sail July 26 for Pompeii, Italy. On our way we passed close to the Isle of Capri. We anchored in the harbor of Pompeii for a short while and then weighed anchor and proceeded to Naples with our cargo of shells, ammunition and different types of supplies. While unloading at Naples that evening, we had another air raid. After being unloaded, we practiced making landings to perfect the techniques and iron out the bugs. With all of these drills, we surmised something was going to happen within a few short weeks. Leaving Naples we went to Nisida, Italy, and were loaded with tanks, trucks, troops, and supplies. We now knew for sure the invasion would take place shortly. We left on August 12 in a large convoy. We saw Winston Churchill ride through the convoy in his cabin cruiser giving the 'V' for victory sign with his fingers as we passed by. On board our ship was Jean Pierre Aumont, a movie actor who was now in the army with the troops to make the landing. He came aboard as an infantryman. I did get to talk to him and he seemed like an ordinary guy, just doing his job. There was no fanfare accorded him as we were there for the same cause on our way to France. On August 14 we were told that D-day was to be the 15th of August and H-hour 0800."[118]

Clyde L. Bond was aboard the LST 1010 for the invasion of southern France. He recalled that "being a Pharmacist Mate Second Class, we were on GQ all day of the 15th [of August 1944]. My quarters were in the mess area, so I didn't see or know much that was going on. I have been under the impression all these years that the 1012 was hit pretty hard. We took on 48 wounded, some Navy from the hit ship and some Army, one German with a stab wound to the chest—he died that day. I moved to the tank deck to administer saline drips and blood plasma. We had one doctor for the group of LSTs. His name was Dr. George Bowles. The wounded were mostly burn cases, so he ordered the drips and left our ship. We had one known Navy officer with both legs broken. We returned to Naples and shuttled tanks and trucks to northern Italy and several trips to Marseille, France. We had a damaged prop and got to Palermo for dry-dock."[119]

Bob Wilson, commanding officer of the LST 1011, reported that "LST 1011, as a unit of Task Force 87, proceeded to transport area off Red Beach, Camel Assault Area, according to Commander Naval Western

Task Force Operation Plan #4-44 for the invasion of southern France. Mission was to land personnel and equipment of 36th Infantry Division, U.S. Seventh Army. Immediate senior in command—Lieut. Commander F.M. Perrin, Commander Task Unit 87.3.4."[120]

Wilson's ship, LST 1011, and the LST 1012 were commissioned about the same time and place. He and the commanding officer of the LST 1012, Marshall J. Flowers Jr. (nicknamed Buck), became friends and went out on liberty together. Flowers died many years ago; but Wilson was willing to relate to the author his navy experiences before, during, and after Operation Dragoon. Bob Wilson wrote,

Before joining the Navy in the middle of 1942, I had been the personnel director of a Baltimore industrial plant that refused to hire Afro-Americans or Jews even after FDR's fair employment proclamation. Assigned to the Officer Appointment Section of BuPers, I was told orally to appoint only those applicants who had graduated from a Navy-approved list of colleges and to assign any qualified Jew to the Armed Guard, a unit that manned the 3" guns the Navy had placed aboard freighters. But I had joined the Navy for sea duty, not desk work, so after various training schools I came into being CO of LST 1011 at her commissioning in Quincy Navy Yard at the same time that Buck Flowers became CO of the 1012.

The Navy had used Filipino boys as stewards' mates since the Spanish-American War but now the Japanese cut off the supply line and Afro-Americans began to fill the need though they had not been part of a naval crew until then. As we left the States, we had a very black man from Georgia leaving five children at home and a light-skinned boy from New York serving us in the wardroom, making our beds, caring for our laundry. Some in the crew rumbled a bit but gradually came to accept them. They went on liberty with their crewmates, drank at the same bars, shared the same prostitutes. So as we moved from Italy into France, they were experiencing a freedom they had not had before.

For several weeks prior to D-day, we shuttled around between Civitavecchia, Nisida, Bastia, Oran . . . having minor shipboard events, but for Buck and Bob without watch duty it was Capri, Rome, Pompeii, Leghorn, Amalfi, Naples in a jeep that our crews had liberated. Learned that the British

PT boaters were "fearless" in making forays against German outposts and ships, and that Italian and French women offered a hospitality that may have been offered to the Germans as well. In Marseille, the professionals had to be registered and regularly examined by medicos. Was all quite legal and the contract was by the evening rather than by the trick. The foreigners seemed way ahead of us in their treatment of sex and race with the judgment depending, no doubt, upon individual concepts of morality as indoctrinated by different cultures.

Through part of June, all July and the first two weeks of August 1944, it was constant shuttling between North Africa and Sicily. On our last trip before invasion, we brought a contingent of WACs from Oran to Civitavecchia, which helped to remind us that women were into this thing too. A smoke pot went off in our tank deck as Italian workmen were unloading us, temporarily suggesting that the whole load of ammunition was about to blow. We were still making the Atlantic crossing on June 6 when the Normandy invasion began. But we knew that Churchill's choice of an invasion at the "soft underbelly" of Europe was coming.

We visited (with Buck) Pompeii with its phallic pieces outside and descriptive murals inside (you pay your money and take your choice), rode the funicular up Capri to drink Marsala wine and leer at the buxom girl singer, drank wine at an outdoor bistro overlooking the hundreds of ships anchored in the Bay of Naples, in a "liberated" jeep we drove north to Leghorn to observe the results of carpet bombing, visited the Colosseum whose ruins now had plenty of company, went underground in the Catacombs to view hundreds of skulls lined up row by row, drove along the beautiful Amalfi coast, danced off an afternoon at the USO with another lovely Italian but we were marked for departure in the morning . . . and for several nights it was Broadway Bills jammed with uniforms different from the ones two weeks before but all looking for something more than a beer. Young Italian urchins hawked for their "blonde, 18-year-old sisters" and there were tales of assignments being made while family watched.

There was a flurry between the two stewards' mates, both black (black and light brown) which resulted in sending the attacker to the beach for psychiatric examination. These two incidents were the only ones of which I am aware. We had I think a most harmonious crew, but then I might have been naïve in assuming that all in the crew's quarters was milk and honey. From my perspective the job as CO of an LST was a real plus. Much that in hindsight I could have done to have been a better skipper but from my previous experiences the assignment fit and I enjoyed the cruise more than could have been expected under such compelling circumstances.[121]

Robert Wilson, commanding officer, LST 1011

The LST 1012, on which this author served, was one of the twenty-eight LSTs en route to the invasion of southern France, having arrived from the United States late in June 1944. General Eisenhower released an additional forty-eight amphibious vessels, some minesweepers, and a strong force of rocket craft late in July. Naval reinforcements for the bombarding squadrons mostly arrived from Britain in late July or early August. That the great agglomeration of ships and craft in the Gulf of Naples did not trigger any enemy attack was a sign of ineffectual German air forces.[122]

German prisoners of war were the LST 1012's passengers. When the dozen or so of them started singing their national anthem on the ship's tank deck, they were told to stop. They ignored the sentry and continued singing. After his second cease order was ignored, the sentry smashed his rifle butt stock into the face of the choir leader. The singing ended.

The LST 1012's commanding officer, Marshall J. Flowers Jr., provided the secretary of the navy the following history of the ship as it pertains to the invasion of southern France:

Oct. 19, 1945   History of USS LST 1012 (Reference: AlPac #202-45)

1. The USS LST 1012 was built by the Bethlehem Steel Co., Ship Building Division at Quincy, Massachusetts during the spring of 1944 and underwent Commissioning ceremonies on April 30, 1944.
2. Brief fitting out at New York City and shakedown in the Chesapeake Bay area were followed by loading at Norfolk, Virginia, Navy Base and onward routing to the Mediterranean Theater of Operations. The ship sailed from the United States in convoy on June 2, 1944 as a unit of LST Flotilla Twenty, assigned to the Eighth Amphibious Forces.
3. First port of call and base for future operations was Bizerte, Tunisia, where the ship arrived on June 21, 1944. Brief training followed in preparation for the part she was to play in the forthcoming invasion of southern France.
4. Operations in the Mediterranean fell into three periods: (a) preliminary preparations for invasion; (b) invasion; (c) follow-up and support of American and French forces in France.
5. During the preliminary preparations, which began when LST 1012 sailed from Bizerte on June 30, 1944,

for Naples, Italy, the ship engaged in the movement of American and British Air Corps out of Civitavecchia, Italy, to Porto Vecchio, Corsica, and independent runs into Calvi and Ajaccio, Corsica.

6. Staging for the invasion began early in August at Nisida, near Naples, Italy. LST 1012 took on combat cargo and personnel and sailed for the invasion beach on August 12. The invasion was participated in without mishap, the 1012 discharging her combat load on H-plus-13 hour of D-day at Cap Drammont, near Saint-Raphael, in southern France.

7. The follow-up began immediately during which trips were made between Naples and southern France and Oran and southern France, moving personnel and equipment of the Allied Forces, including American, British and Colonial French. During this period, a casualty was suffered by the 1012 in a grounding at Cap Drammont which resulted in a week dry-docking at Palermo, Sicily. When again ready for duty the ship served in hauling varied cargo and personnel to such ports as Ajaccio, Corsica; Naples, Italy; Bizerte, Tunisia; Oran, Algeria; Bastia, Corsica; Port du Bouc and Marseille, France.

8. Termination of duty in the Mediterranean Theater came in Oran, Algeria, on Dec. 28, 1944, when LST 1012 was assigned in convoy with other amphibious craft to sail for the United States where she arrived on Jan. 17, 1945, at her home port of Norfolk, Virginia; 85 percent of the original crew and officers were still on board and she had suffered no serious casualties.

9. The month of February was spent in overhaul and refitting at the Norfolk Navy Yard, Portsmouth, Virginia. During this period a nucleus crew of thirty men and three officers remained on board with their equivalent reliefs while the remainder of Ship's Company enjoyed a welcome thirty-day leave.[123]

Harold Larsen, an LST 1012 crew member in its engine room as a motor mechanic, recorded the following in his diary:

On July 7, 1944, at 1334 hours, the LST 1012 moored at Civitavecchia, portside to LST 394, to unload equipment and supplies. "Civitavecchia is located on Italy's west Thenian Sea coast, forty miles northwest of Rome. A few miles south of this port city was a temporary military camp and salvage depot. One day Lt. (jg) A. Evans took Schoenberger and me to this salvage depot. We picked up damaged stock and equipment for use aboard ship.

Movies shown on board ship while at this port were exchanged with other ships in our task force or obtained from a film exchange facility at this camp. This base is probably where Seabees[124] performed their temporary shore duties.

The Free French troops stationed in Corsica were part of the Allied forces that would participate in the landings on the shores of southern France. LST 1012 and several other similar class vessels made six short trips to Porto Vecchio, transporting American and British Air Force replacements. On our return to Civitavecchia we ferried the Free French Air Force.

Most all port landings were made bow-to or perpendicular to a long stone-concrete platform along the shore. Ship would drop stern anchor while approaching platform. Before lines were finally secured, bow doors would open and landing ramp would be brought down. Army and Air Force personnel and equipment would exit ship on this ramp. Ship retracted from platform after the bow ramp was raised. Then the Captain would order reverse engines while winch pulled on stern anchor.[125]

A few days later, several crew of the LST 1012 (three officers and ten enlisted men) traveled southward to Rome. Larsen observed,

Rome looked deserted. Only thirty-seven days have passed since the Allies first entered the Eternal City. Very little business activity and not many people were walking around. There was no public transportation and no civilian vehicles were on the streets—only U.S. Army trucks and jeeps. Our driver parked the vehicle at a U.S. Army post near Vatican City. We all stayed together at the beginning of our tour but later we went in different directions. Rome had many places of interest to see.

Outside St. Peter's Square, peddlers were selling religious medals and picture cards. The square was empty when we entered. St. Peter's Basilica and the Sistine Chapel were closed. Roman Catholic crewmen were disappointed when they learned that an audience with Pope Pius XII was held earlier. We viewed the Basilica outside from the center of a huge oval-shaped square. Large statues of Christ's disciples were on top of a parapet wall. A covered perimeter walk enclosed most of the square. Large pillars on both sides of walk supported a flat stone cornice roof. Many statues were on top of this roof also. Opposite the Basilica was a wide entrance for public access. I wished we had found a guide during our visit.

Our next stop was the Coliseum. We located a guide who described the history of this ancient arena. Later, when I was thirsty I paid a boy 100 lire ($1) for a small bottle of watered-down vino. The child wanted the empty bottle back. All restaurants were closed because of Italy's food shortage. Nothing available to eat or drink. We should have brought canteens of water with us and sandwiches too. We did much walking this day. I was impressed viewing King Victor Emanuel III Memorial (Italy's last king). Leading up to the memorial were 30 or more wide steps. Memorial and steps were constructed entirely of dazzling white marble. A black ornamental wrought-iron fence along the base of stairs restricted visitors. The memorial was open only on certain holidays.

There were many other places I wanted to visit but by sundown I was tired, hungry, and ready to return to the good old LST 1012. After waiting at Civitavecchia Harbor for three hours, our small boat (LCVP) finally arrived. We boarded ship the next day at 0145 hours.[126]

Larsen also visited Pompeii a couple of weeks before the invasion of southern France and recorded his recollections of that liberty.[127]

Nine days in the port of Naples would be fun. I had visited Naples on July 26 when ship was moored off Nisida Island. I had a good time then. During this liberty one of our officers learned that a tour agency in Naples organized a Pompeii excursion for American servicemen. Trip included train fare and guide. Printed on the ticket was the following: Special tours organized for the Allied Forces. Fee: two pounds English or $10 American.

A dozen other crewmen and myself signed up for this tour. Lt. R.C. Steeple was in charge, assisted by Lt. (jg) A.J. Evans. After an early lunch we walked to the tour agency located near the Central Post Office and not far from the train station. We boarded a train and traveled fifteen miles southeast to Pompeii. Our guide was very good and sometimes comical. He spoke perfect English with an Italian accent.

He began the tour by informing us that at noon on Aug. 24, 79 AD, long dormant Mt. Vesuvius erupted, burying the Roman cities of Pompeii and Herculaneum in volcanic ash. An estimated 20,000 people died. Herculaneum, City of Roman Heroes, was eight miles west of Pompeii. People died from burns caused by hot ash and gas in a pyroclastic flow speeding down the mountainside. Similar to an avalanche. This flow buried both cities. Many buildings collapsed from the weight of volcanic material. Some remained upright. Much of Pompeii has been excavated, revealing many structures, household furnishings and human bones. Excavation in Herculaneum began three hundred years ago. Many bones were found.

The last major eruption of Mt. Vesuvius was in 1631. There was a minor eruption in 1944 but damage was minimal. There is a large volcanic field in Pozzuoli, where heat from deep down in the earth forces material to the surface constantly.

The area we visited must have been the brothel section. Excavations had shown that runoff from heavy rains flowed down through the streets. Large, high stepping-stones were placed at crossings to walk on during rainfall. Etched in these stones were symbols directing person to a specific building or place. One stone had a penis chiseled on top, pointing to a popular ancient whorehouse. I use the word popular because chariot ruts in road along this building were the deepest. The interior of this building had sex illustrations painted on the walls.

Our guide led us to this area for one reason, a sales pitch. He showed us a small shiny metal fob that he was selling. This Greek ornament, a phallus with spreading wings, signified the generative power of nature. Archeologist found a large version of this object among these ruins long ago. I purchased one for 200 lira ($2) to show my friends back home. On my return home, I thought, "What will mother say if she discovers this fob?" Later, I threw this ancient symbol of virility in the ocean. Besides, I didn't want to raise a large family anyway.[128]

From August 7 to 9, the LST 1012 was moored outside the Torre Annunziata jetty. Men from Navy Construction Battalion Detachment 1040, Platoon 18, came aboard the ship. In command was Lt. (jg) Thomas C. Barnett. Another officer, Neil N. Salo, and thirty enlisted men joined Barnett. Men assigned to the construction battalion (Seabees) loaded pontoon causeways on both sides of the 1012. Rear Adm. R. L. Conolly had commanded the invasion for the Licata Beach during the July 1943 Sicily invasion. An offshore sandbar at Licata prevented LSTs from coming right up to the beach. Tank motors stalled when they entered deep water. To avoid this problem in future invasions, Admiral Conolly had designed and fabricated pontoon sections that were carried outside of the LSTs' hull. These sections were assembled into a causeway over which tanks could roll to reach water.[129]

The LST 1012 entered the port of Nisida, Italy, at 0802 hours on August 10. At 1011, army food supplies were brought aboard. A caterpillar crane was removed from the ship at 1020. The first army vehicle to board the ship arrived at 1028. At 1415, fresh fruits and vegetables, dry provisions, and other supplies were brought aboard. They were inspected as to quantity by the ship's supply officer, Ens. James A. Duplessis, and for quality by a medical officer on board for the invasion, Lt. M. McCue. The net weight of the supplies was six tons. At 2030, the last of the army vehicles were loaded. At 2150, all army personnel were aboard. The LST 1012 war diary entry for August 10-11 notes that the loading onboard ship was in accordance with Commander Navy Western Task Force Operation Plan 4-44 for the invasion of southern France.

At midnight on August 11, the LST 1012 moved head-on at Berth 14 Nisida. By 0550, preparations were made for getting under way. LST 1012 was maneuvered at various speeds en route to anchorage in Bay Castellammare.

The convoy, including the LST 1012, set sail from Naples at 1600 on August 12, in accord with Admiral Hewitt's Plan 4-44. The captain, Lt. Marshall Flowers Jr., was at the conn. Maneuvering through the Bay of

Naples, the LST 1012's speed was ten knots. At 2205, general quarters was sounded; and at 2245, general quarters was secured (or ended).

August 13 was the day on which the remaining ships and craft of the Western Naval Task Force were to get under way for the assault. Quartermasters Gruntkowski, Hickey, and Sussna of the LST 1012 recorded in the deck log that the weather was fine. The barometer readings of height in inches ranged from 29.91 to 29.97, the temperature from 73 to 84 degrees Fahrenheit, the sky blue, the visibility from 0800 to 2000 hours at thirty miles. The winds were gentle and waters smooth. Enemy air reconnaissance was active. Admiral Hewitt's staff on the flagship *Catoctin* intercepted reports of Allied shipping. Intelligence reports informed Hewitt and his staff that the German Nineteenth Army generals were expecting an attack in the Genoa area. On board were Hewitt's distinguished American and French military and civilian passengers. At 1400 Adm. Spencer Lewis, who had replaced Adm. Don Moon, was on his flagship, *Bayfield,* under way from Naples at a speed of twelve knots, en route to the Camel Beach assault area. LST 1012 was proceeding toward the same destination at a speed of six knots, changing course intermittently, but slightly.

Other Ships and Aircraft

On August 9, 1944, all the assault ships, landing craft, escort vessels of the three major assault forces, and the Sitka Force were in the Bay of Naples. The flagship *Catoctin* and forty-eight merchant vessels for the army corps follow-up and the Sitka Gunfire Support, consisting of the *Augusta,* the French battleship *Lorraine,* the British cruiser *Dido,* and the U.S. destroyers *Somers* and *Gleaves* and the British *Lookout,* were also present. Admiral Hewitt's records indicate that 307 landing craft, 75 assault transports, assault cargo ships, and merchant vessels were loaded in the Naples area. Protecting these ships were 165 escorts. This concentration of shipping provided the enemy with a clear target. Air reconnaissance alerted the Germans, but no attack was undertaken— probably because German air power had been mostly wiped out.

French Moroccan and Algerian troops were loaded on forty merchant transports at Brindisi and Taranto. Twelve escorts protected them. The Delta Gunfire Support was also at Taranto, consisting of the battleships *Texas* and *Nevada,* the cruiser *Philadelphia,* the French cruisers

Montcalm and *Georges Leygues,* and eight U.S. destroyers. Survivors of the Casablanca action, the French destroyers *Fantasque, Malin,* and *Terrible,* joined the armada later.

An Aircraft Carrier Force was at Malta. It had completed a deceptive movement to Alexandria and returned. The Alpha Gunfire Support Group consisted of four British cruisers, the French cruiser *Gloire* and the American cruiser *Quincy,* and two British and four American destroyers. Later, the British battleship *Ramillies* was to join the armada. The gunfire support group of the Camel Attack Force consisted of three U.S. cruisers; the battleship *Arkansas;* the British cruiser *Argonaut;* the French cruisers *Duguay*—Trouin and *Emile Bertin;* and eleven U.S. destroyers. It is useful to remember that the general plan comprised three main assault forces. Each was under the overall command of a rear admiral, United States Navy, and each landing force consisted of one American combat division of troops with its division commander. Left to right along the invasion coast of southern France the three assault forces were assigned as follows: on the left of the Alpha Attack Force, Rear Adm. F. J. Lowry; in the center, Delta Attack Force, Rear Adm. B. J. Rodgers; and on the right, Camel Attack Force, Rear Adm. Spencer S. Lewis. H-hour for these three landings was set for 0800. It was the first occasion in which zero hour was made after daylight.

Preparations undertaken by the Allied Air Force for the invasion of southern France were reported in a 1992 publication[130] as follows:

> The night of Aug. 14, 1944, was clear and cool in the take-off areas. The troop carrier units waited at their stations on 10 airfields extending some 150 miles along the Italian peninsula from Ciampino near Rome to Fallonica. Lack of transportation had compelled the bulk of the force to commence moving to dispersal airfields as early as D-minus-5. The shift was completed by D-minus-2. Now, with preparations complete, an air of confident expectancy prevailed.
>
> Anxiously the weather was watched. The date had been unalterably set for Aug. 15, and weather meant everything. Hill masses and coastal features must be readily identified. A portion of a high-pressure area, broken off from its North Sea center, had settled over the main target zone, with its threat of accumulating fog or stratus. The forecast was for clear weather to Elba, followed by decreasing visibility until the DZs[131] were

reached, where it was expected to be two to three miles. Actually the visibility was less than half a mile. The valley fog, which completely blanketed the early parachute operation, did however lift by 0800 hours in time for the morning glider mission. To make navigation difficulties tougher, the wind was almost 90 degrees off the forecast direction, and infrequent checkpoints over the water route were the navigators' only means of correction. Luckily, the wind did not reach high velocity and was less than 6 mph over the DZ.

Shortly after midnight of 14-15 August the real show began. With everything ready for the green light, the first troop carriers with their load of three pathfinder units took off at 0030. The pathfinder platoons proceeded as a group on a direct line to southern France, making their first landfall just south of Cannes. The pathfinders proceeded inland as planned, located the drop zones and dropped their teams at 0323, 0330, and 0334 hours, respectively.

Approximately one hour after the pathfinders, the main parachute lift, composed of 396 aircraft in nine serials averaging 45 aircraft each, took off and proceeded on their courses, using amber downward recognition lights until the final water checkpoint had been crossed. Wing formation lights were also employed, and no instance of friendly naval fire on our planes was reported. No enemy aircraft was encountered. Of particular interest is the fact that some 400 troop carrier aircraft flew in relatively tight formation, under operational strain, for some 500 miles without accident. Training in night formation flying had paid off.

Undoubtedly the radar, radio, and other marker installations were responsible for this flying accuracy. Eurekas had been installed at each wing departure point, the command departure point, the northeast tip of Elba, Giroglia Island (North Corsica), and on three marker beacon boats spaced 30 miles apart on the course from Corsica to the first landfall checkpoint at Agay, France. These worked perfectly, with an average reception of 25 miles. Holophanes lights, also placed at these positions, aided the navigators to correct their courses against contrary wind currents. Their reception averaged 8 miles until the DZs were reached, when haze and ground fog made them invisible. Beacons (the Radio Compass Homing Devices) were installed at Elba, on North Corsica, and on the center marker beacon boat, and were also dropped on the DZs along with the Eurekas and Holophane lights. Many pilots reported that they received these signals up to 30 miles. The beacons often kept the aircraft on beam when they occasionally lost the signal on their Eurekas. In many cases the signals exhibited a tendency to drift off the frequency despite constant operational checking. Such evident functional defects may jeopardize a whole mission.

In general, the parachute drop was fully successful. Approximately 85 percent, a far larger proportion than had been accomplished in previous operations in the European theater, landed on the DZs or in their immediate vicinity, in areas contiguous to the drop zones, from which terrain the parachute forces could carry out their assigned missions. All this was despite the handicaps of no moon, general haze, and heavy ground fog. An estimated 45 aircraft completely missed their DZs. Some of these dropped their troops as far as 20 miles from the selected areas.

Since the ships of the Allied armada had different characteristics and speeds, it was not feasible for the three main assault units to proceed to the assault area as a single unit. The ships had to be dispatched in convoys by types; LSTs, among the slowest, had to depart first to arrive at their destination approximately simultaneously with the much-faster ships. Each of these convoys was formed in three sections at ten-mile intervals. The first section consisted of Camel Assault Force vessels, the second of Delta vessels, and the third of Alpha vessels. This arrangement permitted the convoys, after proceeding on a northern course up to the west coast of Corsica, to turn left simultaneously by sections, with each section in its proper final approach lane. The convoy routes were designated to promote deception. Proceeding along the Corsica coast, the convoys made it appear that they were headed toward Genoa. Not until the last moment did they turn northwest toward their real destination. For the slowest types, the turn had to be executed a little before nightfall of the eve of the attack.

The Expeditionary Force for Operation Dragoon consisted of ten reinforced divisions. In addition, rear echelon personnel resulted in a total of four hundred fifty thousand men who participated in Dragoon. American forces provided the initial main strength of the invasion. But thereafter, the proportion of French troops increased to 70 percent of the total force.

The Allies had about five thousand aircraft. There were fourteen airfields established in Corsica that served as an advance base for about forty squadrons. Each aircraft carrier had twenty-four planes. The mobility of aircraft carriers multiplied the impact of ship-borne aviation.

The enemy had strongly reinforced coast defenses. But they had to defend all of France against sabotage and resistance and overwhelming naval and air superiority. The Germans expected an invasion. However, they did not know where it would occur. They were deceived by aerial bombing and various diversions. Admiral Hewitt's last-minute movement of his armada's convoys was organized to deceive the enemy into believing that the Gulf of Genoa was to be the invasion site. The choice of the Dragoon landing beaches also surprised the Germans, but not a prominent American civilian.

A Distinguished Witness—James V. Forrestal

Arriving in Europe by air on August 6, 1944, the secretary of the navy, James V. Forrestal, observed Dragoon rehearsals. Then he inspected the Italian front. He boarded the *Catoctin* just before it left for the invasion area. Forrestal was one of FDR's midwar appointments. He had done exceedingly well financially. In the late 1920s and 1930s, he was responsible for many big investment banking successes that led to his becoming president of the Dillon, Read investment firm. One deal that he engineered resulted in a $900,000 profit. It ensured his family's financial future, and Forrestal was hailed as "the boy wonder of Wall Street." He mastered the financing of industry, transportation, and exploitation of mineral resources in foreign countries. His individually derived profits from his securities transactions for the year 1929 called for a tax of more than $95,000. Although Forrestal had not done anything illegal, he had engaged in transactions that raised questions from an ethical point of view; what he had done was to straddle the line separating avoidance of taxes from evasion of taxes. He did not claim that he was badly advised, and he did not transfer responsibility from himself to his accountant or other advisor. Instead, he arranged an income-tax settlement with the Internal Revenue Division of the Treasury Department. Even though he was not a New Dealer and not an admirer of President Roosevelt, Forrestal supported some major New Deal financial reforms. High-ranking officials in the Roosevelt administration, such as Harry Hopkins and Thomas Corcoran, admired Forrestal's support of the Securities and Exchange Act. In June 1940, as France was being overrun by the Germans, Forrestal had concluded that the United States government could use his services in the forthcoming war against totalitarianism, and Roosevelt's key advisors realized that an American rearmament program would require Forrestal's financial abilities and dedication.

His usefulness to the defense of the United States was exemplary. After two months of service in summer 1940 as an administrative assistant to Roosevelt, Forrestal became navy undersecretary. By 1944, he and the top naval officer, Admiral King, had vastly improved the navy's strength. After the death of Frank Knox, Roosevelt announced Forrestal's appointment as secretary on May 10, 1944, on the basis of his excellent record. Forrestal quickly recruited a first-rate staff of men and women who helped him deal with procurement, tax, contract negotiation, legal, public relations, intergovernmental, and other problems. By the end of the war, Forrestal had played a major role in the building of 65,999 combat ships and 110,053 planes.

Arnold A. Rogow has described the results of the efforts of Forrestal's leadership in strengthening the U.S. Navy during World War II this way: "On July 1, 1940, the United States Navy consisted of 1,058 vessels of all types, 383 of which were combat vessels. Uniformed personnel totaled 189,000 men. By November 1, 1944, the number of ships had increased to more than 40,000. The additions included 9 battleships, over 70 aircraft carriers, 34,500 planes, 20 cruisers, more than 500 destroyers and destroyer escorts, and over 100 submarines. Altogether there were more than 1,500 combat vessels, and the total of personnel was 3,600,000, of whom 100,000 were women."[132]

Another *Catoctin* Passenger—Gen. Lucian K. Truscott Jr.

On Saturday, August 12, 1944, General Truscott came aboard the *Catoctin* at 2100 hours. Since the ship was at anchor in Naples and its ventilating system was not operating, Truscott's cabin was a Turkish bath. But the weather outside was delightful. Truscott and Gen. Alexander Patch were eager to see one another. Years later, Truscott remembered their conversation. Patch, "Truscott, I am coming along on the *Catoctin* but I want you to know I do not want to embarrass you in any way. I am not going to interfere with the way you fight your battle. I want you to know it."[133] In his book *Command Decision*, Truscott noted, "I thanked General Patch, and assured him that I had no desire but to work in the closest possible cooperation and that I would always be glad to have his advice."[134] Entries in the journal of General Truscott's aide describe the *Catoctin* voyage as follows:

Sunday, Aug. 13, 1944

A rather sleepless night for all in the hot staterooms. General Truscott—up for leisurely breakfast at 0800. General H.M. Wilson aboard to wish party good luck, with Adm. Morris, RN, Secretary of Navy and Adm. Hewitt aboard. General Truscott on deck to watch proceedings as ship pulls out of harbor to anchor out in bay. Prime Minister Churchill sails in a speedboat with Adm. Morris to wave goodbye and good luck. Ship finally underway after lunch and General Truscott spends afternoon reading. Heat still most oppressive, with ventilating system broken. General is eating at Flag mess.

Monday, Aug. 14, 1944

Another bad night in oven-like cabin. Day quiet and almost uneventful, with ship passing through Sardinia-Corsica strait at noon and skirting western coast of Corsica all afternoon. General Saville in during morning to straighten out question of bombing enemy. Destroyer alongside. General Somerville [*sic*], Secretary Patterson [Assistant Secretary of the U.S. War Department, Robert Patterson] request permission to come aboard tomorrow. Messages from General H.M. Wilson and Adm. Cunningham wishing all good luck. In late evening begin to pass through LCIs. Some 1,001 ships making this invasion. Largest in history. Jitters cooling off a little, and General Truscott—writes letter to wife before starting to bed.[135]

The *Catoctin*, Admiral Hewitt's flagship

Vice Adm. H. Kent Hewitt, USN (right), points out salient
features of the assault sector to Navy Secretary James Forrestal
(center) and Maj. Gen. Alexander M. Patch aboard ship on
D-day minus 1, August 14, 1944.

Secretary of the Navy James Forrestal gets a firsthand experience of the workings of an invasion as he accompanies the Allied force that landed in southern France on August 15, 1944. On August 14, seated below a porthole aboard a U.S. navy ship on route to the objective, Mr. Forrestal holds a press conference for newspapermen covering the story of the mighty assault. At the Secretary's left is Vice Admiral H. Kent Hewitt, USN.

Before and after the Dragoon assault by the U.S. Army's VI Corps, its commander, General Truscott,—dreaded a repetition of the Anzio campaign's failure. That D-day, on January 22, 1944, was sunny and warm; and the Allied troops easily overran the Italian prewar resort town of Anzio, located thirty miles from Rome. But while Allied troops consolidated their positions and prepared to leave the beachhead, the Germans assembled their troops and, for the next four months, carried out a devastating offensive. The Anzio campaign resulted in 29,200 Allied VI Corps combat casualties—4,400 killed, 18,000 wounded, 6,800 prisoners or missing, and 37,000 noncombat casualties. The Anzio campaign failed in outflanking the Germans, providing mobility to the Italian campaign, expediting the capture of Rome. Because of the insufficient provision of Allied troops and supplies, the ambitious objective desired by British planners was frustrated for four bloody months.[136]

Maj. Gen. John P. Lucas was the U.S. Army commander of the Fifth Army VI Corps. It was Lucas who was to lead the Anzio invasion. He has been criticized for being unduly cautious, using precious time digging in and permitting the Germans to counterattack and frustrate a bold Allied behind enemy lines. Lucas's critics claim that an imaginative and aggressive commander such as General Truscott—would have succeeded in achieving Allied goals by a fast and daring offensive from the beachhead. On February 23, 1944, Lucas was relieved of his duties. His successor was Major General Truscott. On May 23, 1944, his VI Corps took out the Anzio bridgehead.[137]

Truscott's apprehension about having his troops trapped on a Riviera beach stemmed from his Anzio experience. On July 12, 1944, he attended a meeting of air, naval, and ground military commanders. Dragoon planners made it clear to him and the others that a thorough accounting had been taken of German troops and other dangers. He was assured that precautions were taken and that Anzio mistakes would not be repeated. Allied air planning officers concluded that the German Luftwaffe was practically nonexistent as a threat. German communications and enemy submarine bases were destroyed. Principal German coastal batteries and radar stations were rendered impotent. To confuse the enemy, Allied attacks were extended from Séte to Genoa, Italy. But not all dangers were removed.

Audie Leon Murphy and Other Soldiers

Despite the various precautions taken, other dangers remained. One brave soldier who participated in Operation Dragoon and was exposed to its danger was Audie Leon Murphy, a twenty-year-old from Hunt County, Texas. His father was a sharecropper, and the shack that Murphy was born in was in the center of a cotton field. In June 1942, Murphy enlisted in the army. By August 11, 1944, when he left Naples on his way to southern France, he was no longer a poor boy from the Texas backwoods. He had grown up fast in Italy and was a man who laid three Neapolitan women in one night. By the end of his army service, Murphy had been wounded in action three times, won the highest awards for bravery, and was no longer an enlisted man. He became an officer and received a battlefield commission. As the most decorated soldier in the history of the United States, he was world famous. On the night of August 9, 1944, the 141st Infantry Regiment of the Thirty-sixth Infantry Division and Murphy had left for the southern French coast. That regiment sailed out to Salerno and lay offshore as the invasion fleet was built around it.

At dawn on the twelfth, the 141st Infantry Regiment was moving north along the coast. Its soldiers were lined up at the rails of LST, taking their last look at Italy. Some may have thought about the first day they arrived in Italy, others about the comrades they left buried there. To some soldiers, Italy meant difficult days of fighting in mountains and mud. Ahead of the 141st Infantry was the job of assaulting hostile places that had been designated by Allied military planners as the Camel Beaches. The high mass of ground projecting out to seas was Cap Drammont. Outlined against the shore was a small island known as Ile d'Or. Dominating it was a stone tower that the soldiers had been told held enemies with weapons ready to kill them. There were other potential sources for death at Cap Drammont.[138]

By the afternoon of August 14, the *Catoctin*'s decks and ladders were jammed with nearly one thousand people, including airmen, sailors, soldiers, generals, admirals, and war correspondents. As mentioned previously, Assistant Secretary of War Patterson was also on board. Born in 1891, Patterson made his name as a federal judge. As Secretary of War Stimson's assistant, Patterson led the army's procurement program and played an important role in the administration of a liberated France. Nicknamed "Old Thorough," he was widely known throughout Washingtonian circles for his administrative ability.[139]

On that Sunday in August, all the elements of the Western Naval Force were at sea and converging on the assault area. Admiral Hewitt reported that ten divisions of troops were afloat, with their equipment and supporting services. The portable number of men was almost a quarter of a million. Transporting them, protecting them, and landing them safely were nearly a thousand ships and many types of small landing craft. Most were navy ships, the remainder operated by merchant marine crews. Of the naval ships and craft, 543 were American, 266 were British, 35 were French, and 7 were Greek. On that lovely summer afternoon, Churchill appeared relaxed and jovial. He looked grand in a white linen suit aboard Adm. John Morris's Royal Navy barge. The prime minister directed the helmsman to go around the ships in the Bay of Naples. Churchill stood in the stern, waving and giving the V-sign to men gathered on the decks of the ships. The sailors waved back and shouted, "It's Winnie! It's the old man himself!"

A few days after Churchill became prime minister on May 2, 1940, Sir Charles Wilson, later Lord Moran, was appointed his physician. It was not that Churchill wanted a doctor but because some of his cabinet members decided that somebody ought to keep an eye on the health of the sixty-five-year-old. Lord Moran was a highly qualified physician, dedicated to keeping his famous patient well and functioning. This was a difficult task, since Churchill, who undermined his health over many years, was afflicted by dyspepsia, coronary problems, melancholia and depression, hernia, and other maladies. Churchill's temperament, egotism, and obstinacy did not make for a good patient-physician relationship. After their first professional meeting on May 24, 1940, Dr. Wilson recorded in his diary, "I do not like the job and I do not think the arrangement can last." But it did last, until Churchill's death on January 25, 1965, at the age of ninety.

To his invaluable medical services from 1940 to 1965, Lord Moran added a good book on Churchill. The material taken from his diaries and a few entries, circa August 1944, merit attention. On August 4, 1944, the prime minister burst out to his physician, "Good God, can't you see that the Russians are spreading across Europe like a tide? They invaded Poland, and there is nothing to prevent them from marching into Turkey and Greece."[140] Lord Moran was concerned that Churchill ignored medical advice. Before going to Italy, the prime minister needed malarial protection, yet Churchill chose to shun medical specialists. He relied on the opinion of King George VI and Gen. Harold Alexander not to take antimalaria precautions. It was only when Moran wrote Churchill a letter that read, "General Alexander suggests the doctors keep their pills. I venture to wonder if General Alexander's views on medical matters have the same value as mine on military affairs,"[141] that Churchill finally took the much-needed pills and avoided malaria.

Lord Moran wrote that on August 14, Churchill spoke to him at length about his depression, his fears, and his worries. Churchill said it helped for him to write down a half a dozen things that worried him. He said that two worries would disappear, about two nothing could be done, and the last two could be settled. Lord Moran told his patient that his depression came from his ancestors. Churchill fought against it all his life and disliked visiting hospitals, always avoiding anything that was depressing. Nevertheless, Churchill buoyed the British and their Allies to be indomitable in their struggle against Nazi evil. That afternoon, Churchill flew in Gen. Henry Maitland Wilson's Dakota plane to Corsica. Then he boarded the destroyer *Kimberly* to see the landing on the beaches of southern France.

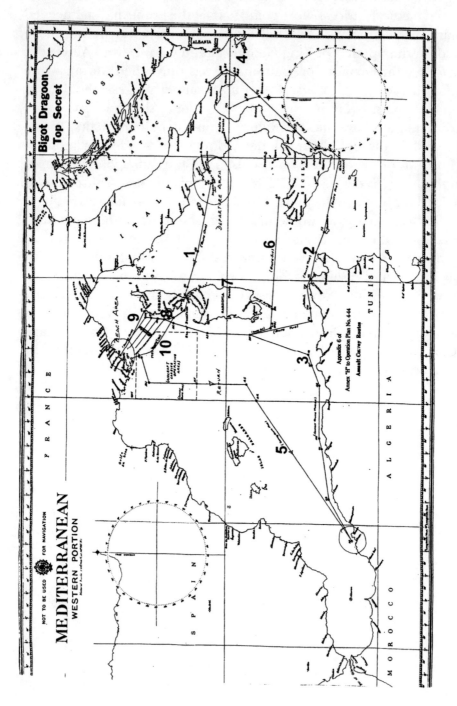

Convoy map from R. C. Steeple Jr. (Executive Officer/Navigator, LST 1012)

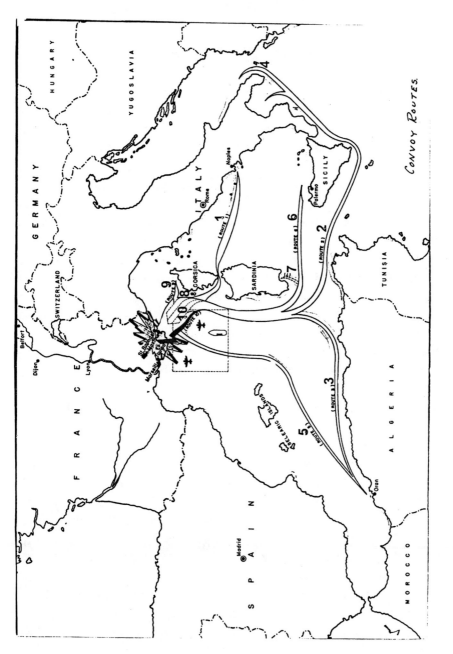

Convoy routes

CHAPTER 9

AUGUST 15, 1944

Thousands of teenaged American soldiers and sailors were busy on Napoleon's birthday. Some of them parachuted into southern French towns while others were stationed throughout the various sections of ships—engine rooms, gunnery stations, wheelhouses, radar and radio shacks, and conning towers. Some sailors in small boats transported frightened, huddled, seasick soldiers to attractive but deadly Riviera beaches. Many of these young men prayed with and without the help of military chaplains before boarding the landing boats. It's unlikely that these young invaders knew much about the controversial history, planning, and preparation for a campaign that might kill or maim them. Some would risk their lives to rescue others. Congressional Medal of Honor winners Audie L. Murphy of Texas and James P. Connor of Delaware should be remembered for their self-sacrifices, as should a seventeen-year-old sailor from southern New Jersey, Ferris C. Burke, and the commanding officer of LST 282, Lawrence E. Gilbert of Brooklyn, New York. Both saved drowning shipmates. But Gilbert did even more; a superb ship handler, he steered his fire-ravaged vessel away from other nearby ships.

One of these fortunate ships was the LST 1012, whose commanding officer, Marshall Flowers Jr., was not an exceptional seaman. A compassionate and quiet gentleman, Flowers was, however, prone to running the 1012 aground, causing it to damage other ships, and taking unwarranted credit for the ship's gunnery performance during the Dragoon invasion. Luckily, the Dragoon invaders were led by generals and admirals of extraordinary competence. Not only did Rear Adm. Spencer S. Lewis perform well under the tragic and difficult circumstances into which he was placed by his predecessor's suicide, he also provided a very useful post-Dragoon analysis. Adm. Harold R. Stark, commanding officer of naval forces in Europe, claimed that Admiral Hewitt was lucky to have the help of Admiral Lewis.

Rear Adm. Spencer C. Lewis

The commanding general of the German forces defending southern France from Allied invasion, Gen. Johannes Blaskowitz, was also exceptional but not fortunate. Repeatedly, he demonstrated courage in criticizing Nazi atrocities as well as great ability in delaying Allied victory and withdrawing his troops in an orderly fashion so that they could continue to fight another day. However, given the potency of the Normandy and Dragoon invasions of France, the formidable Russian victories, and the revival of French strength, it was apparent that the fate of Blaskowitz and millions of his compatriots was defeat and the devastation of their homeland. For actor-soldier Jean-Pierre Aumont and thousands of other French citizens who participated in Dragoon, August 1944 signified an end to bitter exile and a return home.

Dropping into France

Parachutist J. K. Horne Jr. reported the following:

> Sometime shortly after midnight on Aug. 15, 1944, we loaded our equipment and bundles for the early morning jump into southern France known as the Operation Dragoon. Each trooper had his personal equipment: two bandoleers of .30 cal. ammo and enough field rations for three days. The rations included K-rations, C-rations, and concentrated chocolate bars, an M-1 rifle, a .45 pistol, a full musette bag, a bayonet, 3 knives, a main parachute, a reserve parachute, and one telephone switchboard. Every one of us was overloaded.
>
> A short time after crossing the French coastline, we could see troopers jumping from other planes, but the only action light we had was red (that is the ready light). We flew for several minutes more before our green light finally came on and out we went anxious to get going. Being the tallest man in our plane, I was designated as the pusher. The pusher was to be the last trooper out of the plane and made sure everyone else had jumped. I put my shoulder into the back of Roger Bennett, from Albany, Ind., and began to push. We cleared the plane in record time and immediately after the opening shock, I hit the ground. The jump could not have been more than 400 to 500 feet high—should have been at least twice that height.

Having a razor sharp trench knife on my right leg, I dumped my reserve chute and cut the chute harness off, sticking my trench knife in the ground and assembled my M-l rifle for immediate action. Bennett and I landed close together and we started out in the dark to find the rest of our group. After about two running steps, we fell face down from a 6-7' terrace that the French farmers had put in so they could farm the mountainside. Some ten to fifteen minutes later I remembered just where I had left my trench knife—well I'd just have to do without it until I could get another one. As it developed, we were in the same area as our battalion commander, Colonel Melvin Zais. We assembled about 400 troopers within a two-hour period. As soon as Zais determined our location, we proceeded toward our objective near Les Arcs.

The second morning, Aug. 16, rifle fire awakened me from a very short sleep. I was in a ditch on the edge of a town called Callian. I was cold, hungry and of course I was scared. Breakfast was a C-ration of corned beef hash. The hash was cold and a fire to heat it was out of the question. Cold corned beef hash does not make a tasty breakfast. Later that same day, we heard the weirdest music coming our way. It turned out to be British paratroopers playing their bagpipes. I've often wondered if they played the pipes on the way down. It was extremely tiring climbing up and down the mountain trails with the overload of equipment. We had extra ammunition and a half belt of .30 cal. machine-gun ammo, extra batteries for the telephone equipment, three miles of telephone wire and one six-jack telephone switchboard. During the first morning we discovered that with all this telephone equipment, we did not have a telephone. The switchboard was the heaviest of all this, so it fell over the side of the mountain . . . all by itself.

On the way to Les Arcs we played havoc with one German convoy plus several small groups of Germans. We were following a high-tension power line toward Les Arcs, when the colonel decided we needed to cut those lines to disrupt power to any of the enemy that might be using it. Being a wireman, I carried wirecutters and had one pair of large, heavy-duty insulated cutters. Of course I was tasked with climbing a very tall pole to cut the high-tension wires. As I started climbing the pole, I immediately drew rifle fire. So I came back down and asked for a sniper rifle. My plan was to shoot the glass connectors, thereby breaking the wire. This only partially worked. I am sure the German rifle fire saved my life, 'cause the insulation on those cutters was not enough protection from the high voltage. Another trooper lost his life trying to cut the wire with a pick.

Somewhere during these first few days we were stopped by a small force of Germans using a 6' drainage ditch in the same manner as the WWI soldiers used trenches. This was the first time I saw our men use their mortars. They fired a barrage right down that ditch. All that was left were hands, feet and other body parts—no Germans survived.[1]

The First Special Service Force (FSSF) was assigned to Lt. Gen. Alexander M. Patch's Seventh Army for the invasion of southern France. He ordered it to seize German batteries on three rocky landmasses on the left bank of the invasion beach, known as the Iles d'Hyères. The men of the FSSF used rubber boats to land on the shores of Ile de Port-Cros and Ile d'Or (during the night of August 14-15). The defenders of these islands were taken by surprise and surrendered within two days. After this success, the FSSF troops joined the main army and guarded the right flank of the Seventh Army's advance along the Riviera. The FSSF unit established a defensive position in the mountains along the French-Italian border by the beginning of September 1944.

Robert E. Pettit was a member of the FSSF Fourth Company, Second Regiment, and landed on Ile du Levant on August 14-15. His account of the invasion follows:

We began disembarking from the APD *Tattnall* (U.S. Navy destroyer converted to troop carrier) at approximately 2300 hours August 14. We landed via rubber boats at approximately 0130 hours August 15 on the beach with only a searchlight beam coming from the high ground above the beach sweeping across the rubber boats, but the light was immediately switched off and was not seen again.

Moving up from the cove to the NW we encountered an occupied pillbox which was taken with one German killed and four taken prisoner. My company moved to the west end of the island where we captured an outpost in Fort Arbousier. The defenses were quite formidable consisting of pillboxes and mortars in concrete.

We then turned to the NE toward Port del Avis which was the site of the remaining German resistance on the island. A short but vicious firefight ensued and the German commander sent out a surrender party at about 2300 hours and the fight for Ile du Levant ended. However, German batteries from the mainland continued to shell both Levant and Port Cros throughout the night.[2]

D-day on the Riviera: U.S. Navy Responsibilities

On August 15, 1944, the U.S. Navy was charged with establishing the U.S. Seventh Army firmly ashore on the Cavalaire-Fréjus sector by clearing the surrounding waters of German mines and underwater barriers, reducing the effect of German shore batteries, and ensuring that the required troops and equipment landed according to plan on the chosen beaches.[3]

In accordance with the army's plan for the invasion, pre-H-hour bombing began as Allied guns opened fire on the French coast. Once daylight hit, the beach defenses started their scheduled attacks. Admiral Hewitt noted that both were "executed with precision." He added that "it was beautiful to watch. Having had the misfortune of having to combat the French Navy at Casablanca, it was particularly heartening to see their fine cruisers, now under my command, flying their largest *tricouleur* battle flags, heavily engaged in this drive to liberate their own country from the heel of the invader."[4]

Airborne task force troops were dropped from 396 troop-carrier aircraft near Le Muy at around 0400 on the fifteenth. The aircraft were "guided to their objective by carefully stationed beacon vessels," Hewitt added. "How different from Sicily! A few of these troops, dropped in error near St. Tropez, were joined by French Resistance forces, who later led them in a successful attack on that city."[5] These early morning landings went according to plan, thanks to the painstakingly crafted strategy for invading the Riviera. There was little German resistance.

Following the pre-H-hour activities, the first wave of landings along the Alpha, Delta, and Camel Beach sectors went ashore at 0800 hours.

"Such precision," observed Hewitt, "could only have been the result of experience, thorough training, and careful planning on the part of all concerned."[6] But even for battle-tested army veterans of the Italian campaigns, the Dragoon landing was no picnic.

Audie Murphy recalled the invasion on August 15 and his landing on Camel Green Beach this way: "Technically, it was called a perfect landing. The vast operation designed to crack the enemy coastal defenses . . . had been calculated and prepared to the smallest detail, and it moved with the smooth precision of a machine . . . But we do not know, we do not see, the gigantic pattern of the offensive as we peer over the landing boats . . . The battleships have given the beach a thorough pounding . . . The rocket boat guns take over . . . The men huddled in the boat . . . look as miserable as wet cats . . . Suddenly I see the comedy of little men . . ."[7] He spelled out the steps taken by Allied Navy ships to wipe out enemy dangers—the beach pounding by battleship cannons and rockets firing missiles, detonating mines, and cutting barbed-wire entanglements. Under a deafening barrage, Murphy and his fellow landing boat passengers huddled in the boat. "Though the water has been smooth enough, several are seasick; and others have the lost, abstract expression of men who are relieving their bowels," he wrote.[8]

Camel Green Beach. Another wave of infantrymen
and medics hit Green Beach.

As soon as Murphy and other soldiers jumped from the landing craft and waded ashore, they were welcomed by enemy gunfire from the hills above the beach. They quickly learned that the beach had mines that were easily detonated. Murphy saw a buddy's dismembered body. The medic who attended the victim dismissed four approaching litter bearers. Their help was not required.

By the morning of August 15, the *Augusta* arrived in her position at the Sitka Assault Group, where she fired upon Port-Cros Island. During the Dragoon invasion, she fired more than seven hundred rounds of eight-inch projectiles and substantially helped the Allied invasion troops.

On the same day, the LST 1012 landed at Cap Drammont, France. The ship's forward draft, after entering port, was 6 feet forward and 11 feet 1 inch aft. It expended 1,600 gallons of fuel en route to Dragoon and had 9,800 gallons left. The freshwater supply was 11,360 gallons. The temperature of the gun magazines, where ammunition was stored under the supervision of Gunner's Mate Charles Earle, was a minimum of 74 degrees and a maximum of 89 degrees. The weather varied from 72 to 84 degrees. At 0500 hours, the LST 1012 arrived in the transport area off the invasion beach. At 0625, general quarters (emergency warning) was sounded. Crew members went to their battle stations. The author's battle station was helmsman of the ship. Harold Larsen, who was stationed in the engine room, recalled the following: "0625 hours General Quarters. I was on the main deck and 'Ready,' wearing my life jacket and steel helmet. I entered the Starboard deck hatch and descended to the Auxiliary Engine Room four decks below. Two generators were on line essential for landing machinery. I put on my headphone set and called topside that my station was manned. I sat on a stool with my head in soundproof cover watching gauges on electric power panels. The only word that I heard over the phone all day was 'secure.'"[9]

The 1012 deck log that day recorded that the bow doors and ramp were opened at 0930. At 0952, two army DUKWs (amphibious trucks) were launched in accordance with operation orders from LST 1011. At 0955, Chaplain Keenan held Catholic services.[10] The deck log entry for the noon to 1600 watch indicated that during this period the LST 1012 was in the transport area keeping station. Although the ship prepared for beaching as of 1441 hours, the log entry noted at 1500, "Have to wait for further orders."

At 0930 hours on August 15, the first and second wave LSTs were ordered by Commander Alpha Attack Force to unload. Shortly thereafter, the LST 265 received forty-six army casualties wounded on the beach.[11]

Gen. John Dahlquist was eager to leave the *Bayfield* to lead his Thirty-sixth Infantry Division troops ashore. Not only was he the first division commander to set foot in Provence, but he also found himself in the midst of a battle zone. The town of Saint-Raphael was five miles to the left, and Antheor was five miles to the right. Luckily for Dahlquist's Thirty-sixth (also known as the Texas Division), the German defense for the Camel Zone was hardly a model of efficiency, depending heavily on the fighting ability of sprawling units of varying caliber. The German troops were not under any centralized control and were subjected to sabotage and harassment by the French Resistance. The invading troops had plenty of DUKWs (amphibious trucks), jeeps, trucks, ambulances, and bulldozers. Silvery antiaircraft balloons were used over the land and sea. The time was 1015 on August 15.

Allied air and naval firepower blanketed the Germans and their 75-mm gun battery, trapping the enemy gunners in the middle of the invasion sector. Allied tanks tried to neutralize all the defenses at Le Drammont. A few feeble, stray German shells appeared in the air, but there was no effective resistance as the tanks awkwardly proceeded through the village of Le Drammont. German soldiers disappeared from the quarries near the beach, fleeing the invading forces. One of the Allied tank units heading toward the road to Le Drammont overtook twenty-two German prisoners who had been captured near the Camel Green sector by French Resistance members.[12]

Dahlquist's troops were assigned the difficult task of advancing along the Camel sector beaches, from the mouth of the Argens River to the rocky mass of Cap Roux. The mission was treacherous because the Argens Valley was deemed to be the primary zone of action by the Allied staff. The Thirty-sixth Infantry Division had lost many soldiers on the bloody fields of Salerno, Monte Cassino, and Rapido, in Italy. They had been in rough situations before and expected nothing less of this assignment. But when they jumped ashore under enemy fire, they were amazed to find a French civilian, Mario Falco, a Resistance fighter, waiting for them on the beach; and he guided the Americans through the wooded paths of Le Drammont. Thanks to Falco's knowledge of the terrain, Dahlquist's men avoided minefields as he guided them to the radar station and signal tower abandoned by the Germans. Other Resistance fighters and code breakers also helped Allied troops.

The Allies' ULTRA code-breaking ability to intercept and decrypt the enemy's communication system provided Allied air commanders with crucial information to demolish the opponent's transportation routes. Both the British and American air commanders, Generals Arthur Tedder and Carl Spaatz, used their air forces to implement an overall strategy. That strategy called for destroying Germany's fuel plants and its economic and military power, and for deception.

Radar operators who had been trained for the Normandy invasion were sent to the Mediterranean for the invasion of southern France. German reaction to the Allied tactic of transmitting false radar signals is described in a report issued in the intelligence division of the chief of naval operations (Monograph Index Guide No. 701-700, dated October 3, 1944): "It has been reported that a German radio station put out the story that, during the landings in France, a convoy twelve miles long had been repelled in an area that was not invaded. This would seem to indicate that the simulation was successful."[13]

Hewitt observed around 1100 hours that the Allied minesweepers trying to clear the approaches to Camel Red Beach, in the Golfe de Fréjus, came under heavy enemy fire from the northeastern shore of the gulf. This action meant that the Allied troops that landed at the Camel sector might be unsuccessful in advancing and overtaking the enemy to the northwest as quickly as had been hoped.[14] At 1140, the first LST of the Red Beach Assault Group started to unload.[15] Red Beach was longer than Green Beach. The workable length of Green Beach was about 230 yards. Here is Admiral Hewitt's description:

> Our heavy bombers attacked Red Beach, as scheduled, between 1220 and 1300. From then, until near the hour of 1400, the beach was under bombardment by the Camel Gunfire Support Group. It was difficult to see how any of the defenses in that vicinity could still be functioning. During this bombardment, two demolition units with scout boats and twelve explosive drone boats were sent in to attack the underwater beach obstacles. These did not meet with the same success as in the Alpha area. Three drones exploded

as intended, two hit without exploding, one was last seen circling off the beach, one exploded off the left flank of the beach, two were boldly reboarded underway to regain manual control, one was sunk by a destroyer when it reversed course and threatened our own ships, and two were withheld for fear that they also might run wild.

The wildly circling drone boats were observed from the *Catoctin* without our being able to know exactly what was going on, since the communication circuits were very heavily loaded. We also observed the rocket-launching LCTs approach the beach and turn back without firing, and the first wave of assault boats waiting near the line of departure without advancing as scheduled.

The Beach Assault Commander at 1400 reported to the Camel Force Commander that he was held up, and why, but stated that he would carry out the assault at 1430. Admiral Lewis, fully informed of the difficulties, knowing that the enfilade fire from the vicinity of Saint-Raphael was continuing with unabated intensity, and unable to consult General Dahlquist who was out of reach on shore, made the decision on his own responsibility of placing in effect the alternate plan of landing the Red Beach Regimental Combat Team on narrow Green Beach, where its predecessor had landed at 0800. This unit was safely ashore without loss by 1515 and immediately joined the advance on Saint-Raphael and ultimately on Red Beach from the flank. Admiral Lewis was faced with a most difficult situation. The decision he made undoubtedly saved many American lives without hindering the final accomplishment of the 36th Division's mission. He was thanked for this action by General Dahlquist.[16]

RCT 142 was unable to land at Red Beach because of the failure of demolition boats to destroy the underwater obstacles—most notably, mines—and thus landed on Green Beach, starting around 1515 hours. The alternate plan was placed into operation, and RCTs 141 and 143 took their first objective by 1600 hours. Yellow Beach was secured within the hour, and orders were issued at 1700 hours for RCT 142 to attack Fréjus from the northeast at 2000 hours, and for RCT 143 to attack via

Saint-Raphael and Red Beach to Argens River and rendezvous with the Forty-fifth Infantry. However, the difficult coastline provided for a delay in RCT 142's planned attack at 2000 hours.[17]

The Germans heavily mined Camel Red Beach, located at the head of the Gulf of Fréjus, and strongly defended it with coastal gun batteries. Some of these batteries were masquerading at Saint-Raphael as waterfront bars, kiosks, and bathhouses. Sixteen American and British minesweepers had swept the boat channels but could not complete their cleanup task because heavy German gunfire forced their retreat. Even though the minesweepers were out of range of this firing, the Apex drone boats that were sent to explode underwater obstacles behaved erratically. It appears that German radio operations stole the radio direction of the explosive units from the directing boats, causing the drones to go berserk and run around madly. Two drones ran aground, and a destroyer sank one to avoid disaster. Two others were boarded and made inoperable. Only three exploded as planned.

Once he learned that the minesweeping operation was ineffective—that efforts to remove underwater obstacles on Camel Red Beach had failed—Admiral Lewis realized that the lanes leading to Red Beach 264A would signal disaster. His attempts to contact Gen. John Dahlquist failed, as Dahlquist was isolated on a cliff observation post after he and his commando group came ashore on Camel Green Beach. Lewis was in a difficult position because Dragoon's entire tactical plan might be ruined if Red Beach was not used in accordance with the original plan. He decided that Green Beach (264B) was safer and proceeded accordingly. This decision was responsible for the LST 1012 and other craft going in circles for hours. Lewis's order to change landing plans displeased General Truscott—who claimed that by not landing on Camel Red Beach, Dahlquist's 142nd Regiment had delayed clearing the beach for supplies and had prevented the fast capture of the airfield near Fréjus. In thanking Admiral Lewis for his decision, Dahlquist so infuriated Truscott that he requested that his superior, Gen. Jacob Devers, relieve Dahlquist of his command—which Devers declined to do.

Enemy pillboxes along the Camel and other invasion area beaches were under the supervision of German officers and noncommissioned soldiers. Russians, Ukrainians, and other captives were compelled to serve the Germans as low-level privates. Despite the entire coastline being fortified, Lieutenant General Devers considered Saint-Raphael the only area where American troops would meet serious resistance. Allied military planners wanted to assault Camel Beach at the head of the Gulf of Fréjus because it offered good access into the interior. The beach was so strongly defended, however, that attacking it from the front was suicidal. Therefore, the decision was made ultimately to have the Thirty-sixth Division land at smaller beaches farther east first and then Camel Red Beach later. The shores of the Gulf of Fréjus were important to the U.S. Army. Before the war, the French had built a small airfield and a seaplane base behind the beach—the only one on the water's edge in Provence. The Argens Valley was used for at least one thousand five hundred years as an invasion route; aware of this, German commanders had strongly defended Camel Red Beach.

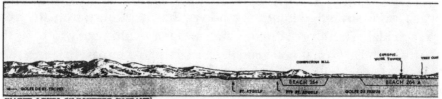

WATER LEVEL SILHOUETTE (DISTANT)

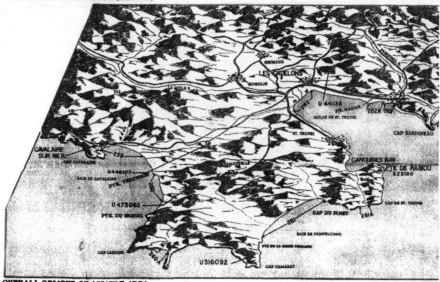

OVERALL OBLIQUE OF ASSAULT AREA

BEACH No. 264 a (North)

CENTER OF BEACH: LAT. 43° 26 N.´ LONG. 06° 45´ E.

COORDINATES: U-564890 — U-588845

NATURE OF SEA BOTTOM: SAND

ANCHORAGE: 500 YARDS OFFSHORE IN 5 TO 7 FATHOMS: BOTTOM OF MUD AND WEED.

LENGTH OF BEACH: 2,750 YARDS

WIDTH: 20 TO 40 YARDS

SUITABILITY FOR CRAFT: NORTHEAST OF "SEAPLANE" PIERS: ALL CRAFT AND LSTs, IF OBSTACLES REMOVED. SOUTHWEST OF PIERS: LCAs, LOVPs, LCMs, LCT (5)s (WET LANDINGS IN-PLACES); LARGER LCTs AND LSTs WITH PONTOONS.

AF 4472

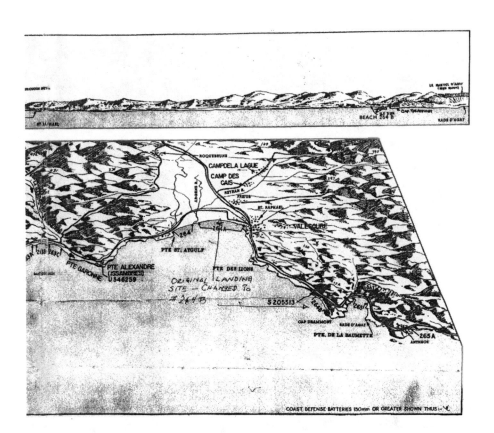

OF ROADS

as of july 20 1944.
EVERSE SIDE OF THIS SHEET

H-DAY = AUG. 15, 1944

TOP SECRET—BIGOT

(Until departure for combat operation
when this sheet becomes Restricted)

PREPARED BY COMMANDER U. S. EIGHTH FLEET
N-2 SECTION

Printed by 19th. Field Survey Coy., R.E., July 1944.

Overall oblique of assault area

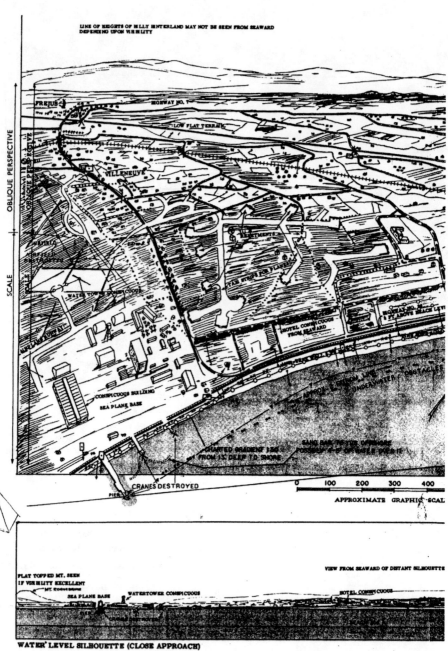

LINE OF HEIGHTS OF HILLY HINTERLAND MAY NOT BE SEEN FROM SEAWARD
DEPENDING UPON VISIBILITY

FREJUS

HIGHWAY NO. 7

LOW FLAT TERRAIN

VILLENEUVE

WATER TOWER CONSPICUOUS

CONSPICUOUS BUILDING
SEA PLANE BASE

HOTEL CONSPICUOUS
FROM SEAWARD

CRANES DESTROYED

PIER

UNDERWATER OBSTACLES

0   100   200   300   400

APPROXIMATE GRAPHIC SCAL

VIEW FROM SEAWARD OF DISTANT SILHOUETTE

FLAT TOPPED MT. SEEN
IF VISIBILITY EXCELLENT

SEA PLANE BASE   WATERTOWER CONSPICUOUS   HOTEL CONSPICUOUS

WATER LEVEL SILHOUETTE (CLOSE APPROACH)

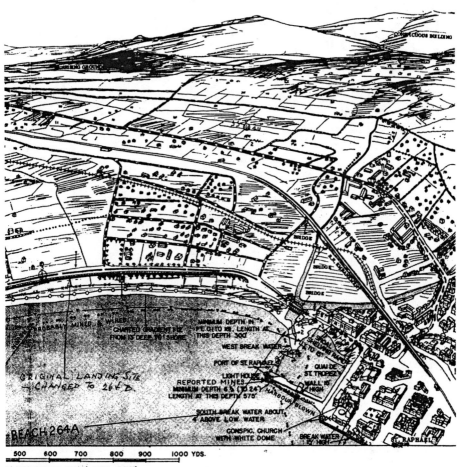

Panoramic sketch of Camel Beach 264A (north)

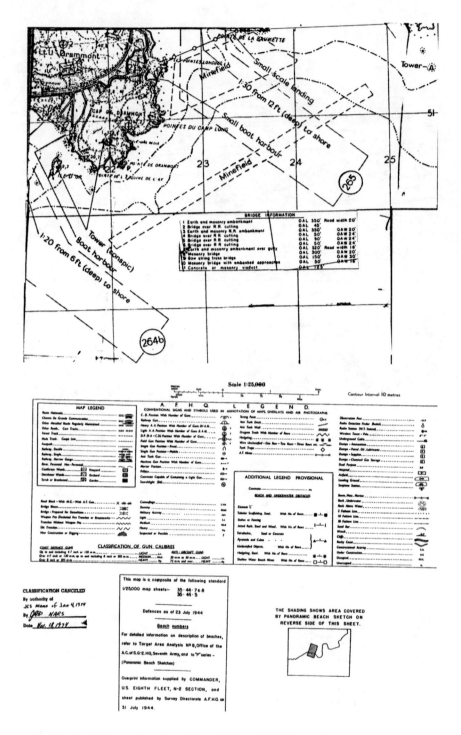

Rade D'Agay showing Camel Beach 264B and Map Legend

Captain Moreno's Revelations

Admiral Hewitt had placed Rear Adm. Spencer Lewis as commander of the Camel Beaches, following Admiral Moon's tragic suicide. Explaining his decision, Hewitt wrote that Lewis was familiar with Moon's Dragoon assignment. Capt. John Moreno (U.S. Navy), who served on Hewitt's staff as air advisor, later revealed some facts about that decision. He pointed out that Lewis undertook the new assignment reluctantly, perhaps because he had just married a British Navy woman who was in Naples. As Moreno put it, "He wanted to make love. He went to sea with us and stipulated that as soon as the touchdown came, I would fly him back from southern France to Naples to be with his bride. Of course he knew nothing about the specifics of the operation."[18]

Another Moreno revelation concerned Lewis being credited with the decision to redirect the Camel Beach landing from the Red (264A) to the Green (264B) Beach. According to Moreno, when Lewis's chief of staff, Capt. Rutledge Tompkins, realized that American radio-controlled small landing craft loaded with explosives were being turned around by the Germans' control of radio frequency and were headed toward American ships rather than those of the enemy, Tompkins initiated the rerouting of ships from Camel Red to Camel Green Beach, even though its small width made it a problem for twenty thousand troops. Green Beach had only one outlet, but it was a lot safer than Camel Red. Dahlquist personally deployed his entire Thirty-sixth Division that transferred to Green Beach. For this, and for thanking Lewis, Dahlquist was threatened with removal from command by General Truscott. —Moreno's account of Captain Tompkins's role in the decision to land the Thirty-sixth Division in the much more hospitable Camel Green Beach differs from all other versions that give Lewis sole credit for the beach-change decision. Tompkins was a quick-witted, brilliant, funny, and not-too-hardworking officer who remained in southern France. He was in charge while Admiral Lewis returned to his wife in Naples.[19] Later, Moreno held the post of naval attaché in London. From July 1, 1945, through August 1, 1946, Admiral Lewis served as chief of staff to the commander of naval forces in Europe. On August 1, 1945, Hewitt took command of the U.S. Naval Forces in Europe, and Lewis was again his chief of staff.

Col. Vincent M. Lockhart has explained why Truscott was so furious at Lewis's decision to divert LST 1012 and other vessels from landing and unloading the 142nd Regimental Combat Team at Red Beach, at Saint-Raphael, to Green Beach, Cap Drammont, instead. Lockhart, who served as an officer in General Dahlquist's Thirty-sixth Infantry Division during Operation Dragoon, wrote that "thirty-five years later, discussing the landing, Maj. Gen. George E. Lynch Jr., then a colonel commanding the 142nd, was to applaud the (Admiral Lewis) decision to change beaches."[20] Lynch's study of intelligence reports from southern France before Dragoon led him to conclude that the Red Beach should not be attacked and to request Generals Dahlquist and Truscott—to change the beach from Camel Red to Camel Green. Truscott summarily denied the request, replying, "A determined regiment can land on any defended beach." Dahlquist said later that Truscott was unhappy with the change and threatened to relieve Dahlquist and have Lynch court-martialled.[21] Lockhart's authoritative accounts conclusively demonstrate that both Lynch and Lewis were correct and Truscott was wrong. Lockhart's final comment was "The huge success that was to follow in the next fifteen days (of Operation Dragoon) probably could not have been accomplished if one Regimental Combat team—the 142nd—had been brutally mauled at the landing. The diversion was correct, the decision to do so was sound, and the results were more than satisfactory."[22] Hewitt also concluded that Lewis's decision "was very fortunate because there would have been heavy losses if they had continued to land (on Camel Red Beach) . . . he'd done absolutely the right thing."[23]

Threats to LST 1012

As LST 1012 approached Camel Green Beach, it came under enemy attack from two sources—a German shore battery and an aircraft bomber that came over the nearby mountains. The shore battery projectile landed in the water in front of the ship, about seventy-five feet away, and an aircraft bomb dropped a considerable distance from the ship's stern (or rear).[24]

The LST 1012 and the LSTs 1010 and 1011 waited in the transport area from 0500 to 2000 hours, far from an invasion landing beach. R. C. "Chuck" Steeple Jr., who was second in command of the 1012, recalled, "We were supposed to go and beach at Camel Beach Red 264A (with the 1010 and the 1011) when the bombardment ceased but someone (thank God!) was not convinced that it was safe enough. We lay to for hours on end, going in circles until we finally got orders to proceed to Camel Beach at Cap Drammont."[25] According to Gunner's Mate Charlie Earle, the LST 1012 was the first in line to get to Camel Green Beach. The LST 282 was about six hundred feet from the 1012, but it never reached the beach, as it was sunk by a radio-controlled glider bomb.

At 2015 hours, the LST 1012's commanding officer, Lt. Marshall J. Flowers Jr., reported that "orders were received to proceed to Green Beach off Cap Drammont to unload cargo. All three vessels [LSTs 1010, 1011, and 1012] proceeded to beach area. At 2058, two enemy planes were sighted overhead—identified as Junker 88s. All three LSTs and vessels in immediate vicinity were firing. At 2059, ceased firing. All 20mm and 40mm guns had opened fire engaging the enemy for the first time. The crew's performance was highly commendable. Good marksmanship was evident and obedience to commands was prompt."[26] Hewitt's chief of staff, John N. Opie III, evaluated the LST 1012's performance differently: "It appears from the sketchy report that fire discipline on board (gunnery on board LST 1012) was poor. Apparently fire was opened even though the planes were out of range. By copy of this endorsement, the Commanding Officer of the LST 1012 is directed to train himself and his ship in judging range to prevent reoccurrence and to improve discipline."[27]

Before and after navy service, Flowers was a headmaster and teacher in Tennessee. From the author's personal observation and the comments of other LST 1012 crew members, Flowers did not direct or implement continuing education concerning gunnery, navigation, seamanship, engineering, or any other nautical specialty. There were a few instances of emergency drills, such as for fires, but there were no abandoning-ship drills, nor was there any special training or rehearsals for invasion landings. To improve their skills, crew members who were ambitious and wanted promotions turned to navy manuals and to other clearly written and well-illustrated educational materials dealing with navigation and other subjects. While standing watch at sea for many hours each day, there was opportunity to learn one's craft. Chuck Steeple taught quartermasters how to use a sextant and the wisdom of Bowditch's treatise on navigation. Before and after his navy service, Steeple was a salesman for his father's company in San Mateo, California, which manufactured and sold outdoor ornaments for building exteriors.

While Steeple was an excellent teacher, Flowers, by contrast, was no communicator although a kind man. Once when Gunner's Mate

Earle slipped on grease and injured his ankle, Gunnery Officer Jack Rushing immediately came to his aid and carried him to a comfortable berth. Shortly thereafter, Commanding Officer Flowers visited and comforted Earle, telling him that during his days as a football coach, he had experienced similar injuries and that the pain would be of short duration. Flowers visited Earle each morning for several days and massaged his ankle.[28]

Reports Concerning a Terrible Night

On the evening of August 15, 1944, Charlie Earle was busy supervising LST 1012 gunnery. Near nightfall, four enemy planes—the type equipped to carry radio-controlled armor-piercing and glider bombs—approached the Camel area from overland at an altitude of fifteen feet, later dropping to eighteen thousand feet for the attack.[29] Rear Admiral Lewis's flagship, the *Bayfield,* was near-missed by several bombs. At about 2010, an enemy bomber released a glider bomb that struck the LST 282 as it waited a short distance off Camel Green Beach to land a large detachment of the Thirty-sixth Division Artillery. The ship burst into flames, and casualties were heavy. The ship and its cargo were destroyed.[30] By 2017 hours, the *Bayfield* finished unloading her wares and departed to report to Return Convoy Controller.[31]

LST 282 commanding officer, Lawrence E. Gilbert, submitted the following report on the sinking of his ship:[32]

> The LST 282, as part of the Camel task force, moved pursuant to Green Beach Assault Group Commander Captain Morris's orders. At approximately 2020 the LST was ordered to proceed immediately. The numbers one, two, five, and six LCVPs and their boat crews had been lowered. All stations were reported manned and ready. All army personnel had been ordered to their vehicles to prepare for disembarking.
>
> A red alert was received via radio at approximately 2030. Gun control and battery officers were alerted. LST 282 proceeded toward Green Beach at standard speed on course. The Captain instructed a signalman to try and contact beach master for instructions. The distance off the beach was approximately twelve hundred yards at 2045; slowed to two-

thirds speed at 2050. An aircraft was reported. The Captain was on the conn. Also on the conn station were a talker, a signalman, the Executive Officer, the Communications Officer, the Medical Officer, and the Gunnery Officer.

The Executive Officer reported what appeared to be a single rocket fired at the plane from the beach. Upon examination with binoculars, a bright red, flaring, rocket-like object was seen about one hundred feet directly under a twin-engine, twin-rudder plane. The object was apparently motionless. The object began to move ahead of the plane and downward on the same course as the plane until its elevation was approximately 25 degrees. At this point it turned approximately 90 degrees to starboard and apparently headed for the LST 282. Bright red flame and white smoke were seen coming from the tail of the object, which resembled a miniature plane. The speed of the object was exceedingly fast. The Captain told the Gunnery Officer it was a radio-controlled bomb and to open fire. The 140mm located on the bow opened fire. It appeared to be about to cross the ship when suddenly it turned about 45 degrees to port and dove into the ship. An explosion followed immediately. Several guns in the forward battery had opened fire on the bomb and plane just an instant or so before the bomb dove. The bomb apparently hit a few feet forward of the superstructure, to the left of the centerline, penetrating the main deck and exploding below. All guns were firing after the bomb hit, until the plane was well out of range.

The crew's quarters aft, officers' country, and tank deck were almost completely ablaze within approximately one minute. Within five minutes the forward and after portions of the ship were completely cut off from each other by fire and explosions. The elevator platform was collapsed in such a way that it was inclined downward and aft, providing a means of exit for troops on the tank deck. Its downward side rested on vehicles parked below it. There was no fire main pressure and the auxiliary pump, capable of pumping five hundred gallons of water a minute, located just forward of the superstructure on the starboard side of the ship on the main deck, was destroyed by the blast. The ship had immediately listed to port as the explosion blew out the port side of the hull. The cargo hatch was partly blown open. Fire-fighting attempts by the forward repair party under the direction of the First Lieutenant were futile.[33] The abandon ship order was given by the Executive Officer from the starboard bridge wing and by the First Lieutenant forward. Attempts to operate the landing machinery forward were useless as all power leads forward were instantaneously destroyed. An attempt to operate the bow doors was unsuccessful. Abandon ship discipline was excellent! Sufficient lines were available on both sides of the ship and debarkation ladders were employed forward on both port and starboard sides. The four after life rafts on the starboard side were successfully launched, the number ten raft burned and the number eight raft was jammed by the explosion and could not be launched. Nothing is known of the other rafts on the port side except that one raft was found floating by the port side. The ship was on the bottom with her bow approximately forty yards from the beach when abandon ship was given forward. Attempts to trip the life rafts forward failed due to the fact that army personnel already in the water were directly below the rafts. The auxiliary engines were left running by the auxiliary engine room detail, which escaped through the use of gas masks. All lights were out.

All hands assisted in the evacuation of injured of both ship's company and army personnel. Boats standing by were the LST 282 LCVPs numbers one and two, six LCVPs from the LST 283, at least one LCVP from the LST 50, several LCVPs from the LST 491, and one U.S. Navy tug which remained well off. The ship was abandoned approximately fifteen minutes after the fire started. Ammunition in ready boxes and in gun tubes had already started to explode as had explosives and gasoline in the vehicles.

Commanding Officer Lawrence Gilbert commended the crew as a whole for its work in assisting the injured off the ship. He made special mention of two LST 282 pharmacist mates—May, H. D., PhMlc, and Sullivan, L. J., PhM2c—and the exceedingly prompt and valuable aid rendered by the Commanding Officer of the LST 283 who personally conducted his small boats in picking up survivors close aboard the LST 282.

There was the complete lack of anti-aircraft fire from any point on the beach or from any ship previous to the actual flight of the bomb. A flight of P-38 Lightnings was said to have passed over the assault area about five minutes before the enemy aircraft was sighted; however, this was not seen by anyone on the conn or reported to the conn. As far as is known, there was no air cover visible during the period from sunset to evening twilight although air cover had been markedly visible during the day. The great quantities of smoke being made by small craft and by units on the beach hampered rescue operations considerably. At the time of the attack, this smoke laying had barely started. What little wind there was, was easterly to northeasterly.

The ship drifted over to the left flank of the Green Beach area and the bow settled on the rocks. At the time of impact, the rudders were jammed at hard left. The ship was still burning the next day and was almost totally destroyed by fire.

LST 282 crew member **Tom Aubut** was rescued and brought aboard the LST 1012. There he was treated for burns to his hands.[34]

Hans E. Bergner, from Texas, was an officer on the LST 282. His parents were from Germany, and he spoke German. After navy service, Bergner served as an educational administrator in his home state. His article "Taking the Fight to France"[35] described the important role that the LST 282 played in the invasion of Normandy. It reached Utah Beach to provide initial medical care to wounded personnel and then transported them back to England. During that invasion, the LST 282 had three surgeons and twenty-four pharmacist's mates onboard. The bulkheads on the sides of the ship's tank deck were equipped to mount litters. The wardroom was set up to handle the most serious cases of surgery. The 282 got some of the wounded from Utah Beach, but then it moved and began receiving casualties from Omaha too because the fighting was much fiercer there. All types of craft brought the casualties to the LST 282. Bergner wrote,

> The LST 282 was relatively safe from enemy fire during her participation in the Normandy invasion. Enemy shore batteries had been a big concern to us beforehand. We wouldn't have been in range of anything except the largest guns, but the

Allies knew that the Germans had them on Pointe du Hoc, on the bluff between Omaha and Utah. Rangers under Lt. Col. James Rudder were assigned to scale those cliffs and silence the guns. The several trips we had made safely between the beachheads and England following the invasion had given me a sense of confidence that I could withstand another operation. After Normandy, we went to the Mediterranean so the ship could take part in the invasion of southern France. We knew that this time we would be beaching on D-day itself.

When we were loading north of Naples, I talked to my close friend and roommate who was the ship's Gunnery Officer, Peter Hughes. I said, "Pete, I feel quite different about this one. I'm not as concerned." He turned to me and said, "You know, it's strange you should say that. I really wasn't so afraid in Normandy, but this time I have a bad feeling."

It appeared that we would have an easy day of it on August 15. We waited offshore after watching the H-hour bombing of the beach and saw our LCVPs return safely after landing assault forces on Green Beach. We saw no enemy planes. With our binoculars we could see resort homes and the hills behind them. In a sense, we sunbathed on the Riviera that day as the ship circled and waited in the transport area for our turn to go in. Our turn came late because there was no immediate requirement for the primary cargo we were carrying: 155mm Long Tom artillery pieces of the 36th Infantry Division. The main deck and tank deck of the LST 282 was jam-packed with those guns and their trailers full of ammunition.

My own first conscious memory is of being on the main deck rather than on the elevated gun tubs. Whether I was knocked down by the concussion or jumped because of fear, I don't really know. I looked back at the conn and could see that it was all crumpled. There was no sign of life. Flames were starting. The next 10 to 20 minutes were terrible. The Long Tom artillery ammunition began cooking off and exploding, as did the ammunition in the ship's own magazines.

There was never any formal order to abandon ship, but people saw the obvious and jumped overboard. I tried to warn some soldiers to stay on board, because we had been taught in midshipman school not to leave the ship until directed because

394

conditions might be even worse in the water. But soldiers get nervous on board ship, where there were no foxholes, so they said to me, "F—you," and off they went.

The first lieutenant had the bow doors halfway open when the bomb hit and all power failed. The bow ramp was still closed, and all the troops manning their vehicles on the tank deck would have been trapped. The rear cables of a large cargo elevator on the main deck were parted, however, causing the rear portion of the elevator to fall onto trucks in the tank deck. That formed a ramp from the tank deck to the main deck. Many injured soldiers, some with their uniforms on fire, scrambled up that ramp to safety. It was similar to the way red ants escape from an ant hole when someone pours in gasoline.

By now the ship had moved to within about half a mile of the beach. Lt. Gilbert, the skipper, got the Navy Cross for his actions that night, and he deserved it. He ordered hard left rudder, which kept the exploding LST 282 from moving in among the LSTs already lined up on the beach. As it was, we careened off the port, and eventually ran aground on some rocks in front of a beautiful resort home.

In addition to his ship handling, the skipper rescued a signalman, George Heckman, who had a badly broken leg. He carried Heckman down three flights from the bridge to the water's edge, and there someone else took over and began pulling him ashore. Then the captain went back and got the engineer officer, Edward Durkee, who was unconscious and had a back full of shrapnel. The captain secured him by his life belt to the rudder post. Both were later recovered in an unconscious condition by rescue craft. The skipper himself had been wounded severely in one arm, so he did those rescues with one arm.

The last people who left the ship swam ahead, trying to beat the hulk ashore. The engines had stopped running as soon as the bomb exploded, but momentum continued to carry the ship toward shore. I myself finally jumped off the port bow. I think I let myself down to the anchor so I wouldn't have to jump so far. In midshipman school I was a non-swimmer and had to go to swimming class when the other guys went to physical education. All I had learned during my youth in the Texas hill country was dogpaddling in various creeks. But I beat that LST ashore. I had an inflatable life belt around my waist, and it worked well. The Army had criticized those belts after so many men were lost in Exercise Tiger in April 1944, claiming that men were pitched forward, forcing their faces into the water. I have to say that my life belt was effective when it came to the test.

When we got ashore, we got behind a large rock on the beach. As the ship got closer, the good swimmers went out and helped the wounded men get ashore. We dragged them behind the rock because we were afraid the exploding ammunition might send shrapnel onto us. Eventually, when we couldn't find any more shipmates or army men, we went up a road to Green Beach. Others, in the water astern of the ship, were rescued by boats from the other ships in the area.

We boarded a sister LST and backed off that night. At that point I panicked and began having what might be called hallucinations. I wanted to get off and go back to my own ship, worried that Pete Hughes might still be alive and I could save him. I calmed down when a shipmate said he had seen Pete lifeless on the deck. It was a horrible night for many of us. Our ship was still burning and, I have been told, smoldering for several days. In those hours afterward I didn't want to look at the LST 282 but somehow I kept doing so.

Bob Beroth, an LST 282 crew member from North Carolina, participated in both the invasions of Normandy and southern France. His recollections follow:

The beach chosen for the landings was a narrow sandy area, located along a rocky shoreline and only about six to eight LSTs could be on the beach at one time. The 282 lay at anchor all day, awaiting orders to proceed to the beach for off-loading. While awaiting our orders, we observed the German artillery located on the mountain overlooking the beaching area, shelling the invasion fleet, but not inflicting any damage. There was a higher range of mountains located north of the coastline mountains. Destroyers and light cruisers were returning the artillery fire coming from the lower mountain range. Late afternoon we received our orders to proceed to the beach for off-loading. For aligning to the beaching area, a starboard turn had to be negotiated. We were ready to make the turn, when a plane was observed flying over the second higher range of mountains and was at a high altitude, but the evening sun was glaring on it, which gave cause for tracking it. Soon a red flame was observed at the rear of the object and it was detected as a radio controlled bomb. It descended in the direction of the invasion fleet and leveled off over a light cruiser, the *Marblehead*. Ships began firing at the descending object as it continued on a course towards the LSTs being beached.

The bomb dived into the cargo hatch of the 282 and exploded in the tank deck. The explosion caused the 282 to roll to her port side and almost turned over. The explosion blew a hole through the port side large enough to drive a large truck through. The blast buckled the bulkheads of the wheelhouse, trapping several Navy personnel there. The conning tower was badly damaged and Captain (Lieutenant) Gilbert was blown into the water with a broken arm. The ladder escape hatches for the engine room buckled and the personnel in the engine room perished. Sailors were manning the 20mm anti-aircraft gun along the port and starboard sides and were killed or blown into the water. The equipment in the tank deck caught fire and the ship was disabled so that no fire fighting equipment was workable and there was no water pressure for the fire-hoses. Our ship drifted to the rocky beach on the western side of the beaching area and continued burning as the exploding ammunition blew holes in every direction.

I was located on the bow. After making certain that there were no rocks to damage our bow doors, I transferred the controls for the ramp and doors to the control section located top-side. As the bombs neared the 282, I grabbed a forward chock and held on as the ship rolled. Ropes were thrown over and starboard side for the army and navy personnel to abandon the ship. No officer was able to give an abandon ship order. I was one of the last crewmembers to leave the ship and swam ashore, scaled a rock wall and hid behind a garage. A coastline road ran along the beach area, about a quarter mile from the beach. An army jeep came by and I hitched a ride to the beaching area, boarded an LST, and the next day was taken to the island of Corsica. At Corsica, some of the survivors of the 282 were placed together in a rest camp for about two weeks. We were then taken to Naples, Italy aboard an LCI. We learned that approximately fifty crewmen had been lost and about a hundred army personnel were lost. In Naples, Italy, we spent a week in a rest camp and were then transported to Bizerte, Tunisia, aboard an English transport, spending several days in Bizerte. We were placed aboard an LST and transported to Algiers, Algeria. Here a convoy was formed for the return trip to New York City."[36]

George Narozonick served on the LST 501 during the invasions of both Normandy and southern France. Concerning August 15, he recalled that

the USS *Marblehead* was called on to knock down a tall transmitting tower. It was a sight I will never forget. After getting the range a shell made a perfect hit, and down it came. Once on our way to the beach, everyone at General Quarters, high above (not seen by our crew before) a radio-controlled bomb missile struck the LST 282 right next to our ship. It hit with a terrific explosion, and the fully loaded ship was being torn apart with all the ammo, gas, etc. that the army had on board. We could see the bomber that dropped the bomb, and we fired back in vain. It was much out of our reach with our 20-, and 40mm. guns. We never knew what the final casualties were, but one after another explosion all night. It was a disaster.

Our then-Deacon of our church, Larry Sullivan, who we knew for many years unknown to each other, was a Pharmacist Mate on the 282. He lucked out because he is still with us to tell what happened aboard ship that day. Anyway, several years ago at an outdoor musical, he sported a LST 282 cap. To the surprise of each other, we recognized that our ships were next to each other that memorable day.[37]

LST 1011 commanding officer **Bob Wilson,** in his diary entry from August 15, 1944, wrote,

In convoy to station off Cap Drammont, southern France. Guide boat lined us up for beaching as LST 282 ahead of us was struck by a radio-controlled bomb from aircraft flying well beyond the range of hundreds of 40mm shells. Searchlights found the bomb but shells, no. Loaded with trucks, jeeps, artillery, and troops, we moved around the 282 as she burned and eventually sank. Back in Norfolk, we had passed white-glove inspection by multiple brass but we had never practiced hitting a beach. On Aug. 15, 1944, we did so, hoping it would be sandy rather than rocky.

We found a batch of wounded waiting to get to the litters on our tank deck and then out to a hospital ship. Concerned that all enemy shore batteries might not have been taken out, we were eager to get into deeper water. The petty officer on duty at the bow doors came up to the conn shouting that the exec would not load the wounded—claiming that they were "niggers." We had gone in behind an all-black company and they had taken quite a beating. The exec had been a soap salesman for P&G in Atlanta; he had no objections when we took on Nazi prisoners. I supposed I could have called for a court martial. My rationale for not doing so came out of the realization that, for some Americans, the hate for blacks might be greater than that for Nazis."[38]

LST 1012 radioman **Charlie Cullen** e-mailed the author this recollection:[39]

I was close to being the youngest person on the ship. On the invasion, I thought we'd be sunk. I spent the night on the boat deck with a life jacket on. I was flat scared. All my valuables were encased in condoms to waterproof them, just in case. At GQ, my station was with Dulaney[40] in the radio room. He and I agreed that we would switch off listening to the frequencies. We both had on our helmets and life jackets. When the JU88 flew over, it was his turn and I was outside looking around. When we started firing, he ran out of the radio shack to see what the hell was going on . . . . When we hit the beach, I went ashore to look around. On the port side, I noticed a skull and cross bones sign reading "Terrain Minen" and an unexploded rocket lying on the ground. It was a pretty little thing, but I had been trained not to touch [it]. May have saved my life—who knows.

The night before the invasion I slept on a bin outside of the wheelhouse. I thought something would happen to the ship, and I slept with my life jacket on. When the JU-88 flew over the next day, I was outside the wheelhouse since it was Dulaney's time on-line. I kept thinking one of our 20mm bullets was going to hit the mast; it never did.

LST 1012 gunner's mate **Charles Earle** was the petty officer on the LST 1012 in charge of all 40-mm twin anticraft pom-pom guns from the ship's bow (front) to its bridge. At that time, Earle had earned the rating of gunner's mate first class (GM 1/C). In August 1944, he was twenty-one years old, and his GM 1/C rating was substantially higher than most of the LST 1012 sailors. The reason was that before coming aboard the LST, he had survived the dangerous duty of serving as a gunner's mate on a merchant marine vessel that had been torpedoed by the enemy.

On the LST 1012, an older and more experienced gunner's mate than Earle did not want the responsibilities assigned to Earle, who had to supervise a crew of five to ten gunner's mates who had to examine different types of ammunition and weapons and supervise demolition devices and equipment for underwater frogmen. Safe ammunition storage required regular reading of temperatures and humidity. Guns and ammunition had to be prepared for the crews of the small boats that were hoisted on the 1012. Spoiled lots of ammunition were to be thrown overboard. It was crucial that different types of friendly and enemy aircraft be spotted and identified with utmost care. A gunner's mate's mistakes were likely to be fatal, and so Earle took aircraft identification teaching seriously.

Earle recalled that sometime between 0300 and 0400 hours on August 15, the general quarters alarm was sounded, summoning the crew to battle stations. A group of army demolition engineers was dropped left four miles from the designated French Riviera beach. They arrived there by small boats. As the 1012 moved in closer to about a mile from the beach, a single file of LSTs systematically fired salvos of rocket bombs on both sides of the beach. About four hundred to five hundred feet away, the LST 1012's captain Marshall Flowers dropped anchor using a two-inch cable. The LST 1012 went up the beach twice. The first time, it turned back because it was being fired upon by a German JU-88 airplane. The beach upon which it was to land and unload was dangerous, and the ship turned back. Ultimately, the beach was made safe by a squad of bombers and naval shelling. According to Earle, the LST 1012 was the first in line to get to the beach. The LST 282 was about six hundred feet away, but it never made it to the beach, falling victim to a German radar station atop a hill that signaled its destruction by an enemy JU-88 plane manned by a crew of four. The JU-88 released a rocket in front of the 282, hitting its main deck. The gasoline on its main deck caused an inferno that spread to the trucks that were to disembark, the stored ammunition, and the ship's bridge. Earle saw sailors jump off the doomed ship. When the JU-88 aimed at the LST 1012, however, the rocket landed in the water, a short distance from the ship's stern (or rear). Earle and his crew of gunner's mates returned fire and could see the sky full of tracers, or projectile powder, which started out as red then turned white. Although it appears that the JU-88 crew that destroyed the LST 282 flew away unscathed, another German airman was not so lucky. Earle reported seeing a German frantically jerking the harness, having been shot down by an American anticraft gunner.[41]

LST 1012 radarman **Frank Lovekin** manned the LST 1012's portside anticraft guns. He and his friend, Charlie Earle, picked up LST 282 survivors and brought them to the LST 1012. Lovekin had received radar and radio navy training and so was often on the bridge.[42] The two men were on the 1012 from its commissioning at the end of April 1944 until its decommissioning in June 1946. Lovekin was assigned to man the anticraft guns during general quarters or emergencies such as invasions, under the supervision of Earle. Both hailed from New Jersey—Lovekin from Tinton Falls and Earle from Newark. Although the term "dysfunctional parents" was not in vogue in the 1940s, Earle's parents clearly qualified by virtue of their alcoholism, their abuse of him, and his abandonment. He did not want to return home when he was discharged from the navy, and so Lovekin volunteered to take him into his maternal grandparents' home. Lovekin's own father had abandoned his wife and son at an early age. After the two men were discharged, Lovekin's grandfather, Walter Dennis, who owned a small and struggling general store in Tinton Falls, New Jersey, took them in. Both married New Jersey girls, and each fathered three daughters. Earle had four grandchildren, and Frank had five. Lovekin lived long enough to enjoy the birth of a great-grandson. He died in spring 2005.

Charlie Earle—crew member LST 1012

At one LST 1012 reunion, Lovekin and Earle recounted more August 15, 1944, stories: about a young officer from a wealthy and prominent family who hid in a cabin and that the LST 1012 won a special naval commendation for its laudable performance during the landing but that the award was rescinded because of Captain Flowers's subsequent bad seamanship. Flowers ran aground a number of times and maimed his ship and others. But on August 15, 1944, he performed well, for the most part, as did nearly all of the crew.

LST 1012 quartermaster **Stephen Sussna** recalled that the LST 1012 landed in Camel Green Beach (264B) at 2140 hours. The stern anchor was out with five hundred feet of cable. The unloading of army personnel and equipment started at 2143 and was completed by 2317. At midnight on August 16, the bow of LST 1012 was still on Green Beach, Camel Section. Army casualties and survivors of the LST 282 were aboard.[43] Later, two French women boarded the ship. Stephen Sussna was on the bridge and saw these neatly dressed women, one wearing black. They appeared to be in their thirties and walked briskly. They were greeted by Capt. Marshall Flowers and his second in command, Chuck Steeple. All four adjourned to the officers' quarters. As a lowly enlisted man, Sussna was not privy to what took place between them and didn't know the purpose for this gathering. Flowers and Steeple were not the type to indulge in any hanky-panky aboard ship, and the women just didn't look as though their presence on the LST 1012 was related to anything but official business. Captain Flowers died in 1987. In 1994 when the author questioned Steeple, he did not remember the two visitors. Now Chuck Steeple is also dead, and the world will never learn what services these women rendered.

Steve Sussna—crew member LST 1012

Admiral Hewitt submitted, on September 2, 1944, a report on the loss of LST 282 in which he outlined the course of how the 282 was destroyed. He wrote,

> LST 282 was the only naval loss from enemy air action during the entire southern France operation. It was destroyed off the Green Beach (near Saint-Raphael) of the Camel Assault Area by a radio-controlled bomb about 2055 on D-day (August 15, 1944). The following peculiar defense difficulties were presented by the attack:
>
> a) Time of the attack (dusk on d-day);
> b) Approach of attacking planes from over hilly terrain behind the beach;
> c) Location of the LST, 1,200 yards offshore, outside both the beach and transport area concentrated defense zones.
>
> At the time all inshore fighter cover was provided by the Army from Corsican bases. A total of from 28-32 fighters for daylight patrols and six night fighters for dusk patrols were scheduled for the assault area. No interception of this attack was reported. Additionally, efforts were made to jam this attack. Regarding the smoke screen that was to cover the Allied ships' landing, the smoke plan for the Camel area provided for three units afloat, composed of small patrol craft and landing craft (LCMs and LCVPs), to smoke to the windward of the transport area and for the assigned Beach Battalion to make smoke during an offshore wind (which existed at the time of this attack). Smoke was to be made "automatically" from one-half hour before sunset to one-half hour after sunset. Sunset on d-day was at 2031, almost simultaneous with receipt of the red alert. The thick smoke screen generated on the beach as well as the small craft hampered rescue operations. Also noted was the negligible force of the wind then blowing, which, though offshore, was of small assistance in spreading the smoke. The most significant factor under those conditions was the position of the LST midway between the beach and transport area and, thus, where it was not under the full protection of the planned smoke screens for either of those two places.[44]

—At Normandy

—Sinking from radio-controlled bomb attack

LST 282

The Bravery of Lawrence E. Gilbert and Ferris C. Burke

Lt. Lawrence E. Gilbert's heroic service on that day in August 1944 earned him the Navy Cross. Secretary of the Navy Forrestal sent Gilbert the following announcement:

> For extraordinary heroism as Commanding Officer of the USS LST 282 when that vessel was subjected to an enemy aerial attack and completely destroyed during the amphibious invasion of southern France on Aug. 15, 1944. Seriously injured and momentarily stunned when thrown to the bridge deck from his conning station by the blast of an enemy glider bomb, Lieutenant Gilbert unhesitatingly struggled through exploding ammunition and heavy black smoke from fires ignited in the cargo of motor trucks loaded aboard to carry a severely wounded signalman below, adjusting the man's life preserver and helping him over the side. Disregarding the grave danger to himself, he continued his valiant efforts by assisting a helpless officer into the water and, after securing him by a life belt to the rudder post, risked his life amid fire and explosions to search for help, remaining in the water for two hours until both men were recovered in an unconscious condition by rescue craft. His courage, fortitude and heroic spirit of self-sacrifice in the face of great peril reflect the highest credit upon Lieutenant Gilbert and the United States Naval Service.[45]

He was born on September 16, 1927. At age fourteen, Ferris C. Burke from the Camden, New Jersey, area served as an oiler in the engine room of a U.S. Army Corps of Engineers ship. During the Depression, his father worked for the Work Projects Administration, the WPA, for $18 per week to support seven children and a wife. From 1913 to 1921, Burke's father served in the navy as a first class petty officer (machinist), assigned to the battleship *South Carolina*. In the 1920s, he used his navy background to work as a railroad engineer.

As a lad, Ferris Burke picked up the small snakes that the WPA workmen saved after digging roads. He would then let the snakes loose and terrify the girls. His elder brother William joined the navy in July 1942, at age twenty. William was a member of the armed guard (navy gun crew on the merchant ships) and served for three years before getting a medical discharge as a seaman first class in 1945. Three of Burke's uncles were also in the navy—Uncle Joseph Burke served from 1910 until 1930; Uncle Ross Ferris retired as chief machinist mate but was recalled when World War II broke out; Uncle John Ferris retired as a chief bosun's mate, and he too was recalled to duty and served through the end of the war.[46] Both of his maternal uncles were navy men.

The only choice for Ferris Burke, therefore, was the navy. On May 24, 1943, Burke went to the draft board rather than the navy recruitment office to enlist, because he knew the draft board would allow him to enlist without attempting to verify his real age. When asked his date of birth, he answered, May 24, 1925.[47] Burke served onboard the LST 285 under Captain Hunt. Before the war, Hunt was an enlisted petty officer (signalman first class) in the navy and therefore a "mustang"—a navy term for an officer who had served as an enlisted man.[48]

In a letter dated December 12, 1945, Admiral Hewitt wrote the following to Ferris Burke, seaman second class, U.S. Naval Reserve:

> Your heroic action in connection with the rescue of three survivors of a sunken LCVP on Aug. 15, 1944, during the invasion of southern France, is deemed worthy of special commendation.
>
> After landing assault troops on the coast of southern France and upon starting back to your control vessel, you saw an LCVP hit by heavy machine gunfire and sink. After the LCVP had sunk, the enemy kept firing at the men in the water. You and the men in your boat in cooperation with another LCVP, turned back in the midst of heavy enemy machine gunfire and without regard for your personal safety, effected the rescue of the three survivors. Expert seamanship and splendid tactics enabled one LCVP to draw the enemy's fire while the other LCVP accomplished the rescue.
>
> I commend you for your courage, seamanship and outstanding devotion to duty, which reflect credit upon yourself and the United States Naval Service.
>
> You are hereby accorded the privilege of wearing the commendation ribbon pursuant to the authority delegated by ALNAV 179-44.[49]

U.S. NAVY MEMORIAL FOUNDATION
⌂ HOME

| Navy Memorial Foundation | Naval Heritage Center | Upcoming Events | FAQ | Links |
| Ships Store | Become a Shipmate | Veterans & Reunion Groups | The Navy Log |

The Navy Log - Use the Online Search

FERRIS CREAMER BURKE

CAMDEN, NJ - 1944

Rate / Rank
BM3

Service Branch
USN

Service Dates
6/1943 - 8/1949

Born
9/16/1927
MAPLE SHADE, NJ

NAVY LOG

SIGNIFICANT DUTY STATIONS

- NAB LITTLE CREEK, VA
- USS LST-285
- USS LCI-570
- NAB FORT PIERCE, FL

SIGNIFICANT AWARDS

- NAVY COMMENDATION MEDAL
- COMBAT ACTION RIBBON
- AMERICAN CAMPAIGN MEDAL
- EUROPEAN-AFRICAN-MIDDLE EASTERN CAMPAIGN MEDAL W/2 STARS
- WORLD WAR II VICTORY MEDAL

Ferris Creamer Burke, Camden, NJ—1944

Trouble at Alpha Beach

The Camel Beach was not the only site of Allied casualties on August 15. The commanding officer of LST 173, Lt. Broughton J. Barber, reported in his action report concerning amphibious operations against the enemy that his ship made a successful landing on Alpha Beach 259 in Cavalaire Bay. The ship acted as an assault troop carrier, landing troops and vehicles of various units of the U.S. Third Army Infantry Division. The assault troops were landed on the designated beach under moderate to light opposition from shore batteries and machine-gun emplacement. One of the most seriously injured sailors suffered compound fracture of both legs and a shattered right foot. By 1350 hours, LST 173 was proceeding at eight knots for the beach. When it was some four hundred yards away, and only a towline to the pontoons, the beachmaster signaled to the LST 173 that the beach was not clear.

By this time, recalled Barber, the ship was within three hundred yards of the beach—too short a distance to retract with the pontoons. He therefore ordered letting go of the stern anchor and full reversal of the engines. The pontoons tipped. When the ship was 250 feet from the beach, the pontoons made excellent momentum, beaching without any damage.

At 1359, Captain Barber received orders to stand off while the beach was being cleared. The beachmaster signaled at 1430 that the beach was ready and to make landing. The pontoons were placed, unloading started at 1540, and 150 prisoners were taken aboard at 1740 hours.

According to Barber, twelve prisoners had minor injuries. The ship's doctor inspected the wounds and dressed them. At 1753, the ship retracted from the beach. An additional forty-three prisoners from Levant Island were brought aboard at 1843. At 2030, the LST 173 received orders to join the convoy at Cape Camarat. At 2032, a red alert was received, and antiaircraft fire off the port bow was observed in the vicinity of the beach at Saint-Tropez (where the LSTs 282, 1012, and others were). Two enemy planes were observed flying about two thousand feet above the flack. A smoke screen was laid by 2111, and it concealed the LST 173. Two enemy planes were sighted passing overhead at about fifteen thousand feet and headed seaward. At 2215, the sailor who suffered the compound fracture of both legs and a shattered right foot had it amputated. Twelve hours had passed since he was brought aboard from a small amphibious craft, LCI 42.

The Third Army and Jean-Pierre Aumont

Battle tested, the Third Infantry Division had landed in North Africa, Sicily, and Anzio. Reinforced with numerous armor, chemical, medical, and ordnance units, this division was to land in the vicinity of Saint-Tropez and Cavalaire, in southern France. Its soldiers had orders to clear the enemy from the high ground and move rapidly inland and prepare to assist the Seventh Army's attack against the ports of Toulon and Marseille. The LST 914 landed the Third Infantry Division and Lt. Jean-Pierre Aumont, a popular French actor, on Alpha Beach.[50]

LST 914 and others land on Alpha Beach

Just as his acting career started to flourish in the United States, Aumont had joined the Free French forces fighting in Tunisia, Italy, and France. Born in Paris as Jean-Pierre Salomons, and of Jewish heritage, he escaped Nazi-occupied France. He went to Hollywood and entered a seven-year Metro-Goldwyn-Mayer (MGM) contract, starting at $2,000 per week. Soon thereafter, he was engaged to marry actress Hedy Lamarr. That engagement didn't last long, but Aumont did not lack for beautiful female company that included Lana Turner and Gene Tierney. Later, he complained of this period in Hollywood, explaining, "I couldn't stand this endless parade of wealth any longer, this assembly of rich foods and entertainment. These women who were too well dressed. I couldn't keep raking in money for smiling in front of a camera while many of my friends and countrymen were either dead, hunted, deported, or without food. As for my contract and my newfound success, at that moment I didn't give a good goddamn for them. I ran back to the hotel. There I gave the porter a telegram: 'Captain de Manziar, Free French Forces. New York. Have decided to join the Free French Forces.' I went up to my room and slept like a log."[51]

On August 8, 1944, Aumont boarded LST 914 en route to Cavalaire, France. On August 13, he asked American General Shepperd permission to disembark with the first elements of the U.S. Third Infantry Division. The general replied, "I know what that means to you, I'll see what I can do." But when the lists were posted, Aumont's name was missing. At midnight he woke up and added his name to the list.

At 0600 hours on August 15, Aumont saw a red rim on the horizon and heard the roar of Allied naval cannons. At 0620, the LST 914's loudspeaker announced an imminent raid by German planes. Ten minutes later, the chaplain said mass. By 0700, it was daylight, and the ship's crew was working the winches to put small landing craft into the water. During the initial landing, the LST 914 was prevented from landing three times, due to loose mines and gunfire, and thus had to turn back to sea. Aumont climbed into the bow of one of the landing craft. It was easy for him to see the beach and its pine trees and thick white smoke. As the small landing craft lowered its ramp, he heard the sound of artillery. Aumont and the other soldiers waded into the water up to their shoulders. They reached a road across from Hotel Pardigon by running through a lane surrounded by trees. An Allied tank was ablaze, and invading soldiers were quiet. Seeing a group of German prisoners walk by, Aumont was consumed with hatred. He later wrote,

"In Italy the Germans were our opponents, but here on this beautiful [French] roadway they are thieves."[52]

Aumont's assignment was to contact members of the local Resistance and provide information for the army intelligence section. On his way to General O'Daniel's headquarters that beautiful day, he met a young French couple and a little boy. When Aumont asked them whether they expected the invasion, they answered that with Allied planes dropping bombs on them for more than a week, only a fool would not have expected an invasion.

Aumont's account of his adventures on August 15 and the two weeks that followed is fascinating. Some of the Var department peasants that he met that day complained about American soldiers who stole their wine. Some French were unhappy that a young woman whom they accused of sleeping with a German officer didn't have her cheeks tattooed with the word "whore."[53] A woman in Cogolin kissed Aumont, and others were overjoyed to see the first French soldier since the 1940 disaster. While some laughed, others cried out, "We've been waiting so long!" Cogolin had been secured by midafternoon of August 15 by the U.S. Third Infantry Division soldiers and Lieutenant Aumont who established contact with the French Commandoes.[54]

James P. Connor, a Congressional Medal of Honor recipient, also took part in the invasion on August 15 on Alpha Red Beach in Cavalaire. A twenty-six-year-old sergeant from Wilmington, Delaware, he served with the Seventh Regiment, Third Infantry Division. Connor's mission was to take out the German fortifications of Cavalaire. He was seriously wounded by a hanging mine, which killed his lieutenant, but he refused medical attention and kept his patrol on task. He was struck a second time, in the shoulder, and again refused to be evacuated, believing that the duty to fulfill his platoon's objective was more crucial than seeking medical treatment.[55]

Overview of Operation Dragoon—Rear Admiral Lewis

Previously unpublished reports by Rear Adm. Spencer S. Lewis and Col. Gen. Johannes von Blaskowitz provide overviews of Operation Dragoon. One of the many virtues of these reports is their candor. Both men acknowledged errors and problems. But the fates of these two men and of their nations were quite different. The Allies overcame their inadequacies and mistakes and ended with overwhelming victory over the Axis. Their failures in southern France expedited the downfall of Nazism. Admiral Lewis's account follows:

The Operation proceeded largely as planned, although enemy resistance was less than anticipated. One outstanding incident was the cancellation of the assault on Red Beach by the Naval Assault Force Commander without prior consultation with the Commanding General, 36th Division (who had already landed but with whom communication had not been established). The Red Beach landing was not attempted because of heavy fire from the beach defenses (in spite of excellent pre-assault naval and air bombardment), because of failure to control the Apex boats and the subsequent failure to pierce the beach obstacles. This contingency had been foreseen and the rapid diversion, with little or no confusion, of the entire Red Assault Group over the already established Green Beach speaks extremely well for everyone concerned in the assault. When communication was finally established, the Commanding General, 36th Division, was in thorough agreement with the change in plans. His [General John Dahlquist] only regret was that the entire Red Assault Group had not been originally scheduled to land over Green Beach, thereby saving the six hours lost in the attempted Red Beach Assault. From the planning viewpoint, such a procedure would hardly be chosen deliberately. It involved landing an entire combat division, less one battalion landing team, over a 230-yard beach with one unpaved exit. The excellence of the beach, permitting dry landings from all types of craft, the weather, and the comparatively light enemy resistance combined to make this landing a success.

Relative immunity was enjoyed from enemy air opposition, due to the preponderance of the Allied Air Forces and their pre-D-day operations. Although enemy air attacks were conducted against the Transport Area from D-day until D+ 8, they were in very small numbers and were largely confined to the dusk period. Only one vessel, LST 282, was lost as a result of enemy air attack. So far as known, no enemy aircraft were shot down by Task Force 87, although one was shot down by a destroyer of the Area Screen in the Camel Area.

The effectiveness of the Area Screen was outstanding. In addition to its anti-aircraft defense, mentioned above, the Screen was completely successful in repelling determined night attacks by enemy boats and other light forces. At least seven boats were destroyed and over fifty prisoners and one light craft were captured.

At 0320, the *Bayfield* passed to the port side of the Camel LCT convoy instead of the starboard side as planned. At 0446, the *Bayfield* was two miles south of its planned position. At 0650, commenced pre-arranged fire on targets assigned in the Gunfire Plan. At 0800, the *Bayfield* was in position.

H-hour had been set for 0800. The boat control circuits were effectively jammed by the enemy, but shortly after 0800 reports began to come in on the landings. The landings on Green and Blue Beaches were proceeding according to schedule and the resistance to the first few waves was slight. Only slight machine gun fire was reported. Soon, however, enemy batteries got the range on Green Beach and the approaches to that beach. LCT 339 and LCT 625 were hit by shellfire in quick succession. The shellfire continued in fair strength throughout the day, and in the afternoon LCT 610 and LCT 51 were hit. The only craft casualties reported during the landings on Blue Beach were 2 LCVPs sunk by machine-gun fire and one beached.

At 0740 Commanding General 36th Division reported that landing on Red Beach had been set for 1400 and requested that the Red Beach assault forces be landed at that time. The beach was one of the best defended in southern France.

At 0800 Beach drenching carried out on schedule but poor visibility caused by dust and smoke after air bombing prevented observation of targets. Believed all active batteries neutralized with exception of two.

A sweeper was shelled while engaged in sweeping the approaches to Red Beach. At 1234, Allied boats left for Red Beach to do the shallow sweeping. When the craft were 1700 yards offshore, the Germans fired a heavy barrage. One vessel continued in to 1,500 yards and then returned to the Line of Departure, while another advanced to within 400-500 yards of the beach. At 1300 they returned to the Line of Departure still under fire.

At 1415, I ordered the Navy Assault boats, scheduled for Red Beach, to land on Green Beach. The change to Green Beach was carried out effectively, and the Red Assault Waves were successful landed there despite shelling of the beach. The Green Beach master had reported early in the day that landing conditions on the beach were excellent. LSTs were landing dry, vehicles were experiencing little or no difficulty in crossing the beach, and the troops were advancing quickly inland.

At 1500 communication indicated progress ashore good. Only thirteen fire missions requested from naval ships throughout day. All batteries in immediate Assault Area neutralized or destroyed.

At 1740, Commanding General 36th Division sent me the following message: "I appreciate your prompt action changing plan when obstacles could not be breached. Expect to take Red Beach tonight, no matter how late. Opposition irritating but not too tough so far."

At 1425, the 36th Division reported that only snipers and minor resistance remained in the vicinity of Rade D'agay, and that it believed it was safe to proceed with removal of the net across the mouth of the bay leading to Yellow Beach. At 1847, craft were engaged in clearing the boom and sweeping the Yellow Beach channels. The boom was sunk at 1915. Fifteen minutes later the LCI (L) 951 struck a mine in the Yellow Beach Area and sustained damage underwater forward. At 2015, Yellow Beach was open for traffic.

During the day there were several reports of aircraft in the vicinity, but there was no direct air attack on the Transport Area, approaches or beaches until 2050 when four unidentified aircraft closed from the NW. At 2100, the AA batteries of the ships in the Transport Area opened up, and at 2100, a JU-88 passed over the Transport Area at about 3,000 feet coming from the beach.

At 2225, LST 282, fully loaded, was hit by a bomb and lost on her approach to the beach.

In the morning the 1ˢᵗ Airborne Task Force and the 2ⁿᵈ Paratroop Brigade had established headquarters at Le Mitan several miles inland. By nightfall the troops landed by Task Force 87 had established a line extended from Boulouris to Amttelle to Les Caoux to Rastel D'Agay to the right flank of Blue Beach.[56]

Citing Dragoon's troubled history, Lewis wrote,

> Considerable difficulties were encountered in the planning for Operation Dragoon because of (a) the unavoidable delay in the receipt of the basic plan. This plan was not received until August 2; (b) the unavoidable delay in the final assignment of ships and craft due (i) to overriding commitments which continued in some cases to within 48 hours of the sortie; (ii) lateness of arrivals of craft from the United Kingdom; (c) Difficulty in obtaining an adequate number of suitable charts. No chart indicating the 100 fathom curve was available. Overlays had to be made in charts which most of the units of this force did not hold. The 1 in 50,000 gridded map-charts were not available in sufficient quantities."[57]

Lewis also described problems in carrying out the convoy and routing plan:

> The necessary separation of each type convoy into three sections, spaced at intervals too great to allow for effective visual communication, did not permit the close tactical control by convoy commanders which would have been desirable. (Nevertheless all convoys made the passage without incident, and this did not prove an actual handicap.)
>
> The assault convoy approached the Transport Area on an 82-mile run after taking their final departure from Corsica. As could be expected, the combination of the relatively slow speeds of the convoys and unpredictable currents resulted in considerable navigational error by the time the convoys reached the Assault Area. These errors were corrected by use of the destroyer reference vessels, and all vessels and craft were correctly positioned in the Transport Area in proper time.

The Defenders' Perspective of Operation Dragoon—Blaskowitz

The German Nineteenth Army, which was responsible for defending southern France, was commanded by Gen. Johannes Blaskowitz who was headquartered in Avignon. At first the news that the German defenders received concerning the Dragoon invasion was from Marseille, a considerable distance from the two areas decided upon by the Allied planners. The alleged landing sites turned out to be deceptions and were, instead, Allied bombing target decoys and dummies dropped by parachutes. Within hours the Germans learned that fierce air attacks and continuous Allied naval bombardment were directed at the actual target area that encompassed beaches near Saint-Tropez, Saint-Raphael, and Le Drammont. French Resistance agents disrupted German Army communications; but their chief, General Blaskowitz, did all he could to mount an effective delaying action against the invaders, realizing that a counterattack was impossible. On the ground and in the air, German military forces were substantially inferior to Allied strength to even undertake a successful withdrawal. The choices facing Blaskowitz were all bad: a retreat of his troops in the direction of Lyon was fraught with the danger of having Gen. George Patton's troops destroy Blaskowitz's army; and if the Germans tried to retreat to upper Italy through the Alps, they were confronted with a geographic nightmare. However, the terrain of the beaches chosen for Operation Dragoon was far from ideal for invasion purposes: the Riviera's coastal area is serrated and rocky and dangerous for navigation; small deepwater bays and gulf alternate with small semicircular sandy beaches. The unsuitability of the Delta area for invasion purposes was due to abundant low-lying swampy areas traversed by channels of the Rhone River. Tank use was an important issue.

The Germans were not completely surprised by the landings. Allegations that they were unaware of the invasion site and that their troops were too far west of the assault beaches, as the *New York Times* of August 16, 1944, claimed, were wrong. Because the planned invasion of southern France was to a large extent based upon the experiences of Normandy two months earlier, the Germans should not have been as surprised by the tactics and devices employed by the Allies on August 15, 1944, as they were. By August 1944, the Germans had constructed extensive offshore obstacles to deter Allied invasion convoys.[58] Additionally, the conglomeration of shipping into the Naples area in the days leading up to the attack, combined with the limited area of French coastline that was available to be invaded, helped to reduce German surprise. Military historian Donald Taggart claims that the Allies "could not depend on surprising the enemy with small, scattered landings, but would have to plan on stunning him with all the firepower and concentrated mass of men and material that the Allies could direct against a small number of closely grouped beaches. The naval gunfire and air support plans were coordinated with the [army's] own attack plan to achieve this effect . . . ."[59]

The Germans were substantially weaker than the invaders and without anticraft air force and troop strength. Haphazard defensive measures, such as hastily built obstructions and weak local counterattacks, were insufficient to stop the Allies. When General Blaskowitz wired headquarters in Berlin about the dire condition of his army's defense, his messages were intercepted by the Allies using the ULTRA code-breaking system. Nevertheless, the Allies were unable to benefit completely from the feeble condition of the enemy because of the unsuitability of the landing beaches which restricted the capacity to land troops, equipment, and supplies. Before August 15, these Riviera beaches and nearby hotels had served as playgrounds for the rich to enjoy splendid views from attractive terraces while drinking tasty aperitifs and ogling nearly nude torsos. Starting on August 15, these same beaches were used to land Allied troops, vehicles, and tons of supplies.[60]

Allied encirclement of Germany's Nineteenth Army was a distinct possibility. Such an event would probably have ended the European war much earlier than May 1945. Blaskowitz made a fast, difficult, and risky decision. First, he ordered his troops to retreat northward through the Rhone Valley to Lyon. From there they were to turn eastward and establish a security line all the way to the Swiss border and to gain time for an orderly retreat to German lines. To avoid unpredictable human errors, and to be certain that his orders would be fully understood and not intercepted, Blaskowitz risked the dangers of frontline combat fire to personally instruct his troops on how to follow his orders. Luckily for the Germans, the danger of encirclement posed by General Patton's Third Army connecting with General Patch's Seventh Army vanished because of the shortage of fuel available for Third Army vehicles.

Among Blaskowitz's achievements was the difficult task, after the Dragoon invasion, of evacuating a sizable portion of the German Army under exceedingly difficult circumstances. The Allied forces were much stronger; and Blaskowitz's troops were at the mercy of enemy air bombing, intelligence interception, and decoding that afforded the Allies advance knowledge of his plans. A combination of military leadership and skillful and imaginative direction of forces resulted in an incredible German retreat of about two hundred forty thousand men over distances varying between three hundred and five hundred miles in about twenty-eight days.

In a report dated September 27, 1944, Blaskowitz described the German plight in southern France, as follows:

By August 15, the German Army Group's forces had been depleted to nine Divisions. As a result of the evacuation of troops from southern France, the French underground movement began to flare up and it was impossible to prevent the Allies from equipping and supplying them by air. The French Resistance was most effective in threatening and handicapping our rear communications on rail and roads as well as in hampering more and more our freedom of action and movement. This resulted in an increasing deterioration of the communication system, which depended on the French postal and cable network and which finally bogged down on Aug. 15, aside from the technically inadequate radio communications. The Resistance movement was centralized in the Garonne Valley on both sides of the important communications-line Bordeaux-Toulouse, in the Pyrenees on both sides of the Rhone Valley from Lyon downwards, in the Central Massive and the Alps. An additional consequence was the release of further forces out of the defensive front for the maintenance of supply and troop-movements as well as for the security of transmission of orders.

The greatest setback to Army Group G was the decisive change of the operational situation in the combat area north of the Loire. After the Allied breakthrough at Avranches (early August), the enemy attack spearheads were approaching the Orleans-Chartres line and thus interrupted the supply line which, leading from Paris via Orleans-Tours, served the elements remaining south of the Loire. What German forces could become rallied on Aug. 10 had been moved to Fontainebleau in order to prevent an enemy breakthrough in an eastern direction. There were also enemy forces pressing towards the south against the Loire Sector of Nantes-Tours. This caused a direct threat to the right wing and the flank of the Army Group. The security of the Loire line was of crucial importance for limited freedom of movement of the Army Group. Authority was granted for the transfer of security forces from that weak front to the Loire. Just what the operational, economical and political reasons were for this stubborn adherence to the yet unattacked seacoast could not be recognized by a military commander who, of course, was lacking the necessary insight.

Had the recommendation of the Army Group found approval, then by Aug. 20 it would presumably have been located in the area around Dijon, in proper strength and ready for new missions and completing the withdrawal systematically and without any great losses of material. This requirement of time became even more critical in the latter part of August, when the actual withdrawal movement had to be carried out under considerably more difficult march-conditions and in the midst of the most serious combat conditions. The proposal for an early withdrawal from the coast would also have secured its supply-line leading from Belfort to Dijon. For the Third U.S. Army could have reached the Seine above Paris already by Aug. 20, which, as a matter of fact, was proven later by the actual events.[61]

Blaskowitz reported that on August 10 he had noticed a "large-scale embarkation of Allied troops in Algerian ports" and, on August 13, a "substantial convoy of Allied naval craft and transports west of the southern tip of Corsica with course to the north." As of August 14, the German general had "confirmation of this naval movement with course to north."[62]

Thus when, on the morning of Aug. 15, the U.S. Seventh Army, assisted by heavy coastal fire and bombing attacks, was landing in the Cannes-Tropez sector, the calculations of the Army Group were only being confirmed. The landings by airborne troops around Draguignan pointed to the intended direction of the enemy thrust. Owing to lack of reserves, immediate action had to be taken. These could no longer be drawn from another sector. The lack of mobility of the forces there and the fact that the communications had been paralyzed by the Maquis moreover no longer permitted such measures. The Division fighting to the east of the Rhone Estuary was tied down locally through the Marseille and Toulon fortresses as well as through the flank-protection towards the Italian Theater of War. It was therefore necessary to push the divisions located between Perpignan and the Rhone Estuary together on the baseline to the left, in order to move the battles closer to the landing area. Appropriate orders were issued by me on the spot as I was passing through.

In accordance with proven customs, the Army Group during the night of Aug. 15-16 immediately moved into the center of events to Avignon, thus establishing contact with other German forces. There, by personal contact with the fighting front, it was found that, in view of the German inferiority on the battlefield both on the ground and in the air, a counterattack would no longer be possible against the bridgehead which the enemy landings had meanwhile established. The battle therefore could merely amount to a time-saving device until the Supreme Command would, perforce, decide to discontinue the battle and to initiate the withdrawal from southern France. The withdrawal had to be safeguarded frontally by stubborn combat.[63]

Much of the German infantry equipment was transported by horses. Reserves and supplies were transported to battle by railroad. Systematic destruction of rail networks was disastrous for the Wehrmacht. Once the Normandy and Dragoon invasions occurred, it was difficult for the Germans to redeploy their forces. The Allies, however, were able to move large numbers of troops into the invasion areas and exact massive pressure on the enemy. German infantry was compelled to fight without enough artillery support and ammunition.

The *Atlantic Monthly*'s "European Front" report of September 1944 stated that "German casualties in dead, missing, wounded, and prisoners approximate 20,000 a day on the combined Russian, Balkan, Aegean, Italian and French fronts. An additional 1,000 a week are being put out of action by guerrillas, by partisans in the occupied countries, and by the French Army of the Interior . . . This meant that one third of the entire German combat strength as it existed was destroyed."[64] Two German Army divisions that were transferred from Poland to France had to walk because of the fuel shortage. An Albanian oil-production facility was captured by the Russians in June 1944. They also captured an important strategic area in Poland in August. Tanks and a variety of German vehicles were surrendered. Churchill summed up the role of his eastern Ally as follows: "It is the, Russian Army which has done the main work of tearing out the guts of the German Army."[65]

German defeat in France had dire consequences: no longer would France be a main source of food, labor, and raw resources for Hitler's minions; no longer would French seaports be used by German submarines; and no longer would radar sites in France provide early warning of Allied aircraft attacks.

American logistical failures and Blaskowitz's professional competence and personal integrity saved the German war machine from being totally crushed by Dragoon. Nevertheless, this invasion contributed greatly to Allied victory over the European enemies in May 1945. Once the port of Marseille was in Allied control, critical supply routes could be established to provide fresh troops, provisions, and equipment for the invading forces. It would also help to secure the southern portions of the Dragoon invasion forces.

Normandy and Dragoon

Historian Alan F. Wilt has compared the invasions of Normandy (Operation Overlord) and southern France (Operation Anvil/Dragoon). He found that the two "were exceedingly important to the Allied war effort," in addition to being closely similar. He provided the following comparative table:

A Comparison of Overlord and Anvil/Dragoon

Overlord	Allied Forces	Dragoon
155,615	Initial Landing Forces	60,150
36	Combat Divisions	10
1,440,000	Total Number of Troops	250,000
6,993	Ships and Landing Craft	2,250
12,837	Aircraft	4,056

Western Europe	German Forces	Southeastern France
58	Combat Divisions	8-2/3
1,873,000	Total Number of Troops	210,000
561	Ships and Craft	75
919	Aircraft	175

The figures indicate that although the magnitude of Normandy was much greater than Dragoon, the southern France invasion was still a big undertaking. The value of Dragoon is attested to by the fact that French Mediterranean ports were able to provide one-third to one-fourth of the supplies needed by the Allies until the end of the war in Europe.[66]

Although the Germans had 942 permanent defense cannons, 600 artillery forces, 62,486 land and sea mines, and 75 tanks in southern France, the Allies were far stronger on land, sea, and air. Wilt found that the Germans were deceived and surprised by the Allied invasion of Normandy. However, Wilt wrote, "By Aug. 7, reports from Army Task Force G, the German headquarters in command of southern France, indicated that 'systematic, especially heavy air attacks on the transportation links over the Rhone and Var rivers point to a landing between these two rivers.' This reduced the area of probability to 150 miles of Provençal coastline, and the invasion took place within this sector."

Wilt concluded his analysis by noting that "to the where was added the when. By the 12th, numerous rumors from sources within the Resistance and from the populace at large pointed to Aug. 15th, Napoleon's birthday, as the day of the attack. Additional information from agents, increased Allied air activity, and the forming up of convoys in Italy and Corsica only tended to confirm, in German eyes, their earlier reports. The Allied landing on the French Riviera therefore came as no surprise. The problem for the Germans was that they had neither the manpower nor the firepower to deal with it.

"As for the German reaction, it was much stronger in the north than in the south, where the Allies advanced up the Rhone River valley at a rapid rate. But Anglo-American forces could not sustain their brilliant summer offensives into the fall of 1944. The pace had been too hectic, the distances for supply too great to overcome."[67]

Allied military leaders in command of Operation Dragoon benefited from the experience of the earlier Mediterranean invasions and Normandy. Adm. Harold R. Stark, in command of United States Naval Forces in Europe during World War II and previously chief of naval operations, played a big role in the planning of the Normandy invasion. In his July 5, 1944, report, Stark analyzed naval versus army air force bombardment:

> Of particular advantage to the invasion troops was the great
> mobility of the vessels, by which artillery concentrations could

be achieved at any point of the coast and the place could be changed according to the exigencies of the situation. The attackers have made the best possible use of this opportunity. Strong formations of warships and cruisers were repeatedly used against signal coastal batteries, thus bringing an extraordinarily superior firepower to bear on them. Moreover, time and again they put an umbrella of fire (Feuerglocks) over the defenders at the focal points of the fighting, compared with which very heavy waves of air attackers have only a modest effect. It is no exaggeration to say that the cooperation of the heavy naval guns played a decisive part in enabling the Allies to establish a bridgehead in Normandy . . . At present, however, fighting at many points has been taking place for several days on the periphery of the range of the heavy and very heavy naval guns.[68]

Stark concluded his letter to Admiral Hewitt by saying, "My every good wish to you and all the gang, never forgetting my old shipmate and pal, Spence Lewis. You are lucky to have him."

French Revival

The French armed forces had a greater role in the invasion of southern France than in any preceding joint Allied force. They had the intimate knowledge of the southern coastline and could thus serve well in combat. "As a result the French representatives were accorded a voice far out of proportion to the strength of the French forces that would be involved—especially on the naval side, where France could contribute 50 ships."[69]

French historian Robert Aron reported that the number of French troops under General de Lattre's command numbered two hundred eighty-six thousand, and the American troops under the command of General Truscott—were less than one hundred thousand.[70]

Maj. Gen. Alexander M. Patch, commanding general, U.S. Seventh Army, inspecting men of the French Forces of the Interior, August 1944

Men and women of a French medical unit join other troops coming ashore from the U.S. Navy's LCI(L) 38 during the August 1944 invasion of southern France. These medical personnelhave standard U.S. "steel pot" helmets, American-style "webbing," uniforms, and mess gear (*Imperial War Museum*)

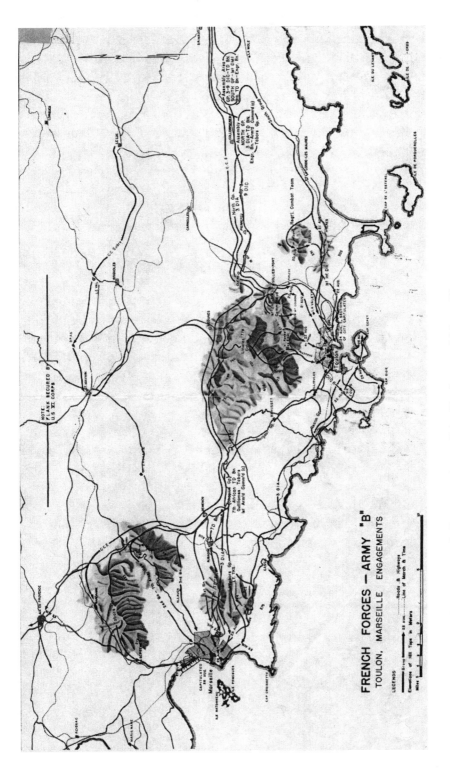

French Forces—Army B in Toulon and Marseille engagements

In the midst of the Dragoon campaign, General de Gaulle convinced General Eisenhower that French troops should gain control of Paris. Eisenhower's decision was based on his acceptance of two de Gaulle claims that (a) ridding the French capitol of German domination was important for French morale and (b) the control of Paris by de Gaulle's forces would diminish the growing prestige of the French Communist Resistance forces.

During the night of August 24-25, French troops marched into Paris with some American help. The German general von Choltitz surrendered on August 25. Later that day, de Gaulle set up headquarters in the War Ministry and appointed Gen. Joseph Pierre Koenig as military governor.

To demonstrate his primacy to his competitors for power to govern France, de Gaulle ordered a victory parade in the Champs-Elysées for August 26, despite the advice of the American commander in the area, General Gerow, that the parade might erupt in violence and disorder. But the march received an enormous ovation. When shots were fired at Notre Dame, de Gaulle remained calm, and Parisians were thrilled. De Gaulle's authority to lead the French people was clear. To further bolster his authority to govern, he had a French army division remain in Paris. Eisenhower did not grant de Gaulle's request to place two additional U.S. divisions in Paris to further reinforce his authority. However, he did assist de Gaulle's emergence as the undisputed leader of France by the beginning of September 1944. De Gaulle was stubborn in his insistence that every French sovereign right be respected by the Allies, even though France was defeated and without power. Ultimately he prevailed. This persistence also brought him the leadership and the everlasting gratitude of his people.

CHAPTER 10

REVERSALS

At the end of World War I, the French could claim that they were the strongest military power in Europe, that they governed the second largest colonial empire in the world, and that they had the world's fourth largest navy. Although they were well aware that they were exposed to attack in the 1930s from Nazi and Fascist militarists, nearly all French military and political leaders were certain that their fortifications and alliances enabled them to thwart enemy attack. This belief in French strength and security was demolished in spring 1940. By June of that year, the French were at the mercy of invaders who had bypassed their Maginot Line, decimated their military forces, and plunged them into a nightmare. To a large extent, the horrors that befell the French were caused by the superiority of German morale, strategy, and armament. Mobility was stressed by German military leaders who used tank and air warfare to the utmost.

After the French debacle, some Americans woke up to the fact that it was dangerous to depend on the Atlantic Ocean for national security. American seamen and ships rushed guns and ammunition left over from World War I across the Atlantic to reequip the Allied troops whose weapons had been lost at Dunkirk. Conscription for the army was started, and the building of a magnificent navy was initiated.

Within four years, the fate of the German people had changed dramatically. At the end of 1940, either through military supremacy or political and economic influence, Germany controlled nearly all of Europe except the European part of the Soviet Union. Their military leaders expected to culminate a series of spectacular victories in an attack on Great Britain. The Germans had gained the help of their Axis partner, Italy. On September 12, 1940, Benito Mussolini had initiated a drive into Egypt against the British, and Hitler also hoped to get the help of Spain and Portugal after Francisco Franco and António de Oliveira Salazar were promised British possessions in Africa. But even before the Pearl Harbor attack, German domination of Europe was challenged in the active resistance of Britain and the logistical support of the United States.[1]

Before the start of World War II, French military leaders underestimated the crucial role of aviation in modern warfare. One important reason that German military aviation was better than the French was that the Germans had more warplanes and pilots. An analysis by Pierre Cot showed that the French pilots were better than the enemy; that every time they engaged in combat with German aviators, one against one, the French were victors; and that German superiority was the result of greater quantity of planes.[2] By August 1944, French pilots were playing a significant role in an Allied air force that was vastly superior to its foe. There was no doubt as to the quality and quantity of air domination.

By the end of summer 1944, the still-dangerous German military machine was seriously damaged after a series of defeats in the Mediterranean and elsewhere. Hitler's erstwhile Italian and Iberian allies were eagerly soliciting Anglo-American favor. About fifteen thousand men under the Free French flag were followers of Gen. Charles de Gaulle in 1940. However, by the end of that year, "35,000 men had joined the 'Free French.'"[3] Volunteers continued to come. They came from Nazi-controlled parts of France, the unoccupied area under Vichy control, German prison camps, French colonies, the United States, and elsewhere. Once they arrived, they were supplied and paid by the Americans despite Churchill's and Roosevelt's strong dislike and distrust of de Gaulle.[4]

Without facilities to communicate with their headquarters, and lacking air reconnaissance and other necessities, German troops could not hold back Dragoon forces. The invaders also faced problems, but these were not on scale with those faced by the Germans. Unloading of equipment and supply delays, foul weather, and shortages of gasoline due to the unanticipated speed of success did not obscure the reality that the enemy occupiers were routed and that Pétain, Laval, and the Vichy regime were doomed.

American, British, and French navy crews bombarded enemy shore batteries without much fear of retaliation. A German submarine crew of fifty was ignominiously caught trying to escape on a fishing boat. Fifteen thousand well-armed German troops, protected in a strong fortress, surrendered to a French force of eight hundred. Nevertheless, the U.S. Office of Naval Intelligence reported that German morale remained remarkably strong. Even more incredible was the resurgence of de Gaulle and his movement that sought, with considerable success, to regain the power and prestige of pre-World War II France. By the end of summer 1944, it was clear that the French were their own political and social masters notwithstanding the smuggling in of forbidden American movies during the Dragoon invasion. Dependence on American aid for necessities did not subject the French to U.S. domination. Also that summer, Marshal Pétain's 1940 hope of having the count of Paris (Henry VI in the Bourbon-Orléans succession) become king of France came to nothing, as did the count's aspiration to establish a "popular social monarchy" in which he would assume the role of monarch-führer.[5]

With the help of their Allies, the French had regained their freedom. But the transformation that was achieved in France because of the invasions of North Africa, Sicily, Salerno, and in France itself was not bought at a bargain price. The successes of these invasions repaired many of the military intelligence, logistic, and diplomatic disasters of 1940-41. Vichy politicians then tried to assassinate de Gaulle—the man who sought to energize the French—and they honored Pétain who played a major role in their defeat.

An atmosphere of stupor had descended upon the French when their nation was overwhelmed by defeat in spring 1940. Slowly, and gradually, they realized that the Germans would not treat them as a free and independent people. The posters on the walls of French municipal buildings beseeching the local population to trust German soldiers soon proved to be snares and delusions. Once this became apparent, the resistance accelerated.[6]

In the autumn of 1918, a shortage of food in Germany exhausted the fighting stamina of the nation and was an important factor in their leaders suing for peace. In their planning for World War II, the Nazis were determined to avoid shortages of food or raw materials and did not hesitate to appropriate these commodities from the French or other people they subjugated.[7] A reversal of fortune was apparent in 1944 over food and other necessities—favoring the French and not the Germans.

In his 1942 examination of the forces of collaboration in France, one analyst found that the silent consent of the highest French bureaucrats was largely responsible for the collaboration with the Germans. But even before the Allied invasion of North Africa, Louis R. Franek claimed that the overwhelming majority of French people hoped for an Allied victory.[8] In August 1944, it was clear that this goal would be realized.

The Drive into France

After their initial successes on the beaches of the French Riviera on August 15, 1944, Allied troops continued to drive further into occupied France, dashing the Axis myth of the "Fortress Europe" and of German invincibility.

On August 16, the USS *Omaha* arrived at the Dragoon assault area. The Thirty-sixth Infantry Division consolidated its position on the right flank near Theoule-sur-Mer and started to move toward Vidauban and Camp des Cais. French combat command troops landed on their nation's beaches at noon and proceeded to assemble in the area of Gonfaron. They were joined at 1800 by other French troops who landed on the beaches in the area of Saint-Tropez-Cavalaire. "By mid-afternoon on Aug. 16, enemy resistance in the entire Fréjus area was broken. The battalions, having completed their various assigned missions, assembled west of Fréjus and moved to Puget."[9]

Allied forces targeted highway and railroad bridges in the lower Rhone Valley with both medium and heavy bombers in order to impede the enemy. Supplies were dropped by 112 C-47s to Allied troops. The major elements of the Third Infantry Division were able to press forward twenty miles inland thanks to the thin German defense in the landing area. This was proven by the interception of a German High Command radio transmission that said, "No counterattack will be launched against the invasion forces until they have driven inland far enough so as to be out of effective range of the support of their own naval gunfire."[10]

Despite their serious reverses in summer 1944, the German military forces were still dangerous. However, the reasons given for their inability to more effectively defend the immediate coastal areas of Operation Dragoon were ominous signs of serious weakness. These omens were German troop deployment that was thinly stretched along the invasion beaches; inability to commit additional troops because of transportation shortages; coastal areas that could not be defended because of inadequate air support, armor, and heavy artillery; isolation and the far distance of the German Army Headquarters; and the harassing effects of the French Resistance, which plagued the Germans from the rear.[11]

Gen. Johannes Blaskowitz reported that a preliminary order came through for the surrender of southwestern France on August 17 up to Orléans-Bourges-Montpellier. That night, he recalled,

The Army Group received the final instructions by radio for cessation of the battle at the Riviera, evacuation of southern France and taking up contact with Heeresgruppe B in the area north of Dijon.

Army Group had been prepared for this order since the enemy breakthrough at Avranches, having recommended it for the last time on Aug. 16. Could the plan still be carried out? All communications—including radio—with HQ, the command authority for all units and agencies located in the Atlantic area between Loire and Pyrenees, had become disrupted, and an up-to-date command had therefore become impossible. The result would be a blind command with its obsolete, tedious command-system, with the road-tied command receivers, heavily escorted on account of the Maquis. In that case, success could become assured only by means of an intelligent independence of the subordinate commanders in a far-flung area of command. Accordingly, troops were instructed to withdraw via Bourges towards Dijon, to secure the northern flank along the Loire and later near Auxerre and try their utmost to maintain contact with the newly organized army in the area around Paris.

The personal knowledge of the combat area, its proximity as well as the fact that the Army was beginning to be consolidated in the direction of the Rhone Valley, lessened the difficulties of speedy and secure transmission of orders. The moving-in of all the elements of the 19th Army into the narrow Rhone Valley—handicapped through the French Resistance movement—had to be (and was) regulated and safeguarded by means of locally designated lines of resistance. The direction of the Army's withdrawal movement via Lyon towards Dijon was, perforce, determined by the situation.

A surprising factor was the orders for troops to turn into the Alps Passes. As a natural result of this order, the road leading over the Digne towards Grenoble was opened up to the landed enemy forces for outflanking movements at an early time. This could only be adjusted in time by the German Army through moving up its only motorized combat units with extreme efforts. For the time being, orders were given independently, tying down the division until such time as the withdrawal movements of the Army could be started. In view of the local proximity of German command-staffs, all these matters could be straightened out through personal contacts.

The Army Group concentrated its attention to the preparatory and potential measures for security and reception of the 19th Army in the area around Lyon after its move out of the Rhone Valley, and then also proceeded there.[12]

D plus 3 of the Dragoon operation started under partly cloudy skies that gave way to thunderstorms in the afternoon. Admiral Hewitt reported that enemy land resistance was "fairly light except in scattered areas."[13] Camel Red Beach (264A) was cleared of obstacles, mines, and roadblocks and opened at 1900, though Alpha Yellow Beach was closed. Some of the beaches still had the smoke screens in operation at dusk in order to divert enemy attention from Allied ships that were unloading. Admiral Hewitt noted that the smoke screen delayed the actual unloading of the ships themselves. Allied crews continued to clear the waters of mines, especially in the Gulf of Fréjus.

On August 18, the headquarters of the German XLII Corps was captured at Draguignan. Hewitt stated that "enemy capabilities at this time were (1) to exert maximum delaying action, (2) to reinforce present troops in the area, (3) to harass the Seventh Army by limited counterattacks, and (4) to delay our advance to the west and maintain a stubborn defense of Toulon and Marseille. The last was believed to be the capability most likely to be adopted."[14]

At dusk, five enemy JU-88 planes passed over Camel Beach 264, one of which descended to six thousand feet and dropped antipersonnel bombs in the Delta area. The bombs straddled the USS *Catoctin*, two hit the ship, resulting in six dead and forty-two wounded. At the same time, one of the JU-88s fired a torpedo in the Delta area, which exploded 250 yards short of target. Reports of objects falling into the water at this time were also reported in the Alpha Beach area. "All areas were blanketed by smoke at the time of the raid," reported Hewitt, with the USS *Plunkett* taking down one of the attacking aircraft.

Despite some difficulties from enemy interruptions, by the end of D plus 4, a total of 90,055 personnel, 13,404 vehicles, and 55,660 tons of supplies were unloaded on the Alpha, Delta, and Camel beaches. Four days after landing, under mostly clear skies, "forward elements had pushed past Sisteron, more than 100 miles from the beaches," according to a Seventh Army report. "Gasoline continued to be the most critical item of supply. Gasoline dumps captured at Draguignan, Le Muy, and later at Digne were exploited to continue the advance and overcome shortages within the units."[15]

Hewitt confirmed that on the same day, August 19, "enemy resistance north towards Digne was negligible . . . Enemy resistance appeared disorganized." The next day, it was observed that "enemy resistance continued light and scattered; at Aix and Durance enemy opposition was fairly stubborn. Enemy capabilities were: (1) to withdraw north up the Rhone Valley, fighting strong delaying action; (2) to launch a local counterattack; and (3) to launch a strong counterattack employing the bulk of the 11th Panzer Division. Our strong advances to the west beyond Aix had outflanked Marseille. The only capability, therefore, left to the enemy, appeared to be to withdraw up the Rhone Valley."[16]

That same day, French troops surrounded Toulon and started to move westward toward Marseille, capturing Le Beausset and Bandol to the west of Toulon. In the meantime, U.S. forces captured Aix and were able to move north. Strong reconnaissance elements north of Sisteron captured Gap, noted Hewitt. Normal fighter cover was maintained by the Allied air forces while fifty-nine convoys arrived and another fifty-eight departed.

The postlanding proceedings continued at a rapid pace. On August 24, the rail link that connected Fréjus and Sainte-Maxime was rehabilitated, allowing the initial forward supply dump to be opened by the army quartermaster. With this action, rations, ammunition, and gasoline could now be stocked at Sainte-Maxime until the major ports of Toulon and Marseille could be cleared and reopened by the Allies.[17] To this end, French troops successfully captured Toulon and La Ciotat on August 25 while continuing to clear out pockets of enemy resistance around Cap Sicie, Saint-Mandrier, and the Marseille ports. Allied bombers and fighters were also now operating in the upper Rhone Valley.

On August 28, Reuters's correspondent Reginald Langford reported that Pierre Laval, premier of Vichy, was arrested by the Gestapo in the French border town of Belfort, near the French-Swiss frontier, and that Marshal Pétain, Vichy chief of state, was also arrested. Langford cabled the full text of Pétain's protest to Hitler about being forced to leave Vichy. The message, dated August 29, read,

In concluding an armistice with Germany, I showed my irrevocable decision to play my part with those of my countrymen and never leave its territory. I have thus been able, in loyal respect of conventions, to defend the interests of France.

On July 16, before persistent rumors concerning certain German intentions with regard to the French government and myself, I had to confirm my position to the diplomatic corps specifying that I should oppose by every means in my power a forced departure to the east.

Your representatives have furnished me with arguments contrary to the truth to make me decide to leave Vichy. Today they wish to compel me by violence and in disregard of all engagements to leave for an unknown destination.

I raise solemn protest against this act of force, which makes it impossible for me to exercise my prerogatives as chief of the French state.[18]

Meanwhile, Allied warships, including battleships, cruisers and destroyers, continued their intensive bombardment of enemy strong points and ran positions along the southern French coast from Marseille to Nice, reported the *ONI Weekly* on August 30, 1944. According to that publication,

The principal effort was directed against enemy fortifications on the peninsulas southwest and south of Toulon, particularly at Fort Six-Cours, Cape Sicie, Cape Cepet, and Saint-Mandrier. This area was shelled every day from the 18th through the 27th August; the bombardment reached its height on the 26th when 2,700 rounds, of which 497 were of major caliber, were fired in an attempt to destroy German resistance in Saint-Mandrier, where extensive underground defense positions had been prepared. On the morning of the 28th, Saint-Mandrier, the last of the enemy positions to hold out, surrendered unconditionally. Among those captured was Rear Admiral Rufus, who had succeeded Vice-Admiral Wever in command of German Naval Forces in southeast France. Admiral Rufus said that Allied bombing and naval gunfire had completely destroyed surface installations on the Saint-

Mandrier Peninsula, forcing the garrison to take shelter in tunnels. Admiral Wever, who was reported to have died of a heart attack at about the time of the Allied landings, was responsible for naval coast defense and is believed to have had his headquarters at Aix-en-Provence.

Among the ships bombarding enemy batteries at Saint-Mandrier on the 25th were the French battleship *Lorraine,* the French light cruiser *Gloire* and the British light cruisers *Aurora* and *Sirius.* The British battleship *Ramillies* and the French light cruiser *Emile Bertin* and destroyer *Terrible* were also identified as being in action this week.

At Marseille a German force of 850 men on an island sent word to an American ship that they would surrender to U.S. forces. The men were evacuated on four LCI's. A small force of Marines from an American cruiser was ready to go ashore to enforce surrender terms.

Other areas shelled by Allied warships included targets at Marseille (on the 22nd and 25th), at Gien (on the 21st, 22nd, and 23rd), in the Cannes area (on the 22nd and 23rd), and near Nice (on the 24th and 25th). Near Valbonne, outside Cannes, an American cruiser, aided by air spotters, destroyed two groups of gun emplacements on the 23rd; the FFI rendered valuable assistance in locating targets for naval gunfire in this area. At Nice on the 24th a bridge across the Var River was damaged by naval gunfire and a cargo vessel in Nice Harbor hit.

The island of Porquerolles, south of Hyères, was shelled on the 21st and on the morning of the 22nd. At 1130 on the 22nd the German garrison on the island surrendered to a United States cruiser; more than two hundred prisoners were taken. The island is now garrisoned by French troops.

Allied minesweeps have been active clearing approaches to French ports now in Allied hands as well as sweeping mines from the operational areas. On the 24th an American battleship and two cruisers bombarded targets in the Gulf of Fos in support of minesweeping operations in that area. Various parties of enemy troops attempting to escape by motor boat and fishing vessel were rounded up by Allied naval vessels throughout the week. On one fishing vessel, four officers and 46 men from a U-boat were captured.

Allied carrier-based aircraft continued to harass enemy communications. On the 20th the naval aircraft claimed to have destroyed nine locomotives and 118 motor transports; on the 21st a merchant vessel and minelayer were destroyed in the Toulon area and eight enemy aircraft shot down; on the 25th two bridges in the Rhone Valley were successfully bombed.

The enemy attempted an attack with explosive boats on Allied naval units on the right flank of the landing area on the night of the 25th. The explosive boats were driven off by screening destroyers; eight of them are reported to have been destroyed.

Allied coastal craft torpedoed two ships of unknown type in the Gulf of Genoa on the night of the 24th. One of the ships was sunk and the other damaged. On the 26th, off Imperia, an enemy torpedo boat was attacked by Allied aircraft; one torpedo hit was claimed.

Additional information on the American naval forces which covered the invasion of southern France was revealed this week by Secretary of the Navy James Forrestal. The ships participating in the operations included the battleships *Texas, Arkansas,* and *Nevada;* the heavy cruisers *Quincy, Augusta,* and *Tuscaloosa;* the light cruisers *Brooklyn, Marblehead, Philadelphia, Cincinnati,* and *Omaha;* and two escort carriers, the *Tulagi* and the *Kasaan Bay.*

Forty-seven American destroyers were employed in the operations, Mr. Forrestal said, in addition to 12 troop carriers; 5 APDs; 76 LSTs; 78 LCTs; and numerous other amphibious craft. Among the destroyers in action were the *Plunkett,* which had her stern blown off at Anzio last spring but is now fully repaired.

Although there were some minor German successes on D-day, the Germans, "broadly speaking, never were able to bring their many threatened air attacks to any substantial fruition." Additionally, since D-day, approximately 25 German generals and an admiral were killed, wounded, captured, or replaced in France.[19]

On August 27, a fishing vessel holding a crew of forty-six men and four officers from an enemy U-boat was captured by the USS *Ericsson.*

These captives reported that they had tried to escape in a submarine from Toulon but had grounded on an island off Toulon and had destroyed the U-boat. Additionally, thirteen men were captured by the USS *MacKenzie* while trying to escape from Saint-Mandrier in a small boat. Near Cap Antibes, three German officers and two men were caught trying to escape to Genoa.

After the August 15 landings, facilities were set up to attend to the wounded and bury the dead. A municipal theater was used as a morgue. Brave French men and women risked their lives to report on German dispositions. Captured high-ranking German officers provided crucial information. One holdout, German Admiral Ruhfuss, commander of the Toulon Garrison, vowed to fight the Allies until the last round of ammunition. After he surrendered and was told that he would be killed if he did not produce a detailed plan of underground minefields, Ruhfuss divulged all. While many were risking their lives to liberate the French Riviera, others were enjoying themselves at hotels such as the Madeleine in Marseille. De Lattre and other French generals used this hotel as their headquarters. They were fulfilling military responsibilities, and their soldiers were fighting and dying nearby as hotel guests were indulging themselves in a variety of pleasures.

German General Schaeffer, who commanded fifteen thousand men behind the concrete walls of Saint-Jean Fort in Marseille that contained two hundred guns, plenty of ammunition, and other necessities, was persuaded by a French general with eight hundred men and not much armaments to unconditionally surrender. Schaeffer rejected a humanitarian plea to give himself and his troops up as prisoners so that further bloodshed would be stopped. After being reminded that he had been condemned to death by a Soviet court martial for atrocities against civilians, Schaeffer turned ashen. He subsequently disobeyed Hitler's orders to resist to the last round, claiming his honorable resistance and his capitulation to the superiority of French forces.

Another indication of the deteriorating force of the enemy in southern France was Hewitt's report that enemy forces gave some resistance north of Montélimar but prepared to withdraw from the Var River area and that since the beginning of Dragoon, the Seventh Army had captured 40,211 prisoners.[20] The *Atlantic Monthly*'s "European Front" report of September 1944 indicated that "German casualties in dead, missing, wounded, and prisoners approximate 20,000 a day on the combined Russian, Balkan, Aegean, Italian and French fronts.

An additional 1,000 a week are being put out of action by guerrillas, by partisans in the occupied countries, and by the French Army of the Interior . . . . This means that within the past sixteen weeks one third of the entire German combat strength, as it existed this spring, has been destroyed."[21]

Two German Army divisions that were transferred from Poland to France had to walk because of the fuel shortage. The Russians captured an Albanian oil production facility in June 1944 and an important area in Poland in August. Tanks and a variety of German vehicles were surrendered. Churchill summed up the role of his eastern ally, as follows: "It is the Russian Army which has done the main work of tearing out the guts of the German Army."[22] German defeat in France had dire consequences: no longer would France be a main source of food, labor, and raw materials for Hitler's minions; no longer would French seaports be used by German submarines; and no longer would radar sites in France provide early warning of Allied aircraft attacks.

On August 28, German forces surrendered in Toulon and Marseille, leaving the Allies with some twenty thousand prisoners of war to contend with. By the end of that month, Hewitt observed that the First Airborne Task Force had moved out of range of naval operations, having advanced to the east beyond Nice "more rapidly than had been expected."[23] "The enemy," he wrote, "was withdrawing hastily northward from Valence, and from the area of southwestern France. Mines and demolitions covered the enemy withdrawal eastward from Nice. The French, by this time, had reportedly taken Montpellier and Séte, and the U.S. Seventh Army had captured Lyon. With these areas under Allied control, the rehabilitation of the railroad system in southern France was begun in earnest, though important operations could not be conceived of until a major terminal, such as Marseille, was also in Allied hands. By September 1, the Allies had captured 59,931 prisoners."[24]

"The French Forces of the Interior have now freed almost all of the territory of southern France not occupied by Allied troops," reported the *ONI Weekly* on August 30, 1944. "The Germans hold only the Biscay coast, a narrow strip south of the Loire and the upper Rhone Valley. Even in these areas a number of large towns have been taken by the FFI. It is reported that about 12,000 Germans in the Landes area, south of Bordeaux, are prepared to surrender to British or Americans."[25]

General Blaskowitz noted the following on September 1, 1944:

The enemy picture remained unclarified due to our own lack of air reconnaissance. Armored spearheads of the Third U.S. Army had pushed up to the Upper Seine around Troyes. The enemy threat remained, owing to the lack of all our communications being cloaked in darkness. To what extent the outflanking movement of the U.S. Seventh Army—aiming, by way of Grenoble, to the Upper Rhone—and Doubs Valleys— was already showing its effects, could not be recognized due to the lack of suitable reconnaissance facilities of the ground forces there. The French Resistance movement in the Jura became noticeably more active.

The supply of the troops also required increasingly greater uniformity of control. Despite the fact that the Army Group thought its mission for the coastal defenses on the Atlantic and the Mediterranean was between 700 and 1,000 km. removed from the supply base in the interior, it had, when being activated, not received a supply section. Anticipating the coming supply difficulties, several recommendations had been made, which were rejected.

On Sept. 1, a liaison officer, who had been sent ahead, had managed to get through, by way of the Maquis-held road, to the Army Group at Dijon; thus the Army Group for the first time had an opportunity to gain an overall impression regarding the present state of the Corps which was about 100,000 men . . . .

Could it be possible that all the forces of the Army Group could, in the last moment, still become united in the Dijon area? The 19th Army had, under heavy sacrifices, been able to move up the Rhone Valley and was advancing smoothly further to the north, protected on the eastern flank by the particularly flexible 11 Panzier Division which, however, was unable to prevent the U.S. Seventh Army from moving up towards Pontalier. In order to shorten our crisis, instructions were issued to immediately send all mobile elements ahead to Dijon without delay. The fact that this would worsen the fate of the immobile, and especially the unarmed, columns had to be taken into the bargain, aside from the necessity to reorganize the entire march-system of the Corps.

The course of subsequent events has justified both arrangements. There still remained the question unsolved as to how the frontal gap between two German armies could be closed in time. For it was obvious that this gap would invite the Third U.S. Army for a breakthrough there and, by means of a drive in the direction of Saarbourge, to paralyze the Saar Region which was of even greater importance to the war-economy. Such a thrust over the Moselle also offered the enemy a final opportunity of taking the 19th Army with a pincer-attack before the latter would gain complete contact with the Vosges Mountains and would be able to seal-off the Mountains' approaches to the Rhine Valley.

This great danger which, even in the last moment, could foil the formation of a coherent defensive front at the German border in the west, had also been recognized by the command of the Wehrmacht. The troops earmarked for this, however, were only beginning to move up. The exact time of their arrival could not be estimated owing to the enemy air superiority which, during daylight, permitted only cautious movements by single vehicles and which more or less brought to a standstill the rail-traffic west of the Rhine.

Meanwhile the crisis in that sector was mounting. The northern-flank cover of the 19 Army on the Plateau de Langres along the line Charmes-Neufchateau-St. Blin-Chaumont was, during the days of 11-14 Sept., broken through and put out of action through French and American armored forces. At the same time, the Third U.S. Army took possession of Nancy. It was out of this situation that the fluctuating battles of the German Army, which lasted one month, were developing for the closing of this dangerous gap. In conclusion, it can be noted that we had accomplished the mission—which had been issued too late—to evacuate southern France.

Its accomplishment was bought with unnecessarily high losses of personnel and matériel. Its success was carried by the skillful coordination of the leadership as well as the stubborn determination of the part of the humble German man to place himself in front of home and hearth, wife and child, parents, brothers and sisters. In true masculine spirit—as it can be found whenever we occupy ourselves with the history of mankind and as it may be encountered with all the creatures of the universe—they could not think or act otherwise.

In any case, it had been possible for the time being to screen off the southwestern border of Germany, for which the necessary forces would have been lacking otherwise. To what extent the greatly worn-out troops—composed in full unison of all components of the *Wehrmacht* and all age-groups (from youths to old men)—should be able to cope with additional battles, depended on the developments. Their reconditioning as well as refurnishing them with weapons and equipment was, aside from supplies, dependent above all upon the further intentions of the enemy who was holding the reins. To analyze these intentions and, if possible, to look through them and meet them, was now up to the commanding authorities, of which I was relieved at that time. The events just described were immediately followed by an evaluation through the Supreme Authority, as a result of which I was, without prior announcement and without being given any reasons, relieved of my assignment on Sept. 22 and replaced through General Black.[26]

With the German evacuation of southern France, the Allies were free to start clearing the way for supplies to enter the country. The first Liberty ships were able to berth in Toulon by September 7 and prepared to unload their supplies. However, one problem that faced the Allies was how to distribute these supplies—for, as the *ONI Weekly* observed, the occupied territories had been stripped of all the locomotives; from France, for example, three thousand to four thousand had been taken by the Germans.[27]

Overall, 2,250 ships and craft took part in the invasion of southern France between August 9 and September 25. Allied losses numbered 13 craft[28] and 48 damaged while the enemy suffered at least 50 craft sunk or destroyed, the loss of 13 human torpedoes, and another 6 damaged craft, and 3 captured. The ability of the Allies to move personnel and equipment off their craft and onto mainland France contributed greatly to the success of Dragoon. From August 15 through September 25, a total of 324,069 personnel, 68,419 vehicles, 490,237 tons of dry supplies, and 325,730 barrels of wet materials were unloaded.[29]

As Admiral Hewitt reported, "During the 40 days following the first assault, the entire south coast of France had been either swept free of mines or remaining minefields located and declared as dangerous areas. Six ports had been cleared. No major loss was sustained due to the enemy mining effort and approximately 550 mines were swept."[30]

Hewitt commented that his responsibility for Dragoon was great but that he had the feeling that

> we had worked things out as well as we could. I could rely on my very fine staff and on my subordinate naval commanders. I didn't worry. I mean that. I had the attitude that we'd done our best and that everything would be all right.
>
> I'm one of these double-acrostic addicts. It's a great relaxation. But sometimes some of my staff would have a fit because we'd be going into one of these landings and I'd be sitting up on the bridge of the flagship *Catoctin*, ready to take action if anything unexpected came up, working out some of these puzzles. I had to concentrate my mind on that. It took it off other worries.
>
> The French—and you couldn't blame them—were extremely eager to be the first to land on their own soil. General Jean de Lattre de Tassigny was insistent about that. He was a very fine man, very pleasant, very volatile. I had to convince him, and General Charles de Gaulle too, that it was hard enough to get soldiers and sailors working together in the same boat in the first place, but with the language barrier it would be absolutely impossible. It would be chaotic. Fortunately, I had my friend Rear Admiral André Lemonnier, head of the French Navy, to back me up on that completely. So they agreed to it, finally. As it worked out, the American troops took the beachhead, and then the French army landed in behind them and started inland.[31]

Maj. Gen. Robert T. Frederick receives the flag of Le Muy from its mayor after the liberation of the town, August 17, 1944.0

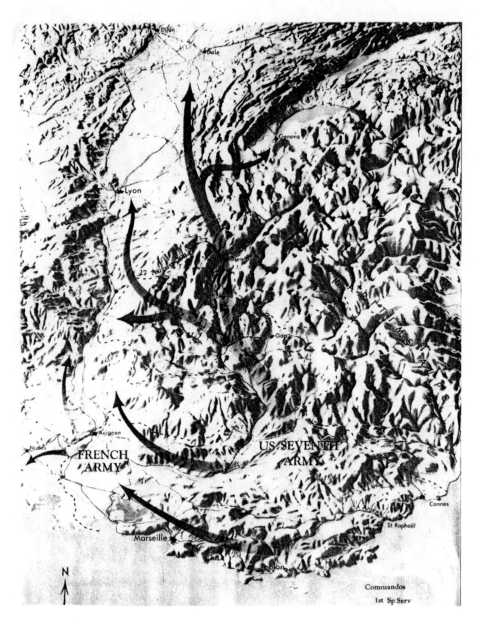

Operation Anvil
(from Gen. George C. Marshall's WWII report)

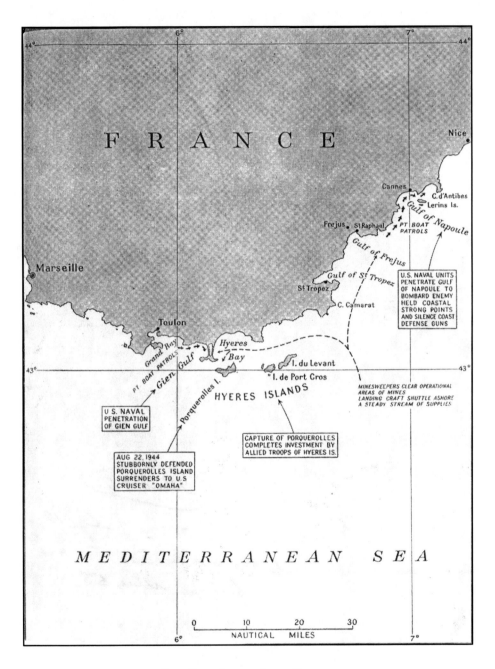

Landings in southern France

French WACS assembling on the beach after landing at Saint-Tropez, France, August 17, 1944

Captured enemy troops

The cost for success was not light: 35 U.S. Navy men killed in action, another 36 missing, and 243 wounded. Approximately 4,500 American battle casualties (slightly more than 2,000 killed, captured, or missing) resulted from Operation Dragoon. French losses were a little higher, and it is also difficult to estimate French Resistance losses. Estimates concerning German losses are 7,000 killed and three times that amount wounded. More than half of the 250,000 German troops surrendered. According to *The Oxford Companion to World War II*, the French casualty loss was 4,000 people and the Americans 2,700.[32] The sacrifices of the men and women involved in the Dragoon invasion significantly helped to weaken the German forces in France. However, they did not eliminate the enemy completely; the Germans still held the north of France in summer 1944, despite the approximate buildup of 20,000 FFI troops in the Seine department by that time.[33]

Dragoon and Paris

Military historian John Keegan claimed that Operation Dragoon allayed Hitler's plans to use Paris as a battleground after the Allies' Normandy advance inland. Hitler intended to use Paris as a major bridgehead on which the German Army could inflict devastating losses on the Allies. He was intent on the destruction of the French capital. But according to Keegan, Dragoon "made nonsense of any hope of holding Paris when a new Allied thrust menaced the rearward communications of the capital with Germany from the south."[34] As evidence that the population of Paris "was not overly resistant" to the German occupiers, Keegan observed that Parisians in March 1944 "welcomed Pétain with tumultuous popular demonstrations" and that as late as August 13 (1944), "Laval had returned to Paris in the hope of reconvening the Chamber of Deputies to accord him powers as legitimate head of government who might treat on sovereign terms with the liberating armies." However, once it became apparent that the Germans were going to lose, armed French Resistance fighters overwhelmed the streets of Paris.[35]

As Allied troops of the Normandy invasion got closer to Paris, some of its people demonstrated their eagerness to destroy the twenty thousand German troops in their midst. Parisian rail and post office workers and police went on strike from August 10 through 16. The Communists within the French Resistance had a majority on the important committees and their leader, Rol-Tanguy, called for the strikes to weaken the Germans despite General de Gaulle's pleas that such action was premature and that the resisters only had six hundred weapons larger than revolvers.[36] Nevertheless, resistance persisted, as was demonstrated in the Var department and elsewhere in southern France.

Professor Jean-Marie Guillion collected photographs of posters and circulars that were distributed throughout southern France during the summer of 1944. Their messages sought to use words as weapons:

- No bread no work.
- Demonstration. July 14, 1944. Hyères.
- Open letter to Prefect. Criticism for Belittling Demonstration.
- Letter complaining that works of art destroyed.
- Communication to Mayor of Sainte-Maxime. Maquis are not thieves.
- Complaint about promised help that did not arrive.
- Description of accomplishment of Resistance guards.
- Areas mined to confuse Germans.[37]

Huge anti-German demonstrations took place on Bastille Day, July 14, 1944, in the eastern districts of Paris. Communist members of the trade union confederation, the *Union des Syndicats*, organized a rally with the support of other Resistance groups. Anti-German demonstrations dominated the streets of Paris for nearly an hour before the Germans clamped down on the protest. Some Frenchmen were arrested, and a few were killed.[38]

It was not just the Communists who were organizing resistance to the Germans; by summer 1944, the French Resistance movement had gained momentum throughout the country, with their stronghold located in southern France. The destruction of German lines of communication and troops proved to the world that the Resistance was serious in attempting to reclaim France. "From its fragmentary, isolated beginnings, at a time when secrecy was of the essence, the Resistance had emerged as a full-scale, nationwide military movement. The Maquisards traversing all of France with such ardor were no longer guerrillas. Their groups had gradually become regular, solidly organized units."[39] Their disruption of German supply and logistics transport was massive. Author Alan Wilt observed that "the rail line between Toulouse and Saint-Gaudens, a distance of some sixty miles, had been cut in thirty-eight places."[40]

Emmanuel d'Astier helped contribute to the success of the Resistance. Born in Paris in 1900, d'Astier was a poet and journalist. Though he was head of French naval intelligence, he was dismissed after the French armistice with Germany in 1940.[41] D'Astier then joined up with a small band of the Maquis in Lyon in unoccupied France. This group became one of the lead members of the Resistance of the Libération-Sud and was the first of the major Resistance groups to oppose the German occupation of France. It began a publication, *Libération*, in July 1941. In 1942, the Libération-Sud joined with other Resistance groups to form the Conseil National de la Résistance (CNR) under the overall direction of Jean Moulin. The CNR proved critical in providing the Allied Armed Forces with crucial information on German troop movements and strength in the preparation for the invasion of southern France. D'Astier died on June 12, 1969.

The Liberation of Paris

General de Gaulle had returned to French soil on August 18, 1944, flying from Algiers to the Allied-controlled airbase at Cherbourg. On August 20, he rallied an audience of seven thousand people, and the populace's support for him was widespread and enthusiastic. Marshal Pétain's attempts to enter a relationship with de Gaullle and his Free French Committee were rejected.

General Eisenhower preferred to bypass Paris. From the perspective of his overall strategy to defeat the Germans, Paris was of little strategic importance, but de Gaulle convinced Eisenhower that a long-drawn-out struggle between the Germans and the Resistance could strengthen the prestige of Communist Resistance fighters and that this should be avoided. The emotional importance of their capital to the French also had to be considered. During the night of August 24-25, French troops marched into Paris with some American help. As the Germans withdrew their grip, the French Second Armored Division of the U.S. First Army marched into Paris on August 25. The German General von Choltitz surrendered the same day. Later that day, de Gaulle set up headquarters in the War Ministry and appointed General Koenig as military governor.

To demonstrate his primacy to his people and his competitors for power, de Gaulle ordered a victory parade on the Champs-Elysées, which took place on August 26, against the advice of the American commander in the area, General Gerow, who was concerned about potential violence and disorder. De Gaulle's march received an enormous ovation. When shots were fired at Notre Dame, he remained calm. Parisians were thrilled. De Gaulle's authority to lead the French people was clear. To further bolster his authority to govern, he had a French Army Division remain in Paris. While Eisenhower did not accede to de Gaulle's request for the placement of two additional U.S. divisions in the French capital to reinforce de Gaulle's authority, Ike did assist de Gaulle's emergence as the undisputed leader of France by the beginning of September 1944. Ultimately, de Gaulle's stubborn insistence that every French sovereign right be respected by the Allies prevailed.

By the end of August 1944, there were few Parisians who did not have a relative or friend in a concentration camp somewhere in France or elsewhere.[42] There were at least thirty-one camps in the unoccupied zone of France, fifteen in the occupied zone, and several in North Africa.[43] By September 1944 most of France was liberated, although parts of the country remained under German control until 1945. De Gaulle visited key French municipalities and was accorded the leadership honors he deserved. Mallory Browne served as a Paris correspondent for the *Christian Science Monitor* several years prior to the war's outbreak. Though he had to leave Paris during the war, Browne quickly made his way back to the city just a few days after its liberation. He wrote,

> The atmosphere of Paris today—make no mistake about it—is the atmosphere of latent revolution . . . Certainly Paris wears its intense atmosphere of potential revolution with the same casual air of gaiety and charm with which Parisiennes wear their huge Revolutionary and Directoire hats . . . No one will ever be able to describe adequately the mad ecstasy of those first days of joyous, triumphant freedom, nor the welcome which the people of Paris gave to both the French and American troops who first entered the city.
>
> There are flags everywhere: the French Tricolor, the Stars and Stripes, the British Union Jack, sometimes Russian, Belgian, and Polish flags as well. The Champs Elysées and the boulevards are alive with fluttering color.
>
> The Gestapo had their principal headquarters in a number of the luxurious apartments along the Avenue Foch and Parisians still hadn't quite got over their four-year habit of keeping away from it.

I saw an old mutilated veteran of the last war, with the Tricolor band of the FFI on his arm, looking at it just the way a mother looks at a new baby. The Champs-Elysées is unchanged . . . . Its cafés still spread their little tables out on the broad sidewalks, and there on Sunday afternoons especially, but every day if it's fair, it is still as true as ever that half Paris sits sipping its aperitifs or coffee and watching the other half stroll by in search of a seat. Only there are no aperitifis—the Germans have drunk them all—and the coffee is a frightful, undrinkable ersatz; so most people sip imitation fruit juices or inferior beer . . . . Unlike London, where there are long lines for everything, liberated Paris appears to have only two kinds of lines. There are long lines of people trying to buy bread at the bakeries. Bread is rationed but even so is hard to get. The food situation is improving, however, and should be nearly normal as soon as it is possible to restore traffic on the railways.

Other queues are of Parisians lining up to see newsreels of the liberation of Paris. There are only one or two movie houses showing these, and no other movies or theaters at all, so the people of Paris gladly stand in line to see pictures of themselves in an epic of heroic resistance—an epic which might well make the rest of the world say of the people of Paris, as Churchill said of the people of Britain in 1940, "This was their finest hour."[44]

Continuing the Fight

The war was not over. As the Germans retreated eastward, they left behind substantial numbers of troops to defend the more critical ports that they did not want falling into Allied hands: Brest, Saint-Nazaire, Lorient, Dieppe, and Le Havre. This was done in attempts to prevent the Allies from developing a firmer chain of logistical supply in the north. Despite these obstacles, by September 5, 1944, there were 2,086,000 Allied troops and 3,446,000 tons of supplies in France.[45]

In his report on the liberation of France, Gen. George C. Marshall noted that

> on Sept. 5 the Ninth U.S. Army under the command of Lt. Gen. William H. Simpson began operations under the Twelfth

Army Group for the reduction of Brest and other French ports, where four German divisions were bottled up. Dieppe fell on Aug. 31; Le Havre on Sept. 11; Brest on Sept. 19. The most strenuous efforts were made to put these ports into operating condition. Tonnage began moving through Dieppe on Sept. 7 and through Le Havre on Oct. 9. Brest was too heavily damaged and too distant from future fields of operations to justify immediate reconstruction.

The defeated German armies now were streaming across France, heading for the shelter of the Siegfried Line. They were under constant air attack. On the ground General Bradley's First and Third Armies, driving northeast from Melun and Troyes reached the Aisne and the Marne, sweeping aside the German rear guards. On crossing the Aisne, the 7th Corps of the First Army turned northward and raced on to Mons in a brilliant stroke that cut off five of the retreating German divisions. The pocket thus formed yielded over 22,000 prisoners with heavy additional losses of killed and wounded.

On Sept. 11 elements of the Third Army contacted Seventh Army columns northwest of Dijon. Four days later on the 6th Army Group passed to operational control of Supreme Headquarters, Allied Expeditionary Forces, severing its fighting connection with the Mediterranean theater, though its supply was continued for some time from Italy.

To the north, our First Army had crossed the Belgian frontier on Sept. 2, captured Liege on the 8th, crossed Luxembourg, and entered Germany on the 11th. The enemy had been kept completely off balance. As the Allies approached the German border, supply lines were stretched to the limit and the marching columns of the armies were maintained only by the full use of air transportation, fast double-lane, one-way truck routes, such as the famous Red Ball Express from the Normandy beaches to Paris, and other emergency measures. Logistical difficulties now began to slow down the advance. Time was needed for the opening of additional ports and for the relaying and repair of hundreds of miles of French railroads.

The ports of southern France were vital to the U.S. Seventh Army and the French First Army in the Southern Group of Armies. Toulon and Marseille were in operation late in September. Since then, 14 divisions were moved through southern French ports, in addition to an average daily unloading of over 18,000 tons of supplies. Two railways were placed in early operation, including the double-track main line through Lyon and Dijon, and thousands of tons of supplies moved daily over these lines and by truck to forward railheads. Port capacities and transportation facilities were sufficient to meet the requirements of the entire Southern Group of Armies until the stubborn defense of the water entrance to Antwerp was reduced.[46]

While the Germans retreated from southern France, they were far from being defeated. German morale and support was still strong. The September 6, 1944, edition of *ONI Weekly*, issued by the Office of Naval Intelligence, evaluated the strength of the German forces and reported that many of the German fighting forces were willing to fight to the death rather than be captured by the Allies. It warned readers of the potential that the Nazi Party could go underground once the Allied occupation was complete. "The Nazi Party, of course, is well schooled in the tactics of underground opposition—it has been combating them over most of Europe for the past four years and it was itself engaged in many illegal practices in Germany prior to Hitler's accession to power in 1933."[47]

As to the party's actual strength, in December 1943 U.S. intelligence estimated the total membership of the Nazi Party to be 6.5 million.[48] Of this number, roughly 600,000 were estimated to be members of the elite guard (*Schutzstaffel*, or SS), both in its general branch (*Allgemeine SS*) and its militarized branch (*Waffen SS*). "The General SS numbered between 200,000 and 240,000 before the war, but is believed to have decreased somewhat in size since then because of enlistment by its members in the Militarized SS and, to a lesser extent, in the Army."[49] The SS was the faction that supplied trustworthy personnel to staff the many policing, intelligence, and military units of the Reich. "The second branch of the SS," the *ONI Weekly* explained, "has expanded from a total of 40,000 men in September 1939 to a strength now estimated at 250,000 to 300,000, organized into 18 to 20 well-equipped and generally well-trained frontline divisions. It seems clear that pro-Nazi officers, especially SS officers, will continue to be favored in respect to promotions. Furthermore, they have been systematically indoctrinated with the most violent Nazi fanaticism ideas, ideas of racial superiority and the Nazi superman, hatred of traditional religion, scorn of slave races as opposed to the master race, veneration of Hitler, and belief in physical force as the solution to every problem. SS men are all the more disposed to 'fight to the last man,' for the additional reason that they have been convinced, by a systematic propaganda, that SS men are always killed if they attempt to surrender. The feeling encouraged in the SS is that they must hang together or they will hang separately." In addition to the SS, it was estimated that there were 1.4 million Storm Troops (*Sturmabteilung,* or SA); 400,000-500,000 National Socialist Motor Corps (*NS Kraftfahrerkorps,* or NSKK); 600,000-800,000 Order Police (*Ordnungspolizei*); 60,000 Railroad Militia (*Bahnschutz*); 1 million to 1.2 million members of the Todt Organization (*Organisation Todt,* or OT); 250,000 men and 150,000 women in the German Labor Service (*Reichsarbeitsdienst*); and 6 million to 8 million in the Hitler Youth (*Hitlerjugend,* or HJ) and the German Boys' Association (*Deutsches Jungvolk,* or "Pumpfe")—all of these corps comprising a strong number of Germans who were still fully indoctrinated in the Nazi wartime propaganda.[50]

Transformation

The withdrawal of German troops freed the French people from the ordeal of life under German occupation. An important reason for this reformation was explained by Gen. George C. Marshall, as follows:

> Orderly civil administration was maintained in support of military operations in liberated and occupied territories. In previous wars, the United States had no prepared plan for this purpose. In World War II it was necessary to mobilize the full resources of both liberated and occupied countries to aid in defeating the enemy. The security of lines of communication and channels of supply, the prevention of sabotage, the control of epidemics, the restoration of production in order to decrease import needs, the maintenance of good order in general, all were factors involved. It was important to transform the inhabitants of liberated countries into fighting allies.

The Civil Affairs Division was created on March 1, 1943, to establish War Department policies designed to handle these problems. In joint operations, the Division worked closely with a similar agency in the Navy Department, as well as with related civilian agencies to determine and to implement United States policies. The Army and Navy were represented on the Joint Civil Affairs Committee under the Joint Chiefs of Staff which was charged with planning for civil affairs in both Europe and the Pacific. In combined operations, United States policies were coordinated with those of the British through the Combined Civil Affairs Committee of the Combined Chiefs of Staff.

Army officers were trained at the School of Military Government established at the University of Virginia and at Civil Affairs training schools to serve in military government and civil affairs activities in the field. The operation of these schools was a responsibility of the Provost Marshal General, under directives prepared by the Civil Affairs Division. In French North Africa the civil administration was conducted by the French Government.

The War Department coordinated negotiations on the United States military level with the French Committee of National Liberation. They drew up agreements for the administration of civil affairs and, after approval by the U.S. Joint Chiefs of Staff, these were signed by General Eisenhower for the United States and General Koenig for the French Committee. The British executed a similar agreement on a governmental level.

A French civil administration cooperated effectively and it was unnecessary for General Eisenhower to invoke his paramount powers of control even in forward areas. So well did this understanding work that, as early as Oct. 24, 1944, a zone of interior was proclaimed in France, which had the effect of formally restoring practically complete control over all governmental problems to the French Provisional Government. The United States and the United Kingdom officials had the aid of French officers in helping the armies keep their lines of communication open and supplies flowing forward. The French Provisional Government furthered the campaign in a variety of ways. During the autumn rains, "duckbill" type tread extensions were needed to give tanks better traction on muddy terrain. The French contributed 600 tons of their sparse steel stocks to make 400,000 "duckbills". They provided storm boats for the spring campaign requiring river crossings. It has been estimated that by the end of February 1945 the French Provisional Government had made available to the Allies supplies, labor, services, installations, transportation, and other facilities valued at approximately 225 million dollars.[51]

In southern France, the French no longer had to answer to the German system of military justice. But everyday interactions between the Germans and the French were complex. As Robert Gildea noted in his work *Marianne in Chains*, "The Germany of Goethe and Beethoven was never quite eclipsed for many French people by the Germany of Hitler, that the clash of Latin and Teuton was disturbed by Germans fluent in French and by Germans descended from French stock, and finally that the German officer, cultivated and honorable as well as virile, exercised a magnetic attraction, particularly over French women."[52] Gildea also found that the transfer of power between the German authorities and the French was, on the whole, peaceful. "In about a quarter of French departments the handover of power at the Liberation lasted for less than a week, and where the departure of the Germans was followed quickly by the arrival of the Allies there was little violence."[53]

Slowly, France began the painful process of renewal. "Real wages went down."[54] Yet it was also a time of entrepreneurship for those who had surplus—albeit, scarce—supplies to sell. Among the profiteers were the grocers. Their "grocer's dictatorship" decided who could purchase what. Most French people survived hunger, but not the seventy-six thousand French and foreign Jews who were deported by French government officials, often cooperating with the Germans. Less than 3 percent survived the camps.[5]

A French government ordinance issued December 26, 1944, was an attempt to determine what constituted collaboration with the enemy. Trials for French collaborators would extend into the early 1950s, and cases were even brought to court as late as the 1990s, such as the trial of M. Papillon. One way to grapple with such divisive matters was often to issue amnesties in order to try to salvage torn neighborly and personal relations. "In general," Professor Tony Judt of New York University found, "the amnesties, the first of which was declared in 1948, reduced rather rapidly the number of people who stayed in prison. An initial 32,000 persons were incarcerated, but that number was down to 13,000 by December 1948, to 8,000 by the following year, and to 1,500 by October 1952. At the end of the Fourth Republic, there remained in French prisons at most 19 persons sentenced for their wartime activities or writings."[56]

Many French mayors had resigned their jobs and tried to shed their collaborationist pasts. Some started contacting Resistance groups. Robert Gildea concluded that "[French] officials who wanted to survive needed to play a double game giving the appearance of loyalty while working in the dark to protect French interests."[57] He found that French responses to Allied bombing of industrial areas that resulted in mostly civilian casualties was regretted but not criticized. Once southern and other parts of France were liberated, General de Gaulle's agents hastily confirmed the continuance in office of most officials who had served the Vichy regime. Only the most despicable Vichyites were removed from their positions. There were some lynchings, and many women were humiliated for "horizontal collaboration" by having their hair shaved. But there were many more pressing concerns that needed attention, such as overcoming food shortages, blocking a Communist takeover, rebuilding destroyed infrastructure, and supplying crucial public services.

The role of women changed under the Vichy regime and under German occupation. With husbands, fathers, sons, and brothers away fighting, many women found that their lives were accorded a new degree of independence, regardless of the often paternalistic policies that the Vichy government tried to impose upon them. As such, women were now able to make independent decisions based upon their own beliefs and thoughts. Such decisions came into play in their role as Vichy collaborators or resisters. Hanna Diamond pointed out that this gave women "an almost unique opportunity to act politically, whether it was by entertaining a German officer or hiding a Jewish family." She also noted that "the events of the purges and the re-establishment of the peace also suggests that men recognized that women had experienced a measure of newfound independence, be it political or otherwise, which was somewhat threatening to them and which in any case could not be allowed to continue."[58]

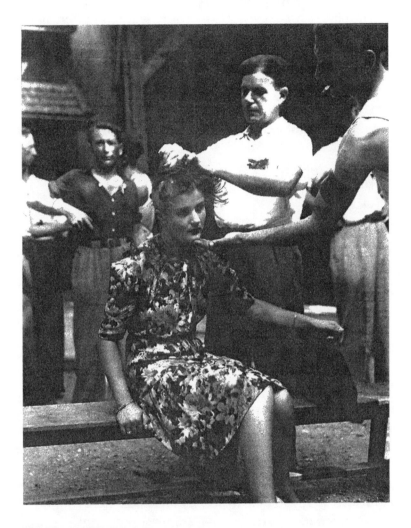

In August 1944, French civilians shave the head of a French woman to punish her for having personal relations with members of the German occupation force.

Many women were targeted as having helped or slept with the German occupiers—some of them unjustly accused. They were rounded up and sent to internment camps or were disgraced. For some Frenchmen, just seeing a woman with a German was enough to condemn her. Some women in the Resistance movement considered German soldiers "nice-looking boys."[59] With the passage of time, fewer collaborators were imprisoned, as statistics concerning the purges that followed the exit of the German occupiers show:[60]

Year	Number of individuals imprisoned for collaboration
1945	40,000
1948 (Dec.)	13,000 (amnesty 1947)
1949 (Oct.)	8,000
1950 (Apr.)	5,587
1951	4,000
1952	1,570 (amnesty 1951)
1956	62 (amnesty 1953)
1957	19
1964	None

Vichy's Despicable Record

The Vichy record has been studied by Henry Rousso in his excellent work *Vichy Syndrome.* He provided this accounting: the Vichy regime and the collaborationist were directly responsible for the imprisonment of 135,000 people, the internment of 70,000 suspects (including numerous political refugees from Central Europe), and the dismissal of 35,000 civil servants. As victims of exclusionary laws, 60,000 Freemasons were investigated, 6,000 harassed, and 549 (of 989) died in the camps.[61]

They sent sixty-five thousand workers to Germany as conscript labor and waged unremitting battle against the Resistance and all other opponents of the regime. Admittedly, Vichy and the collaborationists were not directly responsible for all the executions, extortions, and deportations. Today, however, there can be no doubt that many victims of the era were claimed not by the foreign occupation or military conflict but by internal struggles in which Vichy figured as the initial issue: this is a fact, not an ideological prejudice.

The invading Allied forces were warmly welcomed by the French. Admiral Hewitt wrote,

> We received an amazing welcome, perfectly wonderful, on the part of the French people. I went ashore with General Patch the first day to go around and see what was going on. We took Admiral Lemonnier with us. He had begged to be taken along. He had no part, no command in the operation, but he went about with us. He was the junior, but we all stood aside and said he was to be the first one to land on his own soil. We went around in a Jeep. We had a marvelous reception everywhere. We'd go through a little town and crowds would rush out from cafés with wineglasses and bottles of wine held up for us to partake of.
>
> I remember the first five or six hundred yards in this Jeep after we landed. We went along on the road toward Saint-Raphael, and there was a French girl riding a bicycle ahead of us with her skirts ballooning out. We overtook her, and Lemonnier said something to her. I don't know what he said, but she was so surprised that she promptly fell off her bicycle. We stopped and she came rushing up to the Jeep and gave the admiral a kiss. That was his first welcome to France.[62]

Forbidden American movies were smuggled into France during the Dragoon invasion. They were shown at black market theaters that charged one thousand francs per ticket. One such movie was *Gone with the Wind*, which was shown in an apartment that was converted into a temporary theater.[63] Vichy leaders were too busy trying to escape to enjoy movies.

Throughout the summer of 1944, German control over the French was rapidly ending. Sgt. Len Smith, a staff correspondent for the *Stars and Stripes*, reported that French troops with navy help brought an end to all organized German resistance in the Toulon and Marseille area. American troops and French Resistance fighters encountered some opposition from Nazi German forces that were trying to reach the Franco-German border before the U.S. Seventh Army had closed all escape routes. American soldiers in France were moving so fast that they did not have time to spend their pay, causing the U.S. Secretary of the Treasury Henry Morgenthau to announce that the troops were spending only 10 percent of their earnings. Before the Normandy and Dragoon invasions, the French were warned that their liberation would result in wild spending by the GIs and inflation. By the end of August 1944, they were convinced that the Yanks were not spending enough.[64]

The warm reception that the French extended to the Allied military became cooler as the summer turned to autumn and the war and its hardships continued for the French people. They complained to American military leaders that German prisoners of war were being treated better than their French victims, and disillusionment and resentment replaced the earlier frenzied welcome. The prefect of the Var department suggested that there was a connection between the mutinous behavior by French Senegalese troops in Toulon and Hyères and the influence of black American soldiers. In his report on Franco-American relations in southern France, OSS agent David Rockefeller observed that some French resented black American troops, especially black military police. Authors Footitt and Simon conjectured that there was a correlation between the numbers of foreign troops in southern France and their popularity and that the great warmth shown for Russian troops was due to their small numbers.[65]

But it was American multiracial military might that played the dominant role in French liberation. Evidence of that role and the sacrifices made in freeing the French from German occupation can be found in ten French cemeteries. Buried or missing in France are 66,003 Americans, some 1,555 of whom lie buried in the Rhone Draguignan Cemetery. Thousands more who died fighting in France are buried in the United States. France also owed a debt to troops from other European and African countries.

The question of how much to let the French engage in the fight against their occupiers remained unanswered even after Operation Dragoon. In a 1959 report prepared for the War Department, Maurice Matloff wrote the following:

> The problem of French rearmament was complicated during early 1944 by the involved relations between the Americans and British on the one hand and the French Committee of National Liberation on the other. With the President reluctant to recognize the committee as the provisional government of France and determined to stay out of French postwar problems, most of the guidance received

from him was of a negative character. As he instructed Eisenhower in March, the defeat of Germany was his first aim, but he desired that democratic methods be fostered during the coming liberation of France so that favorable conditions could be established for the eventual formation of a representative French government. He refused to treat with the FCNL on a political level and insisted that any discussions regarding the future employment of the existing French forces be carried on with Eisenhower.

This, among other things, may have contributed to the failure of the negotiations to have de Gaulle broadcast an appeal to the French people on D-day for their cooperation with Overlord. Although de Gaulle's visit to Washington in early July did serve to clear the atmosphere somewhat, the role the French forces would play in the liberation of France and in the defeat of Germany was still not certain.[66]

Costs, Gains, and Predictions

The successful invasion of southern France cost the Wehrmacht fifty thousand soldiers at the same time that the Allies gained possession of almost one-third of French territory, including the valuable port of Marseille through which almost one million additional troops were brought over from England.[67] Dragoon's triumph played a big role in the ultimate success of the Allied forces. Troops from the French colonies were an important part in the success of the French armed forces, with African soldiers serving the cause of French liberation well. But once they had completed their work, they were rounded up into camps and returned to Africa. They were not allowed to participate in the euphoric victory celebrations and parades because of a new French policy of "whitening" its army. Compounding this racism was the fact that many of these African soldiers "had to fight to obtain their pay at the end of the war or had not been granted their full pensions."[68] Despite French and American racism, their troops continued to work together. On August 26, 1944, American artillery sharpshooters teamed up with French infantrymen to close rear approaches to Toulon that could be used by Germans to aid their army. Allied bombers delivered devastating blows to the dreaded Toulon submarine base used by the Germans.[69]

Churchill's dislike for and distrust of the leading French leader continued. In June 1945, Norman Brook, Churchill's deputy cabinet secretary, recorded the prime minister's comments concerning de Gaulle. Churchill portrayed de Gaulle as "the greatest living barrier to reunion and restoration of France"[70] After the war in Europe ended, Churchill claimed that there was "no hope of trustworthy relations with France until we are rid of De Gaulle."[71]

Mary Burnet, of *Harper's* editorial staff, was a specialist in French political affairs. In her September 1944 article entitled "France: The Pieces in the Puzzle," she asked the following questions: Can France reestablish freedom? Will American policy work to that end, or against it? In answering them she found that by the time Allied forces landed in Normandy, General de Gaulle, as head of his French Committee of National Liberation, had gained control of the French Empire with the exception of Indochina, which was controlled by Japan. It was the second biggest empire in the world and wealthy, had control of an army of about twenty-five thousand men, won access to Lend-Lease funds and substantial funds from the French Empire, and secured authority over the French Empire and power to adopt and enforce legislation in France. De Gaulle's Committee—he appointed nineteen of its twenty-one members—appointed special courts to try suspected Vichy and German collaborators. It gained control of a carefully organized propaganda, censorship, and intelligence agency. This included a radio station that was the only channel through which news from Free France was broadcast to the outside world. De Gaulle's intelligence service was headed by Colonel Passy, a reactionary who was accused of being a secret member of a Fascist organization.

De Gaulle's political power was derived in part from the fact that increasing numbers of his followers were given better-paying jobs by joining him than they had before. His Committee of National Liberation paid its staff well and operated in an expensive manner. Its representative in Washington, D.C., received a larger salary than the president of the United States. Not only did de Gaulle's followers benefit financially, according to Burnet, they also received more imposing jobs than ever before. They had a stake in keeping the general in power. Many of these men, however, had not suffered the starvation, bombing, and other hardships that their compatriots had endured during the Vichy years, having spent the time outside the country. These émigrés were looked down upon by those who had stayed behind and stuck things out in

Vichy France. Some of de Gaulle's people had switched sides during the war. In 1944, followers of Pétain shed their allegiance to join de Gaulle. One was Henri Hoppenot.

In autumn 1942, Hoppenot was the Vichy government's representative in Monteudeu. By July 1944 he was de Gaulle's representative in Washington. Of the seven French Army commanders who landed with General de Lattre during the invasion of southern France in August 1944, four had been prominent proponents of the June 1940 armistice that led to the Vichy regime.[72]

Reversals of allegiances also included people who were de Gaulle followers but who later repudiated him. Some men gave up their loyalty to de Gaulle because of their doubts concerning his devotion to democracy and republican government. There were even doubts by anti-Vichy French about de Gaulle's relationship with underground resistance groups. Before 1942, communications between de Gaulle's headquarters in London and the Resistance groups were almost nonexistent. Communications did improve, but it took nearly three years before they became good. Throughout this period, the policy pursued by the Roosevelt administration was directed by FDR's friend Sumner Welles, the State Department's second in command. Under that policy, no action was to be taken by the United States that would in any way influence or limit the rights of the people of France and that the liberated French should freely choose their own political leaders. Roosevelt's distrust of de Gaulle was rooted in his suspicion that de Gaulle was usurping the power of leadership before the French electorate had an opportunity to democratically express their choice. The French did reestablish freedom after their humiliating defeat and the ignominious Vichy regime. American policy helped achieve that end; and imperious, patriotic General de Gaulle, with a prickly personality, fulfilled his promise to reestablish and strengthen French democracy.

In August 1944, fearmongering propaganda from Hitler, Goebbels, and other Nazi leaders predicted that the defeat of the fatherland would result in the castration of German men, enslaving of German women and worse, and the destruction of Germany's economy.[73] A comparatively short time after the unconditional surrender to the Allies in May 1945, democracy and prosperity reemerged in Germany.

Another prediction of interest was made in Prime Minister Churchill's speech to the House of Commons on August 2, 1944, after lauding the Soviet Army's mauling and breaking the German Army. Churchill stated,

"I salute Marshal Stalin, that great champion of his country, and I firmly believe that our twenty years' treaty with Russia will prove to be one of the most lasting and durable factors in preserving peace and order and progress in Europe."[74] Late in August 1944, there were plenty of reasons for the depression-afflicted prime minister to be pleased.

The front-page headline of the *Stars and Stripes* Mediterranean Theater of August 25, 1944, heralded "Allied Victories Rock Hitler's Axis Empire." Nine of the ten columns on this first page also proclaimed Allied triumphs—reporting the liberation of Paris and Bordeaux; the Russian drive on Warsaw and Cracow, Poland; and German reverses resulting in their Bulgarian, Hungarian, Romanian, Turkish, and Vichy coalition partners abandoning the Nazi losers. On the eastern front, the Russians were approaching the Prussian border; on the western front, other Allied troops, now at Grenoble, France, were only 167 miles from Germany.

Only Priv. George Dorsey, a *Stars and Stripes* staff correspondent, in an article entitled "Marseilles: City of Violent Death"[75] reported the pain, death, destruction, and privations that descended upon the French before the national rebirth occurred and grave lessons were learned.

CHAPTER 11

EVALUATION AND LESSONS

The French poet Paul Valéry (1871-1945) went too far when he claimed that history is the science of what never happens twice. Historians do repeat themselves more than history does. Nevertheless, there are lessons from history that should be learned but are not. Operation Dragoon is replete with such instruction: the prevention of looting following an invasion, the installation of competent and honest civil administrators in a foreign nation, and the effective interrogation and humane treatment of prisoners of war—these are just a few of Dragoon's lessons.

If it is the fate of men and women to make mistakes, then such mistakes should be new ones. Unfortunately, too often they are repeated. The lessons from the invasion of southern France are described in the following pages in detail because reliance on "big picture" generalizations is of questionable utility.

An exemplary trait that many of the Dragoon commanding officers shared was the noncomplaining and intelligent use of deficient resources such as inexperienced LST crew members prone to shooting down Allied planes, igniting dangerous galley fires, and colliding with other ships. These were just a few of the mishaps committed by LSTers and other sailors and soldiers. But they did not have a monopoly on inexperience; millions of American soldiers, sailors, and airmen were given big responsibilities after very little training.

Adm. Henry Kent Hewitt, Gen. Alexander M. Patch, and Gen. Lucian K. Truscott—were among the many commanders who had extensive teaching experience before the Pearl Harbor attack. The two men who taught this author about navigation, signaling, and other facets of serving as a navy quartermaster were petty officers on ships destroyed on December 7, 1941. They were men who had decades of seagoing experience. They were good teachers who impressed their students with the seriousness and prestige of serving. More than sixty-two years have passed since this author was one of their students at the Bainbridge Naval Station in Perryville, Maryland, but he still has a vivid recollection of these two first-class teachers. The name of one of them has been forgotten, but he is remembered with respect. The other was Quartermaster First Class Petty Officer Codd. On board the LST 1012, Executive Officer and Navigator Lt. R. C. Steeple Jr. endeavored to teach the author how to use a sextant and the intricacies of Bowditch's treatise on navigation.

General Truscott Assesses Operation Dragoon

Gen. Lucian K. Truscott Jr. described Operation Dragoon as being "characterized by the coordinated violence of the initial assault and by the speed and energy with which success was exploited. These are essentials for victory in any military operation, which commanders and staffs do not always recognize." "Dragoon," he continued, "was fortunate in this respect because the corps and division commanders and staffs had wide experience in assault landings. They had been thoroughly indoctrinated with the value of speed in military operations and the divisions had attained high standards in speed techniques."[1] Another helpful factor, wrote Truscott,—was "that the French forces which followed the assault were equipped and organized on an American scale, and used American equipment, weapons, and supplies. This made the command and logistical problems in southern France far simpler than they had ever been in Italy."

"In one month," Truscott continued, "American and French forces of the Seventh Army had almost completely destroyed the German XIX Army, captured some 80,000 prisoners and inflicted other heavy losses in personnel, equipment and supplies. The Allied Armies had driven nearly five hundred miles north from the beaches to the Vosges Mountains and had joined hands with General Patton's Third Army on the right flank of the Overlord forces. This junction of Dragoon and Overlord cut off many additional thousands of German troops in southwest France, and caused them to surrender without further resistance. Dragoon was therefore responsible for clearing the Germans from all of southern and southwestern France south of the advancing flank of General Eisenhower's Overlord forces. These were already extended over a large area and on supply lines of extreme length. Moreover, Dragoon held down large German forces which would have posed a serious threat to the Overlord forces and compelled General Eisenhower to counter them. No secondary attack in history ever attained greater results. And from a political point of view, the question as to whether or not Dragoon was a mistake involves the strategy of the Italian campaign and the overall strategy of the conduct of the war in Europe."

Truscott—considered another course that the Allies might have taken—"leaving the VI Corps in Italy while the seven French divisions undertook Dragoon, thus enabling the Allied armies to clear the Germans from Italy and thrust into the Balkans during the fall of 1944." He was confident "that the French forces could have established a beachhead in southern France and captured the ports of Toulon and Marseille. But it is highly debatable whether they would have been able to exploit northward as the VI Corps was able to do, because they lacked the experience in assault landings and the technical and practical skill to utilize transport, which was essential. The existence of these French divisions in the Rhone Valley would have served to protect the flank of Overlord, but certainly they would have inflicted less damage on the enemy. In this event it might have been possible, by the early months of 1945, to have cleared Italy of the enemy, and established Allied forces in the Balkans without jeopardizing Overlord in any material way. While the decision to undertake Dragoon was undoubtedly sound under the circumstances, the course of postwar events makes one wish that some Balkan thrust had been attempted."[2]

Generals Truscott,—Patch, and Devers

Should Dragoon Have Happened? An Evaluation

The Allied invasion of southern France was both successful and controversial. This exemplary operation contributed greatly to the winning of the war in Europe. But it has been ignored because it happened between two much bigger and more dramatic Allied campaigns in France and Italy. Although its success is unanimously heralded, to this very day there are still arguments as to whether Operation Dragoon should have been undertaken. Even now, there are many who claim that Prime Minister Churchill, his generals—Alanbrooke, Alexander, and Henry Maitland Wilson—and General Mark W. Clark were correct in opposing Anvil/ Dragoon. Their arguments were that the invasion of southern France was responsible for weakening the main Allied campaign in the Mediterranean. Another complaint that persists is that an Allied thrust up the Italian Peninsula toward Austria and Hungary would have changed the east-west balance of postwar Europe and prevented Soviet dominance over Eastern Europe. In his study *Operation Dragoon: The Allied Invasion of the South of France*, William B. Breuer quoted General Clark as claiming that Stalin was one of the strongest boosters of the invasion of southern France, that he knew exactly what he wanted; and what he wanted most was "to keep us out of the Balkans, which Stalin had staked out for the Red Army." Breuer added, "Not long before his death in April 1984, Mark Clark told the author that 'after the fall of Rome [on June 4, 1944, two days before the Normandy invasion] Field Marshal Kesselring's army [in Italy] could have been destroyed—had we been able to shoot the works in an all-out offense. Then it would be on to Vienna, Budapest, and Prague.'"[3]

Despite the astonishing successes of Dragoon, the question has remained: should Operation Dragoon have been undertaken by the Allied forces in August 1944? Proponents of Dragoon counter with a variety of arguments: they stress the operational and logistical problems of crossing the Italian Alps and challenge Churchill's assertion that a quick thrust could have easily subjugated German-dominated Europe's underbelly. Mountainous terrain and German defensive abilities presented a tough gut and not a flabby belly.

Allied control of France's largest port, Marseille, and of the port of Toulon was much more important and immediate to ending the war in Europe. Shortly after the Dragoon D-day, troops and equipment were able to use these two ports. The Third Allied Army Group was able to reach the German border because of the southern France invasion.

Although there was considerable debate among military and political leaders throughout 1943 and 1944 over whether the campaign in southern France should be pursued, subsequent reports prepared by Adm. Henry Kent Hewitt and others help shed light on the necessity of Dragoon—an invasion that led to the "most successful series of campaigns during World War II," according to historians Jeffrey J. Clarke and Robert Ross Smith. They also claim that without Dragoon, it is doubtful that the Allies would have defeated the Germans in as little time as they did. They wrote, "Perhaps the greatest contribution of the southern invasion was placing a third Allied Army Group—one with two army headquarters, three corps, and the equivalent of ten combat divisions—with its own independent supply lines, in northeastern France at a time when the two northern Allied Army Groups were stretched to the limit in almost every way. It was not the weakness of their [the German] forces, but their inability to best use what they had that made the Anvil landings such a success and made the German withdrawal north such a harrowing one."[4]

The Allied forces benefited from the lack of German preparedness and coordination. The enemy's intelligence system did not anticipate Dragoon properly. Evidence from Col. Gen. Johannes von Blaskowitz's report suggests that although German intelligence foretold of an Allied assault on the southern French coastline, the German High Command was unwilling to devote strength in terms of the numbers of troops to defending this long and rugged stretch along the Mediterranean. As early as 1943, the Germans suspected that an Allied attack on France would be conducted in a dual-prong gesture, with one point of invasion located along the northeastern Atlantic coastline and the second occurring along the country's southern Mediterranean coastline. Blaskowitz noted that "on 6 June the Allied invasion began at the anticipated location, while the expected secondary landing south of the Loire did not come about."[5]

Blaskowitz explained how German troops in southern France were reassigned to the north in order to thwart the Allies there, leaving the southern portion of the country severely understaffed. One German commander, Gen. Georg von Sodenstern, was quite vocal about the futility of launching a successful defense of southern France and was relieved of his duties "for reasons of health," at the end of June 1944.[6] Thus, between understaffing and low morale, German coastal defenses were quickly penetrated by the Allied assault. The U.S.

Seventh Army raced up the Rhone River valley, chasing enemy forces. The pros and cons to Dragoon are numerous. However, the evidence for understanding this invasion outweighs the objections against it.[7] Professor Samuel E. Morison found that "Operation Anvil/Dragoon, the landings on the coast of Provence, was in some respects unique. An almost perfect performance which contributed heavily to victory over Germany was preceded by a difference of opinion between the British and American high commands as to whether it should not take place; a controversy which still continues in the histories of war."[8]

In addition to the arguments in favor of undertaking Anvil/Dragoon presented by Brig. Gen. Frank N. Roberts, and cited in chapter 5, Dragoon directly contributed to Allied successes in the following ways: enemy resistance was so slight as to permit immediate exploitation northward through Grenoble toward Lyon, allowing a linkup with the Third Army twenty-eight days after the landing; the creation of a diversionary effect to assist Overlord; protection of the right flank of the Third Army; and another major port on the continent fell into Allied hands.[9]

Dragoon was justifiably heralded as a triumph that offers many lessons in terms of military planning, intelligence gathering, safeguarding information, logistical preparations, and achieving effective multilateralism. An examination of Dragoon's mistakes is also useful.

Dragoon highlighted the usefulness of amphibious warfare and the critical role played by the numerous LSTs used. But the story did not stop there. Many LST crews incurred problems before and after Dragoon. For example, LST 1012's predilections for mishaps persisted after the invasion of southern France. Capt. Marshall Flowers's war diary entry of October 15, 1944, contains a notation for September 21, 1944: "0751: Underway to proceed to beach at Cap Drammont, France. 0848: Ran aground on shoal-basses Ile d'Or, Cap Drammont, France. 0850 to 1308: Undergoing salvage operations with USS *Naragansett.* 1308: Attempting to get ship off rocks. 1308: ship freed from rocks and proceeded to beach upon orders from beach master. Complete information on damage sustained and action taken during grounding is contained in report submitted to Commander in Chief of Naval Operations letter LST 1012/A9-8/FWs Serial 108 dated Sept. 29, 1944."[10] By September 27, the LST 1012 was moored in a dry dock in Palermo, Sicily; and work on its hull began. What actually happened was that while in the Gulf of Fréjus, a week earlier, the LST 1012 suffered damage after hitting an underground boulder that punctured a large hole in the hull, on the forward, starboard side. This caused flooding in two of the ship's tanks, and the hull was dented with its seam gaping open at frame 41 in the port shaft alley. There was also a hole in the freshwater tank at the lower inboard corner.[11]

In the invasion of Sicily, Allied landing troops did not get crucial assistance against the enemy from the Allied Air Force. When asked if naval gunfire could assist his troops, Gen. George Patton, at first, dismissed the offer. Responding angrily to Admiral Hewitt's chief of staff, Rear Adm. Spencer S. Lewis, and deputy chief of staff, Capt. Jerauld Wright, Patton said, "I don't want any support. Ships float around on water, they never know where they are, they bob around and can never hit anything. Just land me and I'll take care of myself." When it became apparent that his troops were being subjected to tremendous enemy gunfire, Patton relented and received naval bombardment support from Hewitt's armada. Patton subsequently became a true believer in the efficacy of naval gunfire support during daytime.[12]

Another tactic that proved crucial to the invasion was the implementation of smoke screens. As Admiral Lewis noted in his assessment report on Dragoon, "Smoke was most effective in protecting the Transport Area from enemy air attacks particularly during the dusk period. The only loss from enemy air attack occurred to a vessel (LST 282) which was not under the cover of a protective smoke screen. Smoke, undoubtedly, did interfere to a certain extent with the unloading, but only for limited periods. The system of smoking set up by the Smoke Patrol, Landing Craft Smokers, Inner Screen, and ship's boats functioned well but the Beach Battalion and Army smoke-laying organizations did not operate as well as anticipated. The use of smoke automatically, without further orders, at dusk and dawn appears to be sound doctrine although it is not believed necessary to smoke for the half-hour period of full daylight, immediately preceding sunset, and following sunrise. This period should be reduced to ten minutes, at most. The half-hour periods of semi-darkness following sunset and preceding sunrise are appropriate times for smoking. The British LCM Smokers were, by all means, the most effective source of smoke used and their design should be copied by our service for future operations where smoke is required. Control of smoke is admittedly difficult but the use of whistle signals from the flagship appears to be the most satisfactory method for the initiation of the screen. No satisfactory method has yet been evolved for discontinuing smoke before the smoke tanks run dry. Whistle signals cannot be heard above the noise of the smoking craft particularly the LCM Smokers."[13]

Overcoming Failures

General Truscott—selected the Thirty-sixth Infantry Division for the proposed Dragoon assault because after its setbacks at Salerno and Rapido, the Thirty-sixth performed well. He wisely observed that the Thirty-sixth, "having tasted the bitter cup on two occasions, and having more recently eaten the fruits of victory, could be expected to equal and keep pace with its more experienced teammates."[14]

The Allies of World War II overcame major internecine conflicts and achieved substantial military coordination. The Germans and Italians did not achieve the same level of effective coordination with their Axis partner, the Japanese. Gen. George C. Marshall found that "not only were the European partners of the Axis unable to coordinate their plans and resources and agree within their own nations how best to proceed, but the eastern partner, Japan, was working in even greater discord. The Axis, as a matter of fact, existed on paper only. Eager to capitalize on the occupation of the Western powers in Europe, Japan was so greedy for her own immediate conquests that she laid her strategy, not to help Germany defeat Russia and Great Britain, but to accumulate her own profit."[15] Contrast this with the Allied record and the cooperation and coordination demonstrated in Operation Dragoon.

Difficult problems were overcome by the Allies. Joint inter-Allied security measures were extremely tight during the operations to penetrate the European continent. Several explanations for this were cited by the *ONI Weekly* bulletin of September 6, 1944, including "the close proximity of the British Isles to the European mainland, the dense population of Britain, the large numbers of various national groups present in the United Kingdom at that time, the fact that the marshalling areas and the routes to the ports and often even the actual embarkation 'hards'[16] themselves were located in thickly inhabited areas."[17]

Operation Dragoon also had logistic problems. The rapid progress enjoyed by the Seventh Army, resulting from the successful landings at Cap Drammont, was unexpected; and so no logistical plans were in place to provide arms, food, and transportation for troops on such short notice and at such long distances. One example cited by the *CSI Battlebook* was the case of Air Force P-47 planes, which operated out of Corsica, and which, by August 20, were encountering range problems. "Fighter bombers were unable to operate in the northern sector near Grenoble. Logistic operations were supported from the assault beaches until mid-September when Marseille and Toulon were seized. This created a supply line of 175 miles. Although Allied forces took advantage of the opportunities offered them by the successful assault, they were unable to capitalize fully on them because they did not anticipate the extent of their success.

"The immediate effect of the battle's outcome to Allied forces was the ejection of German forces from southern France and the interjection of Free French forces into the fighting. The benefits to the Allies were palpable: (1) the availability to the Allies of a major port complex (Marseille/Toulon); (2) the benefit deriving from two fronts in France; (3) and the morale-enhancing factor of a truly successful major operation. As far as the Germans were concerned, the impact of the operation was severe. The seven German divisions opposing the invasion were eliminated as fighting units. Most Axis troops in southwestern France were surrounded and Germany was forced to divert its attention from Normandy."[18]

Military planners were offered a legacy of lessons, bestowed upon them by their Dragoon planning predecessors. An in-depth study of Dragoon pinpointed several of the advantages:

> (a) Operation Dragoon confirmed the soundness of our known doctrine and techniques in the planning and mounting of an amphibious operation . . . Few, if any, new strategic principles were employed and no important new doctrine was developed. The main lesson was a re-emphasis of the fact that when sound principles are applied to a sound plan, and both are aggressively implemented, the results, far outreaching those anticipated, may be obtained.
>
> (b) The necessity for additional emphasis on inter-theater liaison in planning was brought out. It appears that Operation Dragoon suffered in its early stages from a lack of complete knowledge of the plans for Overlord [the Normandy invasion].

(c) The French Forces of the Interior were utilized to good advantage. Their control was turned over to the French Commander. Prior to D-day they were invaluable in their assistance, and demonstrated that their sabotage work, when properly directed, could in some cases be more effective than air bombardment and certainly less odious to the civilian population.

(d) Command to local commanders, always a characteristic of American operations, permitted sound local decisions to be made, with a resultant aggressive pursuit of the enemy.

(e) More flexibility is needed in logistical planning to provide for changes in the situation. The rapid advance north demonstrated that although great effort on the part of all services can continue the support of any army beyond its normal expectations, that there are, nevertheless, physical limitations to the support which can be obtained across the beaches.

(f) Guerrilla assistance was exploited more than ever before, and proved to be an invaluable asset, rather than a bonus as it had been previously considered.

Various tactical lessons learned from Operation Dragoon are available from the Army Ground Forces after-action report submitted by the European Theater of Operations War Department Observers Board. The War Department Board found that

(a) The longer the division (36th) stayed in the line, the greater the incidence of disciplinary problems and psychosis cases, as reflected in the increasing number of court-martials, stragglers, and hospital admissions for exhaustion. It was observed that sending a small group of men and officers on rotation and temporary duty to the U.S. during the latter part of this period caused a lift in the morale of the entire division out of all proportion to the number who actually benefited.

(b) The enemy booby-trapped stockpiles of engineer materials. On one occasion personnel of this battalion (48th Engineer) sustained injuries when they attempted to fill holes in the road from a conveniently located gravel stockpile, which exploded when a shovel was thrust into it.

(c) Operation Dragoon conclusively proved that it is impractical to load bulk supplies on LSTs on initial lifts.

(d) There was never enough army labor. It was imperative that a civilian labor—procuring agency be set up immediately—on D-day, if the beaches are clear. It was learned that only by offering C Rations as part payment could labor be procured. Food was the incentive—not money.

(e) Political problems in any liberated country should be entirely resolved locally by the inhabitants themselves with allied support of a central government to which local officials can look for authority and general administration.[19]

Adm. Spencer Lewis too noted other military pitfalls. He found that "although Dragoon was an improvement over previous invasions, the anti-aircraft rules prescribed for Dragoon were still too complicated to be effective. They should have been written from the viewpoint of gunners in small landing craft, stressing simplicity and effectiveness. Fire discipline, on the whole, was good and no friendly aircraft was shot down. Air-raid warnings were generally broadcast prior to the arrival of enemy aircraft, although there was one instance in which enemy aircraft were plainly visible directly over the Transport Area at intermediate altitudes before the red alert was received. There was one other instance in which a vessel of the screen reported visual contact with a low-flying enemy aircraft, although no alert of any color was broadcast."[20]

Rear Admiral Lewis was also critical about the use of balloons: "Balloons were not considered worthwhile and it is felt that their use only betrayed otherwise concealed positions. They were known to be directly responsible for the shelling of Green Beach on the afternoon of D-day. Throughout the operation they were flown above the level of the smoke screen, thereby revealing the positions of the Transport and Beach Areas. Particularly in merchant vessels, no effort was made to adjust the height of balloons for existing conditions. A severe electrical storm on 2 September quickly destroyed some twenty balloons, but this solution to the problem cannot always be depended upon. It is recommended that they be used only when enemy air opposition is so strong that low-level enemy bombing and strafing may be expected."[21]

Intelligence and Communications

Allied intelligence services relied upon cooperation and recruitment from all facets of society within occupied Europe. Communists were sought out in order to help unify partisan or resistance groups on the continent. Italians were tapped as reliable unofficial sources, even though the U.S. Army still suspected them as late as 1943. The Rome bureau chief, James Angleton, provided important information concerning German movement within the Italian Peninsula that was relayed to Allied planners.[22]

To protect secret information from the Axis, the U.S. Joint Chiefs established the Joint Security Control (JSC) agency in March 1943, consisting of the heads of the U.S. Army, Gen. George C. Marshall; the U.S. Navy, Adm. Ernest J. King; and the U.S. Army Air Force, Gen. Henry A. Arnold. It was charged with two tasks: (a) preventing information of military value from falling into the hands of the enemy and (b) timing the implementation of those portions of cover and deception plans that had to be performed by military and nonmilitary agencies in the United States.[23]

The functions of the JSC were also to "recommend to appropriate officials the security measures to be carried out within the Joint Chiefs of Staff organization and the War and Navy Departments. These included measures to determine who should be furnished information concerning specific places, dates, and plans for current and projected operations, and when information was to be given." Its task was also to "veto publicity which might jeopardize the success of current or projected operations or procedure incident thereto; control the reference to current or projected operations; guard the secrecy of new weapons, inventions, projects and other military secrets directly or indirectly connected with military and naval materiel and operations."

Concerning the timing and implementation of those portions of cover and deception plans that had to be performed by military and nonmilitary agencies in the United States, the JSC was authorized to

1. Inform military and nonmilitary governmental agencies within the United States of missions assigned to them by

the Joint Chiefs of Staff in carrying out portions of cover and deception plans prepared by the Joint Staff Planners or the commanders of the operation concerned.

2. Follow up on the execution of the mission assigned in (1) above.

3. Recommend to the Joint Staff Planners any action which it (Joint Security Control) believed would further the cover and deception desired for current or projected operations. Various procedures were developed to implement Joint Security Council responsibilities.[24]

Various forms of intelligence provided the Allies with a critical upperhand in Operation Dragoon. In his critique of Dragoon, Admiral Lewis observed the following:

Prior to D-day, photographic sorties were flown frequently enough to keep the interpreter well informed of the changes that occurred from time to time in enemy defenses. Several excellent low oblique sorties and one color photographic sortie proved outstanding in giving detailed intelligence in the assault areas. The color photographs were particularly good in representing the true color of terrain features and landmarks which when passed on to the boat coxswains gave them confidence in knowing what to look for.

From thoroughly studying the defenses of the assault area after capture, it was found that the information received from photographs was essentially correct in every case.

Intelligence concerning the assault beaches presented comparatively few difficulties during the planning phase of Operation Dragoon. Information was available from many sources, and its final evaluation was, in general, quite accurate. In the target area, the range of tide was negligible, and the known underwater gradients were definitely favorable.

It was estimated, and proven during the operation, that all landing craft could beach successfully on the principal h-Hour assault beach, Green.[25]

In preparation for the assault on the Fréjus-Saint-Raphael area to be attacked by the Thirty-sixth Infantry Division, Lewis wrote,

Air spotting proved invaluable in locating active batteries located in wooded and well suited defensive terrain. Army Piper Cubs were used to excellent advantage in destroying in-land strong points, moving troop columns, and reinforcing motorized units. Air control over the assault areas enabled the use of air spotting planes at any desired time.

Communications between naval firing ships, shore fire control parties, air spotters, and Army artillery spotters were well coordinated and permitted a flexible interchange of requests from all of the participating units.

Naval bombarding ships were designated sectors of responsibility in which any active batteries were to be put under intermittent neutralization fire until the strong points could either be destroyed or captured. Piper Cubs in the air proved invaluable for picking out these active batteries and directing fire on them.

White phosphorous projectiles were used to good advantage as a marker for initial salvos, to facilitate spotting, and also as a marker to designate the lifting of fire in a definite area; this permitted our own troops to move in immediately after the last salvo.

Naval bombardment was used in conjunction with Army artillery fire to lay down a prolonged barrage fire in the town of Saint-Raphael. This fire was called for late in the evening of D-day and subsequently all fire was lifted to enable our troops to advance into the town."[26]

Logistics

Dragoon was successful because of the accumulated logistic experience gained from the previous three Mediterranean invasions—North Africa, Sicily, and Salerno—and the planners had ample information on which to draw. In-depth planning for Dragoon commenced in early 1944, with revisions continuing throughout the spring and summer months.

The Allied invasion of southern France on August 15, 1944, relied upon the strength of a well-supplied force. Below is a breakdown of the armada that was placed in the hands of Admiral Hewitt that supplied men and equipment to carry out the assault:[27]

Naval Control, Attack & Convoy Escort Forces	British & Allied	French	USA
Battleships	1	1	3
Cruisers	7	5	8
Destroyers & Escorts	27	19	52
Other Warships	69	6	157
Attack Transports & LSIs	9	—	23
Landing Craft & Ships (major only)	141	—	369
Totals	**254**	**31**	**612**
Grand Total	**897**		

What factors are to be considered in determining logistic adequacy? In his *U.S. Naval Logistics* treatise, Duncan Ballantine wrote, "Logistic requirements must be determined in the light of strategic aims, and for that purpose logistic planners must have firm guidance and accurate information as to strategic plans. Yet for almost half of the war logistic planners lacked the information essential to their task . . . . Another persistent weakness of the logistic planning performed under the Chief of Naval Operations was its lack of comprehensiveness. The Navy entered the war with no clear understanding of the function of logistic planning and with even less organization to perform it. Strategic and logistic planning was for some time mixed together to the detriment of both. Much of the high-level planning passed by default to the bureaus, the implementing agencies whose programs, set in motion without adequate reference to each other, were ultimately to determine the character of the Navy's logistic effort.

"Even without comprehensive planning, procurement programs could be set in motion. Bureaus had the necessary authority and funds to procure, and only in occasional cases could they be accused of setting their sights too low. When the logistic problem shifted, however, from one of procurement to one of distribution, the Navy's lack of centralized logistic control became a matter of greater importance."[28]

By refusing to reallocate the supplies and equipment that had been gathered for the southern France landing and directing them elsewhere, General Devers used his authority as commander of the U.S. Service Supply in the Mediterranean to keep Dragoon alive. He prevented Churchill and the other opponents of Dragoon from aborting the operation. Devers ordered the recently arrived leader of the Guadalcanal campaign in the Pacific, Gen. Alexander Patch, to continue preparations for the southern France landing. General Patch, along with the new head of the Seventh Army and Army Air Force, Brig. Gen. Gordon P. Saville, and Vice Adm. Henry Kent Hewitt continued their planning for Dragoon despite the uncertainty over whether it would happen. After the Allied forces had bogged down in the hedgerows of Normandy, the need for Anvil/Dragoon reemerged. Churchill's tenacious opposition notwithstanding, the Allied command resurrected Dragoon on June 24, 1944. But it was only on August 11, four days before the actual landing (August 15, 1944), that the Allied High Command gave its final approval for Dragoon.

The invasion of southern France would not have been nearly as successful if the logistical lessons were not implemented sufficiently to be of use to the Allied troops. When Operation Dragoon was undertaken, the United States was deeply involved in global operations elsewhere, fighting major battles in Italy, northern France, and the Pacific. The invasion of southern France was an assault on a new front. A study of Operation Dragoon offers the opportunity to learn about the challenges of logistically supporting a new front while waging war in other theaters. Ammunition supply and support for Dragoon was an important issue. According to a War Department Field Manual, "Adequate and timely supply of ammunition to combat troops is crucial for the successful preparation of any military operation. No other single item of supply is so vital to combat."[29]

The lessons learned from Dragoon concerning the supply of proper ammunition are well documented. "Plans must be flexible," wrote Lt. Col. James W. Boddie Jr. in his March 1987 assessment entitled "Ammunition Support for Operation Dragoon, the Invasion of Southern France—Could We Do It Today?" Boddie wrote that "Dragoon planners had anticipated stiff enemy resistance from the German 19th Army that never materialized. This changed the initial assault from an ammunition intensive operation directly into a pursuit/exploitation operation that results in low ammunition consumption but is petroleum intensive.

"Later," he observed, "when the 6th Army Group had pursued the enemy some 400 miles, they reached the 'west wall.' In order to breach the wall, large quantities of ammunition were required. The planning did account for these changes. Initially, ammunition was on the top of all shiploads. When the operation bypassed the assault phase and went directly into pursuit, the ammunition had to be moved in order to get to more urgently needed supplies. Upon reaching the 'west wall,' combat operations had to be delayed until ammunition stocks could be brought forward in the required quantities. Plans should have provisions to exploit success as well as provisions to handle setbacks."[30]

Admiral Lewis stressed the following:

> Noteworthy is the fact that ships and craft allocated to CTF-87 were 100% operative as of dates of departure from assembly areas.
>
> Special provisions were made in basic plans for maintenance of personnel and material in the assault area by means of "mother ships." This method is considered very effective and particularly beneficial to the morale of small boat crews. The mother ship LST 47 assigned to Camel area was amply provisioned and supplied with reserves of such items as smoke pots, floats, lubricating oils, and repair items. Especially heavy demands were made on smoke reserves by reason of defense measures in the area, and special requests had to be made for re-supply.
>
> Repair facilities provided by basic plan were ample and effectively employed in response to the limited demands made upon them.
>
> The provisions made in the plan for salvage and fire-fighting proved adequate and the units performed most creditably. These units, in addition to regular duties, assisted in the removal of the defense net across the entrance to Yellow Beach.
>
> Inshore salvage accomplished its mission without mishap and assisted in attempts to fight fires on LST 282 when latter was hit and destroyed by glider bomb.
>
> Offshore salvage assisted in rescue of personnel both from LST 282 and the four small vessels lost in minefield off Red Beach.

Beach gradients on all beaches in the Camel Area proved to be satisfactory for the beaching of all landing craft including LSTs. The weather was highly favorable for unloading and no craft were broached or lost because of the sea action. Green and Blue Beaches were used for unloading assault personnel and only Green Beach for assault vehicles. Yellow Beach was subsequently opened for unloading small quantities of supplies. The difficulty experienced at Red Beach delayed the unloading of follow-up shipping by an estimated 36 hours.

The discharge of large quantities of bulk cargo into small vessels proved to be more than the Beach Group could cope with initially. Inadequate numbers of trucks and unloading personnel on the beaches were reported by the Beach Group as the cause of the slow unloading. The transportation problem was not solved until the D-5 convoy arrived and then only partially. Labor was procured by hiring civilians to work on the beaches. Cranes and mechanical unloading gear were used on the beaches and in dump areas. Some ships were moved close inshore following clearance of minefields on D-2, D-3 day and DUKWs were used as intended. The unloading situation was summarized by the following dispatch:

CONFIDENTIAL   191340B

Rate of unloading has been limited to date to capacity of Army to unload craft over beaches. This is about half of capacity of craft to unload ships. Principal bottlenecks due to truck and DUKW and labor shortage. CO 540 Engineers has been continuously advised and is fully cognizant of situation. Additional transport expected today. French labor being hired.

The unloading of equipment and supplies based upon pre-determined priorities worked out in a satisfactory manner. Priorities were used only as a general guide and ships were unloaded simultaneously as landing craft were available. Army troops were not familiar with loads and in a number of cases sent towed loads ashore ahead of the prime movers. Large boxes, crates, piling, and dunnage proved to be exceedingly hard to handle in the unloading of MT [merchant] ships. The assignment of landing craft to ships for unloading was well handled by the Unloading Control organization.

Generally, instructions to merchant ships were carried out satisfactorily. One notable exception was lack of proper display, at all times, of identifying signboards. Some MT ships arriving in Camel area had not been provided with these boards as called for, with consequent difficulty of identification and delays in unloading and unnecessary signaling.

While the basic plan called for MT ships to discharge fuel and water to service craft before leaving assault area, "Instructions to Merchant Vessels" did not contain such orders. Consequently, it was necessary to issue special instructions in each case when it was desired to effect transfer of fuel or water from merchant ships.

Some confusion was caused to merchant ships by directives mentioning Task Group and Unit numerical designations and operational code names in place of geographical locations. This is an understandable error, but should be avoided.[31]

Dealing with Casualties and Other Issues

Casualty evacuation was effected in a very satisfactory manner for the most part. The casualty load was not as large as was anticipated, nor was it sufficiently large to offer a real test of the evacuation organization. Casualties were evacuated from and across Camel Beaches as follows:

D-day-D-4 total of 1,404 casualties.

On D-5 and thereafter no casualties were evacuated across Camel Beach as all casualties were evacuated from Delta Beach.

Transports received 121 patients from the beaches on D-day. The employment of [various ships] for hospitalization and evacuation of casualties is sound and is good practice.

The USS *Bayfield* (APA 33) (Flag) [Rear Admiral Lewis's flagship] was used to treat casualties in the absence of hospital ships and of other transports and to furnish medical supplies to other activities.

Loading of casualties into the hospital ships appeared very slow, resulting in patients waiting in small boats an undue length of time awaiting embarkation, and tying up of the small boats urgently required for other functions for an unwarranted length of time.[32]

Inspection of the medical portions of the 8th Beach Battalion on D/2, revealed complete uncoordination between the different medical elements, no coordination between the medical services of the different beaches, no overall medical supervision, no overall compilation of records and submission of reports. This situation arose because the 8th Beach Battalion medical elements were not organized as a medical section with a senior medical officer functioning as a department head. The concept of organization into platoons, with platoons supporting companies is necessary during the assault phase, but in the assault phase only. Before preparation for an operation, the senior medical officer should have the status of a department head to advise and consult within battalion commander, coordinate the medical platoons, supervise their training and equipment, and be responsible to the commanding officer for the medical department. This need is even greater after the Beach Battalion has landed. Here it is imperative to have a responsible medical officer to coordinate the work of the different platoons, coordinate the medical activities of the different beaches, and to exert overall supervision of medical functions, supply, employment of personnel, and the preparation and number of records. A senior medical officer is necessary for contact with his opposite in the Army casualty evacuation organization to assure smooth coordination.[33]

Lewis reported that "communications within the Task Force were generally satisfactory, although the 8th Beach Battalion failed to receive its radio equipment as sched-uled. The following deficiencies were noted:

"(a) One ship broke radio silence to communicate with the USS *Somers*.

"(b) After silence was broken the circuit became overloaded and circuit discipline was poor. This later improved and then again deteriorated, eliciting several reprimands.

"(c) Difficulty was encountered in establishing the radio teleprinter circuit, but once established, this circuit handled a large volume of traffic and proved its worth.

"(d) The Task Force Commanders circuit was again badly overloaded and it was extremely difficult to clear traffic and controlling and clearing high priority traffic.

"The problem of Radio Counter-Measure equipment was a difficult one, and on the whole, appeared fairly well handled. The constant employment of minesweepers prior to the operation added to the difficulty of the installation of their equipment, but this was solved by flying technicians to the staging area to complete these installations. Counter-guided missile equipment functioned well, although one LST was sunk in Camel Area from this type of bomb. Only three guided missile signals were recorded on the Force Flagship.

"The LST 47 was designated as mother ship and equipped with radio material sets, batteries, tools, replacement parts, aligning equipment, etc. All defective equipment in the Task Force was immediately repaired or replaced. This service proved invaluable and such an organization should be provided in every amphibious assault."[34]

However, of utmost importance, Lewis found that every effort must be made toward simplification of amphibious communications, that unnecessary complex communication systems caused problems. Reduction in the number of circuits guarded, and improvement in circuit discipline, was necessary. This applied particularly to the assault forces, since landing craft in general had limited equipment and personnel. High command channels needed to be increased to handle the large flow of traffic. It was imperative that all task force commanders be able to receive and transmit high priority traffic immediately.

Based upon his report, Lewis arrived at several conclusions as to the lessons learned from Dragoon concerning landing plans:

1. Standard Operating Procedures which had been issued in the theater were based on sound principle, but were intended primarily as a basis for night assault operations for which considerable different control and identification technique are required.

2. Special boats provide a heavy and tremendously effective beach fire pounding just prior to touchdown. Although the actual physical damage they can inflict on concrete fortifications is negligible, the shock effect they cause is of such magnitude as to render enemy personnel

ineffective for a long enough period to permit assaulting infantry to reach overpowering positions.

3. Complete tactical surprise was gained on Green Beach, since nearly all the defending forces had been withdrawn to reinforce the Red Beach defenses.

4. Naval gunfire support was insufficient to neutralize enemy artillery during the minesweeping operations against Red Beach. Unswept mines would have caused serious losses had the landing on Red Beach been made.

5. Apex boats were wholly ineffective in this assault.

6. Delayed and erratic operation of Apex boats forced the delay of Camel Beach, resulting in the loss of the full effect of invasion air and naval bombardment.

7. By 1400, the initial shock of action was over for Red Beach defending forces, tactical surprise was completely lost; therefore, much heavier naval fire support was required than would otherwise have been necessary.

8. Consideration of the sequence of events prior to 1430 on D-day and the subsequent intelligence obtained of defenses prepared on Red Beach indicated that at 1430 assault against this beach would very likely have resulted in a near-disaster.

9. The principles laid down regarding the assault of a series of beaches are sound.

10. It was found possible, in good weather, to land and support an entire division over narrow beaches for two days.[35]

The French Contribution

In his 2004 work, *Armageddon: The Battle for Germany 1944-45*, Max Hastings wrote that French contributions to the U.S. Seventh Army's drive north from the Mediterranean during the Dragoon operation "was small and almost entirely symbolic" and that their formations suffered chronic problems of discipline." Hastings supported this contention by alleging that "French colonial units in Italy and later in Germany were responsible for mass rapes on a Russian scale" and that "the French left to the Americans the mundane tasks of providing supply and support for their fighting units."[36]

Hastings was a foreign correspondent for BBC TV and the *Evening Standard*. There is ample evidence to question his statements concerning the involvement of the French in Operation Dragoon. First of all, it was Allied policy for the U.S. military to supply and support French fighting units. The French were hardly as expert in using American supply and support systems as those who developed them, namely, the Americans themselves.

Douglas Porch, professor of national security affairs at the Naval Postgraduate School in Monterey, California, has provided an evaluation of the French Army's role in the Mediterranean during World War II that is more balanced and fair. He presented considerable evidence that British military leaders, such as Generals Bernard Montgomery and Alanbrooke, did not hold too high an opinion of French forces before their mountain forces terrified the Germans in Italy. British and American admiration for these French mountain units composed mostly of goums and other North African soldiers was diminished after reports of their raping rampages in Italy. After the Dragoon landings, de Gaulle replaced many of the veteran North African troops with up to one hundred forty thousand inexperienced white civilian Resistance fighters. Their inadequate training, said Porch, caused "a dip in military efficiency and speed. It also ignited quarrels between de Gaulle and Americans over equipping this force. French field commanders in France and Germany were apt to treat orders from their Anglo-American supervisors as mere suggestions to be disobeyed if they failed to further de Gaulle's stiff-necked crusade to uphold French 'rights' and 'honor.' This added tension to an already brittle relationship."[37]

Following Dragoon, some Allied military leaders issued hostile judgments on the quality of French troops. But considering that the French reentered World War II with the stigma of their disasters of June 1940, that as late as 1943 they had a substantial number of troops consisting mostly of outdated colonial policemen lacking modern warfare training, and that rampant French political rivalries and power struggles soured the attitudes of British and American observers of French military prowess, Porch's contention that the successes of the French troops were considerable merit attention. His chapter on "The Mediterranean Road to France's Resurrection, 1940-1945" stated that the French produced some of the most skilled military leaders—Philippe

Leclerc de Hauteclocque, Jean de Lattre de Tassigny, and Alphonse Juin[38]—two of them, Juin and de Lattre, being former Vichyites. By 1945, there was nearly breakable tension between de Lattre and the more diehard military men who had been de Gaulle's followers since the beginning. But even this serious dispute could not check the effectiveness of the French First Army as it made its way across the German frontier in mid-March 1945. This was a crucial development for the French, for, as de Gaulle rightly foresaw, the French needed to play an integral role in the ultimate German defeat if they were to rest their postwar claims for power upon anything.

The Germans met the invading French forces along the Rhine with considerable resistance. However, divisions of Moroccan soldiers were able to maintain the offensive lines to regain the French homeland. By April 21, 1945, the French had crossed the Danube River and were able to embark upon a series of occupations of key German cities in order to further their claims to be a part of the postwar Allied occupation zones. After their initial occupation of Stuttgart on April 24, French forces proceeded onward to Ulm and Constance.

Another argument against Hastings's contention about "the small and almost symbolic French contribution to the U.S. Seventh Army's drive north from the Mediterranean" was the fact that the French were assigned other major responsibilities, such as fighting the Germans for Marseille and Toulon. The French did, indeed, help themselves. The return to Cap Drammont was for many of paramount importance—both to physically and emotionally return to their homeland. The Seventh Army's report on its actions in France and Germany during the years 1944 and 1945 clearly points out the strategic importance of French troops. "To the French," the report observed, "it was of vital importance that in a campaign for France's liberation, their own forces should be under French command. They agreed, however, that though it meant placing a full French general under an American general of lower rank, they would be willing for the Americans to handle all administration, supply, and the overall tactical planning. During the uncertain periods, they were 'seriously perturbed' to hear that alternatives to Anvil were being considered."[39] National pride and honor required a French army under a French general on French soil.

Gen. Jacob Devers wrote that the major goals of the French fighting in Dragoon were capture Toulon by the end of August, capture Marseille by the end of September, and advance north from the Durance River by mid-October. Generals Devers and Patch agreed that since Toulon and Marseille were French ports and cities of such great importance, the honor of their capture should go to the French army.[40]

Patch expected considerable difficulty in capturing Toulon and Marseille. He also knew that there was a serious threat from the north. If the effort to seize and hold the Durance line failed, a long winter campaign was likely to result. Patch had therefore decided that Truscott,—with his veteran Third, Thirty-sixth, and Forty-fifth Divisions, should be in this decisive area. De Lattre's response was, "I will capture both Toulon and Marseille. Let Truscott protect my right and I'll have them both in two weeks." Actually, it took him only ten days.

In General Devers's opinion, the capture of these two ports by the French in such a short time would go down in history as one of their greatest feats in the war. Half of the French II Corps was engaged in fighting at Toulon while the other half was bogged down in Marseille.[41] Capturing both cities was difficult, and Admiral Hewitt had to send part of his armada to help the corps. Fighting in both cities was characterized by door-to-door struggles before the Germans were finally subdued. By August 24, the eastern part of Toulon was under French command; and following a French breakthrough four days later, the western half soon joined the Allies. Marseille also fell to French hands on August 28.

De Lattre's troops then slogged northward to Grenoble to rendezvous with Truscott's—right flank. De Lattre's contingent was carried across the Rhone River via ferryboat and pontoon bridges and by August 31 had moved toward Lyon in the north. Devers noted that by "September 14 we had accomplished in thirty days the mission of Dragoon—assisting Overlord and clearing the whole of central and southern France. The stage was now set for a new phase of operations in Europe. During the period, French Army 'B' had captured 47,717 prisoners and Truscott had captured 31,211. No time had been taken to count the German dead, which ran into the thousands, nor the captured and destroyed German equipment.

"This was accomplished at a cost of 1,146 French killed, captured, and missing and 4,346 wounded, while the Seventh Army had suffered 3,000 Americans killed, captured, and missing and 4,419 wounded. No operation in our history had up to then produced more decisive, dramatic, swift, and far-reaching results at so little cost.

"On Sept 3rd General Eisenhower had decided that the 6th Army Group Headquarters should assume tactical command of the French

Army 'B' and the Seventh Army as soon as contact with General Patton was established. It was further decided that, concurrently with this, tactical command of the Dragoon forces should be passed from General Wilson to General Eisenhower. Administrative and supply responsibility should remain with General Wilson until it could be assumed by the Americans in the European Theater of Operations. On September 9th we moved to Lyon. On September 14th word was received from General Wilson that the 6th Army Group was now in command of French Army 'B' and the Seventh Army."[42]

The French fleet was rebuilt from the smoldering ashes of Mers-El-Kebir, in North Africa, where the British had bombed the French Navy in July 1940 rather than risk the chance that this strong flotilla could undermine British dominance of the seaway. But during Dragoon, thirty-one French ships joined a British and American flotilla. French ships ceremonially entered the harbor in Toulon in advance of foreign ships. This maneuver was symbolic because Toulon was the main naval base for the French Navy in the Mediterranean, and it was also where the French Navy wrecked many of their ships in November 1942 rather than risk their capture by the Germans as they occupied the rest of France following Operation Torch.

Historian M. R. D. Foot argued that "one reason for mounting Dragoon has been touched on lightly, if at all, by English-speaking commentators, and deserves notice here. Whether the operation was necessary or not, for political or for military reasons, to the Americans or the British, it was indispensable for de Gaulle and for French national self-assurance. Seven of Patch's eleven divisions were French, the revivified French North African Army combined with some of the best of the Gaullist volunteers, and commanded by de Lattre de Tassigny whom SOE had brought out of captivity. De Gaulle alone of the leading Allied political commanders looked at the war from Algiers; seen from there, a formal reoccupation of French soil by French troops was something that simply could not be done without. SOE's part in this necessary operation was to ensure that it went through with the minimum of friction."[43]

French Redemption

The French staged a comeback from the devastation of the June 1940 defeat to glorious victory. French military fortunes had been revived, thanks in no short part to logistical help from the Allies. Inadequately supplied French troops were given the means and leadership to avenge German domination. In Professor Porch's opinion, "Anvil offered an artery through which to tap France's manpower resources and prepare France for a postwar role. De Lattre's task had been especially complex, because he had to fight a series of bitter winter battles in Alsace while at the same time rebuilding and reorganizing his army. That reorganization was vital not only to maintain the combat efficiency of the French First Army, but also France's internal stability and its credibility as an ally. De Gaulle used his military contribution and France's geographic position as leverage to stake out France's claim to an important role in postwar Europe. This was critical to the Allied cause and the stability of postwar Europe. Even if the Allies were reluctant to acknowledge France's contribution to victory at the surrender ceremony of May 8, 1945, the Mediterranean theater allowed them to reap the significant benefit of France's revival."[44]

The planners of Operation Dragoon estimated that 500,000 French and American troops would be landed in the southern French ports by the end of the war in Europe. The actual number was 905,512 personnel, 172,331 vehicles, and 4,122,081 tons of equipment that were debarked.[45] The French Army units that embarked upon Dragoon included a variety of Frenchmen waiting to return home. The French I Corps contained the Third French Algerian Division, the Fourth Moroccan Mountain Division, and the Second Moroccan Infantry Division. Additional units were prepared to lend assistance should the need arise: composing the French II Corps were the First French Armored Division, the Fifth French Armored Division, and the First Infantry Division, all of which were based in North Africa; and the Ninth Colonial French Infantry Division, stationed on the island of Corsica.[46] The French colonial troops spoke six different languages, and the conglomeration of nationalities and different cultures did not facilitate military operations. Complications also arose when the Headquarters Sixth Army Group was secretly organized on August 1, 1944. This group was a mélange of the two armies, American and French, and therefore had to overcome the language barrier. For many staff members, this presented a challenge and made work more difficult.[47]

General Devers posed this question: "Since there was a French army under our command, why was Headquarters 6th Army Group not an Allied Headquarters, composed of French and Americans in equal numbers, instead of being purely American?" This was the sort of arrangement that was utilized with the British, he pointed out, so why not with the French?[48]

Answering his own question, General Devers believed that "there were several compelling reasons why an integrated headquarters was neither possible nor desirable in this case, although there was no desire to deny the French representation. The French did not understand American staff organization and procedure, and there was no time to teach it to them. They also did not understand American supply and evacuation systems and methods. But there were sufficient numbers of American officers who understood French systems and methods to integrate theirs with America's and make them work.

The French Army also did not have sufficient experienced commanders and staff officers to fill their own essential positions, and this fact the French thoroughly appreciated. As a result, they did not insist on French representation in the Headquarters Sixth Army Group. Devers added, "Furthermore, full representation was neither necessary nor desirable from an operational point of view. Experience has shown that in an integrated headquarters of even two nationalities, duplication of effort and high wastage of manpower are inevitable—the result of an effort by each side to insure that the other has its proper counterpart on the staff. The French army commander detailed to us a fairly large mission of liaison officers for each staff section. Indicative of the acute shortage of experienced French officers is the fact that the French were never able to maintain the mission at full strength."[49]

However, French assistance was still substantial. General de Gaulle's account of the French military contribution to the Allied forces in Europe included (a) a campaign army of 230,000 men; (b) sovereignty forces amounting to 150,000 soldiers; (c) a fleet of 320,000 tons manned by 50,000 sailors; (d) 1.2 million tons of cargo vessels and steamships, of which two-thirds were operated by French crews; and (e) an air force of 500 fighter airplanes manned by 30,000 Frenchmen. To this inventory should be added provision by the French of ports, transportation, communications, labor, and other facilities and services.[50]

But it was not all adulation between the French and their Allies. Professor Paul Fussell, who had served as an American infantry soldier in France during World War II, described the relationship between the French and American troops as follows: "Some French civilians tried to repress their instinctive contempt for the Americans while the war was not yet won, but afterward there broke out what one soldier recalled as 'an endless battle between native and GI.' The locals sold the troops 'dishonest bottles of wine.' The GIs countered by throwing from their vehicles, in answer to begging cries for cigarettes and candles, used and ripe old condoms."[51]

Professor Fussell observed that the death and destruction caused by British and American bombs that killed many French people and obliterated their property in 1944 generated hatred against Allied forces, and sometimes they were viewed as invaders of France. He also noted that from the period invasion of Normandy to the May 8, 1945, victory over Germany, 135,000 Americans were dead and 586,628 wounded.[52] A sizable percentage of the American dead are buried on French soil.

The U.S. Navy Department's Office of Naval Intelligence, in its news bulletin, *ONI Weekly*, on September 6, 1944, described the role of the French forces as critical to the defeat of Germany as follows:

> The contribution of the FFI [French Resistance] to the Allied victory in France was considerable and has greatly exceeded many pre-invasion estimates of the help which could be expected from the resistance groups. Since the very beginning of the German occupation there has been an active underground in France, whose principal functions were intelligence and sabotage. At great cost, regular contacts were maintained by means of radio transmitters and couriers were transported to and from France by the RAF. In this way, the Allies were enabled to follow German troop movements in France in detail and, as the date of the invasion grew closer, this served and naturally became more and more important to our plans. Sabotage in the early days was on a small scale and, left in the hands of isolated groups, lacked coordinated direction. Apart from active sabotage, such as bombing transformer stations, pylons carrying high-tension cables and factories thought to be working on the German account, there was much passive sabotage. Factory workers were encouraged to slow up on their jobs; railroad employees held up the turn-around for freight cars or sent them off in a direction opposite to their intended destinations; government clerks "lost" important dossiers and bogged down the Germans in a mass of red tape and paperwork.

In general, one of the principal difficulties for the underground was the problem of combining and coordinating the efforts of many small groups scattered not only by geography but by divergent political views. Another problem was the need for learning the techniques of undercover operations. In this the Communist cells had a head start since they were already accustomed to carrying out their activity underground.

At first the underground was composed chiefly of persons who maintained, at least ostensibly, some legal employment and a fixed place of residence. They were professional men, workers in industry and officials, who continued to work at their usual jobs and on the side spread word of German military movements or committed acts of sabotage. Before long the Germans managed to create a new kind of resistance group. This they did by demanding from the Vichy government huge quotas of young men for deportation to the Reich as forced workers. Rather than go to Germany, many of these men fled their homes and disappeared. These men (called "les gens duMaquis"—men of the bush, or more simply, Maquis) became in effect outlaws; they lived a wild, hand-to-mouth existence, fighting off detachments of Vichy police sent to seize them in their mountain hideouts. When the Vichy police failed to break up these gangs, German formations were sent against them, but such was the nature of the mountainous country in which they hid—especially in the Haute Savoie—that all of these operations failed, and the Maquis was still flourishing when our troops landed in France.

Gradually, and despite heavy losses as the Gestapo and Vichy informers sought to destroy the underground, the activities of separate and isolated groups were coordinated and given a fairly well unified structure. Now all the various resistance organizations—totaling some thirty-three separate organizations—are represented on a *Conseil national de la Resistance* (CNR). This supreme national council is supposed to be the final authority which directs all operations. With it sits a delegation from the Provisional Government (FCNL).

Almost immediately after the landings, sabotage on a very extensive scale and attacks on enemy troops began in many parts of the country. Supplies were dropped to the

Resistance in substantial quantities; equipment of all kinds, including jeeps, was either flown in or parachuted to them, and British, American, and French officers were dropped, who cooperated with the Resistance and assisted in coordinating their operations with those of the Allied armies. Inevitably there were some defects in liaison—both between the various groups operating in the field and their local chiefs and between these chiefs and the higher echelons. The premature announcement of the liberation of Paris seems to be an example of this failure.

The French Resistance also served substantially in delaying and obstructing German troop movements, especially from the Mediterranean coast and the Bay of Biscay, by derailments and the demolition of bridges. It is now clear that one of the principal causes of the German defeat in Normandy was the enemy's inability to bring reinforcements in rapidly. So slowly did replacement proceed that at no time were the Germans able to build up a strategic reserve; troops had to be thrown into the fighting as they arrived, and units which might have prevented our breakthrough, if employed in their full strength, were consumed in driblets without affecting the course of operations. It is not possible to distinguish precisely how much of the delay forced on the Germans was the work of the Allied Air Forces and how much the work of the Resistance, but enough is known to make it certain that the accomplishment of the latter was considerable.[53]

Adm. Henry Kent Hewitt did his best to help soothe the feelings of the French military commanders. In a letter dated June 18, 1944, he wrote to Lieutenant Colonel Caldamaison, general director of public service, to thank him for a present of a spahis uniform that was presented to Hewitt: "It is a gift that I will always hold dear and which will always remind me of my days in North Africa, days that seem good now with the announcement of the liberation of France."[54] After landing on Camel Green Beach on August 16, both Hewitt and General Patch let French Admiral Lemonnier be the first to touch French soil. "I think that I have never seen a happier man," wrote Hewitt.[55]

Admiral Hewitt's sensitivity to problems of protocol helped strengthen French-American friendship. He wrote, in his memoirs, about the period following the American naval victory in North Africa: "We had defeated a gallant French Resistance and were more or less taking charge. But Admiral Micheller (the French naval commander) was a Vice Admiral, I a Rear Admiral. Furthermore, we (the Americans) had not come as conquerors, but as friends and Allies. It was important to restore that relationship." Hewitt, therefore, inquired when it would be convenient for Admiral Micheller to receive his visit. This courteous gesture led to a lasting friendship between the two men.

In August 1944, emotions ran rampant throughout the French forces. General de Lattre recorded that "on all the ships it was the same. On the *Sobieski*, the goal they had dreamed of since 1940 was within their reach. The survivors of June 1940 gathered and were joined by natives of French Equatorial and West Africa, Somalis, New Caledonians, Tahitians, Antilleans, Indo-Chinese, Pondicherians, Syrians and Lebanese, Algerians, Moroccans, Tunisians, Legionnaires, the veterans of Massaouah, Bir-Hakeim, El Alamein and Zaghouan, the soldiers of Koenig, Legentilhomme, Cazaux, and Larminat. All of them were gazing hungrily towards France, for the love of which they had carried the cross of Lorraine under many skies.

"It was to the recovery of the homeland that the hopes of the First Armored Division were eagerly turned. Its history was yet only a history of hope, kept alive by General Touzet du Vigier of the Light Mechanized Brigade and shared by all the men, whether North African French or men who had escaped from France, who formed this large and magnificent armored unit, the first of its kind that the French Army could boast. All these divisions, each with its own characteristics which gave it a clear individuality, shared the same fervor. France was there."[56]

Amidst the joys of ridding France of German occupation, there remained serious problems. For example, Vichy's policies toward women tended to be paternalistic and conservative. Marriage and breeding of larger families and allegiance to Catholicism were the goals that were set for women. This ideology was in conflict with the realities of German occupation that severely limited marriage opportunities and wartime economic facts. Thousands upon thousands of young French people were prisoners of war in German or forced labor camps. Food and other necessities were in short supply for the vast majority of the French. To survive and sometimes prosper, women resorted to a variety of vocations frowned upon by Vichy reactionaries who did not suffer the same economic woes. The many less fortunate did what they could to continue living—and this included selling themselves as collaborationists and prostitutes. But there were significant differences throughout France. For example, women were more concerned about how their behavior was viewed in a small village than women living in a large city. Hanna Diamond found that daughters might also have been influenced by the World War I experiences of their fathers. Those who suffered because of the participation of fathers in the Great War were less tolerant about accepting a second German invasion. Many remembered that the German armies had destroyed their homes and their families and who, since childhood, had heard stories of German cruelty.[57]

Many brave French women did more than just sacrifice themselves by joining the Resistance; they also endangered their children and their parents. Diamond found that most were so delighted to be involved, or so scared, that they rarely questioned what they were asked to do in any case.[58]

Obviously, not all French women were Resistance heroines. A forty-eight-year-old widow who cleaned for German administrative officers in 1942 was responsible for the deaths of five men—one British parachutist and four Frenchmen who helped shelter the parachutist. She had denounced these men to the Germans because she believed that but for the job that the Germans had provided her, she would not have survived. On November 3, 1949, she was condemned to death.[59]

Evaluation

Anvil/Dragoon succeeded because of methodical planning, thorough training programs, talented and seasoned leadership, and the element of surprise.[60]

General Marshall, in his report, "The Winning of the War in Europe and the Pacific," observed that it was the landing of the U.S. Seventh Army, under the command of Lt. Gen. Alexander M. Patch, along the Mediterranean coast of France on August 15, 1944, that greatly aided the continued deterioration of the German Army's position in France. He wrote, "The very threat of such a landing had held substantial German forces of the First and Nineteenth Armies immobilized in the south of France, preventing their deployment against our forces in Normandy. A naval force, comparable in size to the one which participated in the American landings in Normandy, had been assembled. An air offensive, conducted chiefly by the Allied Strategic Air Forces, prepared the way for the invasion by sustained attacks on vital enemy communications and installations in southern France."[61] Samuel E. Morison concluded that Dragoon was the nearly faultless large-scale amphibious operation of World War II.[62] It was this combination of forces and planning that enabled men such as General de Lattre and Jean-Pierre Aumont to return to their homeland, and to Cap Drammont, in mid-August 1944.

The French defeat of June 1940 and the attack of Pearl Harbor on December 7, 1941, were due to failures of military coordination, improper evaluation of intelligence, decentralization of responsibility, and an absence of imagination on the part of military and political leaders. The record of the invasion of southern France was a reversal of prior failures. It is replete with evidence of successful intelligence gathering and analysis, competent military planning and operations, strong logistical support, and effective inter-Allied cooperation.

A spirit of innovation, courage, and sacrifice defined and described many of the Allied leaders and their followers. According to Gen. George Marshall, the Dragoon campaign "was a success in that it enabled the Supreme Allied Commander to consolidate his position in late 1944 and it is unlikely that Allied forces in France would have been able to mount their final offensive into Germany in 1945 without the heavy contribution of ammunition and other supplies through southern France."[63]

Much has changed since August 1944. For one thing, the scope of geographic breadth of logistical planning has enlarged to encompass a truly global agenda. Today, logistical planning, even more so than when planning for Dragoon, must be undertaken in a detail-oriented way, with careful consideration given to what this worldwide stretch means in terms of timing and supplies.

Changes have taken place in the arena of intelligence. In 1944, the OSS was a wartime organization that was established to assist in the defeat of mighty national enemies in a conventional war. However, the OSS was anything but conventional in its recruitment and methods. At an OSS Society banquet held on June 8, 2002, the then-CIA deputy director for operations, James L. Pavitt, observed that "the OSS is still there—in the shadows, and in the innovations that today's clandestine service finds its inspiration."[64] The world in which crucial intelligence is spread is vastly different now than it was in 1944. Dean Joseph S. Nye of Harvard's Kennedy School of Government, wrote that "suppressing terrorism is very different from a military campaign. It requires continuous, patient, undramatic civilian work and close cooperation with other countries. And it requires coordination within our government,"[65] referring to the coordination of intelligence agencies and resources.

Other forms of intelligence and surveillance made themselves useful and integral parts of the Dragoon operation. High-resolution images of German military positions in France, collected by satellites and spy planes to guide the Allied warfare, were not available during World War II. Human intelligence gathering, communications intercepts, and analysis were used in the 1940s. But even after human intelligence gathering, the use of small intelligence teams is crucial.

The shortage of Arabic linguists has been mitigated in Iraq by technological innovations that were not available during World War II. Allied troops and small unit Allied teams did not have the palm-sized computer organizers and digital cameras to scan documents and photograph people for expeditious translation and identification. Now information can be transmitted to headquarters over secure systems that will distinguish an enemy's armored vehicles from friendly ones.

The importance of human virtues has not changed since August 1944. The intelligence, courage, and sacrifices of James V. Forrestal, Henry Kent Hewitt, Alexander M. Patch Jr., Robert T. Frederick, Geoffrey M. T. Jones, Spencer S. Lewis, Samuel Kimmel, Lawrence E. Gilbert, Irving Noyes, Isabell Pell, Helene Gagliano, Lisa Fittko, Jean de Lattre de Tassigny, Antoine de Saint-Exupéry, and countless others are still in the shadows of Cap Drammont and Operation Anvil/Dragoon.

CHAPTER 12

REMEMBRANCE

The man who was supposed to lead the United States Seventh Army into southern France but did not, Gen. George S. Patton, was a great soldier who delighted in war. His colleagues, Generals Alexander Patch Jr., Lucian K. Truscott Jr.,—and Robert T. Frederick, who did command troops in Operation Dragoon, were also great soldiers but did not delight in war. Patton's postwar record was short and tragic; he was dismissed from his command as administrator of Bavaria for impolitic comments and died in December 1945, the victim of an automobile accident. His replacement as administrator was his friend, General Truscott,—who died at age seventy, full of well-deserved honors. Another of Patton's friends, General Patch, was ordered back to the United States after the war to undertake a most important assignment—to prepare a plan for the reorganization of the United States Army. Patch, in his midfifties, did not complete this task, for he contracted pneumonia and died in November 1945.

General Frederick's post-Dragoon career included service as military administrator of Nice and environs. He later desegregated African-American troops when he was placed in command of Fort Ord, in California. The European edition of *Army Times* (May 15, 1951) reported that the U.S. Senate Committee on Armed Services Preparedness considered the Fort Ord training to be superior and commended its system of faculty instruction that rotated classes between listening and watching and actual practice. According to the Senate Committee's report, the superb quality was due to the "outstanding and brilliant military personality of Major General Robert T. Frederick—a personality reflected throughout his command."[1] Later, Frederick served as commander of the U.S. military delegation to Greece in 1951. His World War II wounds compelled Frederick to retire from the army at the age of forty-four. In retirement, he supervised his family's financial interests, escorted his mother to gambling casinos, and regularly responded to requests for help from his former troops. He died at age sixty-three.

Democracy of the Dead

On twelve acres near the eastern edge of the city of Draguignan, at the foot of a hill clad with the characteristic cypresses, olive trees, and oleanders of southern France, sits the Rhone American Cemetery and Memorial. Draguignan, in France's Var department, is a mere sixteen miles from the seacoast. Across the street from the cemetery are schools and playgrounds; to the west is the civilian cemetery of the city of Draguignan.

Buried at the Rhone American Cemetery are 861 U.S. military dead, most of whom died during the landings on the southern coast on August 15, 1944, and the advance northward. The cemetery takes its name from the Rhone River, whose watershed was the scene of these operations.

There are 837 Latin crosses and 24 Stars of David grave markers at the cemetery. Burials at the Rhone American Cemetery are classified as 799 known, 62 unknown, and missing commemorated 294. The tablets of the missing give name, rank, and organization and state the circumstance under which death occurred. The inscription on the tablets of the missing reads, "Here Rests in Honored Glory a Comrade in Arms Known but to God."[2] Those that are attributed to missing, dated August 16, 1945, include LST 282 crew members:

> LTJG Sidney Blustain—0224286, USNR
> ENS Element L. Cassell—0330120, USNR
> MOMM 1C Harold A. Bryan—06212908, USNR
> S2C Robert L. Griffith—07124480, USNR
> GM2C John J. Dunleavy—02444880, USNR
> SF2C Harry H. Hall—08336684, USNR
> MMO3C George T. Irwin—08780781, USNR
> PHM2C Joseph A. Panaccio—02452530, USNR
> MOMM 1C Ernest J. Sadosky—08072724, USNR
> MOMM 2C Warren E. Wagner—07557260, USNR

The remains of the following LST 282 decedents were repatriated to the United States for permanent interment:

> ENS Peter T. Hughes—267150—private cemetery in New York
> QM 2C James E. Kaye—2851263—Arlington National Cemetery,
>   Ft. Myer, Va.

MOMM 1C Lincoln G. Plimpton—6079851—private cemetery in Massachusetts

S1C Bertil H. Noyd—8030363—private cemetery in Massachusetts

S2C John H. Deel Jr.—8351106—private cemetery in Idaho[3]

American Cemetery at Draguignan

The graves of young Americans who answered the call to military service during World War II are found not only in Draguignan but throughout the world. Below are commentaries concerning the post Operation Dragoon lives of some people previously discussed.

Aubut, Tom

After his ship LST 282 was bombed, Thirty-sixth Infantry Division soldiers helped survivor Tom Aubut get aboard the LST 1012, where he was treated for burns to his hands.[4] Aubut was transferred to a hospital in Naples and, after shore leave in the United States, was assigned to the LST 550 and participated in the invasion of Okinawa. His obituary reads as follows:

> Thomas "Frenchy" Aubut, of Citrus Heights, CA, formerly of Duluth, MN, passed away Thursday, Jan. 13, 2005, in California. Tom worked for Minnesota Power for 10 years then he and his brother, Joe, operated Frenchy's Service Station in downtown Duluth for many years. A member of St. Johns Church, Tom served in the U.S. Navy Amphibious forces in World War II and was awarded three bronze stars for action at the Normandy, Southern France, and Okinawa invasions, also the Purple Heart, Cold War Medal, and many battle ribbons. He was preceded in death by his parents, Delima Rose and John Clement Aubut, brothers Wilfred, John, Joseph Clement, and Emil, and sister Mary Jane Sykes. He is survived by his wife of 56 years, Donna Mae (Lindberg) Aubut of Citrus Heights CA, sisters Bernadette Waller and Ethel Beals of Duluth, sons Sheldon, Houlton, WI, and Mitchell, Birmingham, AL, and daughters Autumn Adele Aubut, Carlton, MN, and Nanette Aubut (David Husid), Citrus Heights, CA, 10 grandchildren, and 8 great-grandchildren.[5]

After World War II, while he was vacationing lakeside with his family, Aubut saved the life of a drowning person.

Aumont, Jean-Pierre

A popular French actor who served in the war, Jean-Pierre Aumont's acting career endured some sixty-five years, including roles in Hollywood-based films and Broadway plays. His military distinctions with the French Army earned him the Croix de Guerre and Légion d'honneur awards. He was honored by French President Jacques Chirac as being a "formidable actor who marked the history of the French theater and cinema and who also conquered Hollywood and Broadway with panache."[6]

After World War II, Aumont's film and stage career kept him in his homeland, where he made such films as *Day for Night*, directed by François Truffaut, and *Cat and Mouse*, directed by Claude Lelouch. He also starred with Vivien Leigh in the 1963 Broadway musical *Tovarich*.

Aumont organized a benefit for the survivors of a Fréjus disaster in 1960. A dam had broken there, and hundreds of people had been killed. Aumont and fellow actors Rex Harrison, Claudette Colbert, and Lawrence Olivier participated in the program where $300,000 was raised for the Fréjus victims.[7] Aumont died on January 30, 2001, at his home in Saint-Tropez, France, at age ninety.

Coigney, Rodolphe Lucien

On June 6, 2005, a French Resistance hero died in New York at the age of eighty-nine. Near the end of World War II, Dr. R. L. Coigney helped persuade SS chief Heinrich Himmler to release French women imprisoned in the Ravensbrück concentration camp. Dr. Coigney served as a medical adviser to Gen. Charles de Gaulle's headquarters in London. As a Resistance fighter, he helped other French people and refugees leave the Nazi-occupied French zone and move into the Vichy-controlled area.

In 1952, Coigney was appointed director of the World Health Organization's New York office and served the WHO until 1972. He was an avid fisherman and, in 1989, published his detailed bibliography of more than 460 citations dealing with Izaak Walton's *Compleat Angler or the Contemplative Man's Recreation*, the first edition of which was published in 1653.[8]

Connor, James P.

After receiving the Congressional Medal of Honor for conspicuous gallantry and intrepidity at the risk of life above and beyond the call of duty during Operation Dragoon, Sgt. James P. Connor of the Third Infantry Division was sent to a military hospital in Italy to recover from serious wounds. Through sheer grit and determination, he had led his platoon in clearing an enemy force vastly superior in numbers and firepower from entrenched positions on Cape Cavalaire on the morning of August 15, 1944. He thereby ensured safe and uninterrupted landings for the huge volume of men and equipment that followed.

After receiving the Medal of Honor, honoring him for heroism and his prior exemplary military service during the African and Italian campaigns, Connor was erroneously sent back to combat duties. His new captain was not informed of Connor's record. Connor carried the Medal of Honor in his pocket but did not speak about it. Someone else, however, did tell the captain, who then called headquarters and mentioned that he had a Sergeant Connor with him. A frantic mission ensued to extricate Connor from danger. The captain returned, flustered, and ordered Connor to get down into the cellar of an abandoned home and to stay there, shouting, "If you get killed, it'll be too damned bad for me." Just then a shell came through the house, but no one got hurt. A jeep showed up, driven by an officer. Connor climbed in and was taken back to headquarters, and the captain was spared the serious offense of losing a Medal of Honor winner. "Apparently, the Army officers up the line had been looking for me and somehow my papers got lost and they did not know where I was," Connor later recalled.[9]

While recovering from his wounds, Connor wrote to his father that he had received a medal but without any explanation. He asked his father to keep it a secret and never mentioned any action that he had seen. What Connor stressed in his letters home was about how well he was.[10] However, the U.S. War Department later published the story of Connor's heroism.

When Connor returned home in May 1945, more than six thousand five hundred children who attended parochial schools in the Diocese of Wilmington, Delaware, paraded in his honor, along with cadet nurses and several bands in the Memorial Day parade. Gray skies and a threat of rain did not prevent a massive turnout. Governor Walter Bacon of Delaware accepted a portrait of Sergeant Connor.[11]

Connor's efforts to avoid publicity were repeatedly frustrated after his return to civilian life. He was employed at the Wilmington Veterans Administration regional office, where his job was to counsel World War II, Korean, and Vietnam veterans. He and his wife, Betty, raised four sons at 112 Olga Road, in Elsmere, a small municipality adjacent to Wilmington.[12] Connor was invited to visit with every president from

Truman to Carter and to attend their inaugurals. From 1980 onward, he declined presidential invitations because he wanted to avoid the limelight that had been growing in intensity.[13] Under military protocol, as a Medal of Honor holder, he was entitled to a salute from anyone in military service, regardless of rank. President Truman and Connor were visiting in the Oval Office when the German supreme commander called to surrender. Truman then took Connor with him to announce that the war in Europe was over. When asked why the Nazis gave up, Truman's answer was, "Because I threatened to send Jim Connor back to Europe."[14]

As the years went by, Connor continued to live modestly, devoted to his job of serving fellow war veterans and his family. As a boy, he had played a lot of baseball, and the love for the game continued throughout his life. He and his wife enjoyed watching horse races at the Delaware Park Raceway. They watched but did not bet, according to their son, Jim Junior, because Jim Senior was "very conservative."[15]

As young children, his sons would gather in their parents' bedroom very early during Christmas, and they would all sing Christmas carols. One Christmas morning, Jim Connor showed his sons the scars from the wounds he sustained during Operation Dragoon. "Inquisitive as we were, we would feel the wounds and noticed something hard under the scar," wrote Jim Junior. "Dad told us it was shrapnel from mortars. We asked: 'Why didn't the doctors remove them?' He said they were too deep at the time and eventually the metal would dissolve."[16]

On July 27, 1994, about two weeks short of the fiftieth anniversary of Dragoon, Jim Connor died at the age of seventy-five. In accordance with Connor's preference, his funeral service was simple, with fewer than one hundred mourners at St. Elizabeth Ann Seton Catholic Church. An article by Jim Parks in the Wilmington *News Journal*, dated August 1, 1994, reported,

> The funeral procession did not have a police escort as it wound its way to the Delaware Veterans Memorial Cemetery near Summit.
>
> The only pageantry occurred at the cemetery, where a squad from the 3rd Infantry, the Army's honor guard unit, escorted the casket. The eight soldiers, wearing dress blue uniforms and white gloves, fired a three-volley rifle salute and played Taps beneath gray skies.

513

Following the graveside service, members of the honor guard solemnly folded an American flag and presented it to Connor's wife, Elizabeth.

There were no eulogies or speeches, but during a short sermon, the Rev. Clemens Manista said Sgt. Connor "in service to his country was willing to lay down his life for his friends." After the war, he said, Connor returned home "to help his fellow veterans" while working for the Veterans Administration.[17]

The photos of Sgt. James P. Connor wearing the Congressional Medal of Honor and the presidential commendation follow:

James P. Connor

The President of the United States
in the name of
The Congress
takes pleasure in presenting the
Congressional Medal of Honor
to

CONNOR, JAMES P.

Rank and organization: Sergeant, U.S. Army, 7th Infantry, 3d Infantry Division. *Place and date:* Cape Cavalaire, southern France, 15 August 1944. *Entered service at:* Wilmington, Del. *Birth:* Wilmington, Del. *G.O. No.:* 18, 15 March 1945. *Citation:* For conspicuous gallantry and intrepidity at risk of life above and beyond the call of duty. On 15 August 1944 Sgt. Connor, through sheer grit and determination, led his platoon in clearing an enemy vastly superior in numbers and firepower from strongly entrenched positions on Cape Cavalaire, removing a grave enemy threat to his division during the amphibious landing in southern France, and thereby insured safe and uninterrupted landings for the huge volume of men and materiel which followed. His battle patrol landed on "Red Beach" with the mission of destroying the strongly fortified enemy positions on Cape Cavalaire with utmost speed. From the peninsula the enemy had commanding observation and seriously menaced the vast landing operations taking place. Though knocked down and seriously wounded in the neck by a hanging mine which killed his platoon lieutenant, Sgt. Connor refused medical aid and with his driving spirit practically carried the platoon across several thousand yards of mine-saturated beach through intense fire from mortars, 20-mm. flak guns, machineguns, and snipers. En route to the Cape he personally shot and killed 2 snipers. The platoon sergeant was killed and Sgt. Connor became platoon leader. Receiving a second wound, which lacerated his shoulder and back, he again refused evacuation, expressing determination to carry on until physically unable to continue. He reassured and prodded the hesitating men of his decimated platoon forward through almost impregnable mortar concentrations. Again emphasizing the prevalent urgency of their mission, he impelled his men toward a group of buildings honeycombed with enemy snipers and machineguns. Here he received his third grave wound, this time in the leg, felling him in his tracks. Still resolved to carry on, he relinquished command only after his attempts proved that it was physically impossible to stand. Nevertheless, from his prone position, he gave the orders and directed his men in assaulting the enemy. Infused with Sgt. Connor's dogged determination, the platoon, though reduced to less than one-third of its original 36 men, outflanked and rushed the enemy with such furiousness that they killed 7, captured 40, seized 3 machineguns and considerable other materiel, and took all their assigned objectives, successfully completing their mission. By his repeated examples of tenaciousness and indomitable spirit Sgt. Connor transmitted his heroism to his men until they became a fighting team which could not be stopped.

Congressional Medal of Honor awarded to James P. Connor

On April 5, 2001, a military peacekeeping base camp in Bosnia was opened for returning Muslim refugees who fled when Serbs murdered their families and friends. This hillside base was named Forward Operating Base Connor; it accommodated 150 soldiers to protect Bosnians.[18]

De Lattre De Tassigny, Jean

After World War II, General de Lattre signed the document recognizing the defeat of Germany. He became a national hero. However, during the war, fellow aristocrats looked upon him as a traitor to Marshal Pétain when de Lattre ended his service to the Vichy collaborationist regime after the Germans occupied all of France in November 1942 in violation of the armistice terms of 1940. The French government in 1950 sent de Lattre to serve as commissioner and commander in chief to an unwinnable war in Indochina. His son Bernard, also an army officer, volunteered to fight in Indochina and was killed in 1952. The general died of cancer in Paris shortly after his son. Posthumously, de Lattre was promoted to the rank of marshal. His widow, Simone de Lattre de Tassigny, died in June 2003 at the age of ninety-six.[19]

Fittko, Lisa Ekstein

Lisa Fittko rescued Jews and anti-Nazis from occupied France in the early 1940s. Germans honored her after World War II. At the age of ten, after World War I, she and her family had moved to Berlin. She fled Germany in 1933 and continued her anti-Nazi activities in Prague, where she married Hans Fittko, a fellow exile. They went to Paris in 1938. Evading Vichy authorities after the defeat of France, they ended up in Marseille.

Fittko died on March 12, 2005, at the age of ninety-five. Her death was announced on German radio and television, and obituaries appeared in the major national newspapers. Douglas Martin wrote this about her achievements:

> In 1986, the President of West Germany awarded her the Distinguished Medal of Merit, First Class.
>
> In the United States, Ms. Fittko's story was eventually documented in several novels and films, including the 1998 documentary *Lisa Fittko: But We Said We Will Not Surrender.*
>
> She wrote two books about her experiences. One, *Escape Through the Pyrenees*, which was first published in West

Germany in 1985, won that country's award for the best political book of the year. It was translated into French, Spanish, Italian, Portuguese, Japanese, and, in 1991, into English by Northwestern University Press. The same press, in 1993, published her *Solidarity and Treason: Resistance and Exile, 1933-40.*[20]

Forrestal, James V.

He saw for himself. On the afternoon of August 15, 1944, James Forrestal went ashore at Camel Beach, in Fréjus, to see how the invasion of southern France was faring. At a temporary field hospital, he talked with wounded soldiers of the Thirty-sixth Infantry. The next day, he again left the *Catoctin* and went to Saint-Raphael. Forrestal along with Admiral Lemonnier and Admiral Hewitt were honored by the local populace. At the public square of Saint-Raphael, they joined in singing "The Marseillaise," the French national anthem. Forrestal later checked out the condition of a home near Cannes because of his concern that naval gunfire had damaged the home of playwright Philip Barry, a close friend. When Forrestal returned to the *Catoctin*, he notified Barry, "Villa Lorenzo Intact."[21]

Forrestal continued to visit battlefronts. In February 1945, he observed the marine assault on Iwo Jima, in the northwestern Pacific. His exposure to the horrors of warfare was unusual for an American official of his rank during World War II. Forrestal learned the terrible results of modern warfare and devoted an enormous amount of time and energy to his responsibilities in managing the United States Navy. Later, he applied his considerable ability and energy to the administration of the newly created problem-ridden Department of Defense. He used his great intellectual ability to fulfill his primary task—to support and serve military people who defended the United States. The entries in his diary, *The Forrestal Diaries*, reflect this concern.

Less than a week after Harry S. Truman was sworn in as president of the United States, Forrestal met with him. "I told him that I had got Admiral Hewitt back to pursue the investigation into the Pearl Harbor disaster . . . I felt that I had an obligation to Congress to continue the investigation because I was not completely satisfied with the report my own court had made."[22]

About two years after Operation Dragoon, Forrestal noted, "We have a very large number of vessels in the active fleet which cannot go to sea because of the lack of competent personnel. When Vice Admiral Daniel E. Barbey wanted [in August 1946] to move the *Catoctin*, the command ship at Dragoon for maneuvers, Admiral Barbey had to get personnel from other ships in Norfolk in order to proceed."[23]

At a White House meeting on February 18, 1948, dealing with U.S. military strength, it was concluded that the total U.S. Army shortage would be one hundred sixty-five thousand by the end of 1948. The navy also had an acute shortage of personnel, which required the immobilization of 107 ships until the situation improved. The personnel situation in the air force was considered to be satisfactory.[24]

Forrestal's thinking in strategic global terms led to the establishment of United States naval squadrons in the Mediterranean. The Mediterranean Task Force was the result of Forrestal's leadership. Walter Millis, the historian who edited Forrestal's *Diaries*, concluded that the initiative by Secretary Forrestal in February 1946 "was to have a greater influence on the history of the succeeding years than is realized. It was to buttress Turkish resistance to the advance of Soviet power. It was important for President Truman's foreign policies, and played a role in saving Italy from Communist engulfment."[25]

When Forrestal met with Churchill on March 10, 1946, the British leader told the secretary that he was pleased about the sending of the USS *Missouri* to the Mediterranean but bitterly disappointed that the ship was not accompanied by a substantial task force. Churchill claimed "that a gesture of power not fully implemented was almost less effective than no gesture at all."[26]

Forrestal directed that a statement to the American people be published on October 1, 1946, spelling out U.S. American naval policy concerning the presence of units of United States fleet in the Mediterranean. These units would continue to be there, first of all, to carry out American policy and diplomacy and, secondly, to provide experience, morale, and education to fleet personnel.[27]

Forrestal suffered a sad end. His tragic decline into mental illness and his suicidal fall during the early morning of May 22, 1949, at the age of fifty-two, from a window in the naval hospital at Bethesda, Maryland, have been the subjects of many books, articles, a play, and much talk.[28] This gifted, decent, and patriotic man was a victim of unknown forces that compelled him to destroy himself by overwork.

Frederick, Robert Tryon

After an illustrious military service, Maj. Gen. Robert T. Frederick retired from the army in March 1952. He was still a young man, in his midforties, and different accounts exist as to why he retired. One is that he was forced to leave Greece because of a political dispute with some of that nation's leftist government leaders. A more credible explanation of why Frederick was discharged from the U.S. Army was his medical record; he received many injuries. After his discharge, he was seriously injured in an automobile accident. Nevertheless, Frederick spent the two decades of his retirement in Palo Alto, California, often responding to requests for help from his former troops and attending to his family's financial and other interests.

This heroic man, who lived a life replete with adventure that included serving in the merchant marine and traveling to Australia at age fourteen, looked like a retired high school principal in his later years. He died on November 29, 1970, at the age of sixty-three. His decorations included two Distinguished Service Crosses, two Distinguished Service Medals, the Silver Star, two Legions of Merit, two Bronze Stars, the Air Medal, and eight Purple hearts.

Gilbert, Lawrence Edwin

Admiral Hewitt commended LST 282 commanding officer Lawrence E. Gilbert for his bravery in steering his burning ship from the LST 1012 and other nearby ships. He swam with burned hands and an injured shoulder to rescue two drowning crew members. Gilbert, Ferris C. Burke, and some others dove into the dangerous Mediterranean Sea to save drowning men. There were many others—also good swimmers—who did not take the risk.

Gilbert's first son, Terry, was born in Havana about a month before the LST 282 was blown up. Of course, he does not have any recollection of that period; and as he put it, probably his only thought in the summer of 1944 was where his next meal was coming from. He could only imagine what his mother and his grandparents went through when they first thought that Gilbert was missing in action. Eventually, he was sent to the Walter Reed Hospital for shoulder surgery and rehabilitation. Terry's mother told him that she moved to the hospital during that period to be with her husband. Terry and his sister Grace were left in Havana with their maternal grandparents. Many years later, Terry's mother told him that when she received the telegram from the navy about her husband being MIA, she went dry and could not breast-feed him. Terry wrote that "obviously, the stress at first was very intense for that to happen. I guess there was no long-lasting effect on me as there must have been alternatives to feed me."[30]

520

After he recovered from his injuries, Lawrence Gilbert was assigned to Havana as a naval attaché in 1946. A year or two later, he was reassigned to the U.S., and the family moved in with his parents. Norman Green, a former neighbor and friend, recalled that Gilbert and his wife missed life in Havana and that he never complained about that, his injuries, or anything else. He continued to receive physiotherapy from the Veterans Hospital in Fort Hamilton, New York. Despite shoulder injuries, he had a sunny disposition. His children Terry and Lauren, granddaughter Kirsten, sister Susie, neighbor Norman Green, and crew members Bob Beroth and Tom Aubut all stressed Larry Gilbert's positive outlook. A life-engaging personality, concern for others, and a rich sense of humor were his characteristic trademarks.

U.S. Navy Commodore R. G. Tobin, the port director of New York, wrote the following letter to Gilbert dated February 4, 1947:

> Dear Lieutenant Commander Gilbert:
>
> On the occasion of your release from active duty, I desire to express my appreciation of the services you have rendered to the Navy in time of war, and at this command.
>
> You were assigned to the Office of the Port Director as Ship Movements Officer from July 22, 1946 to Nov. 26, 1946. In this billet, you were the principal aide of the Operations Officer, and as such you supervised the administration and clerical work of all personnel attached to the Operations Office and furnished executive coordination of all the services provided by the Operations Office. Your duties included the screening and providing for the disposition and routing of all dispatch correspondence coming into or emanating from the Operations Office.
>
> At all times you displayed the marked qualities of sound judgment, dependability, resourcefulness and leadership which are in keeping with the high standards of the Naval Service. Your conscientious devotion to duty, and your initiative and energy, has added greatly to the successful performance of this command.
>
> It is my hope that you will meet with every success upon your return to civilian life.[31]

After the brief postwar period in New York, spent regaining his health, working in the insurance industry, and completing a year of New York

University School of Law at night, Gilbert returned with Grace and their children, Terry, Grace, Michael, and Lauren, to pre-Castro Cuba. He continued working as an insurance broker, representing, among others, the Rockefeller interests in Central and South America, and traveling extensively. Gilbert's Spanish was superb, and he mastered the argot of Havana's streets. Norman Green visited Gilbert in Havana and wrote that he was well-known and respected in the expatriate and business communities there. According to Green, "Larry was a formidable presence, genuine, all heart, must have been a fantastic leader."[32]

In New York, Gilbert had worked for Rollibec, a Rockefeller firm that was the main handler of the family's interests in Latin America. He structured insurance programs for properties in Venezuela and reported directly to Laurence Rockefeller. Gilbert also worked for Corroon & Black, an insurance brokerage firm that represented major U.S. corporations with overseas operations. The London insurance market was his main outlet for insurance placements, though he had some U.S. clients with operations in Taiwan.[33]

As a young child, Larry Gilbert was taught to swim and trained to be an expert seaman. His parents were members of a yacht club in Sheepshead Bay, Brooklyn, New York, near their home. In addition to swimming and seamanship skills, he taught himself meteorology. His granddaughter Kirsten, who lived with him and her grandmother Grace from age four to sixteen, wrote that Gilbert "took a liking to tracking hurricanes and projected where they would make landfalls."[34] He had used a map of the Caribbean to calculate that Hurricane Andrew would hit his retirement home in Homestead, Florida. He and his wife fled to Miami and escaped. As he had predicted, the hurricane ripped through their home when it hit. The house was rebuilt, and he lived there with Grace until his death.

Gilbert's reading interest included much more than meteorology and encompassed a great variety of fiction and nonfiction, periodicals, and newspapers. He was addicted to completing the *New York Times* crossword puzzles speedily. Kirsten believes that his record was fourteen minutes. She wrote, "He also absolutely loved to cook. Everything from Polish Stew to traditional Cuban Rice and Black Beans. He had a hibachi in a fireplace in the kitchen and a huge grill on our back patio. He used it as often as he could and especially loved to rotisserie poultry. My grandparents enjoyed entertaining and had many get-togethers. Jumping back a bit, I think I recall someone telling me that they won a jitterbug contest back in Havana at some point."[35]

In 1992, LST 282 crew member Marion E. "Jack" Bowers requested a statement for the Veterans Administration from his commanding officer, Lawrence Gilbert, concerning injuries he had suffered on August 15, 1944. The recommendation for approval of service-connected disability helped Bowers gain additional benefits. The letter that Gilbert wrote begins,

> This will certify that Marion E. Bowers was wounded in action on Aug. 15, 1944, while serving under my command during the invasion of southern France. A brief description of the action appears on the enclosed copy of a page from a book entitled *Battle Report—The Atlantic War*.
>
> As the Captain's "talker," Bowers was one of the people present with me at the conning station during General Quarters when the radio-controlled bomb struck our ship immediately forward of the wheelhouse and exploded below. An officer next to me was killed and Bowers and I were blown off the Signal Bridge.
>
> I learned the next day that he had been rescued, together with the ship's doctor, that he was aboard an Army Hospital Ship and had suffered neck, hip, and back injuries and burns. Subsequently he was transferred to the same Army General Hospital in Naples, Italy, where I was taken.[36]

In a letter dated October 5, 2002, Edward Yungck, a member of the LST 282 crew, asked his former ship's captain, Laurence Gilbert, for a favor. Yungck wrote, "I do not remember a specific date of my standing before you to explain why I was caught in the sack beyond the prescribed 'roll-out' time. The M.A. [master-at-arms] took names three mornings in a row. My guess would be that this occurred in July 1944. I was the last of four or five crewmembers to face you for judgment."[37]

The MA had reported Yungck for the offense of not getting out of the flat canvas contraption that was used for sleeping by enlisted men on LSTs. Yungck did not get up at the required time of 0600 hours. At the July 1944 disciplinary hearing before Captain Gilbert, Yungck said that he was exhausted because he had to do his work and that of "Pop Myers." He continued,

> Pop was about thirty-two years old and I was just nineteen years old. I liked Pop but he was a "goof off" and he had a way of having me do his work as well as mine. I was not getting

enough rest. Evenings I could hardly find time to write home and take a shower before "lights out." You understood but had punished those ahead of me, and so you could not let me off without punishment.

At that time I was a 2nd Class motor mechanic. You reduced me to third class and said that if I was not caught sack-in beyond roll-out time for two months that my 2nd Class rating would be reinstated.

We were sunk before the two months were up and all records were destroyed. As a result I never did get my second class rating back. I was discharged in July 1945 as third class.

If by chance you do remember (and only if you do remember), would you send me a short statement verifying my predicament. I would like to have the Navy Department issue me a new discharge paper showing me as a Motor Machinist Second Class.[38]

It's not known whether Gilbert answered Yungck's letter. Gilbert was ill when he received the letter; and he died on his birthday, November 13, 2002, at age eighty-five. He was survived by his sister Susan of New York, a sister-in-law of Columbia, South Carolina, two sons, two daughters, six grandchildren, and two great-grandchildren. On May 23, 2003, Gilbert and his wife were laid to rest at Arlington National Cemetery, following a military service and a brief sermon by a navy chaplain. Gilbert received a twenty-one-gun salute in recognition of his concern for his fellow human beings. It was a rainy day in Virginia, but that did not keep the many Gilbert friends and family away.[39]

Hall, Virginia

OSS agent Virginia Hall returned to France in March 1944, where she was instrumental in preparing other agents for the invasions of Normandy and southern France. She was awarded the Distinguished Service Cross by Gen. William Donovan in September 1945 and earned the distinction of being the only civilian woman to be awarded that honor.

An article in the *New York Times*, dated December 11, 2006 (p. A10) noted that Virginia Hall continued to keep secret her important role as an Allied spy in World War II until her death in 1982 at age seventy-eight. The British government could not fully honor her because it could not locate her. In 2005 Ms. Hall's biography by Judith L. Pearson, *Wolves at the Door: The True Story of America's First Female Spy* was published.

Hewitt, Henry Kent

By September 27, 1944, Admiral Hewitt's role in Dragoon was nearly completed. There was still a need for U.S. Navy vessels to sweep mines off the French coast and support the Allied campaign in Italy. Allied forces in France were moving toward the Italian border supported by a small Franco-American force of cruisers and destroyers.

As indicated previously, Secretary of the Navy James Forrestal informed President Truman in April 1945 that he believed that he owed Congress a continuance of the Pearl Harbor attack investigation. Dissatisfied with prior investigations, Forrestal called Admiral Hewitt back to the United States to undertake another inquiry of the disaster.[40] Promoted to four-star rank on August 1, 1945, Hewitt assumed command of U.S. Naval Forces in Europe, replacing Adm. Harold Stark. In September 1946, Hewitt was ordered to the Naval War College at Newport, Rhode Island, to serve in an advisory capacity. In April 1947, he was named representative of the chief of naval operations on the Military Staff Committee of the United Nations Security Council. Upon reaching the age of sixty-two, he was transferred to the retired list of the navy. He named his home in Orwell, Vermont, "Foretop."

Mary Kent Norton, Admiral Hewitt's younger daughter, wrote the following:

> Some memories of Dad include the trees he planted, and his wish to cooperate with various environmental efforts. His home of "Foretop" was named after the first sailing ship he served on as a midshipman during the summer cruises. He was captain of the foretop highest mast to furl and unfurl. I am not sure of my accuracy about this detail of the sails.
>
> He did love crossword puzzles and especially the double crossticks that came out in the years after his retirement. And he was a horseman. When he commanded the Naval Ammunition Depot in Bremerton, Washington, the marine battalion stationed there had a stable of horses for patrolling the fences of the ammunition depot. When the patrol was done for the day, my father would ride as often as possible, and I with him.

Dad and Admiral Lord Andrew Cunningham would ride
with the Spahi Regiment and their beautiful Arabian horses.
The cloak given to him by the Spahis is in the Smithsonian
collection in Washington, D.C. He would ride any chance he
could get![41]

Mrs. Norton also recalled that after the war, her father lectured naval
groups about the Mediterranean invasions.

Before retiring, Hewitt received many decorations and awards from
the governments of the United States, Great Britain, France, Russia,
Italy, Brazil, Ecuador, Tunisia, Greece, and the Netherlands. For the
invasion of North Africa, Hewitt received the Distinguished Service
Medal.[42] Through his care, foresight, and leadership, the forces he
transported were landed on November 8, 1942, on a hostile and
unknown shore, during hours of darkness, in a heavy sea, at the proper
time and places. In subsequent tactical action, he handled his forces
to prevent interference by hostile naval units with the landing of U.S.
forces as planned. His services contributed in marked degree to the
success of the enterprise.

Hewitt also received the Gold Star, which was awarded in lieu of
the second Navy Cross. This was earned for his role in the invasion of
Salerno and his extraordinary heroism against German forces. He was
in command of more than six hundred Allied men-of-war ships and
large landing craft responsible for the safe seaborne movements of the
Allied Fifth Army to the Gulf of Salerno, Admiral (then Vice Admiral)
Hewitt brought them skillfully through mine approach courses and
developed a sea frontier length of approximately fifty miles, despite
limited maneuvering space. As the second wave of Allied landing
boats reached the shore, strong German armored elements, deployed
along selected beaches, launched heavy counterattacks. They raked
the sands where Allied troops were trying to dig in; tanks rolled out of
the valley and charged; hostile artillery continually shelled ships in the
anchorages; enemy air forces attacked with high- and low-level bombings,
dive bombing and strafing, and with radio-controlled and rocket-glider
bombs. The entire operation was in jeopardy. Aware of the narrow
margin of success, Admiral Hewitt went ashore. He made a personal
reconnaissance of the situation and learned of the peril in flat coastal
plains where Allied formations were enveloped in low small detached
areas pounded by artillery fire from rugged high ground inland and

requested immediate air and sea reinforcements. His flagship was marked for destruction by the German High Command and pursued as a vital target, so he shifted his flag to a less important unit. His long-range naval guns blasted enemy formations without respite. German penetration was sealed off and rendered an immobile target for heavy strikes by Allied bombers, thus ensuring the success of the Salerno campaign. By his courage, initiative, and inspiring leadership under fire, Admiral Hewitt upheld the finest traditions of the United States Naval Service.

Hewitt was also awarded the Oak Leaf Cluster in lieu of a second Distinguished Service Medal for Operation Dragoon. This award was given for exceptionally meritorious service to the government in a position of great responsibility. As naval commander, Western Naval Task Force, from August 13 to September 27, 1944, Admiral Hewitt was responsible for all naval activities in connection with the invasion of southern France. Displaying great technical skill, efficiency, and a broad knowledge of the tremendous task entrusted with him, he coordinated all naval activities of both United States and Allied forces involved in the operation. His wide professional experience, sound judgment, and energy were of the greatest service in executing combined operations. His forces engaged in amphibious offensive operations with marked effectiveness and made an invaluable contribution to the success of the invasion of southern France. His initiative and tact enlisted the enthusiastic cooperation of all forces under his command. Hewitt died on September 15, 1972, at age eighty-five.

A reading of Admiral Hewitt's history convinces the reader that the pursuit of glory was not a concern to him. That is why his recognition only by historians is inadequate. Attempts to spread better and wider understanding of his achievements should be undertaken.

Kimmel, Samuel

Born on June 10, 1906, Samuel Kimmel received his law degree from the University of Baltimore School of Law in 1935. He served as the commanding officer of the LST 551 and was nearly forty when he returned to his family and law practice. After serving four years in World War II, he spent four more years on active duty during the Korean War. In 1960, Kimmel was promoted captain, U.S. Naval Reserve.

When Maryland Governor Spiro T. Agnew appointed him to the Baltimore County People's Court in May 1967, Judge Kimmel had been a practicing attorney for many years with diversified legal experience that included real estate, zoning, and criminal law. He was an active member of several professional and civic associations.[43]

Kimmel died on March 13, 1982, of Alzheimer's disease. His wife, Viola (née Pearce), died before him. Daughter June V. Webb and son Joseph S. Kimmel, five grandchildren, and a great-granddaughter survived him.[44]

Lewis, Spencer S.

Before his retirement from the navy in October 1947, he was promoted to vice admiral. During thirty-five years of service as a naval officer, he had earned many decorations for bravery, competence, and good judgment. These included the Navy Cross, two Distinguished Service Medals, and three Legions of Merit. Vice Admiral Lewis died on June 26, 1952, in Morocco at age sixty-four.

Murphy, Audie L.

The most decorated soldier in the history of the United States, Audie L. Murphy, received medals before and after August 15, 1944. For his courageous action during Operation Dragoon, when the Third Infantry Division landed and headed inland, Murphy was awarded the Distinguished Service Cross, the second highest U.S. Army medal for valor. Advancing a mile inland, he encountered a steep cliff that rose above the forested and bouldered landscape. The enemy had dug a large pillbox and had placed a coastal gun there. This installation had to be destroyed if Allied troops were to advance. Murphy and his men came under fire, and two were killed. All alone after his best friend, Lattie Tipton, was killed by a German who tricked Tipton into believing that he was about to surrender, Murphy threw a grenade at the enemy dugout and killed its occupants. He found the German machine-gun nest and the man who had betrayed Tipton, and he fired repeatedly. After his killing spree, Murphy calmed down, went downhill where Tipton lay, and wept.

After Tipton's death, Murphy volunteered for many dangerous assignments. By September 1944, his reputation for fearlessness and luck was established. He earned a battlefield commission to second lieutenant. He did not want to be an officer because he was embarrassed by his lack of a formal education, and he wanted to continue fighting the enemy with his men. However, on October 14, 1944, he was compelled to serve as a commissioned officer. He was told that he was a gentleman by an act of Congress and to shave and take a bath. He went back into the front lines of battle. Between August 1944 and January 1945, his hatred of the enemy propelled him to continue fighting, getting wounded three times, and earning the three highest United States military honors.

Life magazine was interested in publishing an account of Murphy's wartime exploits. However, the magazine cancelled printing the Murphy story and replaced it with a story about a lavish party financed by Elsa Maxwell. The site of this extravaganza was the Riviera, near the Dragoon landings, where Murphy had found many impoverished French people.[45]

Opportunities for enrichment through publication of his story and movie acting were available to Murphy when he returned to the United States, and he took them. He coauthored a book, *To Hell and Back*, which was published in February 1949. It received excellent reviews and was a big moneymaker. This success was enhanced by Murphy's career as a Hollywood actor. Though he made nearly fifty movies and was invited to many Beverly Hills parties, he did not enjoy himself.[46] Murphy did not drink, dance, or feel comfortable with Hollywood backbiting and phoniness, preferring friendships with unpretentious working people; and he avoided the social scene. His biographer, Don Graham, quoted Murphy as saying, "I have seen too many good men die to humble myself before people whom I do not respect."[46] He died in a private plane crash in 1971 at the age of forty-six.[47]

Nakano, Lane

Actor Lane Nakano, who starred in the 1951 film *Go for Broke!*, a movie about a Japanese-American soldier's experience during World War II, crystallized the historical experiences of war-torn Europe for many Nisei. Despite the fact that the U.S. government interned his family at a camp in Wyoming following the attack upon Pearl Harbor in December 1941, Nakano served the United States Armed Forces well in France and Italy. After the war, he gained fame as a singer, in addition to his acting. Another of his films, 1965's *Three Weeks of Love*, was also well received. Nakano died in May 2005 at age eighty.[48]

Noyes, Irving "Chet"

LST 494 commanding officer Irving Noyes was released from active duty in March 1946. As a civilian, he demonstrated a diversity of talents—starting and operating a forest products company, teaching high school and college students, founding and operating an educational skills center, and writing music and lyrics for musical plays.

Noyes had six children, many grandchildren, and great-grandchildren. He died on September 7, 2005 at the age of eighty-nine. He was a resident of Jefferson City, Tennessee.[49]

Patch, Alexander M. Jr.

Born into a family of military men, Alexander M. Patch's son, army captain Alexander M. Patch III (known as Mac), followed in his father's footsteps. He served in the army during World War II but was killed in action on October 22, 1944, at age twenty-four, while in an assault near the forest of Parroy, east of Luneville, France. Despite his father's plea that nothing special be done for his son, members of General Patch's staff contributed money for his coffin. Patch continued fulfilling his responsibilities until the end of the war in Europe, leading the Seventh Army through a difficult battle against the strongly defended Vosges and Meurthe line. Bitter cold, rain, and snow demoralized his men while benefiting the defending Germans. Patch tried to keep morale high. His grief-stricken wife received frequent letters from her husband, assuring her that he would take good care of himself. Patch mentioned that General Eisenhower had sent him a large Packard that contained a heater. Gen. Jacob Devers sent Patch a detailed letter of commendation stating that "there could be no greater commendation of your leadership of the Dragoon forces than the regained one-third of French soil in a month, the capture of more than 90,000 prisoners, the decimation of the enemy and the destruction and capture of masses of materials."[50] Indeed, by D plus 3, Patch's troops managed to advance more than five hundred miles into the interior of southern France.

Truman R. Strobridge and Bernard C. Nalty wrote that following the D-day Dragoon landing, the path that Patch took in his lightning dash northward at times mimicked the very same route taken by Napoleon on his north-bound march in 1815 when the emperor escaped from exile on the island of Elba.[51] It was Patch's careful assessment of the situation on the ground in southern France and subsequent successful execution of Allied plans that enabled Dragoon's success.[52]

Recognition of his superb leadership did not mean that General Patch was able to send money to his wife so that she could visit her recently widowed daughter-in-law and infant grandson. Adding to his financial straits was the need for Patch, as an army commander, to spend money before receiving his army paycheck. He was concerned about the welfare of his own soldiers and German prisoners of war. Upon witnessing a traffic accident at Grand Villers that resulted in injury to enemy prisoners, Patch stopped to telephone for doctors and ambulances.

As of August 1945, Patch was assigned to serve in Washington on a special committee known as the Patch Board, where he was responsible for examining the War Department's organization and how to best adapt it to postwar conditions.[53] He was the commander of the Fourth Army from June 1945 until his death on November 21, 1945. He died two days before his fifty-sixth birthday after succumbing to pneumonia, which he had suffered numerous times during the war. Patch had also been afflicted with malaria.[54] On November 23, 1945, the *New York Times* published an editorial page obituary of Patch. His congratulatory message to Seventh Army troops on their victory was reprinted. It read, "The courage and ability of the American citizen under arms needed no proof. You have been true to this most glorious tradition challenged by the Nazi braggart. You dropped your peaceful pursuits and beat him magnificently at his own bloody game. You have met him with the weapons of his own choosing and you have laid him low finally and completely." He was promoted to the rank of general posthumously in July 1954. Among his military distinctions are four Distinguished Service Medals, awards from the Belgian government (Grand Cross of the Order of Leopold II with Palm and the War Cross), and the British government (British Order of the Companion of the Bath [Military]). Another of his distinctions was witnessed by General de Lattre. Patch played "Poet and Peasant" on the accordion like a virtuoso.[55]

Pell, Isabel

Known as Fredericka during her four years of service in the French Resistance and also as the girl with the blonde lock of hair, Isabel Pell returned to Manhattan after World War II. In June 1952, while eating dinner with a friend at La Reine, an eastside Manhattan restaurant, Ms. Pell collapsed, fell off her chair, and died. The *New York Times* obituary of June 6, 1952, reported that Ms. Pell had received the French Legion of Honor for her courageous services in aiding French underground workers and outwitting the Gestapo. She repeatedly risked her life to safely guide American soldiers through German lines. After Ms. Pell returned to the United States, ill health prevented her from working. She was fifty-one when she died.[56]

Isabel Pell, in uniform, at extreme right. Major Geoffrey M. T. Jones, center. Colonel Kenneth Wickham, Chief of Staff of the First Airborne Task Force, standing between Jones and Pell.

Rol-Tanguy, Henri

One of the principal Communist agitators who organized resistance during the war and weakened the moral of German troops, Henri Rol-Tanguy led the final wave of resistance in Paris shortly before its liberation on August 25, 1944. Rol-Tanguy witnessed the German governor of Paris surrender to Allied forces. Following liberation, he served the French Army as a colonel and continued to fight through the final stages of the war. He retired from the army in 1962. From 1964 to 1987, he was a leader in the French Communist Party. In later years, he penned several works on the liberation of France, most notably *The French Communist Party in the Resistance* (1967) and *The Truth About the Liberation of Paris* (1971). For his courage, Rol-Tanguy received many military decorations, most notably the Croix de Guerre. He died on September 8, 2002, at age ninety-four.[57]

Truscott, Lucian K.

The opportunity for a new army command came on September 23, 1945, as a complete surprise to General Truscott and also placed him in an awkward position. That morning, Gen. Dwight Eisenhower offered him Gen. George S. Patton's command in Germany. Patton's reckless comments had ignited severe criticism. At a press conference, he had urged using former Nazi officials in the postwar German civil government. Patton had equated the German Nazi political era with the political struggles between Democrats and Republicans in the United States. To compound his political ineptness, Patton showed a lack of sympathy for the survivors of German concentration camps, criticizing their unkempt appearance.

General Truscott—had wanted to be of service as a good soldier and accept Eisenhower's offer, but as a close personal friend of Patton, he did not want to supersede him. However, since it was clear that Patton had to go, Truscott reasoned that Patton would rather have him as his replacement rather than someone who might be less sympathetic to a great fighting general who had contributed much to the Allied victory in Europe.

Truscott—relieved Patton as commanding general of the Third Army and Eastern Military District of Bavaria in early autumn of 1945. He studied background material and files and met with members of General Eisenhower's United States Forces European Theater staff and their civilian political advisors. In addition to Allied military responsibilities, Truscott was confronted with a variety of issues of postwar administration: feeding and sheltering German civilians and displaced persons, repatriation of Soviet nationals, and prosecution of war criminals.

On October 4, 1945, Truscott met with Patton and received a warm welcome; and over the next two days, they reviewed occupation procedures. Truscott—later described the occasion: "The only sign he [Patton] ever gave of the blow which he must have felt came when he said, 'Lucian, if you have no objection, I want to have a big formal ceremony and turn over the command to you with considerable fanfare and publicity. I don't want Ike or anyone else to get the idea that I am leaving here with my tail between my legs.' I assured him that I was perfectly willing to participate in any ceremony he wished to arrange. The occasion, which took place on Sunday, October 7, turned out to be quite simple, but very moving."[58]

Truscott—remained with the army until his retirement in July 1954. He died on September 12, 1965. Among his awards are the Distinguished Service Cross, the Distinguished Service Medal, and the Legion of Merit.

Pain, Death, and Rebirth

Priv. George Dorsey's *Stars and Stripes* article of August 25, 1944, "Marseilles: City of Violent Death," reported that six thousand people lost their lives by Allied air attacks. He witnessed four men walking fast around a street corner in Marseilles carrying a sagging white blanket containing an old man's dead body. He had entered the lobby of a nearby hotel, the Noailles, wearing a tricolor armband and was shot. The men who carried the victim's body hailed a Red Cross ambulance. Moaning inside the vehicle was a woman who was about to give birth and who was distraught that the dead man was a fellow traveller.[59]

The rebirth of the French people did not arrive free of pain or quickly after the invasion of southern France. It was not until the war in Europe ended that France was completely free of German occupation forces. There were many pockets along the Atlantic coast and in other parts of France that contained enemy troops. Before full liberation came, one hundred twenty-five thousand French people were at risk of being killed or maimed. We do not know the names or fates of the more than two hundred fifty thousand French people who actively assisted the Allies in defeating Nazi Germany, nor do we know the names of thousands of people who were killed as a result of their sacrifices to liberate France. Unnamed opponents of Nazism deserve to be remembered, as well as those mentioned in this book.[60] These people who did not receive recognition and/or medals for their bravery also helped bring about the rebirth of France. That was prophesied by American historians shortly before Operation Dragoon.

More than six decades have passed since the American Historical Association prepared a pamphlet entitled *Will the French Republic Live Again?* It was made available to the U.S. War Department for use by Army Information Education officers in conducting group discussions or forums as part of an education program. The pamphlet provides a prescient answer to the question raised by the Historical Association, "Will the French Republic live again?" It is worth reflection:

> When the German power is broken and France is again free, it is likely that the now silent voice of the repressed French at home will dominate the discussion and the decision over the nation's political future. No government which does not have the support of the French people can long rule France—except by the use of machine guns. The traditions of popular government are too strong to allow disregard of the people's will.[61]

Notes

CHAPTER 1: RETURN TO CAP DRAMMONT

1. Paul Auphan and Jacques Mordal, *The French Navy in World War II*, trans. A. C. J. Sabalot (Annapolis, MD: U.S. Naval Institute, 1957), 352.
2. Alan F. Wilt, *The French Riviera Campaign of August 1944* (Carbondale, IL: Southern Illinois University Press, 1981), 164.
3. John Keegan, *The Second World War* (New York: Penguin Books, 1989), 356.
4. Cap Drammont has been spelled in different ways by different writers, for example, "Cape Dramont," "Le Dramont," etc.
5. American Battle Monuments Commission, *Rhone American Cemetery and Memorial*, 9.

CHAPTER 2: FRANCE BEFORE AND AFTER JUNE 1940

1. A. J. Toynbee, *Survey of International Affairs, 1931* (London: Royal Institute of International Affairs, 1932), 22.

2. Vera Micheles Dean, "Europe under Nazi Rule," *Foreign Policy Reports,* 15 Oct. 1940, 190.

3. Philip Ouston, *France in the Twentieth Century* (New York: Praeger, 1972), 192.

4. "Historical Atlas: Population of Germany," *http://www.tacitus.nu/ historicalatlas/population/germany.htm.*

5. Peter Duignan and L. H. Gann, *World War II in Europe: Causes and Consequences* (Palo Alto, CA: Stanford University, Hoover Institution on War and Peace, 1995), 7.

6. Hans Schmidt, "Germany—The Voice from Within," *Harper's,* June 1940, 96.

7. Ernest R. May, *Strange Victory: Hitler's Conquest of France* (New York: Hill and Wang, 2000), 7.

8. Peter F. Drucker, "Germany's Plans for Europe," *Harper's,* November 1940, 597.

9. Douglas Martin, "Lisa Fittko, 95, Helped Rescue Many Who Fled the Nazis," *New York Times,* 21 Mar. 2005, B7.

10. Ibid.

11. A. J. Liebling, "Letter from Paris," *New Yorker,* 8 June 1940, 38.

12. Jenny Vaughan, *http://www.channel14.com/history/microsites/H/history/c-d/degaulle.*

13. Auphan and Mordal, 71.

14. Auphan and Mordal, 73.

15. Robert de Saint Jean, "The Failure of France," *Harper's,* October 1940, 449. Emphasis in the original.

16. Duignan and Gann, 13.

17. Liebling, *The New Yorker War Pieces* (Albuquerque, NM: University of New Mexico Press, 1994), 38. A biographical statement concerning Henry L. Stimson (1874-1950) is available at *http://www.spartacus.schoolnet. co.uk/USAstimson.htm.* The Department of the Navy-Naval Historical Center at 805 Kidder Breese SE, Washington Navy Yard, Washington, D.C. 20374-5060 has provided a biographical statement of Frank Knox at *http://www.history.navy.mil/photos/pers-us/uspers-k/f-knox.htm.*

18. "France Faces the Attack," *Economist,* 18 May 1940, 898.

19. Keegan, 60.

20. Liebling, "Paris Postscript," in *The New Yorker War Pieces* (3-10 Aug. 1940), 41, 42, 49.

21. Duignan and Gann, 13.

22. Duncan H. Hall, *North American Supply* (London: Her Majesty's Stationery Office, 1955), 133.

23. William L. Shirer, *Collapse of the Third Republic: An Inquiry into the Fall of France in 1940* (New York: Simon & Schuster, 1969). Shirer wrote on page 975, "I do not find it [Hart's statement] in the French edition."

24. May, 248, 249.

25. May, 5, 6.

26. *Time,* 3 June 1940, 22.

27. Ibid.

28. Ibid.

29. George C. Marshall, *The Winning of the War in Europe and the Pacific* (Washington, DC: U.S. War Department, 1945), 2.

30. Henry Rousso, *The Vichy Syndrome: History and Memory in France, 1944,* trans. Arthur Gold Hammer (Cambridge, MA: Harvard University Press, 1991), 6.

31. Peter Leslie, *The Liberation of the Riviera: The Resistance to the Nazis in the South of France and the Story of Its Heroic Leader, Ange-Marie Miniconi* (New York: Wyndham Books, 1980), 57.

32. Adlai E. Stevenson II, "Different Man, Different Moment," *New York Times,* 7 Feb. 2003, A25.

33. Robert Aron, *France Reborn: The History of the Liberation, June 1944-May 1945* (New York: Charles Scribner's Sons, 1964), 465.

34. Translated as "We have been sold" or "We have sold ourselves."

35. Kay Boyle, "Defeat," *New Yorker,* 17 May 1940.

36. Pierre Laval was premier of the Vichy government and had a notorious record as a political opportunist.

37. H. Kent Hewitt, Introduction to *The French Navy in World War II,* by Auphan and Mordal (Annapolis, MD: U.S. Naval Institute, 1958), ix-x.

38. From report by Capt. P. A. P. Ortoli, commander of the *Emile Bertin,* in Admiral Hewitt's Library of Congress Document Archives, 30 Sept. 1944, 13.

39. Robert Murphy, *Diplomat among Warriors* (Garden City, NY: Doubleday, 1964), 54.

40. William D. Leahy, *I Was There: The Personal Story of the Chief of Staff to Presidents Roosevelt and Truman* (New York: McGraw Hill, 1950), 450.

41. Julian Jackson, *France: The Dark Years, 1940-1944* (New York: Oxford Press, 2001), 178; Leahy, 8.

42. Jackson, 223.

43. Hewitt, *Oral History* (New York: Butler Library, Columbia University Press, 1961), 478.

44. Warren Kimball, ed., *Churchill and Roosevelt: The Complete Correspondence,* vol. 2, *Alliance Forged November 1942-February 1944* (New York: Princeton University Press, 1984), 5.

45. Murphy, 62.

46. Edward L. Bimberg, *The Moroccan Goums: Tribal Warriors in a Modern War* (Westport, CT: Greenwood Press, 1991), 21.

47. Robert O. Paxton, *Parades and Politics at Vichy: The French Officer Corps under Marshal Pétain* (Princeton: Princeton University Press, 1966), 43-54.

48. Philippe Burrin, *Living with Defeat: France under German Occupation, 1940-1944* (London: Arnold, 1966). American title: *France under the Germans: Collaboration and Compromise* (New York: New Press, 1996), 73.

49. Julian G. Hurstfield, *America and the French Nation, 1939-1945* (Chapel Hill: University of North Carolina Press, 1986), 31-66. The book describes in detail the complex relationship between the United States and the Vichy government.

50. David Schoenbrun, *The Three Lives of Charles de Gaulle* (New York: Athenaeum, 1966), 123.

51. Leahy, 24-26.

52. On an early June evening in 1954, the author was one of thousands of people attending Fordham University's commencement exercise. We listened to a lengthy statement introducing one of the recipients of an honorary degree, who was also the featured speaker. The author was there at Rosehill in the Bronx to get a law degree. The sixty-year-old honoree that evening was a career diplomat, counsel general in Paris from 1930-36, counselor in the Paris Embassy in 1940, chief civil affairs officer, American Forces Headquarters, the president's special representative in North Africa 1942-43, and American representative to the Italian Advisory Council 1943-44. It is highly unlikely that in 1944 he knew anything about LST 1012, its crew, and its journeys; but the author now realizes that this diplomat played an important role in making the Mediterranean area safer for Allied soldiers, sailors, and airmen. More than fifty years after that 1954 commencement, he regrets that he was ignorant of the diplomat's efforts during World War II. The author wishes that he had thanked Ambassador Murphy.

53. Jackson, 36.

54. Schoenbrun, op. cit.

55. Jackson, 36.

56. Attaché's report on 27 Sept. 1939, serial no. 521, file 800.

57. Hurstfield, op. cit.

58. Gaddis Smith, *American Diplomacy during the Second World War, 1941-1945* (New York: John Wiley and Sons, 1965), 12.

59. Chester Wilmot, *The Struggle for Europe* (New York: Harper, 1952), 143.

CHAPTER 3: UNITED STATES—BEFORE AND AFTER PEARL HARBOR

1. These accounts reveal a good conclusion. The sullying of Stark's reputation by his successor as chief of naval operations, Fleet Adm. Ernest J. King, was repudiated later by the foul-tempered King and by others who knew the full story. Stark received a host of American and foreign commendations and enjoyed a happy and long retirement.

2. President Roosevelt's letter of 14 July 1943 to Navy Secretary Frank Knox, obtained from the National Archives, microfiche, March 2002.

3. Navy Secretary Frank Knox's memo to the director of U.S. Naval Intelligence, Rear Adm. H. C. Train, obtained from the National Archives, microfiche, March 2002.

4. Wyman H. Packard, *A Century of U.S. Naval Intelligence* (Washington, DC: Office of Naval Intelligence and the Naval Historical Center, 1996), 1.

5. "Selected Naval Attaché Reports Relating to the World Crisis, 1937-1943," Microfilm Publications M1975, the National Archives and Record Service General Services Administration (Washington, 1974). Naval Attaché Reports: a) U.S. Naval Attaché Report I-I-36 on German-American relations, 12 Sept. 1938; b) U.S. Naval Attaché Report DIS (c) "Axis People Believe United States Will Not Enter War unless Directly Threatened," May 1941; c) U.S. Naval Attaché Report DIS (c) "Sabotage Reported Planned Attack against United States Army; American Codes Believed to Have Been Broken," June 1941; d) U.S. Naval Attaché Report K-2-76. This report says that Mussolini and Hitler have planned and ordered the murdering of Roosevelt in addition to sabotage activities especially in New York, 16 Jan. 1941.

   Joseph E. Persico, *Roosevelt's Secret War: FDR and WWII Espionage* (New York: Random House, 2001), 7-9. Franklin Delano Roosevelt's reliance on naval intelligence started when he was assistant secretary of the United States Navy during World War I.

6. "Selected Naval Attaché Reports Relating to the World Crisis, 1937-1943," U.S. Naval Attaché Report K-2-76, translation of unsigned note left at American Consulate, Rome, 16 Jan. 1941. See also U.S. Naval Attaché Report DIS (c), which reported intention to sabotage British warships repairing in New York, July 1941.

7. From U.S. Naval Attaché Tokyo Report, 22 Sept. 1941.

8. François Genoud, ed., *The Testament of Adolf Hitler, The Hitler-Borman Documents, February-April 1945* (London: Cassell, 1961), 68.

9. Gerhard Weinberg, *World in Balance* (Hanover: University of New England, 1981), 60; quoting Hitler's comments to Japanese diplomat Matsuoka

Yosuke, 4 Apr. 1940, in *Documents on German Foreign Policy 1918-1945*, no. 266; see also Trevor Roper, *Hitler's Table Talk*, 5 Jan. 1942, 181.

10. Geoffrey P. Megargee, *Inside Hitler's High Command* (Lawrence, KA: University Press of Kansas, 2000), 137.

11. Ian Kershaw, *Hitler: 1936-1945* (New York: W. W. Norton, 2000), 444-45

12. From U.S. Naval Attaché Tokyo Report, 22 Sept. 1941.

13. Eric Larrabee, *Commander in Chief* (Cambridge, MA: Harper & Row, 1987), 115.

14. Dwight D. Eisenhower, *Crusade in Europe* (New York: Doubleday, 1948), 2.

15. See U.S. Naval Attaché Report N-2-97, "Rear Admiral Matsunaga Claims United States Is Weak in Orient," 22 Sept. 1941. Matsunaga said that the Allied powers had only three hundred thousand army troops, one hundred fifty warships, and one thousand planes in the Far East. He also claimed that the inferior quality of American planes precluded their reaching Japan from Kamchatka or the Philippines.

16. Mario Toscano, "Machiavelli Views World War II Intelligence," *The International Journal of Intelligence and Counterintelligence* 1, no. 3 (1986): 45.

17. Toscano, 5.

18. Copy of letter dated 27 Nov. 1936 was obtained from the Library of Congress, Manuscript Division.

19. Copy of letter dated 10 Dec. 1936 was obtained from the Library of Congress, Manuscript Division.

20. Copy of letter dated 11 Sept. 1940 was obtained from the Library of Congress, Manuscript Division.

21. Ibid., 2.

22. Rear Adm. H. Kent Hewitt to Rear Adm. W. S. Anderson, 3.

23. According to Bruce Schulman of the *New York Times*, "In 1937, Roosevelt traveled to Chicago, a hotbed of isolationism to deliver his famous 'Quarantine the Aggressor' speech. War is a contagion, he warned, isolation or neutrality could not protect the United States. There must be positive endeavors to preserve peace." From Schulman's "Building National Resolve by Talking about It," *New York Times*, 15 Sept. 2002, "News of the Week," 5.

24. I. C. B. Dear and M. R. D. Foot, eds., *The Oxford Companion of World War II*. (New York: Oxford University, 1995), 871, 872.

25. Gary Cohen, "The Keystone Kommandos," *Atlantic Monthly*, February 2002, 46-59.

26. The author, at age fifteen in 1940, was fascinated with Willkie; and this fascination still persists.

27. For information about Knox, visit *http://www.answers.com/topic/frank-knox.*

28. Dear and Foot, 1066.

29. Douglas Porch, *The Path to Victory: The Mediterranean Theater in World War II* (New York: Farrar, Straus and Giroux, 2004), 208.

30. Winston S. Churchill, *The Second World War,* vol. 2, *Their Finest Hour* (London: Cassell, 1949), 23.

31. See *The Mediterranean and the Middle East,* vol. 2 (London: Her Majesty's Stationery Office, 1956), 233.

32. Robert H. Connery, *The Navy and Industrial Mobilization in World War II* (Princeton: Princeton University Press, 1951), 107.

33. Porch, 146.

34. Porch, 663, 676.

35. Maurice Barber, letter, "Joy in Europe," *Time,* 8 Jan. 1941.

36. Dear and Foot, 65.

37. U.S. Army, *Mobilization: The U.S. Army in World War II—The 50th Anniversary* (Washington, DC: Government Printing Office, 1995), 9-10.

38. From a copy of the admiral's prepublished *Memoirs* provided to the author by the Hewitt family in September 2001.

39. Ibid.

40. Dear and Foot, 47. See also Kenneth S. Davis, *FDR: The War President, 1940-1943* (New York: Random House, 2000); W. Prange, *At Dawn We Slept* (New York: McGraw Hill, 1981); and R. Wohlstetter, *Pearl Harbor: Warning and Decision* (Larkspur, CO: Pinetree Press, 1962).

41. Rebecca R. Raines, *Getting the Message Through: A Branch History of the U.S. Army Signal Corps* (Washington, DC: U.S. Army Center of Military History, 1996), 243.

42. Raines, 244.

43. Hewitt, *Memoirs,* 136-138.

44. Henry C. Clausen and Bruce Lee, *Pearl Harbor: Final Judgement* (New York: Crown Publishers, 1992), 51.

45. Clausen and Lee, 50.

46. Annual report of the comptroller general of the United States for the fiscal year ended 30 June 1942, 105-106.

47. Ibid., 111-112.

48. Annual report of the comptroller general of the United States for the fiscal year ended 30 June 1943, 79. The *Progressive* magazine of 28 Aug. 1944 noted the following: "Overcharge: Government officials asserted last week that American railroads have overcharged the Government $50,000,000 for hauling war freight in 1943."

49. Duncan S. Ballantine, *U.S. Naval Logistics in the Second World War* (Princeton: Princeton University Press, 1947), 89.

50. William Harlan Hale, "After Pearl Harbor," *New Republic,* 15 Dec. 1941, 816.

51. Benjamin Mitchell Simpson III, *Admiral Harold R. Stark: Architect of Victory, 1939-1945* (Columbia, SC: University of South Carolina Press, 1989), 229, vii-xii.

52. Simpson, "Political Consultations between the United States and the French National Committee, 1942-1943: The Embassy of Admiral Harold R. Stark, USN" (dissertation, Tufts University, 15 Apr. 1968), 1-4.

53. Ibid., 162, 163, 230, 241.

54. A. Timothy Warnock, *Air Power versus U-boats: Confronting Hitler's Submarine Menace in the European Theater* (Washington, DC: Air Force History and Museums Program, 1999), 1.

55. Warnock, 2.

56. Kathleen Broome Williams, *Secret Weapon: U.S. Frequency Direction Finding in the Battle of the Atlantic* (Annapolis, MD: Naval Institute Press, 1996), 232.

57. William Hackmann, *Seek and Destroy: Sonar Anti-Submarine Warfare and the Royal Navy* (London: Her Majesty's Stationery Office, 1984), 238.

58. Kathleen Broome Williams, 5.

59. Alan L. Gropman, *Mobilizing U.S. Industry in World War II: Myth and Reality* (Washington, DC: Institute for National Strategic Studies, National Defense University, 1996). This study is identified as McNair Paper 50.

60. Dear and Foot, 32, 33.

61. Thomas B. Buell, *Master of Sea Power: A Biography of Fleet Admiral Ernest J. King* (Boston: Little, Brown, 1980), 213.

62. Hewitt, *Memoirs,* 38.

63. Ibid.

64. For example, the author crossed the Atlantic Ocean on LST 1012 in the spring of 1944 and in the summer of 1945 was on the way toward the Pacific Ocean on a Landing Ship Dry Dock, or LSD. This LSD carried small landing vessels that were to be used for short shore-to-shore trips. Other types of landing craft included LBW (Landing Barge, Water) and LCA (Landing Craft, Assault).

65. See Jerry F. Strahan, *Andrew Jackson Higgins and the Boats That Won World War II* (Baton Rouge, LA: Louisiana State University Press, 1994).

66. Strahan, 172.

67. *Ships' Data, U.S. Naval Vessels,* vol. 2, *Mine Vessels (LESS CM & DM), Patrol Vessels, Landing Ships and Craft,* Bureau of Ships, Navy Department (Washington, DC: United States Government Printing Office, 1946), 168-9, 188.

68. Claude Miller, "LST," *LST Scuttlebutt,* January-February 2003, 23.

CHAPTER 4: THE STRUGGLE FOR THE MEDITERRANEAN

1. "Our War," *New Republic,* 15 Dec. 1941, 812.
2. For a discussion of the Mediterranean as an Axis theater, see George F. Howe's *The Mediterranean Theater of Operations: Northwest Africa, Seizing the Initiative in the West* (Washington, DC: U.S. Army Center of Military History, 2001), 3-9.
3. Evelyn Cherpak, ed., *The Memoirs of Admiral H. Kent Hewitt* (Newport, RI: Naval War College, 2004), 121.
4. E. B. Potter and Chester W. Nimitz, eds., *The Great Sea War: The Dramatic Story of Naval Action in World War II* (New York: Branhall House, 1960), 39-68.
5. Charles R. Anderson, *Algeria-French Morocco* (Washington, DC: U.S. Army Center of Military History, 1993), 15.
6. See Samuel E. Morison's *History of the United States Naval Operations in World War II,* vol. 2, *Operations in North African Waters: October 1942-June 1943* (Urbana, IL: University of Illinois Press, 2001), 184-87.
7. Pulitzer Prize winner Rick Atkinson portrays Murphy's role in the Operation Torch invasion. See Atkinson's *An Army at Dawn: The War in North Africa, 1942-1943* (New York: Henry Holt, 2003), 251, 252, 531. An example of Ambassador Murphy's advocacy can be found in the appendix section.
8. Morison, 25. Morison cites Cmdr. L. A. Bachman's "Intelligence for Amphibious Operations," *ONI Weekly Bulletin* 2, 3 Mar. 1943, 605-610; lecture by Col. L. B. Ely, USA, on the same subject.
9. David W. Hogan Jr., *U.S. Army Special Operations in World War II* (Washington, DC: U.S. Army Center of Military History, 1992), 29.
10. James Dougherty, *The Politics of Wartime Aid: American Economic Assistance to France and French Northwest Africa, 1940-1946* (Westport, CT: Greenwood Press, 1978), 4 and 125.
11. Monro MacCloskey, *Rearming the French in World War II* (New York: Richard Rosen Press, 1972), 180.
12. Approximately twenty thousand of these were refugees from mainland France; see MacCloskey, 181.
13. Marcel Vigneras, *The U.S. Army in WWII: Rearming the French* (Washington, DC: U.S. Government Printing Office, 1958), 400.
14. MacCloskey, 181.
15. Morison, 4. Professor Morison was a rear admiral in the U.S. Naval Reserve, as well as a friend of President Roosevelt, Fleet Adm. William D. Leahy, and Adm. H. Kent Hewitt.
16. William Langer, *Our Vichy Gamble* (New York: Alfred A. Knopf, 1947), 290.

17. Arthur L. Funk, *Charles de Gaulle: The Crucial Years, 1943-1944* (Norman, OK: University of Oklahoma Press, 1959), 34.

18. Buell, 213. Admiral King was not alone in opposing the invasion of North Africa. The American Joint Chiefs of Staff advised President Roosevelt to concentrate on beating the Japanese; see Morison's *Operations in North African Waters: October 1942-June 1943* (Urbana and Chicago: University of Illinois Press, 2001), 14.

19. Dear and Foot, 814.

20. Thaddeus J. Tuleja, "Admiral H. Kent Hewitt," in *Men of War: Great Naval Leaders of World War II*, ed. Stephen Howarth (New York: St. Martin's Press, 1992), 319-20; letter from Admiral Hewitt; and Lt. Cmdr. R. G. Steere's report of 7 Nov. 1942. Tuleja's biographical profile of Admiral Hewitt provides another version of the North African invasion weather dilemma. According to Tuleja, two days before D-day, Hewitt received disturbing weather reports. Waves of fifteen feet were rolling along the coast of Morocco. The contingency plan in the event of bad weather was for Hewitt to lead his fleet to Gibraltar. Patton was to land his troops and invade the Mediterranean. Lt. Cmdr. Richard C. Steere, Hewitt's staff aerologist, climbed to the flag bridge at night on the day before the invasion, 8 Nov. 1942. Steere awoke Hewitt, who was trying to get some rest on a cot at his command post. The aerologist predicted that sea conditions would moderate for the landings. The admiral's dilemma was acute; should he trust Steere's prediction or the dire earlier weather reports from Washington and London? Hewitt's letter of 11 Aug. 1961, to the director of Naval History, Rear Adm. E. M. Ellen, provides the answer.

21. WNTF is the Western Naval Task Force.

22. Murphy, 141. Murphy's defense of the Darlan-Clark agreement appears in the appendix of this book.

23. Charles de Gaulle, *The War Memoirs of Charles de Gaulle: Unity, 1941-1944* vol. 2 (New York: Simon & Schuster, 1959), 241.

24. Dougherty, 7.

25. Raines, 292-93.

26. Hewitt, "Torch Operation Comments and Recommendations," Commander Amphibious Force, U.S. Atlantic Fleet, serial 00299, 22 Dec. 1942, Appendix C, 16.

27. Ibid., 4.

28. Ibid., 5.

29. Ibid., 29.

30. Author's comment: From my observation in the LST 1012 where I was a short distance from our radar room during Operation Dragoon, I can attest to the fact that no radar problems were encountered on our ship during this invasion.

31. Hewitt, Appendix C, 14.

32. Ibid., 15.

33. Ibid.

34. Ibid., 19.

35. Ibid., 15.

36. Williamson Murray, *Strategy for Defeat: The Luftwaffe, 1933-1945* (Maxwell Air Force Base, AL: Air University Press, 1983), 160.

37. Murray, 163.

38. Tuleja, 321.

39. George F. Howe, *Northwest Africa: Seizing the Initiative in the West,* U.S. Army in World War II: The Mediterranean Theater of Operations (Washington, DC: U.S. Army Center of Military History, 2001), 173.

40. Edward T. Russell and Robert M. Johnson, *Africa to the Alps: The Army Air Forces in the Mediterranean Theater* (Washington, DC: Air Force History and Museums Program, 1995), 33.

41. From Library of Congress—Manuscript Collection.

42. Wilmot, 10.

43. *ONI Weekly Bulletin,* 8 Mar. 1944, 748-49.

44. Stratagem No. 56, "Hush Most Secret," 17 Jan. 1943; cabinet papers, 120/76; quotes by Martin Gilbert, *Winston Churchill,* vol. 7, *Road to Victory* (Boston: Houghton Mifflin, 1986), 297.

45. For more, see Porch's *Path to Victory,* 419.

46. C. J. Molony, F. C. Flynn, H. L. Davies, and T. P. Gleve, *The Mediterranean and the Middle East,* vol. 5, *The Campaign in Sicily and Italy* (London: Her Majesty's Stationery Office, 1973), 121.

47. Potter and Nimitz, 133.

48. Ibid., 135.

49. U.S. Naval Attaché Report D-2-85 entitled "Brief Resumé of Italian Naval Strength," 30 Sept. 1941, 24, reported the following: "Low Italian naval morale; misplaced belief in submarine strength; lack of cooperation between air and naval units, and lack of port aircraft defense detected." Six weeks later, another U.S. Naval Attaché Report, D-2-87, entitled "Relations between Army and Fascist Party," 15 Nov. 1941, 24, contained evidence of growing weaknesses of Italy's Fascist party, such as refusal of the Italian Regular Army officers to join the party and compulsion of reserve officers to do so.

50. For a comprehensive discussion of the Allied landing operations of Sicily, see Molony et al., *The Mediterranean and Middle East,* 1-76.

51. Potter and Nimitz, 138.

52. Bernard Fergusson, *The Watery Maze: The Story of Combined Operations* (New York: Holt, Rhinehart & Winston, 1961), 245.

53. Potter and Nimitz, 140.

54. See Potter and Nimitz map, p. 141. Among Admiral Hewitt's papers deposited in the Library of Congress are identification photos of Allied aircraft.

55. Potter and Nimitz, 143, 149.

56. Robert Jagers, *Whales of World War II: Military Life of Robert Jagers, June 1942 to October 1945* (Farmington, MI: Robert Jagers, 2003), 54.

57. Charles Hakl and Charles Muscatine, crew members of LST 335, "A History of the USS 335 World War II—Sicily, Salerno, Normandy," *LST Scuttlebutt,* May-June 2003, 54. The procedural steps used in beaching an LST may be of interest: (1) when the ship was about two and a half lengths from the beach (or about 820 feet), the command was given to let the anchor go; (2) when the anchor was grounded, the cable winch was allowed to run free; (3) during the beaching and unloading, the ship had to be held at a right angle to the beach; (4) the bow of the ship had to be kept on the beach at all times; (5) this required the anchor cable to be slack and the ship continually driven into a sandy beach; (6) it was important to keep enough tension to avoid letting the stern swing freely. The procedure had to be completed expeditiously so that the ship could leave the beach before it became vulnerable to enemy attack.

58. George H. Sweet, with Donald H. Sweet, *Lightning Strikes: A Story of Amphibious Actions during World War II: The Adventures of LST 358 in the Mediterranean Sea during World War II* (Ridgewood, NJ: DoGo Publishing, 2001), iv-36.

59. Ibid.

60. Ibid.

61. From Fleet Adm. Ernest J. King's *U.S. Navy at War, 1941-1945: Official Report to Secretary of Navy* (Washington, DC: U.S. Government Printing Office, 1946), 294-95.

62. Hewitt, "Torch Operation Comments and Recommendations," serial 00299, 19, obtained by the author from the Office of Naval Records and Library.

63. Porch, 485, 486.

64. Hewitt, *The Allied Navies at Salerno: U.S. Naval Proceedings,* September 1953, 96.

65. Truscott, L. K. Jr., *Command Missions: A Personal Story* (New York: E. P. Dutton, 1951), 249.

66. Fergusson, 255.

67. Eisenhower, 187.

68. Ibid.

69. Wilmot, 121.

70. Wilmot, 137, 135.

71. Potter and Nimitz, 150.

72. Sweet and Sweet, iv-37, iv-38.

73. Raines, 295.

74. *ONI Weekly,* July 23, 1943, 2085. Additional descriptions of the Sicilian and Salerno invasions are to be found in *The Oxford Companion to World War II* edited by I. C. B. Dear and M. R. D. Foot (New York: Oxford University Press, 1995), 945, 1001-1005.

CHAPTER 5: THE LAST AND BEST

1. Prepared by Staff Group 3D under the direction of Maj. Duncan Stewart, submitted to the Combat Studies Institute, U.S. Army Command and General Staff College, Ft. Leavenworth, KS, May 1984, 4.
2. Norman Polmar and Thomas B. Allen, *World War II: The Encyclopedia of the War Years 1941-1945* (New York: Random House, 1996), 2.
3. Leahy, 215.
4. Eisenhower, 282.
5. Forrest C. Pogue, *United States Army in World War II: The European Theatre of Operations* (Washington, DC: U.S. Army Office of Military History, 1954), 228.
6. James Parton, *Air Force Spoken Here: General Ira Eaker and the Command of the Air* (Bethesda, MD: Adler & Adler, 1986), 415.
7. James W. Boddie Jr., *Ammunition Support for Operation Dragoon, the Invasion of Southern France—Could We Do It Today?* (Carlisle Barracks, PA: U.S. Army War College, 1987), 2, 3.
8. Roberts to Handy, "What Shall We Do about Anvil?" memorandum, 23 Mar. 1944; book 16, extract quoted in Maurice Matloff, "The Anvil Decision: Crossroads of Strategy," in *Command Decisions* (Washington, DC: U.S. Army Center of Military History, 1960), 396.
9. De Gaulle, 2.
10. Sweet, iii-22.
11. Carl R. Morin Jr., "The Strategic Consideration of the Allied Invasion of Southern France, 1944" (master's thesis, University of Florida, 1968), 63-77.
12. Morison, 228.
13. Ibid., 230.
14. Thomas M. Barker, "The Ljubljana Gap Strategy: Alternative to Anvil/Dragoon or Fantasy?" *Journal of Military History* 56, no. 1 (1992): 57-85.
15. Matloff, "The Anvil Decision," 393.
16. Field Marshall Lord Alanbrooke, *War Diaries, 1939-1945,* eds. Alex Danchev and Daniel Tudman (London: Weidenfeld and Nicolson, 2001), 450, 515, 521, 532.
17. Morison, *History of United States Naval Operations in World War II,* vol. 2, *The Invasion of France and Germany, 1944-1945* (Boston: Little, Brown, 1975), 225-230.
18. Christopher Hitchens, "The Medals of His Defeats," *Atlantic Monthly,* April 2002, 129.
19. Morin, 105.

20. Morin's commentary is worth notice because of its novelty.

21. Morin, 106-09.

22. Pogue, 224.

23. Hewitt, "Planning Operation Anvil-Dragoon," *United States Naval Institute Proceedings* 80, no. 7 (1954): 745.

24. Hewitt, 911.

CHAPTER 6: IT HAPPENS

1. See radiogram from CINC to commanding general, Seventh Army, ref. no. 16248, 19 Dec. 1943. From Seventh Army Plan as edited by the author.
2. AFHQ to Gen. Mark S. Clark, 1 Jan. 1944.
3. MC 446-E, ref. no. 21956, Commanding General, Seventh Army from CINC, 31 Dec. 1943.
4. Stanley P. Hirshon, *General Patton: A Soldier's Story* (New York: HarperCollins, 2002), 269.
5. William K. Wyant, *Sandy Patch: A Biography of Lt. Gen. Alexander M. Patch* (New York: Praeger, 1991), 22. We are in William Wyant's debt for a first-rate description of Gen. Alexander Patch's character and personality.
6. Porch, 49.
7. Historical Record Anvil, Summary of Events, 18 Jan. 1944.
8. Force 163 was the team responsible for planning Anvil/Dragoon.
9. Historical Record Anvil, Summary of Events, 10 Feb. 1944.
10. AFHQ to General Clark, 28 Feb. 1944.
11. Hirshon, 432.
12. Wyant, 2. See also Strobridge, Truman, and Nalty, "From the South Pacific to the Brenner Pass: General Alexander M. Patch," *Military Review,* June 1981, 47.
13. Williamson Murray and Allan R. Millett, *A War To Be Won: Fighting the Second World War* (Cambridge, MA: Harvard University Press, 2000), 300.
14. Porch, 109-110, 117, 474, 509.
15. Message from General Wilson to General Eisenhower, no. B12995, 19 June 1944.
16. North African Theater of Operations-USA (NATOUSA).
17. Richard C. Fattig, "Reprisal: The German Army and the Execution of Hostages during the Second World War" (dissertation, University of California at San Diego, 1980), 106.
18. *Foreign Relations of the United States: Diplomatic Papers, 1944,* vol 3, *The British Commonwealth and Europe* (Washington, DC: Government Printing Office, 1965), 683.
19. Ibid., 699-700.
20. Ibid., 707-708.
21. Memorandum defining the French point of view in Operation Anvil, Algiers, 11 Mar. 1944.
22. Minutes of conversation between General Wilson and General de Gaulle, 15 Mar. 1944.

23. Official Diary, 19 Apr. 1944.
24. David Schoenbrun, *Soldiers of the Night: The Story of the French Resistance* (New York: E. P. Dutton, 1980), 406.
25. Official Diary, 15 June 1944, Anvil Plan.

CHAPTER 7: FINAL PLANNING

1. From the Library of Congress collection of Adm. H. K. Hewitt's papers.
2. Ibid.
3. By an agreement of the Combined Chiefs of Staff, 24 Oct. 1942.
4. Ernest J. King, *U.S. Navy at War, 1941-1945* (Washington, DC: U.S. Government Printing Office, 1946), 143, 144.
5. Navy term for toilets.
6. The others were Captains Stone and Simpson.
7. Navy terms for kitchens.
8. Admiral Hewitt's schedule 11-17 May 1944; obtained from the Library of Congress collection of Adm. H. K. Hewitt's papers.
9. B. V. McCandlish to Vice Adm. H. K. Hewitt.
10. Flint Whitlock, "Hells Commando," *http://www.thehistorynet.com/WorldWarII/ARTICLES/2000/0100_text.htm*, 1.
11. Anne Frederick Hicks, "Fighting Bob Frederick: The War Made Him, Peacekeeping Broke Him," *Army,* September 1982, 50.
12. Ibid.
13. Ibid., 54.
14. Whitlock, 11.
15. Official Diary, 25 June 1944.
16. Gen. Lucian K. Truscott to Gen. Alexander Patch, 27 June 1944.
17. Gen. Lucian K. Truscott to Gen. Alexander Patch, 21 July 1944.
18. Message from General Wilson to General Eisenhower, 4 July 1944.
19. Admiral Hewitt to General Truscott, 4 July 1944.
20. Admiral Hewitt to Admiral Cunningham, memorandum, 27 July 1944.
21. Official Diary, Force 163, 29 July 1944 and 1 Aug. 1944; General Truscott to General Patch, memorandum, 21 July 1944.
22. General Truscott to Admiral Hewitt, 1 Aug. 1944.
23. Admiral Hewitt to General Truscott, 2 Aug. 1944.
24. Official Diary, Force 163, 14 Aug. 1944.
25. Author's comment: In September 1943, after I had completed boot camp training at the Sampson Naval Station in Geneva in upstate New York, I was given a week's liberty to return home. My parents, sixteen-year-old brother, and I lived in a small $20-a-month four-room apartment in Brooklyn that faced an elevated train line. That is where I spent that seven-day leave. Early in the morning, before my mother left for her job as a poorly paid seamstress in a small Lower East Side factory loft that manufactured pillowcases, she had scrubbed the apartment. When I arrived that evening, the linoleum

and everything else glistened, especially the candles lit to celebrate the Jewish New Year. I was in my sailor's uniform, and seeking my comfort, my mother asked me to remove the top (or blouse) of my uniform. As a pulled it over my head, a package of condoms fell on the floor in full view of all of us. My mother started shrieking in Yiddish that I was becoming a navy bum. My father was a short man who rarely spoke. But this time, to quiet my mother's carrying on about my licentious future, Pop did a brilliant job defending me. He concocted a story told in Yiddish that I had been issued the condoms, that I had not solicited them, and that I had no choice in having them. The condoms were never used. To please me, my mother bought some smoked fish that resulted in food poisoning during that week, which left me without any appetite—neither for food nor for sex.

26. Robert H. Adelman and George Walton, *The Champagne Campaign* (Boston: Little, Brown, 1969), 108.

27. Gerard M. Devlin, *Paratrooper: The Saga of U.S. Army and Glider Combat Troops during World War II* (New York: St. Martin's Press, 1974), 449.

28. Devlin, 455-457.

29. Jim Phillips, *The Devil's Bodyguard* (Williamstown, NJ: Phillips Publications, 1986), 47, 61-73. Descriptions of Duff Matson's Operation Dragoon parachute jump, his injury, and subsequent activities shortly thereafter were provided by Jim Phillips.

30. Parton, 417.

31. William B. Breuer, *Operation Dragoon: The Allied Invasion of the South of France* (Novato, CA: Presidio Press, 1987), 200.

32. First Airborne Task Force, Operation, 15-16 Aug. 1944.

33. Breuer, 200.

34. Ibid., 162, 163.

35. File no. A16-3, serial 101568, 15 Nov. 1964.

36. See Hewitt's "Final Plan for Dragoon," 26.

37. Douglas Fairbanks Jr., *Memorandum for the Admiral—Special Operations Summation Report,* January 1943 to September 1944, 3.

38. Ibid., 4.

39. Author's comment: In the beginning of September 1939, when I was fourteen, my parents took my brother and me to see the World Fair in Queens, New York. My memories of that special day include the pleasure of seeing attractive and immaculately clean buildings and landscaping. It was a delightful escape from the blight of other days. Handsome Douglas Fairbanks Jr. was the featured celebrity guest at the fair. Toward the end of that day, as I enjoyed a last look at the multicolored lighted fountains

and exquisite landscaping, the news spread that Poland had been attacked by Germany. My mother, whose parents, sisters, brothers, nieces, and nephews were in Warsaw, was frightened. I did not know then that Douglas Fairbanks Jr. and I would participate in the invasion of France, nor did I know that our family in Poland would all be killed during the war.

40. Jon Latimer, *Deception in War* (New York: Overlook Press, 2001), 180.

41. Report of the Mediterranean Allied Air Forces (MAAF) Operations in Support of Dragoon.

42. Admiral Hewitt's papers include aircraft identification.

43. Report, AC of S, G-4, Seventh Army, "Oran Notes."

44. Letter, 21 June, Headquarters Force 163 and Memo, 27 July, AC of S, G-4, Headquarters Force 163.

45. Historical Report, AC of S, G-4, 8 Jan. 1945.

46. The author has records detailing Donovan's undergraduate and law school grades from Columbia University.

47. Daniel C. Pinck, Charles T. Pinck, and Geoffrey M. T. Jones, eds., *Stalking the History of the Office of Strategic Services: An OSS Bibliography* (Boston: OSS / Donovan Press, 2000), 118J, 118K.

48. Alfred H. Paddock Jr., *U.S. Army Special Warfare: Its Origins, Psychological, and Conventional Warfare, 1941-1951* (Washington, DC: National Defense University Press, 1982), 27-29.

49. M. R. D. Foot, *SOE in France* (London: Her Majesty's Stationery Office, 1966), 413.

50. Ibid., 47, 50.

51. Margaret L. Rossiter, *Women in the Resistance* (New York: Praeger, 1986), 181.

52. BBC News, 11 Apr. 2006.

53. Kermit Roosevelt, *The Overseas Targets War Report of the OSS,* vol. 2 (New York: Walker, 1976), 12.

54. Ibid., 13, 14.

55. Joseph E. Persico, *Piercing the Reich: The Penetration of Nazi Germany by American Secret Agents during World War II* (New York: Viking Press, 1979), 11.

56. See R. Harris Smith, *The OSS: The Secret History of America's First Central Intelligence Agency* (Berkeley, CA: University of California Press, 1971).

57. 11 Dec. 2001, 9.

58. Quoted in Hillary Footitt and John Simmonds's *France 1943-1945* (New York: Holmes and Meier, 1980), 84.

59. Anthony Cave Brown, *Last Hero: Wild Bill Donovan* (New York: Times Books, 1982), 24-59.

60. "Report on Operation Rabelais," obtained from the National Archives.

61. Critique by Geoffrey M. T. Jones, given to the author. OSS agent Captain Jones was given a forged identity card in July 1944. His carte d'identité indicated that he was a Frenchman from Avignon named Paul Georges Guillot. To explain why Paul Guillot was not drafted into military service, a disability was invented for him—he was mute.

    When Jones parachuted behind German lines in the French Alps to prepare the way for Operation Dragoon in the dead of night, he missed the mountain plateau, but his parachute snagged on an outcropping. Luckily, this kept him from smashing against the mountainside. However, the parachute swung his head into a rock hard enough to cut through the metal covering of his helmet.

    The next day, Jones/Guillot rendezvoused with the local Resistance group dressed in the blue suit of a typical French laborer. He found an underground radio operator who was in contact with Allied Headquarters in Algiers. Jones distributed guns and explosives to the Resistance fighters and organized them for the pending invasion. Having grown up in southern France, he was able to communicate easily. To gather intelligence, Jones went to small towns in the area. These trips were dangerous—capture by the Germans could lead to his spilling of secret Dragoon plans, his death, and the lives of many Allied soldiers, sailors, and airmen. Jones told the author that "in 1944 the Germans already had drugs that would make anyone divulge their secrets, so if captured I had to take a poison pill."

    While Jones and his French resisters headed toward the Dragoon landing beaches, they had to pass a few German roadblocks and avoid being bombed by "friendly" (Allied) air attacks. After Jones completed his mission, he left his blue peasant suit and false papers in a farmhouse.

62. This section is based on Southern France (I-Physical Landscape, II-Coastline Features, III-Climate), Topographic and Intelligence Study, Office of Strategic Services, Research and Analysis Branch, and Mediterranean France, vol. 2 (Terrain Intelligence), prepared by U.S. Geological Survey, Dept. of Interior, for Chief of Engineers, U.S. Army.

63. Target Area Analysis No. 9, Headquarters Force 163, 15 May 1944, E-1.

64. G-2 Information Bulletin No. 1, Headquarters Seventh Army, 16 July 1944, 1, and Target Area Analysis No. 9, F-1.

65. Ibid.

66. Annex F to Operations Plan No. 4044, 3.

67. "Intelligence Summary," Operation Order No. 1, Headquarters XII Tactical Air Command, 31 July 1944, 13.

68. "Order of Battle of German Forces in France," G-2 Information Bulletin No. 2, Headquarters Seventh Army, 20 July 1944.

69. Ibid.

70. The Germans had a grave shortage of vehicles and fuel.

71. G-2 Information Bulletin No. 1, 11.

72. The foregoing analysis is based on Target Area Analysis Nos. 4, 6, 7, and 9.

73. Information on beaches was drawn from ISIS Report on France, zvo. 5 (Mediterranean France), Interservice Topographical Service, March 1943; Target Area Analysis No. 8; Western Naval Task Force Intelligence Plan, 2 Aug. 1944.

74. Diary, Anvil, March 1944.

75. Col. John A. Chambers, Office of the Engineer, Seventh Army, to Historical Section, 22 Sept. 1944.

76. Diary, Anvil, April to July 1944. Letter, Supreme Allied Commander to Commanding General, Invasion Training Center, 15 Apr. 1944.

77. Reports of 36th, 40th, 540th, and 48th Engineers, July and August 1944.

78. Historical Record, Forty-eighth Engineer Combat Battalion, August 1944.

79. Mark W. Clark, *Calculated Risk* (New York: Harper and Brothers, 1950), 306.

80. *Dictionary of American Military Biography* (Westport, CT: Greenwood Press, 1984), 1112.

81. Forty-fifth Division Report, August 1944.

82. Report for Operation Dragoon, Headquarters, Prov. Troop Carrier Air Div., 22 Aug. 1944.

83. Author's comment: When I underwent basic training in the summer of 1943, one of the requirements was to see who could swim and who could not. My father's brother, Morris, drowned at age eighteen; and as a result, my brother and I were kept far away from the water. Thus, when my turn came to climb the tower at navy training and jump into the swimming pool, I told the officer in charge that I couldn't swim. I was petrified when I was pushed off the diving board and later rescued. I eventually took required lessons on how to swim later that winter in bitterly cold water. There, the emphasis was upon floating, which I ultimately mastered. Several months later, I was a full-fledged sailor on a ship that cruised the Atlantic, not knowing fully how to swim. Strangely, this was not an uncommon phenomenon. The executive officer / navigator of the LST 1012, Mr. Steeple, admitted to me in 1994 that he did not know how to swim or float.

84. First Special Service Force, Journal, August 1944; and FO No. 1, DR, Operation Bruno.

85. Field Order No. 1, VI Corps, 29 July 1944.

86. Preliminary Report, Western Task Force, Navy, 9 Aug. to 25 Sept. 1944.

87. Naval Operation Anvil, 29 July 1944.

88. Beach Operation Report, Transportation Officer, Seventh Army, September 1944.

89. Diary, Anvil, August 1944; journals, units of VI Corps, August 1944.

90. XII Tactical Air Command, Operation Order No. 1, 8 Aug. 1944; Preliminary Report, Navy, 9 Aug. 1944.

91. Mediterranean Allied Air Force, Operation Dragoon, vol. 1, August 1944.

92. Mediterranean Allied Air Force, Report on Dragoon Operation, vols. 1, 5, 8, and 10, August 1944. Navy, Operation Dragoon, 14-15 August. Special Service Force Report, August 1944.

93. Sitrep, Navy, 15 Aug. 1944; Preliminary Report, Navy, August 1944.

94. U.S. Eighth Fleet, Operation Support Force, August 1944.

95. First Special Service Force, Operations Journal, 17 and 18 August; Preliminary Report, Navy, 14 and 15 Aug. 1944; and U.S. Eighth Fleet, Operation Support Force, August 1944.

96. Verbal report, Capt. George C. Bartlett Jr., Seventh Army Headquarters.

97. French Commandoes, Operation Journal, 17 and 18 Aug. 1944; Anvil Plan, 29 July 1944.

98. Third Division Report, August 1944; French Commandoes Operation Journal, 17 and 18 Aug. 1944.

99. 141st Infantry Report, August 1944; French Commandoes Operation Journal, 17 and 18 Aug. 1944.

100. Mediterranean Allied Air Force, Operation Dragoon, vol. 1.

101. Lord Wilson (Henry Maitland), *Eight Years Overseas* (London: Hutchinson, 1950), 220, 223.

CHAPTER 8: EN ROUTE TO DRAMMONT

1. Auphan and Mordal, 318.
2. John Davis, "Fifty Years Ago—July 1944," *jbd@netcom.com/jbd@osbm.state. nc.us*, originally posted in Usenet newsgroup soc.history.war.world-war-ii and on the World War II mailing list. Sources: *2194 Days of War*, by Cesare Salmaggi and Alfredo Pallavisimi; *The World Almanac Book of WWII*, by Peter Young; *United States Naval Chronology, World War II*, by Naval Historical Division-United States Navy; *Facts on File Yearbook 1944, Person's Index of World Events*, edited by R. L. Lapica, *http://www.biblio. org/pub/academic/history*.
3. *ONI Weekly*, 9 Aug. 1944, 2552.
4. "Operation Anvil/Dragoon: The Invasion of Southern France by the Third Infantry Division and of the Seventh Army Unit" (unpublished), prepared by Staff Group 3D under the direction of Maj. Duncan Stewart, submitted to the Combat Studies Institute, U.S. Army Command and General Staff College (Ft. Leavenworth, Kansas, May 1984), 27, henceforth referred to as the "Staff Group 3D Operation Anvil/Dragoon Study of May 1984."
5. Alec Guinness, *Blessing in Disguise* (New York: Warner Books, 1985), 139-140.
6. Schoenbrun, *Soldiers of the Night*, 1980.
7. Col. Gen. Johannes Blaskowitz, Commander, German Army Group G, "Fighting by Army Group G, May 10-Sept. 27, 1944," record English copy, Historical Division Headquarters United States, Europe, Foreign Military Studies Branch (Allendorf, May 16, 1947), D739, F6713, No. B-800, fgn ms, 2.
8. Richard Giziowski, *The Enigma of General Blaskowitz* (London: Leo Cooper, 1997).
9. Blaskowitz, 2-4.
10. Ibid.
11. Ibid., 5-7.
12. Jean de Lattre de Tassigny, *The History of the French First Army*, trans. Malcolm Barnes (London: George Allen and Unwin, 1949), 50.
13. De Gaulle, 299.
14. De Lattre, 51.
15. Parton, 415.
16. Morison, *Invasion of France and Germany*, 411.
17. Ibid.

18. Ibid., 415.
19. Warnock, 1.
20. Ibid., 2.
21. Ibid.
22. Kathleen Broome Williams, 29.
23. Hackmann, 238.
24. Kathleen Broome Williams, 30, 232.
25. *ONI Weekly*, 31 May 1944, 1723.
26. *ONI Weekly*, 17 May 1944, 1564.
27. Alan Riding, "Henri Rol-Tanguy, French Resistance, Dies at 94," *New York Times*, 11 Sept. 2002, C12.
28. Dear and Foot, *Oxford Companion*, table 3, 408. One estimate is that one hundred fifty thousand French people were killed because of aerial bombings, German atrocities, and Resistance losses.
29. Porch, 565, 592.
30. Parton, 473-475.
31. W. G. Sebald, "An Attempt at Restitution," *New Yorker*, 20 Dec. 2004, 114.
32. *ONI Weekly*, 22 May 1944, 1625.
33. Ibid.
34. "The French Underground," *ONI Weekly*, 17 May 1944, 1560.
35. Ibid., 1532.
36. *Foreign Relations, 1944*, vol. 3, 723, 724.
37. The details concerning de Gaulle's visit to Washington, D.C., in July 1944 are from

    (a) "The President and the General," *Time*, July 17, 1944, 1, 2.
    (b) "Facts on File," *http://www.biblio.org/pub/academic/history/marshall/military/wwii/50.years*, July 1944; TX 25 June 2002, 5, 7, 9.
    (c) See also "Prime Minister Reviews the War," *ONI Weekly*, 9 Aug. 1944, 2582.
    (d) In July 1944, in Washington, D.C., General de Gaulle's host, President Roosevelt, was suffering from "hyper-tension, hypertensive heart disease, cardiac failure and acute bronchitis" according to FDR's cardiologist, Dr. Howard G. Bruenn. See Carl M. Cannon, "Untruth and Consequences," *Atlantic Monthly*, January-February 2007, 56.

38. Oral History of Columbia University, 1972, 388.
39. According to a report by OSS Jedburgh Teams II. Bradley F. Smith, *Covert Warfare: OSS Jedburgh Teams* (New York: Garland Publishing, 1989), 749.

40. Ibid., xii.
41. Ibid., xiii.
42. Geoff Jones interview with the author, April 2004.
43. Ibid.
44. Elizabeth P. McIntosh, *The Women of the OSS: Sisterhood of Spies* (Washington, DC: United States Naval Institute, 1998), 145.
45. Foot, 412.
46. Jeffrey J. Clarke and Robert R. Smith, *From the Riviera to the Rhine: U.S. Army in World War II* (Washington, DC: U.S. Army Center of Military History, 1993), 88.
47. Kermit Roosevelt, xii.
48. Ibid., 13, 14.
49. Lt. Col. Kenneth Baker, "Final Report on Special Projects Operation Center of the U.S. Army," 4; William Grimes, "Woman on Hunt for Spies Who Didn't Come Home," *New York Times,* 30 Aug. 2006, E6. (This article is a book review of *A Life in Secrets: Vera Atkins and the Missing Agents of WWII* by Sarah Helm [Nan A. Talese / Doubleday, 2006]). British intelligence was not immune from incompetence. F Section was the French division of the British Special Operations Executive. Of the four hundred agents it sent to France, more than a hundred were missing by September 1944. Twelve of these agents who were sent from Britain to France were women who were to serve the Resistance movement as radio operators and couriers. The French pilot who flew these agents from Britain to France betrayed them. After the Nazis took the agents' money, radios, and other equipment, their captors requested the F Section to send more agents and supplies. Maurice Buckmaster, the SOE official supervising this operation, refused to believe it had been usurped by the Germans and continued to send them more agents, money, and equipment. Only when Hitler ordered facetious messages thanking the F Section for its largesse and asked for more did this SOE fiasco end.
50. *Stars and Stripes,* 25 Aug. 1944, 6.
51. Ibid.
52. De Lattre, 51.
53. From Library of Congress collection of Admiral Hewitt's papers.
54. Resistance fighters performed well in the landing phase of Dragoon. Later, they were sent to Grenoble to prevent the retreat of German troops into the lower Rhone Valley. They achieved the important objective of clearing the road to Grenoble.
55. *Foreign Relations, 1944,* vol. 3, 697, 698.

56. Massigli and Puaux were de Gaulle's associates.

57. *Foreign Relations,* 698-699.

58. History Project, Strategic Unit, Office of the Assistant Secretary of War. (Washington, DC: War Department, 1947), 238.

59. Fleet Adm. Ernest J. King, *U.S. Navy at War, 1941-1945* (Washington, DC: U.S. Government Printing Office, 1946), 143.

60. Douglas Fairbanks Jr., *The Salad Days* (New York: Doubleday, 1988), 368.

61. Ibid., 382, 282.

62. Schoenbrun, 411.

63. Jacob L. Devers, "The Invasion of Southern France," *Military Affairs* 10, no. 2 (Summer 1946): 26.

64. Ibid.

65. Rear Adm. Spencer S. Lewis, "Action Report: Assault on the Beaches of Southern France—Report Concerns Operations in the Saint-Raphael-Antheor Area, Mediterranean Area, on Aug. 15, 1944," 7 Sept. 1944, available in the Office of Naval Records and Library, Washington, DC.

66. The report uses the name of Neptune as a code for Normandy.

67. Lewis, 1.

68. W. R. Carter and E. E. Duvall, *Ships, Salvage and Sinews of War* (Washington, DC: U.S. Government Printing Office, 1954), 420.

69. Author's comment. As far as LST 1012 was concerned, I know that Admiral Moon's contention about the absence of a "dry run" or rehearsal was correct. The captain of our sister ship, LST 1011, Bob Wilson, corroborates this.

70. Admiral Hewitt's report on Dragoon, 144.

71. Buell, 201.

72. Ibid., 230.

73. John A. Moreno, "The Death of Admiral Moon," in *Assault on Normandy* (Annapolis, MD: Naval Institute Press, 1994), 230.

74. Ibid., 227.

75. "Wrong Way Pigeon Story," at the Thomas Aubut LST 282 site, *http://www.landingship.com/282/pigeon.htm.*

76. Gilbert entered the navy on 22 Dec. 1941 and was discharged on 26 Jan. 1947. He received the Navy Cross, Bronze Star, Purple Heart, and the Croix de Guerre (Silver Star).

77. Grace Ellen was born 3 Sept. 1942, followed by two boys: Terrance Edwin, born 17 July 1944, and Michael John, born 15 Apr. 1949. A second daughter, Lauren, was the youngest.

78. L. E. Gilbert to Bertram R. MacMannis, 23 Dec. 1942.

79. Dots was Dorothy, Lawrence E. Gilbert's sister.

80. Gilbert to MacMannis, quoting son Larry E. Gilbert.

81. Bob Beroth to the author, 10 Dec. 2004.

82. Author's comment: On the LST 1012, we were also well fed. I did not eat the nonkosher items, but there were plenty of other things to eat. In less than a year onboard the ship, my weight increased from 150 to 180 pounds.

83. Menu from LST 282 at the Thomas Aubut LST 282 site, *http://www.surfacepro.com/lst/menu.htm*, sent via e-mail by Sheldon Aubut, 21 Mar. 1999, after receiving a photocopy of the original from Dick Wagner. Aubut stated that "the spelling errors above were as on the original."

84. Author's comment: During a liberty in Norfolk, Virginia, with Charlie Cullen, I had my first taste of Chinese food. It was not at a kosher restaurant; but I did avoid eating pork and shrimp, lobster, and other forbidden food in the Jewish diet. My mother kept kosher, and but for one exception, I did not eat the forbidden food or mix meat and dairy dishes. The one and only occasion when I intentionally violated the Jewish dietary law happened on the LST 1012 after I got tired of being ridiculed by the nasty gibes of some shipmates who had noticed my practice of not eating pork, bacon, or ham. I was also curious, and so one evening when pork chops and gravy were being served in the galley, I asked for a portion and enjoyed every morsel. My recollection is that the pork chops tasted like chicken, and I didn't miss a drop of the gravy. Shortly after I went to sleep, however, all hell broke loose; and that night I suffered the worst case of the runs in my life. More than once during this misery, I was certain that the wrath of God was upon me for my sin. It was only later that I found out that a laxative had found its way into my gravy. Since then, I have eaten bacon, shrimp, ham, lobster, scallops, etc., and mixed meat and dairy food. But from that terrible night on, I have not eaten another pork chop.

85. Carter and Duvall, 433.

86. Ibid., 433-439.

87. Jackson, 250, 276, 277, 290. The people of the Var department where the Anvil/Dragoon landings took place were dependent on others for edibles other than salt, oil, and wine. Countess Frances Gucciardi and her children were not the only ones desperate for food during the German occupation of France.

William Grimes, "Amid the Rubble, After London Took It," *New York Times,* 27 Apr. 2005, E6 (This is a book review of Maureen Waller, *London 1945: Life in the Debris of War* (St. Martins, 2005). The British people were also subjected to severe food shortages. The average city resident was limited to three eggs a month. To provide more food for their children, many British women gave them their food and smoked to alleviate their hunger.

88. "Revised Phasing of Maintenance in Initial Requirements Subsequent to Maintenance and Supply—All Classes except Air Force, Navy, and Civil Supplies unless Specifically Mentioned." In Annex A—Administrative Instructions #1, 15 Apr. 1944, Seventh Army Plan.

89. Circular Letter No. 362, signed by BuPers, L. E. Denfeld, 222.

90. For information concerning other religious ceremonies, see Circular Letter, 228.

91. Hawser: a heavy rope for mooring or towing.

92. Bob Beroth to the author, 24 Apr. 2002.

93. E-mail from Mike Sgaglione, 25 Mar. 2004.

94. See Action Report, Commander LST Group Two, Alpha Attack Force, Task Unit 84.2, 29 Aug. 1944.

95. Sweet and Sweet, 22.

96. USS LST 494 Association, "Irving 'Chet' Noyes, LST 494's ETO Skipper Passes Away," *http://LST494.FREEYELLOW.com*; *LST Scuttlebutt*, March-April 2006, 32.

97. Mike Guarino, "A Look at 494 in the European Theater during World War II," *LST Scuttlebutt*, March-April 2006, 14, 15.

98. Ibid., 15.

99. Lou Leopold to the author, responding to questions of 16 Oct. 2000.

100. Lou Leopold to the author, 1 Feb. 2004.

101. Lou Leopold to the author, responding to questions of 16 Oct. 2000.

102. On LST 1012, a few desperate sailors drank shaving lotion. Many 1012 crew members got drunk on liberty, but aboard ship sobriety reigned.

103. Information from Lou Leopold given to the Military History Museum.

104. The term "under hack" means punishment for officer involving restriction to his quarters.

105. Churchill's personal physician, Lord Moran, insisted that the prime minister take malaria pills when they visited the area before Dragoon.

106. From the diary of Lou Leopold, obtained by the author.

107. As a teenager, the author sold newspapers on the streets of Brooklyn, New York, and Good Humor ice cream on a Coney Island beach.

108. June Webb, daughter of Capt. Samuel Kimmel, to the author, 3 Aug. 2003.

109. E-mail from Jeff Shatley to the author, 31 Oct. 2003.

110. E-mail from Jeff Shatley to the author, 29 Oct. 2003.

111. E-mail from Jeff Shatley to the author, 27 Oct. 2003.

112. Theodore C. Dunn, Commander, USNR (Ret.), to the author, 26 Jan. 2004.

113. An Italian also tiled the showers of LST 1012.

114. Diary of Theodore Dunn sent to the author.

115. Theodore Dunn to the author, 26 Nov. 2004.

116. E-mail from John T. McCrea, *http://www.landingship.com/282guestbook.htm.*

117. A boatswain's mate is a petty officer responsible for a variety of seamanship tasks, such as mooring, anchoring boat, and ship maintenance.

118. From the diary of Thomas J. Kronenberger.

119. Clyde L. Bond to the author, 23 Apr. 2002.

120. Memo from R. M. Wilson to the cominch, U.S. Fleet on Action Report, Document 145795, 25 Oct. 1944.

121. Bob Wilson to the author, Christmas 2000.

122. Great Britain Admiralty Report, *Invasion of South of France: Operation Dragoon* (London: Her Majesty's Stationery Office, 1994), 16.

123. M. J. Flowers Jr., "Ship's History—Submission of Reference A1Pac #202-45"; Lieutenant Commander Flowers to the secretary of the navy, serial 262, 25 Oct. 1945.

    LST 991 crew member Phil Schreiber of Iselin, New Jersey, covered the fate of his LST and twenty-one other LSTs. The LST 1012 and the others were procured by the United Nations and delivered to the Chinese government in March 1947. They were used by *the* China water transport company, which renamed the LST 1012 the "Wan Pu." According to Phil Schrieber, when new, the cost of an LST was $1,920,000; and the price charged to the United Nations Relief and Rehabilitation Administration was $387,000 for each LST.

    In addition to his extensive research concerning the fate of these LSTs, Mr. Schreiber wrote a history of the LST 991, which was published in England by the Forces Postal History Society. It won the award for the best piece published in 2004. His article "What Happened to your LST" appeared in the *LST Scuttlebutt*, March-April 2006, 23.

124. "Seabees" is a navy construction battalion.

125. Harold Larsen, "A Slow Ship to Shanghai: USS LST 1012 World War II Log Book with Comments and Narrations by Harold Larsen," 8.

126. Ibid., 9.

127. The author also visited Pompeii in the summer of 1944.

128. Larsen, 9.

129. David M. Key Jr., *Admiral Jerauld Wright: Warrior among Diplomats* (Manhattan, KS: Sunflower Press, 2001), 194; LST 1012 Daily Log for 7-9 Aug. 1944.

130. "The AAF in the Invasion of Southern France" (Washington, DC: U.S. Army Air Forces Center for Air Force History, 1992), 32, 34.

131. DZ refers to designated zone.

132. Arnold A. Rogow, *James Forrestal: A Study of Personality, Politics and Policy* (New York: Macmillan, 1963), 95.

133. Lucian K. Truscott Jr., *Command Decision* (New York: E. P. Dutton, 1954), 409.

134. Note previous account dealing with relationship between LST 551 commanding officer Sam Kimmel and superior-ranked officers on LST 551.

135. Ibid.

136. Clayton D. Laurie, *Anzio* (Washington, DC: U.S. Army Center of Military History), 3, 25, 26, 27.

137. Ibid.

138. 141st Infantry Regiment, *141st Infantry Regiment, 36th Infantry Division: Five Years, Five Countries, Five Campaigns, http://www.kwanah. com/txmilmus/36division/archives/141/141/154*. This World War II history site is sponsored and maintained by Gary Butler.

139. Patterson succeeded Henry Stimson as secretary of war.

140. Lord Moran, *Churchill: Taken from the Diaries of Lord Moran—The Struggle for Survival, 1940-1965* (Boston: Houghton Mifflin, 1966), 173.

141. Ibid.

CHAPTER 9: AUGUST 15, 1944

1. A report by Parachutist J. K. Horne Jr., *http://www.thedropzone.org/europe/ Southern%20France/horne.html.*

2. Robert E. Pettit, First Special Service Force, "Robert E. Pettit: Operation Dragoon" (on web), 13 Oct. 2003; first published in the French magazine *Genista.*

3. One indication that Allied forces were subject to enemy fire is the "Statement Concerning Finding of Enemy Death," 17 Aug. 1944. Pers-5 326-GS, by Capt. A. C. Jacobs, USNR, director of Dependents Welfare Division.

4. Hewitt, "Executing Operation Dragoon," *Proceedings of the United States Naval Institute,* no. 8 (August 1954), 903.

5. Ibid.

6. Ibid. The timing was as follows: Alpha 0800 hrs, Delta 0802 hrs, and Camel 0803 hrs.

7. Quoted in Gerald F. Linderman's *The World within War: America's Combat Experience in World War II* (Cambridge, MA: Harvard University Press, 1997), 252. See also Audie Murphy's autobiography, *To Hell and Back* (New York: Holt, Rhinehart & Winston, 1949), 169.

8. Audie Murphy, 170.

9. Harold Larsen, interview by the author, 30 Apr. 1994.

10. Author's comment: In observance of the navy's religious tolerance, R. C. Steeple Jr., executive officer and navigator of the LST 1012, ordered me to take the ship's other Jewish sailor, Dan, to Yom Kippur service in 1944 while we were moored in Naples. Dan was a deckhand seaman, second class—the equivalent to a private. He was a rough and tough kid from the Greater Boston area of Massachusetts, who did not put up with any nonsense from the anti-Semites onboard. On Yom Kippur, we went ashore in Naples to one of the Catholic churches, where our services were conducted by a Protestant chaplain. They passed by relatively quickly, more so than the ones I attended at home in Brooklyn. After they concluded, I wanted to get back to the ship. I had a tendency toward prudence. Danny, on the other hand, had a different idea as to our next move. He had an urge and wanted to get himself a wench. I tried to convince him that two Jewish boys caught by the shore patrol at a whorehouse on Yom Kippur wouldn't look so good. It would be ridiculous. However, he was bigger and stronger than me; there was no convincing him, so there was no use arguing the point. Instead, I made a deal with him: we'd go to the whorehouse and he'd do his thing, after which we'd immediately go back to the ship. He was an honorable

man, and he did what he had to do—I did not indulge—and then we returned to the ship. Nobody else onboard heard a lick of our story; and it was forgotten until April 1994, at the fiftieth reunion commemorating the commission of our ship, when it was recalled.

11. "Task Unit 84.1.2 Action Report," prepared by Commander Task Unit 84.1.2, Commander LST Group Two, 29 Aug. 1944, 2.

12. John Davis, "Fifty Years Ago—August 1944," *jbd@netcom.com, http://www. ibiblio.org/pub/academic/history/marshall/military/wwii/50yearsA/Aug.ix* (25 June 2002). On 15 Aug. 1944, approximately five hundred of the one thousand eight hundred German prisoners of war working at the U.S. Army ordnance depot in Stockton, California, ended a strike that had started the previous day. The strikers were protesting the U.S. War Department's order increasing the work to nine hours. On 16 Aug. 1994, the Operation Dragoon flagship *Catoctin* was damaged by bombing.

13. C. G. Mayer, Lieutenant Commander, USNR, "Radar Moonshine Operations in the Mediterranean," formerly top secret report, 3 Oct. 1944, 3.

14. Hewitt, "Executing Operation Dragoon," 903.

15. "Task Unit 84.1.2 Action Report," prepared by Commander Task Unit 84.1.2, Commander LST Group Two, 29 Aug. 1944, 2.

16. Hewitt, op. cit., 904.

17. Headquarters Thirty-sixth Infantry Division, AP #36, U.S. Army Narrative, L-1009, August 1944, 3.

18. Moreno, 229.

19. Ibid.

20. Vincent Lockhart, *T-Patch to Victory* (Canton, TX: Staked Plains Press, 1981), 58.

21. Lockhart, 59.

22. Ibid., 63.

23. Adm. H. Kent Hewitt's statement to Dr. John Mason of the Columbia Oral History Center, 399.

24. From the author's 2003 interview with Charles Earle, who was in charge of LST 1012's gunnery on 15 Aug. 1944.

25. Chuck Steeple to the author, 29 July 2000.

26. LST 1012 Commanding Officer, Lt. Marshall J. Flowers Jr. action report of 16 Oct. 1944, that was submitted to the Commander Amphibious Force, U.S. Eighth Fleet, Vice Adm. Henry Kent Hewitt.

27. Captain John Opie's post-Dragoon report concerning LST 1012's gunnery performance on 15 Aug. 1944 was acquired from the Naval Historical Library.

28. Charlie Earle, interview by the author, 18 Feb. 2005.
29. Hewitt, "Executing Operation Dragoon," 905.
30. Jacobs, "Statement Concerning Finding of Enemy Death."
31. "Task Unit 84.1.2 Action Report," 2.
32. Lt. L. E. Gilbert, Commanding Officer of USS LST 282, "Report on the Destruction of LST 282," file no. A4-1, serial 005, 2 Sept. 1944, 1-4.
33. "First Lieutenant" is a navy term for officer in charge of ship main-tenance.
34. Telephone interview with the author, 10 Nov. 2003.
35. Hans E. Bergner, "Taking the Fight to France," *http://www.landingship. com/282/bergner.htm* (retrieved 5 Mar. 2002).
36. Bob Beroth to the author, 24 Apr. 2002.
37. George Narozonick to the author, 13 Mar. 2002.
38. Diary of Bob Wilson. Wilson also sent a letter to the author in June 2002 on the subject of navy bigotry.
39. E-mail from Charlie Cullen to the author, July 18, 2001.
40. Lester Dulaney was another radioman on the LST 1012.
41. The Charlie Earle account is based on an interview with the author during an LST reunion in April 2001.
42. Author's comment: My station was in the wheelhouse, which adjoined the radio-radar room. Frank and I often stood watches near to one another, and we had plenty of opportunities to talk in 1944. Starting in 1993 to 2002, Charlie Earle, Frank Lovekin, our wives, and I have met at most LST 1012 annual reunions throughout the United States and became good friends. The relationship between Charlie Earle and Frank Lovekin went beyond friendship—it became a brotherhood.
43. According to the log entry of LST 1012, by R. C. Steeple Jr., 15 Aug. 1944.
44. Adm. H. Kent Hewitt, "Dragoon Operation: Report on Lost Ship while Operating in the Camel Assault Area during the Invasion of Southern France," declassified, serial 005, 2 Sept. 1944.
45. Commendation sent to Lt. Lawrence E. Gilbert, U.S. Naval Reserve, from James Forrestal on behalf of the president.
46. E-mail from Ferris Burke to the author, 22 May 2004.
47. This happens to be the author's birthday.
48. The author too is a mustang; he was commissioned as an officer in 1949 after serving as a petty officer during World War II.
49. H. K. Hewitt, Admiral, U.S. Navy, Commander Twelfth Fleet, to Ferris C. Burke, S2C, U.S. Naval Reserve, 12 Dec. 1945.
50. Gen. L. K. Truscott Jr., "Report to Adjutant General" (Washington, DC: Historical Record Headquarters VI Corp, July & August 1944), 2.

51. Jean-Pierre Aumont, *Sun and Shadow*, trans. Bruce Benderson (New York: W. W. Norton, 1977), 77.

52. Aumont, 100.

53. Ibid., 101.

54. Truscott, "Report to Adjutant General," 2. Aumont served with distinction in the French Army and earned a Croix de Guerre and the Legion d'Honneur. His sixty-five-year acting career included romantic parts in Hollywood and dramatic roles on Broadway. He made his film debut at age twenty-one, and his final performance was in a television miniseries adaptation of *The Count of Monte Cristo* in 1998. Aumont died on 29 Jan. 2001 at his home in Saint-Tropez on the French Riviera, near the Alpha Beach upon which he landed on 15 Aug. 1944.

55. Tom Malone, "Hero James Connor Earned His Medal," *Wilmington News Journal,* 11 Nov. 1968, 30.

56. Rear Adm. Spencer S. Lewis, "Report Concerning Operations in Landing in Saint-Raphael-Antheor, Mediterranean Area, August 15, 1944" (Washington, DC: U.S. Navy Historical Library), 4-5.

57. Ibid., 10.

58. Donald G. Taggart, *History of the Third Infantry Division in World War II* (Washington, DC: Infantry Journal Press), 201.

59. Ibid., 202.

60. Giziowski, 2.

61. Col. Gen. Johannes Blaskowitz, Commander, German Army Group G, "Fighting by Army Group G, 10-22 September 1947," record English copy, Historical Division Headquarters United States, Europe, Foreign Military Studies Branch, trans. R. J. Herman, 16 May 1947, D739, F6713, No. B-800, fgn ms, 7-10.

62. Ibid., 12.

63. Ibid., 12-13.

64. From *Atlantic Monthly*, September 1944, 3.

65. Ibid.

66. Alan F. Wilt, "The Summer of 1944: A Comparison of Overlord and Anvil/Dragoon," *Journal of Strategic Studies* 4, no. 2 (1981): 185-190.

67. Ibid., 191, 193.

68. Letter to Adm. H. Kent Hewitt, 5 July 1944.

69. Auphan and Mordal, 329.

70. Robert Aron, *France Reborn: The History of the Liberation, June 1944-May 1945* (New York: Charles Scribner's Sons, 1964), 309.

CHAPTER 10: REVERSALS

1.   Vera Micheles Dean, "Europe under Nazi Rule," *Foreign Policy Reports*, 15 Oct. 1940, 178.

2.   Pierre Cot, "The Defeat of the French Air Force," *Foreign Affairs* 19 (July 1941): 790-805. Pierre Cot was a French left-wing politician who served as air minister. See also Julian J. Jackson's *France: The Dark Years, 1940-1944* (New York: Oxford Press, 2001), 54, 92, 395, 396, 427, 428.

3.   Winifred N. Hadsel, "Struggle for a New France," *Foreign Policy Reports*, July 1944, 98.

4.   Ibid., 101. Historian and *Newsweek* managing editor Jon Meacham noted that Stalin's antipathy toward de Gaulle was due to some extent to his lack of respect toward the French because of their devastating military collapse. Stalin was not alone; the French were held in contempt by many others. See Meacham's *Franklin and Winston: An Intimate Portrait of an Epic Friendship* (New York: Random House, 2003), 250.

5.   See *Foreign Policy Reports*, 189, citing the *New York Times*, 7 Sept. 1940. In August and September 1944, German control of the French was evaporating.

6.   Victor Vinde, "The Spirit of Resistance," *Foreign Affairs* 21 (October 1942): 59-70.

7.   Karl Brandt, "How Europe Is Fighting Famine," *Foreign Affairs* 19 (July 1941): 806-817.

8.   Louis Franek, "The Forces of Collaboration," *Foreign Affairs* 21 (October 1942): 44-58.

9.   "The Seventh United States Army in France and Germany, 1944-1945," vol. 1, 100-101, 142.

10. *Combat Studies Institute Battlebook 3-D: Operation Anvil/Dragoon* (Ft. Leavenworth, KS: Combat Studies Institute, May 1984), 49.

11. Ibid.

12. Blaskowitz, op. cit., 14-15.

13. Hewitt, "Invasion of Southern France: Report of Naval Commander, Western Task Force," file no. A16-3, serial 01568, 15 Nov. 1944, 59.

14. Ibid., 60.

15. "Seventh United States Army in France and Germany," 317.

16. Hewitt, "Invasion of Southern France," 63, 67.

17. Ibid.

18. Reported in *Stars and Stripes Mediterranean*, 29 Aug. 1944, 2.

19. *ONI Weekly*, 30 Aug. 1944, 2690-2693, 2699.

20. Hewitt, "Invasion of Southern France," 81.
21. *Atlantic Monthly*'s "European Front" report, September 1944, 3.
22. Ibid.
23. Hewitt, "Invasion of Southern France," 82.
24. Ibid., 91.
25. *ONI Weekly*, 30 Aug. 1944, 2703.
26. Blaskowitz, 18-30.
27. *ONI Weekly* 2, no. 29 (21 July 1943): 2097. Publications Branch for the Officers of the United States Navy.
28. One U.S. LST, one British minesweeper, two U.S. minesweepers, two U.S. patrol boats, five landing craft, two British landing craft.
29. Hewitt, "Invasion of Southern France," 133.
30. Ibid.
31. Hewitt, "A Warm Welcome in Southern France," in *Assault on Normandy: First-Person Accounts from the Sea Service*, ed. Paul Stillwell (Annapolis, MD: Naval Institute Press, 1994), 221.
32. Dear and Foot, 422.
33. Claude Chambard, *The Maquis* (New York: Bobbs-Merrill Company, 1970), 195.
34. Keegan, 411.
35. Ibid., 411, 414. After its liberation, Paris became the Allies' European communications center, second only in size to Station "War" in Washington, D.C. WACs (Women's Army Corps) operated the Paris center's switchboards. Rebecca Raines noted that "the Eiffel Tower served as a radio relay terminal." (See her valuable *Getting the Message Through* [Washington, DC: Center of Military History 1996], 302).
36. From "Paris Rising," in Dear and Foot's *Oxford Companion to World War II*, 865.
37. Jean-Marie Guillion, *Le Var: La Guerre, La Resistance 1939-1945* (Nouvelle Edition, 1999), 215-241.
38. Ibid., 195.
39. Ibid., 223.
40. Wilt, 43
41. "Emmanuel d'Astier," *http://www.spartacus.schoolnet.co.uk/Frastier.htm* (retrieved 24 Aug. 2003).
42. Rousso, 82.
43. Jackson, 633.
44. Mallory Browne, "Paris Again," *Harper's*, November 1944, 499-506.

45. "General Marshall's Report: The Winning of the War in Europe and the Pacific" (Washington, DC: U.S. War Dept. General Staff, 1 July 1943-30 June 1945), 37.

46. Ibid., 38.

47. "The Core of German Resistance," *ONI Weekly*, 6 Sept. 1944, 2821.

48. Ibid.

49. Ibid., 2822.

50. Ibid., 2823-2828.

51. From General Marshall's Report, 90-91.

52. Robert Gildea, *Marianne in Chains: Everyday Life in the French Heartland under the German Occupation* (New York: Henry Holt, 2003), 45.

53. Ibid., 318.

54. Paxton, *Vichy France: Old Guard and New Order, 1940-1944* (New York: Alfred A. Knopf, 1972), 375.

55. Rousso, 7.

56. Tony Judt, *Past Imperfect: French Intellectuals, 1944-1956* (Berkeley, CA: University of California Press, 1992), 58-59.

57. Review of *Marianne in Chains*, by Robert Gildea, *New York Times Book Review*, 13 Aug. 2003, E6.

58. Ibid., 127.

59. Ibid., 82, 83.

60. Rousso, 53-54; "France: Railway Fine for Holocaust Deportations," *New York Times*, 7 June 2006, A6. In June 2006, Ariane Bernard of the *New York Times* reported the following: "A court in Toulouse ordered the state and the national railroad company SNCF to pay $80,000 to a Jewish family whose members were delivered to the World War II transit camp at Drancy, outside Paris, that sent Jews off to Nazi concentration camps. It was the first time that the state and the railway had been found liable for their role in the wartime deportation of thousands of French Jews. The suit was brought by two brothers in 2001. They were arrested by the Gestapo and transported to Drancy in 1944, where they remained until it was liberated by the Allies a few months later. According to the plaintiffs' lawyer, Rémi Rouquette, the court found that the state did nothing 'when it had a chance to' and that the railway did not object and in fact billed the state for third-class travel although it used freight and cattle cars."

61. Rousso, 7.

62. Hewitt, "A Warm Welcome in Southern France," 223.

63. *Stars and Stripes Mediterranean,* 29 Aug. 1944, 3; Dan Halpern, "Prince of Saint-Germain," *New Yorker,* 25 Dec. 2006 and 1 Jan. 2007, 138. After the demise of the Vichy regime and its hostility to American culture, there was a huge French appetite for Jazz and other American products. Writing for the *New Yorker* magazine, Dan Halpern offers the cogent argument that perhaps this "helped France reshape its sense of self after the shame of the Occupation."

64. Ibid.

65. Hilary Footitt and John Simmonds, *France 1943-1945* (New York: Holmes and Meier, 1988), 176.

66. Matloff, *Strategic Planning for Coalition Warfare, 1943-1944* (Washington, DC: Office of the Chief of Military History, Department of the Army, 1959), 502-503. While the subjects of French rearmament and postwar forces were being discussed, the Allies had completed their sweep across France; and thousands of eligible Frenchmen, many of them already armed, were made available for employment in the war. The questions of how many could be used and how best they could be used continued to plague the Allies during the balance of the summer.

67. "Facts on File," August 1944.

68. See Tony Chafer, "African Perspectives: The Liberation of France and Its Impact in French West Africa," in Kedward and Wood's *The Liberation of France: Image and Event* (Washington, DC: Berg Publishers, 1995), 246.

69. *Stars and Stripes Mediterranean,* 29 Aug. 1944, 3.

70. Thomas Vinciguerra, "The Private Thoughts of a Public Man," *New York Times,* 22 Jan. 2006, wk5.

71. Ibid.

72. Mary Burnet, "France: The Pieces in the Puzzle," *Harper's,* September 1944.

73. *Progressive,* 14 Aug. 1944, 14.

74. "Prime Minister Churchill Reviews the War," *ONI Weekly,* 9 Aug. 1944, 258.

75. George Dorsey, "Marseilles: City of Violent Death," *Stars and Stripes,* 25 Aug. 1944.

CHAPTER 11: EVALUATION AND LESSONS

1. Truscott, *Command Missions,* 382, 551.
2. Ibid., 552-553.
3. Breuer, 249.
4. Clarke and Smith, 561-562.
5. Blaskowitz, "Fighting by Army Group G in Southern France until the Middle of September 1944," trans. R. J. Herman (U.S. Army Military History Institute), MS No. B-800, 16 May 1947, 7.
6. Georg von Sodenstern, "Southern France—Preparation for Invasion," *CSI Battlebook: Anvil/Dragoon,* OCMH MS-B-276, 1946, 43.
7. Truscott, *Command Missions,* 551.
8. Morison, *Invasion of France and Germany,* 224.
9. *CSI Battlebook: Anvil/Dragoon,* 59, 425.
10. From the LST 1012 diary.
11. USS LST 1011 and 1012 newsletter, June 2002, 7.
12. Jerauld Wright, *The Life and Recollections of a Supreme Commander,* 186, 187.
13. Spencer Lewis Report, Camel Beach Landing, September 1944, 3.
14. Truscott, *Command Missions,* 382. The more experienced troops were the Third and Forty-fifth Infantry Divisions.
15. General Marshall's Report, 1.
16. A strip of stone built on a beach to ease the landing of small craft.
17. "Embarkation Security Officer for the Invasion of France," *ONI Weekly,* 6 Sept. 1944, 2829.
18. *CSI Battlebook,* 9. Quotes from Command and General Staff School, First Command Class, *Operation Anvil (Dragoon) Southern France, 15 Aug. 1944* (Ft. Leavenworth, KS, 1946), E-10.
19. *CSI Battlebook: Anvil/Dragoon,* 62-67; edited quotes from AFG Board; *Report C-639: Combat and Staff Lessons, 7th Army, Invasion of Southern France* (Washington, DC, 1945).
20. Ibid., 6.
21. Spencer Lewis Report, Camel Beach Landing, September 1944, 6.
22. "X-2," *http://www.cia.gov/csi/books/oss/art07.htm* (retrieved 12 Feb. 2004).
23. "Joint Security Control," *Organization* (formerly secret document mailed to the author by the National Archives at College Park, MD), 6-9.
24. Ibid.
25. Lewis Report, 4.
26. Ibid., 5.

27. "World War II at Sea," *http://www.naval-history.net/WW2194406.htm,* 12 (retrieved 14 Aug. 2000).

28. Ballantine, 289-291.

29. FM 9-6, *Ammunition Supply;* War Department Field Manual, 15 June 1944, 5.

30. Boddie, 28.

31. Lewis Report, 7-8.

32. LST 282 Commanding Officer Lawrence E. Gilbert wrote that it took about five hours before he was aboard a rescue ship.

33. Lewis Report, 9.

34. Ibid., 10-11.

    (a)   Frank Graeber of Santa Rosa, California, who served as a quartermaster first class on LST 454 reported in the *LST Scuttlebutt* of March-April 2006, 25, on a visual communication device that used an infrared innovation. It was introduced in April 1943. According to Mr. Graeber, "A rough sea made this transmission a nightmare for signalmen and quartermasters on watch."

    (b)   The lead editorial of the *New York Times* of 14 Dec. 2006 (page A40) complained that radios placed in small United States Coast Guard boats were defective. They had not been made waterproof and shorted out.

35. Ibid.

36. Max Hastings, *Armageddon: The Battle for Germany, 1944-1945* (New York: Alfred A. Knopf, 2004), 69.

37. Porch, 565.

38. Ibid.

39. "Report of Operations: The Seventh United States Army in France and Germany, 1944-1945," vol. 1, 15-16.

40. Devers, 30-31.

41. Ibid., 31-34.

42. Ibid., 41.

43. Foot, 413.

44. Porch, 612-613.

45. "Consolidated Statistics of Transportation Corps Operation in the European Theater of Operations," *The Historical Report of the Transportation Corps,* vol. 7, 3; cited in the "Administrative and Logistical History of the ETO," pt. 8, "Supplying the Armies" (MS Office, Chief of Military History, 1946), 42.

46. Devers, 10.

47. Ibid., 11.

48. Ibid., 14-15.

49. Ibid., 15, 16.

50. De Gaulle, 281.

51. Paul Fussell, *The Boys' Crusade: The American Infantry in Northwestern Europe, 1944-1945* (New York: Modern Library, 2003), 40-41.

52. Ibid., xii.

53. "The French Forces of the Interior," *ONI Weekly,* 6 Sept. 1944, 2832-2837.

54. Adm. H. K. Hewitt to Lieutenant Colonel Caldamaison, Directeur Generale de I'intendance (Aux bons soins du Colonel Regnault), June 18, 1944; from Admiral Hewitt's papers in the Library of Congress, translation from the French. Spahis were native Algerian cavalrymen in the French military service.

55. Hewitt, "Executing Operation Dragoon," *Proceedings of the United States Naval Institute,* no. 8 (August 1954), 906; Noam Cohen, "For British Troops, Help Crossing the Channel," *New York Times,* July 2, 2006, wk5. British soldiers were provided with a manual before the invasion of Normandy that urged civility toward the French. This successful publication dealt with the characteristics of French men and women, their domestic life, and differences between the French and British.

56. De Lattre, 67-69.

57. Diamond, 116.

58. Ibid.

59. Ibid., 90.

60. Devers, 7.

61. General Marshall's Report, 35, 36.

62. Morison, *The Invasion of France and Germany,* 221.

63. Boddie, 30.

64. "Remarks by CIA Deputy Director for Operations James L. Pavitt, OSS Society Banquet, 8 June 2002," *http://www.cia.gov/cia/public_affairs/speeches/ossbanquet_ddo_06082002.html* (June 27, 2002).

65. Joseph S. Nye, "How to Protect the Homeland," *New York Times,* 25 Sept. 2001, A29.

CHAPTER 12: REMEMBRANCE

1. "Major General Robert T. Frederick," *http://en.wikipedia.org/wiki/ROBERTTFREDERICK.*

2. Anthony N. Corea, Colonel, U.S. Air Force (Ret.), Director of Operations and Finance, the American Battle Monuments Commission, to the author, 5 Feb. 2002. See also American Battle Monuments Commission, *Rhone American Cemetery and Memorial,* 20, 25.

3. American Battle Monuments Commission to author, 20 Feb. 2002.

4. Telephone conversation with the author, 10 Nov. 2003.

5. Sheldon Aubut, Thomas Aubut's LST 282 site, *http://www.landingship.com/282/thomas_aubut.htm.*

6. Alan Riding, "Jean-Pierre Aumont, Film Star and Stage Hero, Dies at 90," *New York Times,* 31 Jan. 2001, A19.

7. Aumont, 192, 193.

8. Paul Lewis, "Dr. Rodolphe, 89, Hero of the Wartime French Resistance," *New York Times,* 22 June 2001, B8.

9. *Wilmington (DE) News Journal,* 17 Nov. 1979, 33.

10. *Wilmington (DE) Journal-Every Evening,* 8 Mar. 1945.

11. *Wilmington Journal,* 1 June 1945, 1, 6.

12. In the early 1970s, the author completed a master plan for Elsmere and visited that lovely town often.

13. *Wilmington Journal,* 10 Mar. 1994, 4.

14. Robin Brown, Bear Bureau Reporter, in *Focus,* 14 Nov. 2002.

15. Jim Connor Jr. to the author, 29 Sept. 2003.

16. Ibid.

17. Jim Parks, "Medal of Honor Winner James Connor Buried," *Wilmington News Journal,* 1 Aug. 1994.

18. Adam Ramirez, "Returning Refugees Hope New Base Camp in Bosnia Will Provide Them with Safety," *http://ww2pstripes.osd.mil/01/apr01/ed04060ID.html.*

19. Douglas Johnson, "Simone de Lattre," *Guardian,* 12 June 2003. *http://www.guardian.co.uk/france/story/0.11822,975546.html.*

20. Douglas Martin, "Lisa Fittko, 95, Helped Rescue Many Who Fled the Nazis," *New York Times,* 21 Mar. 2005, B7.

21. Townsend Hoopes and Douglas Brinkley, *Driven Patriot: The Life and Times of James Forrestal* (New York: Alfred A. Knopf, 1992), 196.

22. Walter Millis, ed., *The Forrestal Diaries,* with the collaboration of E. S. Duffield (New York: Viking Press, 1951), 46.

23. Ibid., 196.
24. Ibid., 375.
25. Ibid., 141.
26. Ibid., 145.
27. Ibid., 21.
28. See, for example, C. Arnold A. Rogow's *Victim of Duty: A Study of James Forrestal* (London: Rupert Hart-Davis, 1966), 17-43; Cecilia Stiles, "James Forrestal and American National Security Policy, 1940-1949" (doctoral dissertation, University of Michigan, Ann Arbor, MI, 1989), 438-464; and Hoopes and Brinkley, *Driven Patriot*, 387-487.
29. Ancell R. Manning, *The Biographical Dictionary of World War II Generals and Flag Officers: The U.S. Armed Forces,* with Christine M. Miller (Westport, CT: Greenwood Press, 1996), 108.
30. E-mail from Terry Gilbert to the author, 5 Jan. 2005.
31. R. G. Tobin, Commodore, USN Port Director, to Lt. Cmdr. Lawrence E. Gilbert 4 Feb. 1947.
32. E-mail from Norman Green to the author, 26 Mar. 2005.
33. E-mail from Terry Gilbert to the author, 16 May 2005.
34. E-mail from Kirsten R. Boetcher to the author, 3 Mar. 2004.
35. Ibid.
36. Lawrence E. Gilbert to Veteran Service Office, 15 Sept. 1992.
37. Edward Yungck to Lawrence Gilbert, 5 Oct. 2002.
38. Ibid. Author's comment: I too was charged with the offense of "sleeping in"—of not being awake and out of my sleeping rack before 0600. This charge was made by Petty Officer Bill Finnerin who was responsible for checking and reporting crew members caught sleeping in. As a result, I was punished at a captain's mast by Capt. Marshall Flowers. My punishment was to clean out the holes that were used to secure vehicles on the LST 1012 tank deck. Soldiers often slept on the tank and relieved themselves in the holes. In 1994, at an LST 1012 reunion, Finnerin and I talked about this episode and my claim that Finnerin's accusation was false. After fifty years, Finnerin admitted that I had told the truth but that crew members were needed to scoop out those nasty holes and that the "sleeping in" ploy was one way to get the job done. I was luckier than Ed Yungck, though. A few months after the hole-cleaning episode, I was promoted to petty officer third class. When I was transferred from LST 1012 after we returned to the United States in 1945, my transfer papers incorrectly indicated that I was elevated to petty officer first class. I never claimed this higher rate because I only found out about it in 1994, when

I was belatedly shown the transfer document by crew member Harold Larsen. In 1949, I was commissioned as a U.S. Navy reserve officer. I believe that the "first class" designation on the transfer sheet was an error because I did not merit a promotion from third class to first class.

39. E-mail from Lauren Gilbert Baginski to the author, 13 Nov. 2002.

40. *The Forrestal Diaries*, 46

41. E-mail to the author from Mary Kent Norton, 28 Dec. 2002.

42. The source of citations concerning Admiral Hewitt's decorations and awards is the U.S. History Library.

43. *Baltimore Evening Sun,* 10 May 1967.

44. *Sun,* 15 Mar. 1982.

45. Don Graham, *No Name on the Bullet: A Biography of Audie Murphy* (New York: Viking Press, 1989), 160.

46. Ibid., 170.

47. *New York Times,* 22 May 2005, Television Section, 5; *New York Times,* 31 Jan. 2002, B7. In the late '50s, Audie Murphy nearly died. The war hero became a movie actor. He was in the movie *The Unforgiven*. While in a scene that required him to be in a cold mountain lake, he was saved from drowning by the famous photographer Inge Morath. In 1962 she became the wife of the playwright Arthur Miller. Ms. Morath jumped into the water in her underwear to rescue Audie Murphy. Her obituary by Douglas Martin notes that "she swam a half-mile and dragged Mr. Murphy by her bra strap."

48. "Lane Nakano, 80, a Soldier Turned Actor," *New York Times,* 11 May 2005; Jonathan Mahler, "GI Japanese during World War II; Some Soldiers Were in Internment Camps until They Enlisted," *New York Times Book Review,* 19 June 2006, 17. The 442nd Regimental Combat Team was a segregated unit of Japanese-American soldiers who volunteered to serve in the U.S. Army. They risked their lives fighting in southern France during the summer and autumn of 1944. Under dangerous conditions, they succeeded in rescuing 270 soldiers from a Texas battalion who were pinned down behind German lines in the Vosges Mountains.

Among those who assisted General Clark's Italian campaign achievements were Japanese-American soldiers of the 442nd Regiment. He gave them a chance to fight the Nazis while other American military and political leaders incarcerated and impoverished the families of these soldiers. They repaid Clark for the chance to fight as Americans by phenomenal bravery. The *New York Times* of 28 June 2001 reported that "more than 30,000 Japanese-Americans served in the American military during World War II, earning more than 9,000 Purple Hearts, while more than 120,000 Japanese-American men, women and children were held in remote internment camps or under martial law" (p. A, 24).

49. USS LST 494 Association, "Irving 'Chet' Noyes, LST 494's ETO Skipper Passes Away," *LST Scuttlebutt,* March-April 2006, 32.

50. Wyant, 150.

51. Truman R. Strobridge and Bernard C. Nalty, "From the South Pacific to the Brenner Pass: General Alexander M. Patch," *Military Review,* June 1981, 46.

52. Ibid., 47.

53. Wyant, 210.

54. Ibid., 214.

55. De Lattre, 53.

56. *New York Times,* 6 June 1952, 46.

57. *New York Times,* 11 Sept. 2002, C12.

58. Truscott, 507.

59. George Dorsey, "Marseilles: City of Violent Death," *Stars and Stripes,* 25 Aug. 1944, 1, 8.

60. Gildea, 325; Bernard Schwartz, "The Path of Least Resistance," *Atlantic Monthly,* October 2006, 168, 169. This is a review of Richard Vinen's *The Unfree French* (Yale University Publisher, 2000) and Carmen Callil's *Bad Faith* (Knopf Publisher, 2000). There is also the need to remember that throughout France there were people who indulged in food-ration cheating, black-marketing, profiteering, stealing Jewish property, bearing false witness, collaborating with the Germans, and other evils.

"France: Pensions for Foreign Veterans Raised," *New York Times,* 28 Sept. 2006, A6; Christopher Hitchens, "A French Quarrel," *Atlantic Monthly,* November 2006, 118-122. African soldiers fought for France during Operation Dragoon and in other campaigns to liberate it. But they had to wait until the end of September 2005 before the French government announced that it would pay them the same amount of pension money as their French comrades in arms.

61. American Historical Association, "Will the French Republic Live Again?" (Madison, WI: the United States Armed Forces Institute, June 1944), 36. In addition to winning their freedom from German occupation, the French expected reparations from their enemies for the devastation and theft of their property. Shortly after the end of World War II in Europe, both the French and Russians expropriated industrial and capital resources from the Germans. Historians Robert P. Grathwol and Donita M. Moorhus

have provided an account of subsequent events: "As the expropriations continued, the German economy remained depressed below subsistence level. Great Britain had barely enough resources after the drain of the war to care for its own zone of occupation. Only the United States had the economic strength and the financial resources to reverse Germany's declining economy. The American administrators in Germany faced an unenviable choice: to watch the German population in the west starve slowly; to import food, thereby shifting the cost of Soviet and French expropriation of German resources to the American taxpayers; or to try to stimulate the German economy so it could pay its own reparations and rebuild its resources. Policymakers in the United States chose the last option. In May 1946, the American military governor, General Clay, suspended all deliveries of reparations outside the American zone, hoping to force all four powers to deal with the German economy as a whole." Robert P. Grathwol and Donita M. Moorhus, *American Forces in Berlin: Cold War Outpost* (Washington, DC: Department of Defense, 1994), 28.

Appendices

1.

ATTACHE'S REPORT

Forward seven copies (original and six carbons); this number is necessary because of the limited personnel in O. N. I. and because of the urgency for quickly disseminating information from attachés. These copies will be distributed by O. N. I. as per footnote or elsewhere, according to subject matter.

From .... **Y** .... Date ..**27 Sept**.., 19.**39** Serial No. ......**521**...... File No. **800**
(Commence new series each January first) (Select proper number from O. N. I. Index)

Source of information ....

Subject ....
(Nation reported on)   (Index title as per index sheet)   (Subtitle)

Reference ....

BRIEF.—(The review, indexing, and distribution of reports by O. N. I. will be greatly expedited if a brief summary of the contents is entered in this space. Mention leading geographical, personal, or political names, and the gist of the report.)

Sheet 3

French hopes of Americans joining war (Reliable). It is surprising to hear from many French people, some through ignorance and other through press propaganda, the question, "What is America going to do; when is she going to decide?"

  A good many people mistook the President's address to Congress on the neutrality law for a clear out demand for American participation in the war. This was partly due to the headlines in the French press: "America Pronounces To-morrow!" A member of this office, who went to a nearby store the day prior to the President's message, was immediately accosted by the proprietor, who said, "When is America going to decide — now is the time before it is too late to see Roosevelt has postponed his message until to-morrow." This man actually believed that the President's address was to be a demand for American participation in the war. When I explained that it was merely to remove an embargo so that we could sell war supplies, he nearly keeled over and remarked, "You're out of business."

Source: The National Archives, College Park, MD

583

2.

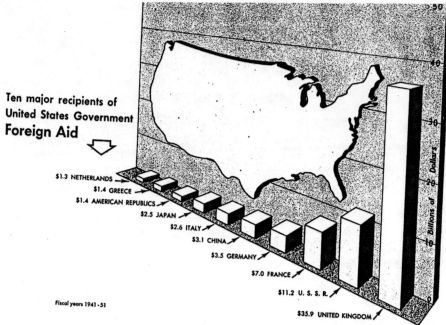

Ten major recipients of
United States Government
Foreign Aid

$1.3 NETHERLANDS
$1.4 GREECE
$1.4 AMERICAN REPUBLICS
$2.5 JAPAN
$2.6 ITALY
$3.1 CHINA
$3.5 GERMANY
$7.0 FRANCE
$11.2 U. S. S. R.
$35.9 UNITED KINGDOM

Fiscal years 1941 - 51

Billions of Dollars

Foreign Aid

by the

United States Government

1940 - 1951

Prepared by the

Clearing Office for Foreign Transactions

OFFICE OF BUSINESS ECONOMICS
Dept of Commerce

U. S. GOVERNMENT PRINTING OFFICE
WASHINGTON : 1952

3.

LEND-LEASE

VALUE OF WAR DEPARTMENT LEND-LEASE TRANSFERS: 1941–49[a]

(IN THOUSANDS OF DOLLARS)

Country	Total	By Method Transfer				By Procuring Agency		
		Direct Shipment	Commanding General Shipment	Theater Transfers		ASF	AAF	Misc Services and Expenses
Total	[b]24,510,915	19,837,425	1,075,800	3,597,690		16,281,511	7,428,397	801,007
Brazil	230,957	155,473	8,452	67,032		143,545	81,084	6,328
British Empire (excluding Canada)	14,296,120	13,291,945	3,337	1,000,838		9,150,923	5,007,040	138,157
Canada	169,825	167,158	0	2,667		93,276	76,024	525
China	1,729,333	270,420	385,867	1,073,046		874,216	291,119	563,998
French forces	2,039,474	15,413	660,905	1,363,156		1,621,777	329,519	88,178
Mexico	31,254	19,702	3,102	8,450		15,198	16,056	[d]
Netherlands	95,421	87,652	0	7,769		16,259	77,929	1,233
Turkey	38,807	32,029	6,754	24		37,723	1,060	24
USSR	5,516,412	5,483,106	505	32,801		4,005,240	1,511,074	98
Other American republics	64,777	60,395	0	4,382		31,572	31,296	1,909
Other countries	59,108	16,882	5,531	36,695		52,623	5,928	557
Not distributed[e]	239,427	237,250	1,347	830		239,159	268	0

[a] Dollar values represent basic costs to War Department plus fixed-percentage allowance for handling charges.
[b] Additional transfers in the amount of $560,051,000 for production facilities completed in the United States.
[c] Of total, material valued at $653,363,000 was directed overseas to United States use or returned to the United States either overseas or in the country.
[d] Less than $500.
[e] Consists of material turned over to the Foreign Economic Administration for retransfer to recipient country and miscellaneous expenses connected therewith.

Source: Whiting, Tod, and Craft, Statistics: Lend-Lease, 15 Dec 52, Table LL-6

585

4. **France vs. Germany**
    Subheadings: Population Problems
    Industry, Limited
    Steel and Aluminum
    Farms and Farmers
    Paying Protection Money

POPULATION PROBLEMS

For almost a century France has had a population problem of increasing acuteness. Since 1880 the French population has remained almost stationary near the figure of forty million. And the birth rate has declined steadily until in recent years it no longer has been sufficient to assure replacement of the population.

POPULATION GROWTH 1830 TO 1930

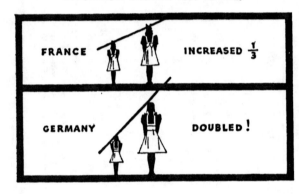

At the same time, France's neighbors were showing very marked increases in population. The French figure rose about one-third in the century from 1830 to 1930 while those for Italy and Germany doubled. Had there been a 1940 census, France would have made an even poorer showing since by that year territorial additions had given Germany a population twice as big as that of France.

Moreover, very significant changes were taking place within the forty million total of French population. Once the most populous country of Europe, France in 1930 was far less densely populated than its neighbors. As a result, immigration from Germany, Italy, and Spain during the interwar years provided France with a population that by 1930 was already about 7 per cent of foreign origin.

Furthermore, the French population was the oldest in Europe and growing older. That is, the proportion of the population com-

posed of people over 60 was large and growing larger; the proportion composed of people under 20 was small and growing smaller.
That kind of situation obviously did not make for a high birth rate.
Neither did another characteristic of the French population: the
marked excess of women over men. In 1930, not counting the
foreign element, there were 111 females in France to every 100
males. This was an unbalance between the sexes greater than in
any other country of Europe and one still further exaggerated since
1940 by the absence of nearly two million Frenchmen held in
German prison and work camps.

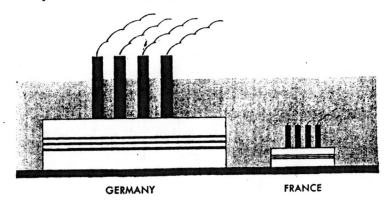

GERMANY   FRANCE

Population statistics reveal another important fact about France.
In comparison with the other industrial nations of the world,
France has not developed as many large factory cities with huge
worker populations. This is partly because French industry is not
geared to mass production so much as it is to small, specialty, and
luxury manufacturing. For generations, Paris gowns and hats set
the style; French perfumes, gloves, silks, and chinaware were eagerly
bought in the markets of the world. The typical French factory
employs less than twenty-five workers, and out of the grand total
of about a million and a quarter industrial establishments the surprising proportion of one-sixth are one-man shops in which the
owner is also the entire labor force.

GERMANY   FRANCE

France has built up several large centers of heavy industry, but it can never approach the industrialization attained by Germany, Great Britain, the United States, and Russia. Unless new advances in science change the picture, France's lack of raw materials and the means of acquiring them in quantity will continue to act as limitations on French industrialization.

First and foremost among these limitations is France's lack of fuel. Insufficient resources of coal, particularly coking coal, have held France back in the industrial race. At no time in the past hundred years has France produced enough coal to supply her own needs. This is significant in view of the fact that, unless and until science is able to discover a substitute, large stocks of coal are vital to industrial production.

Two very important raw materials France does have in abundance. They are iron ore and aluminum ore (bauxite). But the

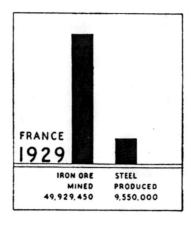

FRANCE
1929

IRON ORE MINED	STEEL PRODUCED
49,929,450	9,550,000

processing of the ores into refined metals requires coal or electricity
—and much of the latter has been produced from coal. Because
its supplies of coal are limited, France has never been able to make
full use of its iron-ore and bauxite deposits.

In the record year 1929, for instance, France produced 49,929,450
long tons of iron ore, about one-fourth of the world production in
that year. But even with that amount of ore and even with the
coal of the Saar Basin, then available to France, only some 9,550,000
long tons of finished steel could be made.

The reason for this lies in the economic fact that it is more
profitable to move iron ore for smelting to areas where coal and
limestone are found in quantity than the other way around. Thus,
most of the iron ore from northern Minnesota flows to the Gary–
Youngstown–Pittsburgh region, where ample supplies of the other
two ingredients necessary to steelmaking are found. For the same
reason much of the ore from French Lorraine normally flows to
Germany's Ruhr Valley.

Modern mechanized warfare requires enormous quantities of steel
in all kinds of arms, munitions, and equipment. A nation's capacity
for producing steel, therefore, is a relatively accurate measure of its
ability to fight a twentieth-century war. In 1939 Germany stood
second among the nations of the world in production of steel;
France was fifth.

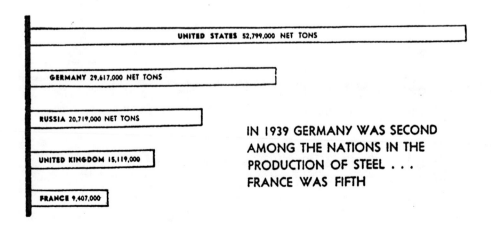

UNITED STATES 52,799,000 NET TONS

GERMANY 29,617,000 NET TONS

RUSSIA 20,719,000 NET TONS

UNITED KINGDOM 15,119,000

FRANCE 9,407,000

IN 1939 GERMANY WAS SECOND
AMONG THE NATIONS IN THE
PRODUCTION OF STEEL . . .
FRANCE WAS FIFTH

BAUXITE
MINED IN
1938

FRANCE   GERMANY

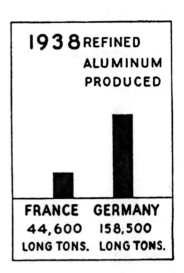

1938 REFINED
ALUMINUM
PRODUCED

FRANCE   GERMANY
44,600   158,500
LONG TONS.   LONG TONS.

For years preceding the outbreak of the war, France had led the world in production of aluminum ore. Yet its position with respect to Germany was even worse for refined aluminum than for steel. In 1938 France mined about thirty-five times as much bauxite as

Germany, which has almost no reserves of that ore. In the very same year Germany, leading the world by a wide margin, manufactured 158,500 long tons of aluminum in refined form, compared with only 44,600 long tons refined in France. Again the explanation is to be found in France's lack of adequate power resources, either coal or hydroelectric, to process the ore.

With the exception of rich potash beds in Alsace, enough to last for centuries at the present rate of use, France either lacks entirely the other so-called "strategic materials" or its supplies are not enough for home consumption. In consequence it depends to an unusual extent for these materials on sources beyond its own frontiers.

In 1925–29—years of great prosperity—France produced exportable surpluses of iron ore, bauxite, chemicals, and potash. But iron and steel production only equaled home use and some machinery was imported. With its industrial plant running at full capacity France produced only a fraction of the output of the industrial giants, and from that time onward its production declined while that of both Germany and Russia was rapidly increasing.

France produces a high proportion of its food requirements, differing in this respect from the other European industrial nations, which normally import much of the food they need. Nevertheless, there are problems connected with French agriculture. The system of landownership in France, a holdover from the feudal days of a thousand years ago, encourages minute subdivision of the farm land rather than its combination into large fields and farms. Of the total 3,966,000 farm units in France, approximately three-quarters are less than 25 acres in size. Nearly one-fourth are less than 2.5 acres. At the other end of the scale only 114,000 farms are larger than 125 acres.

Furthermore, fields belonging to a single owner are as likely to be scattered separately about the locality as to be all next to each other in one place. The result is that tractors and other farm machinery cannot profitably be used, even if the small farmers could afford their purchase. French farmers, therefore, practice a more intensive kind of farming, with greater use of human labor than do American farmers. For instance, in 1929 there were only 20,000 tractors in all of rural France.

The French peasant is a good farmer and he loves the soil. He has tended in the last century more and more toward truck farming, dairying, fruit raising, and the like as the most profitable ways to use his land. Just as French industry is noted for its luxury products, French agriculture is famous for its berries, its wines, its vegetables, and its cheeses. And at the same time, enough wheat, potatoes, sugar beets, and other cereals and root crops are produced to supply the national need of these staples.

However, the production of farm commodities in sufficient quantities to supply the domestic market was not wholly the result of natural fertility. It was partly a result of the national policy of protecting home agriculture as well as home industry from foreign competition behind a high tariff wall. This has assured the French market to the French farmer and the French manufacturer without having to meet direct competition from lower-cost production elsewhere—of American or Canadian or Argentinean wheat, or Cuban cane sugar, for instance.

The tariff has given French economy some of the more undesirable aspects of a hothouse. Enterprises flourish that would die if exposed to the pressure of prices in the world market, and Frenchmen, as consumers, have to pay that much more for the things they buy. The French accept the protectionist argument that the nation's economic life would be destroyed by foreign competition. By and large they seem content to pay the price of artificially stimulating some enterprises and encouraging inefficiency in others behind the protective tariff.

Source: *Will the French Republic Live Again?* Prepared for the United States Armed Forces Institute by the American Historical Association, June 1944.

5. Telegram, Murphy to Hull, January 23, 1943

(To improve the legibility of the copy of this telegram obtained from the National History Division, Office of the Chief of Naval Operations, it has been retyped.)

Author's note:

In this telegram, Robert D. Murphy, U.S. State Department agent in North Africa, sought to refute criticism directed at the president's policies toward the Vichy regime. Roosevelt believed that if the Allies showed goodwill toward the Pétain regime, for example, by providing needed supplies to North African colonists, France would be brought back to fight on the Allied side. This Rooseveltian approach was condemned by American critics of the Vichy regime.

Following President Roosevelt's orders, Murphy promoted an agreement that allowed French officials to use French funds that had been frozen in use in North Africa. This agreement was known as the Murphy-Weygand accord.[1] Murphy also arranged that the British would not invoke their stringent blockade to stop the passage of supplies purchased by the French. Murphy and Weygand also arranged for the use of secret codes and couriers to supply American officials with valuable intelligence information. Murphy's use of American vice counsels as intelligence agents afforded the United States government with the opportunity to oversee what was happening in North Africa, and it also helped in the transmission of uncensored confidential reports to American war leaders.[2]

Murphy's telegram to U.S. secretary of state Cordell Hull spells out American objectives and ways to achieve them. Note, for example, Murphy's comments concerning (1) the American military objective of gaining control of North Africa and the southern shore of the Mediterranean and (2) how a regenerated France would be brought about. Roosevelt and Murphy's prescience are worth remembering and adopting.

For case of reference: Marshal Ferdinand Foch (1851-1928) was the French Army leader during World War I. Georges Clemenceau (1841-1929) was French premier from 1917 to 1920 and France's representative at the Treaty of Versailles.

1. Gen. Maxime Weygand was commander of French forces in North Africa.
2. See Robert D. Murphy's *Diplomat among Warriors* (Garden City, NY: Doubleday, 1964), 90.

Telegram: Murphy to Hull, January 23, 1943

It seems clear to me that the unfavorable press comment results largely from the fundamental mistake of interpreting current events in North Africa in terms of Metropolitan France of other days. This area is not France, but a colonial region that has always been socially, religiously, racially and psychologically different from France.

In the light of events since 1940, the political situation here, always different from that in France, is even less understandable today by those who attempt to do so in terms of the France of 1914-1918.

There is a great shortage of qualified men to fill special positions in Morocco and Algeria. A continued orderly administration is essential and serious consequences to our military operations result from abrupt and radical changes, especially if little known or unqualified personnel were introduced.

Critics have failed to understand: (a) our objective here, and (b)the problems which confronted us on our arrival. We are engaged on a military operation, whose purpose is to gain control of Africa and the southern shore of the Mediterranean.

In order to accomplish this objective we dealt with those Franch whom we found in power here who were willing to aid us by maintaining order and our lines of communication and by putting the French armed forces at their disposal into the fight.

We did not find the ideal Frenchman whom the critics see from the heights of their Ivory Towers. We found Frenchmen who, after being defeated by Germany, had undergone two years of German pressure and propaganda. We found Frenchmen who have changed and who no longer think as did Clemenceau. In working with them we made only one condition: that they showed a wish to fight Germany.

Our critics seem primarily interested, not in the military operation, but in a return to the ideal of France they have in their memories. That is simply impossible in this colonial area. It must wait until the people of continental France are again free. Pressures to accomplish the impossible in French Africa can only have one result: embarrass military operations and make our task harder.

A regenerated France can be brought into being only in France itself. Any attempt to set the pattern for that regeneration before France is liberated is doomed to utter failure and would be inconsistent with the President's declared policy. It must come from within the French, aided by what influence we may be able to exert. It would be fatal for us to try to impose it prematurely from without. We have constantly refrained from assuming the responsibility of forcing people of our choice on local authorities. We deem it wiser to hold them responsible for what they do in respect to the war.

Admiral Darlan had offered before his death to discharge any official if the Allied Staff could offer a qualified and locally acceptable substitute who could be acceptable to the Allies and to the British and American press. We were unable to make useful suggestions. A de Gaullist would have been impossible as they are considered to be extremists by the vast majority here, especially in the armed forces.

Many critics have a tendency to divide all Frenchmen into the sheep and the goats. They feel that all French must be pro-Ally or pro-German. Anyone who held office after the Armistice is labeled "Vichy" which is considered to be equivalent to pro-German.

Such is not the case as many prominent French who hate the Boche and much as Foch ever did, have felt it to be their duty to stick by their government in adversity and do their honest best to resist Germany from within.

It is about time to stop theorizing while there is a desperate fight to win, and allow the light of realism to penetrate the obscurity of ignorance about fundamentals of North African problems.

Source: Algiers 6774, NAF 119231046Z January 3, 1943, in Box 204, File: February 1943, Commander, U.S. Naval Forces in Europe file, Naval History Division, Office of the Chief of Naval Operations

6. Author's note: On January 4, 1937, Capt. H. K. Hewitt, commander of the USS *Indianapolis,* brought the following to the attention of his crew.

U.S.S. INDIANAPOLIS
At Sea 4 January,1937

MEMORANDUM FOR ALL HANDS

  The following letter,from the President of the United States, is quoted:

"THE WHITE HOUSE
  WASHINGTON

23 December, 1936.

 "Dear Captain Hewitt

  "Now that my recent visit to South America in the INDIANAPOLIS is at an end, I retain nothing but the utmost esteem for the fine performance of that vessel so ably commanded by yourself.

  "During the cruise (18 November to 15 December) from Charleston, South Carolina to Rio de Janeiro to Buenos Aires to Montevideo and return (with a stop each way at Trinidad), the ship met every detail of the itinerary with precision and to my complete satisfaction. Furthermore, it was evident that every officer and man in the ship was determined to leave nothing undone that could add to the pleasure and comfort of myself and of those who accompanied me.

  "I feel that this record cruise of approximately twenty-three days at sea, covering something over 12,000 miles opens up new possibilities of drawing us closer to our sister republics of this hemisphere.

  "In sending this letter through the Secretary of the Navy, I am requesting that it be made a part of the official record of yourself, your executive officer, your heads of department and of your communication officer.

 " You have a smart ship.

  "To yourself, to your officers, and to every man in your ship's company -

"Well Done"

/s/ Franklin D. Roosevelt.

Captain H.K.Hewitt, U.S.N.
U.S.S. INDIANAPOLIS,
San Pedro, California"

        H. K. HEWITT

Source: Reproduced from the Collection of the Manuscript Division, Library of Congress, Washington, DC.

7.

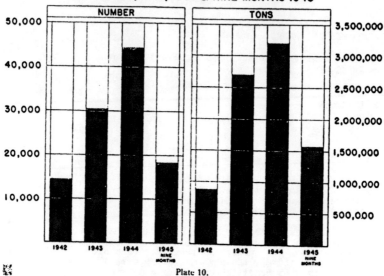

Plate 10.

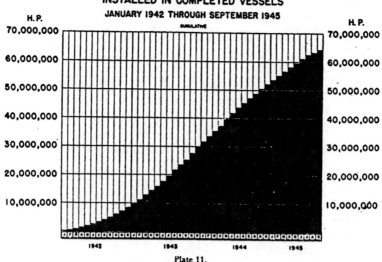

Plate 11.

SOURCE: U.S.Navy at War, 1941-1945: Official Reports to Secretary of the Navy by Fleet Admiral Ernest J. King (Washington, D.C.: U.S. Navy Dept., 1946

8. Excerpts from a letter from Bob Wilson, Commanding Officer of the LST 1011—edited by the author to remove unrelated information

Steve....   January 10, 2001

Pleased that some of the material sent you might be of interest.
Think I've hit the high spots of prejudice observed in the
most exclusive branch of our military at least as practiced
in WWII.   Must comment the obvious that this preference for
male whites of Western European stock was an integral part of
what was done in Philadelphia as of 1787.   The military just
chose to prolong the eliteness of the brotherhood until Harry
Truman ordered some integration that was not in much evidence
during WWII.   Fighting for a democracy that was far from being
one might have helped the Nisei, blacks, Jews, etc. if fulfilling
the "equal justice" objective had been made more obtainable.
(Loved teaching and you trigger the impulse)

My first specific awarenss of anti-semitism didn't come along
until high school when my soon to be brother-in-law who owned
a large swimming pool in N. Baltimore revealed that he "trained"
his help to recognize and reject Jews.   Blacks, too of course.
At Antioch College in Ohio, one of the most "liberal", there
were no blacks and the registrar maintained a quota system for
Jews with or without the approval of the administration.
One of my co-op jobs out of Antioch was in Chicago with the
Illinois State Employment Service.   In 1937 a request for a
non-Jewish counselor for an all-Jewish boys camp crossed my
desk.   It seemed to offer an opportunity to observe close up
what "these people" were like.   I applied, was accepted
and experienced three summers working with other counselors
and campers who, along with their parents, gave me measure of
love not experienced before.

So 10 years later when I reported for duty in BuPers and the
Navy told me not to assign Jews to regular Naval vessels
for they presumably would degrade the service the prejudice
came down hard.   Oswald Jacoby, a renowned expert on bridge
and poker, had written some books, recognized for his mathe-
matical talents, applied for officer ranking.   But he was a
Jew and the unwritten rule was no such on regular naval vessels...but he shouldn't become just a gunner on a freighter.
So he was assigned to a special section where his presence
would not do harm.

By the time I was prepared for sea duty in late 1942 this
discrimination was crumbling but still there as blacks were
assigned as stewart's mates and Jews were assigned to the amphibious force.   Just before departure for overseas we received two Jewish ensigns fresh out of Hunter indoctrination.
Zeik and Zeiburg: One a graduate of St.John's Great Books
program, the other from NYU.   Don't believe I ever did find
a suitable assignment for Zeik even tho he tried to relate what
he knew about Plato to the problems of operating an LCVP.
Zeiburg, also at the end of the alphabet, was an enthusiastic,

10 Jan 2001

lovable kind of a guy who was delighted when we made him our
navigator.   So with a sextant and the HO214 tables he steered
us from New York, across the Pacific, on to Guam and points
beyond.

Even tho the 1011 and the 1012 frequently travelled together
and Buck Flowers and myself enjoyed many "liberties" together
I realize that I didn't get to know much about him.   Think
he ran a "tight" ship with captain's inspections and perhaps
an occasional captain's mast; friendly, good sense of humor
but not all that much fun especially when compared with Zeiburg.
You no doubt know more about his performance as the CO than
do I.

First touch with land after passing through Gibralta under heavy
ship-made smoke was at Bizerte, Algeria where a large inland
sea was entered thru a very narrow channel that seemed only
inches larger than our 50' beam.   The supply officer of the
commissionary was a friend from college days and although all
bottled stuff was supposed to go to the officer's club, Freddie
passed along a couple bottles of bourbon for dollars that I
assume went into his pocket.   A sharp businessman who probably
came out of service with considerably more than when he went
in.

Occasionally when we were designated the flag ship of a convoy
we hosted a regular Navy three striper being disciplined
for some transgression.   Or maybe he was assigned to us to
demonstrate how a Navy ship should be run.   In any case he
would preempt my quarters, provoke my resentment and add to
the existing prejudice.   To his credit however he did not
interfer with the running of the ship even as we landed on D-
Day.   The amphibious force may have been the "dog navy"
but I sincerely believe that our achievements were notable
in part because the regular Navy left us alone.

My ranking as a Lt(jg)upon entry came because, (I presume)of
my age, 28, my experience of one year in the merchant marine,
three summers as a sailing counselor in the Jewish camp, and
my job as Personnel Manager of an industrial plant in Baltimore.
The latter experience got the assignment to BuPers where anti-
semitism and racism were institutionalized.

Bob

Source: Author's correspondence with Bob Wilson

600

9a.

FIGHTING STRENGTH

ENLISTED PERSONNEL U.S. NAVY

1941-1944

FIGURES AS OF 31 DECEMBER

Source: *U.S. Navy at War 1941-1945: Official Reports to Secretary of the Navy* by Fleet Admiral Ernest J. King (Washington, DC: U.S. Navy Dept., 1946).

9b.

Comparative Status of U.S. and Japanese Combatant Ships

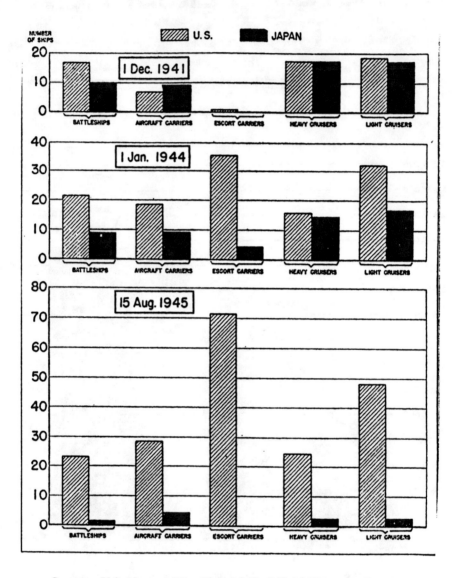

Source: *U.S. Navy at War 1941-1945: Official Reports to Secretary of the Navy* by Fleet Adm. Ernest J. King (Washington, DC: U.S. Navy Dept., 1946).

10.

PRINCIPAL TYPES OF ALLIED LANDING CRAFT, SHIPS, AND VEHICLES USED IN OPERATIONS
1943-45ᵃ

Nomenclature	Builder	Length	Beam	Displacement	Capacity
LCA Landing craft, assault..............	U.K.	41'	10'	8.5 tons (light)	35 troops and 800 lbs. equipment
LCP(L) Landing craft, personnel (large)........	U.S.	36'	10'9"	13,500 lbs. (light)	36 troops or 8,100 lbs. cargo
LCP(L) Landing craft, personnel (large)........	U.K.	36'10"	10'10"	13,000 lbs. (light)	25 equipped troops or 6,700–8,100 lbs. cargo
LCP(R) Landing craft, personnel (ramp)........	U.S.	35'10"	10'9"	13,500 lbs. (light)	36 troops or 8,100 lbs. cargo
LCI(L) Landing craft, infantry (large).......... (1-350)	U.S.	160'	23'3"	194 tons (light)	6 officers and 182 men or 75 tons cargo
LCM(3) Landing craft, mechanized............ (Mark 3)	U.S.	50'	14'1"	26 tons (light)	One 30-ton tank or 60,000 lbs. cargo or 100 troops
LCM(6) Landing craft, mechanized............ (Mark 6)	U.S.	56'	14'1"	26 tons (light)	One 34-ton tank or 68,000 lbs. cargo or 120 troops
LCT(1) Landing craft, tank................. (Mark 1)	U.K.	152'	29'	226 tons (light)	Three 40-ton tanks, or six 25-ton tanks, or six 16-ton tanks, or 250 tons cargo
LCT(2) Landing craft, tank................. (Mark 2)	U.K.	159'11"	31'	296 tons (light)	Approximately same as LCT(1)
LCT(3) Landing craft, tank................. (Mark 3)	U.K.	192'	31'	350 tons (light)	Five 40-ton tanks or ten 3-ton trucks or 300 tons cargo; 24 Army personnel
LCT(4) Landing craft, tank................. (Mark 4)	U.K.	192'	31'	350 tons (light)	Maximum load 240 tons
LCT(5) Landing craft, tank...... .... (Mark 5)	U.S.	114'2"	32'	133 tons (light)	Five 30-ton or four 40-ton or three 50-ton tanks, or 9 trucks or 150 tons cargo
LCT(6) Landing craft, tank.................	U.S.	119'½"	32'	143 tons	Four medium or three 50-ton tanks, or 150 tons cargo; accommodations for 8 troops
LCV Landing craft, vehicle...............	U.S.	36'4"	10'11½"	7 tons (light)	One 1-ton truck or 36 troops or 10,000 lbs. cargo
LCVP Landing craft, vehicle, personnel.......	U.S.	35'9"	10'11½"	18,700 lbs.	36 troops or 8,100 lbs. cargo or 3 tons vehicles
LCC(1) Landing craft, control............... (Mark 1)	U.S.	56'	13'7"	23 tons	Crew only
LCC(2) Landing craft, control............... (Mark 2)	U.S.	56'	14'6"	25 tons	Crew only
LCS(S)(1) Landing craft, support (small)........ (Mark 1)	U.S.	36'8½"	10'11½"	20,000 lbs.	3–4 plus crew and gunners
LCS(S)(2) Landing craft, support (small)........ (Mark 2)	U.S.	36'8½"	10'11½"	22,000 lbs.	3–4 plus crew and gunners
LCS(L)(3) Landing craft, support (large).......... (Mark 3)	U.S.	158'0½"	23'3"	250 tons (light)	Crew only
LCE Landing craft, emergency repair........	U.K.	36'3"	10'10"	23,500 lbs.	Crew and repair gear
LSD Landing ship, dock..................	U.S.	457'9"	72'	4,032 tons (light)	3 LCT (5 and 6)'s each with 5 medium tanks, or 2 LCT (3 and 4)'s each with 12 medium tanks, or 14 LCM (3)'s each with 1 medium tank, or 1,500 long ton cargos or 41 LVT's, or 47 DUKW's; troops: 22 officers, 310 men
LSM Landing ship, medium...............	U.S.	203'6"	34'6"	743 tons (landing)	5 medium or 3 heavy tanks (165 tons maximum payload landing) or 6 LVT's or 9 DUKW's; troops: 48
LST Landing ship, tank.................. (Merchant conversion)	U.K.	382'6"	64'	3,952–4,890 tons (gross)	18 heavy or 22 25-ton tanks or 33 trucks; 2 LCM's or smaller on deck
LST(1) Landing ship, tank.................. (Class 1)	U.K.	400'	49'	2,840 tons (light)	1 LCM or 1 LCS; 13 40-ton tanks or 27 loaded 3-ton trucks (150 tons total); troops: 193
LST Landing ship, tank.................. (U.K. designation: LST(2))	U.S.	328'	50'	1,625 tons (light)	1,600–1,900 tons (ocean-going maximum) (400 tons main deck load); troops: 16 officers, 147 men

PRINCIPAL TYPES OF ALLIED LANDING CRAFT, SHIPS, AND VEHICLES USED IN OPERATIONS
1943–45[a]—Continued

	Nomenclature	Builder	Length	Beam	Displacement	Capacity
LST(3)	Landing ship, tank.................	U.K.	345'10"	54'	3,065 tons (beaching)	5 LCA's, 1 LCT(6), or 14 trucks or upper deck; 27 25-ton tanks or 1. 40-ton tanks on tank deck; troops 168
LSV	Landing ship, vehicle...............	U.S.	45–54'	60'	5,615 (light)	19–21 LVT's, 29–44 DUKW's, 80 troops
LVT(2) (Mark 2)	Landing vehicle, tracked	U.S.	26'1"	10'8"	25,200 lbs. (unloaded)	6,500 lbs. cargo or 24 equipped troop
LVT(3) (Mark 3)	Landing vehicle, tracked............	U.S.	24'1¾"	11'	28,000 lbs. (unloaded)	8,000 lbs. cargo or 24 equipped troop
LVT(4) (Mark 4)	Landing vehicle, tracked............	U.S.	26'1"	10'8"	23,350 lbs. (unloaded)	8,000 lbs. cargo, maximum
LVT(A)(4) (Mark 4)	Landing vehicle, tracked (armored)....	U.S.	26'1"	10'8"	35,100 lbs.	5,000 lbs. ammunition and gear
DUKW	2½-ton, 6x6 amphibian truck.........	U.S.	31'	8'	13,000 lbs. (light)	25 equipped troops, or 12 loaded litters, or 5,000 lbs. cargo
Jeep	¼-ton, 4x4, amphibian truck.........	U.S.	15'7"	5'4"	3,700 lbs. (light)	800 lbs. cargo

[a] Types selected are those identified in ONI 226 as "major operational types." Larger types of landing ships such as the British LSI's of various types, and American AGC's, APD's, APA's, and AKA's are not listed as their characteristics were not standard but varied between individual vessels and classes.
Sources: ONI 226, 7 Apr 44, Allied Landing Craft and Ships, and Supplement No. 1 to ONI 226.

11.

U.S. PRODUCTION OF MAJOR TYPES OF LANDING SHIPS AND CRAFT
1940–45

Date	LST	LSD	LSM and LSM(R)	LCI(L)	LCT (5 and 6)	LCP (L and R)	LCV	LCVP	LCM (2, 3, and 6)	LVT	LVT(A)
Total....	1,041	22	528	921	1,435	4,824	2,366	23,358	11,496	15,501	3,119
1940–41..........	0	0	0	0	0	564	110	0	125	72	0
1942											
January–June....	0	0	0	0	1	553	446	0	84	268	2
July.............	0	0	0	0	1	307	173	0	118	74	0
August..........	0	0	0	0	45	218	382	0	307	94	0
September.......	0	0	0	1	156	222	255	0	131	105	0
October..........	1	0	0	25	152	228	166	0	203	52	1
November.......	18	0	0	59	101	212	254	75	244	133	0
December........	43	0	0	68	9	130	215	140	168	125	0
1943											
January.........	46	0	0	70	5	37	180	205	114	103	0
February........	61	0	0	47	0	44	73	319	156	86	0
March...........	28	0	0	22	0	18	6	655	406	75	0
April...........	17	0	0	10	0	57	1	405	143	35	7
May............	27	0	0	3	0	0	14	416	236	61	47
June............	27	1	0	9	1	0	29	567	146	117	55
July.............	24	0	0	16	0	0	35	1,073	244	174	58
August..........	22	1	0	22	10	0	24	812	401	219	45
September.......	23	2	0	23	32	0	2	943	502	236	68
October..........	16	2	0	25	44	50	1	836	585	243	65
November.......	20	1	0	28	46	50	0	921	563	259	70
December........	25	1	0	30	38	50	0	875	523	246	73
1944											
January.........	28	2	0	35	65	50	0	833	578	341	101
February........	18	1	0	34	84	50	0	932	641	397	114
March...........	28	1	0	54	81	50	0	811	594	604	181
April............	50	0	3	69	100	50	0	744	470	680	194
May............	82	0	39	78	83	50	0	792	487	762	217
June............	37	1	34	60	76	50	0	792	446	696	198
July.............	46	2	39	44	79	100	0	760	441	615	196
August..........	47	0	47	36	71	150	0	712	421	583	176
September.......	46	0	42	27	67	150	0	709	411	510	127
October..........	43	0	46	26	48	217	0	696	293	696	173
November.......	45	0	43	0	28	172	0	753	222	652	151
December........	43	0	43	0	12	163	0	756	206	599	130
1945											
January.........	40	0	45	0	0	150	0	808	135	683	125
February........	28	0	31	0	0	125	0	837	133	727	125
March...........	25	1	36	0	0	125	0	913	120	817	115
April...........	19	2	27	0	0	105	0	816	102	790	70
May............	13	1	22	0	0	125	0	910	93	792	65
June............	5	1	9	0	0	90	0	676	99	785	60
July.............	0	2	11	0	0	80	0	559	104	589	58
August..........	0	0	11	0	0	32	0	307	101	406	52

Source: CPA, Official Munitions Production of the United States, May 1, 1947, pp. 99-104.

12. OSS Application—Geoffrey M. T. Jones

OSS Form 80a   CONFIDENTIAL

OSS REQUISITION BY NAME

(Submit to PPB in duplicate)

TO: CHIEF, PERSONNEL PROCUREMENT BRANCH, OSS   **8 March 1944**
     106 North Building   (Date)

1. FROM: BRANCH CHIEF (OR AREA OPERATIONS OFFICER) **SO** BRANCH, BY *John L Dupree*

2. THRU: THE **N.A.** THEATER OFFICER, BY

3. THRU: BRANCH PERSONNEL OFFICER, **SSO** BRANCH, BY

4. NAME OF REQUISITIONING BRANCH **NA-SO**	5. OSS FORM 80a CONTROL NO., IF ANY.	
6. NAME **Geoffrey Montgomery Talbot Jones**	7. SERIAL NUMBER **O-443912**	8. GRADE **1st Lt.**
9. ARM OR SERVICE **Field Artillery**	10. DATE OF BIRTH **October 12, 1919**	

11. OFFICIAL ARMY ADDRESS & ASSIGNMENT

         Headquarters 11th Airborne Division
         Camp Polk, Louisana

12. INTENDED ASSIGNMENT (Location & Job Description)   **X**   OVERSEAS   U.S.

This man will be used on operations in enemy territory where a fluent knowledge of the French language is required. He must have a proficiency in guerilla and/ or commando warfare, close combat, demolitions and small arms. This is a dangerous and trying mission and he must be a leader and physically able.

13. LANGUAGE FACILITY (Indicate degree of proficiency, and if none required)

     French (fluently). Some Italian

14. WILL SPECIAL OSS TRAINING BE REQUIRED? **Yes**	FOR HOW LONG? **3 weeks**	
15. IS CANDIDATE TO BE INTERVIEWED? **No.**	IF ALREADY INTERVIEWED, BY WHOM? **John L. Dupree**	
16. HAS PERSONAL HISTORY STATEMENT BEEN OBTAINED? **Yes**	17. HAS SECURITY CHECK BEEN ORDERED? **Yes**	
18. THIS REQUISITION IS WITHIN: ( ) A TENTATIVELY APPROVED ALLOTMENT (**x**) ALLOTMENT DATED: **22 January 1944**	AN APPROVED	

19. ADDITIONAL ESSENTIAL & SPECIAL QUALIFICATIONS:
     (If candidate is to be interviewed, indicate any special points to be covered)

     Extensive travel and residence in France and Italy.
     Qualified parachutist

CONCURRENCE IN RELEASE GRANTED BY:

20. SUBMITTED BY:

John L. Dupree

John L. Dupree
(Acting Area Operations Officer, NA)
(For the Requisitioning Branch)

CONFIDENTIAL

CONFIDENTIAL

16. Rating.

	Superior	Excellent	Very Satisfactory	Satisfactory	Unsatisfactory
MOTIVATION, energy, effort, initiative, interest in assignment.	✓				
PRACTICAL INTELLIGENCE, speed and accuracy of judgement, resourcefulness in solving problems.	✓				
STABILITY, emotional control and maturity, absence of nervous symptoms.		✓			
ABILITY TO WORK WITH OTHERS, teamwork, tact, absence of annoying traits.		✓			
LEADERSHIP, organizing ability, ability to win cooperation.		✓			
PHYSICAL ABILITY, agility, daring, ruggedness, stamina.		✓			

17. REMARKS (Be sure to record outstanding accomplishments and weaknesses)_____

_____

_____

_____

_____

18. COMPLETE REASONS FOR RETURN TO U.S. __To be demobilized_____

_____

_____

_____

19. RECOMMENDATIONS (a) Do you recommend his further use in OSS?____No____

(b) If so, in what capacity?_____

20. PAPERS ACCOMPANYING OFFICER (never to include this Form)
    1.   4.
    2.   5.
    3.   6.

21. PAPERS BEING POUCHED TO U.S. - OSS (including this Form)
    1.   4.
    2.   5.
    3.   6.

                          PREPARED BY: _____
                          (Man's immediate superior officer)

                          BRANCH CHIEF _____
                          PERSONNEL OFFICER_____

Source: The National Archives, College Park, MD

13a. OSS Requisition

OSS Form 80a

CONFIDENTIAL

OSS REQUISITION BY NAME

(Submit to PPB in Jual Date)

TO: CHIEF, PERSONNEL PROCUREMENT BRANCH, OSS   8 March 1944
     106 North Building   (Date)

1. FROM: ~~BRANCH CHIEF~~ (OR AREA OPERATIONS OFFICER)   SO   BRANCH, BY *John L. Dupree*

2. THRU: THE **N.A.** THEATER OFFICER, BY _____

3. THRU: BRANCH PERSONNEL OFFICER, **SSO**   BRANCH, BY *N.A. Elmont 9 Mar 44*

4. NAME OF
   REQUISITIONING BRANCH   **NA-SO**   5. OSS FORM 801 CONTROL NO., IF ANY:

6. NAME
   Geoffrey Montgomery Talbot Jones   7. SERIAL NUMBER   8. GRADE
                                        0-443912   **1st Lt.**

9. ARM
   OR SERVICE   **Field Artillery**   10 DATE OF
                                       BIRTH   **October 12, 1919**

11. OFFICIAL ARMY ADDRESS & ASSIGNMENT

                   Headquarters 11th Airborne Division
                   Camp Polk, Louisana

12. INTENDED ASSIGNMENT (Location & Job Description)   **X**   OVERSEAS   U.S.

This man will be used on operations in enemy territory where a fluent knowledge of the French language is required. He must have a proficiency in guerilla and/ or commando warfare, close combat, demolitions and small arms. This is a dangerous and trying mission and he must be a leader and physically able.

13. LANGUAGE FACILITY (Indicate degree of proficiency, and if none required)

   French (fluently). Some Italian

14. WILL SPECIAL OSS
     TRAINING BE REQUIRED?   **Yes**   FOR HOW
                                    LONG?   **3 weeks**

15. IS CANDIDATE
     TO BE INTERVIEWED?   **No.**   IF ALREADY INTERVIEWED,
                                    BY WHOM?   **John L. Dupree**

16. HAS PERSONAL HISTORY STATEMENT
     BEEN OBTAINED?   **Yes**   17. HAS SECURITY CHECK
                                    BEEN ORDERED?   **Yes.**

18. THIS REQUISITION   AN APPROVED
     IS WITHIN: ( ) A TENTATIVELY APPROVED ALLOTMENT (**x**) ALLOTMENT DATED: **22 January 1944**

19. ADDITIONAL ESSENTIAL & SPECIAL QUALIFICATIONS:
     (If candidate is to be interviewed, indicate any special points to be covered)

         Extensive travel and residence in France and Italy.
         Qualified parachutist

CONCURRENCE IN RELEASE GRANTED BY: 20. SUBMITTED BY:

                                           John L. Dupree
    (For PPB, OSS)   John L. Dupree
                                    Acting Area Operations Officer, NA

(28091)   (OVER)   (For the Requisitioning Branch)

CONFIDENTIAL

Source: The National Archives, College Park, MD

13b. **Authorization**

SECRET

OFFICE OF STRATEGIC SERVICES
WASHINGTON, D. C.

5 May 1944

TO: Mr. D. Dimond

FROM: Area Operations Officer, MENA-SO

SUBJECT: 1st Lt. G. H. T. Jones, FA., - French Lessons for,
at Berlitz School.

Authorization is requested for Special Funds to meet the cost of French lessons to be taken by subject officer at the Berlitz School beginning 8 May 1944, and ending immediately prior to his departure for overseas.

Said lessons are essential to the carrying out of subject's duties in the field.

RUSSELL P. PLACE
Area Operations Officer
MENA-SO

APPROVED:

Chief, SC

SECRET

Source: The National Archives, College Park, MD

14a. Commendation—Geoffrey M. T. Jones

HQ 1ST A/B TASK FORCE
Office of the A. C. of S., G-2
APO 758   US ARMY

21 November 1944

SUBJECT: Commendation.

TO   : Capt Geoffry M.T. JONES, OSS, 7th Army.

THRU   : CG 7th Army (Att. CO, OSS Det).

1. I desire to commend you for your splendid performance while attached to First Airborne Task Force as officer in charge of Strategic Services, during period 15 August to 21 November 1944.

2. Your work with the First Airborne Task Force has greatly facilitated the securing of pertinent and vital information for this Headquarters. Entering Southern France alone by parachute prior to the invasion, you efficiently organized a Maquis intelligence net for the Airborne Forces. During the initial landing, and in subsequence operations of the Force, your work has been consistently outstanding: First, you were confronted with the organization of a French Intelligence net whereby information of Ey units operating in France was secured. When the Enemy was subsequently driven from France into Italy, you were then called upon to organize a group of Italian agents in addition to those of the French Intelligence net. This you did without a break in operations.

3. Considering your utilization of the large number of foreign agents necessary, and the outstanding results obtained through your enthusiastic effort, your work in this selected line of endeavor is considered noteworthy and reflects high credit upon you and your training.

/s/ William J. Blythe,
/t/ WILLIAM J. BLYTHE,
Lt Col., GSC,
AC of S., G-2.

CERTIFIED A TRUE COPY.

RAY J. WEICHBRODT,
CWO, USA.

Source: National Archives, College Park, MD

610

14b. Croix de Guerre—Geoffrey M. T. Jones

D E C I S I O N No .679

- - - - - - - - - -

General de GAULLE, President of the Provisional Government of
the French Republic, chief of the armies, makes the citation

IN THE ORDER OF THE ARMY

- Captain Geoffrey Montgomery Talbot JONES, 0143912,
Field Artillery, Hq Det OSS (Main) U.S. Army

American Officer parachuted in FRANCE a few days before the
landing in Southern France with a team whose mission was to establish
the liaison between Resistance Groups and parachuted troops.
Accomplished his mission with complete disregard of danger.

This citation includes the award of the Croix de
Guerre with Palm.

PARIS, 1 Mai 1945

s/ De GAULLE

Source: The National Archives, College Park, MD

14c. Citation—Order of the British Empire—Geoffrey M. T. Jones

C I T A T I O N

MAJOR GEOFFREY M.T. JONES
UNITED STATES ARMY

HONORARY MEMBER OF THE MILITARY DIVISION OF THE
MOST EXCELLENT ORDER OF THE BRITISH EMPIRE

During the summer of 1944, Major (then Lieutenant) Jones was attached to the Subversive Operations element of the United States Office of Strategic Services. In June, 1944, he became a member of the integrated United Kingdom-United States Staff (S.P.O.C.) set up in Algiers by Allied Force Headquarters in order to coordinate subversive operations and liaison with the Resistance Movement in Southern France, in preparation for landing of the United States Seventh Army in the St. Tropez area.

In discharging his Staff duties, Major Jones did a great deal to promote smooth working between the British and United States elements of S.P.O.C. When the planning phase was completed, it was decided that he should himself be parachuted into Southern France in order to establish liaison between the French Resistance and the United States Airborne Division ear-marked for operations in the area. Major Jones was dropped between Draguignan and Grasse on 15th August, 1944, the day on which General Patch's Forces began landings. He was attached to the Airborne Task Force commanded by General Fredericks, which had the task of defending the Eastern flank of the Invasion Forces against German counter-attack from the Nice-Cannes area.

Major Jones fulfilled his liaison mission with great efficiency and distinguished himself under fire. He built up a tactical intelligence-collecting organisation, which greatly facilitated General Fredericks and his forces in fighting their way towards the Italian frontier.

Source: G.M.T. Jones

14d. Geoffrey Jones '42 Recovers WWII False Identity

GEOFFREY JONES '42 RECOVERS WWII FALSE IDENTITY

"GEOFFREY MONTGOMERY TALBOT JONES REQUESTS THE PLEASURE of your company," read the invitation, "at a small cocktail to celebrate the 80th birthday of newly discovered former French resistant Paul Georges Guillot."

It was certainly more exotic-sounding than your average New York social event. When friends of Jeff Jones '42 arrived *en scene* at his brownstone apartment last October for the celebration, however, they were greeted not by a mysterious European visitor, but by the grinning, mustachioed visage of their host, who admitted, in effect, "The Frenchman is me."

In fact, "Paul Guillot" was a nonexistent mute French laborer—the false identity given to Jones in July 1944 when, as a World War II captain in the OSS (Office of Strategic Services, the special operations arm of the U.S. military), he parachuted behind German lines in the French Alps to prepare the way for the massive Allied airborne operation planned in the south of France two weeks later. "Guillot's" forged ID card was only rediscovered last year in a French farmhouse—giving Jones occasion to throw a "welcome back" birthday party for his alter ego (who is actually three years older than he is).

The story of how the ID papers came to light holds as many twists as an OSS cloak-and-dagger operation. It begins with that parachute jump, made in the dead of night. Jones missed the mountain plateau he'd been aiming for, barely escaping serious injury.

"I was lucky, because my parachute snagged on an outcropping, keeping me from smashing against the mountainside," Jones recalls. "Still, the chute swung me in, and I banged my head against the rock hard enough to cut through the metal covering of my helmet."

The next day, dressed in the blue suit of a typical French laborer, Jones/Guillot made his rendezvous with the local French resistance group. After hunting down an underground radio operator who was in contact with Allied headquarters in Algiers, Jones began distributing guns and explosives to the resistance fighters, and organizing them for the upcoming D-day. As the mute "Guillot" (the disability was invented to explain why he had not been drafted into the military—Jones was fluent in French, having lived there as a child) he also made forays into small towns in the area to pick up intelligence on the latest German activities.

The masquerade was anything but frivolous: Jones was replacing an agent who had been caught by the Gestapo. Since he had previously been involved in planning the airborne landing, Jones carried a poison pill to swallow in the event he was captured. "In those days, the Germans already had drugs that would make anyone spill their secrets," he explained. "I couldn't take that chance—too

To prevent his being shot by "friendly fire," Allied troops were given this photo of Geoffrey Jones '42.

PHOTO COURTESY GEOFFREY JONES '42

many lives were at stake."

His closest brush with disaster came just hours before the actual Allied landing, when Jones and his fellow resistants headed south for the landing sights posing as the prisoners of seven local police officers sympathetic to the Allied cause. "We had to go through a number of German roadblocks," he says. "At one in particular, I remember one of the German soldiers studying us a long while before letting us through. He never knew how lucky he was: the .22 silencer in my pocket was aimed straight at his neck the whole time!"

Once past the roadblocks, Jones and his companions still weren't out of the woods: A U.S. plane, under orders to attack any vehicle with headlights on, dropped the bombs that came perilously close to their truck. "We drove the rest of the way with the lights off," Jones recalls.

Leaving his blue suit and false papers in a farmhouse near the town of La Motte (north of St. Tropez), Jones switched to his captain's uniform and finally made contact with the newly arrived U.S. First Airborne Task Force, whose intelligence sections had copies of Jones's photograph.

The operation was a resounding success, thanks in part to the efforts of Jones and his resistance comrades. "A few days later, after we were relieved by the beach-landing troops, I decided it would be nice to retrieve my ID card as a souvenir," Jones says, "so I went back to the farmhouse. But the girl who lived there—she was about 18 years old and had served all of us coffee in a very friendly fashion a few days before—smiled and said she didn't know me, or anything about a blue suit. I figured they were probably just scared that we would come in and take over the house, so I politely walked away and forgot about it."

Until last year, that is. When Jones got a letter from that same woman——who had first served him coffee. While preparing to sell the house she had discovered the ID card packed away in a trunk. Along with the card (which is now on display at the Resistance Museum of Le Muy) she passed along the final clue in the Guillot mystery: She had an identical twin sister! This twin—who had never met Jones—was the one who answered the door on his second visit.

Jones, who continues to be active as president of the Veterans of the OSS and of the William J. Donovan Memorial Foundation (named after the legendary founder of the OSS), was understandably thrilled by the find. "You can see why I had to throw him a party," he says. "It was a very happy occasion. The dress code on the invitation was simply 'tenue joyeux'—wear joyful clothing."

—Royce Flippin '80

Source: Princeton Alumni Weekly

14e. War Department Citation For Legion of Merit—Geoffrey M. T. Jones

WAR DEPARTMENT
THE ADJUTANT GENERAL'S OFFIC
WASHINGTON 25, D. C.

CITATION FOR LEGION OF MERIT

Major Geoffrey M. T. Jones, from August to November 1944, as a member of the Special Operations Branch, Office of Strategic Services on duty with G-3 Allied Force Headquarters, parachuted into France to coordinate French resistance activities in anticipation of the airborne invasion of the southern coast. He then aided in operations of the regional Maquis, and by establishing contact with the Resistance Headquarters behind enemy lines, kept his headquarters informed of enemy movements during early operations in southern France. Through his exceptional leadership and ingenuity in intelligence activities, Major Jones rendered service of outstanding value to Allied operations.

Source: National Archives, College Park, Md.

14f. Citation For Bronze Start Medal—Geoffrey M. T. Jones

CITATION FOR THE BRONZE STAR MEDAL

GEOFFREY M. T. JONES, O-443912, Captain, FA, Office of Strategic Services Detachment 44, for meritorious achievement in connection with military operations in the Maritime Alps Sector, France, from 21 November 1944 to 11 March 1945. As Commanding Officer, Detachment 44, Captain Jones coordinated the activities of eight special agencies in the sector. His imagination, initiative and ability resulted in a highly coordinated intelligence service, thus diminishing the risks involving friendly agents and assuring to the 44th AAA Brigade superior enemy intelligence in relation to installations, movements and probable intentions of the enemy. His diligence, aggressiveness and devotion to duty reflect great credit not only upon himself but upon the armed forces of the United States. Entered the service from New York, New York.

OFFICIAL:

Headquarters, 6th Army Group
US Army

Source: National Archives, College Park, Md.

15. LST Flotilla 10 Enroute to Camel Beach, Operation Dragoon

LST FLOTILLA TEN
c/o Fleet Post Office
New York, N.Y.

From: COM LST FLOT 10

TO :   LSTS IT 87   CLASSIFICATION: SECRET

DATE: 4 AUGUST 44

MAILGRAM

LSTS THIS FORCE WILL PROCEED TO MASIDA FOR LOADING TOMORROW 5 AUGUST X

GROUP 29 UNDERWAY 1100 *1200* X GROUP 30 UNDERWAY 1200 *1300* X FLOT 20 PLUS 525 UNDERWAY

1300 *1400* X ANCHOR OFF MASIDA ON ARRIVAL AND BE PREPARED TO BERTH AT HARDS ACCORDING

TO LOADING PLAN APPENDIX ONE TO A MEX CHARLIE X

CC: LSTS 491, 48, 230, 284, 49, 50, 282, 283, 281 500, 907, 988, 989, 525, 502,

46, 51, 134, 285, 1011 1010, 1012 492.

LCI(L) (C) 951

LCH 240.

Source: The Naval Historical Center

16.

USS LST 1012

PASSENGER - U. S. NAVY - USS LST 282 (SURVIVORS)

(DETACHMENT)

NAME	SER. NO.	RATE	CLASS
DURKEE, Edward Holsey Jr.	140359	Lt. (jg)	USNR
WEILINGER, Rex Frederick	267372	Ens.	USNR
BLAKE, Kenneth Edgar	377 15 27	RT1c	USNR
VANNIER, Edison Donald	800 20 90	MoMM1c	USNR
MAY, Hubert, Doyler	618 56 88	PhM1c	USNR
AUBUT, Thomas, (n)	787 68 90	MoMM3c	USNR
KAMERDZE, John Anthony	817 96 86	S1c	USNR
JUDD, Eldon Neil	868 72 20	EM3c	USN
LAVIGNE, Thomas Frank	645 54 35	S1c	USNR
MULLINEAUX, William Herbert	822 12 68	S1c	USNR
MAUK, Russell Lee	723 37 12	S1c	USNR
HOARD, Jos. Helitt	637 86 40	Cox	USNR
CECIL, Louis Jewell	867 60 12	S1c	USNR
BROOKS, Silas (n)	829 41 58	S1c	USNR
DORSEY, Lester Luke	637 29 16	MoMM3c	USNR
MENIS, Edward Addu	989 99 01	S1c	USNR
RICHTER, Norbert John	869 21 56	S1c	USN
MC KIDDY, William Kenneth	855 87 59	S1c	USNR
JENKINS, Charles Douglas	929 49 66	S1c	USNR
BLACKBURN, William Martin	556 92 10	GM3c	USNR
GRISPINO, Barth Angelo	712 50 65	S2c	USNR
GWYNN, Donald Homer	609 81 17	S2c	USNR
DYER, William James	637 18 82	GM2c	USNR
MAHEK, John (n)	819 10 77	GM2c	USNR
FLEMING, John Paul	711 13 69	GM3c	USNR
NOGLE, Robert Stanley	821 37 62	BM1c	USN

TEMPORARY DUTY FROM USS TEXAS:

BALCH, Richard S.	667 00 47	RM3c	USNR

Source: The Naval Historical Center

17.

USS LST 1012
LST Division 115, Group 58
LST1012/A9-4   Flotilla 20
Serial 119   c/o Fleet Post Office
New York, N.Y.

S E C R E T   16 October 1944

From: Commanding Officer
To :   Commander In Chief - United States Fleet.

Via :   1. Commander LST Flotilla 20.
               2. Commander Eighth Amphibious Force.
               3. Commander Eighth Fleet.

Subject: Action Report.

Reference: (a) ALNAV - 176-43
               (b) COM LST FLOT - 20 - Dispatch Ø81415B Sept.

    1.   The following information is submitted cover-
ing action engaged in by USS LST 1012 on 15 August 1944.

        (a)   LST 1012 was a unit of Convoy SM1 proceeding
               under orders according to Commander Naval
               Western Task Force Operation Plan 4-44 for
               the Invasion of Southern France. Immediate
               Senior in Command - Lt. Commander F. M.
               PERRIN, Commander LST Division 115, Group-
               58, Flotilla - 20.

        (b)   From 0500 to 2000 15 August LST 1012 lay
               to in transport area off Cape Drammont with
               LST 1010 and LST 1011. At 2015 orders were
               received to proceed to "Green Beach" off Cape
               Drammont to unload cargo. All three vessels
               proceeded to beach area. At 2058 two enemy
               planes were sighted overhead - identified
               as Junkers 88's. All three LST's and vessels
               in immediate vicinity commenced firing.
               At 2059 - Ceased firing. At 2103 order was
               given to commence firing on second plane.
               At 2105 - ceased firing. All 20mm and 40mm
               guns had opened fire but planes appeared
               to be out of range and sustained no damage.
               First plane had launched a "robot" bomb prior
               to the opening of fire and shortly thereafter
               LST 282, which was approaching the beach, was
               observed to have been hit by the bomb.

SECRET DECLASSIFIED

She immediately took fire but continued on to beach where she burned completely.

(c) LST 1012 continued on to beach, landing at 2140. No damage or casualties were suffered.

(d) All guns had operated in good order and tracers showed effective concentration of fire. The following ammunition was expanded;

912-rounds - 20mm
161-rounds - 40mm

(e) Being under attack and engaging the enemy for the first time, the crews performance was highly commendable. Good marksmanship was evident and obedience to commands was prompt.

(f) No further appearance was made by enemy aircraft.

(g) LST 1012 retracted from the beach at 0340 16 August, reported to return convoy SRM-1 and Task Unit 87.3.4 was dissolved.

M. J. Flowers Jr.
M. J. FLOWERS JR.

Source: The Naval Historical Center

18a. Commendation letter re: Ferris C. Burke from R. J. Hardy

NAVY DEPARTMENT

BUREAU OF NAVAL PERSONNEL

WASHINGTON 25, D. C.

Pers-68-ejb
tml/812 63 17

2 6 FEB 1945

From: Chief of Naval Personnel.

To :   BURKE, Ferris Creamer, S1c, USN.

Via :   CO, USS LCI (L) 570, New York, N.Y.

Subj: Commendation.

1. The Chief of Naval Personnel takes pleasure in forwarding
with his congratulations the following award made to you for
meritorious conduct as a member of the Naval service:

LETTER OF COMMENDATION WITH COMMENDATION RIBBON

By direction of Chief of Naval Personnel.

R. J. HARDY,
Comdr., USN,
Enlisted Performance Division.

Encl: (2)

(P)

18b. Commendation letter re: Ferris C. Burke from H. K. Hewitt

UNITED STATES FLEET
HEADQUARTERS OF THE COMMANDER TWELFTH FLEET
FLEET POST OFFICE
NEW YORK

12 December 1945.

From: Commander TWELFTH Fleet.
To :   Ferris C. Burke, S2c, U.S. Naval Reserve.

Subject: Commendation.

    1.   Your heroic action in connection with the rescue of three survivors of a sunken LCVP on 15 August 1944 during the invasion of Southern France, is deemed worthy of special commendation.

    2.   After landing assault troops on the coast of Southern France and upon starting back to your control vessel, you saw an LCVP hit by heavy machine gunfire and sink. After the LCVP had sunk the enemy kept firing at the men in the water. You and the men in your boat in cooperation with another LCVP, turned back in the midst of heavy enemy machine gunfire and without regard for your personal safety, effected the rescue of the three survivors. Expert seamanship and splendid tactics enabled one LCVP to draw the enemy's fire while the other LCVP accomplished the rescue.

    3.   I commend you for your courage, seamanship and outstanding devotion to duty, which reflect credit upon yourself and the United States Naval Service.

    4.   You are hereby accorded the privilege of wearing the commendation ribbon pursuant to the authority delegated by ALNAV 179-44.

    5.   A copy of this letter will be forwarded to the Chief of Naval Personnel to be filed in your official record.

H. K. HEWITT,
Admiral, U.S. Navy.

Source: The Naval Historical Center

19. **Letter dated 29 July 1994 from R. C. Steeple, Jr., Executive Officer of LST 1012, to Marian and Steve 4. Personal information removed by the author.**

Saturday July 29th

Dear Steve & Marian

Now, I was surprised to have you inquiring about the invasion that the old LST 1012 was in. Your question, "where was it?" started me delving into old files and coming up with original maps that were part of the stacks of plans, maps and details that we were flooded down with before we sailed from Naples to Southern France. I was able to get excellent one-piece copies and I am enclosing them herewith. We sailed from Naples in the evening of Aug 12th and arrived in the invasion area in the wee hours of the morning Aug 15th. We were supposed to go in and beach at Beach 264A (the 1010, 1011, & 1012) when the bombardment ceased, but some one (thank God!) was not convinced that it was safe enough.

2.

We layto for hours on end, going in circles, until we finally got orders to proceed to Beach 264B at Cap Dramont, where we finally beached around midnight. During this time the LST 282 – on the beach – was hit by a buzz-bomb. She burned badly and had many casualties. Before leaving the beach, we took some of her wounded which we transferred to a Hospital Ship later.

I have marked the pertinent areas on the enclosed copies of the maps and I hope you are able to interpret the markings. It was definitely a "hairy" experience that left life-long memories.

Much love, Fern & Chuck

Source: Author's correspondence with R. C. Steeple, Jr.

20. Action Report from Captain John N. Opie III

U S. EIGHTH FLEET

FILE NO A16-3
    Serial: (Op)

S E C R E T

SECOND ENDORSEMENT to
IST 1012 Secret-ltr.
A9-4, Serial 119 of
16 October 1944.

From:	Commander Amphibious Force, U.S. EIGHTH Fleet.
To:	Commander-in-Chief, United States Fleet.
Via:	Commander U. S. EIGHTH Fleet.

Subject: Action Report.

1.   Forwarded.

2.   This ship was not under the operational command of this Command during the period of this report.

3.   It appears from the sketchy report that fire discipline on board was poor. Apparently, fire was opened even though the planes were out of range.

4.   By copy of this endorsement, Commanding Officer IST 1012 is directed to train himself and his ship in judging range to prevent reoccurrence and to improve fire discipline.

JOHN N. OPIE, III
CHIEF OFFICER

cc:
    ComIST Flot 20
    CO USS IST 1012

21. **Logs USS *Bayfield*, Rear Admiral Spencer S. Lewis's flagship**

15 August, 1944

1. Same as before.

2. Same as before.

3. 0800 - 43° 18'N
          06° 58'E

    1200 - 43° 17'N
          06° 57' 30"E

    2000 - 43° 22' 30"N
          06° 49' 18"E

4. Maneuvering in Transport and Assault Areas (Camel Area) off coast of Southern France. All hands to General Quarters at 0446. All needed boats lowered and away at 0553. Conditions I and IA maintained throughout the day. At 2103 Jones, John W. (7013-898)Cox., and Schultz, Harold W. (695-243)Sea2c, wounded by fragments from shell fired at enemy planes in vicinity. Founard, Robert (725-58-35)B.M.2c, U.S.N. later found to have sustained shrapnel wound. Secured from General Quarters at 2131. Commanding General 36th Division and staff left vessel.

5. No remarks.

6. 290 rounds - 20 m.m.

7. No remarks.

16 August, 1944

1. Same as before.

2. Same as before.

3. 0800 -)
    1200 -) Lying to and anchored - Golfe de Frejus, France.
    2000 -)

4. Maneuvering as before. All hands to General Quarters at dawn and dusk. Fired at enemy aircraft during evening General Quarters. Received casualties aboard.

5. No remarks.

6. 5"/38 cal. - 10 rounds
    1.1"   - 114 rounds
    20 m.m.   - 60 rounds

7. No remarks.

Defeat And Triumph

17 August, 1944

1. Same as before.

2. Same as before.

3. 0800 –
   1200 – Golfe de Frejus, France
   2000 –

4. Standing regular sea watches; carrying out necessary work and using boats for dispatch runs in assault areas and to beaches

5. No remarks.

6. No remarks.

7. No remarks.

18 August, 1944

1. Same as before.

2. Same as before.

3. 0800 –
   1200 – Golfe de Frejus, France
   2000 –

4. Same as before. Fired on enemy aircraft (JU88's) during routine evening General Quarters.

5. No remarks.

6. 5"/38 – 8 rounds.
   1.1" – 126 rounds.

7. No remarks.

Appendices

19-31 August, 1944

1. Same as before. On 29 August, Captain Rutledge B. Tompkins assumed command of Task Force 87, in accordance with C.T.F. 87 dispatch 292130B/August and Naval Commander Western Task Force dispatch 292230B/August. Admiral Spencer S. Lewis left vessel to return to Naples.

2. Same as before

3. 0800 -
   1200 - Anchored in Golfe de Frejus, off St. Raphael, France.
   2000 -

4. Carried out ship's work and duties as flagship. During this period boats were used for dispatch work, smoke patrol, and for close screen against possible human torpedoes. From D-day to D/16, ship's force performed major repair jobs on six (6) Bayfield boats and eleven (11) boats from other ships and authorities in the area. Maintained steam at throttle throughout this period.

5. No remarks

6. No remarks

7. No remarks

L. SPENCER
Captain, USCG.
Commanding.

Source: The Naval Historical Center

22.

L11-1   UNITED STATES EIGHTH FLEET

Serial: 00183

15 FEB 1945

CO USS LST 282 Secret
Serial 005 of 2 Sept. 1944.

From: Commander United States Eighth Fleet.
To :   The Secretary of the Navy.
Via :   Commander in Chief, United States Fleet.

Subject: Loss of USS LST 282 - Report of.

Reference: (a) CTF 87 Operation Plan No. 1-44 of 1 Aug. 1944.
           (b) NCWTF (Com8thFlt) despatch 071627 September 1944.
           (c) Com8thFlt Serial 001205 of 19 Oct. 1944, to CNO only.
           (d) NCWTF Serial 01568 of 15 Nov. 1944, Invasion of Southern France.

1.   Forwarded, concurring in the third endorsement.

2.   LST 282 was the only naval loss from enemy air action during the entire Southern France Operation. It was destroyed off the Green beach (near Saint Raphael) of the Camel Assault area by a radio controlled bomb about 2055B on D-day (15 August 1944). Paragraph 4, page 46, of reference (d) contains a narrative of the enemy's attack.

3.   The following peculiar defense difficulties were presented by the attack:

     (a) Time of the attack (dusk on D-day).
     (b) Approach of attacking planes from over hilly terrain behind the beach.
     (c) Location of the LST, 1200 yards off-shore, outside both the beach and transport area concentrated defense zones.

4.   Comments on defense tactics employed:

     (a) Fighter Cover: At the time all inshore fighter cover was provided by the Army from Corsican bases. A total of from twenty-eight to thirty-two fighters for daylight patrols and six night fighters for dusk patrols were scheduled for the assault area. No interception of this attack was reported. (See pp. 46, 265 and 266 of reference (d)).

     (b) Jamming: Reference (c) is the report on the performance of all jammer ship activities and includes, in paragraphs 1 and 4 of page 11, an account of efforts to jam this attack. Pages 46 and 361 of reference (d) also refer.

2 1546

- 1 -

DECLASSIFIED
L11-1
Serial: 00183

DECLASSIFIED

UNITED STATES EIGHTH FLEET

15 FEB 1945

Subject: Loss of USS LST 282 - Report of.

- -

(c) Smoke: Appendix 1, Annex LOVE of reference (a) contains the smoke plan for the Camel (TF 87) area. It provided for three units afloat, composed of small patrol craft and landing craft (LCMs and LCVPs), to smoke to the windward of the transport area and for the assigned Beach Battalion to make smoke during an off-shore wind (which existed at the time of this attack--see paragraph 8, page 3 of basic letter.) Smoke was to be made "automatically" from one-half hour before sunset to one-half hour after sunset. Sunset on D-day was at 2031B, almost simultaneous with receipt of the "Red Alert". The same paragraph of the basic report mentions the thick "inshore" smoke screen generated by "units on the beach", as well as "small craft", hampering rescue operations. Also noted there is the negligible force of the wind then blowing, which, though off-shore, was of small assistance in spreading the smoke. The most significant factor under those conditions was the position of the LST mid-way between the beach and transport area and, thus, where it was not under the full protection of the planned smoke screens for either of those two places.

5.   The remarks in paragraph 3 of the third endorsement to the basic letter concerning the meritorious conduct of the ships personnel are concurred in, particularly, and suitable rewards have already been made.

6.   Reference (b) recommended that the craft be stricken from the Navy Register.

H. K. Hewitt

H. K. HEWITT

1945 FEB 27 8 09

COMMANDER-IN-CHIEF
FLAG OFFICE
CERTIFIED

2 1546

- 2 -

Source: The Naval Historical Center

23. ## LST 1012 logs

UNITED STATES SHIP	LST 1012	Tues. 15 Aug. 1944,
		(Day) (Date) (Month)

00-04

0000 – Underway in convoy as directed by task force commander. Course 311°(t). Proceeding at various speeds to conform to convoy 0400. Properly relieved O. Engelsen, Lt. (j,g) USNR.

V. A. DUPLESSIS JR. ENS. USNR.

04-08

0400 – Underway as before. Captain at the conn. Manuevering to take position in Transport area. 0625. Sounded General Quarters.

O. ENGELSEN, Lt. (jg) USNR.

08-12

0800 – Manuevering to keep position in Transport Area astern of LST 1011. 0915 Secured from General Quarters. 0930. Opened bow doors and ramp. 0953. Launched two Army Dukws in accordance with Operation orders from LST 101 0955. Chaplain Keenan held Catholic Services. 1027. Sounded general quarters. 1058. Secured from General Quarter.

R. C. STEEPLE Jr. Lt. (jg) USNR

12-16

1200 – Manuevering in Transport area keeping station on LST 1011. 1430. Set Condition I Mike. prepared for beaching. Set course 300°(t). 1441. All engines stopped. 1500. Have to wait further orders. Keeping station on LST 1011.

R. C. STEEPLE Jr. Lt. (jg) USNR.

16-20

1600 – Manuevering as before.

R. C. STEEPLE Jr. Lt. (jg) USNR.

20-24.

2000 – 2015 – In accordance with visual signal from Control vessel, set Condit I Mike, prepared for beaching. 2050. All engines ahead standard. cours 300°(t). 2058. Enemy planes overhead. Commenced firing. 2059. Ceased firing. 2105. Commenced firing. 2105 – ceased firing. 2109. Assumed various courses to approach beach. 2140. – Landed on "GREEN" Beach at course 037°(t). Stern anchor out with 500 feet of cable. 2143. Commenced unloading Army equipment and personnel. 2317. Completed. – unloading. MELVIN, A. M. Pfc. 32 359 677 remained on board at directic of Army Medical Officer. 2320. Secured from Condition I-Mike. set anchor watch.   O. A. FOX, Lt. (jg) USNR. – Officer of the Deck.

R. C. STEEPLE Jr.

Appendices

UNITED STATES SHIP **LST 1012** **Wed. 16 Aug. 1944**
(Day) *(Date)* *(Month)*

00-08

0000 – Beached bow on to Green Beach, Southern France invasion coast as direct
by Task Force Commander, Camel Section. 0045. Casualties from beach-he
(Army) and survivors of USS LST 282 brought aboard, ambulatory and stre
according to attached list. 0140. Pontoon causeways on port and stbd. s
dropped to water and removed by C.B. Crew. 0235. C. B. Detachment detac
from ship. List of personnel is attached. 0320. Sounded Condition "One
0341 Anchors aweigh. Underway proceeding at various courses and speeds
retracting from beach. 0345. Proceeding at various courses and speeds to
to in harbor off invasion beach-head. 0400. Underway at various courses
speeds awaiting orders to reform convoy. -0510. Secured from condition
"one Mike". set condition "3". 0800. Properly relieved by J. A. Dupless
Jr. Ens. USNR.

O. A. FOX, Lt. (jg) USNR.

08-12

0800 – Underway at various courses and speeds awaiting further sailing instruc
0900. Mustered crew at quarters. No absentees. 1200. Properly relieved
O. Engelsen, Lt. (jg) USNR.

J. A. DUPLESSIS Jr. Ens., US

12-16

1200 – Enroute to rendezvous with Camel return convoy at a point bearing 179°.
from Cape Camarat, France, distance 14 miles. 1330. Lay to at rendezvous
point 1544. Manuevering at various courses and speeds to form with conve
Captain at the conn. 1600. Properly relieved by O. A. Fox, Lt. (jg)
USNR.

O. ENGELSEN. Lt. (jg) USNR.

16-18

1600 – Underway as before. Manuevering at various courses, and speeds in convoy
1800. Properly relieved by J. A. DuPlessis Jr., Ens., USNR.

O. A. FOX, Lt. (jg) USNR.

18-20

1800 – Underway as before. 1850. Engines stopped. 1860. Recieved orders from C
Commodore to proceed to U.S. Army Hospital ship, Algenquin to transfer
casualties. 2000. Casualties transferred according to attached list. 2000
Properly relieved by O. Engelsen, Lt. (jg) USNR.

J. A. DUPLESSIS Jr
Ens. USNR.

20-24.

2000 – Underway laying to for transfer of casualties to hospital ship. 2011
Underway to form up with return convoy. Manuevering at various course and
speeds. 2055. Sounded General Quarters upon sighting enemy plane. 2110.
Commenced making smoke screen. 2135. Secured from General Quarters. 2300.
Rejoined return convoy. Course 128°(t). Speed - 7 knots. 2400. Properly
relieved by O. A. Fox. Lt. (jg) USNR.

C. Engelsen

Source: The Naval Historical Center

631

24. **Author's note: A review of the USS *Catoctin* War Diary entries of 13
and 20 August 1944 indicates the dangers confronting Admiral Hewitt's
flagship even after the landings of 15 August 1944.**

IN REPLY REFER TO NO.

COMMANDER-IN-CHIEF
FLAG OFFICE
RECEIVED

U. S. S. CATOCTIN

WAR DIARY

1944 OCT 7   9   58

31 August 1944

1 August 1944   17022

Moored in Berth #16, Naples, Italy. Designated as Amphibious Force Flagship
of the Eighth United States Fleet. Vice Admiral H.K. Hewitt, USN, and staff embarked.

2 – 6 August 1944

Moored as before.

7 August 1944

Moored as before. 0405 Underway and standing out to rendezvous in a position
5 miles south of the Isle of Capri, to carry out scheduled exercises in accordance
with operation plan "Preface". 0600 cleared swept channel and commenced scheduled
exercises. Noon position, 5 miles south of the Isle of Capri. 1231 exercise completed, entered Capri swept channel. 1543 moored to Berth #16, Naples, Italy.

8 – 12 August 1944

Moored as before.

13 August 1944

Moored as before. 0830 The Secretary of the Navy James V. Forrestal arrive
on board. 1459 underway in obedience to Commander Western Naval Task Force operation
plan "Anvil", standing out the swept channel in company with assault formation
SF-1B, OTC and guide in HENRICO (APA 45). 1719 cleared the swept channel and
assumed formation III, standard speed 12 knots, fleet speed 10.5 knots. 2000
position: 40° 41' 00" N, 13° 22' 00" E.

14 August 1944

Steaming as before. 0800 position: 41° 09' 30" N, 10° 35' 45" E. 1155
entered Straits of Bonifacio swept channel. 1200 position: 41° 19' 40" N, 09°
19' 00" E. 1445 HMS KILBERLY with CinCMed embarked, passed down formation. 1611
cleared the swept channel. 2000 formation: 42° 04' 00", 08° 20' 30" E. 2048
arrived at point "GO" and changed course to 312° true, the final course to the
assault area.

15 August 1944

"D" day – Steaming as before, enroute to "Alpha" assault area. 0455 arrived
in assault area and hove to 11 miles south of the Gulf of St. Tropez, France. 0600
fire support vessels commenced pre-landing bombardment. 0755 ceased shore bombardment. 0800 "H" hour, first wave hit the beach with slight opposition. 0914
shifted to "Delta" assault area in obedience to the Admiral's orders. Naval bombardment continued throughout the day. 2100 Major General Truscott, USA, and staff
left the ship.

88253   FILMED

632

IN REPLY REFER TO NO.

U. S. S. CATOCTIN

WAR DIARY (Cont'd)

16 August 1944

Hove to 5 miles south of the Gulf of St. Tropez, France. 1050 the Secretary of the Navy embarked in the PLUNKETT (DD 431). 1310 CinCMed, Lieutenant General Maitland Wilson, RA, and Major General Rooks, USA, came aboard and paid an official visit on Admiral Hewitt. 2019 anchored in the Gulf of Bougnon, France.

17 August 1944

Anchored as before. 1444 the Under Secretary of War Patterson and Lieutenant General Somervell paid an official visit on the Admiral. 2345 enemy E boats attempted to enter the Gulf of St. Tropez but were repulsed by A/S screen.

18 August 1944

Anchored as before. 1057 shifted anchorage to berth R-6. 1547 shifted berth to U-1. 1739 shifted berth to U-7. 2100 some ships present commenced firing at unidentified aircraft. 2105 Vice Admiral Hewitt, USN, Lieutenant General Eaker, USA, and Lieutenant General Devers, USA, came aboard. 2106 enemy aircraft identified as a JU 88 sighted, approaching to port, altitude 15,000 feet. Several missiles (probably small anti-personnel bombs) fell close aboard aft, one of which hit on the after well deck, killing 5 enlisted men and injuring 3 officers and 29 enlisted men and injuring 4 enlisted men from the U.S.S. PT 208 which was close aboard to starboard. About 2110 boat #7 while engaged in laying smoke screen around this vessel, caught on fire 1,000 yards on our starboard quarter. The boat officer later reported that the Besler Smoke Generator caught on fire and spread to 2 oil drums in the stern sheets of the boat. The boat officer ordered all extra hands over the side while he and one man remained to fight the fire. Boat #8 rescued all personnel who abandoned the boat including one man who was immediately killed by striking the propeller when he jumped over the side. 2126 fire in boat #7 extinguished by crew of the barge and was returned to the ship under its own power.

19 August 1944

Anchored as before.

20 August 1944

Anchored as before. 0730 Lieutenant General Devers, USA, Lieutenant General Eakers, USA, Major General Cannon, USA, and Brigadier General Persons, USA, left the ship. 2053 commenced firing at enemy aircraft. 2105 enemy aircraft dispersed after expending 5 rounds of 5"/38, 4 rounds of 40MM and 277 rounds of 20MM ammunition.

21 – 31 August 1944

Anchored as before.

APPROVED: *C. C. Comp*

C. C. COLP,
Commander, USN.,
Commanding.

R. C. Ellenby.

R. C. ELLENBY,
Lieut.(jg), USNR.,
Navigator.

Source: The National Archives, College Park, MD

25.

USS LST 1012
LST1012/A9-4   LST Division 115, Group 58
Serial 116   Flotilla 20
     c/o Fleet Post Office
     New York, N. Y.

15 October 1944

From: Commanding Officer
To :   Commander in Chief - United States Fleet

Subject: War Diary - Submission of -

Reference: (a) ALNAV - 176-43
     (b) Com LST Flot 20 Mailgram Ø81415B Sept.

    1.   The following information covers the movements of USS LST 1012 during the month of August 1944.

    (a)   Aug 1 - Moored at Hard Dock Ajaccio, Corsica - unloading smoke cylinders to be delivered to COM PET DIV ONE, in accordance with orders from NOIC Naples 29164Ø July.
     1236 - Underway for Calvi, Corsica escorted by SC 498.
     1913 - Moored at Hard Dock Calvi.

    (b)   Aug 2 - Unloaded personnel and equipment of LST Advance Base Repair Unit - Flotilla 1.

    (c)   Aug 3 - 0600 - Underway pursuant to orders from SOIS 022229B for Ajaccio, Corsica.
     1600 - Moored along side "Dwight S. Morrow" to unload cargo of seven converted LCP's assigned to COM PET DIV ONE.

    (d)   Aug 5 - 0500 - Underway pursuant to orders from BNLO Ajaccio - Ø41446 Aug. - destination - Naples, Italy - escorted by SC 498.

    (e)   Aug 6 - 1126 - Anchored in Bay of Nisida.
     1916 - Underway for port of Naples to defuel to Tanker "Anarella".

    (f)   Aug 7 - 0352 - Completed transfer of 21,450 gallons of fuel oil to Tanker "Anarella".
     0729 - Underway pursuant to orders from Com LST Flot 20 proceeding to port of Torre Annunziata.

90756

S E **DECLASSIFIED**

(g) Aug 7 to Aug 9 - Moored inside jetty -
Torre Annunziata. Construction battalion
Detachment 1040 - Platoon 18 loaded pontoon causeways on port and starboard sides.
1437 - Proceeded to anchorage - Nisida Bay.

(h) Aug 10 to Aug 11 - Moored at Hard #14
Nisida, U.S. Army Equipment and personnel
loaded on board in accordance with Commander
Naval Western Task Force Operation Plan 4-44.

(i) 0600 - Aug 11 - Underway to anchorage in
Castellamare Bay. 0800. Aug 11 to 1543 Aug 12
Anchored in Castellamare Bay.

(j) 1544 Aug 12 - Underway in Convoy SM-1 as
directed by Com LST Div 115 Flot 20 pursuant
to Commander Naval Western Task Force Operation
Plan 4-44.

(k) Aug 12 to Aug 15 - Underway in Convoy.

(l) Aug 15 - 0500 - Arrival in Transport area
off invasion beach, Southern France.
2100 Proceed to beach with LST's 1010,
1011 and disembarked Army personnel and
equipment.

(m) 0230 - Aug 16, Construction Battalion Detachment 1040, Platoon 18 launched pontoon
causeways. Platoon 18, Lt. (jg) Thomas
C. BARNETT in charge detached from ship. Received on board Twenty eight (28) Naval
Personnel survivors from USS LST 282 and
Ten (10) U.S. Army Casualties from beachhead.
0340. Retracted from beach and proceeded to
assembly area.
1200 - Proceeding to join Convoy SRM-1 pursuant to orders from CTG 80.6.
1600 - Underway in Convoy - destination -
Naples. 2000 - Transferred Army casualties
and one survivor from LST 282 to U.S. Army
Hospital Ship - "Algonquin".

(n) 1840 - Aug 18 - Anchored in Gulf of Pozzuoli.
1900 - Moored to Berth #2 Nisida.

S E C R E T   DECLASSIFIED

(o) Aug 18 to 1900 Aug 20 - Loaded French
Personnel and equipment for transportation
to invasion area, Southern France.

(p) 2300 - Aug 20 to 0600 Aug 21 - Moored to
Ansaldo, Fuel Pier, Pozzuoli. Took aboard
35,600 gallons of fuel and 23,425 gallons
of fresh water.

(q) 1200 Aug 22.   Swung ship for magnetic compass
compensation. 1714 Underway in obedience
to orders from NCSO, Naples to join Convoy
SM-4 in accordance with Commander Naval Western
Task Force Operation Plan 4-44.

(r) 1714 - Aug 22 to 1300 Aug 25 - Underway in
convoy.

(s) 1714 Aug 25 - Moored to pontoon causeway
head of Gulf of St. Tropez; France; Unloaded
all French personnel and equipment.

(t) 1000 Aug 26 - Underway to join Convoy pursuant to orders from CTG 80.6.

(u) 1000 Aug 26 to 1930 Aug 30 - Underway in
Convoy enroute to Oran, Algeria.

(v) Aug 31 - Moored to Pier #13 Port of Oran,
loading French supplies and equipment.

M. J. F lowers Jr
M. J. FLOWERS Jr

CC

Com 8th Phib
Com LST Flot 20
File

Source: The Naval Historical Center

26. Medical Report Concerning First Airborne Task Force

MEDICAL

The following report is a consolidated medical report for the First Airborne Task Force for the month of August, 1944.

A. Total admissions to Hospital for Month of Aug.   1086
    1. Disease   435
    2. Injury   112
    3. Battle Casualty   539

B. Period 1 Aug 44 to 15 Aug 44 (Training period).
    1. Admissions, all cases   132
    2. Disease   110
            Common respiratory disease   4
            Vincent's angina   1
            Common diarrhea   10
            Dysentery, bacillary   15
            F U O   36
            Gonorrhea (new)   19
            Other V D   5
    3. Injuries   22
            Fractures   11
            Contusions   2
            Sprains   6
            Others   3
    4. Battle Casualties   0
    5. Hospital.
            Cases during the training phase were sent to
            the 33rd General Hospital in Rome. Hospital
            facilities were not operated by the A/B TF
            during the period.

C. Period 15 Aug 44 to 31 Aug 44. (Combat).
    1. Admissions, all cases   954
    2. Disease   325
            Common respiratory disease   23
            Common diarrhea   25
            Pneumonia, primary atypical   2
            Dysentery, bacillary   1
            Dysentery, ameobic   5
            Malaria, acquired outside US   20
            Hepatitis   4
            Scabies   8
            F U O   52
            Gonorrhea   26
            Other V D   13
            Vincent stomatitis   1
    3. Injuries   90
    4. Battle Casualties   539

SECRET

(a) Classification
Abdominal	12
Thoracic	22
Maxillo-Facial	14
Neurologic	
Head	17
Spine	4
Nerve	1
Extremities	
Upper	124
Lower	247
Other	98
TOTAL	539

(b) Battle Casualties, <u>caused by</u>:
Bullets	
Unclassified	49
Rifle	76
Machine gun	44
High Explosives	
Unclassified	95
Rifle	46
Mine	22
Booby traps	5
Blast (concussion type injuries)	54
Glider casualties	148
TOTAL	539

D. Number of Patients admitted with multiple wounds   28

E. Number of Patients with self-inflicted wounds   1

F. Number Killed in Action   55

G. During the period from "D" to "D plus 5", many casualties were evacuated directly from units in the 1st A/B TF to the beaches by Port Battalions, the 36th and 45th Divisions.

H. Dental History. There is no dental surgeon assigned to this Task Force. This organization has never operated a clinic. Prior to August 22, only the 517th Parachute Infantry Regiment and the 551st Parachute Infantry Battalion had dental officers. Due to the pending operation these officers were acting as assistant surgeons for their units. However, an extensive program was carried on by all units to have necessary dental work accomplished. This work was completed by the 33rd General Hospital in Rome, Italy, prior to departure from Italy.

August 22 the Special Service Force was attached to the Airborne Task Force. They had two dental officers assigned to that organization.

Appendices

SE⋯

August 28, one platoon of the 638th Medical Clearing
Company was attached to this Task Force. The dental surgeon of
the Clearing Company submitted a negative report for the last
three days of the month.

I.   The following list of units with attached medical
personnel were assigned to the First Airborne Task Force as of
1 August 1944.

1.   509 Parachute Infantry Battalion.
     551 Parachute Infantry Battalion.
     550 Airborne Infantry Battalion.
     517 Parachute Infantry Regiment.
     460 Parachute Field Artillery Battalion.
     463 Parachute Field Artillery Battalion.
     602 Field Artillery Battalion.

2.   The 676 Medical Collecting Company was attached to
     the Task Force to perform second echelon medical
     service in combat.

3.   The 937 Field Artillery Battalion with attached
     medical personnel were attached to the First Air-
     borne Task Force on the 21 August 1944.

4.   The First Special Service Force with medical
     personnel were attached to the First Airborne
     Task Force on 22 August 1944.

5.   The Headquarters Section and first platoon of
     638 Clearing Company was attached to this Task
     Force on the 27 August 1944.

J.   During the Airborne phase of the operations, the period
"D" to "D plus 3", the following casualties were reported to the
A/B TF Surgeon.

1.   Total casualties   300
     (a) Killed in action   6
     (b) Gunshot Wounds   40
     (c) Shrapnel Wounds   26
     (d) Fracture of
               Extremities   94
     (e) Sprains   64
     (f) Other injuries   70

2.   Casualties classified as landing casualties due to
     parachute landings and glider crashes totalled 228.
     Of this total, 148 were classified as glider
     casualties, and 80 were parachute casualties.

3.   Fifty-three glider pilots were reported as casualties
     due to glider crashes. Four deaths of glider pilots
     were reported due to glider landings.

Source: The National Archives, College Park, MD

27. Telegram to U.S. Ambassador Winant

851.01/8–2644 : Telegram

The Ambassador in the United Kingdom (Winant) to the Secretary of State

LONDON, August 26, 1944—5 p. m
[Received August 27—9 :06 p. m]

6934. For Dunn from Phillips. At his request, I called on Massigli this morning accompanied by Reber.[59] After I had congratulated him upon the liberation of Paris,[60] he expressed his sincere appreciation of the way in which this Allied Command had permitted the French forces to take the lead in freeing Paris. He said this would have a profound effect upon the future relations particularly of France and the United States. He has asked me to express the French gratitude to General Eisenhower.

FRANCE   731

He said that General de Gaulle now intends to bring the Committee to Paris as quickly as possible and thus to effect the necessary changes of "government". He hopes that they can arrive from Algiers by August 31 or September 1. Massigli himself expects to proceed to Paris probably August 29 or 30, depending upon results of his conversations here with members of the European Advisory Commission. In this connection he pointed out that it was the French desire to participate from now on in the discussions of great powers and added that this had been made clear ("possibly too clear") by General de Gaulle in his statement of last night. Massigli added that he would discuss this matter with Ambassador Winant.

Great satisfaction is felt by Massigli and others of the French Committee in that when the call to arms was given in Paris, all elements were united under the Resistance Council. The decision to call upon the people to rise was made at the end of last week. Massigli said that this may have been premature from a military point of view but was occasioned by a move on the part of the Communists to assume complete control of the situation in Paris. They had even gone so far as to name their own Prefect of Police. Once the decision to take unified action had been made the Communists however cooperated fully with the Resistance Council and withdrew the appointment. De Gaulle has now appointed Luixet as Prefect of Police.

I have recently returned from a tour of Normandy during which I called upon Coulet the French Commissioner at Bayeux and M. Daure the Prefect at Caen. I was much impressed with the stature of both men and the effective way they were meeting their many problems. British and American civil affairs officers who were in constant contact with both officials seemed entirely satisfied that the affairs of the province and department were being administered as well as possible under the circumstances.

The devastation of towns and villages throughout Normandy largely by our own bombing is far more serious than I had imagined. Phillips.]

Source: *Foreign Relations* 1944 (III): 730-731

28.

MAJOR ITEMS OF EQUIPMENT
FURNISHED BY THE UNITED STATES TO
THE FRENCH FORCES

Item	Quantity
Weapons (Except Combat Vehicles)	
Heavy Field Artillery	85
Light Field and Antitank	851
Antiaircraft Guns	758
Mortars	1,504
Small Arms	
Machine Guns	10,731
Submachine Guns	20,856
Rifles	69,129
Carbines	96,983
Combat Vehicles	
Tanks	1,406
Light	651
Medium	755
Other *	3,941
Ammunition (Rounds)	
Heavy Field Artillery	11,580
Light Field and Antitank	531,079
Antiaircraft	368,500
Mortar	169,172
Small Arms	50,173,000
Trucks	27,176
Light and Medium	20,282
Light-Heavy and Heavy-Heavy	6,894
Trailers and Semitrailers	16,034
Other Vehicles	1,523
Aircraft	1,417
Medium and Light Bombers	330
Fighters	723
Other	364

* Includes carriages for self-propelled weapons.

Source: Theodore E. Whiting et al., Statistics, a volume in prepa-
·ation for the series UNITED STATES ARMY IN WORLD WAR
II, Lend-Lease. MS in OCMH.

In terms of dollar value (value at the time of delivery), the supplies and services furnished by the United States to the French Army, Air Force, and Navy have been estimated at about $1,527,000,000, $457,000,-000, and $310,000,000, respectively, or a total of $2,294,000,000. Of the total, the War Department furnished $2,039,474,000; the remainder, representing items such as vessels and special supplies, was furnished by the Foreign Economic Administration. Comparative figures show that France came third in the list of recipients of War Department lend-lease shipments and transfers: [2]

	Percent
British Commonwealth (excepting Canada)	58
USSR	23
France	8
China	7
Others (approximately 45 countries)	4

In addition the United States furnished the French civilian economy, up to V-J Day, supplies representing another $548,000,000. Thus, for the period 11 November 1941 (when the benefits of lend-lease were first extended to the French) to 2 September 1945 (V-J Day), the total French military and civilian lend-lease account amounted to approximately $2,842,000,000.[3] The account for the immediate postwar period of September 1945 to September 1946 amounted to a further $391,000,000. The French, in return, made available to the U.S. armed forces as reciprocal aid goods and services amounting to $868,000,000.

---

[2] Theodore E. Whiting et al., Statistics, a volume in preparation for the series UNITED STATES ARMY IN WORLD WAR II. Lend-Lease. MS in OCMH.

[3] Unsuccessful efforts were made to obtain from the British War Office statistics on the British contribution to French rearmament. The only figures available are those published by the French Ministry of Finance and Economic Affairs in "Le Prêt-Bail et l'Aide Réciproque Franco-Alliée," Notes et Etudes Documentaires (Paris, 2 and 3 November 1949), which states that the French received from the United Kingdom supplies and services estimated at approximately $435,000,000, and from Canada matériel to the amount of $25,000,000.

Source: Marcel Vigneras, *The U.S. Army in WWII, Rearming the French* (Washington, DC: U.S. Government Printing Office, 1958), 402.

29.

Tonnages Discharged at Continental Ports: June 1944–April 1945

[Long Tons[a]]

Year and Month	Total	Omaha Beach	Utah Beach	Cherbourg	Normandy Minor Ports[b]	Brittany Ports	Le Havre	Rouen	Antwerp	Ghent	Southern France
1944											
June	291,333	182,199	109,134	....	....	....					
July	621,322	356,219	193,154	31,658	40,291	....					
August	1,112,771	348,820	187,955	266,644	125,353	9,499					174,500
September	1,210,290	243,564	150,158	314,431	100,126	75,198					326,813
October	1,309,184	120,786	72,728	365,603	58,816	77,735	61,731	26,891			524,894
November	1,402,080	13,411	12,885	433,301	48,707	64,078	148,654	127,569	5,873		547,602
December	1,555,819	....	....	250,112	50,749	27,327	166,038	132,433	427,592		501,568
1945											
January	1,501,269	....	....	262,423	47,773	....	198,768	157,709	433,094	15,742	385,760
February	1,735,502	....	....	286,591	41,836	....	195,332	173,016	473,463	69,698	495,566
March	2,039,778	....	....	261,492	39,691	....	192,593	268,174	558,066	172,259	547,503
April	2,025,142	....	....	181,043	47,542	....	165,438	240,708	628,227	277,553	484,631

[a] Exclusive of bulk POL and vehicles.
[b] Including Granville.
Source: Historical Report of the Transportation Corps, ETO, Vol. VII, April–June 1945, App. 7, Table 8A.

30.

OPERATIONS
AND PARTICIPATING FRENCH FORCES

MIDDLE EAST AND SOUTHERN TUNISIA ①

June 1941–May 1943

Free French Forces:

Leclerc Column
1st Free French Brigade
2d Free French Brigade
Strength: 13,000
Plus air and naval units

NORTHERN TUNISIA ②

19 November 1942–13 May 1943

French Army Detachment:

19th Corps and supporting troops
Strength: 45,000

SICILY ③

10 July–16 August 1943

4th Moroccan Tabor
Strength: 1,000

CORSICA ④

13 September–4 October 1943

4th Moroccan Mountain Division (—)
2d Moroccan Tabor Group
Shock Battalion
Supporting troops
Strength: 15,000
Plus air and naval units

ITALY ⑤

8 December 1943–23 July 1944

French Expeditionary Corps:

2d Moroccan Infantry Division
3d Algerian Infantry Division
4th Moroccan Mountain Division
1st Motorized Infantry Division
4th, 3d, and 1st Moroccan Tabor Groups
Supporting troops
Strength: 105,000
Plus air units

ELBA ⑥

17–19 June 1944

9th Colonial Infantry Division (—)
2d Moroccan Tabor Group
"Africa" Commando Group
Shock Battalion
Supporting troops
Strength: 12,000

FRANCE ⑦

15 August–15 September 1944

Army B:
1st and 2d Corps

Composed of all units raised in North Africa except 2d Armored Division: [1]

1st and 5th Armored Divisions
1st "Marche" Infantry Division [2]
2d Moroccan Infantry Division
3d Algerian Infantry Division
4th Moroccan Mountain Division
9th Colonial Infantry Division
1st, 2d, and 3d Moroccan Tabor Groups
"Africa" and "France" Commando Groups
Shock Battalion
Supporting troops
Strength: 200,000
Plus air and naval units

[1] 2d Armored Division was transported to the United Kingdom in April 1944 and landed in Normandy on 1 August. The division fought almost continuously under U.S. control except for two periods, 5–31 December 1944 and 20 January–21 February 1945, when it was attached to the 1st French Army.
[2] Formerly 1st Motorized Infantry Division.

FRANCE AND GERMANY ⑧

15 September 1944–7 May 1945

1st French Army:

Components of Army B augmented by units activated in France:

10th Infantry Division
27th Alpine Infantry Division
1st Infantry Division
14th Infantry Division
Also 2d Armored Division (5–31 December 1944 and 20 January–21 February 1945)
Supporting troops
Strength: 290,000
Plus air and naval units

Source: Vigneras, 405.

31.

USS LST 1012
LST Division 115, Group 58
Flotilla - 20
c/o Fleet Post Office
New York, N. Y.

LST1012/A9-4
Serial 118

S E C R E T

15 October 1944

From:	Commanding Officer
To :	Commander in Chief, United States Fleet.

Subject: War Diary - Submission of

Reference: (a) ALNAV - 176-43
(b) COM LST FLOT 20 - Mailgram Ø81415B Sept.

1. The following information covers the movements of USS LST 1012 during the month of September 1944.

(a) Sept 1 - Moored berth #13, Port of Oran loading French equipment and personnel. 1541. Underway to anchorage at Mers El Kebir.

(b) 1600 - Sept 1 to 1100 Sept. 5 - Anchored at Mers El Kebir.

(c) 1100 Sept 5. Underway to join Convoy AM-6 in obedience to orders from COM NOB, Oran Ø41217B Sept., destination - ports in Southern France.

(d) 1600 Sept 5 to 1020 Sept. 9. Underway in Convoy AM-6 according to Commander Naval Western Task Force Operational Plan 4-44.

(e) 1021 Sept. 9. Anchored in Bay of Bougnon, France.

(f) 0100 Sept. 10. Underway proceeding to Anchorage in Gulf of St. Tropez, France. 0220. Anchored in Gulf of St. Tropez. 0735. Underway proceeding to beach west of St. Maxime, France. 0920. Unloaded all French personnel and equipment. 1220. Anchored in Bay of Bougnon. 1624. Underway to join ARM-6 in obedience to orders from Commander LST Division 59, Group 30.

SᴇᴄʀᴇᴛDEᴄGLASSIFIED

(g) 1640 Sept 10 to 1550 Sept 13. Underway
in Convoy ARM-6 - destination - Oran,
Algeria.

(h) 1553 - Sept 13. Entered port of Oran
and moored at berth #18.

(i) 1640 Sept. 13 to 1934 Sept. 14. Moored
at berth #18 port of Oran, loading
French personnel and equipment.

(j) 1934. Sept 14. Underway to fuel pier
#7, port of Oran.

(k) 0740 Sept 15. Underway from fuel pier
to anchorage in outer harbor, Oran.
Received on board 27,185 gallons of
fuel oil.

(l) 1550 - Sept 15. Underway to join Convoy
AM8 pursuant to orders from Routing Officer
NOB, Oran, Algeria in accordance with Com-
mander Naval Western Task Force Operational
Plan 4-44.

(m) 1600. Sept 15 to 1350-20 Sept. Underway
in Convoy AM8 - destination - ports in
Southern France.

(n) 1352 Sept. 20. Let go anchor in Gulf of
Frejus, France. 1723. Commander R. D.
HIGGINS, USNR and Staff reported on board
to establish headquarters for COM LST
FLOT - 20.

(o) 0751 Sept 21. Underway to proceed to beach
at Cape Drammont, France. 0848. Ran
aground on shoal - Basses Isle d'Or, Cape
Drammont, France. 0850 to 1308. Undergoing salvage operations with USS "Naragansett,"
AT 87, attempting to get ship off rocks
1308. Ship freed from rocks and proceeded
to beach upon orders from beach master.
Complete information on damage sustained
and action taken during grounding contained
in report submitted to Commander in Chief

SECRET DECLASSIFIED

of Naval Operations letter LST1012/A9-8/fws
Serial 108 dated 29 September 1944

(p)   Commander R. D. HIGGINS and Staff of LST
       Flotilla 20 detached to LST 1010.

(q)   1600 - Sept 21 to 0600 Sept 22. Remained
       on beach in obedience to orders from Senior
       Salvage Officer - CTF 85. Unloaded
       all French Personnel and Equipment.

(r)   0608 Sept. 22. Underway to anchorage
       in Rade St. Raphaël. 1000 AT 87 USS "Moreno"
       along side to undertake emergency repairs
       to hull.

(s)   1100 Sept. 23 - Underway to go along side
       Tanker HMS "Celerol". 1220 Completed taking
       on fuel from "Celerol" - total received
       38,000 gallons. 1308. Proceeded to anchorage
       in Gulf of Frejus.

(t)   1209. Sept. 24 - Underway pursuant to orders
       from CTU 80.6.10 - 241104A - destination -
       Palermo, Sicily for repairs. Escort vessel
       SC 525.

(u)   1209 Sept 24 to 1400 Sept 26. Underway to
       Palermo, Sicily for repairs. 0915 Sept 26
       Conducted practice firing. Expended 660
       rounds 40mm ammunition Lot #UB 483, S.P.D.

(v)   1404 Sept 26 to 1300 Sept 27. Moored to
       berth "B" North Jetty Palermo.

(u)   1330 27 Sept. Proceeded to dry dock #1
       N.O.B. Palermo.

(x)   1350 27 Sept. to 0000-30 Sept. Moored
       in dry dock #1, N.O.B. Palermo. Repair
       work on hull carried out in accordance
       with work request submitted to Com, N.O.B.
       Palermo.

                                    M. J. FLOWERS Jr.

CC: Com 8th Phib
    Com LST Flot - 20
    File

32.

CIVILIAN SUPPLY

—U.S. SHIPMENTS OF CIVILIAN SUPPLIES
1 JULY 1943–30 SEPTEMBER 1945[a]

(LONG TONS)

Commodity	Total All Areas	Areas of Combined Responsibility			Areas of U.S. Responsibility		
		Total	Mediterranean	Northwest Europe	Total	Philippine Islands	Netherlands Indies
Total.........	6,995,960	6,788,765	3,561,318	3,227,447	207,195	190,946	16,249
Wheat/flour..............	3,132,257	3,081,160	1,267,386	1,813,774	51,097	49,880	1,217
Other foodstuffs...........	1,255,182	1,116,123	483,311	632,812	139,059	127,263	11,796
Medical and sanitary supplies	21,124	16,456	11,093	5,363	4,668	3,853	815
Soap....................	26,572	26,086	8,887	17,199	486	486	0
Coal....................	2,388,743	2,388,743	1,688,279	700,464	0	0	0
Transportation equipment...	22,824	17,313	17,312	1	5,511	4,150	1,361
Communication equipment..	78	0	0	0	78	0	78
Other utility repair equipment and supplies........	367	367	367	0	0	0	0
Clothing, shoes, and textiles.	49,111	44,970	15,443	29,527	4,141	3,615	526
Agricultural supplies and equipment..............	50,954	50,932	49,470	1,462	22	22	[b]
Industrial repair equipment and supplies.............	2,798	2,709	2,709	0	89	56	33
Other equipment...........	11	0	0	0	11	10	1
Miscellaneous manufactured end products............	44,273	42,250	15,459	26,791	2,023	1,601	422
Miscellaneous materials and products................	1,666	1,656	1,602	54	10	10	0

[a] Does not include petroleum products shipped in bulk for combined military and civilian relief use.
[b] Less than 0.5.
Source: International Div, ASF, Civilian Supply, MS, OCMH, general app. D–15.

33.

Casualties (deaths only) incurred by the French armed forces during the entire 1939–45 period are estimated as follows:

```
Total ............................................................ 212,114*
  Army (excluding FFI before Oct 44) ................. 172,613
    (1) Killed in action ............................ 114,613
        1939–40 Campaign of the West ............. 90,000
        1940–45 ...................................... 24,613
            a. Middle East and Northeast Africa
               (Free French) ....................... 1,158
            b. Tunisia (excluding Free French).... 2,300
            c. Italy, Corsica, and Elba............ 6,255
            d. France and Germany............... 14,900
    (2) Died of wounds or illness.................... 14,000
    (3) Died while in POW camps or upon release
        therefrom .................................. 44,000
  Air Force** ...................................... 5,089
  Navy** ............................................ 10,412
  French Forces of the Interior (before Oct 44)** ........ 24,000
```

*Excepting the 1,200 casualties suffered by "Armistice Army" units in the course of operations against Allied forces (Syria, Jun–Jul 41; Northwest Africa, Nov 42).

**No breakdown available.

Source: Lt. Col. P. Santini, "Etude statistique sur les pertes au cours de la guerre 1939–1945," Revue du Corps de Santé Militaire, X, No. 1 (March, 1954).

34.

NEW YORK CROWDS ACCLAIM DE GAULLE IN WHIRLWIND DAY

Victory Now Shines in Skies Over France, He Declares at Official Welcome Here

U. S. ROLE IN WAR LAUDED

His Talks With Roosevelt Are Termed 'Comforting'—Future Cooperation Pledged

By FRANK S. ADAMS

Victory now shines in the skies over France, Gen. Charles de Gaulle declared yesterday in acknowledging a tumultuous welcome from cheering crowds of New Yorkers. Speaking at the official reception in his honor at the City Hall, he characterized the conversations he had just concluded with President Roosevelt as "comforting talks."

Conceding that the impending victory was due in great part to the "stupendous American war effort," to the sacrifices of millions of American men and women and to the courage of American soldiers, sailors and aviators, General de Gaulle said that already reborn French armies, both before and behind the enemy, were playing their part in the decisive battles.

"Tomorrow, when the world will have to be organized for peace and freedom, the United States of America will find France at her side," he declared.

Welcome Here Enthusiastic

His address, far friendlier in tone toward the United States than most of his previous utterances, apparently reflected in part his satisfaction over his conferences with President Roosevelt in Washington.

Source: Frank Adams, *New York Times,* July 11, 1944, p. 1.

Bibliography

BOOKS

Adelman, Robert H., and George Walton. *The Champagne Campaign.* Boston: Little, Brown, 1969.

————. *The Devil's Brigade.* Philadelphia: Chilton Books, 1966.

Alanbrooke, Lord. *War Diaries.* London: Weidenfeld & Nicholson, 2001.

Albion, Robert G., and Robert H. Connery. *Forrestal and the Navy.* New York: Columbia University Press, 1962.

Allen, Frederick Lewis. *The Big Change.* New York: Harper & Row, 1952.

Alsop, Stewart, and Thomas Braden. *Sub Rosa: The OSS and American Espionage.* New York: Reynal & Hitchcock, 1946.

Ancell, R. Manning. *The Biographical Dictionary of World War II Generals and Flag Officers: The U.S. Armed Forces.* With Christine M. Miller. Westport, CT: Greenwood Press, 1996.

Anderson, Charles. *Algeria-French Morocco: The United States Army Campaigns of World War 2.* Washington, DC: U.S. Defense Dept., Army, Center of Military History, 1993.

Aron, Robert. *France Reborn: The History of the Liberation, June 1944-May 1945.* Trans. Humphrey Hare. New York: Charles Scribner's Sons, 1964.

Atkinson, Rick. *An Army at Dawn: The War in North Africa, 1942-1943.* New York: Henry Holt, 2003.

Auphan, Paul, and Jacques Mordal. *The French Navy in World War II.* Trans. A. C. J. Sabalot. Annapolis, MD: U.S. Naval Institute, 1957.

Ballantine, Duncan S. *U.S. Naval Logistics in the Second World War.* Princeton: Princeton University Press, 1947.

Bank, Aaron. *From OSS to Green Beret: The Birth of the Special Forces.* Novato, CA: Presidio Press, 1986.

Battle Stations: Your Navy in Action! New York: Wm. H. Wise & Co. Inc., 1946.

Bennett, Ralph. *Ultra and Mediterranean Strategy.* New York: Morrow, 1989.

Bimberg, Edward L. *The Moroccan Goums: Tribal Warriors in a Modern War.* Westport, CT: Greenwood Press, 1991.

Blum, John Morton. *V Was for Victory: Politics and American Culture during World War II.* New York: Harcourt Brace Jovanovich, 1976.

Blumenson, Martin. *Mark Clark.* London: Congdon & Weed, 1984.

————. *Salerno to Cassini.* Washington, DC: Office of the Chief of Military History, 1969.

Blumenthal, Henry. *Illusion and Reality in Franco-American Diplomacy, 1914-1945.* Baton Rouge: Louisiana State University Press, 1986.

Breuer, William B. *Operation Dragoon: The Allied Invasion of the South of France.* Novato, CA: Presidio Press, 1987.

————. *Secret Weapons of World War II.* New York: John Wiley & Sons, 2000.

Brown, Anthony Cave. *The Last Hero: Wild Bill Donovan.* New York: Times Books, 1982.

————, ed. *The Secret War Report of the OSS.* New York: Berkeley, 1976.

Bryant, Arthur. *Triumph in the West: A History of the War Years Based on the Diaries of Field Marshall Lord Alanbrooke, Chief of the Imperial General Staff.* Westport, CT: Greenwood Press, 1974 (orig. pub. in Garden City, NY: Doubleday, 1959).

Buell, Thomas B. *Master of Sea Power: A Biography of Fleet Admiral Ernest J. King.* Boston: Little, Brown and Company, 1980.

Burnhams, Robert D. *The First Special Service Force: A War History of the North Americans, 1942-1944.* Washington, DC: Infantry Journal Press, 1947.

Burns, James M. *Roosevelt: The Soldier of Freedom.* New York: Harcourt Brace Jovanovich, Inc., 1970.

Burrin, Philippe. *Living with Defeat: France under German Occupation, 1940-1944.* London: Arnold, 1996. American title: *France under the Germans: Collaboration and Compromise.* New York: New Press, 1996.

Calvocoressi, Peter. *Top Secret Ultra.* London: Cassell, 1980.

Carter, Worral R., and Elmer E. Duvall. *Ships, Salvage and Sinews of War.* Washington, DC: U.S. Government Printing Office, 1954.

Chambard, Claude. *The Maquis: A History of the French Resistance Movement.* Trans. Elaine P. Halperin. Indianapolis/New York: Bobbs-Merrill Co., Inc., 1970.

Churchill, Winston S. *The Second World War.* Vol. 2, *Their Finest Hour.* London: Cassell & Co., 1949.

————. *The Second World War.* Vol 5, *Closing the Ring;* Vol 6, *Triumph and Tragedy.* Boston: Houghton Mifflin Co., 1951; 1953.

————. *The Grand Alliance.* Boston: Houghton Mifflin, 1951.

Clark, Mark W. *Calculated Risk*. New York: Harper & Brothers, 1950.

Clarke, Jeffrey J. *Southern France: 15 August-14 September 1944*. Washington, DC: U.S. Army Center of Military History, 1994.

Clarke, Jeffrey J., and Robert R. Smith. *From the Riviera to the Rhine: U.S. Army in World War II*. Washington, DC: U.S. Army Center of Military History, 1993.

Clausen, Henry, and Bruce Lee. *Pearl Harbor: Final Judgement*. New York: Crown Publishers, 1992.

Coakley, Robert W., and Richard M. Leighton. *The United States Army in WWII: Global Logistics and Strategy, 1943-1945*. Washington, DC: U.S. Government Printing Office, 1968.

Cole, Hugh M. *The Lorraine Campaign*. Washington, DC: U.S. Army Center of Military History, 1993.

Cole, Wayne S. *America First: The Battle against Intervention, 1940-1941*. Madison, WI: University of Wisconsin Press, 1953.

Collins, Larry, and Dominique Lapierre. *Is Paris Burning?* New York: Time Warner, 1965.

Connery, Robert. *The Navy and Industrial Mobilization in World War II*. Princeton: Princeton University Press, 1951.

D'Astier de la Vigerie, Emmanuel. *Les dieux et les hommes*. Paris: Julliard, 1952.

Davis, Kenneth S. *FDR: The War President 1940-1943*. New York: Random House, 2000.

Dear, I. C. B., and M. R. D. Foot, eds. *The Oxford Companion to World War II*. New York: Oxford University Press, 1995.

De Belot, Raymond. *The Struggle for the Mediterranean, 1939-1945*. Trans. James Field. Princeton: Princeton University Press, 1951.

De Gaulle, Charles. *The Complete War Memoirs of Charles de Gaulle: Unity, 1942-1944*. Trans. Richard Howard. New York: Simon and Schuster, 1964.

De Gramont, Sanche. *The French: Portrait of a People*. New York: G. Putnam's Sons, 1969.

De Lattre de Tassigny, Jean M. *The History of the French First Army*. Trans. Malcolm Barnes. London: George Allen and Unwin, Ltd., 1949.

D'Este, Carlo. *World War II in the Mediterranean, 1942-1945*. Chapel Hill, NC: Algonquin Books of Chapel Hill, 1990.

Devlin, Gerard M. *Paratrooper! The Saga of the U.S. Army and of U.S. Army and Marine Parachute and Glider Combat Troops during World War II*. New York: St. Martin's Press, 1974.

Diamond, Hanna. *Women and the Second World War in France, 1939-1948: Choices and Constraints.* New York: Longman, 1999.

Dodds-Parker, Douglas. *Setting Europe Ablaze.* Windlesham: Springwood, 1983.

Dorwart, Jeffrey M. *Conflict of Duty: The U.S. Navy's Intelligence Dilemma, 1919-1945.* Annapolis, MD: U.S. Naval Institute, 1981.

Doughtery, James J. *The Politics of Wartime Aid: American Economic Assistance to France and French Northwest Africa, 1940-1946.* Westport, CT: Greenwood Press, 1978.

Duignan, Peter, and L. H. Gann. *World War II in Europe: Causes and Consequences.* Palo Alto, CA: Stanford University, Hoover Institute on War and Peace, 1995.

Dulles, Allen W. *The Craft of Intelligence.* New York: Harper & Row, 1963.

Dunlop, Richard. *Donovan: America's Master Spy.* Chicago: Rand McNally, 1982.

Dysart, Barry J. "The Material Battle in the European Theater." *The Big L: American Logistics in World War II.* Ed. Alan Gropman. Washington, DC: National Defense University Press, 1997.

Eisenhower, Dwight D. *Crusade in Europe.* New York: Doubleday, 1948.

Eisenhower, John. *Eisenhower at War, 1943-1945.* New York: Vintage, 1987.

Fairbanks, Douglas Jr. *The Salad Days.* New York: Doubleday, 1988.

Feis, Herbert. *The Road to Pearl Harbor.* Princeton: Princeton University Press, 1950.

Fergusson, Bernard. *The Watery Maze: The Story of Combined Operations.* New York: Holt, Rhinehart, Winston, 1961.

Finnegan, John P. *Military Intelligence.* Washington, DC: U.S. Army Center of Military History, 1998.

Fisher, Ernest F. Jr. *Cassino to the Alps.* Washington, DC: U.S. Army Center of Military History, 1977.

Fleming, Thomas. *The New Dealers' War: Franklin D. Roosevelt and the War Within World War II.* New York: Basic Books, 2001.

Foot, M. R. D. *SOE in France.* London: Her Majesty's Stationary Office, 1966.

_____. *SOE: An Outline History of the Special Operations Executive.* London: BBC, 1984.

Footitt, Hillary, and John Simmonds. *France 1943-1945.* New York: Holmes and Meier, 1980.

Ford, Corey. *Donovan of OSS.* Boston: Little, Brown and Company, 1970.

Foreign Relations of the United States: Diplomatic Paper, 1944. Vol. 3. Washington, DC: U.S. Government Printing Office, 1965.

Funk, Arthur L. *Charles de Gaulle: The Crucial Years, 1943-1944.* Norman, OK: University of Oklahoma Press, 1959.

————. *Hidden Ally: The French Resistance, Special Operations, and the Landings in Southern France, 1944.* Westport, CT: Greenwood Press, 1992.

Gallico, Paul. *The Zoo Gang.* New York: Coward, McCann & Geoghegan, 1971.

Genoud, François, ed. *The Testament of Adolf Hitler: The Hitler-Borman Documents, February-April 1945.* London: Cassell, 1961.

Gilbert, Martin. *Finest Hour: Winston S. Churchill 1939-1941.* London: Heinemann, 1983.

————. *Winston Churchill.* Vol. 7, *Road to Victory, 1941-1945.* Boston: Houghton Mifflin, 1986.

Gildea, Robert. *Marianne in Chains: Everyday Life in the French Heartland under the German Occupation.* New York: Henry Holt and Company, 2003.

Giziowski, Richard. *The Enigma of General Blaskowitz.* London: Leo Cooper, 1997.

Goldsmith, John. *Accidental Agent.* New York: Scribner's, 1971.

Goodman, Jack, ed. *While You Were Gone.* New York: Simon and Schuster, 1946.

Graham, Don. *No Name on the Bullet: A Biography of Audie Murphy.* New York: Viking, 1989.

Gropman, Alan L. *Mobilizing U.S. Industry in World War II: Myth and Reality.* Washington, DC: Institute for National Strategic Studies, National Defense University, 1996.

Guillon, Jean-Marie. *La Libération du Var: Résistance et nouveaux pouvoirs.* Paris: Centre National de la Recherche Scientifique, 1990.

————. *La Résistance dans le Var* (Doctorat d'Etat, Aix), 1989.

Guinness, Alec. *Blessing in Disguise.* New York: Warner Books, 1985.

Hackmann, William. *Seek and Destroy: Sonar, Anti-Submarine Warfare and the Royal Navy.* London: Her Majesty's Stationary Office, 1984.

Hall, H. Duncan. *North American Supply.* London: Her Majesty's Stationary Office, 1955.

Hastings, Max. *Armageddon: The Battle for Germany, 1944-1945.* New York: Alfred A. Knopf, 2004.

Heinrichs, Waldo H. *American Ambassador: Joseph Grew and the Development of the United States Diplomatic Tradition.* Boston: Little, Brown and Company, 1986.

_____. *Threshold of War: Franklin D. Roosevelt and the American Entry into World War II*. New York: Oxford University Press, 1988.

_____. *Diplomacy and Force*. Chicago: Imprint Publications, 1996.

_____. *Heroes of the Resistance*. Ed. Army Times. New York: Army Times, 1967.

Hewitt, Henry Kent. *Memoirs*. Ed. Evelyn M. Cherpak. Newport, RI: Naval War College Press, 2004.

_____. *Oral History*. New York: Butler Library, Columbia University Press, 1961.

Hirshon, Stanley P. *General Patton: A Soldier's Story*. New York: HarperCollins, 2002.

Hogan, David W. Jr. *U.S. Army Special Operations in World War II*. Washington, DC: U.S. Army Center of Military History, 1992.

Howard, Michael. *Strategic Deception*. Vol. 5, *British Intelligence in the Second World War*. New York: Cambridge University Press, 1990.

_____. *The Mediterranean Strategy in the Second World War*. New York: Praeger, 1968.

Howe, George F. *Northwest Africa: Seizing the Initiative in the West*. U.S. Army in World War II: The Mediterranean Theater of Operation. Washington, DC: U.S. Army Center of Military History, 2001.

Hurstfield, Julian G. *America and the French Nation, 1939-1945*. Chapel Hill: University of North Carolina Press, 1986.

Hymoff, Edward. *The OSS in World War II: The True Story of American Agents behind Enemy Lines*. 2nd ed. New York: Richardson & Steirman, 1986.

Jackson, Julian. *France: The Dark Years, 1940-1944*. New York: Oxford Press, 2001.

Jagers, Robert B. *Whales of World War II: Military Life of Robert Jagers, June 1942 to October 1945*. Farmington, MI: Robert Jagers, 2003.

Jonas, Manfred. *Isolationism in America 1935-1941*. Ithaca: Cornell University Press, 1966.

Judt, Tony. *Resistance and Revolution in Mediterranean Europe, 1939-1948*. New York: Routledge, 1989.

_____. *Past Imperfect: French Intellectuals, 1944-56*. Berkeley, CA: University of California Press, 1992.

Kahn, David. *The Codebreakers: The Story of Secret Writing*. New York: Macmillan, 1967.

Kedward, H. Roderick. *In Search of the Maquis: Rural Resistance in Southern France, 1942-45*. New York: Oxford University Press, 1993.

_____. *Occupied France: Collaboration and Resistance, 1940-1944.* Oxford: Blackwell, 1985.

_____. *Resistance in Vichy France: A Study of Ideas and Motivation in the Southern Zone, 1940-1942.* 2nd ed. New York: Oxford University Press, 1978.

Kedward, H. Roderick, and Nancy Wood, eds. *The Liberation of France: Image and Event.* Washington, DC: Berg Publishers, 1995.

Keegan, John. *The Second World War.* New York: Penguin Books, 1989.

Kershaw, Ian. *Hitler, 1936-1945.* New York: W. W. Norton & Co., 2000.

Kimball, Warren, ed. *Churchill and Roosevelt: The Complete Correspondence.* Princeton: Princeton University Press, 1984.

Lacouture, Jean. *De Gaulle.* 3 vols. Paris: Editions du Seuil, 1984-89.

Langer, William L. *Our Vichy Gamble.* New York: Alfred A. Knopf, 1947.

Larrabee, Eric. *Commander in Chief.* Cambridge, MA: Harper & Row, 1987.

Latimer, Jon. *Deception in War.* New York: Overlook Press, 2001.

Leahy, William D. *I Was There.* New York: McGraw Hill, 1950.

Leslie, Peter. *The Liberation of the Riviera: The Resistance to the Nazis in the South of France and the Story of Its Heroic Leader, Ange-Marie Miniconi.* New York: Wyndham Books, 1980.

Lewin, Ronald. *Ultra Goes to War.* New York: McGraw Hill, 1978.

Lewis, Nigel. *Exercise Tiger.* New York: Prentice Press, 1990.

Liebling, A. J. *The New Yorker War Pieces.* Albuquerque, NM: University of New Mexico Press, 1994.

Lockhart, Vincent M. *T-Patch to Victory: The 36th "Texas" Division.* Canyon, TX: Stakes Plains Press, 1981.

Lottman, Herbert T. *Pétain: Hero or Traitor, the Untold Story.* New York: William Morrow and Co., Inc., 1985.

Lovell, Stanley P. *Of Spies and Stratagems.* Englewood Cliff, NJ: Prentice Hall, 1964.

MacCloskey, Monro. *Rearming the French in World War II.* New York: Richard Rosen Press, 1972.

Markey, Michael. *Jake: The General from West York Avenue.* York, PA: Historical Society of York County, Pennsylvania, 1998.

Marshall, George C. *The Winning of the War in Europe and the Pacific.* Washington, DC: War Department, 1945.

Matloff, Maurice. "Was the Invasion of Southern France a Blunder?" *U.S. Naval Institute Proceedings.* July 1958.

_____. *American Military History*. Army Historical Series. 2nd ed. Washington, DC: U.S. Army Center of Military History, Government Printing Office, 1973.

_____. *Strategic Planning for Coalition Warfare, 1943-1944*. Washington, DC: U.S. Army Office of the Chief of Military History, 1959.

May, Ernest R. *Strange Victory: Hitler's Conquest of France*. New York: Hill and Wang, 2000.

McFarland, Stephen L. *Conquering the Night: Army Air Forces Night Fighters*. Washington, DC: Air Force History and Museums Program, 1998.

McIntosh, Elizabeth P. *The Women of the OSS: Sisterhood of Spies*. Washington, DC: United States Naval Institute, 1998.

McKean, David. *Tommy the Cork: Washington's Ultimate Insider from Roosevelt to Reagan*. South Royalton, VT: Steerforth Press, 2004.

Meacham, Jon. *Franklin and Winston: An Intimate Portrait of an Epic Friendship*.
New York, Random House, 2003.

Megargee, Geoffrey P. *Inside Hitler's High Command*. Lawrence, KS: University Press of Kansas, 2000.

Mendelsohn, John, ed. *Covert Warfare*. vols. 3, 4, 5. New York: Garland, 1989.

Mihan, George. *Looted Treasure: Germany's Raid on Art*. London: Alliance Press, 1944.

Millis, Walter, ed. *The Forrestal Diaries*. With the collaboration of E. S. Duffield. New York: Viking Press, 1951.

_____. *This Is Pearl Harbor*. New York: Morrow, 1947.

Molony, C. J., F. C. Flynn, H. L. Davies, and T. P. Gleve. *The Mediterranean and the Middle East*. Vol. 5, *The Campaign in Sicily and Italy*. London: Her Majesty's Stationary Office, 1973.

Mooney, James L., ed. *Dictionary of American Fighting Ships*. Vol. 7. Washington, DC: Naval Historical Center, 1981.

Moore, Honor. *The White Blackbird: A Life of the Painter Margarett Sargent by Her Granddaughter*. Reed Business Information, Inc., 1997.

Moorehead, Alan. *The Traitors*. New York: Scribner's, 1952.

Moreno, John A. "The Death of Admiral Moon." *Allied Invasion of Normandy*. Annapolis, MD: U.S. Naval Institute, 1994.

Morgan, William J. *The OSS and I*. New York: Norton, 1957.

Morison, Samuel E. *History of United States Naval Operations in World War II*. Vol. 11, *The Invasion of France and Germany, 1944-1945*. Boston: Little, Brown and Co., 1957.

————. *Operations in North African Waters: October 1942-June 1943.* Urbana and Chicago: University of Illinois Press, 2001.

Murphy, Robert D. *Diplomat among Warriors.* Garden City, NY: Doubleday & Co., 1964.

Murray, Williamson, and Alan R. Millett. *A War To Be Won: Fighting the Second World War.* Cambridge: Harvard University Press, 2000.

Murray, Williamson. *Strategy for Defeat: The Luftwaffe, 1933-1945.* Maxwell Air Force Base, AL: Air University Press, 1983.

Nelson, Dennis M. *The Integration of the Negro into the U.S. Navy.* New York: Farrar, Straus and Giroux, 1951.

Nicholas, H. G., ed. *Washington Dispatches, 1941-1945: Weekly Reports from the British Embassy.* London: Weidenfeld and Nicholson, 1981.

O'Neill, William L. *A Democracy at War: America's Fight at Home and Abroad in World War II.* New York: Free Press, 1993.

Ottaway, Susan. *Violette Szabo.* Annapolis, MD: Naval Institute Press, 2002.

Ouston, Philip. *France in the Twentieth Century.* New York: Praeger, 1972.

Packard, Wyman H. *A Century of U.S. Naval Intelligence.* Washington, DC: Office of Naval Intelligence and the Naval Historical Center, 1996.

Paddock, Alfred H. Jr. *U.S. Army Special Warfare: Its Origins, Psychological and Unconventional Warfare, 1941-1951.* Washington, DC: National Defense University Press, 1982.

Parrish, Thomas. *The Ultra Americans.* New York: Stein & Day, 1986.

Parton, James. *Air Force Spoken Here: General Ira Eaker and the Command of the Air.* Bethesda, MD: Adler and Adler Publishers, 1986.

Patton, George S. Jr. *War As I Knew It.* Annotated by Col. Paul D. Harkins. Boston: Houghton Mifflin, 1947.

Paxton, Robert O. *Parades and Politics at Vichy: The French Officer Corps under Marshal Pétain.* Princeton: Princeton University Press, 1966.

————. *Vichy France: Old Guard, New Order, 1940-1944.* New York: Alfred A. Knopf, 1972.

Persico, Joseph E. *Roosevelt's Secret War: FDR and WWII Espionage.* New York: Random House, 2001.

————. *Piercing the Reich: The Penetration of Nazi Germany by American Secret Agents during World War II.* New York: Viking Press, 1979.

Phillips, Cabell. *The 1940s: Decade of Triumph and Trouble.* London: Macmillan, 1975.

Pinck, Daniel C., Charles T. Pinck, and Geoffrey M. T. Jones. *Stalking the History of the Office of Strategic Services: An OSS Bibliography.* Boston: OSS/Donovan Press, 2000.

Playfair, I. S. O., F. C. Flynn, C. J. C. Molony, and S. E. Toomer. *The Mediterranean and the Middle East*. Vol 2. London: Her Majesty's Stationary Office, 1956.

Pogue, Forrest C. *George C. Marshall*. Vol. 2, *Ordeal and Hope, 1939-1942*. New York: Viking Press, 1966.

———. *George C. Marshall: Organizer of Victory, 1943-1945*. New York: Viking Press, 1973.

———. *The Supreme Command: The U.S. Army in World War II*. Washington, DC: U.S. Government Printing Office, 1954.

———. *The United States Army in World War II: The European Theater of Operations*. Washington, DC: U.S. Army Office of Military History, 1954.

Polmar, Norman, and Thomas Ballen. *World War II: The Encyclopedia of the War Years 1941-1945*. New York: Random House, 1996.

Porch, Douglas. *The Path to Victory: The Mediterranean Theater in World War II*. New York: Farrar, Straus and Giroux, 2004.

Potter, E. B., and C. W. Nimitz, eds. *The Great Sea War: The Dramatic Story of Naval Action in World War II*. New York: Branhall House, 1960.

Prange, W. *At Dawn We Slept*. New York: McGraw Hill, 1981.

Raines, Rebecca R. *Getting the Message Through: A Branch History of the U.S. Army Signal Corps*. Washington, DC: U.S. Army Center of Military History, 1996.

Ransom, Harry Howe. *Central Intelligence and National Security*. Cambridge: Harvard University Press, 1959.

Robichon, Jacques. *The Second D-Day*. Trans. Barbara Shuey. New York: Walker Press, 1969.

Rockefeller, David. *Memoirs*. New York: Random House, 2002.

Rogow, Arnold A. *James Forrestal: A Study of Personality, Politics and Policy*. New York: Macmillan, 1963.

Roosevelt, Kermit. *The Overseas Targets War Report of the OSS*. 2 vols. New York: Walker & Co., 1976.

———, ed. *War Report of the OSS*. With the staff, History Project, Strategic Services Unit. Washington, DC: War Department, 1947. 2 vols. New York: Walker, 1976.

Roskill, Stephen W. *The War at Sea, 1939-1945*. 3 vols. London: Her Majesty's Stationary Office, 1954-1961.

Rossiter, Margaret L. *Women in the Resistance*. New York: Praeger, 1986.

Rousso, Henry. *The Vichy Syndrome: History and Memory in France, 1944*. Trans. Arthur Gold. Cambridge: Harvard University Press, 1991.

Russell, Edward T. *Leaping the Atlantic Wall: Army Air Forces Campaigns in Western Europe, 1942-1945.* Washington, DC: Office of Air Force History, 1999.

Russell, Edward T., and Robert M. Johnson. *Africa to the Alps: The Army Air Forces in the Mediterranean Theater.* Washington, DC: Air Force History and Museums Program, 1995.

Schlesinger, Arthur Jr. *A Life in the Twentieth Century: Innocent Beginnings, 1917-1950.* Boston: Houghton Mifflin Co., 2000.

Schoenbrun, David. *The Three Lives of Charles de Gaulle.* New York: Atheneum, 1966.

————. *Soldiers of the Night: The Story of the French Resistance.* New York: E. P. Dutton, 1980.

Sherwood, Robert E. *Roosevelt and Hopkins.* New York: Harper and Row, 1948.

Shirer, William L. *Collapse of the Third Republic: An Inquiry into the Fall of France in 1940.* New York: Simon and Schuster, 1969.

Silverstone, Paul H. *U.S. Warships of World War II.* Annapolis, MD: Naval Institute Press, 1989.

Simpson, Mitchell B. III. *Admiral Harold R. Stark: Architect of Victory, 1939-1945.* Columbia, SC: University of South Carolina Press, 1989.

Smith, Bradley F. Introduction to *Covert Warfare: OSS Jedburgh Teams.* New York: Garland Publishing, 1989.

————. *The Shadow Warriors: OSS and the Origins of the CIA.* New York: Basic Books, 1983.

————. *The Ultra-Magic Deals.* Novato, CA: Presidio Press, 1993.

Smith, Gaddis. *American Diplomacy during the Second World War, 1941-1945.* New York: John Wiley and Sons, 1965.

Smith, R. Harris. *OSS: The Secret History of America's First Central Intelligence Agency.* Berkeley: University of California Press, 1971.

Spector, Ronald H. *At War at Sea.* New York: Viking Press, 2001.

Spiller, Roger J., Joseph G. Dawson, and T. Harry Williams, eds. *Dictionary of American Military Biography.* Westport, CT: Greenwood Press, 1984.

Stafford, David. *Britain and European Resistance.* London: Macmillan, 1980.

Stanton, Doug. *In Harm's Way: The Sinking of the USS Indianapolis and the Extraordinary Story of Its Survivors.* New York: Henry Holt and Company, 2001.

Strahan, Jerry F. *Andrew Jackson Higgins and the Boats That Won World War II.* Baton Rouge, LA: Louisiana State University Press, 1994.

Sweet, George H., with Donald H. Sweet. *Lightning Strikes: A Story of Amphibious Actions during World War II.* Ridgewood, NJ: Dogo Publishing, 2000.

Sweets, John. *Choices in Vichy France: The French under Nazi Occupation.* New York: Oxford University Press, 1986.

————. *The Politics of Resistance in France, 1940-1944: A History of the Mouvements Unis de la Résistance.* Dekalb, IL: Northern Illinois University Press, 1976.

The French Forces of the Interior: Their Organization and Participation in the Liberation of France. French Resistance Unit of the U.S. Army Historical Section, 1945. Microfilm available at Library of Congress, Washington, DC.

Taggart, Donald G., ed. *History of the Third Infantry Division in World War II.* Washington, DC: Infantry Journal Press, 1947.

Toland, John. *But Not in Shame.* New York: Random House, 1961.

Tompkins, Peter. *A Spy in Rome.* New York: Simon and Schuster, 1962.

————. *Intelligence and Operational Support in the Anti-Nazi Resistance: The Italian Partisans in World War II.* Washington, DC: U.S. Central Intelligence Agency, 1998.

Troy, Thomas. *Donovan and the CIA: A History of the Establishment of the Central Intelligence Agency.* Frederick, MD: Aletha Books, 1981.

Truscott, Lucian K. *Command Decision.* New York: E. P. Dutton, 1954.

————. *Command Missions: A Personal Story.* Novato, CA: Presidio, 1990.

————. *The Twilight of the U.S. Cavalry: Life in the Old Army, 1917-1942.* Lawrence, KS: University of Kansas, 1989.

Tuleja, Thaddeus J. "Admiral H. Kent Hewitt." *Men of War: Great Naval Leaders of World War II.* Ed. Stephen Howarth. New York: St. Martin's Press, 1992.

Turner, John F., and Robert Jackson. *Destination Berchtesgaden: The Story of the U.S. Seventh Army in World War II.* New York: Charles Scribner and Sons, 1975.

U.S. Army. *Mobilization: The U.S. Army in World War II.* Washington, DC: U.S. Government Printing Office, 1995.

U.S. War Department General Staff Report to the Undersecretary of War and Chief of Staff. *Logistics in World War II: Final Report of Military History.* Washington, DC: U.S. Government Printing Office, 1993.

United States Seventh Army. *Report of Operations in France and Germany, 1944-1945.* Vol. 1. Heidelberg: Aloys Graf, 1946.

Vatter, Harold C. *The U.S. Economy in World War II.* New York: Columbia University Press, 1985.

Vigneras, Marcel. *The U.S. Army in WWII: Rearming the French.* Washington, DC: U.S. Government Printing Office, 1958.

Vomécourt, Philippe. *An Army of Amateurs.* Garden City, NY: Doubleday, 1961.

Waller, John H. *The Unseen War in Europe.* New York: Random House, 1996.

Warnock, A. Timothy. *Air Force Combat Medals, Streamers, and Campaigns.* Washington, DC: Office of Air Force History, 1990.

————. *Air Power versus U-boats: Confronting Hitler's Submarine Menace in the European Theater.* Washington, DC: Air Force History and Museums Program, 1999.

Weigley, Russell F. *Eisenhower's Lieutenants: The Campaign of France and Germany, 1944-45.* Bloomington, IN: Indiana University Press, 1981.

Whiting, Charles. *America's Forgotten Army: The Story of the U.S. Seventh Army in World War II.* New York: Sarpedon, 1999.

Williams, Chas. *Pétain: How the Hero of France Became a Convicted Traitor and Changed the Course of History.* New York: Palgrave, 2005.

Wilmot, Chester. *The Struggle for Europe.* New York: Harper, 1952.

Wilson, Lord (Henry Maitland). *Eight Years Overseas.* London: Hutchinson, 1950.

Wilt, Alan F. *The Atlantic Wall: Hitler's Defenses in the West, 1941-1944.* Ames, IA: Iowa State University Press, 1975.

————. *The French Riviera Campaign of August 1944.* Carbondale, IL: Southern Illinois University Press, 1981.

Winterbotham, F. W. *The Ultra Secret.* New York: Harper & Row, 1974.

Wohlstetter, R. *Pearl Harbor: Warning and Decision.* Larkspur, CO: Pinetree Press, 1962.

Wyant, William K. *Sandy Patch: A Biography of Lt. Gen. Alexander M. Patch.* New York: Praeger, 1991.

Wylie, Laurence. *Village in the Vaucluse.* New York: Harper & Row, 1957.

Young, Peter, ed. *The World Almanac Book of World War II.* Englewood Cliffs: Prentice Hall, 1981.

DOCTORAL DISSERTATIONS

Brewer, John Clinton. "Lend-lease: Foreign Policy Weapon in Politics and Diplomacy, 1941-1945." Diss., University of Texas, 1974.

Fattig, Richard C. "Reprisal: The German Army and the Execution of Hostages during the Second World War." Diss., University of California, 1980.

Schmidtlein, Eugene Francis. "Truman the Senator." Diss., University of Missouri, 1962.

Simpson, Benjamin Mitchell III. "Political Consultations between the United States and the French National Committee, 1942-1943: The Embassy of Admiral Harold R. Stark, USN." Diss., Tufts University, 1968.

SELECTED ARTICLES

"Allies Drive Inland in Southern France to Join Forces Pounding Nazis in North; Foe's Riviera Beach Defenses Crumble." *New York Times*, 6 Aug. 1944, 1.

"Army-Navy 'Waste' Rapped by Truman." *Stars and Stripes*, 21 Aug. 1944, 3.

"Atlantic Report—European Front." *Atlantic Monthly*, Sept. 1944, 3.

"Battle of Desperation." *Time*, 3 June 1940, 19-21.

"Battle of the Desert." *Time*, 8 Dec. 1941, 22-23.

"Civil Affairs Experts Act as a Vital Link." *Stars and Stripes*, 21 Aug. 1944, 4.

"Crumbling Resistance in France." *New Republic*, 28 Aug. 1944, 235.

"Defense of France." *Time*, 10 June 1940, 24-26.

"Executing Operation Anvil Dragoon." *United States Naval Institute Proceedings* 80, no. 8 (1954): 897-911.

"FDR Saw Pacific Practice Landings; Reports on Hawaii." *Stars and Stripes*, 15 Aug. 1944, 82.

"France Faces the Attack." *Economist*, 18 May 1940, 898.

"France Regained." *Nation*, 26 Aug. 1944, 227-228.

"French Guerrillas Link Two Invasions: Powerful Operation Cited by Allies—FFI Launch Strong Offensive in Savoie." *New York Times*, 19 Aug. 1944, 1.

"High-Ranking Generals Miss Death Off Riviera." *Stars and Stripes*, 21 Aug. 1944, 2.

"Invaders Drive Eight Miles on Riviera, Capture St. Tropez, Resistance Still Slight; U.S. Tanks Race to Block Escape in North." *New York Times*, 17 Aug. 1944, 1.

"Mediterranean Theater: Enter Italy." *Time*, 17 June 1940, 20-23.

"Midwest Truckers Returning to Jobs." *Stars and Stripes*, 15 Aug. 1944, 2.

"Names and Notes in the News." *Progressive*, 21 Aug. 1944, 3.

"Nurses Follow Ashore Shortly after Landings." *Stars and Stripes*, 21 Aug. 1944, 1.

"Obituary of Robert Tryon Frederick." *Army*, Sept. 1982.

"Our War." *New Republic*, 15 Dec. 1941, 811-812.

"Patterson Somervell Received by Pope Pius." *Stars and Stripes*, 15 Aug. 1944, 2.

"Plane Wreck of Prince Is Discovered." *New York Times*, 7 Apr. 2004, A6.

"Prime Minister Churchill Reviews the War." *ONI Weekly Bulletin*, 9 Aug. 1944, 2527-2535, 2578.

"Red Army Masses on Reich's Border for New Assault." *Stars and Stripes*, 16 Aug. 1944, 8.

"Roosevelt at War." *Time*, 29 Dec. 1941.

"Southern France Drive Goes Well." *Stars and Stripes*, 17 Aug. 1944.

"Southern France Land of Hunger." *Stars and Stripes*, 19 Aug. 1944.

"Tactician's Dream." *Time*, 28 Aug. 1944, 22-24.

"The American Mood." *Time*, 14 Aug. 1944, 17.

"The Battle of 1942." *Time*, 1 Dec. 1941, 19.

"The Coming Battle for Germany." *Life*, 28 Aug. 1944.

"The Coming Victory in France." *New Republic*, 28 Aug. 1944, 240-241.

"The Core of German Resistance." *ONI Weekly Bulletin*, 6 Sept. 1944, 2821-2827.

"The Medals of His Defeats." *Atlantic Monthly*, April 2002, 118-129.

"The Presidency: The President's Week." *Time*, 28 Aug. 1944, 16-17.

"The Shape of Things." *Nation*, 15 June 1940, 721.

"The Spy Who Was a Ball Player." *Modern Maturity*, April-May 1983, 96-97.

"The U.S. at War." *Time*, 22 Dec. 1941, 17.

"The War in Review." *Progressive*, 21 Aug. 1944, 2.

"Trouble in Philadelphia." *Time*, 14 Aug. 1944, 21-22.

"U.S. at War." *Time*, 21 Aug. 1944.

"What the Bombing of Paris Means." *New Republic*, 10 June 1940, 776.

Bachman, Leo A. "Intelligence for Amphibious Operations." *ONI Weekly Bulletin*, 3 Mar. 1943.

Bagger, Eugene. "Flight from France, June 17-25." *Harper's*, Nov. 1940, 622-636.

Barber, Maurice. Letter. *Time*, 8 Jan. 1941.

Barker, Thomas M. "The Ljubljana Gap Strategy: Alternative to Anvil/Dragoon or Fantasy?" *Journal of Military History* 56, no. 1, (1992): 57-85.

Bartlett, Vernon. "Invasion Diary: The First Four Days in England." *Harper's*, Aug. 1944, 241-248.

Bergner, Hans E. "One D-Day Story: Half a Century Ago Hans Bergner Took Part in One of History's Greatest Military Operations." *Fredericksburg Standard*, 1 June 1994, 1-11.

Boehm, Philip, trans. *New York Times Book Review*, 14 Aug. 2005. New York: Henry Holt & Company, 2005.

Bolte, Charles. "The War Fronts: The Battle of France." *Nation*, 19 Aug. 1944, 202, 203.

Boyle, Kay. "Defeat." *New Yorker*, 17 May 1941, 18-22.

Browne, Mallory. "Paris Again." *Harper's*, Nov. 1944, 499-506.

Burnet, Mary. "France: The Pieces in the Puzzle." *Harper's*, Sept. 1944, 291-300.

Cohen, Gary. "The Keystone Kommandos." *Atlantic Monthly*, Feb. 2002.

De Saint Jean, Robert. "The Failure of France." *Harper's*, Oct. 1940, 449-460.

Dreher, Carl. "Why Hitler Wins: A Lesson in Technological Politics for Americans." *Harper's*, Oct. 1940.

Drucker, Peter. "Germany's Plans for Europe." *Harper's*, Nov. 1940, 597-604.

Dzwonchyk, Wayne N. "General Jacob L. Devers and the First French Army." MA thesis. University of Delaware, 1975.

Funk, Arthur L. "Churchill, Eisenhower, and the French Resistance." *Military Affairs* 45, no. 1 (1981): 29-33.

Galeano, Eduardo. "Make War, Not Love." *Progressive*, Sept. 2003, 11.

Garvin, William. "A Study of Civil Rights Statutes and Cases." *National Bar Journal*, 1941, 75-86.

Guillon, Jean Marie. "Les Mouvements du collaboration dans le Var." *Revue d'histoire de la deuxième guerre mondiale* 29 (Jan. 1979): 91-110.

Gurley, Franklin L. "Le debarquement en Provence: le 15 Aout 1944." *Guerres mondiales et conflicts contemporains* 44, no. 174 (1994).

Hale, William Harlan. "After Pearl Harbor." *New Republic*, 15 Dec. 1941, 816.

Hamilton, Thomas. "What the Germans Told the French." *Harper's*, Nov. 1944, 342-3.

Hicks, Anne Frederick. "The War Made Him, Peacetime Broke Him." *Army* 32 (Sept. 1982): 48-51, 54-5.

Kanon, Joseph. Rev. of *Eight Weeks in the Conquered City: A Diary*, by Anonymous.

Kohn, Al. "Those First Three Days Like 30 to Paratroopers." *Stars and Stripes*, 24 Aug. 1944.

———. "Nazi General Captured in Southern France." *Stars and Stripes*, 21 Aug. 1944.

Liebling, A. J. "Letter from Paris." *New Yorker,* 24 May 1940 and 1 June 1940, 49-50.

Martin, David. "Lisa Fittko, 95, Helped Rescue Many Who Fled the Nazis." *New York Times,* 21 Mar. 2005.

Michie, Alan. "Policing Germany by Air." *Atlantic Monthly,* Aug. 1944.

Morin, Carl R. Jr. "The Strategic Consideration of the Allied Invasion of Southern France, 1944." MA thesis. University of Florida, 1968.

Nickerson, Hoffman. "The New German Military Theory." *Harper's,* Aug. 1940, 239-246.

ONI Weekly Bulletin, 16 Aug. 1944.

ONI Weekly Bulletin, 25 Sept. 1944.

Pace, Eric. "Obituary of Pierre de Benouville." *New York Times,* 11 Dec. 2001, 9.

Parton, James. "Lt. Gen. Ira C. Eaker, USAF (Ret.), an Aide's Memoir." *Aerospace Historian,* Dec. 1987, 227-235.

Persico, Joseph E. "What Did He Know and When?" *New York Times,* 18 Apr. 1944, 44.

Randall, Willard S. "The Other D-Day." *Journal of Military History* 6, no. 3 (1994): 70-79.

Riding, Alan. "Henri Rol-Tanguy, French Resistance Figure Dies at 94." *New York Times,* 11 Sept. 2002, C12.

Rothstein, Edward. "Contemplating Churchill." *Smithsonian,* Mar. 2005, 91-101.

Schmidt, Hans. "Germany—The Voice from Within." *Harper's,* June 1940, 94-104.

Sebald, W. G. "An Attempt at Restitution," *The New Yorker,* 20 Dec. 2004, 114.

Shanker, Tom. "Army Pushes Human (and High-Tech) Spying." *New York Times,* 15 Sept. 2003, A10.

Sixsmith, E. J. G. "Rome, Anvil and the Ljubljana Gap." *Army Quarterly and Defense Journal* [Great Britain] 99, no. 1 (1969): 51-59.

Smith, Len. "French Captain Was Given Orders to Open Fire on His Own Property." *Stars and Stripes,* 18 Aug. 1944, 2.

Steele, Addison. "Steamshovel at the Treasury." *Progressive,* 14 Aug. 1944, 5.

Stevenson, Adlai III. "Different Man, Different Moment." *New York Times,* 7 Feb. 2003, A25.

Stoler, Mark. Rev. of *Desperate Venture: The Story of the Allied Invasion of North Africa,* by Norman Gelb. *Journal of American History* 80, no. 2 (1993): 743.

Swinton, Stan. "French Patriots Aid Yanks Liberate French Village." *Stars and Stripes,* 21 Aug. 1944, 3.

The Nation, 22 June 1940; 29 June 1940; 6 Dec. 1941; 13 Dec. 1941.

Toscano, Mario. "Machiavelli Views World War II Intelligence." *International Journal of Intelligence and Counterintelligence* 1, no. 3 (1986).

Voorhis, Jerry. "Showdown on the Home Front." *Progressive,* 7 Aug. 1944, 1-2.

Williams, Don. "Riviera Coast Secure, Objectives Taken; Allies Push Ahead." *Stars and Stripes* 58 (1944): 1.

Wilt, Alan F. "The Summer of 1944: A Comparison of Overlord and Anvil/Dragoon." *Journal of Strategic Studies* [Great Britain] 4, no. 2 (1981): 187-195.

MILITARY HISTORIES AND REPORTS

Action Report of LST 1011 dated 25 Oct. 1944, from Commanding Officer R. M. Wilson.

"Air Ground Teamwork on the Western Front: The Role of XIX Tactical Air Command during 1994." An Interim Report. Washington, DC: U.S. Army Center of Military History, 1992.

"Final Report on the SPOC (Special Operations Group) Debriefing Operation." RG 226, Box 135, Folder 767. College Park, MD: National Archives, 1944.

"Loss of USS LST 282—Report from Commander, United States Eighth Fleet (H. K. Hewitt) to Secretary of the Navy (J. V. Forrestal). 2 Sept. 1944. College Park, MD: Naval History Division, National Archives.

"The AAF in the Invasion of Southern France: An Interim Report." Washington, DC: Army Air Forces, 1992.

Allison, David K. *New Eye for the Navy: The Origin of Radar at the Naval Research Laboratory.* Washington, DC: Naval Research Laboratory, 1981.

Army Ground Forces. *Report C-630: Combat and Staff Lessons. 7th Army. Invasion of Southern France.* Washington, DC: 1945.

Blaskowitz, Johannes. "Fighting by Armeegruppe G in Southern France until Middle of Sept. 1944." Trans. R.J. Herman. Allendorf, Germany, 1947. English copy 16 May 1947, Headquarters of U.S. Army, Europe, Historical Division Foreign Military Studies Branch.

————. *German Reaction to the Invasion of Southern France.* Historical Division EUCOM MS-A-868, 1945.

————. *German (OB Southwest) Estimate of the Situation Prior to Allied Invasion of Southern France.* OCMH MS-B-421. 1947.

Boddie, James W. *Ammunition Support for Operation Dragoon, the Invasion of Southern France—Could We Do It Today?* Carlisle Barracks, PA: U.S. Army War College, 1987.

Buhl, Howard. "Diaries of a Motor Machinist, LST 494, from Dec. 22 1943 to June 9, 1944."

Command and General Staff School, 1st Command Class. *Operation Anvil (Dragoon) Southern France.* Ft. Leavenworth, 1946.

Command and General Staff School, 2nd Command Class. *Analysis of Operation Dragoon.* Ft. Leavenworth, 1946.

Congressional Record. Senate. Aug. 3, 1949: 10864.

Deck Log Books, May-August 1944. College Park, MD: National Archives.

Deck Log. Remarks Sheet for 4 June 1944-7 June 1944. College Park, MD: National Archives.

Devers, Jacob L. "Operation Dragoon: The Invasion of Southern France." *Military Affairs* 10 (1946): 3-41.

Flowers, M. J. Jr. M. J. Flowers Jr. to Commander LST Flotilla 20. War Diary of LST 1012. 1 July 1944 to 31 August 1944.

Foreign Relations of the United States: Diplomacy Papers, 1944. Vol. 5. Washington, DC: Government Printing Office, 1965.

Furer, Julius Augustus. *Administration of the Navy Department in World War II.* Washington, DC: Government Printing Office, 1959.

Fussell, Paul. *The Boys' Crusade: The American Infantry in North Western Europe 1944-45.* New York: Modern Library, 2003.

Gilbert, Lawrence E. "Report of Loss of Ship while Operating in the Camel Assault Area during the Invasion of Southern France." Serial 005. 2 Sept. 1944. College Park, MD: Naval History Division, National Archives.

Greenfield, Kent R., ed. *Command Decisions.* Washington, DC: Government Printing Office, 1960. It includes an essay by Maurice Matloff, "The Anvil Decision: Crossroads of Strategy." 383-400.

Hewitt, H. K. H. K. Hewitt to E. J. King. "Torch Operation: Comments and Recommendations," memorandum, 22 Dec. 1942. Serial 00299.

————. *Invasion of Southern France: Reports of Naval Commander, Western Task Force.* U.S. Eighth Fleet, 28 Nov. 1944. ca 400 p., 24 foldouts.

_____. "Torch Operation Comments and Recommendations." Serial 00299. Washington, DC: U.S. Navy Library, Dec. 22, 1942.

_____. "Executing Operation Anvil-Dragoon." *United States Naval Institute Proceedings* 75 (1954): 731-45.

_____. "Planning Operation Anvil-Dragoon." *United States Naval Institute Proceedings* 80, no. 7 (1954): 731-745.

History of the Chaplain Corps, U.S. Navy, 1939-1949. Vol. 2. Philadelphia: Naval Publications and Forms Center, 1995.

Hoopes, Townsend, and Douglas Brinkley. *Driven Patriot: The Life and Times of James Forrestal.* New York: Alfred A. Knopf, 1992.

Ingersoll, R. E. R. E. Ingersoll to E. J. King. "Torch Operation: Comments and Recommendations," memorandum, 22 Dec. 1942.

Jenkins, Reuben E. "Operation 'Dragoon': Planning and Landing Phase." *Military Review* 26 (1946): 3-9.

Kahn, David. "The Ultra Conference." *Cryptologia* 3 (1979): 1-8.

King, Ernest J. *U.S. Navy at War, 1941-1945: Official Reports to the Secretary of the Navy.* Washington, DC: U.S. Navy Department, 1946.

Kirkpatrick, Charles. *Defense of the Americas: The U.S. Army Campaigns of World War II.* Washington, DC: U.S. Government Printing Office.

Laurie, Clayton D. *Anzio.* Washington, DC: U.S. Army Center of Military History.

Lewis, Spencer S. "Action Report: Assault on the Beaches of Southern France, 7 September 1944." Office of Naval Records and Library.

Matloff, Maurice. *Strategic Planning for Coalition Warfare 1943-1944.* Washington, DC: Office of the Center of Military History, 1959.

Mediterranean Army Air Forces. *Operations in Support of Dragoon.* 1944.

Mobilization: The U.S. Army in World War II—The 50th Anniversary. Washington, DC: Government Printing Office, 1995.

Pettit, Robert E. "First Special Service Force," report.

Report from U.S. Naval Attaché in Berlin. 16 Jan. 1941.

Report from U.S. Naval Attaché in Germany. 15 Feb. 1941.

Report from U.S. Naval Attaché in Rome. June 1941.

Report from U.S. Naval Attaché in Tokyo. Mar. 1941.

Report from U.S. Naval Attaché in Tokyo. 22 Sept. 1941.

Smith, John A. "Report of Ship's Assault Boat Unit in Amphibious Operation Conducted against the Enemy in Southern France, 15 August 1944."

Stewart, Duncan, and Staff, Group 3D. "Operation Anvil/Dragoon: The Invasion of Southern France, 15 August-1 September 1944." Ft.

Leavenworth, KS: U.S. Army Command and General Staff College, May 1984.

Strobridge, Truman R., and Bernard C. Nalty. "From the South Pacific to the Brenner Pass: General Alexander M. Patch," *Military Review* 61 (1981).

Syrett, David. "Communication Intelligence and the Battle of the Atlantic." London: British Records Association, Apr. 1995.

Task Unit 84.1.2. Action Report. Prepared by Commander Task Force Unit 84.1.2 Commander LST Group Two, 29 August 1944.

The AAF in the Invasion of Southern France: An Interim Report. Washington, DC: Headquarters, Army Air Forces, 1992.

The Special Committee Investigating the National Defense Program. United States Senate, 77th and 78th Congress. Washington, DC: Government Printing Office, 1943-1945.

U.S. Navy. "Report on the Fitness of Officers." Prepared by Lawrence E. Gilbert. 1 Oct. 1943-31, Dec. 1943. File No. 267150.

U.S. War Department. *To Bizerte with the II Corps.* Washington, DC: Government Printing Office, 1943.

United States Army Signal Corps. "Landings in Southern France, 1944." TV-220, USAMHRC.

United States Comptroller General. *Annual Report of the Comptroller General for the Fiscal Year Ended June 30, 1942.* Washington, DC: Government Printing Office, 1943.

United States Department of Commerce, Office of Business Economics. *Foreign Aid by the United States Government, 1940-1951.* Washington, DC: Government Printing Office, 1952.

United States Forces European Theater, Historical Division. "Supplying the Armies." *The Administrative and Logistical History of the European Theater of Operations.* 1946.

United States. *Hearings before the Joint Committee on the Investigation of the Pearl Harbor Attack.* Parts 36, 37, and 39. (Also referred to as the Hewitt Inquiry concerning the Pearl Harbor Attack.) Washington, DC: Government Printing Office, 1946.

Williams, Kathleen Broome. *Secret Weapon: U.S. Frequency Direction Finding in the Battle of the Atlantic.* Annapolis, MD: Naval Institute Press,1996.

Wilson, Henry M. *Report by the Supreme Allied Commander, Mediterranean to the Combined Chiefs of Staff on Operations in Southern France, August 1944.* Washington, DC: Government Printing Office, 1946.

_____. *Report by the Supreme Allied Commander Mediterranean to the Combined Chiefs of Staff on the Italian Campaign.* Parts 2 and 3. London: His Majesty's Stationary Office, 1948.

MISCELLANEOUS PRINT AND NONPRINT SOURCES

"Report on Operation Rabelais" and "Rabelais—Critique," provided to the author by Geoffrey M. T. Jones.

Boetcher, Kirsten Read. Telephone interviews and personal interview, May 2004.

Burke, Ferris. Telephone interviews and personal interview, Apr. 2004.

Devers, Jacob L. "Operation Dragoon: The Invasion of Southern France." Lecture delivered to American Military Institute, Washington, DC, 27 May 1946.

Earle, Charles. Telephone interviews, 2002-2004.

Gordon, David. "France 1940: National Failure and the Uses of Defeat." Speech to Historical Society and the New York Military Affairs Symposium, 10 May 2002.

Jones, Geoffrey M. T. Telephone interviews, 27 Aug. 2002, 23 Sept. 2002, Apr. 2004, among many.

Lovekin, Frank. Telephone interviews, 2002-2003.

Norton, Mary Kent (Hewitt's daughter). Telephone interview, Oct. 2001.

Norton, Randy (Hewitt's grandson). Telephone interviews, Nov. 2001 and 7 Mar. 2002.

Pavitt, James. Speech to OSS Society dinner, 8 June 2002.

Webb, June. Telephone call, 31 July 2003.

LETTERS AND E-MAILS

Aubut, Tom. E-mail to the author about LSTs, 25 June 2001.

Bellot, Alain. Letter from France's Ministry of Defense to the author about historical research, 8 July 2004.

Beroth, Robert O. Letters to the author about LST 282, 24 Apr. 2002, 9 May 2002, 24 Aug. 2002, 6 Jan. 2003, and 10 Dec. 2004.

Boetcher, Kirsten R. Letters and e-mails to the author, 3 and 10 Mar. and 12 May 2004, 7 and 9 Feb. 2005.

_____. "Memories of Viejo." Letter to the author, 15 May 2004.

Bond, Clyde L. Letter to the author, 23 Apr. 2002.

Buhl, Howard. E-mail to the author, 10 Jan. and 10 Mar. 2005.

Burke, Ferris. E-mail to the author, 2 May 2004.

Chief of Naval Personnel. Letter of commendation to Ferris C. Burke, 12 Dec. 1945.

Clowser, Ed. E-mail to the author, 9 Mar. 2005.

Connor, Jim Jr. E-mail to the author, 29 Sept. 2003.

Cullen, Charles H. E-mails to the author about proposed book, 5 Feb. and 18 July 2001 and 10 Mar. 2005.

Devers, Jacob L. Letter to his wife, Georgie, 3 Mar. 1945.

Dunn, Ted. Letters to the author, 26 Jan. and 26 Nov. 2004 and 8 Mar. 2005.

Frederick, Robert T. Letter to Prince of Monaco, 17 Nov. 1944; copy provided by Hoover Institution of War Revolution and Peace.

Baginski, Lauren Gilbert. Letter to the author, 13 Nov. 2003.

Gilbert, Terry. Letters and e-mails to the author, 5 Apr. 2004, 5 Jan. and 10 May 2005.

Green, Norman. Letter to the author about Lawrence E. Gilbert, 3 and 26 Mar. 2005.

Herzog, Lawrence. Letter to Lawrence E. Gilbert, 1 Jan. 2005.

Hewitt, H. Kent. Letter to Colonel Caldamaison, 18 June 1944; copy obtained from Library of Congress, Admiral Hewitt's Papers.

Hughes, Peter J. Letter to Lawrence E. Gilbert, 20 Nov. 1944.

Lee, Grant. Letter to the author, with extensive list of LST crew members.

Leopold, Louis. Letters to the author, 16 Oct. 2000 and 1 Feb. 2004.

Mueller, Ted. Letter to the author, 4 Jan. 2003.

Naval Historical Center. E-mail to the author about Operation Dragoon, 21 Nov. 2000.

Niewenhous, Beth. Letter to Lawrence E. Gilbert, 5 Apr. 1985; provided to the author by Kirsten R. Boetcher, 1 May 2004.

Norton, Mary Kent. Letter and e-mails to the author, 28 Dec. 2002, among others.

Norton, Randy. E-mail to the author about H. Kent Hewitt's Papers, 10 Oct. 2001.

Narozonick, George. Letter to the author, 13 Mar. 2002.

Peck, Bob. E-mail to the author about Armageddon, 13 Dec. 2000.

_____. E-mail to the author, 18 Mar. 2005.

Prince Louis of Monaco. Letter to Robert T. Frederick, 10 Nov. 1944; copy provided by Hoover Institution of War Revolution and Peace.

Sacco, Pete. E-mail to the author about LST 1012 shipmate.

Sgaglione, Mike. E-mail to the author, 25 Mar. 2004.

Shatley, Jeff. E-mails to the author, 21, 29, and 31 Oct. 2003 and 8 Feb. 2005.

Stark, Harold R. Letter to H. K. Hewitt, 5 July 1944.

Steeple, Chuck. Letter to the author, 29 July 2000.

Webb, June. Letter to the author, 3 August 2003.

Wilk, Jocelyn K. E-mail to the author about naval training at Columbia University, 25 June 2001.

Wilson, Bob. Letters to the author, Christmas 2000, 10 Jan. 2001, June 2002, and 9 Mar. 2005.

ELECTRONIC PUBLICATIONS

Historical accounts of the USS *Brooklyn* (CL-40)—"The Mighty B." *http://www.pittelli.com/ussbrooklyn/brooklyneagle.htm*, posted 6 Apr. 2000.

"Historical Atlas: Population of Germany." *http://www.tacitus.nu/historicalatlas/population/germany.htm.*

Doyle, Charles. Interview, Operation Dragoon. 3 Sept. 2002. *http://www.thedropzone.org/europe/southern%20france/doyle.htm.*

Gans, Bob. "I Would Like to Know." *http://www.kwanah.com/36division/ps/p5038453.htm.*

Horne, J. K. Jr. "A Report by Dragoon Parachutist." *http://www.thedropzone.org/europe/southernfrance/horne.htp* (accessed 24 Jan. 2003).

Johnson, Douglas. "Simonne de Lattre de Tassigny." *The Guardian,* June 12, 2003. *http://www.guardian.co.uk/france/story/0,11882,975546,00.html* (accessed 30 Aug. 2004).

Pearson, Judith L. Synopsis of *Wolves at the Door.* *http://www.judithl.pearson.com/wolves.htm.*

Sprigle, Ray. "LST Crash-Lands in Ohio and Gives Guests 'Battle Thrill.'" *Pittsburgh Post-Gazette* Thursday, 28 Oct. 1943. *http://www.landingship.com/282/news/post.htm.*

Bibliographic Comments

1. The American economic depression, isolationism, and lack of military preparedness are a few of the pre-World War II realities concisely depicted in Frederick Lewis Allen, *The Big Change: America Transforms Itself 1900-1950* (New York: Harper and Brothers, 1952) 146-151, 158-161, 175-176.

2. Cabell Phillips was a journalist associated with the *New York Times* for almost thirty years. His use of the *New York Times* files provides readers with a superb account of the World War II period. He used those files, many governmental records and periodicals, and more than fifty books to complete a chapter dealing with the "Arsenal of Democracy." It is a fact-filled and engrossing description of a stupendous war production record that was seriously flawed by corporate fraud, unconscionable union strikes, and other evils. See: Cabell Phillips, *The 1940s: Decade of Triumph and Trouble* (New York: Macmillan Publishing Company, 1975) 139-170.

3. The anthropologist Margaret Mead wrote the article "The Women in the War." It is one of the twenty-four articles in a book edited by Jack Goodman entitled *While You Were Gone*. Dr. Mead's article and the others provide accounts portraying life in the United States during World War II that are worth remembering. They are well written. Dr. Mead's contribution does not sugarcoat actuality. For example, she distinguishes the circumstances of American women and girls during World War II from the lives of women and girls of the other warring nations. See: *While You Were Gone: A Report on Wartime Life in the United States*, edited by Jack Goodman (New York: Simon and Schuster, 1946) 288.

4. In his admirable book *Among the Righteous Lost Stories from the Long Reach into Arab Lands* (New York: Public Affairs, 2006) 17, Robert Satloff observes that Hitler recognized the significance to the Axis of the Allied victory in North Africa. Hitler equated Germany's loss of North Africa with the loss of the Mediterranean and the ultimate ruin of the German people.

5. Significant and interesting details concerning French Resistance sabotage activities are available in John F. Sweets, *Choices in*

Vichy, France: The French under Nazi Occupation (New York: Oxford University Press, 1986) 212-227.

6. Professor Kedward, *Resistance in Vichy France,* offers interviews dealing with the resistance in southern France during 1940-1942. One interviewee, Joseph Pastor, reported on 13 September 1971 that there was little resistance in *Marseille* between 1940 and 1942. See: H. R. Kedward, *Resistance in Vichy France: A Study of Ideas and Motivation in the Southern Zone 1940-1942* (Oxford: Oxford University Press, 1978) 275.

7. Jacques Robichon, *The Second D-Day,* translated from the French by Barbara Shuey (London: Arthur Barker Limited, 1962) 159-258, wrote a vivid account of Operation Dragoon. In part 3 of *The Second D-Day,* there are descriptions of the activities of the First Airborne Task Force, of Le Drammont beach (Camel Green Beach 264B), of the U.S. Thirty-sixth Infantry Division, and of other dramatic episodes.

8. Events in the United States during the summer of 1944 are well described in *Washington Dispatches 1941-1945: Weekly Political Reports from the British Embassy,* edited by H. G. Nicholas (Chicago: University of Chicago Press, 1981) 387. One example is General de Gaulle's visit to Washington, D.C., and New York City. The British Embassy report of 15 July 1944 indicated that "anxiety to please was considerable on both United States and French sides and [Secretary of State] Hull is said to have expressed his satisfaction with de Gaulle's sentiments and impeccable behavior."

    The *British Dispatch* dated August 20, 1944, noted that Gen. Henry Maitland Wilson stressed the joint role of the British, American, and French troops in Operation Dragoon (p. 403).

9. President Roosevelt's foreign policies toward the major European governments are incisively analyzed by John Morton Blum in *V Was for Victory: Politics and American Culture during World War II* (New York: Harcourt Brace Jovanovich, 1972) 258, 259. According to Blum, even after France was liberated, FDR had serious doubts about de Gaulle's ability to govern France and the general's popularity. Blum wrote that the president supported Mussolini's successor Field Marshall Pietro Badoglio to obtain military advantages from the Italians that did not happen (see Blum, 258, 259).

10.   Hilary Footitt and John Simmonds offer a thorough description of civil affairs planning and administration for southern France. One of the reasons for the success of the Operation Dragoon landing and its subsequent effective civil administration was the excellent quality of Allied intelligence. By the evening of 15 August 1944, an initial group of civil affairs officers had landed on the Dragoon beaches. Another factor was the competence of the French Resistance in liberating Draguignan, Saint-Raphael, Frejus, Saint-Tropez, and other towns before the arrival of Allied troops. Political relationships in southern France between Resistance groups and U.S. Naval Intelligence were mostly harmonious (see Hilary Footitt and John Simmonds, *France 1943-1945* [New York: Holmes & Meier, 1980] 98-100).

Glossary

AA	Antiaircraft guns on LSTs and other ships
AAF	Army Air Forces
AEF	American Expeditionary Forces (World War I)
AFHQ	Allied Force Headquarters
Anvil	The planned 1944 Allied invasion of southern France in the Toulon-Marseille area, later renamed Operation Dragoon
BCRA	Bureau Central de Renseignements et d'Action (Militaire). The intelligence and action network of de Gaulle's France Libre (later France Combattante), run initially from London by Captain (later Colonel) Dewavrin (Passy). It sent French agents to organize Resistance within France, closely allied to the British SOE, which provided the necessary money and arms from the War Office.
Camel	Landing beaches used by U.S. Thirty-sixth Division in the French Riviera campaign
CCS	Combined Chiefs of Staff
CFLN	Comité Français de la Libération Nationale. The governing body of France Combattante established in Algiers under both Giraud and de Gaulle. From the spring of 1944, de Gaulle assumed single leadership.
CG	Commanding General
C in C	Commander in Chief
CO	Commanding Officer
COS	British Chiefs of Staff
D-day	Commencement date of operation: 6 June 1944 for the Normandy (Overlord) landings; and 15 August 1944 for the Anvil/Dragoon landings
Delta	Landing beaches used by the United States Forty-fifth Division in the Dragoon operation
Dragoon	Code name that replaced Anvil, the southern France landings, on July 1, 1944

Drammont	There are a variety of spellings for Drammont; for this book, we have settled on this one—used in official U.S. maps/charts.
Ducroit	Allied air operations after the initial Dragoon landings
DUKW	Churchill's description of the DUKW deserves repetition: "The marvelous duck of American invention is a heavy lorry [truck] which goes between forty and fifty miles an hour along a road, plunges into water and swims out seven miles to sea in quite choppy weather, returning to shore with a load of several tons and going to wherever it is specially needed."
DZ	Designated zone
ETOUSA	European Theater of Operations, U.S. Army
FATF	First Airborne Task Force
FFI	Forces Françaises de l'Intérieur (French Forces of the Interior). According to Generals Montgomery and Eisenhower, the FFI were worth between ten and fifteen divisions to the Allies in the liberation of France.
Ferdinand	Allied deception measure carried out in conjunction with Operation Dragoon
G-2	Military designation of intelligence section (French equivalent of *Deuxième Bureau*)
G-3	Military designation of operations section
GAO	General Accounting Office
H-hour	Time for commencement of an operation
HQ	Headquarters
JCS	U.S. Joint Chiefs of Staff
MAAF	Mediterranean Allied Air Forces
Maquis	French underground agents. Clandestine Resistance groups, many of which had arms and undertook guerrilla operations. An individual member of the Maquis was a *maquisard*.
Milice	Vichy police force, headed by Joseph Darnand, which employed Gestapo-like tactics against the Resistance

Military ranks	*Army*	*Navy*
	Second Lieutenant	Ensign
	First Lieutenant	Lieutenant Junior Grade
	Captain	Lieutenant
	Major	Lieutenant Commander
	Lieutenant	Colonel Commander
	Colonel	Captain
	Brigadier	Commodore
	Major General	Rear Admiral
	Lieutenant General	Vice Admiral
	General	Admiral
	General of the Armies	Fleet Admiral

MTOUSA — Mediterranean Theater of Operations, U.S. Army

MUR — *Mouvements Unis de la Résistance.* A consolidation of three southern Resistance groups: *Combat, Libération,* and *Franc-Tireur*

NARA — National Archives and Records Administration (College Park, MD)

NATOUSA — North African Theater of Operations, U.S. Army

NCO — Noncommissioned Officer (Army)

Nutmeg — Allied air operation prior to Dragoon, from D minus 5 to 0350 hours on D-day

OG — Operational Group (OSS paratroopers, normally consisting of twenty-eight men and two officers)

OSS — Office of Strategic Services

Overlord — Overall Allied plan and operation for the invasion of northwest Europe, spring 1944, including Normandy, June 6, 1944

Petty Officer — Noncommissioned navy rating

RAF — Royal Air Force

RCT — Regimental Combat Team

Romeo — French Commandoes who attacked the French coast west of the main Dragoon invasion force

Rosie — French marines who landed east on the main Dragoon invasion force

Route Napoleon — After his escape from Elba, Napoleon Bonaparte used this route to march to Paris; subsequently, Allies used the same route in August 1944.

Rugby	Allied airborne troops who were dropped behind the Provençal coast in conjunction with Operation Dragoon
Sitka	Allied Commandoes who assaulted the offshore islands of Port-Cros and Levant, 15 August 1944
SAS	Special Air Service (airborne commandoes)
SFHQ	Special Force Headquarters (staff of SOE/SO affiliated with SHAEF in London)
SHAEF	Supreme Headquarters Allied Expeditionary Force (Eisenhower's headquarters for Operation Overlord)
SI	Secret Intelligence Branch, OSS
SO	Special Operations Branch, OSS
SOE	Special Operations Executive
SOE/SO	Joint SOE and SO (of OSS) office in London (later became SFHQ)
SSS	Strategic Service Section (OSS/SI unit attached to Seventh Army)
TD	Tank Destroyer
Texas Division	The Thirty-sixth Division
TF	Task Force
Torch	Allied invasion of North and Northwest Africa, November 1942
T-Patch	Sobriquet for the Thirty-sixth (Texas) Division
ULTRA	Code name for German messages deciphered at Bletchley Park, England
USAAF	United States Army Air Forces
USS *Indianapolis*	President Franklin D. Roosevelt was a passenger on this ship commanded by H. K. Hewitt. The Pan-American Goodwill voyage was undertaken at the end of 1936. This is relevant in that (a) FDR was building up alliances to thwart Axis power in Central and South America and (b) it was the start of the friendship between FDR and Hewitt.
WNTF	Western Naval Task Force
Yokum	Allied air operations immediately prior to Dragoon, from 0350 to 0730 hours on August 15, 1944.

Index

Index

Dakar, 43, 45, 102, 103, 109, 123, 134

Daladier, Edouard, 20, 35

Danube, 494
    upper Danube valley, 276

Darlan, François, 25, 31, 32, 37, 39, 45, 91, 122
    Darlan-Murphy deal, 94, 147
    likes and dislikes, 34
    Murder of Admiral Darlan, The: A Study in Conspiracy (Tompkins), 98
    Operation Torch, 127, 128, 129
    Vichy government, 32, 33

Dartmouth College, 313

Davidson, Lyal A., 77, 112, 248, 257, 303

D-Day, 44, 138, 141, 151, 168, 172, 182, 201, 202, 203, 204, 208, 209, 210, 211, 212, 215, 220, 221, 236, 262, 263, 264, 304, 325, 334, 341, 342, 347, 360, 362, 373, 394, 405, 440, 467, 474, 481, 484, 530
    after, 249
    casualties, 489
    pre-D-Day intelligence, 240, 243, 281
    prior to, 238, 240, 245, 246, 256, 257, 260, 261, 265, 343, 415, 480, 483, 492, 545

De Belot, Raymond
    Struggle for the Mediterranean, 1939-1945, 653

De Benouville, Pierre, 228

de Gaulle, Charles, xii, 24, 31, 32, 38, 40, 44, 59, 70, 91, 94, 166, 178, 179, 193, 200, 223, 279, 286, 287, 302, 324, 430, 446, 453, 454, 455, 462, 468, 493, 496, 497, 498, 511
    Admiral Stark and, 70

    assassination attempts, 433
    broadcasts by, 30, 467
    Churchill's support of, 32
    concerns, 181, 182, 183, 184
    description of de Lattre, 280
    Eisenhower and, 41, 129, 302, 455
    followers, 96, 128, 432, 469, 494
    French National Committee, 289
    influence on the press, 303
    LST inspection, 162
    National Council of Resistance, 283
    Normandy invasion, 182, 301
    Operation Dragoon, 162, 289, 290, 430
    Robert Murphy, 41
    Roosevelt and, 37, 41, 42, 44, 70, 130, 182, 272, 286, 287, 289, 301, 432, 469
    Stalin's antipathy toward, 571
    Vichyites' opinion of, 43
    visit to America, 286
    War Memories, 129

de Lattre, Bernard de Tassigny, 178, 517

de Lattre, Jean de Tassigny, xii, 291, 426, 441, 446, 494, 495, 496, 497, 502, 504, 505
    background and character, 279, 280, 517
    invasion of Elba, 278, 279
    Operation Dragoon, 6, 178, 183, 184, 193, 200, 280, 284, 290, 469
    Patch, Alexander M. Jr., 176, 531

de Saint-Exupéry, Antoine, 4, 285, 299, 505

defeat of France, 1940, 5, 23, 28, 30, 31, 55, 57, 62, 91, 95, 162, 286, 287, 496, 504, 517

I

J

Index

Murphy, Audie L., 4, 363, 368, 374, 376, 528, 580
  To Hell and Back, 529
Murphy, Robert D., x, 4, 32, 34, 39, 40, 41, 44, 91, 94, 98, 127, 128, 147, 229, 230, 330, 331, 332, 593
Murray, Williamson, 133
  A War to Be Won, 174
Mussolini, Benito, 20, 24, 36, 37, 50, 91, 92, 140, 142, 147, 149, 151, 191, 431, 540, 676

N

Nakano, Lane, 529
Nalty, Bernard, 530
Naples, 92, 145, 147, 150, 152, 186, 191, 192, 193, 199, 203, 253, 255, 256, 257, 258, 265, 273, 307, 310, 321, 322, 323, 326, 330, 332, 333, 334, 338, 340, 341, 342, 343, 346, 347, 349, 351, 352, 357, 363, 387, 394, 398, 419, 510, 523, 567
  Bay of, 344, 352, 364
  Gulf of, 304
Narozonick, George, 398
Nation, the (magazine), 668
naval bombardment, 146, 150, 201, 419, 477, 484, 492
Naval Western Task Force, 248, 258, 343
Navy and Industrial Mobilization in World War II, The (Connery), 61
Nazi Germany, 55, 168, 209, 534
Nazis, 1, 8, 21, 22, 30, 32, 35, 37, 39, 63, 95, 122, 223, 228, 229, 275, 280, 370, 399, 431, 433, 458, 465, 469, 470, 531, 561, 580

Nazi Party, 281, 458
  prisoners, 399
  sympathizers, 56, 285
Nazism, 8, 21, 37, 45, 52, 58, 59, 226, 228, 259, 274, 365, 415, 533, 534, 573
  anti-Nazism, 21, 22, 34, 517
  propaganda, 29, 130, 459
Neutrality Act, 67
Neutrality Zone, 65
New Republic, the (magazine), 92
New York Times, the, 5, 6, 21, 228, 419, 522, 524, 531, 573, 576, 580
New Yorker *War Pieces, The* (Liebling), 26
Nice, 4, 24, 30, 234, 237, 238, 241, 244, 261, 304, 438, 439, 442, 506
Niedermair, John, 81
night assault operations, 491
Nineteenth German Army. *See* German Nineteenth Army
Ninth French Colonial Infantry Division, 247, 497
Nisida, Italy, 256, 273, 332, 333, 334, 342, 343, 347, 349, 351
nonintervention, 8, 46, 62
Normandy, 1, 8, 186, 193, 202, 205, 227, 229, 230, 239, 242, 246, 276, 300, 301, 316, 406, 419, 479, 501, 503, 510, 524
  before invasion of, 152, 178, 181, 284
  hedgerows, 486
  invasion of. (*see under* Operation Dragoon
  Red Ball Express, 457
  Utah Beach, 308
Normandy and Dragoon invasions, 313, 370, 423, 424, 425, 466

Index

P

Research and Analysis Branch
(OSS), 220, *See also* Office of
Strategic Services
Resistance in Vichy France (Kedward), 676
Rhine Valley, 444
Rhine, the, 168, 276, 444, 494
Rhone American Cemetery, 7, 507
Rhone River, 167, 210, 214, 215, 236,
240, 280, 290, 419, 425, 443, 476,
495, 507
Rhone Valley, 2, 4, 163, 223, 236,
240, 241, 276, 420, 421, 434, 435,
436, 437, 440, 442, 443, 473, 561
Roberts, Frank N., 476
Rockefeller, David, 227, 301, 466
Rockefeller, Nelson, 68
Rodgers, B. J., 308, 353
Rogow, Arnold A.
*James Forrestal: A Study of Personality,
Politics and Policy,* 357
Rol-Tanguy, Henri, 284, 453, 532
Rome, Italy, 142, 147, 152, 158, 177,
183, 184, 186, 198, 205, 207, 247,
253, 254, 265, 333, 343, 348, 353,
362, 474
Romeo Force, 205, 211, 257, 263
Rommel, Erwin, 1, 93
Rommel's Asparagus, 293
Roosevelt, Franklin D., 31, 32, 38,
42, 45, 46, 47, 50, 53, 56, 57, 59,
61, 62, 66, 73, 94, 105, 112, 127,
129, 164, 168, 176, 195, 217, 219,
357, 540, 541, 545
Churchill and, 34, 58, 60, 63, 93,
136, 147, 157, 159, 160, 163,
181, 182, 196, 287
de Gaulle and, 37, 41, 42, 44, 59,
70, 130, 182, 272, 286, 287,
289, 301, 432, 469

diplomatic style, 62
Dragoon and, 164, 166, 167, 184
health issues, 560
hemispheric defense policies, 52,
54
isolationism, 57
Lend-Lease Act, 60, 61
Murphy Robert D. (*see* Murphy,
Robert D.)
New Deal, 55, 73, 195, 305, 357
North Africa, 39, 40, 94, 97, 98,
103
policies, 39, 41, 44, 45, 97, 128, 676
presidential cabinet of, 26
presidential campaign, 166
Roosevelt administration, 73, 469
Stalin and, 165
Vichy regime and, 33, 37, 38, 39,
44, 593
Roosevelt, Franklin D. Jr., 40, 306
Rosie Force, 210, 212, 264, 305
Ross, Robert, 475
Rossiter, Margaret
Women in Resistance, 224
Rousso, Henry
*Vichy Syndrome, The: History and
Memory in France, 1944,* 30, 464,
573
Royal Air Force, 29, 92, 130, 139,
160, 271, 348
Rushing, Jack, xi, 390
Russell, Edward T.
*Africa to the Alps: The Army Air
Forces in the Mediterranean
Theater,* 134
Russia, 38, 50, 93, 98, 136, 137, 142,
165, 228, 313, 370, 423, 441, 455,
470, 478, 492, 526
Russian Revolution, 18

Index